A Companion to Geoffrey of Monmouth

Brill's Companions to European History

VOLUME 22

A Companion to
Geoffrey of Monmouth

By

Georgia Henley
Joshua Byron Smith

BRILL

LEIDEN | BOSTON

An electronic version of this book is freely available, thanks to the support of libraries working with Knowledge Unlatched. More information about the initiative can be found at www .knowledgeunlatched.org.

Cover illustration: © The British Library Board (Egerton MS 3028, f. 25r).

Library of Congress Cataloging-in-Publication Data

Names: Henley, Georgia, editor. | Byron-Smith, Joshua, editor.
Title: A companion to Geoffrey of Monmouth / by Georgia Henley, Joshua
    Byron Smith.
Other titles: Brill's companions to European history ; v. 22.
Description: Leiden ; Boston : Brill, 2020. | Series: Brill's companions to
    European history, 22127410 ; volume 22 | Includes bibliographical
    references and index.
Identifiers: LCCN 2019057692 (print) | LCCN 2019057693 (ebook) | ISBN
    9789004405288 (hardback) | ISBN 9789004410398 (kindle edition)
Subjects: LCSH: Geoffrey, of Monmouth, Bishop of St. Asaph, 1100?–1154.
    Historia regum Britanniae. | England—Historiography.
Classification: LCC PA8310.G4 C66 2020 (print) | LCC PA8310.G4 (ebook) |
    DDC 936.2007202—dc23
LC record available at https://lccn.loc.gov/2019057692
LC ebook record available at https://lccn.loc.gov/2019057693

Typeface for the Latin, Greek, and Cyrillic scripts: "Brill". See and download: brill.com/brill-typeface.

ISSN 2212-7410
ISBN 978-90-04-40528-8 (hardback)
ISBN 978-90-04-41039-8 (e-book)

Contents

Acknowledgements

We would like to express our gratitude to acquisitions editor Dr. Kate Hammond whose guidance and patience saw this project through from beginning to end. Initially, she had asked for a companion to Gerald of Wales, and we are grateful to her for allowing our vision of a companion to Geoffrey of Monmouth to take precedence. We are also grateful to the anonymous reviewers whose time and expertise went into improving the volume, and to Irini Argirouli, Alessandra Giliberto, and the production team at Brill. We thank our contributors whose dedication, energy, and meticulous research made this volume possible.

A Note on Translations

All of our authors' own translations from primary sources are marked as such. Otherwise, the translations used are always cited. Quotations from secondary sources in modern languages have also been translated, and in these instances the translations are the contributors' own unless stated otherwise. In accordance with the series guidelines, we have translated the titles of works if they are in Latin, Welsh, Irish, or other lesser-known modern languages. However, in some cases in which a translated title would cause confusion, or would require a cumbersome equivalent, we have let the original stand. For example, we have opted not to translate the medieval Welsh titles *Armes Prydein Vawr*, *Brenhinedd y Saesson*, *Brut y Brenhinedd*, *Brut Tysilio*, *Brut y Tywysogyon*, and *Ystorya Dared*, since these texts rarely go by any other name, even in English-language scholarship. Moreover, some Latin titles that are transparent have been left to stand, as well as the *Flores Historiarum* and the *Liber Floridus*, both of which would require explanations of what flowers have to do with history and rhetoric. Similarly, we have opted to leave the *Historia Brittonum* untranslated to avoid any confusion with Geoffrey's own history.

Figures

Abbreviations

AL	*Arthurian Literature*
BAV	Vatican City, Biblioteca Apostolica Vaticana
BBCS	*Bulletin of the Board of Celtic Studies*
Bern, ed. Wright	Geoffrey of Monmouth, *De gestis Britonum*, ed. N. Wright, *The Historia regum Britanniae of Geoffrey of Monmouth, vol. I: Bern, Burgerbibliothek, MS. 568*, Woodbridge, 1984
BnF	Paris, Bibliothèque nationale de France
BL	London, British Library
CMCS	*Cambridge Medieval Celtic Studies / Cambrian Medieval Celtic Studies*
DGB	Geoffrey of Monmouth, *De gestis Britonum*, ed. M. Reeve and trans. N. Wright, *Geoffrey of Monmouth, The History of the Kings of Britain: An Edition and Translation of De gestis Britonum [Historia Regum Britanniae]*, Woodbridge, 2007
Crick, *DR*	J.C. Crick, *The Historia regum Britannie of Geoffrey of Monmouth, vol. IV: Dissemination and Reception in the later Middle Ages*, Woodbridge, 1991
DMLBS	*Dictionary of Medieval Latin from British Sources*, ed. R.E. Latham, London, 1975– <http://logeion.uchicago.edu/> (accessed 16 July 2019)
EHR	*English Historical Review*
Faral, *LLA*	E. Faral, *La légende arthurienne: Études et documents*, 3 vols., Paris, 1929
First Variant Version, ed. Wright	Geoffrey of Monmouth, *De gestis Britonum*, ed. Wright, *The Historia regum Britannie of Geoffrey of Monmouth, vol. II: The First Variant Version: a critical edition*, Woodbridge, 1988
JEGP	*Journal of English and Germanic Philology*
JMEMS	*Journal of Medieval and Early Modern Studies*
PM	Geoffrey of Monmouth, *Prophetiae Merlini*, ed. M. Reeve and trans. N. Wright, *Geoffrey of Monmouth, The History of the Kings of Britain: An Edition and Translation of De gestis Britonum [Historia Regum Britanniae]*, Woodbridge, 2007
Crick, *SC*	J.C. Crick, *The Historia regum Britannie of Geoffrey of Monmouth, vol. III: A Summary Catalogue of the Manuscripts*, Woodbridge, 1989

Tatlock, *LHB*	J.S.P. Tatlock, *The Legendary History of Britain: Geoffrey of Monmouth's Historia regum Britanniae and Its Early Vernacular Versions*, Berkeley, 1950
VM	Geoffrey of Monmouth, *Life of Merlin*, ed. B.F.L. Clarke, *Life of Merlin: Vita Merlini*, Cardiff, 1973
WHR	*Welsh History Review*

Notes on Contributors

Jean Blacker

is Professor Emerita of French, Kenyon College. Her publications include *Wace: The Hagiographical Works*, trans. Jean Blacker, Glyn S. Burgess, and Amy V. Ogden (Brill, 2013) and *Court and Cloister: Essays in the Short Narrative in Honor of Glyn S. Burgess*, ed. Jean Blacker and Jane H.M. Taylor (Arizona Center for Medieval and Renaissance Studies, 2018). Her current book project on the uses of King Arthur in French and Latin historical narrative of the 12th and 13th centuries, focuses on the interconnections between foundation myths, competing claims of identity, and cultural imperialism in the legendary history of Britain.

Elizabeth Bryan

is Associate Professor of English at Brown University. She is the author of *Collaborative Meaning in Medieval Scribal Culture: the Otho Laȝamon* (Ann Arbor, 1999) and numerous articles on Laȝamon's *Brut* and the Middle English Prose *Brut*. Her current research project focuses on illustrated manuscripts of the Middle English Prose *Brut* and how their visual programs interact with their variant *Brut* textual narratives.

Thomas H. Crofts

is Professor of English at East Tennessee State University. Recent publications include "The Old Knight: An edition of the Greek Arthurian poem of Vat. gr. 1822", *Arthurian Literature* 33 (2016), "Writing the *Morte Darthur*: Author, Manuscript, and Modern Editions" (with K. S. Whetter), in *A New Companion to Malory* (D.S. Brewer, 2018), and "Malory's Death Poem", *Arthuriana* 29:1 (2019).

Fabrizio De Falco

is a doctoral student in medieval history at the Università di Bologna and at the Université d'Avignon. His studies focus on courtly literature and its political application. Currently, his research centers on the court of Henry II of England with specific attention to the works of Walter Map and Gerald of Wales.

Siân Echard

is Professor of English at the University of British Columbia. Her work on Geoffrey of Monmouth includes *Arthurian Narrative in the Latin Tradition* (Cambridge University Press, 1998), *The Arthur of Medieval Latin Literature* (University of Wales Press, 2011), and numerous chapters and articles. She is one of the general editors of *The Encyclopedia of Medieval Literature in Britain* (Wiley-Blackwell, 2017), and co-author of *The Book in Britain: A Historical Introduction* (Wiley-Blackwell, 2019).

Michael Faletra

is Professor of English and Humanities at Reed College in Portland, Oregon, where his teaching focuses on the literatures of medieval Britain and of pre-modern Europe more generally. He is the author of *Wales and the Medieval Colonial Imagination* (Palgrave Macmillan, 2014) and has translated Geoffrey of Monmouth's *History of Kings of Britain* (Broadview Press, 2008). Most recently, he has co-translated, with Paul Merchant, *Unless She Beckons: Poems of Dafydd ap Gwilym* (Redbat Books, 2018).

Santiago Gutiérrez García

is a Professor at Santiago de Compostela University (Spain). He specializes in Iberian Arthurian literature and his publications include *Orixes da Materia de Bretaña. Geoffrey de Monmouth e o pensamento europeo do século XII* (Santiago de Compostela, 2002), *A fada Morgana* (Santiago de Compostela, 2003), and "Arthurian Literature in Portugal", in D. Hook (ed.), *The Arthur of the Iberians. Arthurian Legends in the Spanish and Portuguese Worlds* (Cardiff, 2015), pp. 58–117.

Ben Guy

is a Junior Research Fellow at Robinson College, Cambridge. He is the author of a monograph called *Medieval Welsh Genealogy: An Introduction and Textual Study* (Boydell, 2020) which includes a full analysis of Geoffrey of Monmouth's extensive use of Welsh genealogical sources.

Paloma Gracia

is Professor of Romance Philology at the University of Granada specializing in Arthurian literature and historiography of the Middle Ages.

Georgia Henley

is an Assistant Professor of English at Saint Anselm College and a Junior Fellow in the Andrew W. Mellon Society of Fellows in Critical Bibliography. Her research focuses on historical writing, Latinity, and literary transmission in the borderlands between Wales and England. She has published on Geoffrey of Monmouth in *Arthurian Literature* and *Viator* and edited (with A. Joseph McMullen) *Gerald of Wales: New Perspectives on a Medieval Writer and Critic* (University of Wales Press, 2018).

David F. Johnson

is Professor of English at Florida State University. His research focuses on Old and Middle English, Old Norse, and Middle Dutch literatures and their manuscript contexts. Together with Geert H.M. Claassens, he has published three volumes (of six) of Middle Dutch Arthurian romances in facing page text and translation, as well as a volume of essays on King Arthur in the medieval Low Countries.

Owain Wyn Jones

is a lecturer at the School of History and Archaeology, Bangor University. His research focuses on medieval Welsh historical writing, particularly Welsh and Latin chronicles.

Françoise Le Saux

is Professor of Medieval Languages and Literature at the University of Reading (UK). She has published extensively on issues of translation and cultural adaptation in the medieval British Isles. Her publications include *Layamon's Brut. The Poem and its Sources* (Woodbridge, 1989) and *A Companion to Wace* (Cambridge, 2005).

Barry Lewis

is a professor in the School of Celtic Studies of the Dublin Institute for Advanced Studies in Ireland. His research focuses on medieval Welsh literature and hagiography.

Coral Lumbley

is a Postdoctoral Fellow of Arts and Cultures at New York University, where she teaches global premodern studies. Her research brings together Welsh and English literary histories, critical race theory, world literature, and trans/gender studies. Her recent publications include "The 'Dark Welsh': Color, Race, and Alterity in the Matter of Medieval Wales", *Critical Race and the Middle Ages* (*Literature Compass*, 2019) and "Imperatrix, Domina, Rex: Conceptualizing the Female King in Twelfth-Century England", *Visions of Medieval Trans Feminism* (*Medieval Feminist Forum*, 2019).

Simon Meecham-Jones

has lectured for the English Faculty, University of Cambridge in medieval literature and the history of the English language. From 2008 to 2014 he also held a part-time research fellowship at Swansea University. He has researched and published on Chaucer and Gower, 12th-century Latin lyrics, medieval language contact (particularly code-switching), and the representation of Wales and the Welsh people in medieval literature. He edited (with Ruth Kennedy) *Writers of the Reign of Henry II: Twelve Essays* (Palgrave, 2006) and *Authority and Subjugation in Writing of Medieval Wales* (Palgrave, 2008). He is currently completing a two-volume study entitled *Chaucer and Imagination*.

Maud Burnett McInerney

is the Laurie Ann Levin Professor of Comparative Literature at Haverford College. She is presently at work on a monograph about the medieval Troy story.

Nahir I. Otaño Gracia

is an Assistant Professor of English at the University of New Mexico. She specializes in the Global North Atlantic, extending the North Atlantic to include the Iberian Peninsula and Africa. Her recent publications include: "Presenting Kin(g)ship in Medieval Irish Literature", *Enarratio* 22 (2018) and "Vikings of the Round Table: Kingship in the *Islendigasögur* and the *Riddarasögur*", *Comitatus* 47 (2016), among others.

Paul Russell

is Professor of Celtic in the Department of Anglo-Saxon, Norse and Celtic in Cambridge. His research interests include learned texts in Celtic languages (especially legal and grammatical texts), Celtic philology and linguistics, early Welsh orthography, Middle Welsh translation texts, and Latinity in medieval Wales. Recent books include *Vita Griffini Filii Conani. The Medieval Latin Life of Gruffudd ap Cynan* (Cardiff, 2005), and *Reading Ovid in Medieval Wales* (Columbus, 2017).

Victoria Shirley

is a Teaching Associate in the School of English, Communication, and Philosophy at Cardiff University, where she teaches medieval and early modern literature. Her research interests include medieval historical writing in Latin and vernacular languages, national identity, and literary geography. She is currently preparing a monograph on the translation, transmission, and reception of *De gestis Britonum* in England, Scotland, and Wales between 1138 and 1530.

Joshua Byron Smith

is an Associate Professor of English at the University of Arkansas, where he directs the Medieval and Renaissance Studies program. He is also a Senior Fellow in the Andrew W. Mellon Society of Fellows in Critical Bibliography. He is the author of *Walter Map and the Matter of Britain* (University of Pennsylvania Press, 2017). He researches the multilingual literary culture of high medieval Britain.

Jaakko Tahkokallio

is a curator of Special Collections at the National Library of Finland. He holds a PhD from the University of Helsinki and has previously worked as a research fellow in Helsinki and King's College, London. Recent publications include *The Anglo-Norman Historical Canon. Publishing and Manuscript Culture* (Cambridge University Press, 2019) and "Update to the list of manuscripts of Geoffrey of Monmouth's *Historia regum Britanniae*", *Arthurian Literature* 32 (2015), 187–203.

Hélène Tétrel

is an Associate Professor (« maître de conférences habilitée à diriger les recherches ») at the University of Western Brittany in Brest, France, and a member of the Research Centre for Breton and Celtic Studies (CRBC). Her research interests include French and Icelandic medieval literature and more specifically translations from Old French to Old Icelandic. She is currently preparing an edition of the Old Icelandic translation of Geoffrey of Monmouth's *De gestis Britonum*, to be published at Classiques Garnier, in collaboration with Svanhildur Óskarsdóttir (Árni Magnússon Institute for Icelandic Studies, University of Iceland).

Rebecca Thomas

is a British Academy Postdoctoral Fellow at Bangor University. She completed her PhD thesis at the University of Cambridge investigating the construction of ethnic identities in 9th- and 10th-century Welsh texts.

Fiona Tolhurst

is Associate Professor of English at Florida Gulf Coast University, where she is Chair of Language and Literature. She is the author of *Geoffrey of Monmouth and the Feminist Origins of the Arthurian Legend* (Palgrave, 2012) and *Geoffrey of Monmouth and the Translation of Female Kingship* (Palgrave, 2013) as well as the editor of *Theoretical Approaches to Geoffrey of Monmouth*, *Arthuriana* 8:4 (Winter 1998). She is also co-editor, with K.S. Whetter, of *The Stanzaic* Morte Arthur *and the Middle English Tradition*, *Arthuriana* 28:3 (Fall 2018).

Introduction and Biography

Joshua Byron Smith

Geoffrey of Monmouth has suffered a glorious indignity that few writers have ever achieved: his creation has completely outstripped the maker. Few members of the general public, even well-educated ones, recognize the name Geoffrey of Monmouth. (A fact that the personal experience of this chatty medievalist has confirmed on numerous awkward occasions). But his creation is another matter altogether. The names of King Arthur, Guinevere, and their attendant knights perk up the ears of taxi drivers, coal mining fathers and grandfathers, and even scholars of contemporary literature. Medievalists, though we may know Geoffrey's name, have found him hard to contain and classify. So far-ranging is Geoffrey's work that he falls under the purview of several scholarly fields, many of which remain relatively isolated from one another: folklore, history, romance, manuscript studies, Celtic studies, classical reception, and medieval Latin – not to mention the seemingly endless expanse of Geoffrey's *Nachleben*, with its parade of translations, adaptations, and inspirations that continues to the present day. This volume aims to bring together, for the first time, many of these fields and to offer something close to a comprehensive overview of Geoffrey's life and work. It is our hope that this volume will serve as a current snapshot of Galfridian scholarship, incite more interest in Geoffrey and his work, and bring his artistry into greater prominence, all of which – if one is allowed to dream – might ultimately lead to slightly fewer blank stares for some of us.

Geoffrey's fame rests on three Latin works, the earliest of which is the *Prophetiae Merlini* ("The Prophecies of Merlin", hereafter abbreviated *PM*), a collection of prophecies completed before Henry I's death in 1135.[1] With baroque animalistic imagery and apocalyptic fervor, its meaning sometimes seems transparent, and yet at other times playfully obscure. Over 80 copies of this text survive, and it inspired a vogue for Merlin's prophecies throughout

---

1 Orderic Vitalis, *Ecclesiastical History* xii.47 (iv.486), ed. and trans. M. Chibnall, *The Ecclesiastical History of Orderic Vitalis*, 6 vols., Oxford, 1969–80, vol. 6, p. 381. See also Tahkokallio's contribution to this volume. Some of the research for this chapter was presented at the 9th Bangor Colloquium on Medieval Wales on 20 October 2018; I would like to thank the organizers and participants for their helpful discussion on several aspects of this chapter, especially Huw Pryce.

Europe.[2] Geoffrey included the *PM* in his next work, the *De gestis Britonum* ("On the Deeds of the Britons", hereafter abbreviated *DGB*). He had finished this work by January 1139 at the latest, when Henry of Huntingdon reports his astonishment at finding a copy at the abbey of Le Bec.[3] The count of surviving medieval manuscripts of the *DGB* is now 225, making Geoffrey one of the most widely-read secular authors from medieval Britain.[4] Yet even this impressive tally of extant manuscripts falls short of showing the work's reception. The *DGB* was adapted, abbreviated, and translated again and again, making it one of the most influential works of medieval European literature. Its appeal arises from several factors. It filled a gap in the historical record by providing a full account of the earliest history of Britain, from the settlement of the island until the time of the Anglo-Saxon invasion. It also gave the first thorough picture of King Arthur, whose court and conquests are described in such extravagant detail that they inspired generations of future writers. It placed Britain on par with ancient Greece and Rome and made the Britons major players in classical history. Finally, Geoffrey's skill as a writer and his sheer inventiveness make the *DGB* a pleasurable read. Even bare lists of kings are regularly punctuated with marvelous anecdotes.

Until recently, Geoffrey's history was called the *Historia regum Britanniae* ("The History of the Kings of Britain"), but Michael D. Reeve's textual study has confirmed that the title used in the earliest manuscripts, and by Geoffrey himself, was the *De gestis Britonum*.[5] After much debate among contributors, this volume begins the lugubrious process of using the original title in place of the received one. Aside from a desire for greater accuracy, the change is helpful in identifying references to Geoffrey's text and in showing how he framed his own project: the difference between British "deeds" (*gesta*) and British "kings" (*reges*) is not insignificant and shows that Geoffrey conceptualized his own work as being equal to the other great historical works with *de gestis* in their titles. Furthermore, Geoffrey's focus on a people (Britons) instead of a transferrable geopolitical area (*Britannia*) surely bears on critical discussions of Geoffrey's aims in writing his work. Indeed, the emergence of the alternative title might even suggest that many medieval readers viewed his history as providing Britain, not the Welsh, with an ancient, respectable past. Geoffrey's

---

2 For a list of *PM* manuscripts, see Crick, *SC*, pp. 330–32. See also Tahkokallio's contribution to this volume.

3 See Henry of Huntingdon, *History of the English* Letter to Warin, ed. and trans. D. Greenway, *Henry, Archdeacon of Huntingdon: Historia Anglorum. The History of the English People*, Oxford, 1996, pp. 558–83. See also Tahkokallio's and Meecham-Jones's contributions to this volume.

4 Crick, *SC*. For an updated survey, see Tahkokallio's contribution to this volume.

5 *DGB*, p. lix.

third and final extant work is the *Vita Merlini* ("The Life of Merlin", hereafter
abbreviated *VM*), completed around 1150 and extant in only four independent
manuscripts.[6] Written in dactylic hexameter, this poem recounts how Merlin
Silvester goes mad after battle and retires to the woods to live; this enigmatic
and difficult work seems to be deeply in touch with Welsh literature, though
its ultimate sources are unknown. Taken together, Geoffrey's literary output
shows him to be a versatile author: a master of verse and prose, capable of writing forceful speeches and enigmatic prophecy, and a voracious reader and researcher. Although he claimed to be nothing more than a translator – thereby
conforming to medieval literature's aversion to originality, at least outwardly –
he remains one of the most strikingly original writers of the Middle Ages.

A Companion to Geoffrey of Monmouth introduces Geoffrey's oeuvre to first-
time readers and provides a synthesis of current scholarship, all while offering new readings of his work. This volume also seeks to bring Celtic studies
and Galfridian studies into closer dialogue, especially given the importance
of Wales to Geoffrey and his work. To that end, many of the essays are written
by specialists in Welsh history and literature, whose voices have at times been
hard to discern in the general din of Galfridian scholarship. We have also asked
contributors to focus on all of Geoffrey's work, and not merely the Arthurian
sections. Geoffrey has been well-served by Arthurian scholarship, and we have
no desire to replicate many of the excellent recent studies in that field.[7] Instead,
we hope a holistic approach to his work will reveal subtleties often overlooked
in scholarship that concentrates primarily on the Arthurian portions.

The volume is loosely divided into four parts: "Sources", "Contemporary
Contexts", "Approaches", and "Reception". Ben Guy begins the first part with
an investigation of Geoffrey's Welsh sources, showing that Geoffrey not only
acquired but also understood a wide array of Welsh texts. Classical sources
are examined by Paul Russell, who investigates Geoffrey's classical and biblical references, many of which are glancing and difficult to detect. Rebecca
Thomas deals with Geoffrey's early English sources, which he often undermines through his own sleights of hand. Maud Burnett McInerney rounds off
this section by demonstrating that Geoffrey learned how to cultivate prophetic
ambiguity in the *PM* through careful study of his sources, especially Virgil.
Taken as a whole, these chapters show that Geoffrey was an avid researcher,

---

6   Crick, *SC*, p. 333. The *VM* is also found inserted into four copies of Ranulph Higden's
    Polychronicon; see *VM*, pp. 43–44. See also McInerney's contribution to this volume.

7   For example, see the series *Arthurian Literature in the Middle Ages* published by the University
    of Wales Press and S. Echard, *Arthurian Literature and the Latin Tradition* (Cambridge Studies
    in Medieval Literature, 36), Cambridge, 1998, esp. pp. 31–67.

read his sources with discretion, and could manipulate them better than many of his contemporaries.

The next part, "Contemporary Contexts", provides historical and cultural contexts for Geoffrey's work. Jaakko Tahkokallio's chapter surveys the early dissemination of Geoffrey's manuscripts and offers valuable new insights on networks of dissemination, Geoffrey's patrons, and his readership. A few of those early readers are the topic of Simon Meecham-Jones's chapter, which reevaluates early negative reactions to Geoffrey's history. There were, he argues, good reasons for these readers to affect a dislike of the *DGB*. Siân Echard, on the other hand, discusses Geoffrey's Latin readers, many of whom enjoyed his work so much that they felt compelled to interact with the text at length. Françoise Le Saux tackles the difficult question of Geoffrey's influence on the nascent genre of romance, showing how French-language writers quickly took to his work. Welsh speakers, too, also read Geoffrey's work with deep interest, and this Welsh reception is the subject of Owain Wyn Jones's chapter, which demonstrates how his history fits into Welsh historiography. On the other side of the border, Georgia Henley's chapter shows that Geoffrey's work, which is usually seen as an outlier in Anglo-Norman historical writing, actively engages with 12th-century historical methodologies. Wide-ranging and varied, these chapters nonetheless cohere to show Geoffrey's work as both a product of its culture and a cultural force in its own right.

The penultimate part, "Approaches", highlights the dominant trends in Galfridian scholarship and provides a platform for several critical approaches to his work, focusing particularly on Geoffrey's importance to postcolonial theory, feminist theory, critical race theory, and religious studies. Perhaps the most dominant trend in Galfridian scholarship, especially in the past two decades or so, is to read Geoffrey's work in light of Anglo-Norman expansion, and Michael Faletra's chapter does just that, arguing that Geoffrey's work supports colonialist policies. Politics also provides the backdrop for Fiona Tolhurst's chapter, which argues that, because of its pro-Angevin and thus pro-Empress stance, Geoffrey's work displays feminist leanings. Next, Coral Lumbley discusses Geoffrey in light of a growing interest among medievalists in the construction of race, and she demonstrates that Geoffrey's history should be read as one of the controlling texts of medieval racial discourse, especially in the British Isles. Finally, Barry Lewis overturns the long-standing critical commonplace that Geoffrey was simply not that interested in religious matters. These chapters all reveal the versatility of Geoffrey's work, and show that it has much to offer scholars in a variety of fields and with a variety of critical approaches. Of course, these four chapters should not be taken as a definitive list of all that is possible. An eco-critical approach to Geoffrey's work might well prove useful, especially with Geoffrey's intense interest in place. And this volume feels the lack of art historians, many of whom, given Geoffrey's broad reception, could surely produce a chapter on visual representations of his work. For these omissions and others, the editors are heartily sorry, and we offer the same invitation that Geoffrey of Monmouth offered to his contemporary Caradog of Llancarfan: we leave these matters to others to write.

Yet even 14 chapters cannot cover the necessary ground to make any claims to comprehensiveness. Accordingly, this volume limits its focus to Geoffrey's immediate work and life, though our contributors have been permitted occasional forays into other terrain. Nevertheless, Geoffrey's reception posed a challenge for this volume. Given the widespread popularity of the *DGB*, anything that fully treated its reception would transform an already bulky book into several bulky books. Rather than ignore Geoffrey's posthumous appeal altogether, we have thought it better to include as a final part a series of shorter, encyclopedia-like entries on the reception of his work in various linguistic traditions. Only the Welsh, French, and Latin receptions have been accorded their own full chapters, given the importance of these three traditions to Geoffrey. (Nevertheless, we have also thought it best to include Welsh and French reception articles for the sake of thoroughness, especially since these smaller versions offer a more concise bibliographic overview). These shorter articles in the final part are meant to offer points of entry into his reception in as many traditions as we could identify, and they also make for interesting reading regarding the how and why of his popularity (or lack thereof) in different cultural contexts. We encourage readers who have identified other linguistic and cultural traditions into which his work was received to take this volume as a jumping-off point and to continue broadening the critical conversation about the reception of his texts.

One part of Geoffrey's reception that this volume does not cover explicitly – though our authors touch upon it here and there – is the two variant Latin versions of the *DGB*. The First Variant Version has received excellent attention from Neil Wright, and we would direct curious readers to his work.[8] The Second Variant Version has no critical edition, and so for the moment it is difficult to say anything of worth about it.[9] Since companion volumes cover what is normally found in introductory material – sources, methods, and the like – the rest of this introduction concerns Geoffrey's biography, if indeed we can call a life with only a few concrete facts a "biography" at all.

---

8   *First Variant Version*, ed. Wright. Unfortunately, the following work, which provides a revisionist account of the First Variant Version, only became available in the late stages of this book: *The History of the Kings of Britain: The First Variant Version*, ed. and trans. D.W. Burchmore, Cambridge, MA, 2019.

9   See *DGB*, pp. x–xi; Crick, *DR*, pp. 15–16.

For the man who invented King Lear and Arthurian literature as we know it, the details of Geoffrey's life remain largely a mystery.[10] Compared to some of his contemporaries, Geoffrey is not particularly forthcoming about biographical details, and he leaves modern scholars little to work with. Still, he had the courtesy (or perhaps audacity) to sign his works, something that many medieval writers did not feel compelled to do, and this information provides the basis for our knowledge of Geoffrey's life. He calls himself *Galfridus Monemutensis* on three occasions: once in the *PM* and twice in the *DGB*.[11] And in the *VM* he styles himself *de Monemuta*.[12] Some connection with Monmouth is therefore assured, probably implying that he was born in Monmouth and spent his early life there. The local knowledge displayed in his works shows that he was familiar with the region around Monmouth, and so it is probably safe to assume that he was born in or near Monmouth around 1100.[13] The date for Geoffrey's birth "circa 1100", widely repeated in scholarship, works backwards from his appearance at Oxford in 1129, after he had obtained an early education and the title *magister*. However, it is important to remember that nothing is certain in this regard, and Geoffrey could have been born as early as 1070 and died in his eighties. His deep erudition and mastery of Latin points to an early education, and in the first few decades of the 12th century, Monmouth Priory would have been a possible place for a local boy to receive instruction in grammar. Geoffrey may even be the same *Gaufridus scriba*, "Geoffrey the scribe", who witnessed a 1120 charter concerning the priory's property.[14] The early connection with Monmouth priory, however, remains speculative.

Over the last century a broad scholarly consensus has emerged that Geoffrey spent a good deal of his life in Oxford, and that he was a canon of St George's,

10   For Geoffrey's life see: J.E. Lloyd, *A History of Wales from the Earliest Times to the Edwardian Conquest*, 2nd ed., London, 1912, pp. 523–25; H.E. Salter, "Geoffrey of Monmouth and Oxford", *EHR* 34 (1919), 382–85; E. Faral, "Geoffrey of Monmouth: les faites et les dates de sa biographia", *Romania* 53 (1927), 1–42; L. Thorpe, "The last years of Geoffrey of Monmouth", in n.n. (ed.), *Mélanges de langue et littérature françaises du moyen âge offerts à Pierre Jonin*, Aix-en-Provence, 1979, pp. 663–72; M.D. Legge, "Master Geoffrey Arthur", in K. Varty (ed.), *An Arthurian Tapestry: Essays in Memory of Lewis Thorpe*, Glasgow, 1981, pp. 22–27; O. Padel, "Geoffrey of Monmouth and Cornwall", *CMCS* 8 (1984), 1–28, esp. at pp. 1–5; Karen Jankulak, *Geoffrey of Monmouth*, Cardiff, 2010, pp. 5–12; J.C. Crick, "Monmouth, Geoffrey of (d. 1154/5)", *Oxford Dictionary of National Biography*, Oxford University Press, 2004, <http://www.oxforddnb.com/view/article/10530> (accessed 27 June 2018).
11   *DGB*, vii.110.21; Prologus 3.19; xi.177.1.
12   *VM*, l. 1526.
13   Tatlock, *LHB*, pp. 72–77.
14   *Chartes anciennes du Prieuré de Monmouth en Angleterre*, ed. P. Marchegay, Les Roches-Baritaud, 1879, pp. 21–22, no. 8. See also J.E. Lloyd, "Geoffrey of Monmouth", *EHR* 57 (1942), 460–68, at p. 461, n. 2; Tatlock, *LHB*, p. 440.

a short-lived collegiate church inside Oxford Castle, founded in 1074 by Robert d'Oyly and Roger de'Ivry.[15] The central plank of this argument is eight Oxford charters, dating from 1129 to 1151.[16] In these charters, a "Galfridus Arturus" (with slight orthographical variations) appears as a witness. The subjects of these charters and their witnesses make it very likely that the Galfridus Arturus appearing therein was a canon of St George's.[17] This "Geoffrey Arthur" of the Oxford charters has been identified with Geoffrey of Monmouth for the following reasons. First of all, four 12th-century writers call Geoffrey of Monmouth "Geoffrey Arthur", with William of Newburgh helpfully revealing that Geoffrey was nicknamed "Arthur" (*agnomen habens Arturi*).[18] These

---

15   In some scholarship, there is marked confusion as to whether Geoffrey was a secular canon or an Augustinian (thus regular) canon. Augustinian canons lived under a rule, and thus were in some ways akin to monks, while secular canons did not live under a rule. The confusion seems to have arisen in the following manner: there is no evidence that the collegiate church of St George in Oxford Castle was Augustinian. However, the nearby Augustinian house of Oseney acquired St George's as early as 1149. It is difficult to know if Oseney made the previous canons of St George's follow their rule, but they did allow them to possess their prebends for the rest of their lives, which suggests some respect for the status quo and a "friendly" takeover. And even after Oseney assumed its control, St George's remained a parish and employed secular canons. At any rate, it is hardly fair to call Geoffrey an Augustinian if he only became (perhaps unwillingly) affiliated with that order in the last few years of his life. Indeed, if he had chosen an Augustinian house, especially early in his life, it might be an important piece of evidence regarding his religious outlook. It is therefore difficult to see any Augustinian influence in his two earlier works (*pace* Tatlock, *LHB*, p. 82; for a better explanation of some Augustinian connections, see p. 163 of this volume) since he finished them well before St George's was absorbed into Oseney. Tatlock's clumsy phrase, "[t]he Augustinian secular canons' college of St. George" (p. 441), echoed in Thorpe's widely consulted translation "Augustinian canons of the secular college of St. George" (Geoffrey of Monmouth, *De gestis Britonum*, trans. L. Thorpe, *Geoffrey of Monmouth: The History of the Kings of Britain*, London, 1966, p. 12) has given the impression that Geoffrey was an Augustinian. However, if Geoffrey is to be thought of as a canon of St George's – and I am in agreement that the evidence strongly suggests so – he is best thought of as a secular canon. For the collegiate church of St George, see J. Barron, "The Augustinian Canons and the University of Oxford: the Lost College of St George", in C.M. Barron and J. Stratford (eds.), *The Church and Learning in Later Medieval Society: Essays in Honour of R.B. Dobson*, Donington, 2002, pp. 228–54; W. Page (ed.), *The Victoria History of the County of Oxford: Volume II*, London, 1907, pp. 160–61; C. Brooke, R. Highfield, & W. Swaan, *Oxford and Cambridge*, Cambridge, 1988, pp. 49–50.
16   Salter, "Geoffrey of Monmouth and Oxford". The eighth is found in *Facsimiles of Early Charters in Oxford Muniment Rooms*, ed. H.E. Salter, Oxford, 1929, no. 102. Two of these charters Salter identifies as forgeries (no. 2 and no. 102). For a note on Salter's transcription, see *DGB*, p. vii, n. 1.
17   Salter, "Geoffrey of Monmouth and Oxford", p. 385.
18   William of Newburgh, *The History of English Affairs*, ed. and trans. P.G. Walsh and M.J. Kennedy, *William of Newburgh: The History of English Affairs, Book I (Edited with*

references, independent of the charters, are the strongest evidence that the two Geoffreys are the same, but that is not all. Two early families of *DGB* manuscripts append the cognomen "Arthur" to Geoffrey in the title.[19] Moreover, the co-witnesses who appear alongside Geoffrey Arthur in the Oxford charters are also telling: Walter, the archdeacon of Oxford, who is said to have provided the source for the *DGB*, and Ralph of Monmouth, a canon of Lincoln. Ralph was not the only one at St George's with a connection to Lincoln, since Robert de Chesney, who would later become bishop of Lincoln (1148–66), was also a canon there. While Oxford lay within the sprawling medieval diocese of Lincoln, and thus *some* affiliation is unremarkable, these Lincoln connections are nonetheless noteworthy in Geoffrey's case because he dedicated the *PM* and the *VM* to two successive bishops of Lincoln, Alexander (1123–48) and Robert de Chesney. Yet another reason to link the Geoffrey from the Oxford charters and Geoffrey of Monmouth is that in the Oxford charters "Arthur" is unlikely to be a patronym.[20] In the charter collocations, the name "Artur" never once appears in the genitive case, as would be expected if it were a patronym. Instead, in the charters "Arthur" appears to be an *agnomen*, a nickname, and as such indicates that the Oxford Geoffrey had a particular interest, one might even say obsession, with the figure of Arthur.[21] How many budding Arthurian scholars named Geoffrey could there have been in the mid-12th century? Another name also suggests that the two Geoffreys are one and the same – Boso of Oxford, who

---

Translation and Commentary), Warminster, 1988, pp. 28–29. On this passage, see Padel, "Geoffrey of Monmouth and Cornwall", p. 3 and Meecham-Jones's contribution to this volume. For Henry of Huntingdon, see *History of the English*, Letter to Warin. Gerald of Wales, *The Journey Through Wales* i.5, ed. J.F. Dimock, *Giraldi Cambrensis Opera*, 8 vols., London, 1861–91, vol. 6, pp. 3–152, at p. 58; *The Description of Wales*, i.7, ed. J.F. Dimock, *Giraldi Cambrensis Opera*, 8 vols., London, 1861–91, vol. 6, pp. 153–228, at p. 179. For William of St Albans, see William of St Albans, *Life of St Alban*, trans. T. O'Donnell and M. Lamont, in J. Wogan-Browne and T.S. Fenster (eds.), *The Life of St. Alban by Matthew Paris*, Tempe, 2010, pp. 133–65, at p. 139; the Latin text is found in *Acta sanctorum* (June IV, 22). See also Tatlock, *LHB*, p. 439. To Tatlock's count (I have excluded his citation of Matthew Paris because, as he notes, it is late and dependent on earlier sources) can be added *The Waverley Chronicle*, ed. H.R. Luard, *Annales Monastici*, 5 vols., London, 1864–69, vol. 2, pp. 129–411, at pp. 234–35.

19   See the variants on the title for *Q* and *M* in *DGB*, p. 3. Indeed, according to Reeve, *M* (London, British Library, Royal 13 D. ii) has a particularly good textual pedigree: "a transcript of M would be a tolerable substitute for an edition" (*DGB*, p. xvi).

20   See, for example, Padel, "Geoffrey of Monmouth and Cornwall", pp. 1–3. *Pace*, M.J. Curley, *Geoffrey of Monmouth* (Twayne's English Authors Series, 509), New York, 1994, p. 2 and Tatlock, *LHB*, p. 439. See below for more discussion.

21   Padel in "Geoffrey of Monmouth and Cornwall" helpfully suggests the discrepancy in names arose because "Geoffrey himself preferred *Monemutensis*, while others used *Artur* of him; or that in his literary works he preferred to use an epithet which did not show him to have particularly Arthurian connections" (p. 4).

appears as a minor character in the *DGB*.[22] J.S.P. Tatlock believed the name Boso was a pun on the Latin name for Oxford, *Vadum Boum*.[23] (The apparent pun is more easily grasped in the nominative singular, *bos*, "ox, bull"). However, the name Boso would have also had an immediate connotation for Geoffrey's educated contemporaries. In the previous generation, Anselm of Canterbury had explored incarnational theology in his influential *Why God Became a Man*. The form of this work is a dialogue between Anselm and his pupil Boso, who by argumentative necessity is rather dull and dimwitted. The peculiar name Boso therefore would have called to mind a dullard scholar who needed matters explained to him in the simplest of terms. It is not farfetched to read the Boso of Oxford in the *DGB* as a joke directed at Geoffrey's colleagues at Oxford, and thus we would have another connection between Geoffrey of Monmouth and Oxford. Assured that we are dealing with one Geoffrey, we can mine the Oxford charters for two additional pieces of biographical evidence: they tell us that Geoffrey was a *magister* and that he was elected bishop of St Asaph.[24]

The exact connotations of the title *magister* vary in place and time, but in England during Geoffrey's day the title generally means that one had obtained a higher education.[25] As far as we know, this makes Geoffrey one of only four men with the title *magister* who were teaching at Oxford schools around the same time.[26] Where Geoffrey obtained that education is another matter altogether. It is sometimes suggested that Geoffrey went to Paris for advanced study, but this is little more than projecting the attraction that Parisian schools held for later British generations back onto Geoffrey. And while it is plausible that he might have been educated at Paris or another burgeoning proto-university, it is just as plausible that Geoffrey could have received his title "*magister*" from a training in a monastic, collegiate, or cathedral school.[27] Judging by the other three *magistri* at Oxford, all of whom were theologians, it seems that the title might imply he lectured on theology.[28] His skill with the written word, however, shows that he would not have been out of place lecturing on grammar or rhetoric, or perhaps even dialectic. Still, we do not need the

---

22   *DGB*, i.156.338–39: "Boso Ridochensis, id est Oxenefordiae". Boso again appears during Arthur's campaign against Rome.

23   Tatlock, *LHB*, p. 169.

24   Salter, "Geoffrey of Monmouth and Oxford", pp. 384–85.

25   J. Barrow, *The Clergy in the Medieval World: Secular Clerics, Their Families and Careers in North-Western Europe c.800–c.1200*, Cambridge, 2015, pp. 208–10, esp. n. 2. See also Legge, "Master Geoffrey Arthur" and Barron, "Augustinian Canons", pp. 235–36.

26   Legge, "Master Geoffrey Arthur", p. 24.

27   *DMLBS*, s.v. *magister*, def. 5a and 11. My thanks to an anonymous reader for this suggestion.

28   Legge, "Master Geoffrey Arthur", p. 24.

Oxford charters to tell us that Geoffrey was an educated man – his work leaves no doubt – but they do provide one more detail about his biography, and a fascinating one at that. The last two Oxford charters show that in 1151 he had been elected bishop of St Asaph, a newly created diocese in northeastern Wales, itself built on the bones of an older Welsh diocese and apparently designed to counterbalance the preeminence of the diocese of Bangor to its west.[29] He would have been only the third bishop of this new bishopric, and it is difficult to resist speculation of what it might have meant that Geoffrey, a Monmouth man who spent a tremendous amount of energy on the British past, was elected to a Welsh see with strong English leanings.[30] It was not uncommon for clergy who were not yet priests to postpone their ordination into the priesthood until their careers required it, and so on 16 February 1152 he was ordained a priest at Westminster Cathedral, and only eight days later at Lambeth Palace he was consecrated bishop.[31] It is as a bishop that we catch the last documentary evidence of his life as a witness to the Treaty of Westminster in 1153.[32] It has been suggested that the provincial nature of St Asaph "was scarcely suited to a man of Geoffrey's urbane and scholarly character", but a bishopric was a bishopric, and it is unlikely that Geoffrey or his colleagues would have scoffed at the promotion.[33] We probably underestimate his ecclesiastical career at our own peril, if we view his work, as Tatlock did, as indicative of his "secularity of interests".[34] Instead, as Barry Lewis's chapter in this volume shows, Geoffrey

---

29   S. Harris, "Liturgical Commemorations of Welsh Saints II: St. Asaf", *Journal of the Historical Society of the Church in Wales* 6 (1956), 5–24, at pp. 5–7; J.E. Lloyd, "Geoffrey of Monmouth", pp. 465–66.

30   For the early bishops, see "St Asaph: Bishops", ed. M.J. Pearson, *Fasti Ecclesiae Anglicanae 1066–1300: Volume 9, the Welsh Cathedrals (Bangor, Llandaff, St Asaph, St Davids)*, London, 2003, pp. 33–36, *British History Online*, <http://www.british-history.ac.uk/fasti -ecclesiae/1066-1300/vol9/pp33-36> (accessed 6 May 2019).

31   Gervase of Canterbury, *Chronicle*, ed. W. Stubbs, *The Historical Works of Gervase of Canterbury*, 2 vols., London, 1879–80, vol. 1, p. 142 and n. 2; *The Canterbury Professions*, ed. M. Richter, Torquay, 1973, p. 47, no. 95. Now for some chronological housekeeping: In both his profession and Gervase, the year is reported incorrectly. Stubbs explains this error, noting that the only proximate year in which "septimo kalendas Martii" fell on a Sunday was 1152, a leap year. Confusingly, *The Canterbury Professions* is silent on this matter, listing only 1151, an error which is pointed out in *Fasti Ecclesiae Anglicanae*. Even more confusingly, the *Fasti Ecclesiae Anglicanae* itself makes an error while pointing out the error in *The Canterbury Professions*: it lists the day of his consecration and profession of obedience as 23 March, instead of 24 February.

32   *Regesta regum Anglo-Normannorum, 1066–1154*, ed. H.W.C. Davis et al., 4 vols., Oxford, 1913–69, vol. 3, pp. 97–99, no. 272, at p. 98.

33   Curley, *Geoffrey of Monmouth*, p. 5.

34   Tatlock, *LHB*, p. 446.

was very much interested in sacred matters. When the *Brut y Tywysogyon* records his death in 1155, no mention is made of his *DGB*, which would become wildly popular in Wales.[35] Rather, it is his designation as bishop which carries his weight for posterity.

One hotly debated question in Galfridian scholarship, indeed perhaps *the* most hotly debated, also concerns Geoffrey's biography. What was his ethnicity or, to use a medieval term, his *gens*? Intimately bound up in this question is discussion of Geoffrey's attitude toward Wales. Was Geoffrey Welsh, Breton, or Anglo-Norman, or perhaps even a Cornish sympathizer?[36] And did he intend his literary works to support the Welsh cause, to justify Anglo-Norman conquest of Wales, or to play to both sides, allowing supporters of whatever faction to find succor in his spirited account of the British past? There exists, of course, more nuance than this bare summary of over a century of scholarship can suggest, but most scholarship on Geoffrey falls into these categories, either explicitly or implicitly.

Investigations into Geoffrey's ethnicity circle around a few pieces of evidence. First is the name "Geoffrey", which does not seem to have been popular in Wales and had a distinctively continental flavor.[37] Monmouth, moreover, had been under the lordship of Bretons since at least 1086, and a large number of Bretons had settled there. Brittany also looms large in the *DGB*, often appearing as the favored region and providing crucial military support. And

---

35   *Brut y Tywysogyon; or, The Chronicle of the Princes. Red Book of Hergest Version*, ed. and trans. T. Jones (History and Law Series, 16), Cardiff, 1955, 2nd ed., 1973, pp. 132–33: "Yn y ulwydyn honno y bu uarw Jeffrei, escob Lan Daf", "In that year Geoffrey, bishop of Llandaff, died." *Lan Daf* here is a mistake for *Lan Elwy*, the name of the diocese in Welsh. See J.E. Lloyd, *A History of Wales*, p. 525, n. 154.

36   For Geoffrey as Welsh, see J. Gillingham, "The Context and Purposes of Geoffrey of Monmouth's *History of the Kings of Britain*", *Anglo-Norman Studies* 13 (1990), 99–118 (repr. in id. (ed.), *The English in the Twelfth Century: Imperialism, National Identity and Political Values*, Woodbridge, 2000, pp. 19–39). For Geoffrey as a Breton, see J.E. Lloyd, *A History of Wales*, pp. 523–24; id., "Geoffrey of Monmouth", pp. 466–68; Tatlock, *LHB*, pp. 397–400, 443–44. For Geoffrey as a supporter of Anglo-Norman interests, see M.A. Faletra, "Narrating the Matter of Britain: Geoffrey of Monmouth and the Norman Colonialization of Wales", *The Chaucer Review* 35:1 (2000), 60–85; id., *Wales and the Medieval Colonial Imagination: The Matters of Britain in the Twelfth Century*, New York, 2014; M.R. Warren, *History on the Edge: Excalibur and the Borders of Britain, 1100–1300* (Medieval Cultures, 22), Minneapolis, 2000; P. Dalton, "The Topical Concerns of Geoffrey of Monmouth's *Historia Regum Britannie*: History, Prophecy, Peacemaking, and English Identity in the Twelfth Century", *Journal of British Studies* 44:4 (2005), 688–712. For Geoffrey's Cornish sympathies, see Padel, "Geoffrey of Monmouth and Cornwall". For doubt all around, see Jankulak, *Geoffrey of Monmouth*, pp. 11–12.

37   J.E. Lloyd, *A History of Wales*, p. 523; id., "Geoffrey of Monmouth", pp. 466–67.

Geoffrey's intention to write another British history, this time about the flight of the native church into Brittany, has been viewed as another indication of Breton partiality.[38] Finally, his appointment as bishop of St Asaph suggests that he was a candidate of the Anglo-Norman establishment; they would not have chosen a Welshman or a Welsh partisan as a bishop for a newly formed Welsh diocese that was intended to push back against the diocese of Bangor.[39] Taken together, this evidence suggests that Geoffrey felt himself to be Breton, born into a Breton family at Monmouth (or perhaps even in Brittany itself and later brought to Monmouth). The Breton solution has found significant support because it elegantly answers an apparent contradiction: how could a man born in Monmouth (and thus Welsh) narrate his people's fall into disrepute and Insular irrelevance, all while favoring Brittany of all places? The description of Wales at the end of the *DGB* certainly arouses no native pride, and viewing Geoffrey as a Breton, fascinated by but not beholden to the land of his birth, offers a way around this problem. Understandably, many have followed Tatlock's lead in proclaiming Geoffrey to be a "Breton patriot".[40]

However, the Breton solution is not without its difficulties. The idea first appeared in J.E. Lloyd's *A History of Wales from the Earliest Times to the Edwardian Conquest* (1911), in which Lloyd outlined the three major strands of the argument: Geoffrey's name, the Breton settlement at Monmouth, and the work's apparent partiality to Brittany.[41] Before reassessing the evidence, it is helpful to understand the genealogy of this argument by examining Lloyd's own treatment of Geoffrey. Overall, Lloyd's patriotic vision of who counted as Welsh and what counted as Welsh history was heavily informed by his Victorian and Edwardian education and not as capacious as our modern standards might have it.[42] Accordingly, in Lloyd's account Geoffrey was "a foreigner", and whereas we might be prone to viewing Geoffrey as a creative and masterful writer, Lloyd demeaned him as "a mere romancer" – a damning term from an exacting historian.[43] (Lloyd did, however, credit Geoffrey for "giving world-wide currency" to "the ancient traditions of Wales".)[44] It is easy to speculate that

---

38   *DGB*, xi.186.169.

39   J.E. Lloyd, "Geoffrey of Monmouth", p. 465; Tatlock, *LHB*, p. 443.

40   Tatlock, *LHB*, p. 443.

41   J.E. Lloyd, *A History of Wales*, pp. 523–24. Lloyd revisited the idea in "Geoffrey of Monmouth", pp. 467–68.

42   H. Pryce, *J.E. Lloyd and the Creation of Welsh History: Renewing a Nation's Past*, Aberystwyth, 2011, esp. pp. 169–76 for a summary of Lloyd's nationalist project; id., "J.E. Lloyd's *History of Wales* (1911)", in N. Evans and H. Pryce (eds.), *Writing a Small Nation's Past: Wales in Comparative Perspective, 1850–1950*, Farnham, 2013, pp. 49–64.

43   J.E. Lloyd, *A History of Wales*, p. 524; p. 182, n. 82. See also, Pryce, *J.E. Lloyd*, p. 99.

44   J.E. Lloyd, *A History of Wales*, p. 523.

Lloyd, whose own work revolutionized and professionalized the study of medieval Welsh history, saw in Geoffrey much of the same inventive spirit that had gummed up the study of Welsh history in the 18th and 19th centuries.[45] But Lloyd's insistence that Geoffrey was not Welsh does not seem to stem from an inability to recognize that earlier Welsh historians could get things wrong, sometimes disastrously so. Indeed, the fact that Lloyd felt compelled to address Geoffrey's ethnicity, and then returned to the same question some 30 years later, hints at something more, especially since for an earlier generation of critics the major crux of Geoffrey's work was not where its national sympathies lay, but whether Geoffrey's history was a translation or an original work.[46] Lloyd's discomfort with Geoffrey's status as Welsh seems to arise from an inability to accept that one of his own countrymen could end a history of Wales on such an inglorious note. The Breton hypothesis solves a problem that existed for Lloyd, but that did not exist for Geoffrey, at least in the same terms: "the problem of how a foreigner came to be so deeply interested in the legends of the old British time".[47] This phrasing, moreover, neatly avoids the alternative, which was perhaps even more troubling to Lloyd: the problem of how a Welshman came to chronicle, in a specious history, his nation's fall into disrepute. Lloyd's own patriotic reading of Welsh history ended with determined promise, decidedly at odds with Geoffrey's, and I would tentatively suggest Geoffrey's lack of apparent patriotism suggested to Lloyd a decidedly "non-native" feel.[48] At any rate, it is ironic that Lloyd's work, which was written, read, and received as a national panegyric, essentially deprived Wales of its most influential author. Nonetheless, despite the genesis of the Breton argument out of this nationalist framework, Lloyd's scholarly stature meant that others soon followed suit. Edmund Faral's influential study of Geoffrey begins, "In all likelihood, he was born in Monmouth in Gwent, and he was Breton by race".[49]

---

45   Pryce, *J.E. Lloyd*, pp. 95–113 and 116–18.

46   For example, it did not occur to the perceptive critic Thomas Stephens to question Geoffrey's own ethnicity, as his discussion is almost entirely devoted to proving that Geoffrey's history was largely an original work; see T. Stephens, *The Literature of the Kymry: being a critical essay on the history of the language and literature of Wales during the twelfth and two succeeding centuries*, Llandovery, 1849, pp. 307–23. Stephens, however, like other critics before Lloyd, follows Iolo Morganwg's short but fictional biography of Geoffrey (on which see below).

47   J.E. Lloyd, *A History of Wales*, p. 524.

48   J.E. Lloyd, *A History of Wales*, p. 764: "It was for a far distant generation to see that the last Prince had not lived in vain, but by his life-work had helped to build solidly the enduring fabric of Welsh nationality."

49   Faral, *LLA*, vol. 2, p. 1: "Il était né, selon toute vraisemblance, á Monmouth, dans le Gwent, et il était de race bretonne", but see also vol. 2, p. 392.

Tatlock followed this same line of thinking, adding a few other pieces of evidence: an English archbishop would not have appointed a Welsh bishop and Geoffrey seems to only display a superficial knowledge of the Welsh language.[50] This list of evidence has remained static for the last 70 years, and though the Breton argument still has its adherents – some of whom are in this volume – another look at the evidence leaves this editor unconvinced.

First, the name. Lloyd assumed that 12th-century references to "Geoffrey Arthur" meant that his father's name was Arthur, a popular Breton name at the time, but as discussed above the "Arthur" in Geoffrey's name is, to all appearances, a nickname that became attached to him because of his interest in Arthuriana.[51] Nonetheless, it is true that the name Geoffrey was not popular in Wales before the Norman Conquest, but Lloyd goes too far when he claims "a Geoffrey of this time would scarcely be a Welshman."[52] The study of prosopography has progressed a good deal since Lloyd's day, and it now seems clear that, lacking any other evidence, it is difficult to attach ethnicity to Geoffrey on the basis of his name alone. Choosing a continental name 14 or so years after a Breton became lord over Monmouth and some 34 or so years after the Norman Conquest might make Geoffrey's parents nothing more than early adopters of a name that would soon become popular in Britain. There were, after all, social benefits to a trendy name. Consider the case of an Englishman named Alfwy: Alfwy, who would have been around the same generation of Geoffrey of Monmouth, is said to have been "called Geoffrey as a mark of respect", presumably because the continental name carried more cultural caché than his given English name.[53] Moreover, Alfwy and his wife Goda abandoned good English

---

50   *LHB*, p. 443, p. 445.

51   J.E. Lloyd, *A History of Wales*, p. 524; "Geoffrey of Monmouth", p. 467, esp. n. 1. On the basis of chronology, Lloyd dismissed William of Newburgh's convincing explanation of Geoffrey's name, but see Padel, "Geoffrey of Monmouth and Cornwall", pp. 1–4 for a demonstration that "there is no objection to the assumption that William knew what he was talking about" (p. 3). Moreover, Lloyd did recognize that the Latin forms of the name were not in his favor, but he never addresses this discrepancy; see "Geoffrey of Monmouth", p. 467, n. 1. Tatlock in *LHB*, p. 439 recognized the same difficulty, but in response simply asked, "But who can assert how 'mab Arthur' would be Latinized?" It is true that a fuller study of how the English dealt with Welsh names remains a desideratum, but patronymic naming patterns were the norm in the Insular world, where names with *fitz*, *son*, and *mac* were encountered with regularity; *mab/ap/ab* would have presented little difficulty. Many English chroniclers Latinize Welsh patronymics with *filius*, suggesting that they were analyzable and therefore easily understood.

52   J.E. Lloyd, *A History of Wales*, p. 523.

53   K.S.B. Keats-Rohan, "What's in a Name? Some Reflections on Naming and Identity in Prosopography", in A.M. Jorge, H. Vilar, and M.J. Branco (eds.), *Carreiras Eclesiásticas no*

names and named their two sons "Geoffrey" and "Robert".[54] Alfwy, it would seem, knew the benefits of a fashionable name. To be clear, names sometimes are good indicators of ethnicity, but in post-Conquest England and southeastern Wales, where there would have been ample cultural pressure to adapt to the continental elite, especially among the lower nobility, a continental name on its own implies status, or sought-after status, not necessarily ethnicity. I have been writing "continental" instead of "Breton", because the name Geoffrey is itself Germanic and Norman in origin. Any popularity that it obtained among actual Bretons resulted from a similar process of appropriation, wherein Norman names became popular among non-Normans. Thus, even if "Geoffrey" were an infallible marker of ethnicity, it would be difficult to tell whether that ethnicity was Norman or Breton. Finally, there are other Geoffreys lurking in southeastern Wales in the early 12th century. At the Benedictine priory of St Mary in Monmouth, there were no fewer than eight Geoffreys.[55] The brother of Urban, the bishop of Llandaff, apparently had two names, "Stephen" and "Geoffrey".[56] And in an 1146 charter, Bishop Uhtred of Llandaff, "a Welsh bishop of the old school, being married with a daughter called Angharad", had a nephew with the decidedly new-school name, Geoffrey.[57] Are we to identify all of these men as Bretons? Instead, it is safer to say that the prestige of continental names was high in and around southeastern Wales in the late 11th and early 12th century.

As for the matter of the Welsh and bishoprics, Gerald of Wales was certainly under the impression that the Welsh were barred from episcopal office.[58] But Gerald complained about this slight a generation after Geoffrey had died, with a different political situation in place, and with no small amount of personal investment. Certainly, it is not wise to deny that anti-Welsh bias operated in the 12th century, but it is equally wise not to take Gerald's personal grievances at his word. At any rate, as Gerald well knew, his own uncle David fitz Gerald had been elected bishop of St Davids in 1148, just a few years before Geoffrey

---

Ocidente Cristão (séc. XII–XIV). Ecclesiastical Careers in Western Christianity (12th–14th c.), Lisbon, 2007, pp. 331–47, at pp. 335–36.

54   Keats-Rohan, "What's in a Name?" p. 336.

55   See *VM*, pp. 27–28. Clarke calls the popularity of the name Geoffrey "local fashion" (p. 27). He has extracted the names from the charters edited in *Chartes anciennes*, ed. Marchegay.

56   See J.R. Davies, *The Book of Llandaf and the Norman Church in Wales*, Woodbridge, 2003, at pp. 119, 129.

57   J.R. Davies, *The Book of Llandaf*, p. 55. Furthermore, in another example of the popularity of continental names, Uhtred's own son was called "Robert"; "Uhtred" is itself an early English name. For the witness, see *Llandaff Episcopal Acta, 1140–1287*, ed. D. Crouch, Cardiff, 1989, no. 2.

58   Gerald of Wales, *The Rights and Status of the Church of St Davids* i, ed. J.S. Brewer, *Giraldi Cambrensis Opera*, 8 vols., London, 1861–91, vol. 3, pp. 99–373, at pp. 120–23.

became bishop of St Asaph. With a Welsh mother and a Norman father, David could appease both sides, and his case certainly shows that Gerald's complaints do not hold true for the middle of the century (especially since David the uncle could claim to have more Welsh blood than Gerald the nephew, who only had one Welsh grandparent). In the very same year that David was elected, Nicholas ap Gwrgan became bishop of Llandaff, the other southern Welsh diocese. And although Nicholas had been a monk at the abbey of St Peter's, Gloucester for most of his life – it was not unheard of for Welshmen from southeastern Wales to seek out that abbey – he apparently had a Welsh father and acted as a go-between for the Glamorgan Welsh and the earl of Gloucester.[59] Just a few years after Archbishop Theobald had consecrated David and Nicholas, he made Geoffrey bishop of St Asaph. Finally, the archbishop had previously appointed another Welshman, Meurig, as the bishop of Bangor in 1140. Meurig had trouble with both the secular and ecclesiastical leaders of Gwynedd, falling out with his countrymen and fleeing to Canterbury.[60] Far from the impossibility of a Welshman becoming bishop, it seems that Theobald had a policy of appointing Welshmen who showed strong Anglo-Norman leanings: David had a Norman father; Meurig was reform-minded, irked Gwynedd nobility, and even swore fealty to King Stephen; Nicholas had been a monk at Gloucester and had the support of his influential former abbot, Gilbert Foliot; and Geoffrey had resided at Oxford for most of his life and his bona fides as a supporter of the Angevin cause were apparently not in question. Meurig's and David's appointments had setbacks, and their cases suggest that Geoffrey would have had to recognize the supremacy of Canterbury, which, based on how he dismissed St Davids' metropolitan aspirations in his own work, one imagines was freely given in exchange for a bishopric. In sum, I suspect, were he alive today, Archbishop Theobald's face would register astonishment if he were to read that Geoffrey would not have been granted a Welsh see "had he been a Welshman, even a well-affected Welshman", since he had indeed given three well-affected Welshmen sees on earlier occasions.[61]

59   D. Walker, "Nicholas ap Gwrgan (d. 1183), bishop of Llandaff", *Oxford Dictionary of National Biography*, Oxford University Press, 2014, <http://www.oxforddnb.com/view/article/20086> (accessed 26 June 2018). It has sometimes been assumed that Nicholas was the son of the previous bishop of Llandaff, Urban, whose name appears as "Gwrgant" in Welsh. Urban's own ethnicity is uncertain.

60   *The Acts of Welsh Rulers, 1120–1283*, ed. H. Pryce, Cardiff, 2005, p. 323; id., "Esgobaeth Bangor yn Oes y Tywysogion" [The diocese of Bangor in the age of the princes], in W.P. Griffith (ed.), *"Ysbryd Dealltwrus ac Enaid Anfarwol": Ysgrifau ar Hanes Crefydd yng Ngwynedd Ngwynedd* ["Enlightened spirit and eternal soul": essays on the history of religion in Gwynedd], Bangor, 1999, pp. 37–57, at pp. 44–45.

61   Tatlock, *LHB*, p. 443.

Furthermore, the dour ending of Geoffrey's history, at least for Welsh readers, need not imply that he was not Welsh. Geoffrey had a resourceful imagination, but historical exigency forced his hand, and even the most inventive author had to face the fact that the Welsh had lost the majority of Britain and that internecine feuding was rampant in Welsh politics. But more to the point, the assumption that Geoffrey must not be Welsh because he criticizes Welsh leaders and paints a dire picture of their current situation seems to me misguided. For Gildas, Wulfstan, or even commentators on current American politics, criticism of political leaders and the state of the nation does not necessarily imply that one does not belong to that polity. Indeed, the opposite seems more likely. The distance of 900 years tends to flatten out complicated and shifting political beliefs, but it is not too difficult to imagine that Geoffrey could both be Welsh and criticize the Wales of his day. He was not even the only Welsh historian of his generation to give an ambiguous view of his countrymen, as the author of the "Llanbadarn History", who wrote sometime before 1127, has much in common with Geoffrey's approach.[62] Similarly, the author of *Breudwyt Ronabwy* ("The Dream of Rhonabwy") has Arthur praise the ancient Welsh while disparaging the Welsh who defend Britain in later times: "[...] I feel so sad that scum such as these are protecting this Island after such fine men that protected it in the past."[63] Moreover, discussions of the ending of the *DGB* have in general failed to take account of the intellectual climate of the 12th century. Although this period has at times been termed "the Renaissance of the 12th century", it was nonetheless a deeply pessimistic era.[64] Writers decried the fallen state of humanity, and found the idealized past superior to the present, where scholarship, governance, and even love had degraded into a lamentable disarray. The ending of the *DGB* falls completely in line with the dramatic pessimism that marks so many contemporary works.[65]

Still, it is undeniable that Geoffrey does place seemingly undue importance on Brittany in his history, which indeed suggests a Breton partiality of some sort. However, a familial connection to Brittany is not the only explanation.

---

62 O.W. Jones, *"Brut y Tywysogion*: the History of the Princes and Twelfth-Century Cambro-Latin Historical Writing", *Haskins Society Journal* 26 (2014), 209–27, at pp. 222–27.

63 *Breudwyt Ronabwy: allan o'r Llyfr Coch o Hergest* [The Dream of Rhonabwy, from the Red Book of Hergest], ed. M. Richards, Cardiff, 1948, pp. 6–7: "[...] truanet gennyf vot dynyon ky vawhet a hynny yn gwarchadw yr ynys honn gwedy gwyr kystal ac a'e gwarchetwis gynt"; *The Mabinogion*, trans. S. Davies, Oxford, 2007, pp. 214–26, at p. 217.

64 C.S. Jaeger, "Pessimism in the Twelfth-Century 'Renaissance'", *Speculum* 78:4 (2003), 1151–83.

65 A similar sentiment of despair is found in the *VM*, ll. 580–85.

Another possible explanation of this apparent bias relies on the pioneering work of Katharine Keats-Rohan.[66] She has argued that the civil war of King Stephen's reign was, in large part, a war between two feuding Breton kinship groups with long-standing grievances. Her work has demonstrated that, with a few exceptions, the allegiances of the Bretons in the English civil war are entirely dependent on pre-existing kin-groups and their biases. The ins and outs of these two Breton groups are a complicated affair, but what is important for our purposes is that the Empress Matilda had the backing of a group of Bretons whose ancestral allegiances were to eastern Brittany: Dol, Cambour, and Fougères. Stephen, on the other hand, had the support of a group of Bretons led by Alan of Penthièvre, the count of Richmond. Geoffrey, for his part, has been described as a supporter of the Angevin cause during the civil war.[67] He dedicated the *DGB* to Robert, earl of Gloucester, one of the Empress's doughtiest supporters, and the work's portrayal of female rulership would seem to support Empress Matilda's right to rule.[68] Therefore, perhaps his valorization of Brittany owes more to Geoffrey's politics than to any personal connection? Such a view might help explain the favoritism he shows toward Dol, which was the heartland of those Bretons supporting the Empress, and the relative neglect of the rest of Brittany.[69] It might also explain (in part) his devotion to

---

66   K.S.B. Keats-Rohan, "The Bretons and Normans of England 1066–1154: the Family, the Fief and the Feudal Monarchy", *Nottingham Medieval Studies* 36 (1992), 42–78; ead., "William I and the Breton Contingent in the Non-Norman Conquest 1060–1087", *Anglo-Norman Studies* 13 (1991), 157–72.

67   Crick, "Monmouth, Geoffrey of (*d.* 1154/5)"; ead., "Geoffrey of Monmouth, Prophecy, and History", *Journal of Medieval History* 18:4 (1992), 357–71.

68   F. Tolhurst, *Geoffrey of Monmouth and the Translation of Female Kingship*, New York, 2013.

69   Although the Angevin cause did not pick up steam until 1139, after the Empress arrived in England and – importantly – after Geoffrey had written the *DGB*, Keats-Rohan shows that the allegiances of the Bretons in England were almost entirely predictable by their kinship groups and by grievances that went back well into the 11th century. Thus, Geoffrey would have known that the Bretons in England who saw Dol and its environs as their ancestral homeland supported the Angevin cause. For the dating of the *DGB* as a pro-Matilda text even though it was finished before the civil war proper began, see Tolhurst, *Geoffrey of Monmouth*, esp. pp. 54–73. Although Brynley Roberts follows Lloyd in claiming Breton descent for Geoffrey, he fleetingly suggests that Norman and Breton allegiances might have something to do with Geoffrey's praise of Brittany; see B.F. Roberts, "Sylwadau ar Sieffre o Fynwy a'r *Historia Regum Britanniae*" [Remarks on Geoffrey of Monmouth and the *Historia Regum Britanniae*], *Llên Cymru* 12 (1972–73), 127–45, at p. 129: "Mae'n wir fod amodau gwleidyddol y cyfnod yn ei gwneud yn anodd i awdur a geisiai nawdd llysoedd uchaf Lloegr glodfori'r Cymry, a'i bod yn naturiol iddo osod ei bwyslais ar y gangen honno o'r hen genedl a fu, rai ohonynt, yn gynghreiriaid â Normaniaid, ond er hynny, mae'n dra phosibl fod yma gydasiad ffodus o duedd bersonol a gofynion doethineb ymarferol", "It's true that the period's political conditions made it difficult for an author who wanted to

Cornwall, since the leaders of Cornwall and Devon, of West Norman descent and allied to the Bretons of Dol, also supported the Empress.[70] At any rate, space does not permit a full discussion of these matters, and I only wish to suggest that invoking Breton exceptionalism during the conflict between Stephen and Matilda had immediate political ramifications and does not necessarily point to Geoffrey's love of his own ancestral homeland.

Given all this, the idea that Geoffrey was of Breton descent because he favors Brittany and belittles Wales seems more and more like a just-so tautology designed to shoehorn Geoffrey's challenging work into a nationalist paradigm that did not exist in his own day. The central question that Lloyd sought to answer was how a Welshman could create a chronicle that praised the Bretons and offered seemingly little redemption to the Welsh, in stark contrast with Lloyd's own *A History of Wales*. An acceptable patriotic answer was to make Geoffrey a foreigner. This question, undergirded by a clunky nationalism that is ill-suited for a literary work like the *DGB*, still frames the debate on Geoffrey's ethnicity in a manner that constrains interpretations of his work. Instead, I would suggest that we approach Geoffrey's Breton favoritism with a different set of questions. First, what are the political ramifications of writing a history that gives Brittany a prominent role in British affairs during the reign of King Stephen? Does the pessimistic ending of the *DGB* work in the same way as other instances of 12th-century nostalgia and pessimism, as a call to reform and a critique of current institutions? These, to my mind at least, are more promising questions.

Other scholars prefer to see Geoffrey as simply Welsh: he was from Monmouth, gave the Welsh a lavish history, and used Welsh sources.[71] The only piece of roughly contemporary evidence that we have regarding Geoffrey's ethnicity – his origins in Monmouth aside – supports this view. A 12th-century copy of the *DGB* in Oxford, Bodleian Library, Rawlinson C. 152 contains the earliest version of a variant dedication of the *PM* to Alexander, bishop of Lincoln.[72] Here, Geoffrey's usual address to Alexander is replaced by his apology for the

---

gain the support of England's upper nobility to praise the Welsh, and it would be natural for him to emphasize that branch of the ancient race that had allied, at least in part, with the Normans, but in spite of that, it's exceedingly possible that here we are dealing with a fortunate union of personal bias and the demands of practical wisdom."

70 Keats-Rohan, "Bretons and Normans", p. 73. Further investigations along these lines might be profitably combined with the issues raised in Padel, "Geoffrey of Monmouth and Cornwall", pp. 17–20. See also E.M.R. Ditmas, "Geoffrey of Monmouth and the Breton families in Cornwall", *WHR* 6 (1972–73), 451–61.

71 For a representative overview, see Gillingham, "Context and Purposes".

72 See *DGB*, p. ix and Crick, *SC*, pp. 155–56, no. 156.

clumsiness of the prophecies in Latin, and it contains the following clause: "I, a bashful Briton, have not been taught how to sing what Merlin had sung sweetly and in verse in the British language."[73] Although this variant dedication has a decidedly Galfridian ring to it and a good textual pedigree, it is difficult to know if it is to be attributed to a variant from Geoffrey himself, or from a slightly later adapter. Yet even if it is the latter, it would show that an early fan of Geoffrey's work believed, and thought others would believe, that he spoke the same language as Merlin, and that he was thus Welsh. It must be said however that *Brito*, "Briton", is a slippery word in the 12th century, and could mean any of the Brittonic peoples, all of whose languages were most likely still mutually intelligible.[74] For that matter, attempts at uncovering Geoffrey's knowledge of Welsh have proven inconclusive, though it is clear that he had enough knowledge of the language to create Welsh etymologies and possibly access vernacular sources.[75] (As an aside, one wonders whether the reluctance to credit Geoffrey with knowledge of Welsh, in spite of his familiarity with and interest in the language, reflects modern attitudes about which languages are accessible and which are not. All things being equal, knowledge of French or English seems more freely granted to medieval polyglots than Welsh or Irish).[76] The same slipperiness appears at the end of the *VM*, where Geoffrey addresses *Britanni*, "Britons", and asks them to give a laurel wreath to him, since "[h]e is indeed your Geoffrey, for he once sang of your battles and those of your princes."[77] Although it seems as if Geoffrey is claiming that he is a "Briton", the passage is anything but straightforward.[78] However, Owain Wyn Jones, in his contribution to this volume, argues that Geoffrey was careful to distinguish

---

73   *DGB*, vii.110, n. 12–24: "pudibundus Brito non doctus canere quod in Brittannico Merlinus dulciter et metrice cecinit." Translation mine.

74   For an overview of the nomenclature, see H. Pryce, "British or Welsh? National Identity in Twelfth-Century Wales", *EHR* 116 (2001), 775–801.

75   T.D. Crawford, "On the Linguistic Competence of Geoffrey of Monmouth", *Medium Ævum* 51 (1982), 152–62.

76   For instance, Tatlock, *LHB*, p. 445 generously grants Geoffrey knowledge of English based on little evidence, but remains skeptical of Geoffrey's knowledge of Welsh, refusing to state one way or another if he spoke Breton or Welsh, even though the *DGB* shows far greater investment in these. Ben Guy reviews the evidence for Geoffrey's linguistic ability on pp. 39–42.

77   *VM*, ll. 1525–26: "Est enim vester, nam quondam prelia vestra / vestrorumque ducum cecinit."

78   See Guy's chapter in this volume.

Brittany from Britain, and in light of that distinction it would seem that these passages suggest that Geoffrey was Welsh.[79]

Geoffrey's ethnicity is also tied up in another critical debate about the *DGB*. At the beginning of the *DGB*, finding himself contemplating the ancient history of Britain, Geoffrey announces the source for his own study:

> I frequently thought the matter over in this way until Walter archdeacon of Oxford, a man skilled in the rhetorical arts and in foreign histories, brought me a very old book in the British tongue, which set out in excellent style a continuous narrative of all their deeds from the first king of the Britons, Brutus, down to Cadualadrus, son of Cadwallo.[80]

Earlier scholars sought to find Walter's book, or at least identify what texts this book might have contained, but most now recognize this passage and Walter's book as a fictional literary trope.[81] There is, however, much less agreement on how audiences are meant to imagine the origin of this fictional book. When Walter brings the book "*ex Britannia*", does he bring it out of Britain or out of Brittany? From the foregoing discussion, it should be apparent how the origin of the book becomes implicated in larger arguments about Geoffrey's ethnicity and his purpose in writing his history. However, another option for the old book's origin exists besides Britain or Brittany.[82] First, as Paul Russell observes in his contribution to this volume, the *DGB* positions itself as an extension of classical history, picking up where Dares Phrygius's *The Fall of Troy* leaves off. Indeed the opening sentence of the Prologue references the title of Dares' work, making this connection clear to aficionados of Trojan history.[83] But this is not the only reference to Dares. In fact, the passage in which Walter presents

---

79 See Jones's contribution to this volume, as well as Guy's Welsh reception article.
80 *DGB*, Prologus, 2.7–12: "Talia michi et de talibus multociens cogitanti optulit Walterus Oxenefordensis archidiaconus, uir in oratoria arte atque in exoticis hystoriis eruditus, quendam Britannici sermonis librum uetustissimum qui a Bruto primo rege Britonum usque ad Cadualadrum filium Caduallonis actus omnium continue et ex ordine perpulcris orationibus proponebat."
81 For some studies of this trope in the 12th century, see: F. Wilhelm, "Antike und Mittelalter. Studien zur Literaturgeschichte. I. Ueber fabulistische quellenangaben", *Beiträge zur Geschichte der deutschen Sprache und Literatur* 33 (1908), 286–339; M. Otter, *Inventiones: Fiction and Referentiality in Twelfth-Century English Historical Writing*, Chapel Hill, 1996, pp. 81–82; S. Harris, *The Linguistic Past in Twelfth-Century Britain*, Cambridge, 2017, pp. 91–99.
82 I would like to thank Owain Wyn Jones for spurring me to think along these lines.
83 See Russell's contribution to this volume.

the book he brought *"ex Britannia"* is explicitly modeled off the introduction of *The Fall of Troy*. Although it originally was written in Greek, *The Fall of Troy* circulated widely in western Europe in Latin translation, which was purportedly written by one Cornelius Nepos.[84] While Geoffrey has embellished his source, a comparison of the two shows that the found book passage in the *DGB* is indebted to the found book passage in *The Fall of Troy*:

Cum multa Athenis studiose agerem, inveni historicam Daretis Phrygii, ipsius manu scriptam, ut titulus indicat, quam de Graecis et Trojanis memoriae mandavit.[85]

When I was spending my time in a most studious manner at Athens, I found the history of Dares Phrygius, written by his own hand, just as the title makes clear, which he made to remember the Greeks and the Trojans.

Cum mecum multa et de multis saepius animo reuoluens in hystoriam regum Britanniae inciderem, in mirum contuli quod infra mentionem quam de eis Gildas et Beda luculento tractatu fecerant nichil de regibus qui ante incarnationem Christi inhabitauerant, nichil etiam de Arturo ceterisque compluribus qui post incarnationem successerunt repperissem, cum et gesta eorum digna aeternitate laudis constarent et a multis populis quasi inscripta iocunde et memoriter praedicentur.[86]

While my mind was often pondering many things in many ways, my thoughts turned to the history of the kings of Britain, and I was surprised that, among the references to them in the fine works of Gildas and Bede,

---

84   For a discussion the existence of the work in Greek, see A. Beschorner, *Untersuchungen zu Dares Phrygius*, Tübingen, 1992, pp. 231–43.

85   Dares Phrygius, *The Fall of Troy* Prologus, ll. 1–4, ed. F. Meister, *Daretis Phrygii. De excidio Troiae historia*, Leipzig, 1873, p. 1. The lack of a modern edition of *The Fall of Troy* has perhaps rendered Geoffrey's indebtedness to Dares slightly more difficult to detect. Meister's edition begins *"Cum multa ago Athenis curiose"*. However, I have chosen to follow the reading witnessed in several of the earliest British manuscripts; for the English and Welsh reception of Dares, see L.F. D'Arcier, *Histoire et Géographie d'un Mythe: La Circulation des Manuscrits du De Excidio Troiae De Darès le Phrygien (viiie–xve siècles)*, Paris, 2006, pp. 401–23 and pp. 402–03 for a list of British manuscripts. Of the eighteen British manuscripts from the 11th century through the 13th, seven (including the earliest two British witnesses) contain the reading *"studiose agerem"* or its close variant *"studiosissime agerem"*; see D'Arcier, *Histoire et Géographie d'un Mythe*, p. 433, n. 7. See also *First Variant Version*, ed. Wright, p. xc.

86   *DGB*, Prologus 1.1–6.

I had found nothing concerning the kings who lived here before Christ's
Incarnation, and nothing about Arthur and the many others who succeeded
after it, even though their deeds were worthy of eternal praise and are pro-
claimed by many people as if they had been entertainingly and memorably
written down.

First of all, both passages appear at the very beginning of the work. Geoffrey,
moreover, has kept some of the syntax of the first sentence of his source, though
he has added many details in additional clauses: Both passages begin with a
cum clause and an imperfect verb, and both have *multa* toward the beginning
of the sentence. (As Russell shows in his chapter, this type of half-citation is
a hallmark of Geoffrey's style). Both Cornelius and Geoffrey are involved in
studious activity: Geoffrey ponders the history of British kings, while Cornelius
studies at Athens. Both Cornelius and Geoffrey claim to be translating newly
discovered histories that aim to set the historical record straight.[87] They both
pause to reflect on the nature of translation into Latin: Cornelius announces that he has neither added nor omitted anything to his source and that his
translation will be straightforward.[88] Geoffrey, too, claims that his work will
be in a simple style, with no rhetorical embellishments.[89] And they both place
their work in opposition to more established and canonical sources. Cornelius
offers an alternative to Homer, while Geoffrey suggests that Bede and Gildas
do not have the full story either.[90] In writing his revisionist account of British
history, Geoffrey followed Cornelius's discovery of the revisionist account of
Trojan history.

Given this, the imagined source of Geoffrey's British book becomes clearer.
Cornelius claims to have found *historicam Daretis Phrygii, ipsius manu scriptam*,
"the history of Dares Phrygius, written by his own hand". Importantly, the copy
that Cornelius is translating from is Dares' own, from the ancient past. These
few words are important for Cornelius because he directly opposes the authority of Dares, who lived and fought in the Trojan war, to that of Homer, who was

---

87   Cornelius phrases his challenge as a rhetorical question to readers. Dares Phrygius, *The
     Fall of Troy* Prologus, ll. 10–16, ed. Meister, p. 1: "utrum magis verum esse existiment, quod
     Dares Phrygius memoriae commendavit, qui per id tempus ipsum vixit et militavit, quo
     Graeci Troianos obpugnarent; anne Homero credendum, qui post multos annos natus
     est, quam bellum hoc gestum est", "whether they judge what Dares Phrygius passed down
     to be more truthful – he lived and fought during the very time when the Greeks assailed ·
     Troy – or if they should believe Homer, who was born many years after the war had been
     waged."

88   Dares Phrygius, *The Fall of Troy* Prologus, ll. 4–10, ed. Meister, p. 1.

89   *DGB*, Prologus 2.12–17.

90   See note 86 above.

born much later – an eyewitness account versus Homer's poetic retelling. This small detail also accords with the way other uses of this trope function in the late classical world – the book miraculously survives from an antique past.[91] Indeed, other 12th century examples, many of which are indebted to Geoffrey, also imagine that their found books have withstood the wear of time.[92] In other words, these found books are not copies of copies; they are thought to be authentic artifacts from the past, contemporaneous with the events described therein. The *"Britannia"* that produced Geoffrey's book is neither Wales/Britain nor Brittany, but the Britannia that Geoffrey's history describes – the famed ancient kingdom over which Arthur and other kings ruled. That is, after all, why Geoffrey mentions that the book is *uetustissimus*, "very old"; Walter's book has survived from that fabled past to Geoffrey's own day.[93] The *Britannia* of the *DGB*, a sovereign kingdom with a single crown, ruled by the native Britons, is the same as imagined by contemporary Welsh historians.[94] A book surviving from that cherished period would electrify Geoffrey's historically-minded Welsh contemporaries. That is, after all, exactly what happened.

------

91   S. Merkle, "Telling the True Story of the Trojan War: The Eyewitness Account of Dictys of Crete", in J. Tatum (ed.), *The Search for the Ancient Novel*, Baltimore, 1994, pp. 183–96; id., "The Truth and Nothing but the Truth: Dictys and Dares", in G.L. Schmeling (ed.), *The Novel in the Ancient World*, Leiden, 1996, pp. 563–80; K. Ní Mheallaigh, "The 'Phoenician Letters' of Dictys of Crete and Dionysius Scytobrachion", *The Cambridge Classical Journal* 58 (2012), 181–93. I would like to thank Joseph Howley for providing me with these references.

92   *Gesta abbatum monasterii Sancti Albani, a Thoma Walsingham, regnante Ricardo Secundo, ejusdem ecclesiæ præcentore, compilata*, ed. H.T. Riley, London, 1867–69, pp. 26–27; *The Anglo-Saxon Chronicle: a Collaborative Edition. Vol. 7, MS. E*, ed. S. Irvine, Cambridge, 2004, s.a. 963, pp. 57–58 (see pp. xciv–xcvi for a discussion of the 12th-century interpolation of the miraculous discovery of the *"writes"*); J. Byron Smith, *Walter Map and the Matter of Britain*, Philadelphia, 2017, pp. 166–67.

93   At the end of the history, Geoffrey warns his peers to stay silent on the matters of ancient British history, "since they don't possess that book in the British language which Walter the archdeacon of Oxford brought from Britannia ...", "cum non habeant librum illum Britannici sermonis quem Walterus Oxenefordensis archidiaconus ex Britannia aduexit ..." (translation mine). Reeve translates *"ex Britannia aduexit"* as "carried out of Brittany", but I would suggest that *"ex"* here is being used to indicate the source of the book, and that by "brought out of Britannia" Geoffrey asks us to imagine Walter recovering the book from antiquity. See *DMLBS*, s.v. *ex*, def. 6. Of course, Geoffrey could also be imagining a different account of textual transmission at the end of the *DGB*; he does, indeed, seem to delight in ambiguity of this sort.

94   Roberts, "Sylwadau", pp. 139–45; id., "Geoffrey of Monmouth and the Welsh Historical Tradition", *Nottingham Mediaeval Studies* 20 (1976), 29–40. The idea of an ancient, unified British kingdom with a king ruling from London also existed in Welsh law; see R.C. Stacey, *Law and the Imagination in Medieval Wales*, Philadelphia, 2018, pp. 29–55, esp. pp. 34–35.

The Welsh accepted Geoffrey, or at least his work, as their own. Four 13th-century Welsh translations of Geoffrey's *DGB* exist, and more appeared in the following centuries. These translations tend to be on the faithful side, though the only English translation available for a modern audience is the highly idiosyncratic Cotton Cleopatra version, which has given non-Welsh readers the unfortunate impression that the Welsh needed to drastically alter Geoffrey's text to make it palatable; they did not.[95] Moreover, Geoffrey had a pervasive influence on Welsh literature which begins to appear almost immediately after his work circulated. One Welshman, Madog of Edeirnion, produced his own Latin recension of the *DGB*, and provided a prefatory poem that is one of the few surviving direct commentaries on Geoffrey's work produced by the medieval Welsh.[96] For Madog, Geoffrey's history is nothing less than *dulcia*, "sweets", to Welsh readers, providing nourishment and pleasure.[97] Similarly, it would seem that the redactor of the First Variant Version also recognized that the *DGB* could be read as pro-Welsh, and they perhaps even grasped the danger it posed for accepted English historiography, since one of its central adjustments is to make Geoffrey's history fall into line with other English historical sources.[98] Overall, the zeal with which the Welsh took to Geoffrey's history led John Gillingham to observe that "no medieval Welshman made the mistake of thinking Geoffrey anti-Welsh."[99] Those elements in Geoffrey's work that have made modern scholars suspect that it does not support Welsh interests – its Breton favoritism and its ending – seem not to have troubled the medieval Welsh in the least.

Another possibility is that Geoffrey's stance in the *DGB*, or even perhaps in his own life, is one of studied ambiguity, a perspective that other writers from the March of Wales, the borderlands between Wales and England, also adopted.[100] Indeed, he is typically grouped with two other 12th-century Latin

---

95   *Brut y Brenhinedd: Cotton Cleopatra Version*, ed. and trans. J.J. Parry, Cambridge, MA, 1937.

96   The poem appears in Cardiff, Central Library, 2.611, fols. 9v–10r, and was copied into Cambridge, Corpus Christi College, 281. For the edition, see Geoffrey of Monmouth, *De gestis Britonum*, ed. J. Hammer, *Geoffrey of Monmouth. Historia regum Britanniae. A variant version edited from manuscripts*, Cambridge, MA, 1951, p. 18.

97   Geoffrey of Monmouth, *De gestis Britonum*, ed. Hammer, p. 18, l. 24.

98   R.W. Leckie, Jr., *The Passage of Dominion: Geoffrey of Monmouth and the Periodization of Insular History in the Twelfth Century*, Toronto, 1981; *First Variant Version*, ed. Wright, pp. lxx–lxxviii.

99   Gillingham, "Context and Purposes", p. 31.

100 For Gerald of Wales, see R. Bartlett, *Gerald of Wales, 1146–1223*, Oxford, 1982, pp. 16–29 and J.J. Cohen, *Hybridity, Identity, and Monstrosity in Medieval Britain: On Difficult Middles*, New York, 2006, pp. 77–108. For Walter Map, see J. Byron Smith, *Walter Map*, pp. 11–28. For Geoffrey's own ambiguity, see Otter, *Inventiones*.

writers from the Anglo-Welsh borderlands, forming a trio of Marcher writers whose names all happen to begin with the letter *g*: Geoffrey of Monmouth, Gerald of Wales, and Walter Map. All three of these authors engage with Wales and its past in ways that are not easily classifiable. At times, they seem to admire aspects of the Welsh, at others, they denigrate them, and elsewhere they seem to take great joy in explaining the Welsh for a wider audience. In spite of the similarities, Geoffrey's intellectual project remains far different from the other two. His interest in British history is deeper and, in actuality, more serious than Gerald's, whose many talents were often self-serving, and Walter's, who had no aspirations to write something that could pass for serious history. In Welsh matters, if Walter is typically thought of as a brilliant anecdotalist and Gerald as a crafty personal propagandist and sly ethnographer, then Geoffrey of Monmouth might be said to be – paradoxically – the author of both the master narrative and the counter narrative of Welsh history, to use two important terms from postcolonial studies. He provided the Anglo-Norman elite with a master narrative that was used to justify the subjugation of Wales, while at the same time he gave the Welsh an illustrious national pedigree that contained within it the possibility of future glories.

If Geoffrey's intention was indeed to play both sides as a Marcher might, to be both Welsh and Anglo-Norman (as Monmouth itself was), then he succeeded tremendously, since current scholarly opinion of his work is as varied as its medieval British reception. The following essays bear out this ambiguity, especially with regard to Geoffrey's "British book", his ethnicity, and his political leanings. In these matters, we have preferred to let the medley of scholarly opinion stand in the open, rather than hide disagreement through editorial fiat. This policy, however, means that several authors, though they seldom agree, address the same passages and problems. Given the variety that these interpretations bring to the volume, we hope that readers approach these occasional repetitions with forgiving eyes.

Finally, like many popular authors, a few erroneous traditions have arisen about Geoffrey. The most egregious, and interesting, is found in the so-called *Aberpergwm Brut*, a product of Edward Williams (better known as Iolo Morganwg).[101] Iolo was, among other things, a brilliant forger of early Welsh material, and in his *Aberpergwm Brut* one can see his inventive mind at work:

> In the same year, Geoffrey ab Arthur, the family priest of William ab Rhobert, became bishop, but, before he could enter into his office, he

---

101   For Iolo's forgeries, see M.A. Constantine, *The Truth against the World: Iolo Morganwg and Romantic Forgery*, Cardiff, 2007.

died in his house in Llandaff, and he was buried in the church there. He was a man whose equal in learning, knowledge, and every divine virtue could not be found. He was the foster son of Uchtryd, the archbishop of Llandaff, and his nephew on his brother's side, and for his learning and knowledge he was given the archdeaconry in St Teilo's in Llandaff, where he was the teacher of many scholars and princes.[102]

But this is a mess of lies.[103] Somewhat more credible is the occasional suggestion that Geoffrey was responsible for the Book of Llandaff, a gospel book that also contains saints' lives and charters and other material about the history of southeastern Wales, much of it of debatable authenticity.[104] While few scholars today would attribute the Book of Llandaff to Geoffrey, the identification is in truth not so far afield, and it sits uncomfortably here in the same paragraph as Iolo Morganwg's brazen forgery. Geoffrey's supposed authorship of the book is based on some real similarities. Both works show skill in researching and manipulating Welsh historical sources, and both demonstrate a conspicuous ingenuity when it comes to crafting a vision of the past. Indeed, Geoffrey knew material in the Book of Llandaff, but he did not follow it, and he occasionally ridicules the diocese's pretentions in his own work.[105] For this reason, it seems highly unlikely that he had a hand in the Book of Llandaff, though both he and its authors were involved in the same project of pasting together historical sources to create a coherent narrative of the British past.

Even without Iolo Morganwg's romantic biography, modern readers who are approaching Geoffrey and his work for the first time might be tempted to classify Geoffrey as an eccentric, even exotic, figure. After all, a mysterious writer

---

102 *The Myvyrian Archaiology of Wales*, ed. O. Jones, E. Williams, and W.O. Pughe, 3 vols., Denbigh, 1801–07, vol. 2, p. 566: "Yn yr un flwyddyn, y gwnaethpwyd Galffrai ab Arthur (offeiriad Teulu Wiliam ab Rhobert) yn Escob, eithr cyn ei fyned yn ei Ansawdd efe a fu farw yn ei Dy yn Llan Dâf, ac a cladded yn yr Eglwys yno. Gwr ydoedd ni chaid ei ail am ddysg a gwybodau, a phob campau dwyfawl. Mab Maeth oedd ef i Uchtryd Archescob Llan Daf, a nai mab brawd iddaw, ac am ei ddysg a'i wybodau y doded arnaw Febyddiaeth yn Eglwys Teilaw yn Llan Daf lle y bu ef yn Athraw llawer o ysgolheigion a phendefigion." Translation mine.

103 See J.E. Lloyd, "Geoffrey of Monmouth", pp. 462–64.

104 *The Text of the Book of Llan Dâv: Reproduced from the Gwysaney Manuscript*, ed. J.G. Evans and J. Rhŷs, Oxford, 1893, pp. xviii–xxvii; C. Brooke, "The Archbishops of St Davids, Llandaff, and Caerleon-on-Usk", in N.K. Chadwick et al. (eds.), *Studies in the Early British Church*, Cambridge, 1958, pp. 201–42 (repr. in *The Church and the Welsh Border in the Central Middle Ages*, ed. D.N. Dumville (Studies in Celtic History, 8), Woodbridge, 1986, 16–49); Roberts, "Sylwadau", pp. 129–30; *VM*, pp. 31–33.

105 For Geoffrey's knowledge of the Book of Llandaff, see Guy's contribution to this volume.

who called the borderlands home, who possessed deep learning, and who traf-
ficked in ancient stories of a forgotten past certainly exercises a pull upon the
imagination. As attractive as that portrait is, Geoffrey is better understood as a
natural product of multicultural and multilingual 12th-century Britain. Indeed,
as Geoffrey himself wrote, the Britain of his day was "inhabited by five peoples, the Normans, the Britons, the Saxons, the Picts and the Scots".[106] Even
this description falls short of the actual cultural heterogeneity of 12th-century
Britain, since Geoffrey here is constrained by his stylized adaptation of Bede
and he omits Breton immigrants, Flemish settlers, and Jewish inhabitants, to
name just a few. Far from being an outlier, his mélange of Welsh, English, and
Norman influences shows him to be part of the mainstream of the intellectual culture of his day. From Monmouth to Oxford, dying with his eyes turned
toward a bishopric in northern Wales, no doubt still turning over the ancient
British past in his mind, Geoffrey embodies the complex, often vexed, cosmo-
politanism of his day. In turn, we hope that the various essays presented in
this volume, written by scholars at all stages of their careers and from several
disciplines, do justice to Geoffrey's own diverse influences and inspirations.

---

106   *DGB*, i.5.42–44: "… quinque inhabitatur populis, Normannis uidelicet atque Britannis,
      Saxonibus, Pictis, et Scotis".

PART 1

Sources

∵

CHAPTER 1

Geoffrey of Monmouth's Welsh Sources

Ben Guy

Introduction: Britons, Bretons, and the Unworthy Welsh

It has long been recognized that Geoffrey of Monmouth drew on sources originating from the Brittonic-speaking world. This fact is frequently mentioned in scholarly literature, though it is rarely accompanied by detailed supporting evidence. It was, after all, with the Britons, both contemporary and ancient, that Geoffrey was primarily concerned, and it was to the Britons that he looked for source material concerning the history of *Britannia*.[1]

One might legitimately ask whether it is possible, or even necessary, to distinguish between sources that originated from different Brittonic-speaking regions. It would appear that the three surviving Brittonic languages had not yet become mutually unintelligible by the 12th century. Gerald of Wales commented on this matter in the first recension of his *Description of Wales*, completed around 1194, some 60 years after the propagation of the *De gestis Britonum*:

> Indeed, Cornwall and Brittany use almost the same language, which is, nevertheless, still intelligible to the Welsh in many and almost in all cases, on account of their original relationship. Inasmuch as it is less refined and rougher, it is closer to the ancient British language, or so I think myself.[2]

---

1   To avoid confusion, I shall continue to employ the adjective "Brittonic" rather than "British" when referring to the medieval and ancient Britons. I avoid the term "Celtic", which is meaningless in this context.

2   Gerald of Wales, *The Description of Wales* i.6, ed. J.F. Dimock, *Giraldi Cambrensis Opera*, 8 vols., London, 1861–91, vol. 6, pp. 153–228, at p. 177: "Cornubia vero et Armorica Britannia lingua utuntur fere persimili, Kambris tamen, propter originalem convenientiam, in multis adhuc et fere cunctis intelligibili. Quae, quanto delicata minus et incomposita magis, tanto antiquo linguae Britannicae idiomati magis, ut arbitror, appropriata." Translation adapted from Gerald of Wales, *The Journey Through Wales* and *The Description of Wales*, trans. L. Thorpe, *Gerald of Wales: The Journey through Wales / The Description of Wales*, Harmondsworth, 1978, p. 231. For the dates of the recensions of *The Description of Wales*, see R. Bartlett, *Gerald of Wales, 1146–1223*, Oxford, 1982, p. 216.

Modern linguists would agree with Gerald's observation about the mutual intelligibility of Medieval Cornish, Breton, and Welsh, and his consideration of the relationship between the modern languages and their ancient Brittonic precursor furnishes an interesting and early example of philological speculation.[3] But linguistic factors had not forestalled the advent of a divergence in perceived identity and history. While all concerned were aware of their supposed descent from the ancient Britons, centuries of geographical separation and divergent historical development had caused the Britons of Cornwall, Brittany, and Wales to view themselves as distinct groups within the loosening Brittonic family. This process seems not to have been especially advanced by the 9th century. The Welsh Latin *Historia Brittonum*, written in 829 or 830, refers to the Bretons simply as *Brittones Armorici*, "Armorican Britons", and no particular word is used to differentiate the Britons of Wales from Britons elsewhere.[4] The Welshman Asser, writing later in the 9th century, simply uses the word *Britannia*, without further specificity, to describe Wales, just as the same word was used at that time to describe Brittany.[5] Each was unambiguously a "land of the Britons". By the middle of the 12th century, however, circumstances had definitively changed, and Welsh writers were rapidly turning their *Britannia* in the west of Britain into *Wallia*, "Wales", and their fellow Britons into *Walenses*, "Welsh", responding in part to new terminological distinctions introduced by their Anglo-Norman neighbors.[6] On the other hand, the Britons of Brittany, in contrast to the Welsh, were able to continue flourishing successfully within the Anglo-Norman realm as self-identifying *Britones*, preserving the earlier terminology, which remains in use today.[7]

---

3   L. Fleuriot, "Langue et société dans la Bretagne ancienne", in J. Balcou and Y. Le Gallo (eds.), *Histoire littéraire et culturelle de la Bretagne*, 3 vols., Paris, 1987, vol. 1, pp. 7–28, at p. 9; id., *Dictionnaire des gloses en vieux Breton*, Paris, 1964, pp. 13–14; J.E.C. Williams, "Brittany and the Arthurian Legend", in R. Bromwich, A.O.H. Jarman, and B.F. Roberts (eds.), *The Arthur of the Welsh: The Arthurian Legend in Medieval Welsh Literature* (Arthurian Literature in the Middle Ages, 1), Cardiff, 1991, pp. 249–72, at pp. 253–54; J. Loth, *L'Émigration bretonne en Armorique du Ve au VIIe siècle de notre ère*, Rennes, 1883, p. 92.

4   *Historia Brittonum* (Harley 3859) §27, ed. Faral, *LLA*, pp. 2–62, at p. 21 (hereafter referred to as *HB* (Harl. 3859)).

5   E.g. Asser, *Life of King Alfred* §79, ed. W.H. Stevenson, *Asser's Life of King Alfred. Together with the Annals of Saint Neots*, Oxford, 1959, pp. 63 and 65. See too the translation in S. Keynes & M. Lapidge, *Alfred the Great: Asser's Life of King Alfred and Other Contemporary Sources*, Harmondsworth, 1983, pp. 93–94.

6   H. Pryce, "British or Welsh? National Identity in Twelfth-Century Wales", *EHR* 116 (2001), 775–801, at pp. 792–96.

7   P. Galliou & M. Jones, *The Bretons*, Oxford, 1991, pp. 181–82.

During this time, nobody was more keenly aware of such developments than Geoffrey of Monmouth. Had he not possessed an intricate understanding of the cultural self-awareness of different groups of Britons in his own time, he would not have been so careful to distinguish between the origins of the Cornish, Bretons, and Welsh in his history. Most remarkable is the distinction made between the Cornish and the rest of the Britons. Geoffrey attributed to the Cornish an ethnic distinction that arose prior to the foundation of Britain by Brutus. While Brutus and his band of Trojan exiles were navigating the Tyrrhenian sea, they encountered another group of Trojan exiles, descended through four generations from those who had fled from Troy with Antenor:

> Their leader was called Corineus, a just man and a good advisor, of great character and boldness ... When the Trojans realised their common ancestry, they took Corineus and his people with them. Later they were called Cornish after their chief and in every battle proved more helpful to Brutus than the rest.[8]

Geoffrey later explains how, following the establishment of Brutus in Britain and the naming of his people as "Britons" after him, Corineus founded Cornwall, which he called Corineia after himself.[9] Although Cornwall thereafter remains part of Britain for the remainder of Geoffrey's account, the Cornish never lose their unique proclivity for excellence, as has been discussed by Oliver Padel.[10]

The Bretons and the Welsh, on the other hand, are, in no uncertain terms, latter-day Britons. The Bretons are the descendants of those Britons settled in Armorica by Maximianus, then king of Britain, during his campaign of conquest in Gaul:

> He [Maximianus] issued an edict to the effect that a hundred thousand common people should be gathered to be sent to him, as well as thirty thousand knights to protect them from hostile attack in the country they were to inhabit. Once all this was organised, he spread them throughout

---

8   *DGB*, i.17.330–36: "Erat eorum dux Corineus dictus, uir modestus, consilii optimus, magnae uirtutis et audaciae ... Agnita itaque ueteris originis prosapia, associauerunt illum sibi nec non et populum cui praesidebat. Hic, de nomine ducis postmodum Cornubiensis uocatus, Bruto in omni decertatione prae ceteris auxilium praestabat."
9   *DGB*, i.21.462–67.
10   O.J. Padel, "Geoffrey of Monmouth and Cornwall", *CMCS* 8 (1984), 1–28.

all the regions of Armorica, making it a second Britain [*altera Britannia*], which he presented to Conanus Meriadocus.[11]

Thenceforth, the Britons of Armorica in Geoffrey's narrative are called *Armorici Britones*, "Armorican Britons", or more simply *Armoricani*, and Brittany is *altera Britannia*, *minor Britannia*, or *Armoricana Britannia*. The extent to which Geoffrey favored the Armorican Britons over the Insular Britons is well known, and has led to the plausible suggestion that Geoffrey was himself of Breton origin.[12] The contrast between Geoffrey's portrayal of the Insular Britons and the Armorican Britons following the establishment of Brittany is emphasized most starkly in the speech that Geoffrey puts into the mouth of Salomon, king of the Armorican Britons, in his address to Caduallo, the recently exiled king of the Insular Britons:

> When the people of this new Britain of mine lived with your subjects in your Britain, it was the mistress of all the neighbouring realms, and there was no one who could conquer it except the Romans. And although they subjugated it for a time, the Romans were driven out shamefully, their governors lost and slain. But after my subjects came here, led by Maximianus and Conanus, the remaining Britons never again enjoyed the privilege of maintaining uninterrupted control of their land. Many of their leaders upheld the ancient prowess of their fathers, but more proved to be weaker heirs, who forgot it completely when their enemies attacked. Thus I am grieved by the weakness of your people, since we share the same origins and you are called British, just as we are, we who bravely protect this land you see from the attacks of all its neighbours.[13]

---

11   *DGB*, v.86.350–55: "Fecit itaque edictum suum ut centum milia plebanorum in Britannia insula colligerentur qui ad eum uenirent, praeterea triginta milia militum qui ipsos infra patriam qua mansuri erant ab hostili irruptione tuerentur. Cumque omnia perpetrasset, distribuit eos per uniuersas Armorici regni nationes fecitque alteram Britanniam et eam Conano Meriadoco donauit."

12   J.E. Lloyd, *A History of Wales from the Earliest Times to the Edwardian Conquest*, 2 vols., 3rd ed., London, 1939, vol. 2, pp. 523–24; id., "Geoffrey of Monmouth", *EHR* 57 (1942), 460–68, at pp. 466–68; Tatlock, *LHB*, p. 443; B.F. Roberts, "Sylwadau ar Sieffre o Fynwy a'r *Historia Regum Britanniae*" [Remarks on Geoffrey of Monmouth and the *Historia Regum Britanniae*], *Llên Cymru* 12 (1972–73), 127–45, at pp. 128–29. For further discussion of this matter, see the Introduction above, pp. 11–19.

13   *DGB*, xi.194.332–44: "Cum gens huius meae Britanniae una cum uestratibus in uestra Britannia cohabitaret, dominabatur omnium prouincialium regnorum, nec fuit uspiam populus praeter Romanos qui eam subiugare quiuisset. Romani autem, licet eam ad tempus subditam habuissent, amissis rectoribus suis ac interfectis cum dedecore expulsi

Through their continued degeneracy, the Insular Britons did not retain their cherished Brittonic nomenclature for long:

> As their culture ebbed, they were no longer called Britons, but Welsh, a name which owes its origin to their leader Gualo, or to queen Galaes or to their decline ... The Welsh, unworthy successors to the noble Britons, never again recovered mastery of the whole island, but, squabbling pettily amongst themselves and sometimes with the Saxons, kept constantly massacring the foreigners or each other.[14]

Geoffrey therefore emphasizes his claimed historical distinctions between the Cornish, Bretons, and Welsh with clarity and consistency. The Cornish are a special group among the Britons, but their separate origin deep in legendary history serves to underscore their distinction from the Britons proper, and as a result they are not made to bear any responsibility for the Britons of the present. The Bretons and the Welsh, on the other hand, are the direct products of the later stages of Geoffrey's historical arc: the former, the descendants of the Armorican Britons, have courageously maintained the spirit and name of their ancient forebears, whereas the latter, the descendants of the Insular Britons, have grown feeble through civil war, and have lost their right to the Brittonic name, becoming, instead, Welsh. By casting the Cornish as the remote descendants of Corineus's merry band, Geoffrey effectively exonerates them from the charges that he is leveling against the Welsh, making the latter the unique witnesses to the decline of ancient *Britannia*.

It is essential to appreciate Geoffrey's presentation of the various Brittonic peoples in order to interrogate his use of source material emanating from the Brittonic regions properly. For instance, when Geoffrey refers to his infamous "very old book in the British tongue", which, as stated at the very end of the *DGB*, had been brought by Walter, archdeacon of Oxford, *"ex Britannia"*, it

---

abscesserunt. Sed postquam Maximiano et Conano ducibus ad hanc uenerunt prouinciam, residui qui remanserunt numquam eam deinceps habuerunt gratiam ut diadema regni continue haberent. Quamquam enim multi principes eorum antiquam patrum dignitatem seruarent, plures tamen debiliores heredes succedebant, qui eam penitus inuadentibus hostibus amittebant. Vnde debilitatem populi uestri doleo, cum ex eodem genere simus et sic Britones nominemini sicut et gens regni nostri, quae patriam quam uidetis omnibus uicinis aduersatam uiriliter tuetur."

14   *DGB*, xi.207.592–94 and 598–600: "Barbarie etiam irrepente, iam non uocabantur Britones sed Gualenses, uocabulum siue a Gualone duce eorum siue a Galaes regina siue a barbarie trahentes ... Degenerati autem a Britannica nobilitate Gualenses numquam postea monarchiam insulae recuperauerunt; immo nunc sibi, interdum Saxonibus ingrati consurgentes externas ac domesticas clades incessanter agebant."

seems probable, given the overall thrust of Geoffrey's narrative, that *Britannia* here is intended to refer to Brittany rather than Wales.[15] Although Welshmen writing in Latin in the late 11th and early 12th centuries could still refer to Wales as *Britannia*,[16] Geoffrey makes it quite clear that, within the terms of his history, Wales had long forfeited that hallowed name, and that the only remaining Brittonic *Britannia* was *altera Britannia*, or Brittany. It is partly for this reason that efforts to equate Geoffrey's avowed source-book with a manuscript containing a historical compilation similar to the expanded version of the *Historia Brittonum* found in London, British Library, Harley 3859 must ultimately fail.[17] Although Geoffrey certainly did use a compilation of exactly that type, as is discussed below, he is unlikely to have found it in a book brought out of Brittany. Geoffrey's "very old book in the British tongue" is no more than a rhetorical device intended to lend his account credence and mystery, as has long been recognized by scholars.[18] This is not to say that Geoffrey did not use Breton sources, nor even that Walter did not provide Geoffrey with some ancient book to translate,[19] but, as with so many other aspects of Geoffrey's work, one cannot assume that his description of that book was designed for anything other than rhetorical impact; it is not a statement of historical fact. Nevertheless, whether Geoffrey's book existed in reality or merely in rhetoric, there seems little reason to doubt that Geoffrey intended his contemporaries to believe that he had translated a book written in the Brittonic language. William of Newburgh, for one, bemoaned that Geoffrey had sought to translate fictitious accounts of the Britons into Latin.[20]

---

15   *DGB*, Prologus 2.9–10 and xi.208.605. Alternatively, Joshua Byron Smith has suggested that the phrase *"ex Britannia"* refers to ancient Britain, rather than contemporary Brittany or Wales. See Introduction above, pp. 21–24.

16   Pryce, "British or Welsh?" pp. 777–78.

17   E.g. S. Piggott, "The Sources of Geoffrey of Monmouth: I. The 'Pre-Roman' King-List", *Antiquity* 15 (1941), 269–86.

18   See now S. Harris, *The Linguistic Past in Twelfth-Century Britain*, Cambridge, 2017, pp. 91–99. In the Introduction above, pp. 21–24, Joshua Byron Smith argues that Geoffrey borrowed the "ancient British book" device from Dares Phrygius.

19   See also the similar comments in Roberts, "Sylwadau", pp. 134–35 and Harris, *Linguistic Past*, pp. 93–94. Further evidence for Walter's book is provided by Geffrei Gaimar: see I. Short, "Gaimar's Epilogue and Geoffrey of Monmouth's *Liber vetustissimus*", *Speculum* 69:2 (1994), 323–43. See also Le Saux's chapter in this volume.

20   William of Newburgh, *The History of English Affairs* i.3, ed. and trans. P.G. Walsh and M.J. Kennedy, *William of Newburgh: The History of English Affairs, Book I (Edited with Translation and Commentary)*, Warminster, 1988, pp. 28–29; cf. B. Guy, "Gerald and Welsh Genealogical Learning", in G. Henley and A.J. McMullen (eds.), *Gerald of Wales: New Perspectives on a Medieval Writer and Critic*, Cardiff, 2018, 47–61, at p. 52; Harris, *Linguistic Past*, p. 95.

Perhaps it was Geoffrey's chosen presentation of the divergent historical development of the Insular and Armorican Britons that led him to promulgate the idea that his most lauded authority, Gildas, was formerly a resident of Brittany. Geoffrey used Gildas's *The Ruin of Britain* extensively, as has been expertly demonstrated by Neil Wright.[21] In the *DGB*, Geoffrey refers to Gildas by name no less than seven times, usually attributing to him some account or information that can be found nowhere in Gildas's work (nor, for the most part, in the *Historia Brittonum*, which Geoffrey might also have known to be attributed to Gildas).[22] His personal convictions aside, it probably suited the temper of Geoffrey's work to locate such a venerable Briton as Gildas in Brittany rather than Britain; Wales certainly would not do. In the *VM*, Merlin explains to his sister that he wishes to speak with Telgesinus (Geoffrey's version of the legendary Welsh poet Taliesin), who had recently returned "from Armorican parts", where he had been receiving instruction from Gildas.[23] The idea that Gildas resided in Brittany was not invented by Geoffrey. It is found in the earliest *Life of St Gildas*, written in St-Gildas-de-Ruys in Brittany, probably in the 11th century.[24] Not everyone agreed; Gildas does not retire to Brittany in the *Life of St Gildas* composed by Caradog of Llancarfan for Glastonbury Abbey, sometime in the middle of the 12th century, presumably because this would have contradicted his claim that Gildas retired to Glastonbury.[25] In this instance, it would no doubt have suited Geoffrey to follow a Breton view over a Welsh view.

In Geoffrey's terms, it seems, Gildas was no Welsh source. Geoffrey in fact makes no mention whatsoever of having drawn on any source material of Welsh provenance. And yet he most assuredly did so, and to a considerable

---

21   N. Wright, "Geoffrey of Monmouth and Gildas", *AL* 2 (1982), 1–40; id., "Geoffrey of Monmouth and Gildas Revisited", *AL* 5 (1985), 155–63. See also his "Geoffrey of Monmouth and Bede", *AL* 6 (1986), 27–59.

22   See below, pp. 49–50.

23   *VM*, ll. 684–88: "de partibus Armoricanis".

24   *Life of St Gildas* §16, ed. and trans. H. Williams, *Two Lives of Gildas: By a Monk of Ruys, and Caradoc of Llancarfan*, Felinfach, 1990, pp. 36–37 (repr. from H. Williams, ed., *Gildas*, 2 parts (Cymmrodorion Record Series, 3), London, 1899–1901, vol. 2, pp. 315–420, at pp. 346–47).

25   J.S.P. Tatlock, "Caradoc of Llancarfan", *Speculum* 13:2 (1938), 139–52, at pp. 140–42; id., "The Dates of the Arthurian Saints' Legends", *Speculum* 14:3 (1939), 345–65, at pp. 352–53, n. 1; A. Gransden, "The Growth of the Glastonbury Traditions and Legends in the Twelfth Century", *The Journal of Ecclesiastical History* 27 (1976), 337–58, at pp. 340 and 346 (repr. in J.P. Carley (ed.), *Glastonbury Abbey and the Arthurian Tradition*, Cambridge, 2001, 29–53); J. Scott, *The Early History of Glastonbury: An Edition, Translation and Study of William of Malmesbury's De Antiquitate Glastonie Ecclesie*, Woodbridge, 1981, p. 3.

degree. Might it be that Geoffrey deliberately suppressed any acknowledgement of his debt to Welsh materials in order to emphasize the role of his putative "Breton" book as the sole conduit of Brittonic historical authority? How
could Geoffrey's *Gualenses* have accurately preserved the ancient traditions of
their Brittonic forebears when they had become so unworthy, having lost the
very name of Briton? It may have been a problem for Geoffrey's designs that,
although he wished to emphasize the martial prowess and moral dignity of
the Bretons over the Welsh, the overwhelming majority of written sources of
Brittonic origin that he could discover seem to have been written in Wales, and
concerned Wales to a far greater degree than the other Brittonic regions. This
is suggested most persuasively by Geoffrey's spellings of personal and place-
names, which almost invariably display Old Welsh rather than Old Breton
features.[26] The bias toward Welsh displayed by Geoffrey's spellings might be
the product of a comparative dearth of relevant Breton sources available to
him. Such a dearth is certainly apparent today, for there are few native compositions surviving from early medieval Brittany aside from saints' lives and charters. Indeed, the seeming near-absence of extant written sources from early
medieval Brittany relating to the activities of kings, perhaps as noticeable in
Geoffrey's day as it is now, may be more than an accident of textual survival. It
has been argued that vertical power structures in Brittany were relatively weak
during the early Middle Ages and were such as to obviate the need for the types
of king-populated historical texts that provided intellectual legitimization for
medieval states and their rulers. By contrast, texts of this kind were actively
produced in early medieval Wales, where regal authority was much better established throughout the period.[27] The legitimizing historical texts in question include origin legends, chronicles, and genealogies, genres of writing that
gained wide currency during the Middle Ages because of their utility for conferring legitimacy upon contemporary political authority. It was no doubt the
Brittonic purview and linguistic orientation of such texts that made them so

---

26   T.D. Crawford, "On the Linguistic Competence of Geoffrey of Monmouth", *Medium Ævum*
      51 (1982), 152–62, at p. 156. For example, one finds the diphthong /au/ < /ɔ:/ spelled *au*, a
      development peculiar to Welsh among the Brittonic languages, in *Cledaucus, Ebraucus,
      Enniaunus, Gualauc, Kaerebrauc, Maglaunus, Mapcledauc,* and *Rudaucus.* For this
      sound change, see P. Sims-Williams, "The Emergence of Old Welsh, Cornish and Breton
      Orthography, 600–800: the Evidence of Archaic Old Welsh", *BBCS* 38 (1991), 20–86, at
      pp. 63–71.
27   C. Brett, "Breton Latin Literature as Evidence for Literature in the Vernacular, A.D. 800–
      1300", *CMCS* 18 (1989), 1–25, at pp. 19–25; ead., "Soldiers, Saints, and States? The Breton
      Migrations Revisited", *CMCS* 61 (2011), 1–56, at pp. 38–43. For a recent view of the origins
      of this situation in Brittany (with references to earlier literature), see B. Guy, "The Breton
      Migration: a New Synthesis", *Zeitschrift für celtische Philologie* 61 (2014), 101–56.

useful to Geoffrey for his great literary venture. On the other hand, it is worth acknowledging that the bias toward Welsh sources may be illusory: if the lack of comparable texts from early medieval Brittany is indeed an accident of textual survival and does not reflect what would have been available to Geoffrey, then we might underestimate Geoffrey's use of such sources, especially considering the dangers highlighted below surrounding arguments from silence.

The remainder of this chapter examines the sources of Welsh origin that Geoffrey can be shown to have used in his work. The first section considers Geoffrey's linguistic abilities and the extent to which his access to Welsh source material might have been hindered by a language barrier. The second section explores his use of the *Historia Brittonum*, and of the annals and genealogies that accompanied the version of the *Historia Brittonum* at his disposal. The third section briefly draws attention to Geoffrey's access to ecclesiastical texts of Welsh provenance, such as Rhygyfarch's *Life of St David* and *De situ Brecheniauc* ("Concerning the Establishment of Brycheiniog"). The fourth and final section turns to the contentious issue of the relationship between Geoffrey's work and Welsh poetry.

1   The British Tongue

> Brutus named the island of Britain after himself and called his followers Britons. He wanted to be remembered for ever for giving them his name. For this reason the language of his people, previously known as Trojan or "crooked Greek", was henceforth called British.[28]

So Geoffrey describes the origins of the British tongue. It has been pointed out that his designation of British as *curuum Graecum*, "crooked Greek", relies on an etymology of *Cymraeg* (the Welsh word for the Welsh language) that could only arise from direct knowledge of Welsh.[29] *Cymraeg* has here been etymologized as Welsh *cam Roeg*, literally "crooked Greek". The loss of the *G* in *Roeg* (from Welsh *Groeg*) is not a liberty on Geoffrey's part; it is a grammatically regular change in the second element of a compound in Welsh, showing that the person responsible for the etymology had more than a superficial knowledge

---

28   *DGB*, i.21.459–62: "Denique Brutus de nomine suo insulam Britanniam appellat sociosque suos Britones. Volebat enim ex diriuatione nominis memoriam habere perpetuam. Vnde postmodum loquela gentis, quae prius Troiana siue curuum Graecum nuncupabatur, dicta fuit Britannica."

29   Harris, *Linguistic Past*, p. 93; Crawford, "On the Linguistic Competence of Geoffrey", pp. 155–57; Roberts, "Sylwadau", p. 137, n. 45; Tatlock, *LHB*, p. 445, n. 39.

of the language. Unfortunately, one cannot now know whether Geoffrey invented the etymology or was informed about it by another Welsh speaker.

Various attempts have been made to determine Geoffrey's linguistic ability, and in particular his competence in one or more of the Brittonic languages.[30] This has been deemed important for establishing the veracity of his claim that the *DGB* was translated from a "very old book in the British tongue", and for judging the likelihood that he could have employed other vernacular sources with success. However, the value of framing the problem in this way is highly questionable. It has already been noted that Geoffrey's alleged source-book is a rhetorical device, rendering somewhat futile the attempt to establish whether he could feasibly have translated it. Secondly, it is always hazardous to claim that Geoffrey "misunderstood native material" and extrapolate from that that his command of Welsh (or Breton) was less than firm.[31] Geoffrey had no interest in reproducing his source material exactly. At every stage in his works, he crafted the accounts that he found in his sources so that they blended seamlessly with the majestic progression of his imagined history. One underestimates the intimacy between Geoffrey and his sources at great peril.

Geoffrey's self-proclaimed epithet, *Monemutensis*, "of Monmouth", seems to imply that he was brought up in or around Monmouth on the southern border between Wales and England, presumably in the late 11th or early 12th century.[32] This is significant because, by 1075, the lord of Monmouth was Wihenoc of La Boussac, one of the many Breton followers of William the Conqueror.[33] Such a state of affairs might provide a plausible context for Geoffrey's positive portrayal of the Bretons. It is indeed quite possible that Geoffrey's own family arrived in Wales in the wake of the establishment of Wihenoc as lord of Monmouth. As Sir Rees Davies astutely observed, "Geoffrey's father may well have been a first- or second-generation Breton settler in Monmouth, an area

---

30   Tatlock, *LHB*, p. 445; Crawford, "On the Linguistic Competence of Geoffrey".

31   B.F. Roberts, "Geoffrey of Monmouth and Welsh Historical Tradition", *Nottingham Medieval Studies* 20 (1976), 29–40, at p. 36; cf. id., "Geoffrey of Monmouth, *Historia regum Britanniae*, and *Brut y Brenhinedd*", in Bromwich et al. (eds.), *The Arthur of the Welsh*, pp. 97–116, at pp. 109–10; Piggott, "Sources", p. 282.

32   For a good overview of Geoffrey's life, see J.C. Crick, "Monmouth, Geoffrey of (*d.* 1154/5)", *Oxford Dictionary of National Biography*, Oxford University Press, 2004, <http://www.oxforddnb.com/view/article/10530> (accessed 27 June 2018).

33   H. Guillotel, "Une famille bretonne au service du Conquérant: Les Baderon", in *Droit privé et institutions régionals: Etudes historiques offertes à Jean Yver*, Paris, 1976, pp. 361–66; K.S.B. Keats-Rohan, "The Bretons and Normans of England 1066–1154: the Family, the Fief and the Feudal Monarchy", *Nottingham Medieval Studies* 36 (1992), 42–78, at p. 49; ead., *Domesday People: A Prosopography of Persons Occurring in English Documents, 1066–1166. I. Domesday Book*, Woodbridge, 1999, pp. 54–55.

rich in opportunities, formal and informal, for contacts between settlers and natives."[34]

What would such a scenario imply about Geoffrey's linguistic abilities? It might be instructive to indulge in a little speculation, if only to realize the plurality and complexity of the possibilities. If Geoffrey's father were indeed a first- or second-generation Breton settler in Monmouth, it is very likely that T.D. Crawford was correct to assert that Geoffrey's first language would probably have been Anglo-Norman French.[35] Fluency in French would have been an essential tool for enabling Geoffrey to interact with friends and pa-trons in Monmouth and in his later home in Oxford. It is indeed entirely pos-sible that Geoffrey's hypothetical "Breton" ancestors were French- rather than Breton-speaking before they came to Britain.[36]

On the other hand, it is equally possible that Geoffrey's family was Breton-speaking, and that Breton remained the private language of the family for a few generations after they had settled in Monmouth, even though French would have dominated their interactions in the public sphere. One suspects that Geoffrey's perceived competence in Breton is implied in his claim to have translated the "very old book in the British tongue". Although, as discussed above, the claim is unlikely to have been literally true, its rhetorical impact was presumably predicated on its assumed plausibility to contemporaries. The claim was read by those who knew Geoffrey and whom Geoffrey wanted to judge him favorably. Whatever he claimed about the contents of Walter's al-leged Breton book, it is difficult to believe that Geoffrey would have professed himself to his associates as the translator of a long Breton narrative had he no observable familiarity with the language.

Whatever his family's origins, it cannot be doubted that Geoffrey, growing up in Monmouth, would have had a long acquaintance with Welsh. If Geoffrey were a Breton-speaker of any competence, one would imagine that Welsh would not have been unduly challenging for him, and that he could have rap-idly become comfortable reading the written language, especially since the spelling systems of Old Breton and Old Welsh (and indeed Old Cornish) were so similar. Even if Geoffrey knew nothing of Breton, Welsh would not have been inaccessible to him. No more evidence of Geoffrey's linguistic adept-ness is required than the substantial Latin compositions that flowed from his

---

34   R.R. Davies, *The Age of Conquest: Wales, 1063–1415*, Oxford, 2000, p. 106.

35   Crawford, "On the Linguistic Competence of Geoffrey", pp. 152–53. Tatlock similarly com-
      mented that "no doubt one of his vernaculars was Norman-French": Tatlock, *LHB*, p. 445.

36   Cf. Roberts, "Sylwadau", p. 128, n. 9; Crawford, "On the Linguistic Competence of Geoffrey",
      p. 157.

pen, which afford ample testimony to his confident Latinity. Had he applied the same ability to Welsh in support of his academic interests, he might have acquired considerable facility with at least the written language, if not also the spoken. It is likely that Geoffrey received his early education in one of the churches of south-east Wales, and we have other evidence (such as the vernacular description of Llandaff's privileges, known as *Braint Teilo*) for the cultivation of written Welsh in scholarly circles in the south-eastern churches of Geoffrey's day.[37]

Though most of the comments above are ultimately speculative, they should hopefully make the point that Geoffrey was, at the least, multilingual and proficient at linguistic study. Modern scholars will never be in a position to judge Geoffrey's exact knowledge of Welsh or Breton. The only safe assumption is that language would not have been an insurmountable barrier between Geoffrey and the sources that he wished to access. With this in mind, we may venture forth, with Geoffrey, into *Gualia*.

2   The History of the Britons

> He was grieved, however, that his brother Nennius lay between life and death, seriously injured; for the wound Caesar had inflicted in their duel had proved incurable.[38]

It has always been clear to students of Geoffrey that the *Historia Brittonum* was one of the primary sources of inspiration for the *DGB*. The *Historia Brittonum* is an account of the Britons written in Latin and produced in Gwynedd, in North Wales, in 829 or 830. One of the three branches of the *Historia Brittonum*'s textual tradition contains a prologue in which the author of the text identifies himself as one Nennius, but the authenticity of this prologue has been disputed by modern critics.[39] Geoffrey's Nennius, brother of Lud and Cassibellaunus,

---

37   For *Braint Teilo*, see now P. Russell, "*Priuilegium Sancti Teliaui* and *Breint Teilo*", *Studia Celtica* 50 (2016), 41–68.

38   *DGB*, iiii.57.78–81: "Angebatur tamen ex alia parte dolore, quia frater suus Nennius, letaliter uulneratus, in dubio uitae iacebat; uulnerauerat enim illum Iulius in supradicto congressu et plagam inmedicabilem intulerat."

39   David Dumville argued that the prologue was a later concoction in which the work was attributed to Nennius because of his fame as a scholar of the Britons: D.N. Dumville, "'Nennius' and the *Historia Brittonum*", *Studia Celtica* 10/11 (1975–76), 78–95. Others have argued that the prologue is more likely to have been a part of the original *Historia Brittonum*: P.J.C. Field, "Nennius and his History", *Studia Celtica* 30 (1996), 159–65; B. Guy,

is unlikely to bear any relation to the author of the *Historia Brittonum*. Then again, it is something of a pleasing irony to read of Geoffrey's Nennius fighting so valiantly against Caesar. The author of the *Historia Brittonum* was, after all, the first known writer to portray Caesar's assault on Britain from a point of view sympathetic to the Britons, following almost nine centuries of historiographical defamation that began with Caesar's own account in *The Gallic Wars*. As Geoffrey remarks, "Nennius congratulated himself on being able to exchange even a single blow with so famous a man."[40]

The *Historia Brittonum* is a synthetic account of the Britons from their origins to their wars with the English kings in the 7th century, assembled from a variety of sources, including origin legends, saints' lives, and genealogies, as well as popular Latin texts such as Jerome's translation of Eusebius's universal chronicle, Gildas's *The Ruin of Britain*, and Bede's *Ecclesiastical History*.[41] Many of the most famous incidents in Geoffrey's history appear in their earliest recorded forms in the *Historia Brittonum*. These include the settlement of Britain by Britto/Brutus; the foundation of Brittany by Maximianus; the tale of Vortigern, Hengist, and the Treachery of the Long Knives; the account of the two embattled dragons of Snowdonia; and, of course, the catalogue of Arthur's victories against the Saxons. In the *Historia Brittonum*, these events are only loosely connected, and do not act as components of an integrated political narrative. Geoffrey, however, wove the *Historia Brittonum*'s disjointed episodes into a coherent story with uncanny sleight of hand.

It is argued below that Geoffrey did not draw on the *Historia Brittonum* indiscriminately. Instead, he carefully incorporated some episodes, altered others, and left some out altogether. He was nevertheless acutely conscious of the original meanings of the episodes and indicated as much in his renditions of them. There is evidence that Geoffrey was familiar with the "Harleian" recension of the *Historia Brittonum*, as well as with the Welsh annals and genealogies that are interpolated into the copy of the *Historia Brittonum* in the Harley manuscript from which the recension is named. For instance, the annals probably enabled Geoffrey to deduce his famous date for the battle of Camlan, while the genealogies offered Brittonic name forms that were used in many parts of

"The Origins of the Compilation of Welsh Historical Texts in Harley 3859", *Studia Celtica* 49 (2015), 21–56, at pp. 45–54.

40 *DGB*, iiii.56.57–58: "Nennius ultra modum laetatur se posse uel solum ictum tanto uiro ingerere."

41 For general accounts of the text, see D.N. Dumville, "*Historia Brittonum*: An Insular History from the Carolingian Age", in A. Scharer and G. Scheibelreiter (eds.), *Historiographie im frühen Mittelalter*, Wien, 1994, pp. 406–34; id., "The Historical Value of the *Historia Brittonum*", *AL* 6 (1986), 1–26.

the history. Moreover, since Geoffrey's copy of the genealogies corresponded in certain respects to the version used in places and in texts connected to Caradog of Llancarfan, it is suggested that the latter might have provided Geoffrey with his copy of the Harleian recension of the *Historia Brittonum*, interpolated with the relevant annals and genealogies.

A good example of how Geoffrey borrowed episodes from the *Historia Brittonum*, but recrafted them to suit his own designs, is provided by the legend of Vortigern and the two dragons.[42] Many aspects of the story are shared by the versions in the *Historia Brittonum* and the *DGB*. In both, the Saxons rebel against Vortigern, who flees westward to Snowdonia. There he orders a fortress to be built, but on each day the previous day's construction work has mysteriously disappeared. To remedy the situation, his *magi* advise that the foundations of the fortress be sprinkled with the blood of a boy without a father. Such a boy is duly located, but, once he is brought into Vortigern's presence, the boy questions the advice of the *magi* and instructs the king to dig underneath the foundations to discover the real explanation for the problem. The boy had rightly perceived that the foundations of the fortress are unstable because they had been built over a pool of water. Within the pool, moreover, are two dragons, who begin to fight once they are revealed. As the boy explains, one dragon is red, representing the Britons, while the other is white, representing the Saxons. The combat between the two signifies the struggle for supremacy in Britain. The *Historia Brittonum* briefly explains that the red dragon will ultimately be victorious, but in the *DGB* matters are made rather more complex by the introduction of Merlin's long prophecy.

Although the versions told in the *Historia Brittonum* and the *DGB* run in parallel insofar as the elements described above are concerned, Geoffrey's subtle changes of emphasis impart significant new shades of meaning to the tale. In the *Historia Brittonum*, the basis of the story is onomastic. It is obvious that the fortress in question is Dinas Emrys in Snowdonia, since at the end of the story the fatherless boy reveals his name to be *Ambrosius* (the Latin name from which Welsh *Emrys* derives), and consequently, as the narrator explains, "he was seen to be Emrys Wledig", who was presumably a well-known figure of legend in North Wales in the early 9th century.[43] The story thus "explains" how the fortress acquired its name. Furthermore, because it was evidently understood that the Welsh name *Emrys* was equivalent to Latin *Ambrosius*, the name allowed the author of the *Historia Brittonum* to fashion an additional link between the story of the fortress and the period of Vortigern's kingship. The boy

---

42   *HB* (Harl. 3859) §§40–42, ed. Faral, vol. 3, pp. 30–33.

43   *HB* (Harl. 3859) §42, ed. Faral, vol. 3, p. 32: "Embreis Guletic ipse videbatur."

reveals that his father was actually a consul of the Roman people, implying that this Ambrosius was the Ambrosius Aurelianus of Gildas, whose parents are specified to have been Roman nobles.[44] We are then told that Vortigern gave Ambrosius "the fortress with all the kingdoms of the western region of Britain, and he himself with his *magi* went to the northern region".[45] It thus appears that the author of the *Historia Brittonum* used the story to explain the transfer of power in western Britain from Vortigern to Ambrosius.

Geoffrey was certainly aware of the political implication of the *Historia Brittonum*'s version of the story, but he put his own spin on the tale by re-focusing it on the prophet Merlin. In Geoffrey's version, Merlin takes the place of Ambrosius as the fatherless boy summoned to the fortress in Snowdonia. At one point, Geoffrey alludes to the *Historia Brittonum*'s portrayal of events by ambiguously referring to the boy as *Ambrosius Merlinus*; one suspects that he understood the onomastic implication of the *Historia Brittonum*'s story and wished to preserve that feature in his account, even if it no longer provided a central element.[46] But the aspect of the *Historia Brittonum*'s story that most enthralled Geoffrey was the boy's ability to explain the meaning of the warring dragons, for it was this that prompted the introduction of Merlin's prophecy in Geoffrey's version. Geoffrey's Merlin is based on Myrddin, the prophet of Welsh legend, who is discussed in more detail below. It has been suggested that Geoffrey changed the name to "Merlin" in order to evade the unfortunate coincidence in spelling between Myrddin and the French word *merde*, meaning "excrement".[47] Geoffrey inserts a subtle indication of his awareness of the Welsh name by having Vortigern's envoys find Merlin not in *campus Elleti* in Glywysing, as in the *Historia Brittonum*, but in *Kaermerdin*, "Carmarthen", the second element of which in the Welsh version of the name (modern Welsh "Caerfyrddin") is indeed *Myrddin*.

Geoffrey again demonstrates his appreciation of the *Historia Brittonum*'s version of the story in the way that he ends his account. Due to the change in the identity of the boy, the story can no longer end with Vortigern's granting power in western Britain to Ambrosius. However, Geoffrey shapes his narrative so as to preserve the same chronological sequence, and in the first sentence following Merlin's final prophecy he immediately states that "As soon as the

---

44 Gildas, *The Ruin of Britain* §25.3, ed. and trans. M. Winterbottom, *Gildas: The Ruin of Britain and Other Works* (Arthurian Period Sources, 7), Chichester, 1978, pp. 28 and 98.

45 *HB* (Harl. 3859) §42, ed. Faral, vol. 3, p. 32: "arcem ... cum omnibus regnis occidentalis plagae Brittanniae, et ipse cum magis suis ad sinistralem plagam pervenit."

46 *DGB*, Prophetiae 111.31.

47 Cf. Tatlock, *LHB*, p. 175. For an alternative suggestion, see P. Russell, *Vita Griffini filii Conani. The Medieval Latin Life of Gruffudd ap Cynan*, Cardiff, 2005, pp. 125–26.

next day dawned, Aurelius Ambrosius and his brother landed, accompanied by ten thousand knights."[48] Ambrosius had set off, it should be noted, from Brittany; Geoffrey here introduces the Bretons into the story even when they were lacking entirely from his source.

Just as interesting as the episodes of the *Historia Brittonum* that Geoffrey incorporated into his history are the episodes that he silently discarded. These include the *Historia Brittonum*'s account of St Germanus and Cadell Dyrnllug, which in the *Historia Brittonum* was designed to provide an explanation for the origins of the kings of Powys.[49] Germanus is given only very summary treatment in the *DGB*, presumably because Geoffrey did not wish to dwell upon the Pelagian heresy, which the historical Germanus was sent to Britain to eradicate.[50] It is an interesting feature of Geoffrey's history that he omits all mention of Powys, despite his evident enthusiasm for employing authentic-looking names for the various ancient kingdoms, lordships, and peoples in his narrative. Perhaps Powys could not be integrated neatly into the *DGB*'s geopolitical scheme; Geoffrey is quite explicit at one point that the *Venedoti* are the *Norgualenses*, "North Welsh", and the *Demetae* are the *Suthgualenses*, "South Welsh".[51] The *VM* is equally clear about the division of Wales between the *Venedoti* and the *Demetae*, leaving no room for the *Historia Brittonum*'s *Povisi*.[52] Geoffrey's reluctance to grant Powys a place in his history presumably reflects the kingdom's relative lack of importance in the centuries prior to Geoffrey's lifetime; it was probably only during the early decades of the 12th century that Powys re-emerged as a significant Welsh kingdom.[53]

Geoffrey's account of Arthur's early battles against the Saxons owes much to the *Historia Brittonum*, but, again, he has not followed his source slavishly. While the *Historia Brittonum* names nine sites at which twelve battles were fought by Arthur, Geoffrey selected only four: the river Duglas, the province of Lindsey, the forest of Colidon, and the hillside in the region of Bath (*pagus Badonis*).[54] More significantly, Geoffrey added a crucial element to Arthur's

---

48   *DGB*, viii.118.22–23: "Nec mora, cum crastina dies illuxit, applicuit Aurelius Ambrosius cum germano suo, decem milibus militum comitatus."

49   *HB* (Harl. 3859) §§32–35, ed. Faral, vol. 3, pp. 23, 25, and 27.

50   *DGB*, vi.101.369–76. For a recent treatment of St Germanus and Britain, see A.A. Barrett, "Saint Germanus and the British Missions", *Britannia* 40 (2009), 197–217.

51   *DGB*, ix.156.329–30.

52   *VM*, ll. 21 and 26.

53   D. Stephenson, *Medieval Powys: Kingdom, Principality and Lordships, 1132–1293*, Woodbridge, 2016, ch. 1. The idea of a tripartite division of Wales between Gwynedd, Powys, and Deheubarth only emerged from the second half of the 12th century, as witnessed by the writings of Gerald of Wales and the Welsh lawbooks.

54   *HB* (Harl. 3859) §56, ed. Faral, vol. 3, pp. 38–39; *DGB*, ix.143–47.

campaigns that was entirely absent from the *Historia Brittonum*: the Bretons. Here we are confronted with an indication of the potential difficulty that Geoffrey may have encountered while writing a history of the Britons which was favorable to the Bretons but which used primarily Welsh source material. Following the establishment of the Armorican Britons by Maximianus, the *Historia Brittonum* makes no further mention of Armorica or its Brittonic-speaking inhabitants. For Geoffrey, however, the Armorican Britons become a constant source of strength and support for the Insular Britons. Arthur is no exception. Having no choice but to lift the siege of York due to the overwhelming numbers of the enemy, Arthur and his counselors determine to seek the assistance of Arthur's nephew Hoel, king of the Armorican Britons, who dutifully comes to support his uncle with 15,000 men. Only then is Arthur able to continue his campaigns and, together with Hoel, defeat the Saxons in the province of Lindsey.

A more surprising source for the *DGB* is the *Historia Brittonum*'s collection of *mirabilia*, "wonders" or "marvels". Shortly after Arthur's final victory over the Scots and Picts, Hoel finds himself amazed by the 60 rivers, islands, crags, and eagles' nests of Loch Lomond, where Arthur had recently blockaded his enemies for a fortnight.[55] The same features are attributed to Loch Lomond in the *Historia Brittonum*.[56] In a curious aside, Arthur then tells Hoel about two other wonders, which also derive from the *Historia Brittonum*.[57] It is not at all clear why these descriptions have been included in Geoffrey's narrative.

A debt to the *Historia Brittonum* more profound than the sum of the individual episodes transferred into the *DGB* is implicit in the overall scope and conception of Geoffrey's historical project. Geoffrey's account ranges from the fall of Troy to the death of Cadualadrus in 689. Throughout this entire period, Geoffrey's Britons enjoy almost unbridled sovereignty over the island of Britain. Geoffrey's decision to extend the supremacy of the Britons as far as the late 7th century had profound consequences for the ways in which later writers conceived the advent of English rule in Britain.[58] Yet it was a decision that

---

55 *DGB*, ix.149–50.

56 *HB* (Harl. 3859) §67, ed. Faral, vol. 3, p. 58. See A. Woolf, "Geoffrey of Monmouth and the Picts", in W. McLeod (ed.), *Bile ós Chrannaibh: A Festschrift for William Gillies*, Ceann Drochaid, 2010, pp. 269–80, at pp. 273–76. Note that John Morris, in his translation of the *Historia Brittonum*, incorrectly translates *stagnum Lumonoy* as "Loch Leven" rather than "Loch Lomond": *Historia Brittonum*, ed. and trans. J. Morris, *Nennius: British History and the Welsh Annals* (Arthurian Period Sources, 8), London, 1980, p. 40. For a possible source of Morris's confusion, see Woolf, "Geoffrey of Monmouth", p. 275.

57 *HB* (Harl. 3859) §§69–70, ed. Faral, vol. 3, p. 59.

58 R.W. Leckie, Jr., *The Passage of Dominion: Geoffrey of Monmouth and the Periodization of Insular History in the Twelfth Century*, Toronto, 1981.

accorded with his Welsh sources. The *Historia Brittonum*, though written in the 9th century, does not mention any events later than the battle of Nechtansmere in 685,[59] and the latest king of the Britons mentioned is Cadwaladr son of Cadwallon, who was "reigning among the Britons after his father" during the reign of Oswiu, king of Northumbria (642–70).[60] This is the Cadwaladr who appears in the early medieval pedigree of the kings of Gwynedd in North Wales, and indeed the *Historia Brittonum* designates his father Cadwallon as *rex Guenedotae regionis*, "king of the kingdom of Gwynedd", on two separate occasions.[61] The significance of Cadwaladr's terminal position within the context of the *Historia Brittonum* is very difficult to judge, because the part of the text dealing with the 7th century is structured around a collection of early English genealogies and a Northumbrian king-list, and the fragments of narration interpolated therein lack continuity and integration.[62] However, the significance of the *Historia Brittonum*'s reluctance to peer beyond the reign of Cadwaladr should not be overlooked. An important point of comparison is the 10th-century Welsh prophetic poem *Armes Prydein Vawr* ("The Great Prophecy of Britain").[63] This poem is the earliest surviving text in which a certain

---

59   *HB* (Harl. 3859) §57, ed. Faral, vol. 3, p. 39.

60   *HB* (Harl. 3859) §64, ed. Faral, vol. 3, p. 43: "regnante apud Brittones post patrem suum".
      8th-century figures do occur in the *Historia Brittonum* among its genealogies of English
      kings, but they are accorded no attention beyond the simple mention of their names.
      See D.N. Dumville, "The Anglian Collection of Royal Genealogies and Regnal Lists",
      Anglo-Saxon England 5 (1976), 23–50, at p. 45; K.H. Jackson, "On the Northern British
      Section in Nennius", in N.K. Chadwick (ed.), *Celt and Saxon: Studies in the Early British
      Border*, Cambridge, 1963, rev. ed. 1964, pp. 20–62, at pp. 22 and 60–61.

61   *HB* (Harl. 3859) §61 and §64, ed. Faral, vol. 3, pp. 41 and 43. For the genealogy, see *Early
      Welsh Genealogical Tracts*, ed. P.C. Bartrum, Cardiff, 1966, p. 9.

62   D.N. Dumville, "On the North British Section of the *Historia Brittonum*", WHR 8 (1977),
      345–54, at pp. 349–54; K.H. Jackson, "On the Northern British Section", pp. 25–27;
      H.M. Chadwick & N.K. Chadwick, *The Growth of Literature*, 3 vols., Cambridge, 1932–40,
      vol. 1, p. 155.

63   For this poem, see *Armes Prydein Vawr*, ed. and trans. I. Williams and R. Bromwich, *Armes
      Prydein: The Prophecy of Britain from the Book of Taliesin*, Dublin, 1972; D.N. Dumville,
      "Brittany and *Armes Prydein Vawr*", *Études celtiques* 20 (1983), 145–59; A. Breeze, "*Armes
      Prydein*, Hywel Dda, and the Reign of Edmund of Wessex", *Études celtiques* 33 (1997), 209–
      22; H. Fulton, "Tenth-Century Wales and *Armes Prydein*", *Transactions of the Honourable
      Society of Cymmrodorion*, new series, 7 (2001), 5–18; C. Etchingham, "Viking-Age Gwynedd
      and Ireland: Political Relations", in K. Jankulak and J. Wooding (eds.), *Ireland and Wales in
      the Middle Ages*, Dublin, 2007, pp. 149–67; G. Isaac, "*Armes Prydain Fawr* and St David", in
      J.W. Evans and J.M. Wooding (eds.), *St David of Wales: Cult, Church and Nation*, Woodbridge,
      2007, pp. 161–81; N. Tolstoy, "When and Where was *Armes Prydein* Composed?" *Studia
      Celtica* 42 (2008), 145–49; T.M. Charles-Edwards, *Wales and the Britons, 350–1064*, Oxford,
      2013, pp. 519–35.

Cadwaladr appears as one of the two deliverers of the Britons, who are prophesied to return to lead the Britons to victory over the English. The other deliverer
is a certain Cynan. The identities of these two characters are nowhere made
explicit in *Armes Prydein Vawr*, but Geoffrey, who probably knew the poem, or
one very like it (as discussed below), offered a solution in the *VM*: Cadwaladr is
Cambrorum dux, "leader of the Welsh", and Cynan is from *Armorica*.[64] In other
words, he seems to identify the two deliverers of Welsh prophecy with his own
Cadualadrus and Conanus Meriadocus. It is impossible to know if Geoffrey's
assumptions or stipulations matched the ideas of Welsh composers of prophecy, but the position of Cadwaladr son of Cadwallon, upon whom Geoffrey's
Cadualadrus is partially based, as the latest king of the Britons in the *Historia
Brittonum* may well indicate that Geoffrey's identification of the Cadwaladr of
prophecy is correct. If Cadwaladr son of Cadwallon had acquired the role of
prophetic deliverer in Wales no later than the 9th or 10th centuries, one wonders what the perceived historical significance of his reign to the Welsh during
the same early period was. Whatever it was, it seems likely that Geoffrey was
privy to it, and seized upon it as the basis for the final act of his history.

Geoffrey certainly made good use of the *Historia Brittonum*; but which
version of the text did he use? There are five primary Latin recensions of the
Historia Brittonum, each of which had a different pattern of circulation during
the Middle Ages. The five recensions are as follows:
- The Harleian recension: probably best represents the original 9th-century
  text, and circulated in manuscripts particularly in south-eastern England in
  the late 11th and 12th centuries.[65]
- The Gildasian recension: the vulgate text from the 12th century to the end
  of the Middle Ages, similar to the Harleian recension but truncated and attributed to Gildas.[66]
- The Vatican recension: created in England in 943 or 944, during the reign of
  King Edmund; the text was abbreviated and reworded from an English point
  of view, and appears in manuscripts from the 11th century onwards.[67]

---

64   *VM*, ll. 967–68.

65   See Guy, "Origins"; D.N. Dumville, "The *Liber Floridus* of Lambert of Saint-Omer and the
    Historia Brittonum", *BBCS* 26 (1975), 103–22. No critical text of the Harleian recension has
    been published, but for the text of the fullest manuscript witness, see *HB* (Harl. 3859).

66   See D.N. Dumville, "Celtic-Latin Texts in Northern England, c. 1150–c. 1250", *Celtica* 12 (1977),
    19–49, at p. 19. For descriptions of the manuscripts of the recension, see D.N. Dumville,
    "The Textual History of the Welsh-Latin *Historia Brittonum*", 3 vols., unpublished PhD the-
    sis, University of Edinburgh, 1975, vol. 2, ch. 6. The latter is now available online: <https://
    www.era.lib.ed.ac.uk/handle/1842/8972> (accessed 22 June 2019).

67   See D.N. Dumville, *Historia Brittonum 3: The "Vatican" Recension*, Cambridge, 1985.

– The Chartres recension: a fragmentary text related to the Vatican recension, preserved only on flyleaves taken from a Breton manuscript of the first half of the 11th century.[68] The Chartres manuscript, along with the flyleaves, was unfortunately destroyed in 1944.
– The Nennian recension: redacted in its extant form in the second half of the 11th century, possibly in Abernethy in Scotland, and preserved only in extracts added to the margins of Cambridge, Corpus Christi College, 139 between 1164 and 1166; closely related to *Lebor Bretnach*, the Irish version of the *Historia Brittonum*.[69]

It was suggested by Theodor Mommsen that Geoffrey used a copy of the Gildasian recension, because at one point in the DGB Geoffrey states that the miracles of St Germanus were described by Gildas in his book.[70] Gildas's *The Ruin of Britain* does not mention St Germanus, but the *Historia Brittonum* does: it describes a number of miracles performed by Germanus during his sojourn in Britain. The implication might be that Geoffrey used a version of the *Historia Brittonum* ascribed to Gildas. However, as Alex Woolf has pointed out, Geoffrey's account of Germanus actually derives from Bede rather than the *Historia Brittonum*.[71] More significantly, Michael Reeve has adduced textual evidence which shows that Geoffrey cannot have relied solely on a manuscript of the Gildasian recension, because he accurately quotes the *Historia Brittonum* at a point when the extant witnesses to the Gildasian recension are faulty.[72] Therefore, while it is possible that Geoffrey was aware of the attribution of the *Historia Brittonum* to Gildas in some manuscripts, we should not read too much into Geoffrey's direct references to Gildas, especially since, as Neil Wright has cautioned, most such references are spurious and have no basis in any text attributed to Gildas.[73]

---

68   See D.N. Dumville, "An Irish Idiom Latinised", *Éigse* 16 (1975/76), 183–86. For the text, see Faral, *LLA*, vol. 3, pp. 4–28; F. Lot, *Nennius et l'Historia Brittonum*, Paris, 1934, pp. 227–31.

69   See T.O. Clancy, "Scotland, the 'Nennian' Recension of the *Historia Brittonum*, and the *Lebor Bretnach*", in S. Taylor (ed.), *Kings, Clerics and Chronicles in Scotland 500–1297: Essays in Honour of Marjorie Ogilvie Anderson on the Occasion of her Ninetieth Birthday*, Dublin, 2000, 87–107; Dumville, "Nennius". For the *Lebor Bretnach*, see the edition *Lebor Bretnach: The Irish Version of the Historia Brittonum Ascribed to Nennius*, ed. A.G. Van Hamel, Dublin, 1932, and the textual discussion in D.N. Dumville, "The Textual History of the *Lebor Bretnach*: a Preliminary Study", *Éigse* 16 (1976), 255–73.

70   DGB, vi.101.375–76; T. Mommsen, *Chronica Minora saec. IV. V. VI. VII. Vol. 3* [Minor Chronicles of the 4th, 5th, 6th, 7th centuries, Vol. 3] (Monumenta Germaniae Historica, Auctores Antiquissimi, 13), Berlin, 1898, p. 133; Piggott, "Sources", p. 272.

71   Woolf, "Geoffrey of Monmouth", p. 274.

72   DGB, p. lviii (esp. n. 62).

73   Wright, "Geoffrey of Monmouth and Gildas", pp. 22–24.

One distinguishing feature of the fullest manuscript of the Harleian recension is the appearance of a set of annals and a collection of genealogies embedded within the text, between the chronological calculations in chapter 66 and the list of the cities of Britain in chapter 66a. The annals are known as either the "Harleian chronicle" or the "A-text of *Annales Cambriae*", and the genealogies as the "Harleian genealogies".[74] In their extant forms, both the chronicle and the genealogies belong to the middle of the 10th century. It has been argued that the annals and genealogies were a feature of the archetype of the Harleian recension, but that for various reasons they were not included in the few other surviving manuscript witnesses to the recension.[75] Both the annals and genealogies were used by Geoffrey, making it likely that he had access to a version of the Harleian recension of the *Historia Brittonum*.

Geoffrey's use of the annals is less obvious than his use of the genealogies. An event noted in the early section of the *DGB*, during the reign of Riuallo, may contain a textual echo: it is said that "While he was king, it rained blood [*cecidit pluuia sanguinea*] for three days and people died from a plague of flies."[76] This may be compared with the annal for 689 in the Harleian chronicle, which reads *pluuia sanguinea facta est in Brittannia*, "it rained blood in Britain."[77] Another verbal borrowing may be seen in Geoffrey's reference to *Margadud rex Demetarum*, "Margadud king of the Demetae", at the battle of Chester (which Geoffrey places in Leicester); this probably emulates the obituary of *Morgetiud rex Demetorum*, "Maredudd king of the Demeti", in the annal for 796 in the Harleian chronicle.[78]

A chronicle like the Harleian chronicle was almost certainly the source for Geoffrey's famous date for the battle of Camlan. The *DGB* contains only three precise dates: the date of Lucius's death in 156, the date of Camlan in

---

74 Both are edited in E. Phillimore, "The *Annales Cambriæ* and the Old-Welsh Genealogies from *Harleian MS.* 3859", *Y Cymmrodor* 9 (1888), 141–83 (repr. in J. Morris (ed.), *Genealogies and Texts* (Arthurian Period Sources, 5), Chichester, 1995, pp. 13–55).

75 Guy, "Origins", pp. 53–54.

76 *DGB*, ii.33.287–89: "In tempore eius tribus diebus cecidit pluuia sanguinea et muscarum affluentia homines moriebantur."

77 In one particular respect, Geoffrey's copy of this chronicle might have preserved a reading that was closer to the "Breviate chronicle" or "B-text of *Annales Cambriae*", which derives from the same common source as the Harleian chronicle: the Breviate chronicle, like Geoffrey, uses the verb *cecidit* rather than *facta est* in this annal. However, overall it is likely that Geoffrey's copy of the chronicle was closer to the Harleian version than the Breviate version, as argued below. For the three surviving Latin versions of this annal in parallel, see *Annales Cambriae, AD 682–954: Texts A–C in Parallel*, ed. and trans. D.N. Dumville, Cambridge, 2002, pp. 2–3.

78 *DGB*, xi.189.213; cf. xi.200.480; *Annales Cambriae*, ed. and trans. Dumville, pp. 8–9.

542, and the date of Cadualadrus's death in 689.[79] Although Geoffrey's 542 date has attracted a certain amount of rather credulous speculation, such as is inevitable in an "Arthurian" context, no consensus has developed regarding its origin.[80] Fortunately, the two other dates are easier to explain. The date of Lucius's death has been borrowed from Bede, who states that Lucius sent his letter to Pope Eleutherius during the joint empire of Marcus Antoninus Verus (i.e. Marcus Aurelius) and Aurelius Commodus (i.e. Lucius Verus), which Bede says began in 156 (actually 161).[81] Bede was likewise the source for the date of Cadualadrus's death. Geoffrey's Cadualadrus, king of the Britons, is a merger of two historical kings of the second half of the 7th century: Cadwaladr, king of Gwynedd, and Cædwalla, king of the West Saxons. It was the latter who provided Geoffrey with the most convenient way to date the death of the final king in his epic narrative; Bede dated Cædwalla's death to 20 April 689, and so Geoffrey duly transferred this date to his Cadualadrus.[82] However, Geoffrey also had access to a source containing a date for the death of Cadwaladr of Gwynedd: the Harleian chronicle.[83] Although modern scholars have deduced that the Harleian chronicle places the death of Cadwaladr of Gwynedd in the year 682,[84] the chronicle itself does not contain any absolute dates; instead, it simply numbers its annals in groups of ten. This feature, coupled with the relative proximity of the two dates 689 and 682, would have made it easy for Geoffrey to equate the obituary of Cædwalla of the West Saxons in Bede (689) with the obituary of Cadwaladr of Gwynedd in the Harleian chronicle (usually deduced as 682).

The Harleian chronicle was probably the only source accessible to Geoffrey that offered a date for another key moment in his history: the battle of Camlan. Again, although scholars have deduced that the Harleian chronicle places

---

79   *DGB*, v.73.8, xi.178.83–84, and xi.206.585–86.

80   For example, see G. Ashe, "'A certain very ancient book': Traces of an Arthurian Source in Geoffrey of Monmouth's History", *Speculum* 56:2 (1981), 301–23, at p. 317. For an incisive critique of Ashe's methodology, see R.W. Hanning, "*Inventio Arthuri*: a Comment on the Essays of Geoffrey Ashe and D.R. Howlett", *Arthuriana* 5:3 (1995), 96–99, at pp. 96–98.

81   Bede, *Ecclesiastical History* i.4, ed. and trans. B. Colgrave and R.A.B. Mynors, *Bede's Ecclesiastical History of the English People*, Oxford, 1969, pp. 24–25.

82   Bede, *Ecclesiastical History* v.7, ed. and trans. Colgrave and Mynors, pp. 470–71.

83   Additionally, Geoffrey could have worked out a date for Cadwaladr of Gwynedd's death using chapter 64 of the *Historia Brittonum*, which appears to claim that Cadwaladr died in the famous plague during Oswiu's reign (i.e. in 664) (*HB* (Harl. 3859) §64, ed. Faral, vol. 3, p. 43). However, Geoffrey seems to have ignored this claim, which in any case is probably incorrect (cf. Charles-Edwards, *Wales*, pp. 355–56; K.H. Jackson, "On the Northern British Section", p. 35).

84   Phillimore, "*Annales Cambriæ*", p. 159; *Annales Cambriae*, ed. and trans. Dumville, p. 2.

Camlan in 537, the original text does not offer an absolute date.[85] Geoffrey's
only option was to count back the years from an event with a known date to an
event with an unknown date. Counting back from the obituary of Cadwaladr
of Gwynedd in the Harleian chronicle would have revealed to Geoffrey a gap
of 147 marked years between that event and the battle of Camlan. All Geoffrey
needed to do was subtract 147 from his absolute date for the death of Bede's
Cædwalla, in 689, and he had deduced a date for Camlan: 542.

The result is all the more striking because it implies that Geoffrey used a text
of the Welsh annals that contained the same errors as the Harleian chronicle.
All copies of the Welsh annals inevitably contain copying errors, especially because it was so easy to omit or insert year markings in sections of the annals in
which no actual events were recorded. This is why there is a discrepancy between the 147 marked years separating Camlan from Cadwaladr's death in the
extant text of the Harleian chronicle and the 145 years separating the two dates
which scholars have attributed to the chronicle's events, 537 and 682. Only one
other copy of the Welsh annals survives in which the number of years between
Camlan and Cadwaladr's death can be counted: the late-13th-century "Breviate
chronicle", or "B-text of the *Annales Cambriae*", which derives from the same
common source as the Harleian chronicle. By comparing the Harleian chronicle and the Breviate chronicle with one another and with external sources,
it is possible to infer that, between their records for Camlan and Cadwaladr's
death, the Harleian chronicle, by comparison with the Breviate, is missing four
annals and has three additional annals, whereas the Breviate chronicle, by
comparison with the Harleian, is missing four annals and has no additional
annals.[86] The discrepancy means that the Breviate chronicle contains only 144
marked years between Camlan and Cadwaladr's death, and could not have
been used by Geoffrey to deduce the date 542 for Camlan. This strongly suggests that Geoffrey used a version of the Welsh Latin annals that was closer
to the Harleian chronicle embedded in the *Historia Brittonum*, confirming in
turn that he probably had access to a version of the Harleian recension of the
Historia Brittonum.

Geoffrey's use of a text like the Harleian genealogies has been better documented, since the relationship between Geoffrey's work and the genealogies
has been studied by Edmond Faral, Arthur E. Hutson, and Stuart Piggott.[87] One

85   Phillimore, "*Annales Cambriæ*", p. 154.
86   These calculations rely on the excellent work of H. Gough-Cooper in *Annales Cambriae:
      A, B and C in Parallel, from St Patrick to AD 954*, 2016, <http://croniclau.bangor.ac.uk/
      documents/AC_ABC_to_954_first_edition.pdf> (accessed 30 April 2017), pp. 7–16.
87   Faral, *LLA*, vol. 2, pp. 117–18, 137–39, and 276; A.E. Hutson, *British Personal Names in the
      Historia regum Britanniae*, Berkeley, 1940; id., "Geoffrey of Monmouth", *Transactions of the
      Honourable Society of Cymmrodorion* (1937), 361–73, at pp. 368–73; Piggott, "Sources".

of the clearest examples of Geoffrey's deployment of these genealogies comes
in his list of the attendees at Arthur's Whitsun court at Caerleon, among whom
are the following ragtag bunch:

> **Donaut Mappapo**, **Cheneus Mapcoil**, **Peredur Maberidur**, Grifud
> Mapnogoid, Regin Mapclaut, Eddelein Mapcledauc, Kincar Mabbangan,
> *Kinmarc*, *Gorbonian Masgoit*, *Clofaut*, RUN MAPNETON, KINBELIN
> MAPTRUNAT, CATHLEUS MAPCATEL, Kinlith Mapneton[88]

Most of these names have been lifted wholesale from a few adjacent sections
of a text very like the Harleian genealogies. Compare the names in bold, italicized, or set in smallcaps with the following extracts from the genealogies:[89]

> [U]rbgen map *Cinmarc* map Merchianum map Gurgust map Coil Hen.
> [G]uallauc map Laenaec map *Masguic Clop* map Ceneu map Coyl Hen.
> [M]orcant map Coledauc map Morcant Bulc map Cincar braut map Bran
> Hen map Dumngual Moilmut map *Garbaniaun* ...
>
> [D]unaut map Pappo map **Ceneu map Coyl Hen.** [G]urci ha **Peretur
> mepion Eleuther** Cascord maur ...
>
> [R]UN MAP NEITHON map Caten map Caurtam map Serguan map
> Letan map CATLEU MAP CATEL map Decion map Cinis Scaplaut map
> Louhen map Guidgen map Caratauc map CINBELIN MAP TEUHANT ...

This is the only section in Geoffrey's history where he retains the Old Welsh
map ("son (of)") formula found in the genealogies; elsewhere he picks out the
names and epithets but does not explicitly use the patronymics. This is not to
say that he was unaware of them. In the first extract from the genealogies just
quoted may be found the name *Dumngual Moilmut*; this was Geoffrey's source
for the name of his great lawgiver, Dunuallo Molmutius, whose relationship
with his son, Brennius, the conqueror of Rome, was determined by the relationship between *Dumngual Moilmut* and his son *Bran Hen*, "Bran the Old", in
the genealogies.[90]

A high proportion of the Brittonic name-forms in the *DGB* can be found distributed across almost every section of the Harleian genealogies, making it very

---

88   *DGB*, ix.156.340–43.
89   Phillimore, "*Annales Cambriæ*", pp. 173–76; cf. *Tracts*, ed. Bartrum, pp. 10–11.
90   Piggott, "Sources", p. 279. Geoffrey may have had another Welsh source for his Dunuallo
      Molmutius: see Roberts, "Sylwadau", pp. 136–37; M.E. Owen, "Royal Propaganda: Stories
      from the Law-Texts", in T.M. Charles-Edwards, M.E. Owen, and P. Russell (eds.), *The Welsh
      King and his Court*, Cardiff, 2000, pp. 224–54, at pp. 229–30.

likely that Geoffrey used a version of the text similar to that which survives embedded in the *Historia Brittonum* in the Harley manuscript. He seems to have
favored some sections of the genealogies over others. He made good use of the
sections concerning the legendary heroes of the Brittonic north, the subjects
of the first two extracts quoted above. He also made frequent use of the pedigrees of the kings of Gwynedd and Dyfed (his two principal "Cambrian" kingdoms), which are the first two pedigrees in the Harleian genealogies. As many
as nine of the names of Ebraucus's sons and daughters may have been taken
from these two pedigrees: Iagon, Chein, and Aballac from the Gwynedd pedigree (compare *Iacob, Cein*, and *Aballac*) and Margadud, Regin, Kincar, Gloigin,
Tangustel, and perhaps Ragan from the Dyfed pedigree (compare *Margetiut,
Regin, Cincar, Gloitguin*, and *Tancoystl*).

One might question the extent to which Geoffrey understood the genealogies that he quarried for name forms. He knew that the genealogies were
lists of names, but did he know the proper historical contexts to which those
names pertained? Despite the Harleian genealogies containing no dates and
few place-names, Geoffrey does indicate that he could contextualize some of
them. A particularly striking example concerns Geoffrey's King Tenuantius,
successor of Cassibellaunus and father of Kimbelinus. Tenuantius is Geoffrey's
version of the Tasciovanos of history, the father of Cunobelinos and grandfather of Caratacos. But while the latter two are known to us through Roman
writers, such as Suetonius, Dio Cassius, and Tacitus, Tasciovanos is known
solely through his coins. The only written source that mentions the father
of Cunobelinos prior to the *DGB* is the Harleian genealogies, in the pedigree
forming the third extract quoted above, which incorporates the three generations *Caratauc map Cinbelin map Teuhant*, "Caratacos son of Cunobelinos son
of *Teuhant*".[91] According to John Koch, *Teuhant* would be the regular Old Welsh
derivative of Tasciovanos, suggesting that at this point the Harleian genealogies have incorporated accurate information about the family that had been
preserved in oral tradition.[92] Since there is no reason that Geoffrey would
have known the name of Cunobelinos's father from independent sources, he
must have realized that the pedigree's *Caratauc* and *Cinbelin* corresponded
to the pre-Roman kings Caratacos and Cunobelinos mentioned in his other

---

91   Piggott, "Sources", p. 280; J.T. Koch, "A Welsh Window on the Iron Age: Manawydan,
     Mandubracios", *CMCS* 14 (1987), 17–52, at p. 17.
92   J.T. Koch, "*Llawr en asseð* (CA 932) 'The laureate hero in the war-chariot': Some
     Recollections of the Iron Age in the *Gododdin*", *Études celtiques* 24 (1987), 253–78, at
     pp. 266–70.

sources, and then correctly deduced from this that *Teuhant* was Cunobelinos's predecessor.

Arthur's Whitsun court at Caerleon provides other examples of Geoffrey's comprehension of the genealogies. Among the attendees may be found *Caduallo Lauihr rex Venedotorum*, "Caduallo Lauihr, king of the Venedoti", and *Stater rex Demetarum*, "Stater, king of the Demetae".[93] The two names have been taken respectively from the Gwynedd pedigree (*Catgolaun Iauhir*) and the Dyfed pedigree (*Stater*) in the Harleian genealogies, showing that Geoffrey understood to which kingdoms those pedigrees pertained. In the case of Caduallo Lauihr, he is even roughly correct about the implied date; the historical Cadwallon Lawhir of Gwynedd was the father of Maelgwn Gwynedd, who, as we know from Gildas, flourished in the 6th century.[94] Geoffrey demonstrates his thorough understanding of the Gwynedd pedigree later in his history in the conversation between Caduallo and Salomon of Armorica, in which Caduallo, who is himself based on the historical Cadwallon son of Cadfan of Gwynedd (d. 634), explains his descent from Malgo, Geoffrey's version of Maelgwn Gwynedd.[95] Throughout the post-Arthurian section of his history, Geoffrey's successful coordination between the Gwynedd pedigree and other information derived from Gildas, Bede, and elsewhere creates an important element of continuity in the narrative. It does not matter that the pedigree offered by Geoffrey's Caduallo contains a discrepancy when compared with the Harleian genealogies, in listing Ennianus, rather than Run, as Caduallo's ancestor; it would not have satisfied Geoffrey to reproduce his source exactly.

One further example of borrowing from the genealogies might suggest the origin of Geoffrey's copy of the text. At the beginning of his reign, Dunuallo Molmutius, a typically strenuous scion of the house of Cornwall, defeats three kings in order to become king of Britain: Pinner, king of Loegria, Rudaucus, king of Wales, and Staterius, king of Scotland.[96] The names *Pinner* and *Staterius* can only be based on the *Pincr* and *Stater* of the Dyfed pedigree in the Harleian genealogies; they are not, in fact, real names, but rather Latinate titles (*pincerna*, "cup-bearer", and *stator*, "magistrate's marshal") artificially introduced into the pedigree in order to extend it further back in time.[97] The name *Rudaucus*, on the other hand, has been taken from a version of the Gwynedd pedigree.

93   *DGB*, ix.156.329–30.
94   Gildas, *The Ruin of Britain* §§33–36, ed. and trans. Winterbottom, pp. 32–36 and 102–05.
95   *DGB*, xi.195.376–83.
96   *DGB*, ii.34.
97   E.W.B. Nicholson, "The Dynasty of Cunedag and the 'Harleian Genealogies'", *Y Cymmrodor* 21 (1908), 63–104, at p. 81; B. Guy, "The Earliest Welsh Genealogies: Textual Layering and the Phenomenon of 'Pedigree Growth'", *Early Medieval Europe* 26 (2018), 462–85, at p. 484.

In the Harleian genealogies, one of the ancestors of the kings of Gwynedd is called *Patern Pesrut*. However, versions of the same pedigree also appear in the Welsh Latin *Lives* of saints Cadog and Carannog. The *Life of St Cadog* was written by Lifris, archdeacon of Glamorgan, at the end of the 11th century, but the genealogy might have been added during the 12th century.[98] Similarly, the genealogy in the probably 12th-century *Life of St Carannog* may have been inserted at a slightly later point, since it now separates two parts of what may once have been a unitary composition.[99] In both these versions of the genealogy, the same ancestor is called *Patern Peis Rudauc* rather than *Patern Pesrut*. *Rudauc*, which in modern Welsh would be spelt *rhuddog*, is an adjective meaning "red, reddish-brown", but it is not attested independently in any written text until 1707 (unlike the much commoner adjective *rhudd*, on which *rhuddog* is based).[100] This renders it very likely that Geoffrey took the name *Rudaucus* from a version of the Gwynedd pedigree, a version which, moreover, was slightly closer to the version in the *Lives* of Cadog and Carannog than to the one in the extant Harleian genealogies. This is significant because the *Lives* of Cadog and Carannog themselves seem to have taken the genealogy from a text very similar to the Harleian genealogies that was circulating in places connected to Llancarfan, where St Cadog was the patron saint, during Geoffrey's lifetime.[101] There is further evidence for this. For example, Glastonbury Abbey, which at some point in the 12th century commissioned a *Life of St Gildas* from none other than Caradog of Llancarfan,[102] was the place where additional material was added to William of Malmesbury's *The Early History of Glastonbury* from the Harleian recension of *Historia Brittonum* and from genealogies like

---

98 For the date of the *Life*, see C.N.L. Brooke, *The Church and the Welsh Border in the Central Middle Ages*, ed. D.N. Dumville (Studies in Celtic History, 8), Woodbridge, 1986, pp. 72–73 and 89. For the suggestion that the genealogy is a later insertion, see H.D. Emanuel, "An Analysis of the Composition of the 'Vita Cadoci'", *National Library of Wales Journal* 7 (1952), 217–27, at p. 220.

99 For the *Life* (or *Lives*) of St Carannog, see K. Jankulak, "Carantoc alias Cairnech? British Saints, Irish Saints, and the Irish in Wales", in K. Jankulak and J.M. Wooding (eds.), *Ireland and Wales in the Middle Ages*, Dublin, 2007, pp. 116–48.

100 *GPC Online*, University of Wales Centre for Advanced Welsh and Celtic Studies, Aberystwyth, 2014, <http://www.geiriadur.ac.uk/> (accessed 30 April 2017), s.v. *rhuddog*. It does not seem that the addition of the suffix -*og* to *rhudd* altered the word's meaning. Cf. P. Russell, *Celtic Word Formation: The Velar Suffixes*, Dublin, 1990, p. 38.

101 The evidence is set out more fully in B. Guy, *Medieval Welsh Genealogy: An Introduction and Textual Study*, Woodbridge, 2020, pp. 79–100.

102 See above, n. 25.

the Harleian genealogies, possibly at the end of the 12th century.[103] It is quite possible that Caradog of Llancarfan himself, whom Geoffrey describes as "my contemporary", provided Geoffrey with his copy of the Harleian recension of the *Historia Brittonum*, containing versions of the same interpolated annals and genealogies as are found in the extant Harley manuscript.[104]

3   The True Faith

> Religion will be destroyed again and archbishoprics will be displaced. London's honour will adorn Canterbury and the seventh pastor of York will dwell in the kingdom of Armorica. St Davids will wear the pallium of Caerleon, and the preacher of Ireland will fall silent because of a baby growing in the womb.[105]

The quotation above is spoken as part of Merlin's prophecies to Vortigern. The passage appears near the beginning of the prophecies and concerns events due to happen not long after the reign of Arthur. Its subject matter is readily identifiable, within the terms of Galfridian history. According to Geoffrey, when the Britons were converted to Christianity during the reign of King Lucius, three metropolitan dioceses were established, based in York, London, and Caerleon.[106] This prophecy foretells certain events that will befall each one. London's honor will pass to Canterbury during the time of St Augustine, even though Geoffrey does not explicitly mention Augustine's foundation of the church of Canterbury; St Samson, whom Geoffrey has flee from York during Arthur's campaigns against the Saxons, becomes archbishop of Dol by the time of Arthur's Whitsun court at Caerleon;[107] and St David's wearing of the pallium of Caerleon is a reference both to Geoffrey's St David, "archbishop of Caerleon", dying in St Davids during the reign of Constantinus, and to the real 12th-century campaign of Bernard, bishop of St Davids, for the elevation of St Davids to the

---

103   Scott, *Early History*, pp. 187–88, nn. 22 and 24; D.E. Thornton, "Glastonbury and the Glastening", in L. Abrams and J.P. Carley (eds.), *The Archaeology and History of Glastonbury Abbey: Essays in Honour of the Ninetieth Birthday of C.A. Ralegh Radford*, Woodbridge, 1991, pp. 191–203, at pp. 195–96 and 200–01.

104   *DGB*, xi.208.602: "contemporaneo meo".

105   *DGB*, Prophetiae 112.46–50: "Delebitur iterum religio, et transmutacio primarum sedium fiet. Dignitas Lundoniae adornabit Doroberniam, et pastor Eboracensis septimus in Armorica regno frequentabitur. Meneuia pallio Vrbis Legionum induetur, et praedicator Hiberniae propter infantem in utero crescentem obmutescet."

106   *DGB*, iiii.72.418–26.

107   *DGB*, ix.151.194–96 and ix.158.406–09.

status of an archbishopric.[108] But it is the last part of the passage that concerns us most here. This appears to be a reference to two events in Rhygyfarch's *Life of St David*, written late in the 11th century: St Patrick's visit to Dyfed prior to David's birth, and Gildas's being struck dumb by the unborn David, still in his mother's womb.[109] In Geoffrey's typical fashion, he has combined aspects of these two events together so as not to replicate either one too closely. Another reference to Rhygyfarch's portrayal of Patrick's visit to Dyfed occurs later in the history, where Geoffrey explains that St Patrick had founded St Davids and had foretold David's birth.[110] Again, Geoffrey has altered Rhygyfarch's account; in the latter, David's birth is foretold to Patrick by an angel, not by Patrick himself. Still, it is probably fair to deduce that Geoffrey was familiar with Rhygyfarch's *Life of St David*.

It is very likely that Geoffrey knew some of the hagiographical literature generated by the ecclesiastical controversies of South Wales in the first half of the 12th century.[111] The controversies centered on Bishop Bernard of St Davids' (unsuccessful) campaign to establish St Davids as the seat of an independent archbishopric, and Bishop Urban of Llandaff's (successful) campaign to assert the independence of Llandaff as the center of a bishopric subordinate to Canterbury. Each of these campaigns produced saints' lives and accounts of ecclesiastical history to be used as propaganda, culminating most famously in the Book of Llandaff.[112] Some of Geoffrey's passing references to events of ecclesiastical history bear witness to his familiarity with the claims that these dioceses were propagating through their texts. For instance, his reference in the *VM* to St Davids, where "the pall lost for many years will be recovered", shows his cognizance of the claim of the church of St Davids to have been the seat of an archbishop earlier in its history.[113] The claim is found in Rhygyfarch's *Life of*

---

108 *DGB*, xi.179.89–91. For Bernard's campaign, see M. Richter, *Giraldus Cambrensis: The Growth of the Welsh Nation*, Aberystwyth, 1972, at pp. 40–61; *Episcopal Acts and Cognate Documents relating to Welsh Dioceses 1066–1272*, ed. J.C. Davies, 2 vols., Cardiff, 1946–48, vol. 1, pp. 190–208.

109 Rhygyfarch ap Sulien, *Life of St David* §3 and §5, ed. and trans. R. Sharpe and J.R. Davies, "Rhygyfarch's *Life* of St David", in J.W. Evans and J.M. Wooding (eds.), *St David of Wales: Cult, Church and Nation*, Woodbridge, 2007, pp. 107–55, at pp. 110–15; cf. Wright, "Geoffrey of Monmouth and Gildas Revisited", pp. 156–57.

110 *DGB*, xi.179.92–93; cf. Tatlock, *LHB*, p. 246.

111 For more detailed discussion, see Barry Lewis's chapter in the present volume.

112 For the relationship between the Book of Llandaff and 12th-century ecclesiastical politics, see J.R. Davies, *The Book of Llandaf and the Norman Church in Wales*, Woodbridge, 2003. For a diplomatic edition of the whole manuscript, see *The Text of the Book of Llan Dâv: Reproduced from the Gwysaney Manuscript*, ed. J.G. Evans and J. Rhŷs, Oxford, 1893.

113 *VM*, l. 623: "palla sibi reddetur dempta per annos."

St David, and was developed and elaborated as the 12th century progressed.[114] Geoffrey's reference to St Teilo, "a distinguished priest of Llandaff", replacing St Samson as archbishop of Dol probably betrays his familiarity with the version of the *Life of St Teilo* preserved in the Book of Llandaff. Only this version of the *Life*, unlike the other, probably earlier, version preserved in London, British Library, Cotton Vespasian A. xiv, mentions Teilo as bishop of Llandaff and then later as bishop of Dol following St Samson.[115]

De situ Brecheniauc ("Concerning the Establishment of Brycheiniog") is another Latin ecclesiastical text probably produced in South Wales in the first half of the 12th century that may have been used by Geoffrey. This text narrates the conception and birth of Brychan, the eponymous founder of Brycheiniog in south-central Wales, and then lists Brychan's many sons and daughters, most of whom can be identified as saints associated with churches in Brycheiniog and other regions of South Wales. Arthur Hutson suggested that Brychan was the inspiration for Geoffrey's Ebraucus, whose 20 sons and 30 daughters are enumerated in the *DGB*.[116] As Hutson pointed out, some of the more unusual names among Ebraucus's daughters are paralleled only among the names of Brychan's daughters. These include Gorgon (compare *Gurygon/ Grucon*), Kambreda (compare *Kein/Kein breit*), and Claudus (compare *Gladus/ Gluadus*). In each of these three cases, the former of the two bracketed italicized forms has been taken from the version of *De situ Brecheniauc* in Cotton Vespasian A. xiv, while the latter has been taken from the related text known as *Cognacio Brychan*, found in London, British Library, Cotton Domitian A. i.[117] The closer correspondence between the *DGB* and the forms found in *Cognacio Brychan* may suggest that Geoffrey drew on a version of the Brychan tract resembling the latter.

---

114   Rhygyfarch, *Life of St David* §§49–53, ed. and trans. Sharpe and Davies, pp. 142–47.

115   *DGB*, ix.158.406–09: "Teliaus illustris presbiter Landauiae". For the text of the Book of Llandaff's version of the *Life of St Teilo*, see *Life of St Teilo*, ed. J.G. Evans and J. Rhŷs, *The Text of the Book of Llan Dâv: Reproduced from the Gwysaney Manuscript*, Oxford, 1893, pp. 97–117; for a summary of the differences between the two versions of the *Life*, see P.C. Bartrum, *A Welsh Classical Dictionary: People in History and Legend up to about A.D. 1000*, Aberystwyth, 1993, pp. 605–06. It has been argued that Teilo's visit to Dol in the Book of Llandaff is modeled on the Breton *Life of St Turiau*; see G.H. Doble, *Lives of the Welsh Saints*, ed. D.S. Evans, Cardiff, 1971, pp. 183–86; J.R. Davies, *Book of Llandaf*, p. 117.

116   Hutson, *British Personal Names*, pp. 16–22; id., "Geoffrey", pp. 361–68. For Ebraucus's daughters, see *DGB*, ii.27.99–104.

117   Both versions are edited and translated in A.W. Wade-Evans, "The Brychan Documents", *Y Cymmrodor* 19 (1906), 18–48. Both versions were edited again, without translations, in *Vitae Sanctorum Britanniae et Genealogiae: The Lives and Genealogies of the Welsh Saints*, ed. A.W. Wade-Evans, Cardiff, 1944, pp. 313–18.

4   Dark Sayings from a Dark Heart

It is the will of the most-high Judge that the British shall be without their kingdom for many years because of their weakness, until Conanus shall arrive in his ship from Armorica, and that revered leader of the Welsh, Cadwaladrus. They will join together with the Scots, the Welsh, the Cornish, and the Armoricans in a firm league. Then they will restore to their own people the crown that had been lost. The enemy will be driven out and the time of Brutus will be back once more.[118]

This section of Merlin's prophecy to Telgesinus in the *VM* is the closest that Geoffrey comes to paraphrasing a 10th-century Welsh prophetic poem that he almost certainly knew, known as *Armes Prydein Vawr* ("The Great Prophecy of Britain").[119] *Armes Prydein Vawr* foretells of an alliance of Welsh, Irish, Cornish, Bretons, and others who will rise up to defeat the English with the help of the returning leaders Cadwaladr and Cynan, just as in the *VM*.[120] The poem was probably composed in the first half of the 10th century, while either Æthelstan (924–39) or his half-brother Edmund (939–46) were supreme in Britain, and it may have been inspired by the alliance between the Hiberno-Scandinavians of Dublin, the Scots of Alba, and the Britons of Strathclyde at the battle of Brunanburh in 937. The poet specifically recounts how the victory of the Welsh had been prophesied by no less a figure than Myrddin, the Welsh precursor of Geoffrey's Merlin, whose appearance in this context may have been one of the inspirations for Geoffrey's portrayal of Merlin as the chief political prophet of his legendary world.[121]

Prophecy, as a method of political commentary on past events and an expression of desires and anxieties about the future, was a popular literary genre

---

118   *VM*, ll. 964–72: "sententia summi / judicis existit, Britones ut nobile regnum / temporibus multis amittant debilitate, / donec ab Armorica veniet temone Conanus / et Cadualadrus Cambrorum dux venerandus, / qui pariter Scotos Cambros et Cornubienses / Armoricosque viros sociabunt federe firmo / amissumque suis reddent diadema colonis, / hostibus expulsis renovato tempore Bruti." I have altered Clarke's translation following advice from an anonymous reviewer.

119   Cf. D. Edel, "Geoffrey's So-Called Animal Symbolism and Insular Celtic Tradition", *Studia Celtica* 18/19 (1983/84), 96–109, at p. 97; A.O.H. Jarman, "The Merlin Legend and the Welsh Tradition of Prophecy", in Bromwich et al. (eds.), *The Arthur of the Welsh*, pp. 117–45, at p. 137.

120   See above, pp. 48–49.

121   *Armes Prydein Vawr* l. 17, ed. and trans. Williams and Bromwich, pp. 2–3.

during the Middle Ages.[122] It was a literary form that was thoroughly exploited by Geoffrey, whose *PM* achieved fame and popularity as a work in its own
right, in addition to forming the central linchpin of the *DGB*.[123] But to what
extent did Welsh examples of the genre influence Geoffrey's particular brand
of Merlinian prophecy? It is relatively uncontroversial to claim that Geoffrey
may have known *Armes Prydein Vawr*, since the dating of that poem to the first
half of the 10th century is fairly secure. But in this respect *Armes Prydein Vawr*
stands almost alone, because the dating of the majority of early Welsh prophetic poems is contested and uncertain.[124] Included in the latter category are
the early Myrddin poems, the dating of which is inextricably bound up with
the intractable question of their relationship with the *VM*.[125]

It has been persistently claimed that Geoffrey discovered the Welsh legend
of Myrddin between the completion of the *DGB* around 1138 and the writing of the *VM* around 1150.[126] This is because the account of Merlin's life in
the *VM* mirrors various aspects of Myrddin's story in Welsh poetry, whereas

122   For an excellent summary focused on the 12th century, see R.W. Southern, "Aspects of
      the European Tradition of Historical Writing, 3: History as Prophecy", *Transactions of the
      Royal Historical Society*, fifth series, 22 (1972), 159–80 (repr. in R.J. Bartlett (ed.), *History and
      Historians: Selected Papers of R.W. Southern*, Oxford, 2004, 48–65). For the later Middle
      Ages, see the collection of essays in M. Reeves, *The Prophetic Sense of History in Medieval
      and Renaissance Europe*, Aldershot, 1999.
123   See J. Crick, "Geoffrey of Monmouth, Prophecy and History", *Journal of Medieval History*
      18:4 (1992), 357–71; ead., "Geoffrey and the Prophetic Tradition", in S. Echard (ed.), *The
      Arthur of Medieval Latin Literature: The Development and Dissemination of the Arthurian
      Legend in Medieval Latin* (Arthurian Literature of the Middle Ages, 6), Cardiff, 2011,
      pp. 67–82; C. Daniel, *Les prophéties de Merlin et la culture politique (XIIe–XVIe siècles)*,
      Turnhout, 2006; and Maud McInerney's contribution to the present volume.
124   Compare the lack of secure dates for the poems edited in M. Haycock, *Prophecies from the
      Book of Taliesin*, Aberystwyth, 2013.
125   The dominant view of their relationship during much of the latter half of the 20th
      century was that of A.O.H. Jarman: see his "The Welsh Myrddin Poems", in R.S. Loomis
      (ed.), *Arthurian Literature in the Middle Ages*, Oxford, 1959, pp. 20–30; id., *The Legend of
      Merlin*, Cardiff, 1960; id., "Early Stages in the Development of the Myrddin Legend", in
      R. Bromwich and R.B. Jones (eds.), *Astudiaethau ar yr Hengerdd / Studies in Old Welsh
      Poetry: Cyflwynedig i Syr Idris Foster* [Studies in Old Welsh poetry presented to Sir Idris
      Foster], Cardiff, 1978, pp. 326–49; "Merlin legend". Aspects of this view have recently
      been challenged: O.J. Padel, "Geoffrey of Monmouth and the Development of the Merlin
      Legend", *CMCS* 51 (2006), 37–65; N. Tolstoy, "Geoffrey of Monmouth and the Merlin
      Legend", *AL* 25 (2008), 1–42.
126   J.J. Parry, *The Vita Merlini* (University of Illinois Studies in Language and Literature, 10.3),
      Urbana, IL, 1925, pp. 13 and 16; M.E. Griffiths, *Early Vaticination in Welsh with English
      Parallels*, Cardiff, 1937, p. 78; Jarman, *Legend of Merlin*, pp. 24–25; id., "Early Stages", p. 349;
      id., "Merlin Legend", p. 135; Roberts, "Sylwadau", p. 139; *VM*, p. 29; Tolstoy, "Geoffrey of
      Monmouth", pp. 11 and 13.

the account of Merlin in the *DGB* does not. As A.O.H. Jarman put it, "at some time subsequent to 1138, however, Geoffrey must have learnt more about the Myrddin legend and realised that the account given of him in the Historia was contrary to popular tradition."[127] But we have already noted how perilous it is to assume Geoffrey's ignorance or miscomprehension on the basis on his failure to reproduce a source at his disposal exactly. Alignment with popular tradition was not one of Geoffrey's primary concerns. Geoffrey's creation of a new "Merlin" character through the merger of the fatherless boy of the *Historia Brittonum* and the Welsh prophet Myrddin was deliberate and considered, and provides no evidence at all for the extent of Geoffrey's acquaintance with Welsh Myrddin poetry by 1138. This can be judged only through positive evidence, rather than evidence of absence.

It is likely that the *VM* reflects Geoffrey's familiarity with versions of some surviving Welsh poems.[128] The parallels between the *VM* and the Welsh poems are all the more striking in view of the apparent obscurity of the *VM* during the Middle Ages, making it less likely that the Welsh poems have been influenced by the *VM*.[129] One such poem is *Yr Afallennau* ("The Apple Trees"), the earliest extant copy of which is found in the mid-13th-century Black Book of Carmarthen. In this poem, the narrator prophesies political events, including great victories for the Welsh over the English, from underneath an apple tree. Although the narrator remains nameless, references to incidents from his past, including the battle of Arfderydd, his madness, and his sleeping in the forest of Celyddon, align him with Geoffrey's Merlin in the *VM*. Geoffrey may allude to this poem or a poem with a similar theme in his repeated references to Merlin's encounters with apples and apple trees.[130] Another poem that seems to be reflected in the *VM* is *Ymddiddan Myrddin a Thaliesin* ("The Conversation of Myrddin and Taliesin"), also preserved in the Black Book of Carmarthen, which may have provided a model for the long conversation between Merlin and Telgesinus (Geoffrey's Taliesin) in the *VM*.[131] One of the topics discussed in

---

127   Jarman, "Merlin Legend", p. 135.
128   English translations of the Welsh Myrddin poems discussed below may be found in J.K. Bollard, "Myrddin in Early Welsh Tradition", in P. Goodrich (ed.), *The Romance of Merlin: An Anthology*, New York, 1990, pp. 13–54.
129   Tolstoy, "Geoffrey of Monmouth", pp. 25–27 and 34–36.
130   *VM*, ll. 90–95, 567, and 1408–16; cf. Jarman, *Legend of Merlin*, p. 25; id., "Merlin Legend", p. 134; Padel, "Geoffrey of Monmouth and the Development of the Merlin Legend", pp. 57–58; Tolstoy, "Geoffrey of Monmouth", p. 38.
131   *Ymddiddan Myrddin a Thaliesin (o Lyfr Du Caerfyrddin)* [The Conversation of Myrddin and Taliesin (from the Black Book of Carmarthen)], ed. A.O.H. Jarman, Cardiff, 1951, at p. 44; id., *Legend of Merlin*, p. 25; id., "Early Stages", p. 332; Padel, "Geoffrey of Monmouth and the Development of the Merlin Legend", pp. 45–46.

the *Ymddiddan* is *gueith Arywderit*, "the battle of Arfderydd", which in the *VM* turns Merlin mad and drives him into the forest of Calidon. The *VM*'s story may be compared with the final stanza of the *Ymddiddan*, where Myrddin states that, in the battle, "seven score generous men went mad, they perished in the forest of Celyddon."[132] The *VM*'s conversation between Merlin and Telgesinus may also have been inspired by Welsh poems linked with the legendary Welsh poet Taliesin. Telgesinus's role in the *VM* is primarily that of a cosmological commentator, who divulges information to Merlin about the world's waters, islands, and, curiously, fish. A similar range of cosmological expertise, including knowledge of fish, is attributed to the legendary persona of Taliesin in some of the poems preserved in the 14th-century Book of Taliesin.[133]

A final poem that Geoffrey may have drawn upon is *Cyfoesi Myrddin a Gwenddydd ei Chwaer* ("The Prophecy of Myrddin and Gwenddydd his Sister"), which is preserved in manuscripts from the end of the 13th century onwards. This is a long poem in which Gwenddydd questions her brother Myrddin in alternating stanzas about the future rulers of the Welsh. The poem is cast as prophecy, but begins by listing quasi-historical rulers of the Welsh, following first the *Historia Brittonum*'s account of the northern kings who opposed the English and latterly the Gwynedd pedigree up to the reign of Hywel Dda (d. 950). Thereafter the prophetic references become much vaguer, crystallizing only later in the poem in allusions to the 12th-century rulers Gruffudd ap Cynan, Owain Gwynedd, and King Henry.[134] It has been suggested, quite plausibly, that the arrangement of the extant text is due to its being composite: namely, that an earlier prophetic poem, composed perhaps in the 10th century during the reign of Hywel Dda, was later augmented with stanzas referring to the 12th century.[135] Many aspects of the poem, including the prophecy, the references to Arfderydd, Rhydderch, and Gwenddolau, and the role of Myrddin's sister Gwenddydd (called Ganieda by Geoffrey), who in the *VM*

---

132 *Ymddiddan Myrddin a Thaliesin* ll. 35–36, ed. Jarman, p. 58: "Seith ugein haelon a aethan ygwllon, / Yg coed keliton y daruuan." Translation is my own.

133 Cf. M. Haycock, *Legendary Poems from the Book of Taliesin*, Aberystwyth, 2007, pp. 13, 156–57, 443, 515, 521, and 523.

134 M.B. Jenkins, "Aspects of the Welsh Prophetic Verse Tradition: Incorporating Textual Studies of the Poetry from 'Llyfr Coch Hergest' (Oxford, Jesus College, MS cxi) and 'Y Cwta Cyfarwydd' (Aberystwyth, National Library of Wales, MS Peniarth 50)", unpublished PhD thesis, University of Cambridge, 1990, pp. 80–83. It is not clear which son of which Henry is implicated in the phrases *keneu Henri*, "Henry's cub" (l. 209) and *mab Henri*, "Henry's son" (l. 213) (ibid., pp. 53 and 64).

135 Jenkins, "Aspects of the Welsh Prophetic Verse Tradition", pp. 40–41; J. Rowland, *Early Welsh Saga Poetry: A Study and Edition of the Englynion*, Cambridge, 1990, pp. 291–93; Tolstoy, "Geoffrey of Monmouth", pp. 20–25; Charles-Edwards, *Wales*, pp. 337–39.

finally joins Merlin and prophesies with him, imply that Geoffrey was familiar with the *Cyfoesi* or with something like it at the time that he composed
the *VM*.[136] Might he have known a version of the poem at an earlier stage,
when he was composing the *DGB*? There may be a hint that he did in his treatment of Caduan, Caduallo's father and predecessor. It has already been noted
that Geoffrey was familiar with the pedigree of the kings of Gwynedd. It is
possible that this pedigree was Geoffrey's only source for Caduan, father of
Caduallo, who is based on the historical 7th-century Cadfan of Gwynedd, father of Cadwallon; in this case, Geoffrey's attribution of the kingship of the
Venedoti and then of all the Britons to Caduan was solely a deduction from
the pedigree, in light of the more famous position of the historical Cadwallon.
However, if Geoffrey already knew the *Cyfoesi*, which lists Cadfan as king of the
Welsh prior to Cadwallon, his decision would have had a surer foundation, and
his ability to manipulate the pedigree of the kings of Gwynedd would be more
readily explained.

Conclusion: the Laurel Wreath

We have brought the song to an end. So, Britons, give a laurel wreath to
Geoffrey of Monmouth. He is indeed your Geoffrey, for he once sang of
your battles and those of your princes, and he wrote a book which is now
known as the "Deeds of the Britons" – and they are celebrated throughout
the world.[137]

Who are these "Britons", so beholden to Geoffrey of Monmouth? The Welsh,
whom Geoffrey perniciously castigates in his history? The Bretons, who barely
rate a mention in the poem for which this conclusion was written? The Britons
of yore, who could look upon Geoffrey only as some distant, unknowable
Homer? Or some combination of them all, the subject of an ironic paean for a
people who only truly exist in Geoffrey's pages?

   If there is any single conclusion to be drawn from this chapter, it is that
Geoffrey of Monmouth was the master of his source material. He may have
known the limitations of Breton source material, and he certainly knew the

---

136   Tolstoy, "Geoffrey of Monmouth", p. 38.
137   *VM*, ll. 1525–29: "Duximus ad metam carmen. Vos ergo, Britanni, / laurea serta date
      Gaufrido de Monemuta. / Est etenim vester, nam quondam prelia vestra / vestrorumque
      ducum cecinit scripsitque libellum / quem nunc Gesta vocant Britonum celebrata per
      orbem."

challenges presented by the relatively abundant Welsh source material. He understood how to use less tractable sources like bare genealogies and exiguous annals, and he understood how to weld them seamlessly to well-known narratives like Bede's *Ecclesiastical History*. He consulted all the sources from Wales that he could find, in Latin and Welsh, but felt no compulsion to incorporate everything so discovered into his compositions. However, nothing absorbed into his work is left bare. Just as with the classical and biblical sources examined in the next chapter, Geoffrey deliberately sought to exercise the few readers who would have been conversant with the Welsh sources by masking his intertextual debts at every turn. But there was also an essential difference. Within the intertextual discourses of classical and biblical literature, Geoffrey was merely a passing participant; within the intertextual discourse of Brittonic history, Geoffrey was the enduring master architect.[138]

---

138   I would like to thank Paul Russell, Barry Lewis, and Rebecca Thomas for kindly suggesting improvements to various drafts of this chapter.

CHAPTER 2

Geoffrey of Monmouth's Classical and Biblical Inheritance

Paul Russell

1   In the Beginning

The "very old book in the British tongue" brought to Geoffrey by Walter has always been the natural starting point for any discussion of Geoffrey and his sources for the *De gestis Britonum*.[1] But the sentence which follows mention of the book (apart from its reference to translation (*transferre*)) has attracted relatively somewhat less attention:

> Though I have never gathered showy words from the gardens of others, I was persuaded by [Walter's] request to translate the book into Latin in a rustic style [*lit.* stilus], reliant on my own reed pipe.[2]

But this is arguably even more revealing of his sources than the preceding sentence with its much discussed "very old book" and references to the works of Gildas and Bede. The crucial phrase, which could be taken as Geoffrey's nod toward the modesty topos, is *agresti tamen stilo propriisque calamis*, "in a rustic

---

1 *DGB*, Prologus 2.9–10: "... quendam Britannici sermonis librum uestustissimum ..." Translations of the *DGB* are normally Wright's unless it was felt necessary to vary it; for other texts, translations are my own unless otherwise indicated. To a large extent the following discussion focuses in the *DGB*, which provides many more complex examples to consider, but some cases where Geoffrey draws on classical sources in the *VM* are also discussed. His debt to biblical sources in the latter is less easy to pin down; for a discussion of some of the theological aspects of the *VM*, see Barry Lewis's chapter in this volume (pp. 420–23). I am grateful to Ben Guy for reading a draft of this chapter and for the comments of the anonymous referees, and also to the editors for their careful guidance and help.

2 *DGB*, Prologus 2.12–15: "... Rogatu itaque illius ductus, tametsi infra alienos ortulos falerata uerba non collegerim, agresti tamen stilo propriisque calamis contentus codicem illum in Latinum sermonem transferre curaui ..." Wright, and others (Geoffrey of Monmouth, *De gestis Britonum*, trans. L. Thorpe, *Geoffrey of Monmouth: The History of the Kings of Britain*, London, 1966, p. 51; Geoffrey of Monmouth, *De gestis Britonum*, trans. M.A. Faletra, *The History of the Kings of Britain, Geoffrey of Monmouth*, Peterborough, Ontario, 2007, p. 41), render *stilo* as "style" but it may be intended more precisely as *stilus*, "pen, stylus".

style, reliant on my own reed pipe"; on the face of it, he seems to be taking refuge in the rusticity of his Latin as an excuse for a lack of polish. But there is something else going on here. In the longer prologue containing a joint dedication to Robert of Gloucester and Waleran of Meulan, which is preserved in ten manuscripts, the veil is pulled back a little further:[3]

> ... so that I may rest beneath the shade of your spreading branches and my muse can play her melody on my rustic pipe, safe from envious critics.[4]

Under the protection of Robert and Waleran, Geoffrey has had the time and the space to listen to his Muse. But at this point the allusion to (and the partial quotation of) Virgil's first *Eclogue* is unmistakable and was clearly intended for what it was (the relevant phrases are italicized):

Meliboeus:	You, Tityrus, lie *shaded by the spreading branches of a beech*
	and woo the woodland muse with your slender reed;
	but we are leaving the lands of our country and its pleasant fields.
	We in exile from our country; you, Tityrus, at ease in the shade
	teaching the woods re-echo 'Fair Amaryllis'. 5
Tityrus:	O Meliboeus, a god has brought about this peace for us;
	For he shall always be a god to me, and often shall
	a tender lamb from our folds stain his altar.
	He has permitted my cattle to roam, as you can see,
	and *me to play what I like upon my rustic pipes*.[5] 10

---

3   On the Waleran prologue, see *DGB*, pp. ix–x and xix; cf. Geoffrey of Monmouth, *De gestis Britonum*, ed. A. Griscom, *The Historia Regum Britanniae of Geoffrey of Monmouth with Contributions to the Study of its Place in early British History with a Literal Translation of the Welsh Manuscript No. LXI of Jesus College Oxford*, London, 1929, pp. 49–50.

4   *DGB*, Prologus 4.8–10 (n. 23.8–10): "... ut sub tegmine tam patulae arboris recubans calamum musae meae coram inuidis atque improbis tuto modulamine resonare queam"; *improbis* is understood here by Wright as "critics", but others take it to reflect a more general hostility: "envious and malicious enemies" (Geoffrey of Monmouth, *De gestis Britonum*, trans. Thorpe, p. 52); "the jealous and craven" (Geoffrey of Monmouth, *De gestis Britonum*, trans. Faletra, p. 42).

5   Virgil, *Eclogues* i.1–10, ed. R.A.B. Mynors, *P. Virgili Maronis Opera*, Oxford, 1969, my translation; the relevant phrases are italicized: "Meliboeus: 'Tityre, tu *patulae recubans sub tegmine fagi / silvestrem tenui Musam meditaris auena*; / nos patriae fines et dulcia linquimus arua. / nos patriam fugimus; tu, Tityre, lentus in umbra / formosam *resonare* doces Amaryllida silvas.' Tityrus: 'O Meliboe, deus nobis haec otia fecit. / namque erit ille mihi semper deus, illius aram / saepe tener nostris ab ovilibus imbuet agnus. / ille meas errare boues, ut cernis, et *ipsum / ludere quae uellem calamo permisit agresti*.'"

While the reference has been noted, its significance has not been recognized even though it offers an immediate reason for thinking afresh about how Geoffrey was using source material which was probably part of his staple education.[6] It is easy to spot such allusions, but far harder to gauge their import for Geoffrey's audience.

Eclogue I has the form of a dialogue between two standard characters of pastoral, Meliboeus and Tityrus. The former begins with a contrast: while he is leaving his lands (*linquimus arua / nos patriam fugimus*, "we are leaving the lands of our country and its pleasant fields"), Tityrus reclines under a shady tree practicing tunes on his pipes. Tityrus replies that a god (*deus*) has brought him leisure (*otia*); he does not have to leave his land and so can relax and play his rustic pipes (*calamo agresti*). The historical context of the poem is well known and would have been familiar to Geoffrey:[7] the poem refers to Octavian's annexation in the late 40s BC of land in Transpadana (the area of northern Italy north of the Po, near Cremona and Virgil's home, Mantua) to pay off the veterans of the campaigns against Pompey. Despite its pastoral tone, this is a highly political poem about loss of homeland, exile, and finding new lands on the edge of the known world; as such, it encapsulates the themes played out in the *DGB*. The *deus* (l. 6) is of course Octavian (Augustus-to-be) to whom Virgil successfully appealed through his powerful friends to be allowed to keep his *patria*. Just as Tityrus can relax under a tree thanks to Octavian, so can Geoffrey under the protection of Robert and Waleran. But just as they are depicted as displaying the generosity of an Octavian, so is Tityrus at this point to be equated with Virgil and by implication with Geoffrey.

But *Eclogue* I is not to be set aside just yet. In the closing stanzas Tityrus offers a series of *adynata* "impossibilities" (of the pigs-will-fly type):

---

6 The link with *Eclogues* I is noted in Geoffrey of Monmouth, *De gestis Britonum*, ed. Griscom, pp. 49–50 where it is suggested that Geoffrey "modelled his new line on Virgil" (p. 50); the suggestion here is that he is simply making the allusion already present in the main part of the Preface more explicit. On Geoffrey's schooling, see below, pp. 82 and 101.

7 The circumstances of Virgil retaining his land was a standard part of all the antique and medieval lives of Virgil, and from there seem to have been absorbed into Virgilian commentaries; see *Vitae Virgilianae Antiquae*, ed. G. Brugnoli and F. Stok, Rome, 1997; J.M. Ziolkowski & M.C.J. Putnam, *The Virgilian Tradition. The First Fifteen Hundred Years*, New Haven, 2008, pp. 179–403.

... sooner each shall wander in exile far from their lands
and sooner shall the Parthian drink from the Saône or the German from
    the Tigris
than shall his (*sc.* Octavian's) gaze slip from my mind.[8]

In his safety and self-assurance Tityrus can blithely assert that peoples will not have to travel vast distances across the world: the Parthians will not come from the east all the way to Gaul to drink the waters of the Arar (Saône), nor will the Germans travel as far east as the Tigris. But Meliboeus's response is more sanguine, "it is alright for you but ...":

But we shall go from here, some to the thirsty Africans,
others to Scythia, and to Crete's swift Oaxes,
and to those who are completely cut off from the world, the Britons.[9]

In fact, he says, people *will* go into exile and, what is more, they will even go to the ends of the earth, even as far as Britain.

    Geoffrey's *DGB* continues a narrative begun in Dares Phrygius's *The Fall of Troy* (*De excidio Troiae*), a text perhaps of the 5th century AD purporting to be translated from Greek, which relates the whole of the fall of Troy in a single narrative. It ends at the moment when Aeneas abandons Troy, and this is where Geoffrey takes up the story. This is signposted by Geoffrey's allusion to Dares' title in the first line of Book I: "After the Trojan war, Aeneas, fleeing the devastation (*excidium*) of the city ..."[10] Aeneas is like Meliboeus at this point, but not like Tityrus who is allowed to stay; just as the descendants of Meliboeus might end up in Africa or Scythia or even Britain, so the descendants of Aeneas and the Trojans end up scattered across the world. The *DGB* then shares a Virgilian narrative whereby the Trojans become Romans and Italians, but it is a narrative which then branches off onto another tale of exile, finally bringing Brutus and his line to Britain. But it also constantly harks back to Rome – and, moreover, Romans (and those genetically related to them) seem unable to leave Britain

---

8   Virgil, *Eclogues* i.61–63, ed. Mynors, my translation: "... ante pererratis amborum finibus exul / aut Ararim Parthus bibet aut Germanus Tigrim / quam nostro illius labatur pectore uultus."

9   Virgil, *Eclogues* i.64–65, ed. Mynors, my translation: "At nos hinc alii sitientis ibimus Afros, / pars Scythiam et rapidum Cretae veniemus Oaxen / et penitus toto divisos orbe Britannos."

10   *DGB*, i.6.48, my translation: "Aeneas post Troianum bellum excidium urbis ... diffugiens".

alone.[11] In other words, the link between Rome and Britain is never broken but simply re-aligned and re-shaped.

Another theme which *Eclogue* I opens up is that of civil war; the context of the poem is the aftermath of the destructive *bellum ciuile* which tore the Roman empire apart. It can be no accident that one of the few Roman authors that Geoffrey mentions by name in the *DGB* is Lucan, but in addition, as has often been noted, Geoffrey's work is permeated with allusions to the language and imagery of Lucan's *Civil War* – again hardly surprising in a work preoccupied with that most destructive of activity, "war ... worse than civil".[12]

This illustrates a point to which we shall return, namely that Geoffrey's use of such sources is often allusive, potentially elusive, and sometimes illusory; the apparently pastoral image of Geoffrey settled under his tree pondering his great work was not what Geoffrey intended (or at least not all that he intended), and the allusion to *Eclogue* I is made to work harder than might be apparent. It is more explicit in the extended prologue (with the dedication to Waleran), but for those of Geoffrey's audience with the learning to notice, it is present in the original prologue too: *agresti tamen stilo propriisque calamis contentus*, "content with my rustic style, reliant on my own reed pipe".[13] The allusiveness of the reference in the *DGB* recalls Conte's observations (made in relation to the use of allusion in Latin verse) that "a single word in the new poem will often be enough to condense a whole poetic situation and to revive its mood";[14] here, for those who can recognize it, the words *agresti tamen stilo propriisque calamis*, I would suggest, both condense and revive the mood of *Eclogue* I, and bring us immediately into a world of civil war, exile, and migration. Another point well made by Conte is also relevant here and that is what he calls the "epigraphic technique", the use of a quotation of, or allusion to, one poem at the beginning of another poem

---

11   For an impression of the presence of Rome and the Romans in the *DGB*, one need simply look at the Index in *DGB*, p. 303, s.vv. *Roma, Romani, Romanus*; cf. in particular *DGB*, iiii.54–72, but also episodes such as Arthur's abortive attempt to conquer Rome (*DGB*, ix.158–x.176).

12   Lucan, *The Civil War* i.1, trans. J.D. Duff, *Lucan. The Civil War*, Cambridge, MA, 1928, p. 3: "bella ... plus quam civilia" (based on A.E. Housman's edition of the text, *M. Annaei Lucani Belli civilis libri decem*, Oxford, 1950). Geoffrey's reference to Lucan is in the context of Caesar's invasions of Britain where a speech of Pompey is quoted in which he disparages Caesar.

13   *DGB*, Prologus 2.13–14.

14   G.B. Conte, *The Rhetoric of Imitation: Genre and Poetic Memory in Virgil and Other Latin Poets*, Ithaca, 1986, p. 35.

whose development includes that initial poetic retrieval but subordinates it to its own purposes. What is recalled is extraneous to the new poem but it is irrevocably embedded in the other poetic situation. But the previous poetic context necessarily carries over into the new.[15]

Just like Geoffrey's use of Dares' title (*De excidio Troiae*) in the opening line of his main narrative (*excidium urbis*), the signposting of *Eclogue* I in the Preface, however oblique, allows the context and thus the thematic potential of those previous works to "carry over" into his own work. In the preface of Geoffrey's work, then, what seems on the surface to be a pastoral trope is actually highly political. We might also think of that other great poem of the countryside, the *Georgics*, which arguably is again a political poem pretending to be something else. In the light of our discussion of *Eclogue* I, when we turn to the next chapter of Geoffrey's work, "Descriptio Insulae" (*DGB*, i.5), it becomes much easier to recognize that this might not just be a rehearsal of the standard topos of the geographical survey and the *locus amoenus* which we find as a preface to a range of ancient and early medieval writers, such as Tacitus, Bede, and Gildas, but rather, in terms of structure and content, a passage carefully modelled on Virgil's "praise of Italy" (*laus Italiae*) in the second book of the *Georgics*.[16] But for a quirk of fate, Brutus and his people might have been Romans thriving and farming in Italy; instead Geoffrey seems to be offering them a location ideally suited to them and destined to be their homeland.

However, before we go thinking that the *DGB* is an exercise in classical source-spotting, it is also worth noting that, when Brutus and his men eventually reach Britain, it is described as the "promised isle" (*promissa insula*).[17] Viewed from that perspective, the biblical resonances cannot be ignored; after all, the whole of Book I is a narrative of exile, war, and seemingly endless migration.[18] By chapter 20, Britain has indeed become the promised (is)land.

While the Virgilian allusions in the prologue of the *DGB* may have to be teased out, a classical allusion seems to have been handed to us on a plate

---

15   Conte, *Rhetoric of Imitation*, p. 25.

16   Virgil, *Georgics* ii.136–76, ed. R.A.B. Mynors, *P. Virgili Maronis Opera*, Oxford, 1969; see also Faral, *LLA*, vol. 2, p. 69.

17   *DGB*, i.20.451–52.

18   For further discussion, see Barry Lewis's contribution to this volume, pp. 400–1. The concept of the "promised land", which presumably lies behind *promissa insula*, is of course biblical, but the phrase does not occur until later patristic sources. What patristic sources Geoffrey was familiar with is an interesting question which is beyond the remit of this chapter; it is not impossible that he made the same inference from passages such as Genesis 15:18–21 as other writers have done.

in the otherwise conventional opening to the *VM*.[19] Addressing Robert de
Chesney, bishop of Lincoln, Geoffrey invokes the Muses, but at the same time
claims he is not up to the task:

> Indeed, it might well have been yourself whom I would wish to embrace
>   in a
>   [noble poem.
> But I am not the man for it: no, not even if Orpheus and Camerinus
> and Macer and Marius and Rabirius of the great voice
> were all to sing through my mouth and the Muses were my
>   accompanists.[20]

The Muses and Orpheus are standard reference points, but it is noted by Parry
and Clarke that the poets Camerinus, Macer, Marius, and Rabirius are drawn
from Ovid, *Epistulae ex Ponto*.[21] Clarke suggests that Geoffrey could have drawn
on a "stock list" of poets but this seems unlikely since *magnique Rabirius oris*,
"and Rabirius of the great voice", is a direct quotation from Ovid.[22] However,
as we have seen, it pays to take heed of Geoffrey's sources. Ovid's poem is the
final poem in his series of four books, *Epistulae ex Ponto*, composed in Tomis,
his place of exile on the Black Sea. It is a curious poem which has not attracted
very much critical attention.[23] Essentially Ovid provides a list of contemporary
and living poets who he supposes are still composing and thriving in the Rome
from which he has been exiled, and it could be read as a complaint about how
they are successful while he moulders. But by the end of the poem his stance
seems to have shifted to being more concerned about his legacy: "my muse
had a famous name and she was read among such men".[24] That is, he was a
poets' poet. The poem ends with a plea that his "body" (*sc.* of poetry) should

---

19   *VM*, ll. 1–18.

20   *VM*, ll. 13–16: "Ergo te cuperem complecti carmine digno / sed non sufficio, licet Orpheus
     et Camerinus / et Macer et Marius magnique Rabirius oris / ore meo canerent Musis co-
     mitantibus omnes."

21   J.J. Parry, *The Vita Merlini* (University of Illinois Studies in Language and Literature, 10.3),
     Urbana, IL, 1925, pp. 20 and 119; *VM*, pp. 11 and 137; see Ovid, *Epistulae ex Ponto* iv.16.5–
     6, 19, and 24, ed. S.G. Owen, *P. Ovidi Nasonis Tristium Libri Quinque Ibis Ex Ponto Libri
     Quattuor Halieutica Fragmenta*, Oxford, 1915.

22   *VM*, pp. 11 and 137. It is possible that the poet named as Marius is an error for Marsus who
     is named in the same line as Macer and Rabirius.

23   The best discussion is C. Lehmann, "The End of Augustan Literature: Ovid's *Epistulae ex
     Ponto* 4", unpublished PhD thesis, University of Southern California, 2018, esp. pp. 274–341.

24   Ovid, *Epistulae ex Ponto* iv.16. 45–46, ed. Owen: "claro mea nomine Musa / atque inter
     tantos quae legeretur erat."

not be cut up or burnt. Again there seems to be a point to this. It is tempting to read Ovid's poem as having a ring of finality about it, and after all the *VM* is Geoffrey's final work, but we cannot know that Geoffrey intended it to be that. More significant, I suggest, is the link between Ovid's exile and Merlin's intermittent exiles (and the stress and suffering this caused to all concerned) on the one hand and the general anxiety about the nature of poetical and prophetic composition in exile. While this is less easy to pin down and must remain a suggestion, the choice of poets in this list was intended to lead the well-educated reader elsewhere, and that might have been toward reflections on the nature and consequences of exile.

2   Previous Work

In what follows, the classical and biblical elements in Geoffrey's work are considered side-by-side. As will emerge, it is often difficult to disentangle the two, and it is not clear that it would be helpful to do so. But even if we keep them entangled, there are methodological difficulties of several kinds. Recent discussion of Geoffrey's sources has largely focused on his proximate medieval sources, such as *Historia Brittonum*, Gildas's *The Ruin of Britain*, and Bede's *Ecclesiastical History*.[25] But difficulties can arise where Geoffrey is using, for example, a narrative frame from *Historia Brittonum* but then filling it out with allusions from elsewhere.[26] On the other hand, Geoffrey's use of classical and biblical sources is largely nowadays taken for granted and little further thought has been devoted to it. The earliest studies, both dissertations emanating from Halle, Tausendfreund (on Virgil) and Feuerherd (on allusions to the Old Testament) remain useful both factually and methodologically.[27] This work implicitly lies behind all later work and it is important to realize how

---

25   *DGB*, pp. lvii–lix; see also Faral, *LLA*, vol. 2, passim; Tatlock, *LHB*, passim; S. Piggott, "The Sources of Geoffrey of Monmouth: I. The 'Pre-Roman' King-List", *Antiquity* 15 (1941), 269–86; id., "The sources of Geoffrey of Monmouth: II. The Stonehenge story", *Antiquity* 15 (1941), 305–19; D.C. Fowler, "Some Biblical Influences on Geoffrey of Monmouth's Historiography", *Traditio* 14 (1958), 378–85; E. Pace, "Geoffrey of Monmouth's Sources for the Cador and Camblan Narratives", *Arthuriana* 24 (2014), 45–78; and especially N. Wright, "Geoffrey of Monmouth and Bede", *AL* 6 (1986), 27–59; id., "Geoffrey of Monmouth and Gildas", *AL* 2 (1982), 1–40; id., "Geoffrey of Monmouth and Gildas Revisited", *AL* 5 (1985), 155–63.

26   An example of this is discussed below, pp. 87–89.

27   H. Tausendfreund, *Vergil und Gottfried von Monmouth*, Halle, 1913; P.O. Feuerherd, *Geoffrey of Monmouth und das Alte Testament mit berücksichtigung der Historia Britonum des Nennius*, Halle, 1915.

much of the later methodology can be traced back to these works. A particularly helpful illustration of this is Feuerherd's recognition of the notion of "reversal" (*Umkehrung* or *Verkehrung*);[28] while Geoffrey may at times reverse the direction of the biblical allusion, the Old Testament source may still be the source with which Geoffrey was working; a simple example, discussed further below, relates to the giants: while in the Old Testament giants invaded Israel, in Geoffrey Brutus and his men come to Britain, a land inhabited by giants.[29] It is clear, however, through the onomastic links that we are to see this as one of Geoffrey's sources despite the "reversal" in the direction of movement. Since then, Faral's notes to his 1929 discussion of Geoffrey's narrative are full of helpful, and mainly correct, identifications and references.[30] Hammer added more specific references in a 1947 article, and the apparatus to his edition of the First Variant Version identified numerous passages, although he failed to distinguish what was unique to the First Variant and what was in the vulgate version.[31] Most recently, Neil Wright has identified most of the classical and biblical references in his edition of the First Variant Version.[32] Much of this work, however, useful though it has been, has tended to concentrate on quotation-spotting, without exploring how Geoffrey might have absorbed and re-processed such narratives and themes. But even if specific allusion, or even quotations, can be identified, we should be asking how this helps us understand what Geoffrey was doing and how his audiences reacted to these allusions (if indeed they ever spotted them). It is easy to take such work for granted and to assume that such traditional analysis has already been done. But it still remains for us to consider the implications of what can be argued to be a deep and wide-ranging engagement with the classical and biblical knowledge at Geoffrey's disposal.

It is interesting, too, to ask why one should need to argue in these terms for a closer and more engaged reading of Geoffrey. There may be several reasons, which in part have to do with the way we (and our students) read Geoffrey and his sources. There is, for example, a tendency to focus on the Arthurian sections

---

28   For examples, see Feuerherd, *Geoffrey of Monmouth*, pp. 30, 34, and 38.

29   Feuerherd, *Geoffrey of Monmouth*, p. 34; see also below, pp. 94–98.

30   Faral, *LLA*, vol. 2.

31   J. Hammer, "Geoffrey of Monmouth's Use of the Bible in the *Historia Regum Britanniae*", *Bulletin of the John Rylands Library* 30 (1947), 293–311; Geoffrey of Monmouth, *De gestis Britonum*, ed. id., *Geoffrey of Monmouth. Historia regum Britanniae. A variant version edited from manuscripts*, Cambridge, MA, 1951, passim. The former contains much that is debatable. One of the difficulties is that it is much easier to spot poetic diction embedded in prose, and so easier to identify classical allusions (many of which derive from classical verse), than it is to identify allusions to the prose of the Old Testament.

32   *First Variant Version*, ed. Wright, pp. xxiii–xxvi (and especially n. 30 (Bible), nn. 31–37 (classical)).

of the work with less attention paid to the earlier books which are in fact much more indebted to classical and biblical modes of narrative. Furthermore, the same selectivity also applies to Geoffrey's sources: the Bible is now less well known, and the historical books of the Old Testament even less so. Likewise even the *Aeneid* tends to be read selectively, with some books more read than others. Books III and IX, which are highly important for our purposes, tend to be among the least read books. That said, to judge from the density of glossing on medieval manuscripts of the *Aeneid*, medieval readers were not entirely virtuous in this regard, either. Similarly, among other classical sources drawn upon by Geoffrey, Lucan and Statius are nowadays relatively under-read.

The questions, then, which the following discussion seeks to explore center on how an appreciation and understanding of Geoffrey's sources help us to understand the *DGB*: what did a particular verbal or episodic link with the Bible or a classical text mean to his audience? Additionally, we might return to our discussion of *Eclogue* I where we noted that the reference to the *Eclogue* in the shorter prologue was much briefer and more allusive than in the extended version containing the dedication to Waleran. It is not that the reference is indecipherable, but just that Geoffrey requires more work from his audience for them to derive full value from it. Interesting in this context is Wright's observation that one of the features which distinguishes the First Variant from the vulgate is that it contains much more explicit quotation from both classical and biblical sources.[33] Turned around the other way, this example simply highlights how little direct quotation there is in the vulgate version, which begs the question, why does Geoffrey make it so difficult for us (and perhaps also for his medieval audience) to read his allusions? Was the introduction (by someone else) of more obvious quotations in the First Variant (probably within a few years of the vulgate) a silent acknowledgement that Geoffrey had made life overly difficult for his audience?[34]

But we can begin with a more open-ended question: apart from a general expectation that he would be quoting from, and modeling his work on, biblical and classical sources, why should we think he would be? Or perhaps we might ask the question the other way round: why would we *not* think he would be quoting in this way? There is a broad answer which might allow us to make a little progress. In Geoffrey's view, Britons and the history of Britain form a strand of "universal history": they trace their ancestry back to Troy and beyond (like the Romans) and were a race in exile (like the Jews); Feuerherd noted that

---

33   *First Variant Version*, ed. Wright, pp. xxiii–xxvi.

34   On the authorship and date of the First Variant, see *First Variant Version*, ed. Wright, pp. xi–lxxviii (especially pp. lxx–lxxv).

"Das ganze Werk macht den Eindruck, als habe es Galfred in Parallele zu der Geschichte des Judenvolkes geschrieben."[35] One way of embedding Britain and the Britons in this broader historical narrative was to weave into their story the topoi and cross-references which hold all of those earlier narratives together: the rise and fall of kings, the movements of peoples, themes of treachery and deceit, patricides, fratricides, and civil wars. In that respect it might be argued that it does not really matter that a particular episode is based on a narrative attested in the Old Testament or Virgil or Lucan; it was all part of that same heroic and bloody world back into which the Britons' ancestry was to be traced and from which they had emerged.

3   A Digression into North Wales

This is a world which audiences of the mid-12th century would have been familiar. We might gain a firmer grasp on the expectations of a 12th-century audience by stepping back briefly from Geoffrey and looking at a text probably composed with a few years of the *DGB* and whose author almost certainly knew it and drew upon it. Examining this text, which has never before been brought into conjunction with Geoffrey, allows us to avoid getting tangled up in the intertextual problems we encounter comparing Geoffrey's work with that of William of Malmesbury or Henry of Huntingdon, and to get a sense of what an audience might expect from such narratives.[36] In 1137, more or less when Geoffrey was letting the *DGB* loose on the world, Gruffudd ap Cynan, king of Gwynedd, died; within a decade or so of his death, his biography, the *Life of Gruffudd ap Cynan*, was composed, the first and only biography of a medieval Welsh king. The author was probably a cleric, perhaps at least trained at St Davids (if not from there). He was familiar with the standard modes of biography, but also had the Latinity of the Old Testament embedded in his head. The *Life of Gruffudd ap Cynan* offers us a way of thinking about Geoffrey's modes of

---

35   Feuerherd, *Geoffrey of Monmouth*, p. 13: "the whole work creates the impression that Geoffrey wrote it in parallel to the history of the Jewish people"; we might compare the arrival of Brutus and his men in Britain toward the end of Book I (*DGB*, i.20.451–52) where Britain is described as the *promissa insula*, "promised isle".

36   On 12th-century history writing generally, see the discussions by A. Gransden, *Historical Writing in England, c.550–c.1307*, London, 1974, pp. 105–317; J. Gillingham, "The Context and Purposes of Geoffrey of Monmouth's *History of the Kings of Britain*", *Anglo-Norman Studies* 13 (1990), 99–118 (repr. in id. (ed.), *The English in the Twelfth Century: Imperialism, National Identity and Political Values*, Woodbridge, 2000, 19–39).

reference and his weaving together of classical and biblical allusions,[37] for we can observe what another biblically trained cleric from western Britain might do. Gruffudd's ancestry (and therefore his claim to the kingship of Gwynedd) was by no means clear-cut, and so the *Life* is structured to present someone who claimed to be royal in all branches of his kindred. For our purposes, the fact that on his father's side the biographer uses genealogical information derived from Geoffrey is less significant than that the earlier stages unite Trojans with early Old Testament figures, and thence back to Adam and God.[38] The author of the *Life* was well-versed in Old Testament royal narratives: when in the mid-1090s William Rufus decided to campaign in Gwynedd, his aims are summarized as follows: "... and (he) led into Gwynedd various squadrons of cavalry and infantry with which he planned to destroy and < > exterminate the natives so that he might not leave even a dog pissing against a wall".[39] The last phrase is strikingly Old Testament but with a literary twist;[40] in Kings and Samuel, the term is used to describe the destruction of all males, but here not even the male dogs are left alive to cock their legs against any walls that might have been left standing. The next sentence takes the conceit even further: all the trees were cut down so that there was not even shade to succor the people of Gwynedd: "He also embarked upon a scheme of cutting down and destroying the forests and groves so that not even, as it were, a shadow might be left by which the weaker might protect themselves."[41] Likewise, Norman kings are

37   See the *Life of Gruffudd ap Cynan*, ed. P. Russell, *Vita Griffini Filii Conani. The Medieval Latin Life of Gruffudd ap Cynan*, Cardiff, 2005; the text was translated into Welsh perhaps in the early decades of the 13th century (for which see *Historia Gruffud vab Kenan*, ed. D.S. Evans, *Historia Gruffud vab Kenan, gyda rhagymadrodd a nodiadau gan D. Simon Evans* [Historia Gruffudd ap Cynan, with introduction and notes by D. Simon Evans], Cardiff, 1977). This text had been known previously only from this Welsh version (though that was always thought to be a translation of a Latin text), but some twenty years ago the Latin text was discovered and reconstructed from a later manuscript version.

38   For discussion of his genealogy, see D. Thornton, "The Genealogy of Gruffud ap Cynan", in K.L. Maund (ed.), *Gruffud ap Cynan. A Collaborative Biography*, Woodbridge, 1996, pp. 79–108, at pp. 82–87; note that Thornton's discussion is based on the Welsh translation as the Latin text had not been discovered yet.

39   *Life of Gruffudd* §25/1, ed. Russell, pp. 78–79: "et in Venedotiam equitum peditumque varias turmas duxit, quibus incolas omnes funditus destruere et < > pessundare proposuit, ut ne canem mingentem ad parietem relinqueret" (reference is by section and sentence number; < > indicates a gap caused by damage to the Latin manuscript which can sometimes be filled by reference to later copies).

40   For discussion, see P. Russell, *Vita Griffini Filii Conani. The Medieval Latin Life of Gruffudd ap Cynan*, Cardiff, 2005, pp. 25–26, 48, and 155.

41   *Life of Gruffudd* §25/1, ed. Russell, pp. 78–79: "Aggressus est sylvas ac lucos scindere et evertere, ut ne vel umbra quidem, qua se imbecilliores tutarentur, superesset."

described as slaughtering the people of Gwynedd *in ore gladii*, "at sword-point" (*lit.* "at the mouth of a sword"): "so that he might at last root out the realm of Gruffudd and destroy his subjects at sword-point (as it were), slaughter them, and completely wipe them out".[42] The use of *ut dicam* here is the equivalent of putting speech-marks around the phrase and is intended to show that this is a quotation of a common Old Testament phrase used throughout the historical books.[43] However, the most striking amalgam of classical and biblical references is presented when the author digresses on the treachery by which Gruffudd was captured and imprisoned by the Normans:

> No-one should be surprised at the changes in human fortunes that sometimes it is necessary to win and sometimes to flee: indeed usually the cause is treachery. For in this way the unfaithful people of Israel delivered Judas Macabaeus, their king and leader, into the hands of Demetrius, the king; Judas, however, this warrior of God, like a giant or a lion avenged himself on both. Julius Caesar who had subjugated the whole world by continuous warfare was assassinated by treachery and daggers by the senators of Rome on the Capitolium itself. Even Arthur, the outstandingly noble king of the kings of the whole of Britain, worthy of undying fame, waged twelve wars against the Saxons and the Picts. In the first of these he had been totally routed by treachery in the country of Llwyd Coed, which is also called Llwyn Llwyd. But in the remaining battles he took worthy vengeance against the Saxons <...>, the oppressors of his own subjects, and they could not resist even as an old man.[44]

---

42   *Life of Gruffudd* §32/7, ed. Russell, pp. 86–87: "ut iam tandem Griffini principatum funditus eradicaret subditosque eius in ore (ut dicam) gladii perderet, mactaret, et funditus perimeret". For the biblical parallels to this phrase, see *Life of Gruffudd*, ed. Russell, p. 164.

43   *Life of Gruffudd*, ed. Russell, p. 164.

44   *Life of Gruffudd* §14/13–18, ed. Russell, pp. 64–65: "Nemo miretur has humanarum rerum vicissitudines, ut interdum vincere, interdum fugere sit necesse: proditio siquidem cum primis causa est. Sic enim in manus Demetrii regis infidelis populus Israeliticus Iudam Maccabeum regem ac principem suum tradiderunt: verum Bellator hic Dei, ut gygas vel leo seipsum ultus est in utrosque. Iulius Caesar qui continuis bellis orbem terrarum sibi subiugarat, a senatoribus Romanis in ipso Capitolio Romano proditione ac pugionibus confoditur. Arthurus etiam regum totius Britanniae rex praenobilis et fama nunquam intermoritura dignus duodecim bella contra Saxones ac Pictos gessit. In quorum primo fusus fugatusque erat ex proditione in civitate Llwyd Coet quae et Llwyn Llwyt dicitur. At in reliquis de Saxonibus < > subditorum suorum oppressoribus poenas dignas sumpsit, cui ne seni quidem resistere potuerunt." For discussion, see *Life of Gruffudd*, ed. Russell, p. 48.

The line of argument is essentially that all great men are brought down by treachery, as this is the only way they can fall. The triad of great men with whom Gruffudd is compared unites the worlds of the Old Testament, Rome, and Britain: Judas Maccabaeus, Julius Caesar, and Arthur. The reference to the last of these is almost certainly dependent on Geoffrey, as the *DGB* is the earliest surviving source to present a narrative of the fall of Arthur as a result of treachery.[45] But the biographical details relating to the other two are imported from the Old Testament and perhaps Suetonius, respectively, although there are plenty of sources recounting the death of Caesar. A striking feature of the *Life of Gruffudd ap Cynan* is that it uses the career of Judas Maccabaeus as its primary template for the life of Gruffudd: the various successes, setbacks, betrayal, and eventual triumph of Gruffudd are depicted as mirroring Judas's career. The parallels are not just thematic; for example, even the language of *ut gygas uel leo*, "like a giant or a lion", used twice in the *Life of Gruffudd ap Cynan*, is a quotation from 1 Maccabaeus 3:3–4.[46]

When Gruffudd's chief poet, Gellan, is killed at the battle of Aberlleiniog, the author claims he lacks the skills of a Cicero or Homer to recount the deeds of Gruffudd in the way that Gellan would have done:

> With what variety of knowledge, with what splendour of eloquence should he have been, he who could narrate the famous deeds of Gruffudd and his achievements in Wales, Ireland, and the subject isles of Denmark, and among various other peoples; I freely admit that I do not have that ability, nor indeed would I be equal to such a great task even if I had the power of the eloquence of Tullius in oratory or I could defeat Homer in formal <verse>.[47]

The claim reaches back into classical literature to find the parallels which he cannot match.

Although the *Life of Gruffudd ap Cynan* was composed in Wales, it allows us to get a sense of how a contemporary writer, with a similar background and

---

45   The use of the spelling "Merlinus" in *Life of Gruffudd* §8/1, ed. Russell, pp. 58–59, instead of a form based more closely on Welsh "Myrddin", may also have been taken over from Geoffrey.

46   *Life of Gruffudd* §§14/14 and 18/8, ed. Russell, pp. 64–65, 70–71.

47   *Life of Gruffudd* §23/17, ed. Russell, pp. 76–77: "Quanta scientiarum varietate, quanto eloquentiae splendore perpolitum esse oporteret qui Griffini egregia facinora, res praeclare gestas in Cambria, Hibernia, insulis Daniae subiectis, aliisque diversis nationibus enarrare posset; ingenue fateor deesse mihi facultatem, immo nec tanto oneri posse esse parem, si vel soluta oratione Tullii eloquentia pollerem, vel adstricta < > Homerum vincerem."

training as Geoffrey's, would be working; it has the added advantage of not being a text Geoffrey could have used, though it does look as if the author of the *Life* may have been one of the earliest users of the *DGB*. The combination of particular phrases, such as *in parietem mingentem*, "pissing against a wall", and *ore gladii*, "at sword-point", together with strong narrative parallels, seem to have allowed an audience to settle into a familiar world of heroic struggle, but one in which genealogical links were important and everyone was ultimately related. In some respects, the allusions of the *Life of Gruffudd ap Cynan* are closer to those in the First Variant Version than the vulgate, though that might reflect its slightly later date of composition, but at any rate it can reassure us that for narrative compositions of this period what we find in the *DGB* was not out of the ordinary, even if perhaps more allusive.

4   Some Specific Questions

The general question posed above as to why we would expect to find classical and biblical allusions has so far been given a general answer. But there are more specific reasons as well to expect these parallels.

First, we might consider the narrative (and in some instances the manuscript) context. As noted above, the narrative of the *DGB* is explicitly a continuation of Dares Phrygius's *The Fall of Troy*. But Aeneas is a marginal figure in the *DGB*, lasting for all of five lines in the standard edition (I.vi.48–52), and perhaps for very good reasons; unlike the usual version of the fall of Troy involving the wooden horse and so on, Dares depicts Aeneas as the traitor who lets the Greeks in.[48] Dares ends at that point (and so Geoffrey effectively begins) with a catastrophic act of treachery. This would not be the last treacherous act in the *DGB*, and more specifically it is difficult to believe that the depiction of Vortigern as the king who let the English into Britain does not owe something to the Aeneas of Dares. Furthermore, as Julia Crick has noted, 27 manuscripts of Geoffrey's *DGB* (out of a current total of 224 manuscripts) are preceded by a text of Dares.[49] At a later stage, in the Welsh versions of Geoffrey, *Brut y Brenhinedd* ("History of the Kings"), a frequent collocation of texts is *Ystorya Dared* (Dares), *Brut y Brenhinedd* (*DGB*), and *Brut y Tywysogyon* ("History of the Princes", the medieval Welsh continuation of Geoffrey in annalistic form).

---

48   Dares Phrygius, *The Fall of Troy* §XLI, ed. F. Meister, *Daretis Phrygii. De excidio Troiae historia*, Leipzig, 1873; while not the form of the story used by Virgil (for obvious reasons), a similar narrative is suggested in the opening of Livy's *History of Rome* (i.1).

49   Crick, *DR*, pp. 37–39.

Manuscript context then is one way to establish the kind of thematic connections between texts which would give rise to borrowings between them.

We should also consider what little we might know about Geoffrey's education. There is much we do not know, but it is highly likely that in the late 11th and early 12th century the young Geoffrey would have been brought up at school on versions of the so-called *Liber Catonianus*; the contents varied somewhat over time but invariably contained the text called *Disticha Catonis* ("Distichs of Cato") which consisted of a series of moralizing instructions. This evidence gives us some indication of what being well read amounted to. For our purposes, one section is particularly illuminating:

> If by chance you were to want to learn about the cultivation of the land, read Virgil ... If you desire to know about the Roman and Punic wars, you should seek out Lucan who spoke of warfare. If loving pleases you in any way, or by reading it pleases you learn to love, seek out Ovid.[50]

It may not strike us as odd that Virgil is prescribed for reading on agriculture, when the tending of the land was an inherently political activity, but we might have thought that he would have been on the reading-list for war as well. But Lucan is recommended for war and especially for *Romana ... et Punica ... bella*, presumably for the Punic wars and the Civil War, though there is no evidence that he wrote anything about the former; parts of his *Civil War*, however, are set in Africa and that may have given rise to the confusion.[51] Finally there is Ovid for love. We may ask where the prose writers are to be found, but it is likely that what we have here is a reading list for an education in verse rather than all their reading. All three authors appear in some shape or form in the *DGB*; while Virgil and Lucan would not be surprising, given the subject matters and themes, the presence of Ovid is striking. But we perhaps have to recall how many passages there are where the driving force behind the action is a man's desire for a woman, e.g. Silvius and a niece of Lavinia, Uther and Igerna, Vortigern and Rowena, and so on; no doubt the image of Helen as a catalyst of

---

50   *Distichs of Cato*, ed. M. Boas, *Disticha Catonis recensuit et apparatu critico instruxit Marcus Boas*, Amsterdam, 1952, p. 90: "Telluris si forte velis cognoscere cultus, Virgilium legito ... Si Romana cupis et Punica noscere bella, Lucanum quaeras, qui Martis proelia dixit. Si quid amare libet, vel discere amare legendo, Nasonem petito." On the *Distichs of Cato*, see also P. Russell, *Reading Ovid in Medieval Wales*, Columbus, 2017, pp. 218–20, 223.

51   *Punicus* here should be taken to refer to North Africa rather than more specifically to Carthage; a significant element of Lucan's poem is set in Africa.

war lies behind some of this, as is the Dido and Aeneas episode, but there is certainly Ovidian passion built into the narrative as well.[52]

A striking example of Ovid's presence is in the *VM* (in addition to the allusion in the prologue[53]) where a messenger to Merlin in his mountain-top hideaway seeks to soothe Merlin's complaint by singing a lament about Guendoloena, Merlin's wife, and Ganieda, his sister: "One for a brother, one for a husband weeps."[54] By the reference to *cum modulis cithare*, "by the notes of his lute", we are reminded at once of Tityrus under his tree.[55] At one point the laments of the two women are compared to the lamentations of Dido (when abandoned by Aeneas), of Phyllis (when Demophoon never returns), and of Briseis (at potentially losing Achilles):

> So once Sidonian Dido mourned, when the fleet weighed
> anchor and Aeneas hastened on his way.
> So once poor Phyllis sighed and wept
> when Demophoon failed his appointed hour.
> So Briseis cried, Achilles lost.[56]

All three figure in Ovid's *Heroides*, "letters which provide a female critique of male heroism through passionate protests about the men's betrayal and abandonment of their lovers".[57] Clarke observes that "these examples of womanly sorrow are in fact all different from Guendoloena's case and from one another, but it does not matter."[58] However, it is not clear how different they are; it rather depends of the degree of magnification with which they are scrutinized. The common denominator is the loss of a man, husband, lover, or brother:

---

52   The sources for the female characters in Geoffrey are generally understudied; for studies, which are more interested in the contemporary context, and their treatment in later reworkings of Geoffrey, cf. F. Tolhurst, *Geoffrey of Monmouth and the Feminist Origins of the Arthurian Legend*, New York, 2012; id., *Geoffrey of Monmouth and the Translation of Female Kingship*, New York, 2013.

53   See above pp. 72–74.

54   *VM*, ll. 170–97; quotation is *VM*, l. 187: "Hec fratrem flet et illa virum."

55   *VM*, l. 166, ed. Clarke; the translation is mine, as Clarke's rendering "by strumming on the guitar" creates quite the wrong impression; cf. Parry's translation: "with cadences on the cither", Parry, *The Vita Merlini*, p. 41.

56   *VM*, ll. 191–95: "Non secus indoluit Sidonia Dido solutis / classibus Enee tunc cum properaret abire. / Cum non Demophoon per tempora pacta rediret / taliter ingemuit flevitque miserrima Phillis. / Briseis absentem sic deploravit Achillem."

57   Tolhurst, *Geoffrey of Monmouth and the Feminist Origins*, p. 119; see Ovid, *Heroides* VII, II, III respectively, ed. and trans. G. Showerman (rev. J.P. Gould), *Ovid Heroides and Amores*, 2nd ed., Cambridge, MA, 1977.

58   *VM*, ed. Clarke, p. 138.

Aeneas was (in Roman eyes) married to Dido before he left her in Carthage; Demophoon seems to have been married to Phyllis but never came back; Briseis's main concern is that in his sulk Achilles will not do anything about getting her back and may go off home to Greece and leave her behind, but implicit in this is the audience's knowledge that he will be killed by Hector. At this point Guendoloena and Ganieda have no sense of an outcome and so one way of reading these *exempla* is that they are covering all possible options.

So far we have been considering the context of the composition of the DGB and have drawn attention to the importance of drawing parallels between events in Britain and in the classical and biblical worlds. In that respect, the synchronisms are of particular importance. Throughout the early books and occasionally thereafter, Geoffrey provides synchronisms between what is happening in Britain and elsewhere, typically (and, where relevant) in Troy, Greece, Rome, and the biblical world (both Old and new Testament). For example:

> At that time the priest Eli was ruling in Judaea and the Ark of the Covenant had been captured by the Philistines. The sons of Hector were ruling in Troy after the descendants of Antenor were exiled. In Italy there ruled the third of the Latins, Silvius Aeneas, the son of Aeneas and the uncle of Brutus.[59]
>
> At that time King David was ruling in Judaea, Silvius Latinus was king in Italy, and Gad, Nathan and Asaph were prophesying in Israel.[60]
>
> At that time Solomon began to build the Lord's temple in Jerusalem, where the queen of Sheba came to hear his wisdom, and Italy Silvius Alba was succeeded by his son Silvius Epitus.[61]
>
> At that time lived the prophets Isaiah and Hosea; and Rome was founded on April 21st by the twins Romulus and Remus.[62]
>
> In his reign was born Our Lord Jesus Christ, whose precious blood redeemed the human race, bound beforehand in the chains of idolatry.[63]

---

59   DGB, i.22.506–09: "Regnabat tunc in Iudaea Heli sacerdos et archa testamenti capta erat a Philisteis. Regnabant etiam in Troia filii Hectoris, expulsis posteris Antenoris. Regnabat in Italia Siluius Aeneas, Aeneae filius, auunculus Bruti, Latinorum tercius."

60   DGB, ii.27.91–92: "Et tunc Dauid rex regnabat in Iudaea et Siluius Latinus in Italia et Gad Nathan et Asaph prophetabant in Israel."

61   DGB, ii.28.113–15: "Tunc Salomon coepit aedificare templum Domino in Ierusalem et regina Saba uenit audire sapientiam eius, et tunc Siluius Epitus patri Albae in regnum successit."

62   DGB, ii.32.283–85: "Tunc Ysaias et Osea prophetabant et Roma condita est .xi. kl Mai a geminis fratribus Remo et Romulo."

63   DGB, iiii.64.275–77: "In diebus illis natus est dominus noster Iesus Christus, cuius precioso sanguine redemptum est humanum genus, quod anteacto tempore daemonum catena obligabatur."

At that time the apostle Peter, after founding the church of Antioch, came to Rome, became its bishop and sent the evangelist Mark to Egypt to preach the text of his gospel.[64]

The synchronisms occur very frequently in Book II; there are none in Book III, and only two in Book IIII, marking the birth of Christ and the establishment of Peter as bishop of Rome. At the end of Book IIII, Geoffrey states that he has left the Christian mission in Britain to Gildas and he will focus on the history of the Britons. The first of these synchronisms seems to be adapted from *Historia Brittonum*, and it may be that this encouraged Geoffrey to add further synchronisms to his narrative.[65] It is also noteworthy that the synchronisms peter out at much the same point as does Geoffrey's interest in reign-lengths and how the kings are related.[66] In other words, by this point the *DGB* has gradually become more inward-looking and less concerned with the world beyond Britain, though, as emerges in the narrative, that world will not leave Britain alone. But the point of these synchronisms seems to be to mark narrative stages and what is happening elsewhere (and industrious readers could have collated them with copies of the various chronicles they may have had to hand). Not only, therefore, does it give the audience a sense that Britain was part of that wider world, but it created an expectation that matters in Britain might turn out in a similar way. The high frequency of such synchronisms in Book II, especially 26–32, is noteworthy, and creates a sense of events elsewhere moving very quickly; but it is a period where we see the early kings of Rome (all Brutus's relatives, in fact) synchronized with Saul, David, Solomon, and the prophets. But back home, Britain is not missing out; as we shall discuss below, Ebraucus is producing offspring from numerous wives at a biblical rate; Leil is founding Carlisle, and Rud Hudibras Shaftesbury, and a local eagle is producing its own brand of prophecy (though not much to Geoffrey's liking). The allusions need not be obvious, but one only need mention the foundation of Rome by Romulus and Remus to hint both at the dominance of Rome in the coming narrative and at the fratricidal parallels which will be played out in Britain.

---

64   *DGB*, iiii.68.340–43: "Eodem tempore Petrus apostolus Antiochenam ecclesiam fundauit Romamque deinde ueniens tenuit ibidem episcopatum misitque Marcum euangelistam in Aegyptum praedicare euangelium quod scripserat." There are further synchronisms at *DGB*, ii.26.68–69, ii.26.84, ii.29.122–23, ii.30.129–30.

65   *Historia Brittonum* §11, ed. and trans. J. Morris, *Nennius: British History and the Welsh Annals* (Arthurian Period Sources, 8), London, 1980, p. 61. I am grateful to Ben Guy for making this and the following point to me.

66   Cf. Geoffrey of Monmouth, *De gestis Britonum*, trans. Thorpe, pp. 286–88 for list of reign-lengths and synchronisms.

When Cassibellaunus celebrates a victory over Caesar, he does so with a feast of Solomonic proportions:

> Cassibellaunus, overjoyed at having triumphed for a second time, issued an edict that all the British nobles should gather with their wives in the city of Trinovantum to hold fitting ceremonies for their native gods, who had granted them victory over so mighty an emperor. They came without delay and slaughtered animals in various sacrifices. At these were offered forty thousand cows, a hundred thousand sheep, innumerable birds of different species and also a collection of thirty thousand woodland beasts of every kind. After they had completed their offerings to the gods, they refreshed themselves with the left-over food, as was the custom at sacrifices. Then they spent the rest of the night and the following day in various sports.[67]

Feuerherd has noted that this is derived from the account of Solomon's feast in I Kings 8:62–63, though it has also been pointed out that the combination of feast, sacrifices, and games reads more like a Virgilian celebration.[68] Typically, Geoffrey uses it to set the stage for civil strife: the young men fall out, leading to a breakdown in relations between Cassibellaunus and Androgeus, who goes over to Caesar's side and invites him back into Britain with the inevitable result. As is often the case with Geoffrey, episodes early in the narrative find reflexes later in the work: this great feast at which Cassibellaunus behaves like Solomon has close parallels with Arthur's celebration at Caerleon;[69] the reigns of neither ultimately turn out well.

---

67   *DGB*, iiii.61.134–44: "Cassibellaunus autem, secundo triumphum adeptus, maximo gaudio fluctuans edictum fecit ut omnes proceres Britanniae in urbe Trinouantum cum uxoribus suis conuenirent debitasque sollempnitates patriis deis celebrarent, qui uictoriam sibi de tanto imperatore concesserant. Cumque omnes postposita mora aduenissent, diuersa sacrificia facientes occisioni pecudum indulserunt. Litauerunt ibi .xl. milia uaccarum et centum milia ouium diuersorumque generum uolatilia quae leuiter sub numero non cadebant, praeterea .xxx. milia siluestrium ferarum cuiusque generis collectarum. Mox, cum diis suos honores perfecissent, refecerunt se residuis epulis ut in sacrificiis fieri solebat. Exin quod noctis et diei restabat diuersos ludos componentes praeterierunt."

68   Feuerherd, *Geoffrey of Monmouth*, pp. 52–55; Faral, *LLA*, vol. 2, pp. 153–54; Tatlock, *LHB*, p. 261.

69   *DGB*, ix.156–57.

5   Three Case Studies

So as to avoid a piecemeal approach to discussing the multiple allusions in Geoffrey's work, what follows takes the general observations made above and applies them to three case studies. At this point we shall be less interested in identifying direct quotations and more concerned with the bigger episodes and structural themes, since they are more helpful in understanding how all of this might work. The difficulty is that one is then left to fall back on a certain amount of intuition and guess-work; if we leave aside the hard proof of a quotation, what do we have to work with that produces any kind of convincing case? In the end it will come down to likelihoods; can it really be the case that Geoffrey could quote (admittedly allusively and evasively at times) from, and direct our attention to, classical authors and biblical sources and not be aware of the bigger narrative and thematic structures into which he was reaching for those briefer and more glancing allusions? The answer must surely be that he could not have been. A further issue is the tendency to think in binary terms: it is either a classical source or a biblical source? But as we have already seen, sources can easily be both working side by side or even more closely than that; these observations reflect an underlying unease as to whether we should be even separating Geoffrey's classical and biblical inheritance from his use of other materials which themselves draw upon that same inheritance.

6   The Travels of Brutus

It has long been known that the basic narrative and geographical framework of the *DGB* Book I derives from *Historia Brittonum* §10; the short section of text printed below encapsulates the frame of Geoffrey's Book I, which takes up 462 lines in the standard printed edition:[70]

> Aeneas founded Alba and afterwards took a wife and she bore to him a son called Silvius. He married a wife, who became pregnant, and when Aeneas was told that this daughter-in-law was pregnant, he sent word to his son Ascanius, to send a wizard to examine the wife, to discover what

---

70   I follow the text used in *Historia Brittonum* §10, ed. and trans. Morris, pp. 19 and 60. Manuscript variants in Mommsen's edition include *Bruto* and *Brutus* (*Historia Brittonum*), ed. T. Mommsen, *Chronica Minora saec. IV. V. VI. VII. Vol. 3* [Minor Chronicles of the 4th, 5th, 6th, 7th centuries, Vol. 3] (Monumenta Germaniae Historica, Auctores Antiquissimi, 13), Berlin, 1898, pp. 111–222, at p. 150. For further discussion of Geoffrey's use of *Historia Brittonum*, see Ben Guy's chapter in the present volume.

she had in her womb, whether it was male or female. The wizard examined the wife and returned, but he was killed by Ascanius because of his prophecy, for he told him that the woman had a male in her womb, who would be the child of death, for he would kill his mother and his father, and be hateful to all men. So it happened; for his mother died in his birth, and the boy was reared, and named Britto.

Much later according to the wizard's prophecy, when he was playing with others he killed his father with an arrow shot, not on purpose, but by accident. He was driven from Italy, [...] and came to the islands of the Tyrrhene Sea, and was driven from Greece, because of the killing of Turnus, whom Aeneas had killed, and arrived in Gaul, where he founded the city of Tours, which is called Turnis, and later he came to this island, which is named Britannia from his name, filled it with his race, and dwelt there. From that day Britain has been inhabited until the present day.[71]

The source of much of the detail used to fill out this account is Virgil's *Aeneid*, and in particular Books III and IX. The former, dramatically presented as the second part of Aeneas's narrative to Dido, relates Aeneas's storm-tossed journey from Troy to Carthage by way of Thrace, Delos, Crete, and Buthrotum on the Adriatic coast of Greece to visit Helenus, the Trojan seer. The journey is littered with confusing prophecies; the Trojans are driven in different directions by the contradictory whims of Venus and Juno, each at different times capable of turning Jupiter to their will. Throughout the narrative of these early books

---

71   *Historia Brittonum* §10, ed. and trans. Morris, pp. 19 and 60: "Aeneas autem Albam condidit et postea uxorem duxit et peperit ei filium nomine Silvium. Silvius autem duxit uxorem et gravida fuit et nuntiatum est Aeneae, quod nurus sua gravida esset et misit ad Ascanium filium suum, ut mitteret magum suum ad considerandam uxorem, ut exploraret quid haberet in utero, si masculum vel feminam. et magus consideravit uxorem et reversus est. propter hanc vaticinationem magus occisus est ab Ascanio, quia dixit Ascanio, quod masculum haberet in utero mulier et filius mortis erit, quia occidet patrem suum et matrem suam et erit exosus omnibus hominibus. sic evenit: in nativitate illius mulier mortua est et nutritus est filius et vocatum est nomen eius Britto. Post multum intervallum iuxta vaticinationem magi, dum ipse ludebat cum aliis, ictu sagittae occidit patrem suum non de industria, sed casu. et expulsus est ab Italia et arminilis fuit et venit ad insulas maris Tyrreni et expulsus est a Graecis causa occisionis Turni, quam Aeneas occiderat, et pervenit ad Gallos usque et ibi condidit civitatem Turonorum, quae vocatur Turnis. et postea ad istam pervenit insulam, quae a nomine suo accepit nomen, id est Brittanniam et implevit eam cum suo genere et habitavit ibi. ab illo autem die habitata est Brittannia usque in hodiernum diem." The [...] indicates a gap in the translation where Morris omitted to render *et arminilis fuit*, which has admittedly defied interpretation; Mommsen notes the manuscript variants, *arminiis, armil(l)is, armimil(l)is, ariminis, armiger*, and some possible but unlikely emendations (*Historia Brittonum*, ed. Mommsen, p. 152).

of the *Aeneid*, we are constantly reminded of the Trojan diaspora, Helenus and Andromache carried by Pyrrhus, Antenor, the founder of Padua, and so on.[72] Book IX, on the other hand, is set in Italy after they have finally landed on the banks of the Tiber only to find the site of the future Rome already occupied by a Greek king; it relates the early struggles of the Trojans to establish a bridgehead in Italy. Book I of the *DGB* tells of the travels of Brutus after he is sent into exile after accidentally killing his father Silvius. Brutus's journey, like that of Aeneas, is winding and slow, with several abortive attempts to settle before finally reaching Britain – which of course was his onomastic destiny. Geoffrey clearly drew on these books of the *Aeneid* as models. The most striking episode in this respect is his encounter with the descendants of Helenus (Aeneas's host) who had been enslaved by the Greek king Pandrasus. One of the interesting features both in Virgil and Geoffrey are the narrative reversals; just as in *Aeneid* IX the Trojans are at times the besieged (as at Troy), but then on other occasions also the besiegers, so Brutus, as leader of the descendants of Helenus, besieges and outwits the Greeks. Rather than remain with the permanent threat of Greek retaliation, Brutus and his men decide to leave with Brutus accepting the offer of Pandrasus's daughter Innogin as his wife. After a short journey, they land at the deserted island of Leogetia, where in an abandoned temple of Diana, Brutus seeks guidance; she appears in a dream, and in a verse prophecy, directs him to an *insula in occeano ... undique clausa mari*, "an island in the ocean ... surrounded by the sea".[73] This passage, just like the subsequent episode in Aquitania, combines elements from both *Aeneid* III, IX, and elsewhere. The link with Helenus is the obvious signpost that we should look to *Aeneid* III, but the tactics of the warfare in both episodes with Trojans combining with Greeks, and at some points behaving like them, such as the use of deceit and trickery to overcome the enemy, a prophecy delivered on an island, can all be paralleled in these books of the *Aeneid*. We can also track details: Brutus's growing reputation, *diuulgata ... per uniuersas nationes ipsius fama*, "As Brutus's fame spread throughout every land", echoes Virgil's description of the fame of the Trojans and their war, *bellaque iam fama totum uolgata per orbem*, "wars now spread by rumour throughout the whole world", which Aeneas only realizes when he sees the frieze on the temple of Juno in Carthage;[74] Silvius's love for a niece of Lavinia, *furtiuae ueneri indulgens*, "indulging a secret passion", by which Brutus was conceived, is described in the same terms as

---

72   M. Hurley, *Geoffrey of Monmouth*, New York, 1994, pp. 14–18.

73   *DGB*, i.16.306.

74   *DGB*, i.7.75–76; Virgil, *Aeneid* i.457, ed. R.A.B. Mynors, *P. Virgili Maronis Opera*, Oxford, 1969.

Dido's contemplated love for Aeneas.[75] Some of the most striking connections are made, as it were, in transit: as Brutus and his men sail through the western Mediterranean (though the geography is hazy to say the least), they encounter Corineus, a descendant of Antenor, who plays a crucial role in the settlement of Britain; in the *Aeneid*, Venus uses Antenor as an example of a Trojan who was permitted to settle elsewhere, unlike Aeneas, who was still being hounded by Juno.[76] They also encounter Achaemenides in Sicily, who was abandoned by Ulysses in the escape from the cave of the Cyclops.[77] All these cross-references and parallels form part of an intricate weaving together which ties Brutus and the Britons into a bigger story.

One final aspect of the Virgilian flavor is reflected in an interest in onomastics: when Brutus finally lands in Britain,

> Brutus names the island Britain after himself and called his followers Britons. He wanted to be remembered for ever for giving them his name. For this reason the language of his people, previously known as Trojan or 'crooked Greek', was henceforth called British.[78]

Both country and language are to be named after Brutus. In this erasure of the onomastics of Troy, there is an echo of *Aeneid* XII.819–40 where Juno, finally acknowledging defeat, still insists, with Jupiter's grudging agreement, on the name and language of Troy being effaced. But throughout the DGB, just as in the *Aeneid*, there is an interest in the causality of onomastics: *Corineus* : Cornwall; *Turnus* (nephew of Brutus, but echoing Aeneas's rival in Italy) : *Turo* (Tours); *Troia Nova* : *Trinovantum*; *Lud* : London; the sons of Brutus, *Locrinus, Albanactus, Camber* : *Loegria, Albania, Cambria* respectively, etc. Onomastic explanations of this kind were ubiquitous in Geoffrey's world (and we would not necessarily need to seek a model elsewhere) but they are particularly common in the origin-legends of the *Aeneid*; for example, the explanation of the

---

75   DGB, i.6.54; Virgil, *Aeneid* iv.171, ed. Mynors. We might also note that this is one of the many ways in which Brutus prefigures Arthur; both are presented as the product of a "furtive love".

76   DGB, i.17.329–30; Virgil, *Aeneid* i.241–49, ed. Mynors.

77   On giants, see below, pp. 94–98.

78   DGB, i.21.459–62: "Denique Brutus de nomine suo insulam Britanniam appellat sociosque suos Britones. Volebat enim ex diriuatione nominis memoriam habere perpetuam. Vnde postmodum loquela gentis, quae prius Troiana siue curuum Graecum nuncupabatur, dicta fuit Britannica." On "crooked Greek", see Hurley, *Geoffrey of Monmouth*, pp. 11–12, and Ben Guy in this volume, pp. 39–40.

name of Latium as where Saturn "lay hidden" (*latuisset, Aeneid* VIII.322–23);[79] and the names of the noble families of Rome as derived from the eponymous heroes listed in the catalogue of Italian heroes in *Aeneid* VII.640–814.

7   The Passing of Kings and Old Testament Models for "Regime Change"

Given the geographical range and narrative context, the primary frame of reference for the *DGB* Book I is unsurprisingly Virgilian, and no more surprising are the Old Testament models which come to the fore in Books II–III where the succession of pre-Roman kings is narrated. Old Testament kings are usually defined by their heroic stature and courage, their fertility, and their ambitious urban planning. As Feuerherd noticed, the depiction of Ebraucus, which is a composite of Saul, David, and Solomon, does this and more:[80]

> By his twenty wives Ebraucus fathered twenty sons and thirty daughters and ruled the kingdom of Britain with great energy for sixty years. His sons were named Brutus Greenshield, Margadud, Sisillius, Regin, Morvid, Bladud, Iagon, Bodloan, Kincar, Spaden, Gaul, Dardan, Eldad, Iuor, Cangu, Hector, Kerin, Rud, Assarach, Buel; the names of his daughters were Gloigin, Innogin, Oudas, Guenlian, Gaurdid, Angarad, Guenlodee, Tangustel, Gorgon, Medlan, Methahel, Ourar, Mailure, Kambreda, Ragan, Gael, Ecub, Nest, Chein, Stadud, Gladus, Ebrein, Blangan, Aballac, Angaes, Galaes (in her day the most beautiful woman in Britain or Gaul), Edra, Anor, Stadiald and Egron. Ebraucus sent all his daughters to Italy to Silvius Alba, who had succeeded Silvius Latinus. There they wedded Trojan nobles, whom the Latin and Sabine women refused to marry. His sons, led by Assaracus, took ship to Germany, where with Silvius Alba's help they subdued the inhabitants and conquered the kingdom.[81]

---

79   J.J. O'Hara, *True Names. Vergil and the Alexandrian Tradition of Etymological Wordplay*, Ann Arbor, 1996, pp. 207–08. For the use of names in Roman poetry, see O'Hara, *True Names*, pp. 66–73 on proper names, and 115–242 for a catalogue of the etymological wordplay in the *Aeneid*, and the essays in J. Booth and R. Maltby (eds.), *What's in a Name? The Significance of Proper Names in Classical Latin Literature*, Swansea, 2006.

80   Feuerherd, *Geoffrey of Monmouth*, pp. 36–39. We may note too that this paragraph is wrapped around with synchronisms referring to these kings; see above, pp. 84–86.

81   *DGB*, ii.27.95–108 (the following Latin quote omits the lists of names): "[sc. Ebraucus] [g]enuit etiam .xx. filios ex uiginti coniugibus quas habebat nec non et .xxx. filias regnumque Britanniae .lx. annis fortissime tractauit. Erant autem nomina filiorum eius …; nomina autem filiarum …, Galaes (omnium pulcherrima quae tunc in Britannia siue in

Furthermore, like any self-respecting Old Testament king, Ebraucus had territorial ambitions not only in Britain, where he founded York (eponymously *Kaerebrauc*) and Dumbarton, but most of his sons went off and conquered Germany. He also sent his daughters off to marry the Trojans in Italy *quorum cubilia et Latinae et Sabinae diffugiebant*, "whom the Latin and Sabine women refused to marry", thus side-stepping the tale of the rape of the Sabine women.[82] But, like all sensible rulers of Britain, Ebraucus was careful to maintain links with Europe, and the effect of such European integration is, of course, that everyone who then comes back to Britain, whether the Romans or the English (and later the Bretons), is genetically related. So even when Geoffrey is in Old Testament mode, he is careful not abandon the other strands of the narrative.

Not all reigns are explored in such detail. Variation of pace is characteristic of Geoffrey's style. After the long slow narrative of King Lear, in the passage which follows, we run through six generations in as many lines, beginning with the death of Cunedagius, briefly pausing to record (but not to dwell upon) some Old Testament plagues, bloody rain and flies, before slowing for another thematically significant moment:

> When Cunedagius finally died, he was succeeded by his son Rivallo, a peaceful and fortunate youth, who ruled the kingdom well. While he was king, it rained blood for three days and people died from a plague of flies. He was succeeded by his son Gurgustius; next came Sisillius, next Iago, Gurgustius's nephew, then Kinmarcus, Sisillius's son, and finally Gorbodugo. He had two sons, called Ferreux and Porrex. When their father grew old, they quarrelled about which ones of them should succeed to the throne. Porrex felt the greater desire and tried to kill his brother Ferreux by setting an ambush, but the latter discovered the plot and escaped his brother by crossing to France. Aided by the French king, Suhardus, he returned to fight his brother, In the battle Ferreux and all the troops with him were killed. Their mother, named Iudon, was greatly angered by the news of the death of one of her sons and came to hate the other, whom she had loved less. She burned with such fury over Ferreux's death that she desired to take revenge on his brother. Waiting until he was asleep, she and her serving women fell upon him and tore him to

---

Gallia fuerant), ... Has omnes direxit pater in Italiam ad Siluium Albam, qui post Siluium Latinum regnabat. Fuerunt ibi maritatae nobilioribus Troianis, quorum cubilia et Latinae et Sabinae diffugiebant. At filii duce Assaraco fratre duxerunt classem in Germaniam et auxilio Siluii Albae usi subiugato populo adepti sunt regnum."

82   *DGB*, ii.27.106.

pieces. For a long time after that, civil strife troubled the people and the kingdom was ruled by five kings, who inflicted defeats on one another.[83]

One of the major themes of the *DGB* involves brothers falling out over the kingship and the inevitable descent into civil war (*civilis discordia*) which follows.[84] Here Ferreux and Porrex fall out in time-honored fashion. Whether we see the model for this as Cain and Abel, other Old Testament examples, Romulus and Remus, or simply Geoffrey's own experience of 12th-century Britain (where especially in Wales royal siblings were always in dispute), the message is that this is the way it was and always will be, and the consequences are never good.[85] Here we also have a maternal strand to the narrative with their mother Iudon and her maid-servants conspiring to dismember Ferreux.[86] The consequence is civil war, which thematically takes us back into the world of Lucan.

But all is not lost. The last episode of Book II ushers in Dunuallo Molmutius, who is depicted as a Solomonic figure, fearless in battle and wise in peace. Once he has gained control and quelled the civil strife, he sets about handing down laws to the Britons, and generally rules like Solomon.[87] But there are other echoes in this episode as well: in the midst of the battle against Rudaucus and Staterius, Dunuallo dresses 600 of his men in enemy armor and succeeds

---

83   *DGB*, ii.33.286–304: "Postremo defuncto Cunedagio successit ei Riuallo filius ipsius, iuuenis pacificus atque fortunatus, qui regnum cum diligentia gubernauit. In tempore eius tribus diebus cecidit pluuia sanguinea et muscarum affluentia homines moriebantur. Post hunc successit Gurgustius filius eius, cui Sisillius, cui Iago Gurgustii nepos, cui Kinmarcus Sisillii filius, post hunc Gorbodugo. Huic nati fuerunt duo filii, quorum unus Ferreux, alter Porrex nuncupabatur. Cum autem pater in senium uergisset, orta est contentio inter eos quis eorum in regno succederet. At Porrex, maiori cupiditate subductus, paratis insidiis Ferreucem fratrem interficere parat. Quod cum illi compertum fuisset, uitato fratre transfretauit in Gallias sed usus auxilio Suhardi regis Francorum reuersus est et cum fratre dimicauit. Pugnantibus autem illis, interfectus est Ferreux et tota multitudo quae eum comitabatur. Porro mater eorum, cui nomen erat Iudon, cum de nece filii certitudinem habuisset, ultra modum commota in odium alterius uersa est. Diligebat namque illum magis altero. Vnde tanta ira ob mortem ipsius ignescebat ut ipsum in fratrem uindicare affectaret. Nacta ergo tempus quo ille sopitus fuerat, aggreditur eum cum ancillis suis et in plurimas sectiones dilacerauit. Exin ciuilis discordia multo tempore populum afflixit et regnum quinque regibus summissum est, qui sese mutuis cladibus infestabant." On this passage, see Faral, *LLA*, vol. 2, pp. 115–17; on the (rejected) possibility that the plague of bloody rain may derive from William of Malmesbury, see Feuerherd, *Geoffrey of Monmouth*, pp. 44–46.

84   Feuerherd, *Geoffrey of Monmouth*, pp. 16, 21.

85   Tatlock, *LHB*, p. 383; cf. 2 Samuel 5:13–14, 1 Kings 11:1, 3 (Feuerherd, *Geoffrey of Monmouth*, pp. 36–39).

86   For other powerful mothers in the *DGB*, cf. iii.41 (Tonwenna), iii.47 (Marcia), vi.107 (Merlin's mother).

87   Feuerherd, *Geoffrey of Monmouth*, pp. 39–44.

in turning the tide of the battle, but *timens ne a suis opprimeretur*, "apprehensive of being killed by his own men", he changes his armor back again.[88] Tausendfreund has noted the parallel with an episode in *Aeneid* 11.386–437 where Aeneas and his men change into enemy-armor: "*dolus an uirtus quis in hoste requirat?*" "'deceit or valour, who would ask in battle?'" shouts Coreobus.[89] In the *Aeneid*, however, *dolus* is always associated with Greeks and not with Trojans (who are course Romans-to-be);[90] the wooden horse is described as a *dolus*;[91] the trickery of Sinon is characterized as *uersare dolos*, "employing tricks";[92] and the gifts of the Greek should rightly be viewed with suspicion: *aut ulla putatis dona carere dolis Danaum?* "or do you think that any gifts from the Greeks are free from deceit?"[93] The Trojans, of course, fall for it and, as in the episode where they change arms, it all goes wrong; Trojans simply cannot do *dolus*. In the *DGB* Book 11.34, Dunuallo's concern is probably well-placed; as a genetic Trojan he is not well-equipped for this, and as a wise king he knows when to stop.

8   Giant-Killing as a Civilizing Process

In the two preceding sections we have argued that it is possible to identify a primary source for the episode, whether classical or biblical, but it is important not to rule out influences and echoes from elsewhere. Not all instances are so easy to disentangle.

When Brutus received his traveling directions from Diana in the form of a verse-prophecy on the island of Leogetia, Britain is described as:

> Brutus, to the west, beyond the kingdoms of Gaul,
> lies an island of the ocean, surrounded by the sea,
> an island of the ocean, where giants once lived,
> but now is deserted and waiting for your people.
> Sail to it ...[94]

---

88   *DGB*, ii.34.320; cf. Tausendfreund, *Vergil und Gottfried von Monmouth*, p. 50.

89   Virgil, *Aeneid* ii.390, ed. Mynors.

90   Cf. Virgil, *Aeneid* ii.152, ed. Mynors: "dolis instructus et arte Pelasga", "well trained in the Greek art of deceit"; Virgil, *Aeneid* ii.252, ed. Mynors: "Myrmidonum dolos", "the tricks of the Greeks".

91   Virgil, *Aeneid* ii.264, ed. Mynors.

92   Virgil, *Aeneid* ii.62, ed. Mynors.

93   Virgil, *Aeneid* ii.43–43, ed. Mynors.

94   *DGB*, i.16.305–12: "Brute, sub occasu solis trans Gallica regna / insula in occeano est undique clausa mari; / insula in occeano est habitata gigantibus olim, / nunc deserta quidem, gentibus apta tuis. / Hanc pete ..."

It turned out, as often is the case with prophecies in Geoffrey (and also in Virgil), that matters were not so clear-cut; on their arrival in the *promissa insula*, it emerges that the prophecy was premature and that some giants did still exist. However, as soon as they were cleared out into the mountains (*repertos gigantes ad cauernas montium fugant*, "and (*sc.* after) driving off to mountain caves any giants they came upon"[95]), the proper civilization and cultivation of Britain could begin. The expulsion of giants, apparently throwbacks to an earlier age, seems to have been regarded as a necessary preliminary to the establishment of civilization.[96] In the distribution of territory in Britain, however, Corineus, never one to step back from a fight with a giant, was allocated Cornwall, where there were more giants still on the loose than anywhere else. These giants turn up at Totnes, Brutus's landfall in Britain, to gatecrash a feast; they were all eventually killed except for their leader, who was captured so that Corineus could fight him. Predictably the giant was defeated at Corineus's hands, who hurled him off a cliff, which was then named after him.[97] There is nothing overly remarkable about any of that except that the giant went by the striking name of Goemagog. For Geoffrey's audience that name would certainly have brought to mind the Old Testament names Gog and Magog, the names of a people and a place associated with hostility to the Jews:[98]

And I shall send a fire on Magog, and among them that dwell carelessly in the isles: and they shall know that I am the Lord.[99]

And when the thousand years are expired, Satan will be loosed out of his prison, and will go out to deceive the nations which are in the four quarters of the earth, Gog, and Magog, to gather them together in battle, whose number is as the sand of the sea.[100]

---

95   *DGB*, i.21.456–57.

96   On the notion of giants being things of the past, see also *DGB*, viii.129–30 (the Stonehenge narrative), during which it is asked how the stones got to Ireland in the first place; the inevitable answer is that they were brought from Africa by giants (*DGB*, viii.129.244–45). For discussion of Geoffrey's giants in a broader context, see W. Stephens, *Giants in Those Days: Folklore, Ancient History, and Nationalism*, Lincoln, NE, 1989, pp. 39–40; J.J. Cohen, *Of Giants: Sex, Monsters, and the Middle Ages* (Medieval Cultures, 17), Minneapolis, 1999, pp. 29–42; V.I. Scherb, "Assimilating Giants: the Appropriation of Gog and Magog in Medieval and Early Modern England", *JMEMS* 32 (2002), 59–84, at pp. 65–68.

97   *DGB*, i.21.466–89.

98   Cf. Hurley, *Geoffrey of Monmouth*, pp. 18, 83–84, 91–92.

99   Ezechiel 39:6: "Et immittam ignem in Magog, et in his qui habitant in insulis confidenter: et scient quia ego Dominus"; we may also note that they are located *in insulis*.

100 Revelation 20:7–8: "Et cum consummati fuerint mille anni, solvetur Satanas de carcere suo, et exibit, et seducet gentes, quae sunt super quatuor angulos terrae, Gog, et Magog, et congregabit eos in praelium, quorum numerus est sicut arena maris."

While Gog is not specifically described as a giant, Genesis report that giants were regarded as throwbacks, but by interbreeding had been reduced to *viri famosi*, "men of renown":

> There were giants on the earth in those days; and also after that, when the sons of God came in unto the daughters of men, and they bore children to them, they were the mighty men of old, men of renown.[101]

The immediate reaction, then, of Geoffrey's audience would probably have been to interpret these giants in biblical terms, and as another feature which tied Britain to the world of the Old Testament.

But other giants were also available for comparison and to be overcome. We have seen already how aspects of the Arthurian episode in the later books of Geoffrey echo earlier narratives, for example, the "furtive" love by which Brutus was conceived, or Ebraucus's great feast. Arthur, too, had his giants to fight en route to meeting the army of Lucius Hiberius. On hearing that a giant had arrived from Spain at Mont-Saint-Michel and was terrorizing the locals, he goes off to dispatch it single-handed.[102] As such, it has all the elements of the encounter between David and Goliath (1 Samuel 17) and was presumably intended to call aspects of that encounter to mind. However, the general tone of the battle and, in particular, the blinding of the giant, the destruction of boats with boulders, and the devouring of captives alive, would all have suggested another hero-giant encounter: that between Ulysses and the Cyclops, Polyphemus, probably most easily accessible to Geoffrey and audience through the *Aeneid*.[103] This is recounted to Aeneas in Sicily by Achaemenides, a survivor of Ulysses' expedition, and has already been mentioned as an example of how the new and old worlds were tied together in Virgil.[104] However, while Aeneas and Ulysses, in the different layers of this story, succeed in making their escape, Arthur goes one further and kills the giant. Almost as an afterthought, Geoffrey has Arthur refer to another encounter with a giant, Ritho on Mount Aravius, who had a propensity not only for killing his opponents but also for making a cloak out of their beards.

There are, then, classical as well as biblical resonances to these encounters with giants. Two further classical giants and their opponents seem to be

---

101 Genesis 6:4: "gigantes autem erant super terram in diebus illis postquam enim ingressi sunt filii Dei ad filias hominum illaeque genuerunt isti sunt potentes a saeculo viri famosi."

102 *DGB*, x.165.

103 Virgil, *Aeneid* iii.599–683, ed. Mynors.

104 See above, pp. 88–91.

relevant here as well. *Aeneid* VIII opens with Aeneas being given a guided tour of the site of the future Rome. As one part of that tour, Evandrus relates the story of how Hercules, on the way back from Spain with the cattle of Geryon, fought and dispatched the half-human, half-beast Cacus, who had been terrorizing the locality.[105] Here again giants are depicted as throwbacks (Cacus is a son of Vulcan) and as obstacles to civilized development; their extermination is required, especially if a hero like Hercules happens to be on hand to carry it out. We may dwell briefly on *Aeneid* VIII and the presence of Hercules in the Roman epic. Later in the book, Aeneas is shown into Evandrus's cottage, where Hercules also stayed while getting rid of Cacus.[106] Aeneas is invited to sit in the cottage, and the implication is that we are to see Aeneas as a second Hercules bringing safety and civilization to the Rome-to-be. If we accept this reading, we can see a network of implications developing which would allow an alert learned reader of the *DGB* to link Hercules with Aeneas, Aeneas with Brutus, Brutus with Arthur, Arthur with Corineus, and now finally Arthur with Hercules.

Hercules also figures in another giant-killing episode, this time in Lucan, which arguably has a closer link to Geoffrey's concerns. Book IV of Lucan's *Civil War* deals with the campaigns in Libya, and in this section Lucan takes the opportunity to present a range of narratives on items of local interest. One such episode involves Hercules' encounter with Antaeus and their great battle. After a long struggle (depicted as if between two oiled wrestlers), which Hercules looks likely to lose, he realizes that Antaeus, whose mother was Terra, was gaining renewed energy and strength from contact with the earth.[107] So he picked up Antaeus and held him off the ground until he died: *morientis in artus / non potuit nati Tellus permittere uires*, "Earth could not direct strength into the limbs of her dying son."[108] Again Hercules, by removing a local trouble-maker, allowed civilization to flourish. For our purposes, however, there is a significant detail in this narrative. We might wonder whether the image of Antaeus being held off the ground until he died has influenced the depiction of Goemagog lifted off the ground by Corineus before being projected off the cliff.[109] As is often the case with these kinds of parallels, there are no obvious verbal parallels, simply a parallel image which might, in the minds of some of the audience, conjure up the death of Antaeus dangling from Hercules' arms.

---

105   Virgil, *Aeneid* viii.190–275, ed. Mynors.
106   Virgil, *Aeneid* viii.358–69, ed. Mynors.
107   Lucan, *The Civil War* iv.599–660, ed. Housman and trans. Duff.
108   Lucan, *The Civil War* iv.650–51, ed. Housman and trans. Duff.
109   Cf. Faral, *LLA*, vol. 2, p. 88.

Again as with other suggestions of this type, it is difficult to be precise, but the treatment of giants as an obstacle to civilization in the DGB is consistent with what we see both in classical and biblical sources. To what extent Geoffrey was influenced by these different episodes is impossible to gauge, but it is unlikely that his depictions are entirely independent, nor is it surprising to see him using classical and biblical allusions in the same episode. Erich Poppe has noted a similar case in his discussion of the Middle Irish *Imtheachta Aeniasa* ("The Wandering of Aeneas") where the main model is, of course, the *Aeneid*, but where at one point a Virgilian allusion gives way to a biblical allusion about swords being turned into ploughshares.[110]

9   Allusion and Evasion

A substantial industry has grown up over the years in spotting quotations in Geoffrey from classical and biblical sources. Some of the earlier works, such as those by Tausendfreund and Feuerherd (and occasionally Faral), moved beyond a phrasal analysis to consider parallels to particular episodes.[111] At various points, scholars have noted, with varying degrees of frustration and puzzlement, how difficult it is to identify Geoffrey's sources. An early comment in this regard was by Feuerherd:

> Auf den ersten Blick könnte es befremdend erscheinen daß der Geistliche Galfredus Monumetensis in seiner verhältnismässig umfangreichen Darstellung nicht öfter das alte Testament anführt. Doch glaube ich, daß es Absicht des Chronisten war. Er wollte es seine Leser nicht merken lassen, daß er seine Historia der Geschichte der Juden nachschrieb.[112]

Feuerherd's remarks were directed at Geoffrey's use of biblical sources, but could easily be rephrased to apply more generally to his use of sources. As

---

110   E. Poppe, "*Imtheachta Aeniasa* and its Place in Medieval Irish Textual History", in
        R. O'Connor (ed.), *Classical Literature and Learning in Medieval Irish Narrative* (Studies in
        Celtic History, 34), Woodbridge, 2014, pp. 25–39, at pp. 27–28.

111   Tausendfreund, *Vergil und Gottfried von Monmouth*, pp. 16–50; Feuerherd, *Geoffrey of
        Monmouth*, pp. 24–85; Faral, *LLA*, vol. 2; Tatlock, *LHB* was more concerned with themes
        to the extent that his discussion and annotating of sources tended to be patchy and
        scattered.

112   Feuerherd, *Geoffrey of Monmouth*, p. 15: "At first sight it might appear odd that the cleric
        Geoffrey of Monmouth in his comparatively rich presentation does not often quote from
        the Old Testament. But I think this was the intention of the chronicler. He did not wish his
        readers to notice that he was modelling his work on the history of the Jews."

noted above, Geoffrey does not make life easy for us, only emphasized by the fact that the First Variant Version tends to give its audience a slightly easier ride.[113] Geoffrey's evasiveness in this regard has long been recognized. In discussing the Goemagog episode, Faral remarks that it is not that Geoffrey is attempting to conceal his sources that is interesting, but rather that it is so easy to see through him:

> Mais ces emprunts, rélativement très nombreux, Geoffrey a pris grand soin de les dissimuler. Il ne se souciait pas qu'on reconnaît ses larcins ni qu'on découvrît chez lui les traces des légendes dont l'immixtion à son récit ne pouvait que compromettre la reputation d'auteur véridique à laquelle il prétendait. Aussi, tout en empruntant, a-t-il systématiquement déformé, faisant, par exemple, de l'île de Gyaros un devin Gérion ... Toutefois, ses artifices n'ont pas suffi à cacher son jeu; s'il pille, on le prend souvent sur le fait ... s'il allègue des authorités, son imposture est souvent manifeste: ... Et l'on a si vite fait de le connaître, que ses précisions affectées, ces nombres soigneusement determinés, 600 hommes ici, 2,000 hommes là, n'ont pas d'autre résultat que de rendre plus apparents ses déguisements systématiques.[114]

Faral returned to the same theme later in a more general way:

> Sa lecture était vaste; mais il en a porté le poids avec aisance, sans jamais être l'esclave de ses auteurs, et c'est pour cette raison qu'il est souvent si délicat de determiner ses sources. Beaucoup des épisodes de son roman ont de l'analogie avec des themes historiques ou légendaires connus de nous et qu'il a sans doute connus lui-même; mais son imagination a cueilli, transformé et adapté avec tout de dexterité, que ses emprunts sont souvent difficiles à dénoncer. Quand il a transcrit littéralement tel ou tel passage pris à autrui, il semble l'avoir fait par affectation, comme

---

113   See above, pp. 75–76.

114   Faral, *LLA*, vol. 2, p. 92: "But as for these relatively numerous borrowings, Geoffrey took great care to conceal them. He did not worry if anyone recognized his or if anyone caught him out mixing together parts of legends in his narrative even though it could only compromise the reputation he was claiming as a truthful author. Also, in all his borrowings, he would systematically distort them, creating, for example, a divinity Gerion out of the island of Gyaros.... All the same, his tricks were not sufficient to conceal his game; if he plunders, he is caught at it, ... if he claims authority, his bogus claim is often clear: ... And one soon gets to know that his affected precision, his carefully precise numbers, 600 men here, 2000 men there, only have the effect of making his systematic concealments all the more apparent."

pour rendre manifeste qu'il n'inventait pas: ailleurs, quand il le voulait,
même s'il inspirait des auteurs les plus vénérables, Virgile ou d'autres, il
savait rester libre et forger lui-même son expression.[115]

Tatlock's discussion, on the other hand, does not engage directly with these
issues; since his discussion is more thematically based, they only surface spo-
radically, but even then Geoffrey's propensity for evasion is noted: "as so often,
Geoffrey warily paraphrases his borrowing";[116] "here, as usually, Geoffrey's
literary reminiscences are merely vague and disguised."[117] The irritation with
Geoffrey and almost a hand-wringing despair are evident in a comment toward
the end of his work: "useless to guess where Geoffrey got the idea".[118]

The source-hunting and text-combing will no doubt go on and continue to
give rise to further expressions of frustration and imputations of culpability
against Geoffrey. But there is an underlying question that is never really addressed: why does Geoffrey make his audience work so hard? Now this question may be approached in a number of different ways. One is hinted at in
one of Faral's comments quoted above where he observes that Geoffrey seems
unbothered by the fact that one can see through his disguises even though
that might compromise his claim to be writing history. The point is in part that
Geoffrey's sense of writing history involves reference to earlier sources, but at
the same time those sources themselves indulge in imaginative digressions
and reconstructions. One particular instance of this is the use of imaginary
speeches often just before battles, or, an extension of this device, the exchange
of imaginary correspondence, the rhetorician's *sermocinatio*.[119] This has been
part of the historian's tool box from Herodotus and Thucydides onwards and

---

115   Faral, *LLA*, vol. 2, p. 398: "His reading was vast; but he carried its weight with ease, without
ever being slave to his authors, and it is for that reason that it is often so tricky to establish
his sources. Many episodes of his story bear an analogical relationship with the historical
and legendary themes known to us, and he doubtless knew them himself; but his imagination has gathered them in, transformed and adapted them with such dexterity that his
borrowings are often difficult to identify. When he has literally transcribed this or that
passage from somewhere, he seems to have done so for show, as if he was making it clear
that he had not made it up; elsewhere, when he wanted, even if inspired by the most
venerable authors, he knew how to remain free and to craft his own expressions."

116   Tatlock, *LHB*, p. 260, n. 14.

117   Tatlock, *LHB*, p. 342, n. 127.

118   Tatlock, *LHB*, p. 390.

119   See H. Lausberg, *Handbook of Literary Rhetoric*, trans. M.T. Bliss et al., Leiden, 1998,
pp. 366–69, at p. 366: "the fabrication – serving to characterize natural (historical or invented) persons – of statements, conversations, and soliloquies or unexpressed mental
reflections of the persons concerned".

is liberally exploited by Geoffrey. The classical antecedents for such speeches would have been clear for him (his model very probably being Sallust, whom he quotes on several occasions), as also would have been the implied license to create one's own; a subtle nod toward them is offered in Hoelus's reply to Arthur's speech rejecting Lucius Hiberius's demand for tribute in which he describes Arthur's *deliberatio* as *Tulliano liquore lita*, "soaked in Cicero's honey".[120] That the accumulation of speeches in the *DGB* was seen as characteristic of Geoffrey's presentation is suggested by the fact that one distinguishing feature of the First Variant Version is the removal or reduction of some of the speeches found in the vulgate.[121] If then we view Geoffrey's treatment of his classical and biblical models in the light of how he uses speeches, it may not be so surprising that a precise tracking and accounting of sources and quotations is not always possible. Furthermore, it is not clear that Geoffrey was necessarily intending a precise and identifiable references on all occasions; a glancing partial quotation (or even not textual reference at all) may have been all that was needed to direct his audience to the model (or models) he had in mind. As has been argued above, his general aim seems to have been to present the travels of Brutus and the settlement of Britain as emanating from, and forming part of, the same world as depicted in the sources with which he and his audience would have been very familiar. In sum, we may have simply to accept that Geoffrey was often being very vague.

Another approach, which may perhaps prove more satisfying, is to think about the kind of rhetorical training which Geoffrey would have received in the late 11th and early 12th centuries. It has generally been thought that rhetorical training went through significant changes in the 12th century, but Geoffrey's training is likely to have been more "old-school" where ideas of *imitatio* and *aemulatio* figured significantly.[122] While *imitatio* was an important element in rhetorical training, slavish imitation was only acceptable at an elementary stage, and *aemulatio* was the goal: to go beyond simple imitation to create something new but still based on the respected models.[123] However, that connection to the model may well be disguised and dependent on the knowledge of the audience to make the links and to appreciate the subtlety of the

---

120   *DGB*, ix.160.483–84.

121   *First Variant Version*, ed. Wright, p. xxxix (Wright's category H).

122   There is a problem of talking about rhetorical training in the late 11th century and early 12th century; while the 12th century may have been a period of renewal, most rhetorical studies are very silent on the preceding century.

123   Conte, *Rhetoric of Imitation*, pp. 32–39. On *imitatio* and *aemulatio*, see R. Copeland and I. Sluiter (eds.), *Medieval Grammar and Rhetoric. Language Arts and Literary Theory, AD 300–1475*, Oxford, 2009; Lausberg, *Handbook of Literary Rhetoric*, pp. 483–85, 499.

approach. An interesting and potentially revealing illustration of these tech-
niques can be found in the central books of Macrobius's *Saturnalia* in which
this highly literary discussion turns to Virgil's debt to Homer.[124] The crucial
point for our purposes here is the concept of the "well-disguised imitation":

> ... sometimes he conceals the imitation of his model so that he changes
> only the arrangement of the passage he has borrowed and makes it seem
> like something else.[125]

Those who know the texts well enough can see past the *aliud videri*, "the fact
that it seems like something else", and gain added value; for those who cannot, Virgil provides entertainment and interest enough anyway. Slightly later
in the same discussion, Macrobius is more explicit and suggests that part of
being *scrupulosus et anxius*, "thorough and painstaking", was to disguise one's
sources:

> ... for just as our poet's learning was thorough and painstaking so was it
> well-disguised and as it were covert to the extent that it is hard to recog-
> nize the sources for many of his borrowings.[126]

This strand of antique literary criticism runs more deeply; the theme of making
things look other than they are, with the emphasis on ideas of dissimulation
and secrecy so that the audience can take pleasure in seeing through the veil, is
also found in a comment by the Elder Seneca who seems to be offering us the
exception that proves the rule: in a discussion of Ovid's borrowing of Virgilian
phrases, it is proposed that Ovid liked the phrases so much that he made it
clear that it was a borrowing: *non subripiendi causa sed palam mutuandi, hoc
animo ut vellet agnosci*, "not for the sake of stealing but of open borrowing,

---

124   For discussions of this passage, see S. Hinds, *Allusion and Intertext: Dynamics of
      Appropriation in Roman Poetry*, Cambridge, 1998, p. 25, and B. Miles, *Heroic Saga and
      Classical Epic in Medieval Ireland*, Woodbridge, 2001, pp. 143–44.
125   Macrobius, *Saturnalia* v.16.12, ed. J. Willis, *Ambrosii Theodosii Macrobii Saturnalia*, 2nd ed.,
      Leipzig, 1970: "interdum sic auctorem suum dissimulanter imitatur, ut loci inde descripti
      solam dispositionem mutet et faciat velut aliud videri."
126   Macrobius, *Saturnalia* v.18.1, ed. Willis: "... fuit enim hic poeta ut scrupulose et anxie, ita
      dissimulanter et quasi clanculo doctus, ut multa transtulerit quae unde translate sint dif-
      ficile sit cognita." On the sense of *dissimulanter* in these passages, see Hinds, *Allusion and
      Intertext*, pp. 23–24.

with the intention of having it recognized".[127] The point here, it seems to me, is that, while Ovid was pleased to be seen alluding to Virgil, he was more evasive about his allusions to other authors.

As Brent Miles puts it in a recent work on the adaptation of classical epic in medieval Ireland, "the intention was to vary the imitation enough for the source not to be obvious without the exercise of the reader's/hearer's erudition."[128] This is not just an issue for the transmission and adaptation of classical and biblical sources in medieval literature (where sometimes one also has to deal with adaptation into the vernacular). Strategies of intertextuality, the adaption of, or allusion to, the work of one classical author by another, has always attracted critical attention from the scholia on Homer and Servius's commentary on Virgil onwards. But, as Hinds has argued in his exemplary study, "[sc. This] is a relationship between author and reader which can involve indirection as much as direction, concealment as much as revelation."[129] He argues that in many instances it is difficult to discern the precise links amidst the "noise" of intertextual echoes, and "it will be more important to affirm the existence of a shared discourse than to classify the individual voices which make up that discourse."[130] Applied to Geoffrey's use of classical and biblical sources, such an approach would encourage us first to acknowledge the existence of that discourse (and that seems clear from Geoffrey's prologue onwards) and then explore it in a range of different ways. Just as Hinds shows that the precision of an allusion can be illusory when the broader range of verbal echoes are brought to bear,[131] so with Geoffrey we know so little of the chronologically intervening material that we cannot be sure whether he is alluding to a classical or biblical source directly or whether he had encountered it in a different context, or indeed whether he is doing all these things at the same time.

The nature of Virgil's debt to Homer has been characterized in a well-known metaphor, dating from the late antique period as "snatching the club from Hercules".[132] The general import of the metaphor has to do with the quality

---

127 Seneca the Elder, *Suasoriae* 3.7, ed. M. Winterbottom, *The Elder Seneca, Declamations: Controversiae and Suasoriae*, 2 vols., Cambridge, MA, 1974, vol. 2, pp. 544–45; see also Hinds, *Allusion and Intertext*, p. 23, where he takes this as a "reference" rather than as an "allusion" and as functioning as a "guarantee of the author's integrity". On the significance of *subripiendi* here, see below.
128 Miles, *Heroic Saga and Classical Epic*, p. 144.
129 Hinds, *Allusion and Intertext*, p. 25.
130 Hinds, *Allusion and Intertext*, pp. 50–51.
131 Cf. the examples discussed in Hinds, *Allusion and Intertext*, pp. 26–51.
132 For discussion in an Insular context and on the metaphors associated with *subripere* and *extorquere*, see A. Burnyeat, "'Wrenching the club from the hand of Hercules': Classical

and process of the reproduction of epic material. As we have argued, Geoffrey's debt to his classical and biblical sources in the DGB is pervasive but multifarious: not only did he *inter alia* snatch a club from Hercules, but he also stole a sling from David, a shield from Aeneas, and ideas of kingship from Solomon and of civil war from Lucan. In doing so he did his best to conceal his efforts and leave his audiences to work it out for themselves.

———————

Models for Medieval Irish *compilation*", in O'Connor (ed.), *Classical Literature and Learning*, pp. 196–207.

CHAPTER 3

Geoffrey of Monmouth and the English Past

Rebecca Thomas

Geoffrey does not grant much space to the English in the *De gestis Britonum*. In one respect, this is unsurprising: Geoffrey's history extends back to the origins of the Britons in Troy, spending a significant amount of time in pre-Roman Britain, and as such the English enter the narrative rather late in the day. Even after their arrival, however, the English do not appear in the way which we might expect. The traditional narrative of the development of the English kingdoms, pioneered by sources such as Bede's *Ecclesiastical History* and the *Anglo-Saxon Chronicle*, and accepted and reproduced by many of Geoffrey's contemporary Anglo-Norman historians, has no place in the DGB. With his strikingly different version of events, Geoffrey certainly cannot be accused of lacking originality in his treatment of English history. The way in which he approached this subject is highly significant not only for our understanding of his attitude toward the English, but also for the composition of the DGB more generally.

There was no shortage of contemporary historians writing of the English past, such as Henry of Huntingdon, the first version of whose *History of the English*, with which Geoffrey was most likely familiar, was completed by 1130. Henry presents us with a conventional account of English history, drawing heavily on Bede and the *Anglo-Saxon Chronicle*.[1] Hengist and Horsa arrive in Britain in 449, and after recounting their dealings with the Britons, Henry proceeds through the various other Saxon settlers of the 5th and 6th centuries. Battles between them and the Britons are often recorded, and it is only after noting the foundation of the kingdom of Wessex in 519 and the 17-year rule of King Cerdic that Henry inserts a brief account of King Arthur, drawn mainly

---

[1] Diana Greenway notes that about 25 per cent of *History of the English* derives from Bede, about 40 per cent from the *Anglo-Saxon Chronicle*: Henry of Huntingdon, *History of the English*, ed. and trans. D. Greenway, *Henry, Archdeacon of Huntingdon: Historia Anglorum. The History of the English People*, Oxford, 1996, p. lxxxv. Greenway also discusses the relationship between *History of the English* and *De gestis Britonum*, see pp. ci–ii, civ and 24, n. 35. On Henry's presentation of the English past, see J. Campbell, "Some Twelfth-Century Views of the Anglo-Saxon Past", *Peritia* 3 (1984), 131–50, at pp. 134–35 (repr. in id. (ed.), *Essays in Anglo-Saxon History*, London, 1986, 209–28). On the question of Geoffrey's familiarity with Henry's work, see also Tatlock, *LHB*, pp. 5 and 34.

from the 9th-century *Historia Brittonum*.[2] After Arthur we return to a narration of the establishment of the various English kingdoms and their relations
with each other in the 6th century. Henry dedicates a book to the conversion
of the English, drawing heavily on Bede to recount Augustine's mission and the
activities of the Christian kings of 7th-century Northumbria. Moving beyond
Bede, his narrative continues to track the fate and fortune of English kings and
their kingdoms down to the Norman Conquest.

Henry's more conservative narrative helps us see just how different and
inventive Geoffrey's history is. Where Henry tracks the development of the
English kingdoms, Geoffrey relates a period of British supremacy. The *DGB* tran-
sitions from the arrival of Hengist and Horsa to the dominance of the British
kings Aurelius Ambrosius, Uther Pendragon, and Arthur. Arthur is followed by
a series of British kings (drawn from Gildas's *The Ruin of Britain*) who are all
successful in subduing the Saxon threat, until Kareticus, weakened by civil war,
is defeated by an African army in alliance with the Saxons. It is only at this
point that the Saxons gain the largest part of the island, which Geoffrey calls
Loegria, and the Britons retreat to Cornwall and Wales. Geoffrey then relates
the conversion of the English by Augustine before proceeding with an account
of the 7th century, which is, once more, largely a period of supremacy for the
Britons. The British king Cadwallon controls all territory south of the Humber,
a dominance which is only brought to an end when a plague forces his son
and successor, Cadwaladr, to flee the island. The plague, Geoffrey stresses, also
brings the Saxons to their knees, but once it passes, the survivors send word to
their homeland, and a second migration results in the establishment of their
supremacy over the island. Geoffrey ends by naming Æthelstan (893/4–939) as
the first Saxon king to rule *Loegria*.

Where, then, are the English in the *DGB*? When is England? The period
from the arrival of Hengist and Horsa in the 5th century to the conversion
of Northumbria and the successes of its kings in the 7th century is rewritten as a period of British dominance. The establishment of the English kingdoms painstakingly related in Henry's *History of the English* has no place in
Geoffrey's work. While English kings and kingdoms do feature in Geoffrey's
account of the 7th century, their success is halted by the military might of
Cadwallon: the Northumbrian and Mercian kings are subsidiary characters,
rulers only with his blessing. Indeed, in this section of the *DGB*, Northumbria
and Mercia aside, Kent is the only other English kingdom to be mentioned,
and this purely in the context of Augustine's mission. Indeed, there is no need
to refer to any other kingdom: all territories south of the Humber are allegedly

---

2   Henry of Huntingdon, *History of the English* ii.18, ed. and trans. Greenway, pp. 98–101.

under British overlordship. The period from the 7th century onwards is simply absent, summarized in the statement that Æthelstan was the first to rule *Loegria*. Geoffrey's account of English history thus effectively jumps from the 7th century to the 10th.

This is more than simply a tongue-in-cheek re-writing of a traditional narrative. R. William Leckie, Jr. has illustrated how, through his re-casting of events, Geoffrey succeeds in postponing the passage of dominance over the island of Britain from the Britons to the Saxons.[3] Thus, while Hengist and Horsa are undoubtedly important figures in the narrative, their arrival in 449 does not mark the beginnings of a gradually increasing English supremacy. With tales of Arthur and his successors, Britain, in Geoffrey's narrative, does still very much belong to the Britons. It is only after the death of Cadwaladr in the late 7th century that dominance begins to pass to the English, a process completed, according to Geoffrey, by Æthelstan's reign in the 10th century.[4] The *DGB* thus offers a dramatic alternative to the traditional narrative of the history of early medieval Britain.

What purpose Geoffrey harbored in constructing this alternative vision of British history is a contentious issue. It has been suggested that the *DGB* served as a legitimization of Norman power in Britain and was perhaps intended to warn the Anglo-Normans of Geoffrey's day of the dangers of disunity.[5] Conversely, Geoffrey has been labelled pro-British in his sympathies. Thus, John Gillingham has argued that the *DGB* sought to combat the view, commonplace in the works of Anglo-Norman historians such as Henry of Huntingdon and William of Malmesbury, that the Britons were barbarians, and links this agenda to the political significance of the Welsh in the 1030s, which was heightened by the rebellion of 1136–38 and the subsequent alliance with Robert of Gloucester.[6] As will be discussed further in this chapter, Geoffrey can certainly be charged with constructing a narrative of the English past that is more favorable to the Britons than the accounts found in any of his sources or in the work of his contemporaries. However, the complexity of the connection between

---

3   R.W. Leckie, Jr., *The Passage of Dominion: Geoffrey of Monmouth and the Periodization of Insular History in the Twelfth Century*, Toronto, 1981.

4   Leckie, *Passage of Dominion*, pp. 59–71.

5   F. Ingledew, "The Book of Troy and the Genealogical Construction of History: The Case of Geoffrey of Monmouth's *Historia regum Britanniae*", *Speculum* 69:3 (1994), 665–704, at pp. 681–88; P. Dalton, "The Topical Concerns of Geoffrey of Monmouth's *Historia Regum Britannie*: History, Prophecy, Peacemaking, and English Identity in the Twelfth Century", *Journal of British Studies* 44:4 (2005), 688–712; Leckie, *Passage of Dominion*, p. 57.

6   J. Gillingham, "The Context and Purposes of Geoffrey of Monmouth's *History of the Kings of Britain*", *Anglo-Norman Studies* 13 (1990), 99–118 (repr. in id. (ed.), *The English in the Twelfth Century: Imperialism, National Identity and Political Values*, Woodbridge, 2000, 19–39).

Geoffrey's historical Britons and the Welsh of his own day makes it difficult to link this attitude to a clear political agenda. The Welsh may be the descendants of the historical Britons, but, according to Geoffrey, they are *degenerati*, "unworthy successors", who have lost both their name and their claim to the whole of Britain through civil strife.[7] Consequently, that Geoffrey's narrative favors the Britons at certain points does not necessarily translate to support for the contemporary Welsh.

As Monika Otter has noted, that evidence can be found in the *DGB* to support such a wide range of potential motivations "is surely indicative of a purpose beyond simply taking sides in contemporary political struggles".[8] While not dismissing the indications that Geoffrey does, on occasion, show sympathy toward the Britons, Otter argues that, ultimately, the text ought to be understood as a parody in that it takes the same form as other medieval histories, but provides new content which conflicts with these previous works.[9] The referentiality that governs the writing of William of Malmesbury and Henry of Huntingdon, namely, the grounding of their histories in perceived historical reality which is accessed through the works of earlier writers, does not concern Geoffrey. Thus, under the cover of following his alleged source material (*Britannici sermonis librum uetustissimum*, "a very old book in the British tongue"), he produces an original and inventive narrative of English history.[10]

This does not, however, mean that Geoffrey simply ignores all other accounts of English history. What is striking about the *DGB* is that, while producing a dramatically different version of events, Geoffrey is nonetheless in constant dialogue with works such as Bede's *Ecclesiastical History*. It is clear from the broad outline of the work sketched above that Geoffrey does diverge from his sources in key respects. However, this issue requires assessment in

---

7   *DGB*, xi.207.598. For a more detailed discussion of the relationship between the Welsh, Cornish, and Bretons and Geoffrey's historical Britons, see Ben Guy's contribution in this volume.

8   M. Otter, "Functions of Fiction in Historical Writing", in N. Partner (ed.), *Writing Medieval History*, London, 2005, pp. 109–30, at p. 120.

9   Otter, "Functions of Fiction", pp. 119–20; ead., *Inventiones: Fiction and Referentiality in Twelfth-Century English Historical Writing*, Chapel Hill, 1996, pp. 79–80. See also V.I.J. Flint, "The *Historia Regum Britanniae* of Geoffrey of Monmouth: Parody and Its Purpose. A Suggestion", *Speculum* 54:3 (1979), 447–68.

10   *DGB*, Prologus 2.9–10; Otter, *Inventiones*, pp. 79–83. For further discussion of the relationship between history, truth, and fiction in the 12th century, see M. Kempshall, *Rhetoric and the Writing of History, 400–1500*, Manchester, 2011, esp. pp. 428–41, and in the context of Geoffrey of Monmouth specifically, see R.M. Stein, *Reality Fictions: Romance, History, and Governmental Authority, 1025–1180*, Notre Dame, 2006, pp. 106–25.

a more specific context. To this end, the following examination will focus on two key parts of Geoffrey's narrative: the coming of the Saxons in 449 and the relations between the Britons and the kingdoms of Northumbria and Mercia in the 7th century. I will consider what sources Geoffrey was using, and how he adapted these sources to depict the English in a certain way. I have thus far focused on Geoffrey's treatment of the English in the *DGB*, but there is something also to be said about their appearance in the *VM*. Here, Merlin prophesies the overthrow of the Britons by the Saxons until they are driven back by an alliance of Scots, Welsh, Cornish and Bretons.[11] This prophecy, which is heavily reliant on the Welsh prophetic poem *Armes Prydein Vawr* ("The Great Prophecy of Britain"), is considered elsewhere in this volume, and consequently discussion of the *VM* in this chapter will focus on Merlin's account of the interaction between the Britons and Saxons in the time of Vortigern.[12] While the presentation of the English in the *DGB* is the main avenue of investigation here, their treatment in the *VM* will be considered where relevant.

The term "Anglo-Saxons" is conventionally associated with the period of increasing ties between the kingdoms of Mercia and Wessex in the 9th century and thereafter.[13] Asser, in his *Life of King Alfred*, for example, refers to King Alfred as *Anglorum Saxonum rex*, "king of the Anglo-Saxons", and the term is frequently employed in charters of the 10th century.[14] In modern scholarship it is frequently used as a term to describe the English peoples before the Norman Conquest. It is not, however, a term used in Geoffrey's work. For his account of the 7th century he does occasionally employ the term *Angli*, "English". Scholars have noted that this usage is confined to the period after Augustine's mission, and consequently may reflect the increasing influence of Bede's *Ecclesiastical History* on Geoffrey's work.[15] However, for the most part, Geoffrey refers to the kings and peoples of specific kingdoms, for example, *Mercii*, "the Mercians", and *Northamhimbri*, "the Northumbrians". For the period prior to Augustine's mission, Geoffrey consistently uses *Saxones*, "the Saxons". Thus in the following discussion I will either refer to specific kingdoms, or will follow Geoffrey in referring to the Saxons.

11 *VM*, ll. 959–75. Cf. *DGB*, Prophetiae 115.110–16.
12 See Ben Guy's contribution to this volume.
13 For a summary of the evidence see S. Keynes, "Anglo-Saxons, Kingdom of the", in M. Lapidge, J. Blair, S. Keynes and D. Scragg (eds.), *The Blackwell Encyclopaedia of Anglo-Saxon England*, 2nd ed., Chichester, 2014, p. 40.
14 Asser, *Life of King Alfred*, ed. W.H. Stevenson, *Asser's Life of King Alfred. Together with the Annals of Saint Neots*, Oxford, 1959, p. 1, Dedication.
15 N. Wright, "Geoffrey of Monmouth and Bede", *AL* 6 (1986), 27–59, at p. 34; Tatlock, *LHB*, p. 19.

1   The Coming of the Saxons

Our first surviving source to recount the coming of the Saxons to Britain is
Gildas's *The Ruin of Britain*, a text with which Geoffrey was certainly familiar.[16]
Geoffrey makes particular use of Gildas's complaint against the five tyrant kings
to create a succession of British monarchs to succeed Arthur.[17] Neil Wright has
illustrated Geoffrey's practice of borrowing passages from Gildas's account of
the coming of the Saxons and placing them elsewhere in his narrative – to
fashion his account of the defeat of the British king Ceredig, for example.[18]
For the *adventus Saxonum* itself, however, there were other sources to which
Geoffrey could turn, sources which, while themselves drawing on *The Ruin of
Britain*, had developed Gildas's work. Most prominent among these sources
were Bede's *Ecclesiastical History* and the *Historia Brittonum* (attributed to
"Nennius" in certain manuscripts).[19]
    Finishing his *Ecclesiastical History* in 731, Bede related the coming of the
Saxons in greater detail than Gildas, bringing the deal struck between Hengist
and Horsa and the *superbo tyranno*, "proud tyrant", whom he named Vortigern,
to the fore. Developing Gildas's criticism of the Britons, Bede stressed how they
had brought the disaster upon themselves.[20] In 829 or 830 his narrative found a
challenge in the form of *Historia Brittonum*.[21] This history of the Britons is often
viewed by scholars as a reply to Bede, mainly because the author stresses that,

---

16   *The Ruin of Britain* is conventionally dated to the first half of the 6th century, see
      T.M. Charles-Edwards, *Wales and the Britons, 350–1064*, Oxford, 2013, pp. 215–18;
      D.N. Dumville, "The Chronology of *De Excidio Britanniae*, Book I", in M. Lapidge and
      D.N. Dumville (eds.), *Gildas: New Approaches*, Woodbridge, 1984, pp. 61–84. Cf. N.J. Higham,
      The English Conquest: Gildas and Britain in the Fifth Century, Manchester, 1994, pp. 118–41.
17   Geoffrey records the five kings as succeeding one another, in contrast to Gildas's narra-
      tive, where the five kings are presented as contemporaries. See *DGB*, xi.179–86. Cf. Gildas,
      The Ruin of Britain §§28–36, ed. and trans. M. Winterbottom, *Gildas: The Ruin of Britain
      and Other Works* (Arthurian Period Sources, 7), Chichester, 1978, pp. 29–36 and 100–05.
      For discussion of the impact of this alteration on Geoffrey's narrative, see Leckie, *Passage
      of Dominion*, p. 63.
18   N. Wright, "Geoffrey of Monmouth and Gildas", *AL* 2 (1982), 1–40, at pp. 11–12.
19   For discussion of *Historia Brittonum*'s authorship see D.N. Dumville, "'Nennius' and the
      Historia Brittonum", *Studia Celtica* 10/11 (1975–76), 78–95; P.J.C. Field, "Nennius and his
      History", *Studia Celtica* 30 (1996), 159–65; B. Guy, "The Origins of the Compilation of Welsh
      Historical Texts in Harley 3859", *Studia Celtica* 49 (2015), 21–56, at pp. 44–51.
20   Bede, *Ecclesiastical History* i.15, ed. and trans. B. Colgrave and R.A.B. Mynors, *Bede's
      Ecclesiastical History of the English People*, Oxford, 1969, pp. 48–53. Cf. Gildas, *The Ruin of
      Britain* §23, ed. and trans. Winterbottom, pp. 26 and 97.
21   For discussion of the date see D.N. Dumville, "Some Aspects of the Chronology of the
      Historia Brittonum", *BBCS* 25 (1972–74), 246–51.

contrary to Bede's contention, the Britons played a key role in the conversion of the English.[22] Geoffrey was certainly familiar with *Historia Brittonum*: he drew heavily upon the work for various episodes scattered throughout the DGB. While a thorough assessment of Geoffrey's familiarity with *Historia Brittonum* is conducted elsewhere in this volume, it is important in this context to think about the impact upon his presentation of the English.[23] Crucially, in its version of the *adventus Saxonum*, *Historia Brittonum* heaps further detail on to the brief account provided by Bede, and also diverges from the *Ecclesiastical History* at several key points.

It is immediately clear that Geoffrey favored *Historia Brittonum*'s account, and that, as Edmond Faral noted, it was his principal source for this section of the DGB.[24] While there are instances where material is shared between all three texts, Geoffrey overwhelmingly draws on the narrative provided by *Historia Brittonum*. We have roughly the same events in both texts: Hengist gaining the friendship of Vortigern and gradually summoning a greater number of Saxons to Britain; Vortigern falling in love with Hengist's daughter; the battles of his son Vortimer against the Saxons; and the treachery of the long knives.[25] As *Historia Brittonum*'s narrative is longer and more detailed than that offered by Bede it is perhaps unsurprising that this was Geoffrey's chosen source. However, it is not simply *Historia Brittonum*'s pattern of events which Geoffrey borrows: he also keeps the text's attitude toward the Britons and Saxons and its presentation of their role in these events.

We see an example of this immediately as Geoffrey follows *Historia Brittonum* in claiming that the Saxons arrived in Britain as exiles. This is in direct contrast to the narrative provided by Gildas, Bede, and the *Anglo-Saxon Chronicle*, and followed by Henry of Huntingdon and to an extent William of Malmesbury (as discussed below), who claim that the Saxons were invited to Britain. Bede adds that this occurred in 449, and Gildas's *superbo tyranno*, "proud tyrant", is named Vortigern:

> In the year of the Lord 449 Marcian, forty-sixth from Augustus, became emperor with Valentinian and ruled for seven years. At that time the race

---

22   See below for further discussion of the relationship between *Historia Brittonum* and Bede, p. 120.

23   See Ben Guy's contribution to this volume.

24   Faral, *LLA*, vol. 3, pp. 215–16. Robert Hanning has highlighted the influence of *Historia Brittonum* on Geoffrey's work more generally; see R. Hanning, *The Vision of History: From Gildas to Geoffrey of Monmouth*, New York, 1966, pp. 138–39.

25   A more detailed breakdown of the episodes Geoffrey draws from *Historia Brittonum* can be found in Faral, *LLA*, vol. 3, pp. 215–17.

of the Angles or Saxons, invited by the aforementioned king [Vortigern], came to Britain in three warships and by his command were granted a place of settlement in the eastern part of the island, ostensibly to fight on behalf of the country, but their real intention was to conquer it.[26]

While in *Historia Brittonum* Vortigern does later reach an agreement with the Saxons, to begin with they are simply exiles. This is crucial as it changes the role of the Britons in the episode, and the author's attitude toward them: both Gildas and Bede place the blame for the Saxon incursions firmly on the shoulders of the Britons, with Gildas specifically noting the stupidity of the Britons for inviting the Saxons when they already feared them.[27] In *Historia Brittonum*'s account this condemnation vanishes, and the Britons are rather presented as offering the hand of friendship to the Saxons who have nowhere else to go.

Using *Historia Brittonum* as a basis, Geoffrey embellishes this account to explain the reason for the exile of the Saxons: their land was overpopulated and thus Hengist and Horsa were forced to leave to make their fortune elsewhere. This account was in fact taken from William of Malmesbury, who, in his *Deeds of the English Kings*, offered this as an explanation not only for the incursion of the Saxons in Britain, but also the Vandals in Africa, the Goths in Spain, the Lombards in Italy, and the Normans in Gaul.[28] Robert Hanning argued that by describing the Saxons as exiles, and by providing this detailed explanation of their fate, Geoffrey underlines the importance of their migration: they are not mere adventurers, but settlement founders. He notes the similarity to the Britons, who, in both *Historia Brittonum* and the DGB, had arrived in Britain as

---

26   Bede, *Ecclesiastical History* i.15, ed. and trans. Colgrave and Mynors, pp. 48–51: "Anno ab incarnatione Domini ccccxlviiii Marcianus cum Ualentiniano quadragesimus sextus ab Augusto regnum adeptus vii annis tenuit. Tunc Anglorum siue Saxonum gens, inuitato a rege praefato, Brittaniam tribus longis nauibus aduehitur et in orientali parte insulae iubente eodem rege locum manendi, quasi pro patria pugnatura, re autem uera hanc expugnatura suscepit." Cf. Gildas, *The Ruin of Britain* §23, ed. and trans. Winterbottom, pp. 26 and 97; ASC E 449, *The Anglo-Saxon Chronicle: a Collaborative Edition. Vol. 7: MS. E*, ed. S. Irvine, Cambridge, 2004, p. 16; Henry of Huntingdon, *History of the English* ii.1, ed. and trans. Greenway, pp. 78–79; William of Malmesbury, *Deeds of the English Kings*, ed. and trans. R.A.B. Mynors, completed by R.M. Thomson and M. Winterbottom, *William of Malmesbury: Gesta Regum Anglorum, The History of the English Kings*, 2 vols., Oxford, 1998–99, vol. 1, pp. 20–21.

27   Gildas, *The Ruin of Britain* §23, ed. and trans. Winterbottom, pp. 26 and 97.

28   William of Malmesbury, *Deeds of the English Kings* i.5.1–3, ed. and trans. Mynors, vol. 1, pp. 22–23. For further discussion of William's account, and his sources, see Faral, *LLA*, vol. 3, pp. 218–19.

exiles from Troy.[29] However, as noted above, the importance of the migration of 449 is diminished in Geoffrey's work. Indeed, a further migration, after the plague of the 7th century, is required before the Saxons are able to gain dominance over the island.[30] Consequently, it is perhaps of greater significance here that Geoffrey follows *Historia Brittonum* in rejecting the notion that the Saxons were invited by the Britons, thus relieving the Britons of any blame for their initial arrival. This is particularly significant considering that William of Malmesbury, who is, after all, Geoffrey's source for this explanation of the Saxons' exile, also includes the claim made by Gildas and Bede that the Saxons were invited to Britain. In William of Malmesbury's account, the Saxons are invited exiles, while in the *DGB* they are simply exiles.

Geoffrey also follows *Historia Brittonum* in stressing the paganism of the Saxons. As an introduction to the Saxons when they arrive in Britain, *Historia Brittonum* explains that they were descended from Geta, an idol they used to worship as God.[31] While Bede and the *Anglo-Saxon Chronicle* recorded the genealogy of the Saxons as far back as Woden, these texts simply listed the names of the ancestors without further comment.[32] Geoffrey not only follows *Historia Brittonum* here, but also develops its account: in the *DGB*, Vortigern immediately notes that he is saddened by the *incredulitas*, "faithlessness", of the Saxons.[33] While Vortigern, despite this initial query, does not view their paganism as a barrier to the forming of an alliance, it is clear that the rest of the Britons are uncomfortable. Thus, later in Geoffrey's narrative, the Britons ask Vortigern to expel the Saxons from the island, as they are worried about the extent to which the Christian Britons are intermingling with the pagan Saxons.[34] This is particularly interesting in light of what Henry of Huntingdon has to say on the matter. He also stresses the paganism of the Saxons (and reproduces *Historia Brittonum*'s account of Geta), yet he focuses on how, in seeking help from the pagan Saxons, the Britons turned their backs on God and were justly punished as a consequence.[35] In Geoffrey's narrative, not only do the Britons not invite the Saxons, but they are also uncomfortable with their paganism.

29   Hanning, *Vision of History*, p. 170.

30   Leckie, *Passage of Dominion*, pp. 59–71. See discussion above, p. 107.

31   *Historia Brittonum* (Harley 3859) §31, ed. Faral, *LLA*, vol. 3, pp. 2–62, at p. 23.

32   Bede, *Ecclesiastical History* i.15, ed. and trans. Colgrave and Mynors, pp. 50–51; *ASC* E 449, ed. Irvine, p. 16.

33   *DGB*, vi.98.285–86.

34   *DGB*, vi.101.391–96.

35   Henry of Huntingdon, *History of the English* ii.1, ed. and trans. Greenway, pp. 78–79. For discussion of how Henry presents five invasions of the island of Britain (Romans, Picts and Scots, Saxons, Vikings, and Normans) as five punishments from God, see Henry of Huntingdon, *History of the English*, ed. and trans. Greenway, p. lix; A. Galloway, "Writing

The role of Vortigern here also merits comment. It is notable that Vortigern accepts the paganism of the Saxons, while the rest of the Britons protest. Of course, this focus on the actions of specific individuals is a key characteristic of Geoffrey's work, and has been viewed as part of a wider trend in Anglo-Norman historical writing.[36] Thus the history revolves around the actions of individuals such as Brutus, Arthur, Vortigern, and Cadwallon. However, it is nonetheless significant that the Britons as a group are uncomfortable with Vortigern's acceptance of the Saxons. According to Hanning, this illustrates the "separation of individual and nation"; the Britons are not to blame for Vortigern's crimes.[37] This is a pattern which we can already see in *Historia Brittonum*, where every decision made concerning the Saxons is presented as being Vortigern's alone, thus minimizing the responsibility of the Britons as a collective for the ensuing disasters. It is Vortigern who receives the Saxons and grants them Thanet, and Vortigern who falls in love with Hengist's daughter and grants him the kingdom of Kent.[38] While reproducing this focus on Vortigern fits Geoffrey's wider preoccupation with the actions of specific individuals, it nonetheless also gives the impression that it is Vortigern alone who is mainly to blame for the successes of the Saxons. Geoffrey's claim that the rest of the Britons were dissatisfied with Vortigern's actions accentuates this impression.

Hanning argued that a further illustration of this disconnect between Vortigern and the people he claimed to rule was Geoffrey's retelling of the treachery of the long knives.[39] In *Historia Brittonum*, 300 unarmed British elders (*seniores*) are slaughtered by the Saxons at the peace conference, and Vortigern is the only Briton left alive.[40] William of Malmesbury develops this narrative. In his account, the Britons are invited to a feast, and no mention is made of them being unarmed. Hengist goads them into a fight and all are slaughtered.[41] Geoffrey, in contrast to both these accounts, focuses on the resistance and bravery of the Britons: despite being unarmed, they fight bravely and cause significant damage to the Saxons. He relates how Eldol, earl of Gloucester, wards off the Saxons with a staff and eventually manages to

---

History in England", in D. Wallace (ed.), *The Cambridge History of Medieval English Literature*, Cambridge, 1999, pp. 255–83, at pp. 263–64.

36   Hanning, *Vision of History*, esp. pp. 124–44.

37   Hanning, *Vision of History*, p. 151.

38   *Historia Brittonum* §31 and 37, ed. Faral, *LLA*, vol. 3, pp. 23 and 27–29.

39   Hanning, *Vision of History*, pp. 151–52. Faral also points to this episode as an example of Geoffrey attempting to present the Britons in a more positive light, see Faral, *LLA*, vol. 2, pp. 228–29.

40   *Historia Brittonum* §46, ed. Faral, *LLA*, vol. 3, p. 34.

41   William of Malmesbury, *Deeds of the English Kings* i.8.3, ed. and trans. Mynors, vol. 1, pp. 26–27.

escape.[42] These additions present the Britons as playing a far more active role in the treachery of the long knives, and the victory of the Saxons as less swift and straightforward than in *Historia Brittonum*'s account. On the side of the Saxons, their treachery is lifted wholesale from *Historia Brittonum*. As well as the treachery of the long knives, Geoffrey reproduces *Historia Brittonum*'s account of Hengist's scheme to marry his daughter to Vortigern. Indeed, Geoffrey quotes *Historia Brittonum*'s description of Hengist as a *uir doctus atque astutus*, "a shrewd and cunning man", and copies Hengist's speech to Vortigern claiming his right, as his father-in-law, to advise him in all matters.[43]

In relating the coming of the Saxons and their initial settlement in the island of Britain, it is clear that Geoffrey is primarily reliant upon *Historia Brittonum*. To a certain degree this is unsurprising as, of the surviving sources, it is *Historia Brittonum* that provides the most detailed account of these events. However, Geoffrey is also making a deliberate choice: he follows *Historia Brittonum* over Gildas, Bede, and the *Anglo-Saxon Chronicle* in presenting the Saxons as exiles, for example. In choosing *Historia Brittonum*'s narrative over Bede's, which was, as we have seen, favored by his contemporaries William of Malmesbury and Henry of Huntingdon, Geoffrey sides, in this instance, with the account which is most favorable to the Britons. Nor is he content to simply reproduce *Historia Brittonum*'s depiction: he loads the skeletal narrative provided by his source with additional material; but this material accentuates, rather than contradicts, the attitude already present in *Historia Brittonum*. Geoffrey's additions thus stress and develop the negative characteristics of the Saxons, while increasing the agency of the Britons and presenting a sympathetic view of their dealings with Hengist and his followers.

This is not to say that Geoffrey presents a consistently favorable view of the Britons. Influenced by Gildas, he dwells on the destructive tendency of the Britons toward civil war, as in the *PM*, where Merlin prophesies that "then the red dragon will return to its old ways and strive to tear at itself."[44] Indeed, the different presentation of the *adventus Saxonum* in the *VM* illustrates the ambiguity and complexity of Geoffrey's motivations. The Saxons are still presented as treacherous and deceitful, doing damage to Britain through their *prodicione nefanda* "black treachery" and killing the Britons at a peace conference *premeditate fraude*, "by calculated deceit", but the agency granted to the

---

42   *DGB*, vi.104–05.

43   *Historia Brittonum* §37 and 38, ed. Faral, *LLA*, vol. 3, pp. 27 and 29. Cf. *DGB*, vi.99.301–02 and vi.101.378–83.

44   *DGB*, Prophetiae, 113.56–57: "Exin in proprios mores reuertetur rubeus draco et in se ipsum saeuire laborabit." Cf. Gildas, *The Ruin of Britain* §§26–27, ed. and trans. Winterbottom, pp. 28–29 and 98–99.

Britons in the *DGB* is absent.[45] Nor are the Saxons described as exiles in the *VM*, with Merlin instead recounting how Vortigern, unable to withstand rebellion, called for the assistance of foreign warriors, an account closer to that provided by Gildas and Bede than to *Historia Brittonum*. Merlin continues: "Soon bands of fighting men arrived from all over the world and he welcomed them. In particular, the Saxons sailed in in curved ships and brought their helmeted troops to his service."[46] The actions of the Saxons and Vortigern's culpability take center stage in the *VM*'s narrative, as illustrated by the way Merlin introduces the account with the statement "for I have lived long and seen much – our own folk turning on one another, and the chaos the barbarian brings."[47] Thus the *VM* offers a somewhat different perspective on the *adventus Saxonum* to that given in the *DGB*.

As noted above, Geoffrey uses the *liber uetustissimus*, "very ancient book", to provide *DGB* with the appearance of textual authority, to suggest that, although his history diverges dramatically from the conventional narrative of English history seen in the works of Bede and his contemporary Anglo-Norman historians, it is nevertheless operating within a pre-existing framework.[48] However, this did not entail a complete rejection of what had come before, as the influence of *Historia Brittonum* on the account of the *adventus Saxonum* in the *DGB* illustrates. While the above consideration of the *VM* warns against the view that Geoffrey had a straightforward overarching agenda to exonerate the Britons of the past, it remains that, in recounting the *adventus Saxonum* in the *DGB*, he follows the source most favorable to the Britons, and develops this material to create an account which is more sympathetic still.

2   A Narrative of British Domination

As explained at the beginning of this chapter, in Geoffrey's narrative the *adventus Saxonum* is followed by an account of a series of British kings who wage war successfully against the Saxons, the most famous of these being King Arthur. What is a period of formation and consolidation of English kingdoms

---

45   *VM*, ll. 1004 and 1010–11.
46   *VM*, ll. 999–1002: "Mox ex diversis venerunt partibus orbis pugnaces turme, quas excipiebat honore. Saxona gens etiam curvis advecta carinis ejus ad obsequium galeato milite venit."
47   *VM*, ll. 979–81: "nam tempore multo vixi videns et de nostratibus in se et de barbarica turbanti singular gente."
48   Otter, "Functions of Fiction", p. 120.

in the *Anglo-Saxon Chronicle* and Henry of Huntingdon's *Historia Anglorum* becomes a period of British domination in the *DGB*. In the present context it is how Geoffrey's narrative proceeds beyond the history of these kings that is significant, as it once more overlaps with familiar sources. In particular, his account of the conversion of the English in the 6th century, and the subsequent wars between the Britons, Mercians, and Northumbrians in the 7th century, bears signs of being influenced by Bede's *Ecclesiastical History*. This offers a good opportunity to examine how Geoffrey adapted his sources in his depiction of relations between the Britons and the Saxons.

This section of the *DGB* covers Augustine's mission at the end of the 6th century and the reigns of three kings of the Britons: Cadfan (*fl. c.*616–*c.*625), Cadwallon (d. 634), and Cadwaladr (d. 664/682). Geoffrey tracks the passing of supremacy back and forth between these kings of Gwynedd and the Northumbrians. There are certain episodes in this narrative which are entirely unique to Geoffrey's work, for example, Cadwallon's flight to Brittany to seek the help of King Salomon and the mission of his nephew, Brianus, to kill Edwin's augur Pellitus, whose magic was preventing the Britons from returning to the island.[49] There are other episodes which, it has been suggested, may have some grounding in Welsh tradition, for example the claim made by Geoffrey that Edwin and Cadwallon were brought up together at the court of Cadfan of Gwynedd.[50]

However, for the most part, the basis of this section of Geoffrey's work is Bede's *Ecclesiastical History*. Geoffrey uses Bede's work as a skeleton to which he adds further material, much like his use of *Historia Brittonum* discussed above. However, while Geoffrey did not, on the whole, dramatically change the direction and message of *Historia Brittonum*, here he diverges wildly from his source. His treatment of Cadwallon serves as an introductory example of this trend. According to Bede, Cadwallon killed a succession of Northumbrian kings (Edwin, Osric, and Eanfrith), before he himself was defeated in battle and killed by Oswald at Heavenfield in 634.[51] In Geoffrey's narrative, however,

---

49 *DGB*, xi.193–96. For discussion of the reasons behind such additions, see Faral, *LLA*, vol. 2, p. 329.

50 N.K. Chadwick, "The Conversion of Northumbria: A Comparison of Sources", in ead. (ed.), *Celt and Saxon: Studies in the Early British Border*, Cambridge, 1963, pp. 138–66, at pp. 149–51; Charles-Edwards, *Wales and the Britons*, p. 389, n. 52. Cf. V. Tudor, "Reginald's *Life of Oswald*", in C. Stancliffe and E. Cambridge (eds.), *Oswald: Northumbrian King to European Saint*, Stamford, CT, 1995, pp. 178–94, at pp. 182–83.

51 Bede, *Ecclesiastical History* ii.20 and iii.1, ed. and trans. Colgrave and Mynors, pp. 202–05 and 212–15. *Historia Brittonum* also records that Cadwallon was killed by Oswald, at the battle of Cantscaul; see §64, ed. Faral, *LLA*, vol. 3, p. 43.

Cadwallon was not present (and did not die) at Heavenfield. Rather the battle is fought between Oswald and Penda of Mercia. Though Oswald is victorious on this occasion he does not kill the Mercian king, and Penda subsequently kills him at Burne. In Bede's account, Penda does kill Oswald, but this happens some time after the defeat and death of Cadwallon, at the battle of Maserfelth (or Cocboi) in 642.[52] Geoffrey's reference to "Burne" may be an appropriation of Bede's Denisesburn, the name given in the *Ecclesiastical History* for the battle of Heavenfield. The striking point that emerges from a brief comparison of these two narratives is that Geoffrey's Cadwallon remains alive and active for much longer than Bede's account allows. Indeed, in Geoffrey's narrative, Cadwallon remains overlord of the Britons, Mercians, and Northumbrians until his death from illness and old age, after reigning for 48 years.[53]

Of course, as Faral explained, by simply rejecting the notion that Cadwallon and the Britons were ever fatally defeated by the Northumbrians, Geoffrey accords his subjects a far more favorable treatment than that given to them by Bede.[54] In so doing he also naturally diminishes the achievement of the Northumbrians. Rather than dying at Oswald's behest, Cadwallon survives to preside over Oswald's death, the reign of his successor, Oswiu, and the death of Penda, king of the Mercians. As discussed briefly already, it has long been recognized that this extension of Cadwallon's life, and the consequent extension of British dominance, has the impact of delaying the final victory of the Saxons, and the passing of control of the island of Britain into their hands. Leckie draws attention in particular to Geoffrey's account of the agreement between Cadfan and Æthelfrith, whereby the Humber was set as the boundary between their territories. That Cadfan, like Cadwallon after him, is described as ruling the territories south of the Humber dismisses the significance of Saxon settlement in the south. Moreover, while Cadwallon is initially expelled from Britain by Edwin, his eventual victory and subsequent dominance over the Northumbrian kings underlines the weakness of the position of the Saxons north of the Humber. The implication is that the Britons remained a force to be reckoned with throughout the 7th century, and indeed Geoffrey does not allow the Saxons to gain complete control of *Loegria* until the reign of Æthelstan in the 10th century.[55]

Crucially, this diminishing of the dominance of the Saxons is not restricted to the extension of Cadwallon's life and reign. Cadwallon is presented as a more

52   For discussion of the location of Oswald's death and the various place-names used see
      C. Stancliffe, "Where was Oswald killed?" in Stancliffe and Cambridge, *Oswald*, pp. 84–96.
53   *DGB*, xi.201.504–12.
54   Faral, *LLA*, vol. 2, pp. 331–32.
55   Leckie, *Passage of Dominion*, esp. pp. 66–72.

powerful overlord than Bede's Northumbrian kings, three of whom (Edwin, Oswald, and Oswiu) are included in his list of kings who managed to extend their rule over all the southern kingdoms.[56] A brief examination of how Bede and Geoffrey present the affairs of Mercia after the death of Penda illustrates this point. After defeating Penda at Winwaed, Bede tells us that Oswiu gave the Mercian kingdom to the deceased king's son Peada. However, Peada was subsequently murdered, and three Mercian ealdormen, Immin, Eafa, and Eadberht, rebelled against Oswiu, choosing another of Penda's sons, Wulfhere, as king.[57] Geoffrey, in contrast, presents Cadwallon as the constant force behind the development of events. With no mention of Peada, he presents Wulfred (Bede's Wulfhere) as succeeding to the kingdom of the Mercians, significantly with Cadwallon's blessing. While Wulfred subsequently allies himself with the Mercian leaders Eba and Edbert to rebel against Oswiu, Cadwallon orders them to make peace.[58] Geoffrey's Cadwallon thus has a far firmer grip on events in Mercia than Bede's Oswiu.

The extension of Cadwallon's life, and the consequent dramatic re-shaping of events, is an obvious divergence from Bede's narrative. However, Geoffrey's engagement with the version of the English past presented in the *Ecclesiastical History* is multi-layered and in many respects subtler than his treatment of Cadwallon might suggest. Geoffrey is in constant dialogue with Bede, and Neil Wright has produced a thorough survey, highlighting each instance of dependence, but also divergence.[59] I will not reproduce such a list here, but rather will focus on examining one example in detail, which will illustrate the complexity and sophistication of Geoffrey's response to the *Ecclesiastical History*.

3   Conversion and Christian Kings

Focusing in particular on issues of conversion and Christianity allows us to gain an insight into how Geoffrey reacts to this key plank of Bede's work. Much of this relates to his depiction of 7th-century kings, but it is worth starting

---

56   Bede, *Ecclesiastical History* ii. 5, ed. and trans. Colgrave and Mynors, pp. 148–51. For further discussion, see P. Wormald, "Bede, the *Bretwaldas* and the Origin of the *Gens Anglorum*", in P. Wormald et al. (eds.), *Ideal and Reality in Frankish and Anglo-Saxon Society*, Oxford, 1983, pp. 99–129; Charles-Edwards, *Wales and the Britons*, pp. 426–27; S. Keynes, "Bretwalda or *Brytenwalda*", in Lapidge et al. (eds.), *Blackwell Encyclopaedia of Anglo-Saxon England*, pp. 76–77.

57   Bede, *Ecclesiastical History* iii.24, ed. and trans. Colgrave and Mynors, pp. 294–95.

58   *DGB*, xi.200.500–03.

59   Wright, "Geoffrey of Monmouth and Bede".

by moving back to 597 and the Augustinian mission. One of Bede's key complaints against the Britons is that they shunned the duty expected of them as Christians in refusing to assist in Augustine's mission to convert the Saxons. Bede relates how Augustine requested the Britons to do three things: keep Easter at the correct date, perform the sacrament of baptism, and preach to the Saxons. However, the Britons, believing Augustine to be proud as he had not risen from his seat at their approach, rejected these requests, refusing also to accept Augustine as archbishop over them.[60] This appears to be the primary reason for Bede's negative treatment of the Britons in his *Ecclesiastical History*.[61] It proved to be a controversial view. As noted above, *Historia Brittonum*, composed a century or so after Bede finished his *Ecclesiastical History*, appears to present a case in defense of the Britons in claiming that Edwin of Northumbria was baptized by a Briton, Rhun ab Urien, and that Rhun continued to baptize *omne genus ambronum*, "the entire race of the Ambrones (*sc.* English)", for 40 days.[62]

Wright has argued that Geoffrey also answers this charge, but rather than following *Historia Brittonum*'s lead and presenting an entirely different set of events, Geoffrey simply adapts Bede's tale of the meeting at Augustine's Oak to reflect positively upon the Britons. A key part of this adaptation involves careful attention to structure.[63] Geoffrey notes Augustine's arrival in Britain, but then, unlike Bede, turns to provide a description of the ecclesiastical

---

60 Bede, *Ecclesiastical History* ii.2, ed. and trans. Colgrave and Mynors, pp. 134–41. While Bede refers to Augustine as *archiepiscopus*, his status was more correctly that of a metropolitan bishop, see T.M. Charles-Edwards, *Early Christian Ireland*, Cambridge, 2000, pp. 416–20.

61 For more extensive discussion of Bede's view of the Britons, see T.M. Charles-Edwards, "Bede, the Irish and the Britons", *Celtica* 15 (1983), 42–52; W.T. Foley and N. Higham, "Bede on the Britons", *Early Medieval Europe* 17 (2009), 154–85; A.T. Thacker, "Bede, the Britons and the Book of Samuel", in S. Baxter et al. (eds.), *Early Medieval Studies in Memory of Patrick Wormald*, Ashgate, 2009, pp. 129–47.

62 *Historia Brittonum* §63, ed. Faral, LLA, vol. 3, p. 43. *Ambrones* is normally interpreted as a nickname for the English, meaning "robbers", see D.N. Dumville, "The Textual History of the Welsh-Latin *Historia Brittonum*", 3 vols., unpublished PhD thesis, University of Edinburgh, 1975, vol. 1, p. 238, n. 3. It is possible that the author of *Historia Brittonum* came across the name in Gildas's *The Ruin of Britain*, where it is used to describe the Picts and the Irish, see Gildas, *The Ruin of Britain* §16, ed. and trans. Winterbottom, pp. 21 and 94. For scholarship suggesting that *Historia Brittonum* was replying to Bede see D.N. Dumville, "*Historia Brittonum*: An Insular History from the Carolingian Age", in A. Scharer and G. Scheibelreiter (eds.), *Historiographie im frühen Mittelalter*, Wien, 1994, pp. 406–34, at p. 434; N.J. Higham, "Historical Narrative as Cultural Politics: Rome, 'British-ness' and 'English-ness'", in id. (ed.), *The Britons in Anglo-Saxon England*, Woodbridge, 2007, pp. 68–79, at p. 76; Charles-Edwards, *Wales and the Britons*, pp. 446–47.

63 Wright, "Geoffrey of Monmouth and Bede", pp. 35–36.

organization of the British church, stressing the historic division of Britain into three archbishoprics (York, London, Caerleon) since the conversion of Lucius, king of the Britons, in the time of Pope Eleutherius.[64] Not only does this stress the antiquity and continuity of the British church, but it also stresses the novelty of Augustine's position as archbishop of Canterbury.[65] Further to this, Geoffrey focuses purely on Augustine's desire that the Britons submit to his authority, and preach to the Saxons, making no mention of the other two requests (regarding the dating of Easter, and baptism) recorded in Bede. As Augustine's speech outlining his demands is placed immediately following the detailed description of the organization of the British church, Geoffrey succeeds in depicting the request as somewhat unreasonable. Unreasonable, too, the request that the Britons assist in the mission when Geoffrey prefaces the meeting between the British bishops and Augustine with an account of how the Britons were ravaged by the Saxons. Indeed, Abbot Dinoot, spokesman for the Britons, replies to Augustine that the Britons could not possibly preach to a people who were depriving them of their country.[66] Geoffrey continues, "and for that reason the British detested them, despising their faith and beliefs and shunning them like dogs."[67] Wright has pointed out that this is in fact an adaptation of a statement made by Bede elsewhere in his *Ecclesiastical History*.[68] After describing the suffering inflicted upon Northumbria by the Welsh and the Mercians, Bede claims that "indeed to this very day it is the habit of the Britons to despise the faith and religion of the English and not to co-operate with them in anything more than with the heathen."[69] While this statement was formulated by Bede as an attack on the actions of the Britons, in Geoffrey's narrative these actions are made to seem perfectly legitimate.

Neil Wright's examination thus very clearly demonstrates how Geoffrey carefully re-ordered Bede's narrative, emphasizing different points and providing a very specific additional context, resulting in a more favorable depiction

---

64 This tradition is recorded in *Historia Brittonum*, and derives ultimately from the *Book of the Popes* (*Liber Pontificalis*). For discussion see Charles-Edwards, *Wales and the Britons*, pp. 322–23.

65 Wright, "Geoffrey of Monmouth and Bede", p. 36.

66 Wright, "Geoffrey of Monmouth and Bede", pp. 37–38.

67 *DGB*, xi.188–89.193–95: "unde eos summon habebant odio fidemque et religionem eorum pro nichilo habebant nec in aliquo Anglis magis quam canibus communicabant."

68 Wright, "Geoffrey of Monmouth and Bede", pp. 37–38.

69 Bede, *Ecclesiastical History* ii.20, ed. and trans. Colgrave and Mynors, pp. 204–05: "quippe cum usque hodie moris sit Brettonum fidem religionemque Anglorum pro nihili habere, neque in aliquo eis magis communicare quam paganis." See also Henry of Huntingdon, *History of the English* iii.33, ed. and trans. Greenway, pp. 184–85. This passage in Bede's *Ecclesiastical History* is discussed in further detail below, see pp. 123–24.

of the Britons. What this means in this case is a neutralization of Bede's description of the Britons as "bad" Christians. However, in this section I would like to illustrate that Geoffrey does not confine his efforts to defend the Britons against Bede's charges to his account of Augustine's meeting with the British bishops. Rather, his preoccupation with combating Bede's view of the Britons as "bad" Christians influences his presentation of the events of the 7th century more generally, as exemplified by his treatment of the conflict between the Britons and Northumbrians.

Bede's Northumbrian rulers are all pious Christian kings who are harassed by the pagan Mercians. Edwin is the first Northumbrian king to be converted, Oswald is victorious at the battle of Heavenfield after raising a cross and beseeching his army to kneel and pray, and Oswiu's defeat of Penda paves the way for the conversion of the Mercians. While, as already noted, Geoffrey dramatically alters Bede's narrative concerning these kings by extending Cadwallon's life and dominance, it is worth looking more closely at the difference in the depiction of the events by the two authors. In Bede's account, the paganism of the Mercians is stressed. When describing the attacks on Northumbria in the aftermath of Edwin's death, Bede states, "Penda and the whole Mercian race were idolaters and ignorant of the name of Christ."[70] He proceeds to note that Oswald was killed by "the same heathen people and the same heathen Mercian king as Edwin".[71] His successor, Oswiu, was attacked by the heathen people, the Mercians (*pagana gente Merciorum*, "the pagan Mercian people") who had killed his brother.[72] Finally, Bede depicts Oswiu's defeat of Penda as Christian victory, which is followed by the conversion of the Mercians:

> King Oswiu brought the campaign to a close in the district of *Loidis* (Leeds) on 15 November in the thirteenth year of his reign, to the great benefit of both peoples; for he freed his own subjects from the hostile devastations of the heathen people and converted the Mercians and the neighbouring kingdoms to a state of grace in the Christian faith, having destroyed their heathen ruler.[73]

---

70   Bede, *Ecclesiastical History* ii.20, ed. and trans. Colgrave and Mynors, pp. 202–03: "Penda cum omni Merciorum gente idolis deditus et Christiani erat nominis ignarus."

71   Bede, *Ecclesiastical History* iii.9, ed. and trans. Colgrave and Mynors, pp. 242–43: "… eadem pagana gente paganoque rege Merciorum".

72   Bede, *Ecclesiastical History* iii.14, ed. and trans. Colgrave and Mynors, pp. 254–55.

73   Bede, *Ecclesiastical History* iii.24, ed. and trans. Colgrave and Mynors, pp. 292–93: "Hoc autem bellum rex Osuiu in regione Loidis tertio decimo regni sui anno, septima decima die kalendarum Decembrium, cum magna utriusque populi utilitate confecit. Nam et suam gentem ab hostile paganorum depopulatione liberauit, et ipsam gentem

Thus not only are the Mercians depicted as pagans, but this paganism is specifically associated with Penda. Moreover, Oswiu is presented as a glorious Christian king in facilitating the conversion of a heathen people. This is of course in contrast to the Britons, who are, according to Bede, a stubborn, proud people who refused to preach to the Saxons. Bede's description of Cadwallon and the Britons is illuminating in this context. Specifically, in the aftermath of Edwin's death at the battle of Hatfield Chase in 633, Bede describes how the Britons and the Mercians joined forces to terrorize the Northumbrians:

> At this time there was a great slaughter both of the Church and of the people of Northumbria, one of the perpetrators being a heathen and the other a barbarian who was even more cruel than the heathen. Now Penda and the whole Mercian race were idolaters and ignorant of the name of Christ; but Cædwalla, although Christian by name and profession, was nevertheless a barbarian in heart and disposition and spared neither women nor innocent children. With bestial cruelty he put all to death by torture and for a long time raged through all their land, meaning to wipe out the whole English nation from the land of Britain. Nor did he pay any respect to the Christian religion which had sprung up amongst them. Indeed to this very day it is the habit of the Britons to despise the faith and religion of the English and not to co-operate with them in anything any more than with the heathen.[74]

Interestingly, Geoffrey does not shy away from this criticism of Cadwallon; indeed, he incorporates Bede's account almost verbatim. Cadwallon's persecution of the Northumbrians is described thus in the *DGB*:

Merciorum finitimarumque prouinciarum, desecto capite perfido, ad fidei Chrisianae gratiam conuertit."

74   Bede, *Ecclesiastical History* ii.20, ed. and trans. Colgrave and Mynors, pp. 202–05: "Quo tempore maxima est facta strages in ecclesia uel gente Nordanhymbrorum, maxime quod unus ex ducibus, a quibus acta est, paganus alter quia barbarus erat pagano saeuior. Siquidem Penda cum omni Merciorum gente idolis deditus et Christiani erat nominis ignarus; et uero Caedualla, quamuis nomen et professionem haberet Christiani, adeo tamen erat animo ac moribus barbarus, ut ne sexui quidem muliebri uel innocuae paruulorum parceret aetati, quin uniuersos atrocitate farina morti per tormenta contraderet, multo tempore totas eorum prouincias debachando peruagatus, ac totum genus Anglorum Brittaniae finibus erasurum se esse deliberans. Sed nec religioni Christianae, quae apud eos exorta erat, aliquid inpendebat honoris, quippe cum usque hodie moris sit Brettonum fidem religionemque Anglorum pro nihili habere, neque in aliquo eis magis communicare quam paganis."

The victorious Cadwallon passed through all the provinces of the English, persecuting the Saxons so relentlessly that he spared neither women nor children; indeed he wanted to wipe out the whole English race from British soil, and subjected every one of them he could find to unheard-of tortures.[75]

While Geoffrey reproduces Bede's criticisms of Cadwallon's actions, Neil Wright has pointed out that he omits Bede's criticisms of Cadwallon himself: Cadwallon is not here described as *animo ac moribus barbarus*, "a barbarian in heart and disposition", for example. Furthermore, placed alongside the efforts of the Saxons to treacherously steal Britain from its rightful inhabitants, Cadwallon's actions do not appear unjustified.[76] As discussed above, Bede's final statement of this passage, noting the continuing refusal of the Britons to cooperate with the Saxons, is in fact used by Geoffrey, but in a different section of the *DGB*, and in defense of the Britons.[77] As an additional point it is interesting to note that, in the context of Geoffrey's work, Cadwallon's actions are not in fact that unusual. Indeed, prior to Cadwallon's victory, Edwin had inflicted a similar persecution on the lands of the Britons: "The victorious Edwinus led his army through the provinces of the Britons, burning cities and putting town- and countrymen to the torture."[78] Thus we see that Cadwallon is simply acting as Edwin acted before him. There is nothing particularly un-Christian about this (as is the implication in Bede's narrative); rather, it is simply the action of a victorious king.

A key part of Bede's criticism was that Cadwallon aligned himself with the pagan Mercians, when, as a Christian king, he should have known better. For Bede, as seen in the extract quoted above, Penda's actions are, if despicable, nonetheless understandable due to his ignorance of Christianity. However, Cadwallon's actions are inexcusable: he is a Christian, and yet acts like a barbarian, happier to cooperate with the pagan Mercians than with the Christian Northumbrians. Thus we are presented with a fairly clear-cut categorization

---

75   *DGB*, xi.198.433–37: "Habita igitur uictoria, Caduallo uniuersas Anglorum prouincias peruagando ita debachatus est in Saxones ut ne sexui quidem muliebri uel paruulorum aetati parceret; quin omne genus Anglorum ex finibus Britanniae abradere uolens quoscumque reperiebat inauditis tormentis afficiebat." I have modernized the names to aid comparison with the other sources.

76   Wright, "Geoffrey of Monmouth and Bede", p. 42.

77   Wright, "Geoffrey of Monmouth and Bede", pp. 37–38. This is discussed further above, see p. 121.

78   *DGB*, xi.193.289–91: "At Edwinus, ut triumpho potitus fuit, duxit exercitum suum per prouincias Britonum combustisque ciuitatibus ciues et colonos pluribus tormentis affecit."

of the Mercians and Britons in Bede's work: the former are pagans, the latter are Christians in name alone. This is picked up by Henry of Huntingdon, who explains that while Penda and the Mercians were pagans, "Cædwalla was more savage than a pagan."[79]

Geoffrey's take on the matter is strikingly different. He does not seek to deny or diminish the holiness of the Northumbrian kings. As discussed above, he changes certain key details: for example, the battle of Heavenfield now occurs between Oswald and Penda, rather than Oswald and Cadwallon as in Bede. Despite this alteration in personnel, Geoffrey nonetheless repeats the episode of Oswald raising the cross of the Lord and beseeching his soldiers to kneel and pray to God for victory. However, crucially, Penda and the Mercians are never described as pagans in Geoffrey's narrative. Penda is simply *rex Merciorum*, "king of the Mercians", and while he is referred to as a *nefandi ducis*, "wicked leader", his paganism is never mentioned.[80] As a consequence, there are no questions raised over Cadwallon's alliance with Penda. It is simply an alliance between two kings; in Geoffrey's narrative there remains no trace of Bede's presentation of the unnatural alliance between a supposed Christian and a heathen people. This is a subtle shift in perception, but it has a significant impact on the overall tone of the narrative. Cadwallon's actions are viewed in a completely different light, not because the actions themselves have necessarily changed (at least in the case of his alliance with Penda and killing of Edwin), but because these actions are depicted in a subtly different way. Geoffrey's Cadwallon, then, is not the bad Christian portrayed by Bede.

This is not to say that there are no bad Christian kings in Geoffrey's narrative. Bede views Cadwallon as fulfilling this role due to his alliance with the heathen Mercians and attacks on the pious Northumbrians, yet Geoffrey in fact has someone else in mind: Æthelberht of Kent (d. 616?). Here we must return to the meeting between Augustine and the Britons discussed above. In Bede's account, there are seven British bishops and many learned men at the meeting, mainly from the monastery of Bangor Iscoed, under the authority of Abbot Dinoot. When they refuse Augustine's requests, he warns them that refusal to preach to the Saxons will result in death at their hands. Bede immediately relates how this came to pass, as Æthelfrith, king of the Northumbrians, brought an army to Chester to battle against the Britons. When he saw that the priests (most from the monastery of Bangor) had assembled to pray for a

---

79   Henry of Huntingdon, *History of the English* iii.33, ed. and trans. Greenway, pp. 184–85: "... Cedwalla uero pagano seuior."

80   There are several references to Penda as *rex Merciorum*: DGB, xi.196.417; xi.199.443; xi.200.462. For *nefandi ducis*, see xi.199.443.

Northumbrian defeat, he ordered that they be slaughtered first. Their guard, Brocmail, fled, and about 1,200 of the priests were killed.[81]

This episode is once more heavily altered by Geoffrey in a way that reflects more positively upon the Britons. Rather than praying for the defeat of the English, in Geoffrey's account the monks are praying for the safety of their own people, and rather than flee, Brocmail dies trying to protect the city.[82] The monks, who in Geoffrey's account are slaughtered after the battle, are presented as martyrs.[83] What is significant in the present context is the reason given for Æthelfrith's attack. Bede does not tell us what prompted Æthelfrith to march on Chester, he simply presents it as a fulfilment of Augustine's prophecy. Geoffrey, however, states the following:

> Æthelberht, king of Kent, indignant that the Britons had refused to submit to Augustine and had rejected his preaching, incited Æthelfrith, king of Northumbria, and the other Saxon subkings to collect a great army and go to the city of Bangor to kill Dinoot and the other priests who had slighted them.[84]

This is a dramatic departure from Bede's account, and, as Wright notes, "Ethelfrid is represented as the cats-paw of Ethelbert of Kent (and hence indirectly of Augustine himself)."[85] The reframing of this episode has a significant impact on the above discussion of how Geoffrey neutralizes Bede's complaint against the Britons. Bede attacks Cadwallon for supporting a pagan king against a Christian people. Here, Æthelberht of Kent, a Christian king (indeed, the first Christian king according to Bede's narrative), facilitates the killing of the priests of Bangor and their abbot Dinoot. It is not, as in Bede's account, an attack on the Britons that simply happens to end in the slaughter of the priests, but rather a targeted attack against the priests themselves. Nor is it simply the work of a pagan king as in Bede's narrative: here it is a Christian king who gives the order. This has the effect of turning Bede's characterization on its head.

---

81   Bede, *Ecclesiastical History* ii.2, ed. and trans. Colgrave and Mynors, pp. 136–41.
82   *DGB*, xi, 189.206–8.
83   Wright, "Geoffrey of Monmouth and Bede", pp. 39–40.
84   *DGB*, xi.189.195–200: "Edelbertus ergo rex Cantiorum, ut uidit Britones dedignantes subiectionem Augustino facere et eosdem praedicationem suam spernere, hoc grauissime ferens Edelfridum regem Northamhimbrorum et ceteros regulos Saxonum instimulauit ut collecto grandi exercitu in ciuitatem Bangor abbatem Dinoot et ceteros clericos qui eos despexerant perditum irent."
85   Wright, "Geoffrey of Monmouth and Bede", p. 39.

It is perhaps significant that this re-casting of the Britons, Northumbrians, and Mercians is thematically consistent with the treatment accorded to the Saxons in the section of the *DGB* concerning the *adventus Saxonum*, discussed above. In both cases, faith is a defining characteristic which Geoffrey grapples with, whether to stress the paganism of the Saxons or to neutralize Bede's depiction of the Britons as bad Christians. While it is generally recognized that Geoffrey's *DGB* represents a shift away from the providential toward a more secular and national history, with a focus on individuals and the role of fortune, it is clear from this discussion that ideas of conversion and faith remain important to his narrative.[86] Such ideas are prevalent in his source material, especially the *Ecclesiastical History*, and this discussion has illustrated how Geoffrey went beyond simply subverting Bede's chronology in his engagement with this text. To the modern reader, the obvious, bold changes made to Bede's narrative, such as the extension of Cadwallon's life, perhaps deflect attention from the more subtle changes, such as the depiction of Æthelberht of Kent as a villain. The consequence of this adaptation of, and divergence from, the *Ecclesiastical History* is an account of 6th- and 7th-century relations between the Britons and English which is unprecedented in its positive treatment of the former.

4   Conclusions

For Geoffrey, the English only begin to achieve dominance over Britain after the death of Cadwaladr in 689, a trajectory completed by Æthelstan becoming the first Saxon king to rule all *Loegria* in the 10th century. Prior to this, the past was British, and the English only relevant inasmuch as they interacted with the Britons. They may have experienced brief moments of supremacy, but these were never more than moments. Edwin enjoyed a spell of overlordship having expelled Cadwallon from Britain, but Cadwallon returned, and Edwin's overlordship died with him. The domination of the English was never lasting, and the Britons were never permanently subdued. Indeed, in the end, it was not the military might of the English that defeated the Britons, but a plague with the force of God's will.

In creating this original and creative version of history, Geoffrey struck his own path, leaving his sources behind. Consequently, the *DGB* is full of plot twists to shock any reader familiar with the conventional narrative of

---

86   Hanning, *Vision of History*, pp. 138–39. For further discussion, see Barry Lewis's chapter in this volume.

English history: individuals do not live and die at the expected time, and battles are fought at unexpected places and with surprising casts. But despite his
efforts to create something new, Geoffrey remained conscious of what had
come before. Indeed, for his account of the *adventus Saxonum* we have seen
that he follows *Historia Brittonum*'s lead, with his additions, while undoubtedly creative, simply accentuating themes already present in the 9th-century
history of the Britons. His approach to the *Ecclesiastical History* is clearly different: Geoffrey has no problem in turning Bede's narrative on its head to suit his
own purposes. However, even here we see a keen awareness of prior tradition.
In producing his alternative narrative, Geoffrey does not simply ignore Bede;
he takes and carefully alters episodes from the *Ecclesiastical History*, adding
detail, emphasis, and different context to change the fundamental message of
the work.

The past was not viewed as uncharted territory in the 12th century, and it
is in this context that we should understand Geoffrey's careful treatment of
his sources.[87] Monika Otter has illustrated how Geoffrey plays with the principle of textual *auctoritas*: through alleging reliance on the *liber uetustissimus*,
"very ancient book", Geoffrey provides the appearance of textual authority for
the *DGB*, making the same claim to truth as other 12th-century histories, while
simultaneously ensuring that his account is unverifiable.[88] This discussion
has illustrated that his treatment of known sources is equally complex. That
Geoffrey diverges from the received chronology of early medieval British history has long been recognized, but there are also further layers to his engagement with sources such as Bede's *Ecclesiastical History*. Interestingly, in the
instances considered here, every addition Geoffrey makes to his sources, every
event he decides to exclude, or include in a different form, works to present the
Britons in a favorable light. Geoffrey's attitude toward the English past cannot
be understood independently of this context. This is not to say that he sets out
to consistently depict the Britons as the heroes of his history; the influence of
Gildas's criticisms of his countrymen can be felt in the focus on civil war in the
DGB, for example. Neither can this sympathy for the Britons be neatly mapped
on to a 12th-century landscape; indeed, Geoffrey stresses the disconnect between the Britons of the *DGB* and the Welsh of his own time. However, the
DGB's account of the *adventus Saxonum* and 6th- and 7th-century relations between the Britons and the English reflects better on the Britons than the work
of any writer that preceded Geoffrey. In this context, early medieval England
belonged to the Britons.

87   Otter, *Inventiones*, p. 83.
88   Otter, "Functions of Fiction", p. 120.

CHAPTER 4

Riddling Words: the *Prophetiae Merlini*

Maud Burnett McInerney

In Shakespeare's *Henry IV*, Henry Percy, better known as Hotspur, complains to Mortimer about their co-conspirator, Owen Glendower:

> Sometimes he angers me
> With telling me of the moldwarp and the ant
> Of the dreamer Merlin and his prophecies ...
> And such a deal of skimble skamble stuff.
>
> *Henry IV Part I*, III.1.143–49

For Hotspur, Merlin's prophecies are hogwash, inseparable both from Owen's pretentions and from his superstitious Welshness. In the context of Shakespeare's play, they are also, quite simply, false: for all that he boasts of omens, of "fiery shapes / of burning cressets" and earthquakes at his birth, Owen Glendower did not prove to be the long-awaited king who would restore the independence of the Welsh. He escaped the fate of Percy, whose head would hang on London Bridge as witness to his treachery, but only to fade out of history, his date and place of death unknown.[1] Shakespeare's mockery of the *Prophetiae Merlini*, however, only testifies to the extraordinary tenacity of their hold upon the British imagination, some three and a half centuries after they were composed by Geoffrey of Monmouth. In the intervening centuries, the prophecies had taken on a life of their own, circulating independently of the *De gestis Britonum*[2] and revised and reimagined for every possible purpose in England, Wales, and beyond. Many of Geoffrey's contemporaries and successors believed in the prophecies, or wanted to, either as revealed truth or as useful political tools, and much critical energy has been devoted to unmasking such Galfridian curiosities as the boar of trade, the old man in white on

---

1 On Owain Glyn Dŵr, see G.A. Williams, *The Last Days of Owain Glyndŵr*, Talybont, 2017 and I. Mortimer, "The Great Magician", in id. (ed.), *The Fears of Henry IV: The Life of England's Self-Made King*, London, 2007, pp. 226–43. For Owain Glyn Dŵr's own use of prophecy, see R.R. Davies, *The Revolt of Owain Glyn Dŵr*, Oxford, 1995, pp. 156–61.
2 According to Julia Crick, no fewer than 76 independent manuscripts of the *PM* exist; see Crick, *SC*, pp. 330–32.

the snow-white horse, or the city-building hedgehog.[3] In the pages that follow, I argue that such attempts are largely futile (though they would no doubt have delighted Geoffrey); rather, given the always dubious status of Geoffrey's sources, the function of the *PM* is literary as much as it is political. As Lesley Coote points out, "prophecy is not a genre but a discourse" with the capacity to operate independently of the intent of its author or the desires of its readers.[4] Not only does the *DGB* as a whole manifest considerable anxiety about the reliability of prophecy, but the primary operation of prophecy within a text that purports to be history is to create a complex narrative temporality which claims access to past, present, and future. In the creation of such a temporality, Geoffrey is perhaps closer to his great inspiration, Virgil, than to any of his contemporaries.[5]

Medieval prophecy was rooted in both pagan and Judeo-Christian traditions. From the classical tradition, medieval authors adopted the all-knowing Sibyl from the sixth book of Virgil's *Aeneid*; like Virgil himself, who was believed to have predicted the advent of Christ in the fourth *Eclogue*, the Sibyl became an example of pagan prophecy predicting Christian truth.[6] The Bible provided not only the examples of Isaiah, Jeremiah, Daniel, Ezekiel and the so-called minor prophets, but was understood to be inherently prophetic in the sense that the Old Testament predicted the New and the New looked forward to the end of times and the establishment of the kingdom of God on earth. The single most important prophetic text of the Middle Ages was the Revelation of John, which, in the later half of the 12th century, would be enthusiastically channeled by the works of Hildegard of Bingen and Joachim of Fiore. Apocalyptic prophecy always had a political element to it – Joachim himself identified a panoply of antichrists past and present, from Herod and Nero to Saladin – but its primary focus was eschatological: it looked beyond this world and into the next.[7] Geoffrey of Monmouth's prophecies differ in that they are secular rather than religious; while he may draw images from Revelation and other religious texts, his *PM* stand at the beginning of what Rupert Taylor, in 1911, identified as a tradition of primarily political prophecy in England.[8]

---

3 *DGB*, Prophetiae 115.129, 115.108–09, 116.172, respectively.

4 L.A. Coote, *Prophecy and Public Affairs in Later Medieval England*, Woodbridge, 2000, p. 13.

5 See Paul Russell's chapter in this volume.

6 See P. Dronke, "Medieval Sibyls: Their Character and their 'Auctoritas'", *Studii Medievali* 36:2 (1994), 581–615, at pp. 608–09.

7 E.R. Daniel, "Joachim of Fiore's Apocalyptic Scenario", in C.W. Bynum and P. Freedman (eds.), *Last Things: Death and the Apocalypse in the Middle Ages*, Philadelphia, 2000, pp. 124–39. On the multiplicity of antichrists, see R.E. Lerner, "Antichrists and Antichrist in Joachim of Fiore", *Speculum* 60:3 (1985), 553–70, at pp. 562–63.

8 R. Taylor, *The Political Prophecy in England*, New York, 1911; see pp. 27–38 for Taylor's account of the classical and biblical sources of Geoffrey's prophecies.

Geoffrey identifies the *PM*, which comprise Book VII of the *DGB*,[9] as a digression from the central narrative, one imposed upon him by an eager public. In the middle of his account of the reign of the usurper Vortigern, he inserts the following statement: "Before I had reached this point in my history, news of Merlin spread and I was being pressed to publish his prophecies by all my contemporaries, and particularly by Alexander bishop of Lincoln, a man of the greatest piety and wisdom."[10] As in the case of the *DGB* itself, Geoffrey here claims to be translating the prophecies from a language unknown to Alexander (*ignotum tibi ... sermonum*, "a tongue ... unknown to you").[11] The impression he creates is that the scholarly community was in an uproar about the *PM*, inaccessible to the Latinate but French- and English-speaking scholars of Oxford and Lincoln, and that Geoffrey therefore paused in his endeavors at the very moment when he should have been continuing the story of Vortigern to make a quick translation for their sake, which he drops into the larger narrative as the *PM*.

In fact, we know that the *PM* were already in circulation several years before Geoffrey completed the *DGB*. Orderic Vitalis, an English-born monk at work upon his own history, the *Ecclesiastical History*, at Saint-Évroul in Normandy, saw a copy of it before the end of 1135.[12] Orderic had brought his account up to his own days, describing the death of Robert Curthose, eldest son of William the Conqueror and deposed duke of Normandy. Evidently inspired to think of prophecy by Robert's prescient dream of the death of his son, Orderic followed that event with a summary of "the prophecy of Ambrosius Merlin, which he uttered in the time of Vortigern, king of Britain".[13] The *DGB* was not yet in circulation at the time, and Orderic's citation, which is often word for

---

9   In Reeve's edition, they are titled *Prophetiae Merlini* rather than Book VII, reflecting the
     original independent circulation of the prophecies.

10   *DGB*, Prologus in Prophetias Merlini 109.1–4: "Nondum autem ad hunc locum historiae
     peruenceram cum de Merlino diuulgato rumore compellebant me undique contempo-
     ranei mei prophetias ipsius edere, maxime autem Alexander Lincolniensis episcopus,
     uir summae religionis et prudentiae." Translations are Wright's unless otherwise noted.
     See M.A. Faletra, "Merlin in Cornwall: The Source and Contexts of John of Cornwall's
     Prophetia Merlini", *JEGP* 111:3 (2012), 303–38, at p. 312 for the argument that there was a
     pre-existing prophecy in a form of Old Cornish dating to 1070–1130. Faletra argues that
     John of Cornwall (who knew Cornish) certainly drew upon this in his "rich and overtly
     critical response" (p. 305) to the *DGB*, and that Geoffrey (who probably did not know
     Cornish) may also have been aware of it. See also M.J. Curley, "A New Edition of John of
     Cornwall's *Prophetia Merlini*", *Speculum* 57:2 (1982), 217–49.

11   *DGB*, Prophetiae 110.15.

12   See Jaakko Tahkokallio's chapter in this volume.

13   Orderic Vitalis, *Ecclesiastical History* xii.47.1–2, ed. and trans. M. Chibnall, *The Ecclesiastical
     History of Orderic Vitalis*, 6 vols., Oxford, 1969–80, vol. 6, p. 387: "Ambrosii Merlinii prophe-
     tia quam tempore Guortigerni regis Britanniae uaticinatus est".

word, must thus derive from Geoffrey's earlier, independent *PM*.[14] Orderic's own comment, toward the end of his summary, implies also that the work was not easily available; he writes that he has "taken this short extract from the book of Merlin, and ... provided a very small sample of it for scholars to whom it has not been divulged".[15] How exactly the *PM* came into his hands is unclear, but evidently he sees himself as having had rare and privileged access – thus his emphasis on other scholars who have not been so fortunate. The diminutive *libellus* also makes it plain that what he saw cannot have been the DGB as a whole, since it could by no stretch of the imagination be described as a "little book".

Orderic's evidence makes nonsense of Geoffrey's claim that he had to put aside the longer work in order to translate the prophecies in a white heat, but it gives us little insight into the sources upon which Geoffrey may have drawn. Was Merlin indeed already a well-known figure in the early 12th century? Were rumors about him spreading? As early as 1928, James Douglas Bruce pointed out that "Merlin owes his fortune in the history of fiction and popular tradition to Geoffrey of Monmouth. He is virtually the creation of Geoffrey."[16] More recently, O.J. Padel has asserted that "in Merlin's case there is no doubt but that it was Geoffrey who launched him on his international literary career."[17] The figure of Merlin that Geoffrey creates is a composite, partly inspired by the boy-prophet Ambrosius from the *Historia Brittonum* (mid-9th century[18]), and

14   Reeve suggests that the *PM* functioned as a sort of "trailer" for the DGB; DGB, p. viii. See also Curley, "A New Edition", pp. 219–20; C.D. Eckhardt, "The Date of the *Prophetia Merlini* Commentary in MSS Cotton Claudius BVII and Bibliothèque Nationale Fonds Latin 6233", *Notes and Queries*, new series, 23 (1976), 146–47, at p. 146; J. Crick, "Geoffrey and the Prophetic Tradition", in S. Echard (ed.), *The Arthur of Medieval Latin Literature: The Development and Dissemination of the Arthurian Legend in Medieval Latin* (Arthurian Literature of the Middle Ages, 6), Cardiff, 2011, pp. 67–82. For the possibility that the *PM* was circulating in some form as early as the 1120s, see B. Meehan, "Geoffrey of Monmouth, *Prophecies of Merlin*: New Manuscript Evidence", *BBCS* 28:1 (1978–80), 37–46.

15   Orderic Vitalis, *Ecclesiastical History* xii.47.493, ed. and trans. Chibnall, vol. 6, p. 386: "Hanc lectiunculam de Merlini libello excerpsi et studiosis quibus ipse propalatus non est quantulamcumque stillam propinavi."

16   J.D. Bruce, *The Evolution of Arthurian Romance from the Beginnings down to the Year 1300*, Baltimore, 1928 (repr. Gloucester, MA, 1958). See also P. Zumthor, *Merlin le Prophète, un thème de la littérature polémique de l'historiographie et des romans*, Lausanne, 1943, pp. 17–25.

17   O.J. Padel, "Recent Work on the Origins of the Arthurian Legend: A Comment", *Arthuriana* 5:3 (1995), 103–14, at p. 105.

18   The *Historia Brittonum* has been securely dated to 829/30: B. Guy, "The Origins of the Compilation of Welsh Historical Texts in Harley 3859", *Studia Celtica* 49 (2015), 21–56.

partly by the bardic Myrddin of Welsh tradition, who appears in the 10th century *Armes Prydein Vawr* ("The Great Prophecy of Britain").[19]

Ambrosius's appearance in the *Historia Brittonum* is brief; a mysterious boy without a father (although, in typically Nennian contradictory fashion, the author later claims that his father was a Roman consul), he prophesies and then interprets the combat between two dragons, one red and one white, who are preventing the construction of King Vortigern's tower, explaining that the red dragon represents the British and the white the Saxons. Ambrosius predicts that the British will eventually drive the Saxons out of Britain, a prophecy that would become known throughout Welsh literary history as the "Omen of the Dragons" because of the ominous words pronounced by Geoffrey's Merlin Ambrosius, *Vae rubeo draconi*, "Alas for the red dragon".[20] After this episode, which Geoffrey will expand in Book VII of the *DGB*, he disappears from the narrative.

The Welsh sources Geoffrey may have used in creating Merlin are much less clear. Four poems from the Black Book of Carmarthen (*Llyfr du Caerfyrddin*, Aberystwyth, National Library of Wales, Peniarth 1), copied around 1250, are attributed to Myrddin, who is imagined as a 6th-century bard; one, *Ymddiddan Myrddin a Thaliesin* ("The Conversation of Myrddin and Taliesin"), actually names him.[21] These poems may have been in circulation in some form when

---

19   *Armes Prydein Vawr*, ed. and trans I. Williams and R. Bromwich, *Armes Prydein: The Prophecy of Britain from the Book of Taliesin*, Dublin, 1972. T.M. Charles-Edwards argues for a date between 927 and 994; see *Wales and the Britons 350–1064*, Oxford, 2013, pp. 519–35. As long ago as the 1880s, G. Paris, "La Borderie, L'*Historia Britonum*", *Romania* 12 (1883), 367–76, at p. 375 suggested plausibly that Geoffrey altered "Myrddin" to "Merlin" to avoid a name that might recall the French *merde*: "Ce nom est l'invention de Gaufrei de Monmouth, qui sans doute a reculé devant le *Merdinus* qu'il aurait obtenu en latinisant le nom gallois", "The name is the invention of Geoffrey of Monmouth, who no doubt recoiled at *Merdinus*, which he would have gotten by Latinizing the Welsh name."

20   *DGB*, Prophetiae 112.34. See, for instance, the Welsh prose text *Lludd and Llefelys* (dating is problematic; a fragment appears in the White Book of Rhydderch *c*.1350, but the tale is also incorporated into a Welsh translation of the *DGB* in Aberystwyth, National Library of Wales, Llanstephan 1 in the mid-13th century); see D. Huws, *Medieval Welsh Manuscripts*, Aberystwyth, 2000, p. 58 and *Cyfranc Lludd and Llefelys*, ed. B.F. Roberts (Mediaeval and Modern Welsh Series, 7), Dublin, 1975. The story is the origin of the Welsh flag, a red dragon on a green and white ground, which was flown by Henry Tudor before his accession as Henry VII. On Henry as the *mab darogan*, "son of prophecy", see A.L. Jones, *Darogan: Prophecy, Lament and Absent Heroes in Medieval Welsh Literature*, Cardiff, 2013, p. 3.

21   For details of dating and provenance, see Huws, *Medieval Welsh Manuscripts*, pp. 70–72; see also *Llyfr Du Caerfyrddin: gyda Rhagymadrodd, Nodiadau Testunol, a Geirfa* [The Black Book of Carmarthen: with introduction, textual notes, and vocabulary], ed. A.O.H. Jarman, Cardiff, 1982.

Geoffrey was writing.[22] The Red Book of Hergest (*Llyfr Coch Hergest*, Oxford, Jesus College, 111), a collection dated to shortly after 1382,[23] contains three more poems associated with Myrddin, *Cyfoesi Myrddin a Gwenddydd ei Chwaer* ("The Prophecy of Myrddin and Gwenddydd his Sister"), *Gwasgargerdd Fyrddin yn y Bedd* ("The Diffused/Scattered Poem of Myrddin in the Grave"), and *Peirian Faban* ("Commanding Youth").[24] These poems allow for a "feasible reconstruction" of Myrddin as an exemplar of the Wild Man of the Woods, a folkloric motif at least as old as the biblical Nebuchadnezzar, according to A.O.H. Jarman.[25]

The dating of all of these texts, however, is problematic; nor is it clear how much of the Welsh material was familiar to Geoffrey when he was composing the *PM*, although Ben Guy argues, in an essay in this volume, that Geoffrey may have known most of them even as he was composing the *DGB*.[26] Certainly, when he came to write the *VM* a decade or so later, he drew on traditions concerning a mad prophet who lived in the woods. Geoffrey seems to have seen no contradiction between this figure and the magician of the *DGB*; the Merlin of the *VM* refers to his prophecy before Vortigern.[27] Gerald of Wales, however, whose suspicions about Merlin were profound, categorically denies that they can have been one and the same: "There were two Merlins. The one called Ambrosius, who thus had two names, prophesied when Vortigern was king ... The second Merlin came from Scotland ... He went mad ... and fled to

---

22   See N. Tolstoy, "Geoffrey of Monmouth and the Merlin Legend", *AL* 25 (2008), 1–42, at pp. 2–3 for a summary of the debate around Geoffrey's access to these materials.

23   Huws, *Medieval Welsh Manuscripts*, p. 82; see also id., "Llyfr Coch Hergest", in I. Daniel, M. Haycock, D. Johnston and J. Rowland (eds.), *Cyfoeth y Testun: Ysgrifau ar Lenyddiath Gymraeg yr Oesoedd Canol*, Cardiff, 2003, pp. 1–30.

24   *Cyfoesi Myrddin* is edited by M.B. Jenkins, "Aspects of the Welsh Prophetic Verse Tradition: Incorporating Textual Studies of the Poetry from 'Llyfr Coch Hergest' (Oxford, Jesus College, MS cxi) and 'Y Cwta Cyfarwydd' (Aberystwyth, National Library of Wales, MS Peniarth 50)", unpublished PhD thesis, University of Cambridge, 1990, pp. 33–90, although I was not able to consult it for this essay; see also *Peirian Vaban*, ed. A.O.H. Jarman, "Peirian Vaban", *BBCS* 14 (1950–52), 104–08; for translations, see *The Four Ancient Books of Wales Containing the Cymric Poems Attributed to the Bards of the Sixth Century, Volume I*, trans. W.F. Skene, Edinburgh, 1868, pp. 218–40, and *The Romance of Merlin: An Anthology*, ed. P. Goodrich, New York, 1990.

25   A.O.H. Jarman, "The Merlin Legend and the Welsh Tradition of Prophecy", in R. Bromwich, A.O.H. Jarman, and B.F. Roberts (eds.), *The Arthur of the Welsh: The Arthurian Legend in Medieval Welsh Literature* (Arthurian Literature in the Middle Ages, 1), Cardiff, 1991, pp. 117–45, at p. 117. See also N. Thomas, "The Celtic Wildman Tradition and Geoffrey of Monmouth's *Vita Merlini*", *Arthuriana* 10:1 (2000), 27–42.

26   See Ben Guy's contribution to this volume, pp. 62–65.

27   Jarman, "The Merlin Legend", p. 132.

the wood where he passed the remainder of his life as a wild man of the woods. This second Merlin lived in the time of Arthur."[28] Gerald's comment that the "second Merlin" came from Scotland suggests some awareness of the parallel (or perhaps precursor) traditions of another wild man, the Scottish Lailoken.

Like Merlin himself, the *PM* is very much a composite, inspired by Welsh prophetic tradition rather than directly descended from it. It is possible that Geoffrey knew *Armes Prydein Vawr*, the 10th-century Welsh poem in which Myrddin appears, and which predicts the expulsion of the Saxons from Britain; the poem's reiteration of the coupled names Cynan and Cadwaladr is echoed in the *PM*.[29] Other sources are difficult to identify, and Zumthor suggests that Geoffrey was at least as much indebted to biblical prophecy and to the legends around the Tiburtine Sibyl as he was to Welsh material.[30] The related questions of Geoffrey's access to Welsh materials, his knowledge of the Welsh or Cornish languages, and his own ethnic identity have been treated extensively elsewhere, most recently in the introduction to the present volume. Regardless of his ethnicity, Geoffrey was deeply implicated in what Faletra calls "the network of Norman power";[31] he depended upon it for professional advancement within the church, at the very least. In translating or purporting to translate British prophetic material into Latin, Geoffrey was engaged in something more complicated than the glorification of an idealized British or Celtic past; medieval Celtic language speakers did not, in any case, see each other as natural allies, as their modern descendants sometimes strive to. Geoffrey operated in a 12th-century sphere of Norman political and cultural ascendance in which there circulated a lively tradition of Welsh prophecy, but the prophecies he

---

28 Gerald of Wales, *The Journey Through Wales* ii.8, ed. J.F. Dimock, *Giraldi Cambrensis Opera*, 8 vols., London, 1861–91, vol. 6, pp. 3–152, at p. 133: "Erant enim Merlini duo; iste qui et Ambrosius dictus est, quia binomius fuerat, et sub rege Vortigerno prophetizavit ... alter vero de Albania oriundus ... dementire coepit, et ad silvam transfugiendo silvestrem usque ad obitum vitam perduxit. Hic autem Merlinus tempore Arturi fuit", translated in Gerald of Wales, *The Journey Through Wales* and *The Description of Wales*, trans. L. Thorpe, *Gerald of Wales: The Journey through Wales / The Description of Wales*, Harmondsworth, 1978, pp. 192–93.

29 *DGB*, Prophetiae 115.110–11: "Cadualadrus Conanum uocabit et Albaniam in societatem accipiet", "Cadualadrus will summon Conananus and make Scotland his ally." See A.O.H. Jarman, "The Welsh Myrddin Poems", in R.S. Loomis (ed.), *Arthurian Literature in the Middle Ages*, Oxford, 1959, pp. 20–30; D.N. Dumville, "Brittany and *Armes Prydein Vawr*", *Études celtiques* 20 (1983), 145–59.

30 Zumthor, *Merlin le Prophète*, pp. 26–29. See also Paul Russell's contribution to this volume.

31 M.A. Faletra, "Narrating the Matter of Britain: Geoffrey of Monmouth and the Norman Colonization of Wales", *The Chaucer Review* 35:1 (2000), 60–85, at p. 62.

places in the mouth of Merlin need not be read (although they often were, in
the centuries to follow) as pro-Welsh. Rather, as Victoria Flood puts it, they
perform a kind of "paranoid ventriloquism" which "anticipate[s] the terms of
Welsh prophetic opposition during a period of heightened border threats" in
the aftermath of the death of Henry I.[32] While Geoffrey does not appear to
have drawn directly on pre-existing Welsh prophecies, perhaps because he
did not have access to the language in which they circulated, he does incorporate into the figure of Merlin essential elements of the Welsh prophetical
poet. As Williams notes, Geoffrey's Merlin is "a distinctly Taliesinic figure ... an
all-knowing youth, prophesying obscurely",[33] and Taliesin even appears in the
VM, as Telgesinus.[34] The essential feature of the Welsh prophet as embodied in
Taliesin is that he is also a poet: Welsh prophecy was a poetic mode, expressed
in a variety of more and less strict meters.[35] The "continuum of identity between the figures of the poet and the prophet"[36] are perhaps what license
Geoffrey's revision of Virgil's *Aeneid*, a text to which the *PM* is in many ways
more explicitly indebted than it is to any particular Welsh work. The insertion
of the *PM* into the *DGB* operates, in fact, not only to reconfigure the Breton
or British hope for the return of Arthur in pro-Norman rather than pro-Welsh
terms, but also to create a prophetic power for its author, Geoffrey himself,
with roots in both Insular and Virgilian traditions.

Within the larger context of the *DGB*, the *PM* has a problematic narrative
effect. The *DGB* declares itself as history in its opening line: "While my mind
was often pondering many things in many ways, my thoughts turned to the
history of the kings of Britain."[37] What follows certainly looks like one kind of
history; beginning with Brutus, the exiled grandson of Aeneas, Geoffrey traces
the lineage of the kings of Britain down through the ages until 682 CE. The
work constructs an apparently linear chronology, reign by reign, father to son
(or, in some cases, daughter), until the sudden eruption of the *PM* at the end of
the sixth book. An exploration of the past is thus suddenly interrupted by an

---

32   V. Flood, *Prophecy, Politics and Place in Medieval England: From Geoffrey of Monmouth to
      Thomas of Erceldoune*, Cambridge, 2016, p. 35.

33   M. Williams, *Fiery Shapes: Celestial Portents and Astrology in Ireland and Wales, 700–1700*,
      Oxford, 2010, p. 77.

34   On the possibility that the Book of Taliesin (*Llyfr Taliesin*) draws upon Geoffrey and not
      the other way around, see M. Haycock, "Taliesin's 'Lesser Song of the World'", in T. Jones
      and E.B. Fryde (eds.), *Ysgrifau a cherddi cyflwynedig i Daniel Huws. Essays and Poems
      Presented to Daniel Huws*, Aberystwyth, 1994, pp. 229–50, at p. 243.

35   On the variations between metrical prophetic forms, see A.L. Jones, *Darogan*, p. 14.

36   M. Williams, *Fiery Shapes*, p. 76.

37   *DGB*, Prologus 1.1–2: "Cum mecum multa et de multis saepius animo reuoluens in hysto-
      riam regum Britanniae inciderem."

exploration of the future, a phenomenon that threatens to upset the temporality of the text thus far, transforming its focus from the (quasi-) historical past to the mystically glimpsed future.

The question "What is history?" cannot be addressed comprehensively within the scope of this essay, but it is, I hope, fair to say that, in the 21st century, history is still generally understood to have some connection to actual events of the past, to "what happened". We are often admonished to learn from the events of the past, as when the Civil Rights movement of the 1960's is invoked as precedent for the LGBTQ rights movement of the present day. Even if, post-Foucault and Derrida, we are suspicious of empiricist histories that propose to tell us precisely what happened and why, and are more interested in history as discourse, in how history frames what happened, we still assume some connection between that discourse and actual events. *Discipline and Punish*, after all, begins with an event that actually occurred, the torture and execution of Robert-François Damiens on the Place de Grève in Paris, in 1757. For medieval historians, the foundation of history upon fact, and indeed the distinction between history and what we would call fiction, are not particularly relevant. What matters instead is the way in which both history and fiction could point toward truth. Walter Map, writing in the generation after Geoffrey, was keenly aware of the fascination with the past that characterized the time in which he wrote. In *The Courtier's Trifles*, he argues that

> we have histories continued from the beginning down to us; we read fiction [*fabulae*] too; and if we understand the mystical significance of history, we then learn what ought to please us ... Admonitory stories set before us Atreus and Thyestes, Pelops and Lycaeon, and many like them, that we may shun their ends; and the utterances of history are not without their use: one is the method and intention of the story in either case.[38]

For Walter, the distinction between what did and did not happen is of little importance; rather, he makes the point that moral truth can be expressed in different genres; *fabulae* may be as exemplary as *historiae*. Each reveals something profound and monitory about the workings of the universe: "In narratives

---

38   Walter Map, *The Courtiers' Trifles* i.31, ed. and trans. M.R. James, revised by C.N.L. Brooke and R.A.B. Mynors, Oxford, 1983, pp. 126–28: "historias ab inicio ad nos usque deductas habemus, fabulas eciam legimus, et que placere debeant intellectu mistico nouimus ... Fabule nobis eciam commonitorie Atreum et Thiestem, Pelopem et Licaona, multosque similes eorum proponunt, ut uitemus eorum exitus, et sunt historiarum sentencie non inutiles; unus utrimque narracionum mos et intencio."

[*scripturis*] adversity succeedeth in turn to prosperity and vice versa."[39] As Monika Otter puts it, "a neat categorical distinction between fiction and other modes of discourse is not to be expected in twelfth century thought."[40]

Even by 12th-century standards, however, a history that not only appears to have little, if any, relationship to what happened in the past, but also suddenly reverses its own temporality in order to announce what will happen in the future would be an oddity. Emerging in the middle of a document that claims to look into the deepest past, the *PM* not only predicts the future from the perspective of those within the text, it carries on to predict a future that occurs after the ending of that narrative with the fall of Britain to the Anglo-Saxons, and then further still to a future that extends through and beyond the lifetime of the author. The immediate context of the *PM* within the larger narrative helps explain why Geoffrey included it. After the murders of Constantinus and his son Constans, Vortigern usurps the throne. Almost immediately, the Saxon brothers Hengist and Horsa land in Kent with an imposing army. Vortigern, under threat from the Picts, offers the Saxons land in exchange for protection and marries Hengist's daughter, Ronwein. After a series of bloody struggles between Vortigern and his Saxon allies and the native British, Hengist initiates a full-scale invasion of the island, and Vortigern is driven into Wales, where his magicians advise him to build a great tower as refuge against the barbarians. Each day, however, the foundations that are laid are swallowed up by the earth. The magicians instruct Vortigern to find a boy without a father and sacrifice him so that his blood pours over the newly laid stones, promising that this will allow the building of the tower. A boy named Merlin, son of a noble mother and an incubus, is brought before Vortigern, but he challenges the king's magicians:

> Without knowing what is hindering the foundation of the tower that is being built, you have advised that the cement be sprinkled with my blood, whereupon it would almost instantly stand firm. But tell me what is hidden beneath the foundations. There is something beneath which prevents the tower standing firm.[41]

---

39   Walter Map, *The Courtiers' Trifles* i.31, ed. and trans. James, p. 128: "sibique succedunt inuicem in scripturis tum aduersitas prosperitati, tum e conuerso mutacione frequenti."

40   M. Otter, *Inventiones: Fiction and Referentiality in Twelfth-Century English Historical Writing*, Chapel Hill, 1996, p. 14.

41   *DGB*, vi.108.561–64: "Nescientes quid fundamentum inceptae turris impediat, laudauistis ut sanguis meus diffunderetur in caementum et quasi ilico opus constaret. Sed dicite michi quid sub fundamento latet. Nam aliquid sub illo est quod ipsum stare non permittit."

The magicians are confounded, and Merlin orders the king to dig down beneath the foundation, revealing a pool of water. Again he challenges the magicians to explain what lies beneath the pool, and again they fail to answer. Merlin predicts that beneath the pool two dragons will be found asleep; the king, impressed by Merlin's previous prediction, does so, and "all the bystanders too were filled with wonder at his wisdom, thinking that he was inspired."[42]

At this point, before the truth of Merlin's second prediction can be substantiated, but at the very moment when all the witnesses are convinced of his prophetic power, Geoffrey ends the chapter and begins the *PM*, thus leaving his readers hanging just like the king and his counselors, while he pronounces his second dedication, to Alexander of Lincoln:

> Alexander bishop of Lincoln, my love for your noble person compelled me to translate from British into Latin the prophecies of Merlin ... because I was sure that the discernment of your subtle mind would grant me pardon, I have put my rustic pipe to my lips and, to its humble tune, have translated the tongue which is unknown to you. I am surprised that you deigned to entrust this task to my poor pen when your staff of office can command so many men of greater learning to soothe the ears of your intellect with the sweetness of a more sublime song. And to say nothing of all the scholars in the whole of Britain, I readily admit that you alone could sing it best of all with your bold lyre, if your lofty office did not call you to other business. Since it is your wish, therefore, that the reed of Geoffrey of Monmouth pipes this prophecy, please favour his playing and with the rod of your muses restore to harmony anything irregular or faulty.[43]

---

42   *DGB*, vi.108.576–77: "Ammirabantur etiam cuncti qui astabant tantam in eo sapientiam, existimantes numen esse in illo."

43   *DGB*, Prologus in Prophetias Merlini 110.8–9, 13–24: "Coegit me, Alexander Lincolniensis praesul, nobilitatis tuae dilectio prophetias Merlini de Britannico in Latinum transferre ... quoniam securus eram ueniae quam discretio subtilis ingenii tui donaret, agrestem calamum meum labellis apposui et plebia modulatione ignotum tibi interpretatus sum sermonem. Admodum autem ammiror quia id pauperi stilo dignatus eras committere, cum tot doctiores uirga potestatis tuae coherceat, qui sublimioris carminis delectamento aures mineruae tuae mulcerent. Et ut omnes philosophos totius Britannuae insulae praeteream, tu solus es, quod non erubesco fateri, qui prae cunctis audaci lira caneres, nisi te culmen honoris ad cetera negocia uocaret. Quoniam ergo placuit ut Galfridus Monemutensis fistulam suam in hoc uaticinio sonaret, modulationibus suis fauere non diffugias et siquid inordinate siue uitiose protulerit ferula camenarum tuarum in rectum aduertas concentum."

Here, as in the dedication to the *DGB*, a magisterial example of the humility topos, Geoffrey's style is at its most florid. By evoking the pipe of Pan and the Muses, it places both Alexander and Geoffrey within a classical context, as though to balance the very non-classical effect of the prophecies to follow. The claim that Alexander, with his bold lyre, could perform the task better, and the invitation to the bishop to correct anything "irregular or faulty", are disingenuous to say the least, since Geoffrey has already established that the language of the prophecies is unknown to Alexander. The dedication thus invokes the potentially protective authority of Alexander and the church for a literary endeavor which is entirely Geoffrey's own.

The dedication completed, Geoffrey returns briefly to narration: two dragons, one red and one white, emerge from the pool and begin to fight; the white one appears to be winning, but the red one soon gains the upper claw. Vortigern demands to know the meaning of the omen; Merlin's response begins,

> Alas for the red dragon, its end is near. Its caves will be taken by the white dragon, which symbolises the Saxons whom you have summoned. The red represents the people of Britain, whom the white will oppress. Its mountains will be levelled with the valleys, and the rivers in the valleys will flow with blood. Religious observance will be destroyed and churches stand in ruins. At last the oppressed will rise up and resist the foreigners' fury. The boar of Cornwall will lend his aid and trample the foreigners' necks beneath his feet.[44]

The prophecies carry on in this vein for pages, finally coming to a close with a sort of astrological apocalypse, a "baroque fantasy of cosmic collapse", in Mark Williams' words:[45]

> Lightning bolts will flash from Scorpio's tail and Cancer will quarrel with the sun. Virgo will mount on Sagittarius' back and defile her virginal flowers. The moon's chariot will disrupt the zodiac and the Pleiades burst into tears. Janus will not perform his duties, but will close his door and hide in the precinct of Ariadne. In the flash of its beam, the seas will rise and

---

44   *DGB*, Prophetiae 112.34–40: "Vae rubeo draconi; nam exterminatio eius festinat. Cauernas ipsius occupabit albus draco, qui Saxones quos inuitasti significat. Rubeus uero gentem designat Britanniae, quae ab albo opprimetur. Montes itaque eius ut ualles aequabuntur, et flumina uallium sanguine manabunt. Cultus religionis delebitur, et ruina ecclesiarum patebit. Praeualebit tandem oppressa et saeuiciae exterorum resistet. Aper etenim Cornubiae succursum praestabit et colla eorum sub pedibus suis conculcabit."

45   M. Williams, *Fiery Shapes*, p. 92.

the dust of the long-dead will be reborn. The winds will contend with a terrible blast and the stars will hear them howl.[46]

Geoffrey's vision of the future, inserted into a vision of the past, thus ends with a vision of the end of times.

At this point, he returns to narrative mode, noting that these prophecies (and, he teasingly adds, *haec et alia*, "and more", which he evidently did not see fit to transcribe)[47] provoke admiration at the ambiguity of Merlin's expressions: "his riddling words reduced the bystanders to amazement."[48] Vortigern asks Merlin to interpret the prophecy with regard to his own fate, and Merlin responds that he should flee the sons of Constantinus (Aurelius Ambrosius and Uther Pendragon) who are already on their way to retake Britain; each will reign in succession, but each will die by poison, only to be avenged by the *aper Cornubiae*, "the boar of Cornwall".[49] The next day, Ambrosius and Uther do indeed arrive, and not long after, Vortigern is burned to death in his tower. In this way, Geoffrey models for his readers the interpretation of Merlin's prophecies: Ambrosius and Uther are avenged by Arthur, whom any reader must therefore identify as the boar of Cornwall, born as he was at Tintagel.

The prophecies fall into three parts. The first is the "Omen of the Dragons", interpreted for Vortigern by Merlin himself.[50] The version in the *Historia Brittonum* is brief and clear without being explicit when Ambrosius explains it: "the red serpent is your dragon, but the white dragon belongs to those people who invaded many nations and regions of Britain, and held them almost from sea to sea: but eventually, our people will rise up and forcefully cast out the Saxon race from beyond the sea."[51] For the Welsh author, writing in the 9th century, this event was still in the future; his prediction is the origin of the so-called Breton or British hope, the hope that the kingdom of Britain might

---

46   *DGB*, Prophetiae 117.298–304: "Cauda Scorpionis procreabit fulgura, et Cancer cum sole litigabit. Ascendet Virgo dorsum Sagitarii et flores uirgineos obfuscabit. Currus lunae turbabit zodiacum, et in fletum prorumpent Pleiades. Officia Iani nulla redibunt, sed clausa ianua in crepidinibus Adriannae delitebit. In ictu radii exurgent aequora, et puluis ueterum renouabitur. Confligent uenti diro sufflamine et sonitum inter sidera conficient."

47   *DGB*, viii.118.1.

48   *DGB*, viii.118.1–2: "ambiguitate verborum suorum astantes in ammirationem commovit."

49   *DGB*, viii.118.20–21.

50   *DGB*, Prophetiae 112.34–43.

51   *Historia Brittonum* (Harley 3859) §42, ed. Faral, *LLA*, pp. 2–62, at p. 32: "Vermis rufus draco tuus est … at ille albus draco illius gentis quae occcupavit gentes et regiones plurimas in Brittania, et pene a mari usque ad mare tenebunt, et postea gens nostra surget, et gentem Anglorum trans mare viriliter deiciet." Translation mine.

be regained by the Britons themselves, the Welsh or their Breton cousins who had migrated across the channel.[52] Geoffrey's revised version of the prophecy places it in the past, in the days of Arthur, the Boar of Cornwall: "The islands of the ocean will fall under his sway and he will occupy the glades of France. The house of Rome will tremble before his rage, and his end shall be unknown."[53] Arthur's exploits in Europe and his attempted conquest of Rome are described in Book X, and his uncertain end in Book XI, when he is both *letaliter uulneratus*, "mortally wounded", and taken away *ad sananda vulnera sua*, "to have his wounds healed", in the Island of Avalon.[54] For Geoffrey, the hope of Britain has already come and gone, and whether it will come again remains shrouded in several kinds of mystery.

The next section of the *PM* (§§112–13) maps the centuries between the death of Arthur and Geoffrey's own time. Orderic Vitalis found it easy enough to identify the figures in these prophecies:

> Men well read in histories can easily apply his predictions, if they know the lives of Hengist and Katigern, Pascent and Arthur, Aethelbert and Edwin, Oswald and Oswy, Caedwalla and Alfred, and other rulers of the Angles and Britons ...[55]

A reader more skeptical than Orderic will immediately perceive that it is no wonder that the first set of prophecies, covering the period from the Saxon invasion to the death of Cadwaladr, were proven true, since they correspond exactly to the narrative of the *DGB* from this point onward; Merlin, after all, speaks through Geoffrey, who was certainly a "man well read in history", in the very same histories Orderic, too, had read. Indeed, *PM* §112.43–61 describes events that will come to pass in Books XI and XII of the *DGB*; Arthur is succeeded, as predicted, by six kings. The "wolf from the sea who will be accompanied by the forests of Africa" of *PM* §112.45 is revealed in Book XI.184.124 as the king of a tribe of Africans settled in Ireland;[56] the man of bronze

---

52   For the Normans' use of Breton auxiliary forces during the Conquest, see Flood, *Prophecy*, pp. 39–40.

53   *DGB*, Prophetiae 112.41–42: "Insulae occeani potestati ipsius subdentur, et Gallicanos saltus possidebit. Tremebit Romulea domus saeuiciam ipsius, et exitus eius dubius erit."

54   *DGB*, xi.178.81–82.

55   Orderic Vitalis, *Ecclesiastical History* xii.47.493, ed. and trans. Chibnall, vol. 6, pp. 386–87: "Historiarum gnari eius dicta facile poterunt intelligere, qui nouerint ea quae contigerunt Hengist et Catigirno, Pascent et Arturo, Aedelberto ac Edwino, Oswaldo et Osuio, Cedwal et Elfredo, aliisque princibus Anglorum et Britonum ..."

56   *DGB*, Prophetiae 112.45 "aequoreus lupus quem Affricana nemora comitabuntur". This is probably the earliest example of the conflation of Irish and African ethnicities which

(*PM* §112.55) above the gates of London resolves into King Cadwallo, whose embalmed body, encased in bronze, is erected by his people as a "terror to the Saxons".[57] Cadwallo's son, Cadwaladr, the last of the kings of Britain according to the *DGB*, travels to Rome upon the command of an angelic voice, as predicted by Merlin: "A blessed king will prepare a fleet and be numbered among the saints in the palace of the twelfth. There will be grievous desolation in the kingdom ..."[58] At this point, Geoffrey's Merlin has predicted the entirety of the history that Geoffrey was himself engaged in writing, a curious bit of narrative sleight of hand.[59] Inevitably, these prophecies must be read as truth revealed, since they are revealed as such in the books that follow them. They also prepare the ground, and the reader's imagination, for the prophecies of §113.

These prophecies are populated with the same kinds of wildlife and meteorological events as those that came before, but they describe the years leading up until the moment of Geoffrey's composition of the *DGB* in the 1130s, thus becoming involved in the politics of the day, rather than in the history of centuries past. Merlin predicts the Norman Conquest, evoking the characteristic armor of the Normans: "The German dragon will be hard put to keep possession of its caves, since retribution will be visited on its treason. Then it will prosper for a short time, but Normandy's tithe will injure it. A people will come clad in wood and tunics of iron to take vengeance on its wickedness."[60] As Flood points out, Geoffrey here makes a significant addition to the "Omen of the Dragons" when he makes the German dragon guilty of treason; the reference is to Harold Godwinson, who was supposed (by the Normans) to have sworn fealty to Duke William after being shipwrecked on the coast of Normandy, providing one of the excuses for the Norman Conquest.[61] This addition makes the Normans into rightful rulers rather than unjust invaders. Orderic Vitalis was quick to interpret the rest of this passage:

---

was to become popular in English propaganda during the period of the Great Hunger in Ireland in the mid-19th century.

57   *DGB*, xi.510: "in terrorem Saxonibus".

58   *DGB*, Prophetiae 112.60–62: "Rex benedictus parabit nauigium et in aula duodecimi inter beatos annumerabitur. Erit miseranda regni desolatio ..."

59   On prophesying the past, see R. Trachsler, "*Vaticinium ex eventu*, ou comment prédire le passé: observations sur les prophéties de Merlin", *Francofonia* 45 (2003), 91–108.

60   *DGB*, Prophetiae 113.69–73: "Vix obtinebit cauernas suas Germanicus draco, quia ultio prodicionis eius superueniet. Vigebit tandum paulisper, sed decimatio Neustriae nocebit. Populus namque in ligno et rerreis tunicis superueniet, qui uindictam de nequitia ipsius sumet."

61   Flood, *Prophecy*, p. 38.

For clearer than daylight to the thinking man are the words about the two sons of William, which run, "There shall follow two dragons" – that is, licentious and warlike lords – "of whom one will be slain by the dart of envy" – that is, William Rufus by the arrow while hunting – "the other" – that is, Duke Robert, will die "under the shadow of prison, bearing the empty honour of his former title" – that is, of the duke. "Then shall come the Lion of Justice", which is applied to Henry, "at whose roar the towers of Gaul shall shake and the island dragons shall tremble", because by his wealth and power he surpasses all who have reigned before him in England.[62]

Merlin's description of the reign of the Lion of Justice, Henry I, who was still alive as of Orderic's writing, is a masterpiece of ambiguity. It has utopian elements ("in his time gold will be extracted from the lily and the nettle, and silver shall drip from the hooves of lowing cattle",[63] and "the greed of kites will be ended and the teeth of wolves blunted"[64]); these are balanced by more ominous predictions: *Humanitas supplicium dolebit.*[65] Wright translates this last phrase as "men will suffer punishment", which allows the interpretation that they are being justly punished by a king who stands for the rule of law; Faletra's translation, perhaps more literal, is less positive: "humankind will mourn its dire straits."[66] The phrase "the lion's cubs will become fishes of the sea" is taken by Orderic and later writers as referring to the drowning of Henry I's only legitimate male heir, William Ætheling, in the White Ship disaster of 1120.[67]

After this point, the prophecies are, inevitably, increasingly obscure, since they are no longer predicting a future familiar to Geoffrey as his own past, and

---

62 Orderic Vitalis, *Ecclesiatical History* xii.47.493–94, ed. and trans. Chibnall, vol. 6, pp. 387–89: "nam luce clarius patet callenti, quod de duobus Guillielmi filiis dicitur, 'Succedent', inquit, 'duo dracones', domini scilicet libidinosi et feroces. 'quorum alter invidiae spiculo' id est Guillielmus Rufus in venantione sagitta 'suffocabitur, alter' id est Rodbertus dux 'sub umbra' carceris stemma pristini 'nominis' id est ducis gerens perebit. 'succedit leo iustitiae' quod refertur ad henricum 'ad cuius rugitum Gallicanae turres et insulani dracones contremiscent', quia ipse diuitiis et potestate transcendit omnes qui ante illum in Anglia regnaverunt." This passage provides *a terminus post quem*, since Orderic writes as if Henry I, the Lion of Justice, were still alive; Henry died in 1135.

63 *DGB*, Prophetiae 113.79–80: "In diebus eius aurum ex lilio et urtica extorquebitur et argentum ex ungulis mugientium manabit."

64 *DGB*, Prophetiae 113.84: "Peribit miluorum rapacitas, et dentes luporum hebetabuntur."

65 *DGB*, Prophetiae 113.82–83.

66 Geoffrey of Monmouth, *De gestis Britonum*, trans. M.A. Faletra, *The History of the Kings of Britain, Geoffrey of Monmouth*, Peterborough, Ontario, 2007, p. 133.

67 *DGB*, Prophetiae 113.84–85: "catuli leones in aequoreos pisces transformabatur."

their style grows increasingly surreal. This did not prevent 12th-century readers from interpreting them. Étienne de Rouen, writing *The Norman Dragon* (*Draco Normannicus*) in the late 1160s, found in the *PM* references to the marriage of the princess Matilda to the Emperor Henry v, the death of Stephen, the marriage of Henry and Eleanor, and the conflict between Henry and his sons.[68] The Eagle of the Broken Covenant was often identified as the Empress Matilda, denied her rightful place as Queen of England.[69] John of Salisbury, writing to Thomas Becket in the 1170s, refers to Henry II as the Eagle, although Crick notes that he may have been being ironic.[70]

Vernacular writers appear to have been more suspicious of the prophecies. In the first translation of the *DGB* into Old French, composed around 1155, Wace notoriously refused to include them: "I do not wish to translate his book, for I do not know how to interpret them."[71] Laȝamon, translating Wace into English around 1200, follows suit. Blacker suggests that this reluctance may stem from the fact that Wace, as a vernacular writer and self-described *clerc lisant* for the royal family of Henry II, may have been so dependent on Henry's goodwill that he dared not risk antagonizing the king with even a hint of criticism or a less than glorious future, such as that which various of Merlin's prophecies suggested.[72] It is also possible that Wace, engaged in a translation of the story of the British people from Troy to the conquest of Britain by the Anglo-Saxons, saw the prophecies, as modern readers are inclined to do, as a distraction from the larger narrative impulse of Geoffrey's work.[73] Finally, the status of prophecy itself within the larger narrative is extremely dubious, a fact which may have contributed to Wace's unease.

Merlin's prophecies appear as part of the Arthurian section of the *DGB*, the most read and most influential part of the narrative; Merlin is, after all,

---

68   J. Blacker, "Where Wace Feared to Tread: Latin Commentaries on Merlin's Prophecies in the Reign of Henry II", *Arthuriana* 6:1 (1996), 36–52, at p. 37.

69   R. Taylor, *Political Prophecy*, p. 23; Faletra, "Narrating the Matter of Britain", p. 77; M.J. Curley, *Geoffrey of Monmouth* (Twayne's English Authors Series, 509), New York, 1994, p. 77.

70   Crick, "Geoffrey and the Prophetic Tradition", p. 73.

71   Wace, *Roman de Brut*, trans. J. Weiss, *Wace's Roman de Brut: A History of the British: Text and Translation* (Exeter Medieval English Texts and Studies), Exeter, 1999, rev. ed. 2002, p. 191, ll.7539–40 (French text adapted from Wace, *Roman de Brut*, ed. I.D.O. Arnold, 2 vols., Paris, 1938–40): "Nel vul sun livre translater / Car jo nel sai interpreter."

72   Blacker, "Where Wace Feared to Tread", pp. 44–45.

73   It is clear, however, that many scribes saw the *PM* as the main event within the *DGB*; see, for example, Auxerre, Bibliothèque Municipale, 91, fols. 142–53, in which the prophecies are rubricated; see also Crick, *SC*, p. 331.

Arthur's prophet and magician, and Arthur himself, as we have seen, is the subject of the first prophecy, the Boar of Cornwall. As Siân Echard reminds us, however, there is a great deal more to the *DGB* than the Arthurian material;[74] it springs rather from the tale of the Trojan diaspora, and very particularly from the *Aeneid*. As in the *Aeneid*, prophecy is a concern of the text from its first pages. If the *DGB* is read not as a free-standing text but as part of a much larger literary project, a response to or continuation of the *Aeneid*, then its significance is deeply altered. The hinge of the *Aeneid* – the point at which the hero's destiny shifts to assume its full, imperial potential – occurs when Aeneas journeys to the underworld in Book VI and receives Anchises' prophecy about the future of Rome. The *PM*, as Tatlock pointed out long ago, forms a similar hinge in the *DGB*, also coming in the center of the narrative, right before the rise of Uther Pendragon and the birth of Arthur, who is the epitome of imperial British ambition.[75] Reading the *PM* against Books III and VI of the *Aeneid* reveals a slippery quality to prophecy within the text, one which is not apparent in the *PM* read alone.

The *DGB* begins with a prophecy: Brutus will kill both of his parents and wander the world in exile before achieving the highest honor.[76] This prediction is fulfilled in Book I: Brutus's mother dies giving birth to him, and he kills his father accidentally while hunting. The second prophecy is more problematic. On a deserted island, Brutus invokes the goddess Diana, who responds to his prayer:

> Brutus, to the west, beyond the kingdoms of Gaul,
> lies an island of the ocean, surrounded by the sea;
> an island of the ocean, where giants once lived,
> but now it is deserted and waiting for your people.
> Sail to it; it will be your home for ever.
> It will furnish your children with a new Troy.
> From your descendants will arise kings, who
> will be masters of the whole world.[77]

---

74   See S. Echard, "Geoffrey of Monmouth", in Echard (ed.), *The Arthur of Medieval Latin
      Literature*, pp. 45–66, at pp. 45–46, for Geoffrey. On the Virgilian elements in Geoffrey's
      book, see R. Waswo, "Our Ancestors, The Trojans: Inventing Cultural Identity in the
      Middle Ages", *Exemplaria* 7:2 (1995), 269–90, at pp. 279–82.

75   Tatlock, *LHB*, p. 403.

76   *DGB*, i.6.57–59.

77   *DGB*, i.16.305–12: "Brute, sub occasu solis trans Gallica regna / insula in occeano est un-
      dique clause mari; / insula in occeano est habitata gigantibus olim, / nunc deserta qui-
      dem, gentibus apta tuis. / Hanc pete; namque tibi sedes erit illa perhennis. / Hic fiet natis

Diana's prophecy has clear parallels with the oracle her brother Apollo gives in Book III of the *Aeneid*:

> Sons of Dardanus, hardy souls, your fathers' land
> that gave you birth will take you back again,
> restored to her fertile breast.
> Search for your ancient mother. There your house,
> the line of Aeneas, will rule all parts of the world ...[78]

Each promises the hero a homeland from which his descendants may grow to rule the world, in very similar language. The prophecy in the *Aeneid*, however, quickly proves misleading. Anchises interprets it as referring to Crete, but as soon as Aeneas begins to build a city there, it is stricken by plague. In a dream, the Lares and Penates clarify: the "ancient mother" is not Crete, but Italy, and the Trojans sail on. Diana's prophecy, by contrast, does not misdirect Brutus, although it certainly misinforms him. Faletra points out the "great contradiction" of Diana's speech: the giants are still very much alive in Britain, as Brutus will discover when he eventually gets there.[79]

The misleading qualities of Diana's speech should direct our attention to the problems of predicting the future, even within a narrative whose end is known (the foundation of Britain by Brutus is as inevitable as the foundation of Rome by Aeneas). Unlike Apollo's prophecy, Diana's is not merely misinterpreted, it is *wrong*. She does not declare that the island is uninhabited, which might, in a pinch, be understood as uninhabited by humankind; rather, she states explicitly that the island is now (*nunc*) deserted, although it was once (*olim*) occupied by giants. This flat untruth is followed by two predictions capable of bearing multiple interpretations. The first is the promise that Britain will be the eternal (*perennis*) seat of Brutus and his descendants; the second is that Brutus's heirs "will be masters of the whole world".[80] Many readers have taken this to refer to the conquest of Rome by Brennius, or to the conquests of Arthur, but the geography of the narrative itself makes this doubtful, since

---

altera Troia tuis. / Hic de prole tua reges nascentur, et ipsis / tocius terrae subditus orbis erit."

78 Virgil, *Aeneid* iii.94–98, ed. R.A.B. Mynors, *P. Virgili Maronis Opera*, Oxford, 1969: "Dardanidae duri, quae vos a stirpe parentum / prima tulit tellus, eadem vos ubere laeto / accipiet reduces. Antiquam exquirite matrem: / hic domus Aeneae cunctis dominabitur orbis, / et nati natorum, et qui nascentur ab illis." Translation from Virgil, *Aeneid*, trans. R. Fagles, New York, 2006, p. 104.

79 Faletra, "Narrating the Matter of Britain", p. 71.

80 *DGB*, i.16.311–12: "ipsis / tocius terrae subditus orbis erit."

"the whole earth" should encompass those lands east of Rome through which Brutus himself has recently traveled. The only descendant of Brutus whom this part of the prophecy can be said accurately to describe is Constantinus, British through his mother Helen. That Britain will be the everlasting possession of the Trojans is even more problematic, given that the entire thrust of Geoffrey's narrative is directed toward proving that the British no longer rule nor deserve to rule in the island, but have been supplanted by the Anglo-Saxons, and eventually the Normans. In apparent contradiction of the angelic voice that speaks to Cadwaladr at the end of the *DGB*, promising that "through his blessing the British people would one day recover the island, when the prescribed time came", Geoffrey insists flatly at the end of the book that "the Welsh, unworthy successors to the noble Britons, never again recovered mastery over the whole island."[81] If the future promised by Diana's prophecy and reasserted by the angelic voice is to come to pass, in other words, it does not appear to have done so in the narrative circumscribed by Geoffrey's *DGB* – not, at any rate, for Brutus's British descendants. If, however, Diana's prophecy is read as promising Britain perennially to the descendants of Troy, rather than specifically to the British descendants of Troy, the difficulty disappears: the Normans had been Trojan ever since the 11th century, when Dudo of St Quentin provided them with a genealogy extending back to Antenor.[82] Prophecy's slippery nature, its openness to interpretation, is precisely what made the *PM* so variously useful to different audiences throughout the ages. This hermeneutic instability, present already in Diana's prophecy, is simply carried to new heights in the *PM*, and here again the Virgilian intertext is instructive.[83] Indeed, it may well be from Virgil that Geoffrey learned the trick of predicting the past.

---

81   *DGB*, xi.205.568–69: "Dicebat etiam populum Britonum per meritum suae fidei insulam in futuro ademptum postquam fatale tempus superveniret"; *DGB*, xi.205.598–99: "Degenerati autem a Britannica nobilitate Gualenses numquam postea monarchiam insulae recuperauerunt."

82   Dudo of St Quentin, *The Customs and Deeds of the First Dukes of the Normans*, ed. J. Lair, *De moribus et actis primorum Normanniae ducum auctore Dudone Sancti Quintone decano*, Caen, 1865, p. 130.

83   A secondary example of such instability occurs in the case of the prophetic Eagle of Shaftesbury. Geoffrey refers twice to this bird; the first time he dismisses its prophecies (*DGB*, ii.36.32–34), but the second (*DGB*, xi.218.575–78) they provide confirmation of the authority of the Holy Voice that speaks to Cadualadrus. In the decades after the appearance of the *DGB*, a quasi-independent Prophecy of the Eagle evolved, often attaching itself to manuscripts of the *DGB*; see Crick, *DR*, pp. 65–66 and A.F. Sutton and L. Visser-Fuchs, "The Dark Dragon of the Normans: A Creation of Geoffrey of Monmouth, Stephen of Rouen, and Merlin Silvester", *Quondam et Futurus: A Journal of Arthurian Interpretations* 2:2 (1992), 1–19, at pp. 2–4.

The *PM* and the vision of Roman futurity in *Aeneid* Book VI are linked not only by their positions in the two texts, but also thematically and, although this may not be immediately evident, formally. Structurally, each is the major extended prophecy at the center of a book studded with lesser, or at any rate briefer, prophecies. In the *DGB*, as we have seen, Diana's oracle at the beginning and the angelic voice at the end predict the future of the descendants of Brutus. The situation in the *Aeneid* is more complicated. As Sarah Mack notes, "there are two futures in the poem and two sorts of prophecy to express them. First, and most commonly predicted, is the immediate future, which is revealed in short and fairly limited prophecies … The other future in the poem is the distant future centering on Rome from its foundation to Augustan times."[84] Into the first category fall the prophecies of Hector and Creusa in *Aeneid* Book II, those of Apollo (corrected by the Lares and Penates and expanded by Celaeno) and Helenus in Book III, of Tiber in Book VIII, and so forth. Mack identifies these as "directional prophecies" which move Aeneas from one point to the next on his journey toward Italy and the foundation of Rome, and notes that while they do come true, they are in most cases misleading and excessively optimistic.[85] The "Roman" prophecies, on the other hand (Jupiter's in Book I, Anchises' central revelation in Book VI, and the ekphrastic prophecy of Aeneas's shield in Book VIII) "exist outside of the narrative of the poem".[86] They narrate the future not of the individual hero but of Rome, the nation Aeneas will found. They are also, importantly, narrations about the remote future from the point of view of the protagonist, Aeneas; he cannot, indeed, be expected to understand much of what Anchises reveals to him in the underworld. Simultaneously, of course, from the perspective of the author, the prophecies narrate the past, and even the very recent past: the civil wars from which Rome had emerged during Virgil's lifetime.

Anchises' prophecy takes the form of a genealogy, not of a person but of Rome itself; the succession of figures he displays are sometimes father and son, but more often linked by their assumption of *imperium*: all are sons of the Rome that was, fathers of the Rome that will be. The *PM* often also takes this pseudo-genealogical form: "His six successors will wield the sceptre";[87] "The sixth will overthrow the city walls of Ireland and turn its forests into a plain."[88] It is true that the two texts initially appear to have little in common stylistically.

---

84   S. Mack, *Patterns of Time in Virgil*, Hamden, CT, 1978, p. 56.
85   Mack, *Patterns of Time*, pp. 56–57.
86   Mack, *Patterns of Time*, p. 67.
87   *DGB*, Prophetiae 112.43–44: "Sex posteri eius sequentur sceptrum."
88   *DGB*, Prophetiae 114.99–100: "Sextus Hiberniae moenia subuertet et nemora in planiciem mutabit."

Merlin's prophecies are in unruly prose and teem with unidentifiable figures and strange beasts like the hedgehog of §116.175–76, who hides apples and constructs pathways beneath the city of London, while *Aeneid* VI proceeds in dignified hexameters, summoning up an orderly parade of Roman dignitaries. Or so it would seem, but it is important to recognize that the classical past is in many ways much closer to its 21st-century readers than it was to Geoffrey in the 12th. The following passage might have been as opaque to medievals as Geoffrey's prophecies are to moderns:

> But you see that pair of spirits? Gleaming in equal armor,
> equals now at peace, while darkness pins them down,
> but if they should reach the light of life, what war
> they'll rouse between them! Battles, massacres ...
> ... the bride's father, marching down from his Alpine ramparts,
> Fortress Monaco ... her husband set to oppose him
> with the armies of the East![89]

Any modern commentary will identify these two figures as Caesar and Pompey (Pompey was married to Caesar's daughter, and their alliance disintegrated after her death). But would the allusion have been evident to a 12th-century reader? Servius identifies Caesar and Pompey. Fulgentius, whose allegorizing interpretation may have been especially popular in the British Isles, does not. Without commentary, or with a commentary not based upon Servius, this passage is not so different in substance from a passage like the following:

> The island will be soaked in nightly tears, and so all men will be provoked to all things. Their progeny will try to fly beyond the heavens, but the favour of new men will be raised up. The possessor will be harmed by the goodness of the wicked until he dresses himself as his father.[90]

---

89 Virgil, *Aeneid* vi.824–29, ed. Mynors: "illae autem paribus quas fulgere cernis in armis, / concordes animae nunc et dum nocte prementur, / heu quantum inter se bellum, si lumina vitae / attigerint, quantas acies stragemque ciebunt / aggeribus socer Alpinis atque arce Monoeci / descendens, gener adusersis instructus Eois!" Virgil, *Aeneid*, trans. Fagles, p. 197. Fagles supplies the names of Caesar and Pompey, in the places marked by elision in my citation.

90 *DGB*, Prophetiae 114.87–90: "Nocturnis lacrimis madebit insula, unde omnes ad omnia prouocabantur. Nitentur posteri transuolare superna, sed fauor nouorum sublimabitur. Nocebit possidenti ex impiis pietas donec sese genitore induerit."

The contrast between night on earth and heavenly glory marks both passages, as does the reference to fathers and sons. Or, to take another example, Anchises describes the construction of the walls of Rome in the following lines:

> ... watch,
> my son, our brilliant Rome will extend her empire far
> and wide as the earth, her spirit high as Olympus.
> Within her single wall she will gird her seven hills ...[91]

Geoffrey's Merlin describes another city: "London will be filled with envy and will increase its walls threefold. The Thames will form a moat around the city ..."[92] In both of these passages, cities fortify themselves. I do not argue here for direct influence of one passage on the other but simply that the flavor of Anchises' prophecy is not so different from that of Merlin's, if one accounts for the greater un-interpretability of the vision of Roman futurity to its medieval readers. Geoffrey, in other words, may have thought his prophetic text was more like Virgil's than we do. His inspiration is literary as much as it is either prophetic or political, regardless of the uses to which his texts were turned. He was, after all, in some important sense, writing a sequel to the *Aeneid*.

The very indeterminacy of the *PM* proved, finally, to be its greatest strength, the source of its longevity. By creating a text so marvelously open to interpretation, Geoffrey in fact created a magisterial role for himself: the authority of his vision of the British past and future, located in lost books in other languages, finally depended entirely on its own uniqueness, on the fact that it was a vision accessible only through Geoffrey himself. The author himself thus comes to function not only as historian but also as prophet, possessed of privileged access to knowledge about both the past and the future. With regard to his own text, he plays the role of a Merlin, or indeed of a Virgil, who was respected in the Middle Ages as seer, magician, and prophet,[93] an expanded role which recalls the identity of history and prophecy within the Welsh tradition.[94] In the centuries after Geoffrey's death, the *PM* was deployed to legitimize the accession of the Tudors, as we have seen, but also in support of Robert the Bruce in

---

91   Virgil, *Aeneid* vi.781–83, ed. Mynors: "en huius, nate, aspiciis illa inluta Roma / imperium terris, animos aequabit Olympo, / septemque una sibi muro circumdabit arces ..." Virgil, *Aeneid*, trans. Fagles, p. 197.

92   *DGB*, Prophetiae 116.174–76: "Inuidebit ergo Lundonia et muros suos tripliciter augebit. Circuibit eam undique Tamensis fluuius ..."

93   On Virgil's magical powers, see J. Wood, "Virgil and Taliesin: The Concept of the Magician in Medieval Folklore", *Folklore* 94:1 (1983), 91–104.

94   A.L. Jones, *Darogan*, p. 2.

his rebellion against Edward I.[95] Across the Channel, the prophecies were often cited by the French to the detriment of the English during the Hundred Years' War: Eustaches Deschamps composed a ballad "De la prophecie Merlin sur la destruction d'Angleterre qui doit bref advenir"[96] and Joan of Arc was identified with the mysterious girl from the "city of the holy forest", although she herself apparently put little stock in prophecy.[97] A Catalan "Profecia de Merlin" from around 1370 comments on the successors of Alfonso X.[98] In "To the Majesty of King James", Drayton recognized the first Stuart king as the prince who "as their great Merlin prophesied before / Should the old Britons regality restore",[99] while in the 17th and 18th centuries the once lofty tradition devolved into a series of "prophecies of Merlin" which consisted of horoscopes and other popular prognostications.[100] Nor has the phenomenon run its course: as recently as 2010, the American tabloid *Sun* published an article on Merlin's prophecies, recently unearthed by archaeologists and "just translated", predicting everything from the Great Recession to global warming.[101] The *Prophetiae Merlini* continues to speak, even to the 21st century.

95   N. Gallagher, "The Franciscans and the Scottish Wars of Independence: An Irish Perspective", *Journal of Medieval History* 32 (2006), 3–17, at p. 9.
96   Zumthor, *Merlin le Prophète*, p. 68.
97   *DGB*, Prophetiae 116.155–56: "ex urbe canuti nemoris". On Joan, see Zumthor, *Merlin le Prophète*, pp. 69–70 and C. Daniel, "L'audience des prophéties de Merlin: entre rumeurs populaires et textes savants", *Mediévales: Langues, Textes, Histoire* 57 (2009), 33–51, at pp. 42–46.
98   Zumthor, *Merlin le Prophète*, p. 77. See also pp. 432–36 in this volume.
99   A. McRae and J. West (eds.), *Literature of the Stuart Successions: An Anthology*, Manchester, 2017, p. 42.
100 Zumthor, *Merlin le Prophète*, p. 74.
101 "Disasters! War! Recession! More! 7 Forbidden Prophecies: Mystic Merlin's Secrets Come True", *Sun*, 11 September 2010, p. 1.

PART 2

Contemporary Contexts

∵

CHAPTER 5

Early Manuscript Dissemination

Jaakko Tahkokallio

Since its release, the *De gestis Britonum* has been defined by its popularity. The work became successful quickly and the material record of its early reception is exceptional in its extent. The count of surviving manuscripts runs to 225 at the moment, and almost 80 of them can be dated to before *c.*1210.[1] In what follows I shall examine the first stages of the transmission and reception of the *DGB* using these early manuscripts as my primary body of evidence.

The first part of this chapter discusses the earliest dissemination of the work, bringing together evidence from the manuscripts, textual transmission, and narrative and documentary sources. I start from the process of how the text was released and move on to discuss the role of the dedicatees and early documented readers in the circulation of the text. I also suggest circumstances in which the three dedications of the work were probably penned and look briefly at the genesis of the textually idiosyncratic versions of the work, the so-called First and Second Variants. This part depends heavily on Michael Reeve's textual work and the division of the transmission of the *DGB* into two main families, depending on lost archetypes Φ and Δ respectively.

In the second part, I turn to what the manuscripts tell us about the early audience and its attitudes toward the *DGB*. Here, I first provide an overview of what is known about the origins of the early copies and point out the scale of early monastic dissemination, in particular on the Continent. Despite its

---

1 I include manuscripts dated to *s.* xii or *s.* xii/xiii in this count. For descriptions of the manuscripts, see Crick, *SC*; ead., "Two Newly Located Manuscripts of Geoffrey of Monmouth's *Historia regum Britanniae*", *AL* 13 (1995), 151–56; and J. Tahkokallio, "Update to the List of Manuscripts of Geoffrey of Monmouth's *Historia regum Britanniae*", *AL* 32 (2015), 187–203. After the publication of the latest up-date article, a further early-14th-century copy came to surface at a Christie's sale in London (2015, Sale 1568), and was bought by Trinity College, Dublin (now Dublin, Trinity College, 11500). *DGB* remained available well into the modern era as well. The first printed editions are from 1508, when Ponticus Virunius published an abbreviated version (Reggio Emilia, 1508; reprinted twice, in Augsburg, 1534, and London, 1585) and Ivo Cavellatus published the complete text (Paris, 1508, reprinted in 1514). Hieronymus Commelinus re-edited the work and published it in 1587 (Heidelberg). The next full edition of the *DGB* was prepared in London 1844, and reproduced in 1854 (Halle). *PM* has been published separately in 1603, 1608, 1649 (all three editions with the commentary attributed to Alan of Lille), 1837, 1840 and 1853. For the editions, see *DGB*, pp. lxii–lxiv.

---

arguably secular and controversial content, the DGB was widely accepted into institutional libraries and copied alongside respectable historical works. However, I also draw attention to the fact that information about origin is available only for a relatively small part of the manuscript corpus. In the final and more speculative part of the chapter I discuss the possibility that a significant share of the 12th-century copies were originally produced for individual readers outside monastic scriptoria. The chapter closes with a detailed examination of some early continental copies which probably have non-institutional origins and in whose making professional or semi-professional artisans may have been involved.

1   **Release and Early Transmission**

The circulation of the DGB started with the release of a prelude. Geoffrey himself wrote in the DGB that rumors about Merlin had started to circulate before he had reached the point in the DGB to which the *Prophetiae Merlini* belonged. To satisfy the curious, he explained, he had sent the *PM* to Alexander, bishop of Lincoln (d. 1148), with a cover letter that was included in most versions of the DGB as well.[2] We have a *terminus ante quem* for this separate release of the *PM*, thanks to Orderic Vitalis (1075–c.1142), monk of Saint-Evroul (in Normandy). In his *Ecclesiastical History*, Orderic quoted at length from a booklet which he called *Libellus Merlini*, "The Little Book of Merlin". He also speculated on what the *PM* meant to say about Henry I of England whose destiny, according to him, still remained open. This means that Orderic had access to the text before Henry's death which took place in December 1135.[3]

The separate release of the *Libellus* is well attested in the manuscript record as well. The *PM* exists in 13 independent copies datable to the 12th century (including manuscripts dated to c.1200). By comparing their texts to Orderic's lengthy quote from the *Libellus Merlini* – a certain witness to the independently released version – it has been possible to determine whether manuscripts containing only the *PM* really stem from the independently released *libellus* or

---

2   DGB, vii.109.1–7: "Nondum autem ad hunc locum historiae perueneram cum de Merlino diuulgato rumore compellebant me undique contemporanei mei prophetias ipsius edere, maxime autem Alexander Lincolniensis episcopus ... Cui cum satisfacere praeelegissem, prophetias transtuli et eidem cum huiusmodi litteris direxi."

3   Orderic Vitalis, *Ecclesiastical History* xii.47 (iv.486), ed. and trans. M. Chibnall, *The Ecclesiastical History of Orderic Vitalis*, 6 vols., Oxford, 1969–80, vol. 6, p. 381. On the dating of the passage, see Chibnall, "Introduction", p. xviii. See also *Bern*, ed. Wright, pp. xii–xvi, and DGB, p. viii.

were extracted from the complete *DGB* later on.[4] This comparison shows that while some of the independent *PM* are indeed extracts from the *DGB*, at least nine of the surviving 12th-century copies descend from the independently released text.[5]

Orderic was by no means exceptional in having early access to the *PM* on the Continent. In fact, six out of nine of the 12th-century copies belonging to the independent line of transmission are continental.[6] At the same time, chronicle and charter evidence shows that the patron of the work, Alexander of Lincoln, was in Normandy for a substantial period around the time of its probable presentation to him, starting at some point in 1134 and ending before Easter 1136.[7] Furthermore, when the preface to Alexander appears as a part of the *DGB*, Geoffrey introduces it with the words *eidem cum huiusmodi litteris direxi*, for which the most natural translation is "I sent [them] to him with this letter."[8] In the independent *PM* manuscripts, the letter is at times included and at times not, which could indicate that it was originally a separate document.[9] The wide early availability of the *PM* on the continent, combined with what we know about Alexander's movements, suggests the possibility that Geoffrey may have presented the *PM* to Alexander in Normandy in 1134 or 1135, perhaps by sending it to him with a cover letter.

At the same time, the Insular manuscripts hint that, in Britain at least, Alexander played a role in the early transmission of the work, and that its

---

4 See *DGB*, pp. xxix–xxxi.

5 Berlin, Staatsbibliothek, theol. lat. quarto 328; Liège, Bibliothèque publique centrale, 369 C; Lincoln, Cathedral Library, 214; London, British Library, Additional 25014; Oxford, Lincoln College, Lat. 27; Paris, Bibliothèque nationale de France, lat. 2935, lat. 6237, lat. 6274, lat. 7481, lat. 9422, lat. 14465, lat. 15172; and Vatican City, Biblioteca Apostolica Vaticana, Reg. lat. 807. Of these, BL Add. 25014, BnF lat. 7481, and BNF lat. 9422 are extracts, and the affiliation of Berlin, theol. lat. qu. 328 is unclear.

6 The continental manuscripts are Berlin, theol. lat. qu. 328; BnF lat. 2935, lat. 6237, lat. 6274, lat. 15172; and BAV, Reg. lat. 807. The three Insular copies with the independent text are Liège 369; Lincoln 214; and Oxford, Lincoln College, Lat. 27.

7 Alexander went to King Henry's court in Normandy at some point in 1134 to settle a dispute with the archbishop of Canterbury (Henry of Huntingdon, *History of the English* vii.43, ed. and trans. D. Greenway, *Henry, Archdeacon of Huntingdon: Historia Anglorum. The History of the English People*, Oxford, 1996, p. 490). In September 1134 he witnessed a royal charter at Verneuil (*Regesta regum Anglo-Normannorum, 1066–1154*, ed. H.W.C. Davis et al., 4 vols., Oxford, 1913–69, vol. 2, no. 1895) and probably around that date King Henry secured Lincoln's privileges, at Arganchy and Rouen, presumably at Alexander's initiative (ibid., vol. 2, nos. 1899 and 1911). Alexander was back in England by Easter 1136 when he witnessed King Stephen's charter in London (ibid., vol. 3, no. 46).

8 Neil Wright's translation, *DGB*, vii.109.7.

9 Of the 12th-century *PM* manuscripts belonging to the independent transmission, Oxford, Lincoln College, Lat. 27; BnF lat. 2935, lat. 6237, and lat. 15172 exclude the letter.

circulation may even have been restricted to circles close to him there, while it enjoyed wider success on the Continent. Two of the three 12th-century British copies stemming from the independent release have an association with Lincoln: one belongs to the Lincoln Cathedral Library and the other to Lincoln College, Oxford, to which it came from the Gilbertine house of Sempringham, founded by Alexander.[10]

Alexander was one of the great ecclesiastical princes of the day and also the patron of another contemporary English historian, Henry of Huntingdon (c.1088–c.1157).[11] However, for the *DGB* Geoffrey turned to another source of patronage: Robert, earl of Gloucester (d. 1147), Henry I's illegitimate son. Robert was born before the king's marriage and enjoyed a special status among the royal bastards, especially after the death of Henry's only legitimate male heir in 1120. He was highly educated, and not only Geoffrey but also William of Malmesbury dedicated historical works to him.[12] A possible link between Robert and Geoffrey might have been provided by the scholarly connections between Caen, which was Robert's Norman base, and St George's collegiate church of Oxford, of which Geoffrey was a canon.[13]

Whatever the origin of the connection, the earliest version of the *DGB* was dedicated to Robert and he no doubt received a copy of it early on. Just as is the case with the *PM*, this presentation may well have taken place in Normandy. William of Malmesbury's *The Contemporary History* tells us that Robert of Gloucester stayed there from Easter 1137 until September 1139, which is the most likely time window for the work's presentation to him.[14] Furthermore, the earliest report about the existence of the *DGB* comes from the Norman

---

10   Oxford, Lincoln College, Lat. 27 bears a Sempringham *ex libris* datable to c.1200 (fol. 6v) and contains two letters to St Gilbert of Sempringham.

11   D.M. Smith, "Alexander (*d.* 1148)", *Oxford Dictionary of National Biography*, Oxford University Press, 2004, <http://www.oxforddnb.com/view/article/324> (accessed 13 March 2017).

12   For Robert's life and career, see D. Crouch, "Robert, earl of Gloucester and the Daughter of Zelophehad", *Journal of Medieval History* 11:3 (1985), 227–43.

13   See R. Foreville, "L'École de Caen au XIe siècle et les origines normandes de l'université d'Oxford", in *Études médiévales offertes à M. le Doyen Augustin Fliche de l'Institut*, Montpellier, 1952, pp. 81–100. On the canons of St George, see J. Barron, "The Augustinian Canons and the University of Oxford: the Lost College of St George", in C.M. Barron and J. Stratford (eds.), *The Church and Learning in Later Medieval Society: Essays in Honour of R.B. Dobson*, Donington, 2002, pp. 228–54. For Geoffrey's relationship to the college of St George, see E. Salter, "Geoffrey of Monmouth and Oxford", *EHR* 34 (1919), 382–85 and M.D. Legge, "Master Geoffrey Arthur", in K. Varty (ed.), *An Arthurian Tapestry: Essays in Memory of Lewis Thorpe*, Glasgow, 1981, pp. 22–27.

14   For the chronology of Robert's movements, see William of Malmesbury, *The Contemporary History*, ed. E. King, trans. K.R. Potter, *William of Malmesbury. Historia novella: The*

abbey of Le Bec, where Henry of Huntingdon was astonished by finding it in January 1139.[15] We cannot be sure how long before that the work had been put into circulation, but it seems unlikely that Henry, who belonged to the same intellectual circles as Geoffrey and shared his interests, would have remained unaware of it for long afterwards. A presentation of the work taking place in Normandy in 1137–38, or alternatively immediately before Robert's departure from England at Easter 1137, would be very much compatible with Henry's surprise, and, while this scenario remains unproven, it also fits together with the early textual transmission of the work, to which I will come back shortly.

At Le Bec, Henry of Huntingdon was introduced to the DGB by the prior of the house, Robert of Torigni (c.1110–86), a well-known chronicler in his own right. He is also the first person in the history of the dissemination of the DGB with whom we can associate a surviving manuscript. This is the earliest relatively securely dated copy of the DGB, now kept in Leiden, which was produced at Le Bec under Robert's supervision.[16] This manuscript contains several historical works, including Robert of Torigni's redaction of *The Deeds of the Norman Dukes*, and it was copied in two stages. The first one, penned in the 1130s, included *The Deeds of the Norman Dukes*, Einhard's *Life of Charlemagne*, Alexander material, and two brief chronicles. Sometime around 1150, the DGB and the *Historia Brittonum* were added.

On the account of its textual features, the first half of the Le Bec copy of the DGB descends from a manuscript now kept at Bibliothèque Sainte-Geneviève

---

    Contemporary History §466 and §478, Oxford, 1998, pp. 21–22 and 34. See also Crouch, "Robert, earl of Gloucester", p. 232.

15   Henry was on his way to Rome with Theobald, archbishop of Canterbury. The story is reported by Henry in his Letter to Warin, reproduced in Henry of Huntingdon, *History of the English*, ed. and trans. Greenway, pp. 558–83.

16   Leiden, Universiteitsbibliotheek, B.P.L. 20 (number 76 in Crick's *Summary Catalogue*; from here on, I provide references to Crick's *Summary Catalogue* in the form "DGB ms 76"). For Robert's role at the library of Le Bec, see D. Bates, "Robert of Torigni and the *Historia Anglorum*", in D. Roffe (ed.), *The English and Their Legacy, 900–1200. Essays in Honour of Ann Williams*, Woodbridge, 2012, pp. 175–84. Robert's involvement in the production of the Leiden manuscript been suspected for long and confirmed by Benjamin Pohl's recent work; see B. Pohl, "*Abbas qui et scriptor?* The Handwriting of Robert of Torigni and his Scribal Activity as Abbot of Mont-Saint-Michel (1154–1186)", *Traditio* 69 (2014), 45–86. As Pohl explains, Robert did not copy any of the works himself, but the manuscript was corrected and annotated with *nota* monograms by him. Pohl's article does not discuss the monograms, but they are in the same hue of ink as the textual notes which Pohl identifies as being in Robert's hand. They are also very similar to the *nota* monograms seen in two copies of Henry of Huntingdon's *History of the English* associated with Robert: Paris, Bibliothèque nationale de France, lat. 6042, and Cambridge, University Library, Gg.2.21. For the ownership history of BnF lat. 6042, see Pohl, "*Abbas qui et scriptor?*", p. 67.

(henceforth, G).[17] This manuscript is in fact the starting point of all of the early continental circulation and altogether 70 manuscripts depend on it textually. While G may not, on the first look, give the impression of being paleographically quite so early, its position in the continental stemma is beyond doubt because of textual evidence. Its scribe first omitted some words in copying it, and then added them as corrections – but some of them in wrong places. This odd misplacement is seen in virtually all continental copies from before the last quarter of the 12th century, including the Leiden manuscript.[18]

Curiously, however, these continental copies repeat the mistakes of G only for its first half, until *DGB* §108. After this point, they start following directly the exemplar of G, which was a lost copy of the archetype Φ.[19] To account for such a textual situation, we must assume that there existed a copy which descended partly from G and partly from its exemplar. This copy, which we may call post-G, then gave birth to a large number of further copies.

One wonders, of course, why post-G was copied partly from G if its exemplar, a copy with more textual authority, was also available. The structure of G suggests an answer. The point at which post-G stopped following G and reverted directly to its exemplar (§108) coincides with a change of scribal hand in G. This takes place very near the end of the fourth quire, six lines from the bottom of its last verso side. My suggestion is that once the first four quires of G were finished, they were immediately put into use as an exemplar for another copy, while the copying of the rest of G was still taking place from the original exemplar. Once the copying of post-G arrived at §108, G itself was complete and its original exemplar had become available. Preferring it to G would have been an obvious choice, especially since the second half of G, copied by another scribe, is less careful work than the first four quires.

---

17   Paris, Bibliothèque Sainte-Geneviève, 2113 (*DGB* ms 191).

18   See M.D. Reeve, "The Transmission of the *Historia regum Britanniae*", *Journal of Medieval Latin* 1 (1991), 73–117, at p. 84, and also *DGB*, p. xv. The distinctive transpositions occur at *DGB* §6.55 (Cumque id |patri| Ascanio), §8.97–98 (celsitudinem |tue| potentiae), §76.94 (habere captaret |de illo| uenerunt uenedoti), §81.212 (mauricus magnae |et pulchre| staturae), §95.185 (melius potestati |sue| et familiaritati), and §106.523–24 (in ecclesia sancti petri |in eadem urbe| inter monachas). However, for their second half the continental manuscripts follow the exemplar of the Sainte-Geneviève manuscript directly, not repeating its errors. The only continental manuscripts from before the last quarter of the century which have a different progeny are Alençon, Bibliothèque municipale, 12 (*DGB* ms 12) and Paris, Bibliothèque nationale de France, lat. 6232 (*DGB* ms 177), partly following the Sainte-Geneviève manuscript but partly copied from an Insular exemplar.

19   See *DGB*, pp. xiv–xv. London, British Library, Additional 15732 (s. xii, continental) is the only 12th-century manuscript descending directly from G in its entirety.

We know from Henry of Huntingdon's testimony that Robert of Torigni possessed a copy of the *DGB* in 1139, and that the Leiden manuscript was later copied under his supervision from post-G (or its descendant). Given that G was copied at the very beginning of the continental transmission, it may well be a result of scribal activity taking place around Robert of Torigni. Paleographically, the Sainte-Geneviève manuscript appears quite certainly Norman and indeed is not far away from manuscripts that can be associated with Robert himself.[20] Neil Wright has suggested that G itself could have been Robert's personal copy, and this is certainly a possibility.[21] However, since Robert is known to have had an active role in the circulation of texts in Normandy, perhaps an even more likely candidate for his personal copy might be post-G, i.e., the lost manuscript descending partly from G. It was post-G (or its descendant), after all, which he later made the Le Bec scribes use as their exemplar and which was also widely copied by others.

What we know about Robert of Gloucester's later movements and the textual history of the *DGB* is compatible with the hypothesis that the work was released into wider circulation by presenting it to him in Normandy (or in England immediately before his departure in 1137). The whole of the early continental transmission descends from the lost archetype Φ, via G and post-G, as argued above. The descendants of Φ show greater consistency in their chapter markings, rubrics, and initials than manuscripts of other textual branches. Michael Reeve has plausibly suggested that Φ was the presentation copy given to Robert, since in such a copy attention would have been given to these final touches.[22]

In Britain, the majority of the early manuscripts descend from another archetype, the so-called Δ, and overall the textual division between the Continent and Britain is surprisingly sharp. The Channel appears, in this case, to have been more of a barrier than a conduit for the circulation of texts. However, while Δ has no early continental witnesses, Φ has some textually significant descendants that are clearly of British origin. Interestingly, circumstantial evidence suggests a connection to Robert of Gloucester for many Insular copies depending on Φ.

---

20 For manuscripts produced close to Robert, see in particular Pohl, "*Abbas qui et scriptor?*".
21 N. Wright, "The Place of Henry of Huntingdon's *Epistola ad Warinum* in the Text-History of Geoffrey of Monmouth's *Historia regum Britanniae*: a Preliminary Investigation", in G. Jondorf and D.N. Dumville (eds.), *France and the British Isles in the Middle Ages and Renaissance: Essays by Members of Girton College, Cambridge, in Memory of Ruth Morgan*, Woodbridge, 1991, 71–113, at p. 89.
22 *DGB* p. lx, and Reeve, "Transmission", p. 102, n. 5.

London, British Library, Royal 13 D. ii (*DGB* ms 112) is textually the most important of these manuscripts. It was by the 13th century (at latest) at Margam Abbey (Cistercian, Glamorgan), which was Robert of Gloucester's foundation, possibly founded at his deathbed. Furthermore, the manuscript also contains excellent textual witnesses – all copied by the same scribe – of other texts dedicated to Robert of Gloucester, i.e., William of Malmesbury's *Deeds of the English Kings* and *The Contemporary History*, the latter of which is largely a story about Robert himself. Finally, in the Margam manuscript, *The Contemporary History* has rubrication that is not found in any other copy and that casts Robert's character and actions in very favorable light.

Throughout, the textual quality of these works is remarkable. As regards William's *Deeds of the English Kings*, the Margam text has enjoyed a privileged position in its editorial history.[23] For the *DGB*, the Margam text is the best representative of the principally continental Φ family – and also, arguably, the best single witness to the text of the *DGB* overall. In Michael Reeve's words, "a transcript of M [=Margam Abbey ms] would be a tolerable substitute for an edition."[24] Indeed, the editor of *The Contemporary History* has suggested that the compilation of texts and the rubrics were created by Robert's son, Roger, bishop of Worcester (*c*.1134–79).[25] The Margam copy is from the very end of the 12th or the beginning of the 13th century and thus it postdates both Robert and his son Roger. However, one is bound to wonder whether the scribe who copied it used as his exemplar for the *DGB* the manuscript which Robert of Gloucester had been given, probably in Normandy (and from which the continental transmission had started), and which he brought to England and eventually left to his son Roger.

Robert certainly had a copy of the *DGB* in his possession after he returned to England in September 1139, since Gaimar's *Estoire des Engleis* tells us that he provided the text to Walter Espec, a Yorkshire magnate, most likely in the early 1140s.[26] This loan, so it would seem, initiated another English branch

---

23   R.M. Thomson and M. Winterbottom, "Introduction", in William of Malmesbury, *Deeds of the English Kings*, ed. and trans. R.A.B. Mynors, completed by R.M. Thomson and M. Winterbottom, *William of Malmesbury: Gesta Regum Anglorum, The History of the English Kings*, 2 vols., Oxford, 1998–99, vol. 1, pp. xiii–xxviii, at pp. xviii–xix.

24   *DGB*, p. xvi.

25   For the "Robertian" nature of the text of *The Contemporary History*, see E. King, "Introduction", in William of Malmesbury, *The Contemporary History*, ed. King, pp. lxxvii–xciv. For the possible connection with Roger of Worcester in particular, see ibid., pp. xci–xciv.

26   The precise date of Gaimar's *Estoire* remains open. I. Short, "Gaimar's Epilogue and Geoffrey of Monmouth's *Liber vetustissimus*", *Speculum* 69:2 (1994), 323–43, has argued for an early date, in the 1130s, while P. Dalton, "The Date of Geoffrey Gaimar's *Estoire des*

of transmission depending on the archetype Φ. The key manuscript of this group is Cambridge, Gonville and Caius College, 406/627 (*DGB* ms 30), which likewise has substantial textual authority and served as one of the five manuscripts Reeve used for reconstructing archetype Φ. This 12th-century manuscript was kept by c.1300 at Bridlington Priory (Augustinian, Yorkshire) and its 12th-century marginalia suggest that the manuscript was already in Yorkshire in the 12th century.[27] Bridlington Priory belonged to the Yorkshire network of Augustinian houses, in which Walter Espec took interest.[28]

What is more, its decoration merits attention. The manuscript, which contains only the *DGB*, opens with two multi-color initials, one of which shows a long-haired character wearing a crown-like headgear (in the upper lobe of a "B"), and a grumpy-looking clerk (in the lower lobe). The most obvious idea would be to interpret these characters as a patron and an author, but the patron, portrayed with long blond hair, may well be female, unlike the dedicatees of the text. According to Gaimar, Walter Espec provided the *DGB* to Ralf fitz Gilbert, and it was his wife, Lady Constance, who was Gaimar's patron. Gaimar also tells us that he himself made a copy of this manuscript. One wonders whether the persons portrayed could even be Lady Constance and Gaimar, and whether this could have been the copy which Gaimar made, although paleographically the manuscript seems too late for this.[29] Whomever the figures represent, they are exceptional in the transmission of the *DGB* and do not seem to reflect any known tradition of decoration.

Engleis, the Connections of his Patrons, and the Politics of Stephen's Reign", *The Chaucer Review* 42:1 (2007), 23–47, has provided thorough criticism of Short's position. However, if we put together Short's and Dalton's arguments, 1141 would seem to be the moment at which no piece of evidence contradicts another.

27   On the provenance, see Crick, *SC*, p. 50, and the marginalia in the manuscript, on fol. 43r. The hand of the marginalia seems rather early, using for instance *e-caudata*.

28   Walter founded Kirkham Priory in 1130. See D. Knowles, *The Monastic Order in England*, 2nd ed., Cambridge, 1963, p. 229.

29   The main hand of the manuscript seems to date from around the middle of the 12th century, and a dating to the early 1140s is within possible limits. However, another, later-looking hand (using for instance crossed *et nota*) copied the lower half of the first page (and only that), in an ink of different hue. For the manuscript to date from Gaimar's time, the later-looking hand's work would need to be a significantly later addition, which cannot be proved. Certainly, however, the later-looking scribe wrote after the initials had been painted (ink overlaps the decoration), which is not the normal order of work and suggests some unusual history of production.

FIGURE 5.1   Cambridge, Gonville and Caius College, 406/627, fol. 1r

Altogether, there are nine British manuscripts which are related to Gonville and Caius 406/627.[30] Information on early provenance is unfortunately missing for most of them. However, we know that the copy textually closest to Gonville and Caius 406/627 was in Nun Appleton, just outside of York, in the 17th century, where it belonged to the small Fairfax family library, a locally sourced collection.[31] Moreover, it is certain that Alfred of Beverley used a manuscript textually close to Gonville and Caius 406/627 in Yorkshire, c.1143, as he created his epitome of the DGB.[32] All the available evidence thus clusters close to Helmsley Castle (24 miles from York) where Walter Espec kept his copy of

30   Aberystwyth, National Library of Wales, Peniarth 42 (DGB ms 8), Porkington 17 (DGB ms 10); Cambridge, Gonville and Caius College, 103/55 (DGB ms 28); London, British Library, Harley 225 (DGB ms 100); London, Lambeth Palace Library, 188 (DGB ms 199), 454, fols. 124r–204r (DGB ms 123); Oxford, Bodleian Library, Fairfax 28 (DGB ms 141), Rawlinson B. 148 (DGB ms 153); Philadelphia, The Free Library, E.247 (DGB ms 192).

31   For the Fairfax manuscripts, see F. Madan, H.H.E. Craster, and N. Denholm-Young, A Summary Catalogue of Western Manuscripts in the Bodleian Library at Oxford, vol. 2, part 2, Oxford, 1937, pp. 772–89.

32   Reeve, "Introduction", p. xiv.

the *DGB*, and it appears highly likely that Robert of Gloucester's book loan to him was indeed behind this textual group.

Manuscripts of the Φ family – the continental mainstream – also provided the textual starting point of two deliberately revised versions of the text, the so-called First and Second Variants, which were both created in Britain. We may assume that their makers also gained access to the text via Robert of Gloucester or circles close to him. Besides abbreviating the work to some extent, the First Variant recasts the whole text stylistically – it is the *DGB* written in someone else's Latin.[33] The First Variant was known to Wace at around 1150, but the earliest surviving manuscript dates from *c.*1200, and most are later, with Welsh associations. The Second Variant does not depart from the standard (so-called vulgate) version before about the middle of the work, but from then on it starts to abbreviate the text and does so increasingly as we approach its end. Unlike the First Variant, the Second Variant exists in numerous 12th-century copies. The earliest of them, Cambridge, University Library, Mm.5.29 (*DGB* ms 54) is paleographically one of the most conservative of all British copies and may date from Geoffrey's lifetime. While the text of this manuscript represents the Second Variant only for its first half, its early date shows that the Second Variant came to be early in the transmission history of the *DGB*.[34]

Given the early date of the Variants, one wonders whether haste in copying was a factor contributing to their creation. The work became successful quickly and the few existing copies must have been in high demand in the early stages of the transmission. Besides appearing a likelihood, this is indeed suggested by the story of G, post-G, and their descendants examined above. Limited availability combined with high demand could easily have led into situations where an exemplar was available only for a short period. Several early manuscripts show traces of hurried copying. Two of them are among the most important textual witnesses of the other main textual family, the Insular Δ. Cambridge, University Library, Dd.6.12 (*DGB* ms 43), in which the text of the *DGB* occupies 115 folios, was copied neatly by one scribe until fol. 42, but from then on anomalies of quire structure suggest that three scribes worked on the following parts simultaneously.[35] In the last quire, as many as four different scribes participated into the copying and at this stage the aesthetic quality

---

33   For what can be known about its origins, see Wright, "Introduction", pp. lxx–lxxviii.

34   The scribe switched exemplars to a manuscript of another textual family around the point in which the omissions of the original text become substantial. See *DGB*, pp. xv and xxiii.

35   The second scribe, who copied the text until the beginning of the *PM*, needed an additional slip to finish his or her stint, inserted between fols. 60 and 61. The third scribe's stint ends mid-page, on fol. 67v.

of the handwriting deteriorates, probably because of extreme haste. Another copy, Oxford, Bodleian Library, Bodley 514 (*DGB* ms 136), shows probably six different hands, some of which use documentary-style-influenced scripts and write only short stints, which again gives the impression of copying being pushed through within an uncomfortably short span of time by recruiting all possible help. On the Continent, an early manuscript, now in the Palatine collection of the Vatican Library, was copied at least in part simultaneously, as is again indicated by anomalies in quire structure.[36]

Furthermore, poor exemplar availability probably contributed to how a manuscript with a very conspicuous mistake became widely used as an exemplar early on in the continental transmission. In 13 out of the 35 12th-century Φ family continental manuscripts, the name of the dedicatee, Robert of Gloucester, is missing.[37] While dedications could be purposefully suppressed, this does not appear to have been what happened, since most of the dedicatory passage, containing other references to the patron, was left intact. The omission only managed to make the passage textually nonsensical, as is evinced by the various scribal emendations witnessed in most of its several descendants.[38] Certainly, this omission happened very early, since many of the earliest continental manuscripts show it and it is unlikely that an exemplar with such a glaring shortcoming at the very beginning of the text would have been used if the text was already widely available. It has been suggested that the omission was originally a result of leaving the place for the name of the dedicatee empty for later completion in another color.[39] For instance, Robert of Gloucester's half-sister, Empress Matilda, had a copy of Eckehardt of Aura's chronicle in which her name was inscribed in gold letters, and in which such a procedure of production must have been followed.[40] One wonders whether the starting point of the nameless dedication transmission could have been a luxury copy which Robert commissioned in Normandy in late 1137 or 1138, but which remained on

---

36   Vatican City, Biblioteca Apostolica Vaticana, Pal. lat. 956 (*DGB* ms 195).

37   Aberystwyth, National Library of Wales, 11611 (*DGB* ms 2); Auxerre, Bibliothèque municipale, 91 (*DGB* ms 14); Brussels, Bibliothèque royale, 9871–9874 (*DGB* ms 20); Cambridge, University Library, Mm.1.34 (*DGB* ms 53); Madrid, Biblioteca Nacional de España, 6319 (F.147) (*DGB* ms 125); Montpellier, Bibliothèque interuniversitaire, 92 (*DGB* ms 126); Paris, Bibliothèque nationale de France, lat. 5233 (*DGB* ms 166), lat. 6041B (*DGB* ms 173), lat. 6231 (*DGB* ms 176), lat. 8501A (*DGB* ms 183), lat. 18271 (*DGB* ms 189); and Troyes, Médiathèque, 273bis (*DGB* ms 208).

38   On the "nameless dedication", see Reeve, "Transmission", p. 81 (esp. n. 19) and Crick, *DR*, p. 118, n. 38.

39   See Reeve, "Transmission", p. 81, n. 20. As both Crick and Reeve explain, the original idea was presented by Mary Garrison.

40   Cambridge, Corpus Christi College, 373, fol. 95v.

the Continent in an incomplete state when he left Normandy for England in September 1139.

Robert of Gloucester's active role in the early circulation of the *DGB* is suggested by Gaimar's testimony, the characteristics of the textual tradition depending on Φ and, more tentatively, by the nature of the nameless dedication. It is as well a possibility that he was involved in the two other dedications with which the *DGB* is found. The first of these addresses Robert together with Waleran, Count of Meulan, and the second Robert together with King Stephen.

These double dedications have been much debated because Waleran and Stephen were Robert's enemies in the civil war of Stephen's reign. The conflict went back to Henry I's disputed succession. After Henry had died without a male heir, Stephen, Count of Boulougne and grandson of William the Conqueror, swiftly took the English throne which Henry had promised to his daughter, Matilda. Waleran of Meulan's support was essential for Stephen's consolidation of his position. Robert, on the other hand, was Matilda's half-brother and closest ally, and he eventually took up her cause and started a war against Stephen in 1139. Acton Griscom, who discovered the double dedication, considered it to have been the original one, penned before relations between Robert and Waleran became openly hostile, and this idea has had some support until recently.[41] Reeve's work on the textual history has however proved what others have long suspected on the account of internal evidence, namely, that the first dedication was to Robert alone.[42]

One must ask why Geoffrey re-dedicated a work, already presented to Robert, jointly to him and his enemies. Gaimar's testimony and the textual history suggest that the presentation to Robert was actually working in favor of the *DGB*'s circulation. Re-dedication to a bitter rival could have risked good relations with this useful literary promotor, if this action was initiated by the author alone. At the same time, Alfred of Beverley's famous testimony from the early 1140s shows that Geoffrey's work was quickly turning out to be a bestseller,

---

41 See Geoffrey of Monmouth, *De gestis Britonum*, ed. A. Griscom, *The Historia Regum Britanniae of Geoffrey of Monmouth with Contributions to the Study of its Place in early British History with a Literal Translation of the Welsh Manuscript No. LXI of Jesus College Oxford*, London, 1929, pp. 42–98. See as well D. Dumville, "An Early Text of Geoffrey of Monmouth's *Historia regum Britanniae* and the Circulation of some Latin Histories in Twelfth-Century Normandy", *AL* 4 (1985), 1–36, at p. 27; D. Crouch, "Robert, earl of Gloucester", p. 230; Short, "Gaimar's epilogue", pp. 338–39; M. Aurell, *La légende du Roi Arthur: 550–1250*, Paris, 2007, p. 102.

42 Elsewhere in the text (also in the double dedication version) Geoffrey refers to his patron in the singular: *consul auguste*, "most noble earl" (*DGB*, xi.177.1). For example, see Tatlock, *LHB*, p. 436. On the implications of the textual history for the chronology of the dedications, see *DGB*, pp. ix–x, esp. p. xix.

something fashionable people needed to be acquainted with.[43] Presenting tailored copies of the DGB to other men of power, with Robert kept in as the original patron of the work, could have been Robert's way of asserting his status. As we shall see, neither Waleran or King Stephen at least in any way contributed to the distribution of the DGB, while Robert certainly did so. This suggests they may have been less than enthusiastic about the books they received.

The first and by far the more popular of the double dedications was the one addressing Robert jointly with Waleran. Considering the possibility that it was made with Robert's participation, appropriate circumstances would have occurred in the summer of 1141 when Waleran left England and made his peace with Robert. At this point, the two magnates met, witnessing charters by which Bordesley Abbey passed from Waleran to Matilda as part of the process of reconciliation.[44] The charters were written at Devizes, but throughout the period Robert and Matilda's court was based at Oxford, Geoffrey of Monmouth's probable place of residence. The Insular origin of the double dedication is supported by the fact that it is found in eight Insular but only two continental 12th-century manuscripts (including manuscripts dated to s. xii/xiii), in both of which the double dedication has, furthermore, been added to a text originally dedicated to Robert alone.[45] This textual situation – the double dedication receiving relatively wide circulation in Britain but almost none on

43   Alfred of Beverley, *Annals*, ed. T. Hearne, *Aluredi Beverlacensis Annales, sive historia de gestis regum Britanniae, libris IX. E codice pervetusto ...*, Oxford, 1716, p. 2: "Ferebantur tunc temporis per ora multorum narraciones de hystoria Britonum, notamque rusticitatis incurrebat, qui talium narracionum scienciam non habebat ... Quid plura? Quaesivi hystoriam, & ea vix inventa, leccioni ejus intentissime studium adhibui", "At that time many people were telling stories about the history of the Britons and it was a sign of boorishness not to be acquainted with these ... What else? I looked for the history and, once I had found it, I dedicated myself to reading it."

44   *Regesta regum Anglo-Normannorum*, ed. Davis et al., vol. 3, nos. 115 and 116, dated to 25 July–15 September, but in fact predating 12 August. See D. Crouch, *The Reign of King Stephen 1135–1154*, New York, 2000, pp. 183–84, n. 41, and M. Chibnall, *The Empress Matilda: Queen Consort, Queen Mother and Lady of the English*, Oxford and Cambridge, MA, 1991, pp. 134–35. Acton Griscom was aware of the above documents and discussed the possibility of the joint dedication having been made for the occasion, but he dismissed this theory, largely because he was misinformed about the chronology of the dedications (he considered the joint dedication the original one, a theory now discredited). See Geoffrey of Monmouth, *De gestis Britonum*, ed. Griscom, pp. 69–80.

45   Cambridge, Trinity College, O.2.21 (DGB ms 39, Insular); Cambridge, University Library, Ii.1.14 (DGB ms 48, Insular), Ii.4.4. (DGB ms 49, Insular); London, British Library, Lansdowne 732 (DGB ms 107, Insular); New Haven, Beinecke Library, 590 (DGB ms 128, Insular); Oxford, Bodleian Library, Additional A.61 (DGB ms 134, Insular), Bodley 514 (DGB ms 136, Insular); Paris, Bibliothèque nationale de France, lat. 6040 (DGB ms 170, probably Insular); Vatican City, Biblioteca Apostolica Vaticana, Reg. lat. 692 (DGB ms 197, continental; joint

the Continent – suggests that Waleran did not promote the version dedicated to him in any measure. He, after all, left England at the end of the summer of 1141, never to return. Consequently, the source for the dissemination of the double dedication in Britain cannot have been the copy he received.

As it happens, we can locate the precise exemplar from which the (completely Insular) transmission of the double dedication text started. Textually, all the manuscripts with the joint dedication to Robert and Waleran are similar. They represent the Insular Δ branch of transmission, except for one passage (§§114–37) in which they follow Φ, i.e., the other archetype and the probable presentation copy whose descendants dominate the continental tradition. We can be certain that they all descend from Paris, Bibliothèque nationale de France, lat. 6040, of Insular origin, which provides a material answer to this textual puzzle. In Paris 6040, the chapters in which the text follows Φ (§§114–37) form a single quire (fols. 33r–39v), copied by a hand that is different from but contemporary with the main hand. On the final verso side of this quire (fol. 39v), we can, furthermore, see the scribe stretching his letters and spacing them more widely so as to fit the text neatly on the remaining side. In other words, it appears that the whole text of Paris 6040 was originally copied from an exemplar with the Δ type text, but that one quire was soon lost and the missing part of the text was resupplied from a different source.

Indeed, there is material evidence that the manuscript went through an accident, most likely as it was being bound. All of the folios in Paris 6040, except those of the quire copied by the different scribe, soon after their writing lost a triangular piece of parchment from their inner top corner, as if a blade had cut through the whole book, and this is no doubt what actually happened (it is difficult to imagine any other instrument than binder's guillotine causing such neat damage). Every single folio was immediately repaired by carefully gluing a patch of parchment on each bifolium, and the lost text was recopied on these patches, apparently by the original scribe. It appears likely that it was in this process of repair – we must imagine a room full of bifoliums under weights being glued – that one quire went missing. Reeve's conclusion is that Δ and Φ were both authorial versions of the text, and that Δ was probably the later of these, produced presumably by authorial revision of the draft.[46] Considering the possibility that Robert of Gloucester was involved in the making of the double dedication, it is at least a curious coincidence that the manuscript from which all the double dedication copies descend brought together the text as

---

dedication added in the margin but later erased), and Vat. lat. 2005 (*DGB* ms 199, continental; follows the double dedication version only for the first chapters).

46   *DGB*, p. xiii, p. xix.

it had been presented to Robert (Φ) and the authorially revised version (Δ), which was probably in Geoffrey's possession.

A text of the same hybrid type, always descending from Paris 6040, accompanied the second re-dedication, jointly to Robert and King Stephen. This was, however, produced with less effort. It is a lazy reworking of the dedication to Robert and Waleran, created by altering the names and titles so that Robert became Stephen and Waleran became Robert. The text which accompanies it is furthermore quite corrupt, so presumably this second joint dedication came about with an ad hoc modification hastily made to a manuscript with the double dedication to Robert and Waleran that happened to be available, not as a deliberately produced presentation copy. A possible context for its making would have been provided the curious circumstances of September to October 1141. At this point, Robert and King Stephen had both been taken prisoner by the opposing side and negotiations over their exchange were taking place.

2   Monastic Manuscripts

Individual bibliophiles, whether monks like Robert of Torigni, secular ecclesiastics such as Alexander of Lincoln, or lay magnates such as Robert of Gloucester and Walter Espec, played a significant role in the dissemination of the *DGB*. However, despite its secular tone and the evidence for the activity of individual readers in its circulation, monastic libraries were at least as important for the early transmission, especially on the Continent.

We have seen how the *DGB* was incorporated into an already existing codex containing serious historical texts at Le Bec around 1150, and compilations of this kind became the main vehicle of its transmission in institutional contexts. Over the third quarter of the century, we can identify historical compilations containing the *DGB* made at the Cistercian house of Pontigny (Burgundy, c.1164–66),[47] Saint-Germain-des-Prés (Paris, in or soon after 1168),[48] the

---

47   Montpellier 92 (*DGB* ms 126). On the content, see Crick, *SC*, pp. 208–09; on the origin, see M. Peyrafort-Huin, *La bibliothèque médiévale de l'Abbaye de Pontigny (XIIᵉ–XIXᵉ siècles)*, Paris, 2001, pp. 64–65 and 541–42.

48   Paris, Bibliothèque nationale de France, lat. 12943 (*DGB* ms 184). See Crick, *SC*, pp. 286–88 and J. Tahkokallio, "Monks, Clerks and King Arthur: Reading Geoffrey of Monmouth in the Twelfth and Thirteenth Centuries", unpublished PhD dissertation, University of Helsinki, 2013, pp. 190–91.

Benedictine abbey of Anchin (Flanders)[49] and an unidentified monastic scriptorium in Reims.[50] At Pontigny, the DGB was copied in tandem with Bede's *Ecclesiastical History*, while at Saint-Germain-des-Prés, the DGB was joined to an earlier, 11th-century copy of the same work. At Anchin, it was accompanied by Dudo of Saint-Quentin's *The Customs and Deeds of the First Dukes of the Normans* and in Reims by Ademar of Chabannes's *Chronicle*. From the last quarter of the 12th century we find manuscripts of similar content from the Benedictine houses of Marchiennes (Flanders),[51] Fécamp (Normandy),[52] and Saint Evroul (Normandy),[53] and the Cistercian abbeys of Chaalis (Picardy)[54] and Valuisant (Burgundy).[55] Early in the 13th century, further compilations were produced at Jumièges (Benedictine, Normandy),[56] St Martin (Benedictine, Tournai),[57] and, slightly later, Aurillac (Benedictine, Auvergne).[58] By this time, the DGB was transmitted in monastic compilations in German-speaking areas as well, copied at Salem (Cistercian, Konstanz),[59]

---

49   Douai, Bibliothèque municipale, 880 (DGB ms 59). See Crick, *SC*, pp. 93–94 and Tahkokallio, "Monks, Clerks and King Arthur", pp. 169–70.

50   Paris, Bibliothèque nationale de France, lat. 6041B (DGB ms 173). On the content, see Crick, *SC*, p. 273; on the origin, see P. Bourgain, "Un nouveau manuscrit du text tronqué de la Chronique d'Adhemar de Chabannes", *Bibliothèque de l'École des chartes* 143 (1985), 153–59, esp. p. 155.

51   Douai, Bibliothèque municipale, 882 (838) (DGB ms 60). On the content and origin, see Crick, *SC*, pp. 94–98 and Tahkokallio, "Monks, Clerks and King Arthur", p. 170.

52   Bern, Burgerbibliothek, 568 (DGB ms 15). On the content and origin, see Crick, *SC*, pp. 21–25 and Wright, "Introduction", pp. xxxv–xliii.

53   Alençon, Bibliothèque municipale, 12 (DGB ms 12). On the content, see Crick, *SC*, pp. 15–17; on the origin, see G. Nortier, "Les Bibliothèques médiévales des abbayes bénédictines de Normandie. IV. La bibliothèque de Saint-Evroul", *Revue Mabillon* 47 (1957), 219–44, at p. 220.

54   Paris, Bibliothèque nationale de France, lat. 17569 (DGB ms 188). On the content and origin, see Crick, *SC*, pp. 292–93 and Tahkokallio, "Monks, Clerks and King Arthur", p. 191.

55   Auxerre, Bibliothèque municipale, 91 (85) (DGB ms 14). On the content and origin, see Crick, *SC*, pp. 19–21 and F. Bougard, P. Petitmengin, & P. Stirnemann, *La bibliothèque de l'abbaye cistercienne de Vauluisant*, Paris, 2012, pp. 34, 36, 159–61.

56   Rouen, Bibliothèque municipale, U.74 (1177) (DGB ms 200). On the content and origin, see Crick, *SC*, pp. 305–06 and Tahkokallio, "Monks, Clerks and King Arthur", p. 194.

57   Brussels, Bibliothèque royale, II.1020 (DGB ms 21). On the content and origin, see Crick, *SC*, pp. 32–33 and A. Boutemy, "Note sur l'origine et la date du *Status Imperii Iudaici*", *Scriptorium* 1 (1946/47), 66–69, at p. 66.

58   Montpellier, Bibliothèque interuniversitaire, H 142 (DGB ms 222). On the content and origin, see Tahkokallio, "Update", pp. 196–99.

59   Heidelberg, Universitätbibliothek, 9.31 (DGB ms 75). On the content, see Crick, *SC*, pp. 122–24; on the origin see W. Werner, *Die mittelalterlichen nichtliturgischen Handschriften des Zisterzienserklosters Salem*, Wiesbaden, 2000, p. 231.

Allerheiligen (Benedictine, Schaffhausen),[60] and probably at Heisterbach (Cistercian, Nordrhein-Westfalen).[61] This kind of transmission suggests that the *DGB* was taken seriously and seen as a worthy addition to the body of historical information that these religious houses possessed.

In Britain, early institutional readership was more restricted, to judge by the surviving manuscripts. To appreciate the differences, one must keep in mind that over the first century of the *DGB*'s dissemination – before *c.*1250 – the overall numbers of copies attributable to the Continent and to Britain are similar. Excluding the non-localizable manuscripts,[62] there are 49 probably continental and 45 probably Insular copies. However, while 16 of these continental manuscripts have a probable institutional origin, a monastic origin has been suggested for just three Insular manuscripts (Battle, Margam, and St Albans).[63] This paucity of Insular institutional copies does not result from any general lack of monastic historical manuscripts, which is well demonstrated by a simple comparison with William of Malmesbury's *Deeds of the English Kings*. From before *c.*1250, the *Deeds of the English Kings* survives in 16 probably British copies[64] – as compared to the approximately 45 British copies of the *DGB* from the same period. However, nine copies of the *Deeds of the English Kings* (against three of the *DGB*) have a proposed institutional origin. Manuscripts of William's work were probably copied at the Benedictine

---

60   Schaffhausen, Stadtbibliothek, Min. 74 (*DGB* ms 218). On the content and origin, see Tahkokallio, "Update", pp. 188–91 and R. Gamper, G. Knoch-Mund, & M. Stähli, *Katalog der mittelalterlichen Handschriften der Ministerialbibliothek Schaffhausen*, Dietikon-Zürich, 1994, p. 35.

61   London, British Library, Harley 3773 (*DGB* ms 102). On the content and area of origin, see Crick, *SC*, pp. 166–68. My interpretation of its precise origin is based on the presence of several texts attributed to Cesarius of Heisterbach, including what seem drafts for his version of the *Catalogus episcoporum Coloniensium*. A full analysis of the manuscript awaits publication.

62   Cambridge, Trinity College, R.7.6 (*DGB* ms 36); Oxford, All Souls College, 35 (*DGB* ms 132); and Paris, Bibliothèque nationale de France, lat. 6232 (*DGB* ms 177).

63   Battle (Benedictine, Sussex, *s.* xii²): London, British Library, Royal 4 C. xi (*DGB* ms 108); Margam (Cistercian, Glamorgan, *s.* xii/xiii): London, British Library, Royal 13 D. ii (*DGB* ms 112); St Albans (Benedictine, Hertfordshire, *s.* xiii¹): London, British Library, Royal 13 D. v (*DGB* ms 113).

64   Cambridge, Trinity College, R.7.10 and R.7.1; Cambridge, University Library, Ii.2.3; London, British Library, Arundel 35, Harley 261, Cotton Claudius C. ix, Additional 23147, Harley 447, Royal 13 D. v, and Royal 13 D. ii; Oxford, All Souls College, 33, 35, and b. 32, no. 22; Oxford, Bodleian Library, Laud Misc. 548 and Laud Misc. 729.

centers of Bury,[65] Rochester,[66] Battle,[67] Llanthony, and St Swithun (Winchester),[68] at the Cistercian abbeys of Buildwas,[69] Margam,[70] and Merevale,[71] and at the Augustinian house of Newark (Surrey).[72] It is remarkable that a work with a clearly more restricted overall diffusion penetrated institutional collections in Britain so much more efficiently.

Compared to the Continent, the British manuscripts of the *DGB* also more often contain only this work. Before c.1250, 25 of the continental manuscripts of the *DGB* are compilations, but this is the case with just 13 Insular ones. Since there is a strong correlation between monastic origin and compilation format on the Continent, this difference in codicology could well be taken to suggest more limited institutional circulation in Britain.[73]

The situation, however, changed over the second half of the 13th century. Between c.1250 and the beginning of the 14th century (including manuscripts dated to s. xiii/xiv), as many as 14 compilations containing the *DGB* produced in Britain survive,[74] and five of these have a probable monastic ori-

---

65   London, British Library, Harley 447. On the origin, see W. Stubbs, "Preface", in id. (ed.), *Willelmi Malmesbiriensis monachi De gestis regum Anglorum libri quinque*, 2 vols., London, 1887–89, vol. 1, pp. ix–cxlvii, at p. lxxvii; N. Ker, *Medieval Libraries of Great Britain: A List of Surviving Books*, London, 1964, p. 20.

66   London, British Library, Harley 261. On the early Rochester connection, see Stubbs, "Preface", p. lxxiv and Ker, *Medieval Libraries*, p. 161.

67   BL Cotton Claudius C. ix. On the origin, see Stubbs, "Preface", pp. lxxxiii–iv.

68   BL Arundel 35. On the origin, see Stubbs, "Preface", p. lxvii, and Thomson and Winterbottom, "Introduction", p. xv.

69   CUL Ii.2.3. On the origin, see P. Binski & P. Zutshi, *Western Illuminated Manuscripts: A Catalogue of the Collection in Cambridge University Library*, Cambridge, 2011, pp. 59–60.

70   BL Royal 13 D. ii. On the origin, see Crick, *SC* and King, "Introduction", pp. xci–xciv.

71   Oxford, All Souls College, 33. On early provenance, see A. Watson, *Descriptive Catalogue of the Medieval Manuscripts of All Souls College, Oxford*, Oxford, 1997, p. 66. Use of flex punctuation and overall appearance suggest Cistercian origin as well; see M. Parkes, *Pause and Effect: An Introduction to the History of Punctuation in the West*, Berkeley, 1993, pp. 39–40.

72   Oxford, Bodleian Library, Laud Misc. 548 (1377). On the origin, see Stubbs, "Preface", pp. lxviii–lxix. There is some overlap, since two of the manuscripts contain both Geoffrey and William (BL Royal 13 D. ii and Royal 13 D. v).

73   There are 25 continental compilations from before c.1250, 14 of which have a probable institutional origin.

74   Aberystwyth, National Library of Wales, 13210 (*DGB* ms 4), Llanstephan 176 (*DGB* ms 6); Cambridge, Clare College, 27 (*DGB* ms 22); Cambridge, Trinity College, O.2.21 (*DGB* ms 39); Cambridge, University Library, Dd.10.31 (*DGB* ms 44); Dublin, Trinity College, 515 (E.5.12) (*DGB* ms 67); Exeter, Cathedral Library, 3514 (*DGB* ms 70); London, British Library, Arundel 326 (*DGB* ms 88), Cotton Vespasian E. x (*DGB* ms 98), Egerton 3142 (*DGB* ms 99), and Harley 4003 (*DGB* ms 103); Oxford, Bodleian Library, Laud Misc. 720 (*DGB* ms 150); Oxford, Christ Church, 99 (*DGB* ms 160); Paris, Bibliothèque nationale de France, lat. 4999A; and Manchester, John Rylands Library, lat. 216 (*DGB* ms 165).

gin: Robertsbridge (Cistercian, Sussex),[75] St Albans,[76] Whitland (Cistercian, Wales),[77] Abingdon (Benedictine, Oxfordshire),[78] and Holme (Benedictine, Norfolk).[79] The slower take-off of monastic dissemination may indicate that British audiences were more critical of the truth value of the work than continental ones. This does not seem surprising, given that the English church traced its roots back to the late sixth-century Gregorian mission and that Bede's work was the canonical account of its origins. A text that told about late Roman and early medieval Christian society and conflicted with Bede in its details could easily have met with some resistance. Whereas the DGB was quickly accepted as an uncontroversial addition to the corpus of historical information in France and Flanders, it was only over the 13th century that Galfridian facts became historical mainstream in Britain, concurrently with the rise of the Latin and vernacular *Brut* traditions.

3   Books for Individuals?

In all these institutional manuscripts, the text of Geoffrey's DGB comprises part of a compilation containing other historical texts. However, most manuscripts of the DGB are not compilations at all. If we look at all the non-fragmentary copies from before *c*.1300, we see that 66 out of 126 (52 per cent) are single-text manuscripts, containing only the DGB. These single-text copies and the compilations contrast starkly in terms of how much is known about their origins. Whereas 23 of the compilations have been attributed with a probable institutional origin, we do not know the precise origin of any of the single-text manuscripts. There is also a clear difference in format. The single-text copies are less bulky, having an average page area of 359 cm^2 as opposed to the 568 cm^2 of the compilations.

The contrast in origin information suggests that a much smaller proportion of the single-text copies were actually produced for institutional collections.

---

75   NLW 13210 (DGB ms 4). On the content and origin, see Crick, *SC*, p. 7.

76   Cambridge, Clare College, 27 (DGB ms 22). On the content and origin, see Crick, *SC*, pp. 33–34 and N. Morgan, "Matthew Paris, St Albans, London, and the leaves of the 'Life of St Thomas Becket'", *Burlington Magazine* 130 (1988), 85–96, at p. 90, n. 22, and p. 92.

77   Exeter 3514 (DGB ms 70). On the origin and content, see Crick, *SC*, pp. 114–17 and ead., "The Power and the Glory: Conquest and Cosmology in Edwardian Wales (Exeter, Cathedral Library 3514)", in O. Da Rold and E. Treharne (eds.), *Textual Cultures: Cultural Texts*, Cambridge, 2010, pp. 21–42, at pp. 30–34.

78   BL Arundel 326 (DGB ms 88). On the origin and content, see Crick, *SC*, pp. 142–44 and Ker, *Medieval Libraries*, p. 2.

79   BL Egerton 3142 (DGB ms 99). On the origin and content, see Crick, *SC*, pp. 163–64.

The same idea is conveyed by the difference in size, the monastic library books often (if by no means always) being of relatively large format. My suspicion is that many of the single-text copies were produced for individual owners. The writing of the DGB coincided with a great expansion in both the supply and demand of writing, a key feature of the so-called 12th-century renaissance. Cathedral schools were churning out a new educated class, which found employment in royal, episcopal, and comital chapels and chanceries, and sometimes possibly also in lesser aristocratic households. The incipient commercialization of book production was one feature of this new dynamism, both making it easier (for wealthy secular clerks) to commission books and offering opportunities for scribal employment (for their less well-off colleagues). When considered quantitatively, the codicology of the copies of the DGB, put together with information about their origins, appears to reflect these developments.

A manuscript's origin as a book produced for personal use is difficult to prove, however. Not one of the 12th- or early 13th-century century copies of the DGB bears a contemporary *ex libris* inscription indicating private ownership. We are thus left with paleographical, or, more broadly, typological and material criteria for identifying such books, and these are not very helpful at this point in time. In the 13th century, it is possible to recognize books produced on commission by urban craftsmen, often for individuals, on stylistic criteria. Book production had by then become an organized commercial craft, and this development was accompanied by the creation of relatively fixed styles of decoration and layout, at least in the most important centers of production.[80] The 12th-century situation was, however, different. While manuscripts were

---

80   On the emergence of such styles, see e.g. F. Avril, "A quand remontent les premiers ate-
      liers d'enlumineurs laïcs à Paris", *Les Dossiers de l'archéologie* 16 (1976), 36–44; B. Brenner,
      Manuscript Painting in Paris during the Reign of Saint Louis: a Study of Styles, Berkeley,
      1977; P. Stirnemann, *Quelques bibliothèques princières et la production hors scriptorium au
      XIIe siècle*, Paris, 1984; ead., "Fils de la vierge. L'initiale à filigranes parisiennes: 1140–1340",
      Revue de l'Art 90 (1991), 58–73. On early "commercial" book production generally, see, e.g.,
      C. De Hamel, *Glossed Books of the Bible and the Origins of the Paris Booktrade*, Woodbridge,
      1984; M. Rouse & R. Rouse, *Manuscripts and Their Makers: Commercial Book Producers in
      Medieval Paris, 1200–1500*, 2 vols., Turnhout, 2000; id., "The Book Trade at the University
      of Paris, ca. 1250–ca. 1350", in L. Bataillon, B. Guyot, and R. Rouse (eds.), *La Production
      du livre universitaire au moyen âge*, Paris, 1988, pp. 41–114; A. Stones, "Secular Manuscript
      Illumination in France", in C. Kleinhenz (ed.), *Medieval Manuscripts and Textual Criticism*,
      Chapel Hill, 1976, pp. 83–102; and P.M. de Winter, "Copistes, éditeurs et enlumineurs
      de la fin du XIVe siècle: la production à Paris de manuscrits à miniatures", in *Actes du
      Congrès national des sociétés savantes: Section d'archéologie et d'histoire de l'art*, Paris, 1978,
      pp. 173–98.

certainly produced on commission then as well, the styles and arrangements by which they were made were more varied.

Nevertheless, over the century, styles of decoration developed which can be associated with emerging proto-commercial book production, and some manuscripts of the *DGB* reflect them. The earliest of these is Vatican City, Biblioteca Apostolica Vaticana, Pal. lat. 956, datable to around or before the middle of the 12th century.[81] This manuscript has pen decoration which echoes the style seen in books produced in Chartres in the 1130s and 1140s, even though the initials are not "pure" representatives of this style.[82] Still more informal and simplified versions of the Chartrain motifs of penwork can be seen in the initials of Paris, Bibliothèque nationale de France, lat. 6232 (*DGB* ms 177). In this manuscript, probably produced in the north of France, partly from an Insular exemplar, the penwork is in red, blue, and green, in contrast to the red-blue aesthetics of the proper Chartrain flourishes. The Chartres-style decoration is seen in many high-grade manuscripts known to have been produced on commission, and its emergence appears to be one reflection of the incipient professionalization of bookmaking.[83] Its influence on the decoration of these less sumptuous and more quickly produced copies of the *DGB* could indicate that these books, as well, were made in secular contexts, possibly for individual users.

In addition to the pen decoration, the Chartres-style books often have distinctive and very elaborate major initials which are not found in Pal. lat. 956 or BnF lat. 6232. This is not surprising, given the relatively modest quality of these books and the fact that the Palatine manuscript, the finer one, has lost its first quire, in which the only major illuminated initials of the *DGB* are usually located.[84] Another manuscript, however, may point indirectly at the existence of an early, high-grade copy with such major initials. This is Paris, Bibliothèque nationale de France, lat. 8501A (*DGB* ms 183). The manuscript itself is later, from the second half of the 12th century. It contains several texts copied by multiple hands and it is by no means luxurious. Most of its initials are simple, single-color letters, sometimes with modest pen flourishes, but the first two

---

81   BAV Pal. lat. 956 (*DGB* ms 195).

82   I owe this observation to Michael Gullick.

83   P. Stirnemann, "Où ont été fabriqués les livres de la glose ordinaire dans la première moitié du xiie siècle?", in F. Gasparri (ed.), *Le xiie siècle: mutations et renouveau 1120–1150*, Paris, 1994, pp. 257–85, at pp. 272–73 and pl. x, and Stirnemann's pdf, <http://www.manuscrits -de-chartres.fr/sites/default/files/fileviewer/documents/reconnaitre-ms/decor-styles_ chartrains_petit_0.pdf> (accessed 5 October 2017).

84   Major initials are by far the most commonly seen in the beginning of the work, for example, the "C" of *Cum mecum*, *DGB*, Prologus 1.1) and the "B" of *Britannia* (*DGB*, Prologus 5.24).

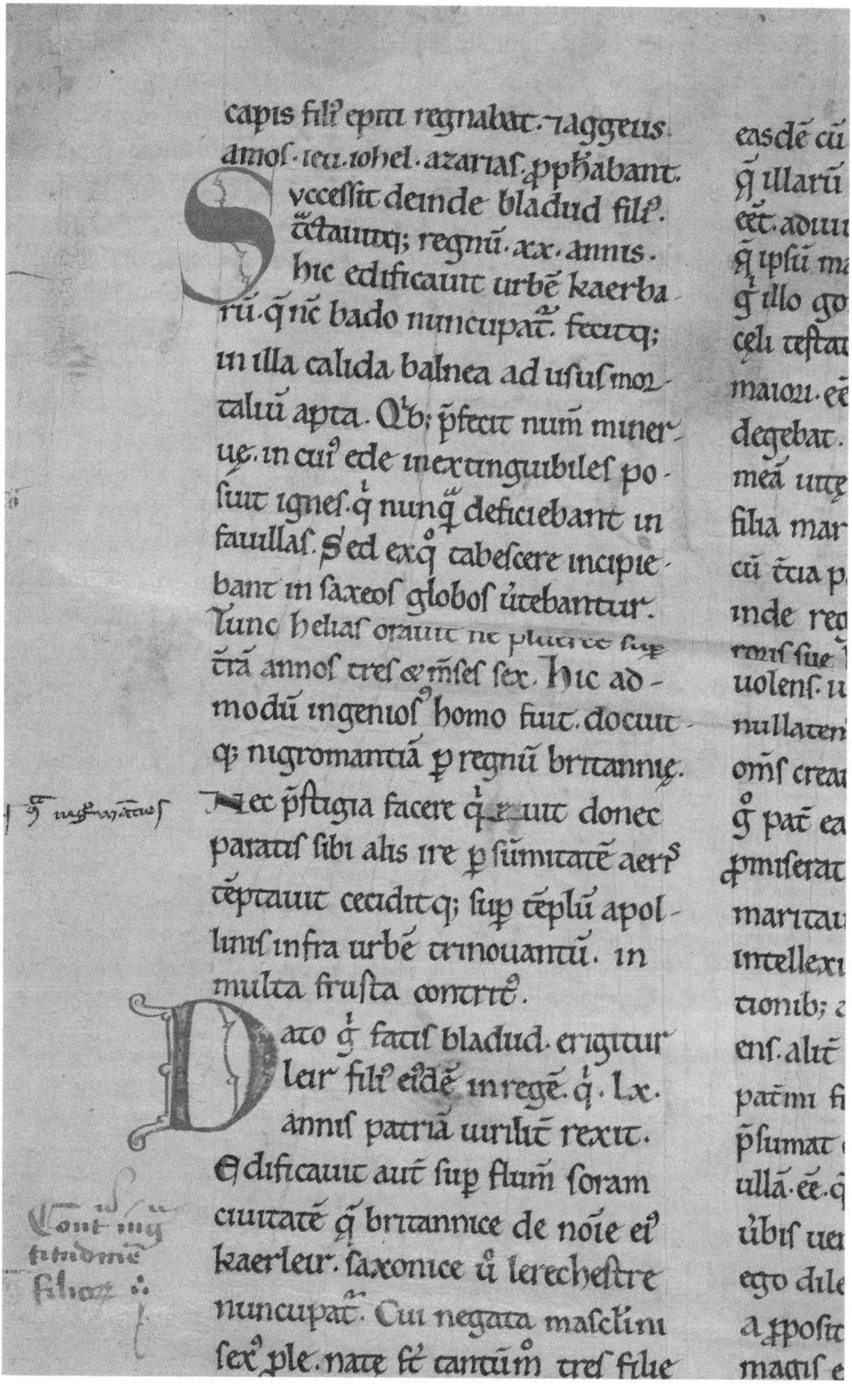

capis fil? epra regnabat. ᚐaggeus.
amos. ᚊeu. iohel. azarias. pphabant.
vcceſſit deinde bladud fil?.
ᚊctautnᛁ; regnũ. xx. annis.
hic edificauit urbē kaerba
rũ. ᚊ nc bado nuncupat̃. fecitᛁ;
in illa calida balnea ad uſuſmoꝛ
talũ apta. Q'b; pfecit num miner
ue. in cui? ede inextinguibileſ po
ſuit igneſ. ᚊ nunᛁ deficiebant in
fauillaſ. s'ed exᛁ tabeſcere incipie
bant in ſaxeoſ globoſ utebantur.
Tunc heliaſ orauit ne plueret ſup
tiã annoſ treſ & mſeſ ſex. hic ad
modũ ingenioſ homo fuit. docuit
ᛁ nigromantiã p regnũ britannie.
[margin: ᚊ nigromancus]
ᚊec pſtigia facere ᚊ uit donec
paratuſ ſibi aliſ ire p ſũmitate aerſ
teptauit ceciditᛁ; ſup teplũ apol
liniſ infra urbē trinouantũ. in
multa fruſta contritē.

ato ᚊ fatiſ bladud. erigitur
leir fil? eidē in regē. ᚊ. Lx.
anniſ patriã uiriliti rexit.
Edificauit aut ſup flum ſoram
ciuitatē ᚊ britannice de noie ei?
kaerleir. ſaxonice ū lerecheſtre
nuncupat̃. Cui negata maſclini
ſex? ple. nate ſt̃ cantũin treſ filie

[margin left: Cont iuᛁ tatione filioꝛ :·]

[right column fragments:]
easdē cũ
ᚊ illarũ
eēt. aduu
ᚊ ipſiu m
ᚊ illo go
celi teſtat
maioꝛi. eē
degebat.
meā uttᚊ
filia mar
cũ ttia p
inde reᚊ
ronſ ſue
uolenſ. u
nullaten
omſ crea
ᚊ pat ea
cpmiſerat
maritau
intellexi
tionib; ᛁ
enſ. altē
patini fi
pſumat
ullā. eē. ᚊ
ubiſ uei
ego dile
a ppoſt
magiſ e

FIGURE 5.2 Vatican City, Biblioteca Apostolica Vaticana, Pal. lat. 956, fol. 1v

at the beginning of the DGB stand out from the rest. These are simply drawn by pen, but they are clearly imitations of elaborate multicolor initials, probably specifically of the type seen in many commissioned 12th-century books from the middle of the century. The large initial "B" beginning §5 of the DGB in particular bears an uncanny resemblance to the elaborate initials produced by an artist active in Chartres in the 1140s, identified by Patricia Stirnemann.[85] Looking at the rendering of the details, this letter appears to be a copy of something resembling the initial found in Tours, Bibliothèque municipale, 93, fol. 2v or Troyes, Bibliothèque municipale, 2391, fol. 34v, a book made for Thibaut II, Count of Champagne (1090–1152), whose son Henry (the Liberal, 1127–81), arguably owned a copy of the DGB.[86] The fact that the manuscript contains one of the two surviving copies of a rare text, *A Poem on Muhammad* (*Otia de Machomete*), known to have been written in Chartres between 1137 and 1155, supports connecting this manuscript with Chartres.[87] It has been suggested that BnF lat. 8501A may have been copied at Mont-Saint-Michel, this association being based on the resemblance of a marginal drawing representing King Arthur (fol. 108v) to the style of pen-drawn illustrations produced at Mont during Robert of Torigni's abbacy (1154–86).[88] While some stylistic similarity can indeed be seen, this does not constitute proof of the manuscript's origin, especially since the marginal drawing could have been supplied later.[89]

In this chapter, I have but scratched the surface of the wealth of information that the manuscripts of the DGB can provide. They not only inform us about the contemporary reception of Geoffrey's work but also open a window into a rare corner of 12th-century book culture. The large number of the manuscripts

85   See Stirnemann, "Où ont été fabriqués les livres", pp. 270–71.

86   See Stirnemann, *Quelques bibliothèques princières*, p. 22, and ead., "Les bibliothèques princières et privées aux XIIe et XIIIe siècles", in A. Vernet (ed.), *Histoire des bibliothèques françaises, Tome 1. Les bibliothèques médiévales du VIe à 1530*, [Paris], 1989, pp. 173–91, at p. 177.

87   Robert Huygens, editor of the text, thought it probable that both surviving copies reflect the same exemplar, which was close to the authorial text. See R.B.C. Huygens, "*Otia de Machomete* [A poem on Muhammad], Gedicht von Walter von Compiegne", *Sacris erudiri* 8 (1956), 287–328.

88   M.-F. Damongeot-Bourdat, "Le roi Arthur et le Mont-Saint-Michel", *Les Amis du Mont-Saint-Michel* 115 (2010), 36–41, at p. 41. For the style of drawing, see M. Bourgeois-Lechartier & F. Avril, *Le Scriptorium du Mont Saint-Michel*, Paris, 1967, esp. pp. 18–19 and p. 46, and figures 44, 81 and 126–28.

89   Since Robert of Torigni's handwriting has recently been identified (Pohl, "*Abbas qui et scriptor?*") it can be observed that his hand does not seem to appear in BnF lat. 8501A. This is of course no proof that the manuscript could not have been copied at or for Mont-Saint-Michel, but given the central role of Robert in the transmission of the DGB, this absence is worth noting.

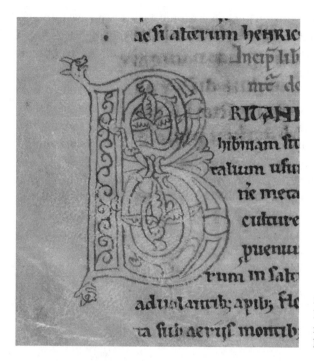

FIGURE 5.3
Paris, Bibliothèque
nationale de France,
lat. 8501A, fol. 63v

FIGURE 5.4
Troyes, Bibliothèque
municipale, 2391, fol. 34v

of the *DGB* is remarkable since its copying cannot have been based on any kind of institutionalized demand or captive audience. Most medieval bestsellers were works which had a specific audience that could not do without them: canon law books were necessary for bishops and episcopal administrators, school books for scholars, and texts on monastic spirituality for monasteries. There were, however, no similarly binding reasons why anyone *needed* to own an arguably newly-translated ancient history. As a literary phenomenon, the *DGB* came as close to what we mean by the word "bestseller" as it is possible to get in a medieval Latin context: it was a work whose success was based on the appeal that the text had to its readers. As such, its manuscripts tell us about the various ways in which books were produced and procured in the 12th century: monastic copying, professional book production, and various kinds of ad hoc arrangements. Much paleographical and codicological work remains to be done on them.

CHAPTER 6

Early Reactions to Geoffrey's Work

Simon Meecham-Jones

Although the 12th century was blessed with a profusion of elegant and idio-syncratic works of erudition, its literary horizon offers no more spectacular or unforeseen comet than the pan-European fascination with Geoffrey of Monmouth's *De gestis Britonum* and *Vita Merlini*. The scale of popularity and influence of Geoffrey's work is made more remarkable by its apparently unpropitious subject matter. Geoffrey adapted (or, some have claimed, invented) the historical triumphs and travails of a barely remembered people living on what was perceived to be the furthest outcrop of civilization:[1]

> While my mind was often pondering many things in many ways, my thoughts turned to the history of the kings of Britain, and I was surprised that, among the references to them in the fine works of Gildas and Bede, I had found nothing concerning the kings who lived here before Christ's Incarnation, and nothing about Arthur and the many others who succeeded after it, even though their deeds were worthy of eternal praise and are proclaimed by many people as if they had been entertainingly and memorably written.[2]

Geoffrey presents his aim modestly, as an act of repair on the historical tradition, but his work immediately and indelibly changed the trajectory of that narrative, while at the same creating a hunger for his subject which crossed geographical and cultural boundaries, and which is by no means spent even

---

1 J. O'Reilly, "The Art of Authority", in T. Charles-Edwards (ed.), *After Rome* (Short Oxford History of the British Isles), Oxford, 2003, pp. 141–90, at p. 141: "The utter remoteness of the islands at the north-westerly limits of the Ocean and the barbarian nature of their inhabitants was a commonplace or topos in the works of Roman poets and historians. They therefore regarded the partial conquest of Britain, the largest in the skein of islands at the furthest end of the inhabited world, as a symbol of Rome's universal dominion and civilizing role."

2 *DGB*, Prologus 1.1–7: "Cum mecum multa et de multis saepius reuoluens in hystoriam regum Britannie inciderem, in mirum contuli quod infra mentionem quam de eis Gildas et Beda luculento tractatu fecerant nichil de regibus qui ante incarnationem Christi inhabitauerant, nichil etiam de Arturo ceterisque compluribus qui post incarnationem successerunt repperissem, cum et gesta eorum digna aeternitate laudis constarent et a multis populis quasi inscripta iocunde et memoriter praedicarentur."

now. For Geoffrey's work to have become so widely sought after and then assimilated as a source and the setter of precedents, the texts must have expressed some quality, or qualities, which spoke eloquently to the preoccupations of contemporary as well as subsequent audiences. Geoffrey's texts, figuratively, had revealed to Europe a nostalgia for an experience of loss which had not previously been recognized.

Geoffrey's ability to speak to issues not addressed by existing literary tradition or writers of his age resulted in the rapid circulation of his work. Within two generations of the completion of the DGB, the figure of a probably mythical British king was being depicted in the mosaic of a cathedral ceilings in Otranto in southern Italy,[3] and the themes of Arthurian literature were embedded in literature in French, German, Spanish, and Welsh, as well as Latin.[4] The copious survival of medieval manuscripts of Geoffrey's texts provides further evidence of the scale of the popularity of his work. In her survey, Crick noted around 215 manuscripts of the DGB which have survived, at least in part, a figure which has continued to rise.[5] Nor was the copying of the texts confined to Britain or the territories allied to the Angevin throne.[6] Crick singles out the Low Countries, for example, as an important center of Galfridian manuscript production.[7] But Geoffrey's importance was not limited to these Latin manuscripts for long. His original texts were swiftly translated into vernacular versions. In Wales, for example, there were at least three distinct translation traditions into Welsh which scribes could copy, amalgamate or extend.[8] The third, and perhaps broadest, sphere of Geoffrey's decisive influence was exercised through the immense number of texts which were, factually or stylistically, indebted to his works and their distinctive ethical climate(s). In this category must be included most of the genre of romance, as well as a great

3 Loomis argues for a pre-Galfridian inspiration for the mosaic at Otranto, but offers no explanation how "the renown of the British hero" had reached Italy by this time: R.S. Loomis, *Arthurian Tradition and Chrétien de Troyes*, New York, 1949, p. 20.
4 For more on Geoffrey's reception in these languages, see the reception chapters at the end of this volume and Siân Echard's contribution to this volume.
5 Crick, *DR*. See Jaakko Tahkokallio's contribution to this volume, p. 155.
6 The early circulation of the work in Britain and on the Continent is considered by Tahkokallio in his contribution to this volume, pp. 155–80.
7 Crick, *DR*, pp. 210–11; see also David Johnson's contribution to this volume.
8 Patrick Sims-Williams has recently argued for a fourth: *Rhai Addasiadau Cymraeg Canol o Sieffre o Fynwy* [Some Middle Welsh adaptations of Geoffrey of Monmouth], Aberystwyth, 2011; id., "The Welsh Versions of Geoffrey of Monmouth's 'History of the Kings of Britain'", in A. Harlos and N. Harlos (eds.), *Adapting Texts and Styles in a Celtic Context: Interdisciplinary Perspectives on Processes of Literary Transfer in the Middle Ages. Studies in Honour of Erich Poppe*, Münster, 2016, pp. 53–74.

range of medieval historical, political, and moral writings, not excluding those which were written to challenge, contradict, or "correct" Geoffrey's work.

The unprecedented circulation of texts by an otherwise obscure ecclesiastwriting on a previously ignored topic draws us to the central paradox of Geoffrey's reception history.[9] The speed and extent of his influence might seem to suggest that his texts were received without reservation or challenge, whereas the survival of admittedly a small number of hostile written comments seems to demonstrate the reverse. Furthermore, the presumption that Geoffrey "remains, however, often misjudged if not condemned, and as controversial as ever" makes it harder to determine how far such comments should be read, not as specks of isolated criticisms but as representative expressions of contemporary reservation about his standing.[10]

There can be no denying Geoffrey's influence in establishing *la matere de Bretagne*, "the matter of Britain", as one of the most productive foundations of medieval literature.[11] It was swiftly accepted into the narrative capital of European vernaculars, undergoing expansion and hybridization, adding new characters and situations (like Lancelot's affair with the queen) that drew the attention of readers across Europe, with a speed and a geographical coverage which was signified, for example, in the excitable but clearly impressed testimony of Alan of Lille:

> What place is there within the bounds of the empire of Christianity, to which has not extended the winged praise of the Arthur of the Britons? Who is there I ask who does not speak of the Britannic Arthur, who is but little less known to the peoples of Asia than to the Britons, as we are informed by our pilgrims who return from the countries of the east. The Easterns speak of him, as also do the Westerns, though the breadth of the whole earth lies between them. Egypt speaks of his name, and the Bosphorus is not silent; Rome, the Queen of the cities sings his deeds, and his wars are not unknown to her former competitor Carthage. His

---

9   Geoffrey's career has been traced by J.E. Lloyd, "Geoffrey of Monmouth", *EHR* 57 (1942), 460–68. See also Introduction, pp. 6–28.

10   R.W. Hanning, *The Vision of History in Early Britain: From Gildas to Geoffrey of Monmouth*, New York, 1966, p. 122.

11   Jehan Bodel's celebrated classification of the three "matters" of romance at the end of the 12th century must itself be considered proof of the widespread influence of Geoffrey's text: "N'en sont que trois materes a nul home vivant / De France, et de Bretaigne, et de Romme la grant", "There are only three matters no living man should be ignorant of; the matter of France, the matter of Britain, and the matter of glorious Rome": Jehan Bodel, *La chanson des Saisnes*, ed. A. Brasseur, *La chanson des Saisnes* (Textes littéraires français, 369), 2 vols., Geneva, 1989, vol. 1, p. 2.

exploits are praised in Antioch, Armenia, and Palestine. He will be celebrated in the mouths of the people, and his acts shall be food to those
who relate them.[12]

So extensive was the vogue for Geoffrey's work that, even if Alan's praise was
intended to be sarcastic, the joke was undercut. Nonetheless, it is inevitable
that such success would cause disquiet, as well as some professional jealousy,
rendering Geoffrey's work contentious for some of his readers. The difficulty
for modern critics, then, is to try to determine how far the surviving contemporary attacks on Geoffrey should be considered minor correctives to a generally positive contemporary reception history, which have been allowed undue
prominence due to the ideological (or even historiographical) priorities of
later critics. Immediately, it is important to enter a caveat. It would be wrong to
presume that the political sensitivity of the implications of Geoffrey's work is
long spent. In his view of Britain as an ancient and indivisible polity, Geoffrey
offered a coherent, but not necessarily welcome, projection of the inevitable
and beneficial closeness of the relationship of Wales and Scotland (and, more
tangentially, Ireland) to the English crown, in his own day and subsequently.
It was a justification that was to be worked hard by those contemptuous of
ideas of "British" identities, such as Edward I, formulating the English claim
to Scotland and Wales. The ability of Geoffrey's texts to serve and support political and cultural campaigns and to draw attention to issues of identity and
rightful authority helps to provide one explanation for the vehemence with
which some commentators have sought to discredit his work.

---

12   Text and translation from T. Stephens, *The Literature of the Kymry: being a critical essay
     on the history of the language and literature of Wales during the twelfth and two succeeding
     centuries*, Llandovery, 1849, pp. 421–22: "Quo enim Arturi Britonis nomen fama Volans non
     pertulit et vulgavit: quousque Christianum pertingit imperium? Quis, inquam, Arturum
     Britonum non loquatur, cum pene notior habeatur Asiaticis gentibus, quam Britannis;
     sicut nobis referunt Palmigeri nostri de orientis partibus redeuntes? Loquuntur illum ori-
     entales, loquuntur occidui, toto terrarum orbe divisi. Loquitur illum Ægyptus; Bosforus
     exclusa non tacet. Cantat gestae ejus domina civitatum Roma, nec emulam quondam ejus
     Carthaginem, Arturi praelia latent. Celebrat actus ejus Antiochia, Armenia, Palaestina.
     [In ore populorum celebrabitur, et actus ejus cibus erit narrantibus]." Loomis makes some
     adjustments to the translation, e.g. he replaces Stephens' "Easterns" with "Eastern People",
     but his translation retains a slightly archaic sound; Loomis, *Arthurian Tradition*, p. 3. Alan
     of Lille's Latin appears as part of a commentary on the *PM: Interpretation of the Prophecy
     of Merlin*, printed by Ioachim Bratheringii, *Prophetia anglicana: Merlini Ambrosii bri-
     tanni ... vaticinia et praedictiones a Galfredo Monemutensi latine conversae una cum sep-
     tem libris explanationum in eamdem prophetiam ...*, Frankfurt, 1603 and 1608, Book I at
     pp. 22–23.

At the heart of much of this dismissal lies the issue of Geoffrey's status as a "historian", but it is important to recall that, as Alan of Lille's remark makes clear, Geoffrey was equally celebrated for his presentation of the *PM* and (presumably) the *VM*. Geoffrey's fame as the broadcaster of prophecy was established almost immediately, as witnessed in comments by Orderic Vitalis, but this element of his achievement remains a phenomenon that skeptical modern critics prefer not to consider. It is important, also, to recognize that the prophecies would demand distinct Insular and Continental readings. In Britain, the prophecies were primarily read as predictions for British history. It is striking how, during the Lancastrian textual campaign to undermine the legitimacy of Richard II's rule, frequent recourse is made to "convenient" interpretations of Merlin's prophecies.[13] It is a tactic which remains potent throughout the Wars of the Roses (and later), in English as well as Welsh prophetic and political poetry.[14] For those unconcerned by who occupied the English throne, or the political condition of the Welsh, the prophecies offered compelling (and reassuring) proof of God's occasional willingness to intervene directly in human affairs. There is no evidence that Geoffrey's authorship of the *PM* and the *VM* was used as a means of discrediting his account of British history, though William of Newburgh perhaps allows his distrust of Geoffrey as a historian to check his respect for the prophecies.

Few modern critics place any credence in Geoffrey's claim to be translating from a *Britannici sermonis liber vetustissimus*, "a very old book written in the British language".[15] Instead it has been assumed that the *DGB* is an exercise of imagination, that is, primarily or exclusively of Geoffrey's imagination. Laura Ashe admits some minimal qualification, before concluding that although "Geoffrey is likely to have drawn on earlier oral as well as written traditions ... his book as a whole is a vast product of the imagination."[16] Yet the implications of such a view have not yet been fully developed. To have created such a prolific cast of characters and such a memorable and affecting sequence of situations would have required a prodigious exercise of imagination. Though

---

13   This process is traced in D.R. Carlson, *John Gower, Poetry and Propaganda in Fourteenth-Century England*, Cambridge, 2012.

14   V. Flood, *Prophecy, Politics and Place in Medieval England: From Geoffrey of Monmouth to Thomas of Erceldoune*, Cambridge, 2016.

15   Interestingly, Southern is a significant exception: R.W. Southern, "Aspects of the European Tradition of Historical Writing, 1: The Classical Tradition from Einhard to Geoffrey of Monmouth", *Transactions of the Royal Historical Society*, fifth series, 20 (1970), 173–96 (repr. in R.J. Bartlett (ed.), *History and Historians: Selected Papers of R.W. Southern*, Oxford, 2004, 11–29). For the claim, see *DGB*, Prologus 2.10.

16   L. Ashe, *Early Fiction in England from Geoffrey of Monmouth to Chaucer*, London, 2015, p. 4.

generally denied the laurels as a historian, Geoffrey has yet to be duly recognized for his accomplishments as an imaginative author. Burrow is one of the few critics to begin to acknowledge the enormity of Geoffrey's achievement:

> The consensus seems to be that, though there may be traces of Welsh legend and genealogy, partly from oral tradition, in Geoffrey's work, it is essentially his creation.... remarkable not only for the important gap it purports to fill in historical knowledge of Britain, but also for the accomplished and assured manner of Geoffrey's narration.[17]

What remains clear is that much about Geoffrey's achievement remains uncertain. It is impossible to recover with any certainty how he viewed his own work, if we doubt the evidence preserved in his introductions. This uncertainty can be refined into three questions:

1.   What was Geoffrey's understanding of "history"?
2.   From where did he derive his source material – assuming he did not invent almost all of it?
3.   What were his motivations in writing this work?

In answer to all three heads of query, critics have been eager to interpret early references to Geoffrey's work to buttress their conclusions. Yet careful analysis of the early witnesses shows how much care is needed in interpreting these early witnesses without prejudice.

Perhaps the most controversial of these topics concerns Geoffrey's understanding of historical method. Hanning distinguishes Geoffrey's writing from the tradition of historical writing as "pseudohistory rather than history" though at the same time he notes that "it is still representative in many ways of the historiographical developments of its day."[18] He interprets Geoffrey's method as being influenced by secular and classical models, as distinguished from the tradition of Bede's salvation history, yet it is Geoffrey's method that is presumed to be pseudo-history. A similar ambivalence can be detected in Burrow, who distinguishes between the (disputed) factual bases of Geoffrey's work and his ability to fulfill a contemporary audience's expectations of a historian:

> The interest of Geoffrey's work is not exhausted by consideration of whether it has any factual basis. Geoffrey clearly knew what his

---

17   J.W. Burrow, *A History of Histories: Epics, Chronicles, Romances and Inquiries from Herodotus and Thucydides to the Twentieth Century*, London, 2008, p. 234.

18   Hanning, *Vision*, p. 4.

contemporaries expected a history to be like, and was talented enough, free apparently from any danger of allowing his narrative to be dominated by its sources, amply to give it to them.[19]

This does not resolve the problem raised by Crick, namely that "Geoffrey's work can be classed as parody, fraud, or history" since "Geoffrey's intentions remain buried in his work and in its relationship to its sources."[20] Though she notes cautiously that "the reaction of the immediate audience for which it was intended is unknown", other critics have been swifter to attempt to enlist medieval references to Geoffrey as proof of his intentions – that is, of an intention to deceive.

Of course, the absence of alternative surviving sources makes it impossible to determine how far Geoffrey had access to unrecorded sources (whether written or oral) and, if so, whether he analyzed them with due rigor. It is important to bear in mind how sparse the survival of early Welsh manuscripts has proved. Daniel Huws suggests that they may have been written in Insular scripts which were becoming obsolete,[21] while Sims-Williams offers additional explanations for their scarcity:

> For some reason such as poor storage conditions, early codices, whether Latin or vernacular, survived badly in Wales, Ireland and Scotland, and most of the famous early Celtic manuscripts are extant because at an early stage they were taken to the Continent or, as in the case of the Juvencus and other surviving manuscripts from Wales, to England. Such manuscripts were preserved abroad for the sake of their Latin contents, rather than for any incidental vernacular glosses and marginalia; and completely vernacular manuscripts would not have warranted preservation.[22]

To these accounts should be added the reminder that medieval Wales was regularly a war zone, from before the Norman Conquest at least until the completion of the Edwardian annexation in 1284, beset by invading English armies which had no incentive to respect documents which might support the legitimacy of Welsh claims to the land. In such a context, Hanning's repeated and pointed references to Geoffrey's powers of imagination offer a judgement

---

19   Burrow, *History of Histories*, p. 234.
20   Crick, *DR*, p. 2.
21   D. Huws, *Medieval Welsh Manuscripts*, Aberystwyth, 2000, p. 212.
22   P. Sims-Williams, "The Early Welsh Arthurian Poems", in R. Bromwich, A.O.H. Jarman, and B.F. Roberts (eds.), *The Arthur of the Welsh: The Arthurian Legend in Medieval Welsh Literature* (Arthurian Literature in the Middle Ages, 1), Cardiff, 1991, pp. 33–61, at p. 35.

which, however plausible, are incapable of proof, but which must inevitably color any readings of contemporary accounts.[23]

This difficulty underlines and potentially threatens to undermine the interpretation of evidence from another leading Anglo-Norman historian, Henry of Huntingdon. In a letter, Henry tells how he was concerned that Bede's *Ecclesiastical History* seemed to lack information about the British past. Seeking help in "filling out the great unrecorded gaps in the British past",[24] Henry expresses delight at being introduced to Geoffrey's work by Robert of Torigni: "But this year, on my way to Rome, I discovered, to my amazement, a history of the above reigns at the abbey of Le Bec."[25] There would, initially, seem to be no reservation in Henry's enthusiasm for Geoffrey's work. But this acknowledgement is not inscribed into the text of Henry's own historical work, but is separately recorded in a letter designed to be circulated with Henry's discrete *History of the English*. It is easy though not inevitable to read this as a sign of Henry's skepticism about Geoffrey's reliability, but perhaps Wright is closer in suggesting that this provides an elegant means to pass over the delicate task of reconciling inconsistencies between Geoffrey and Bede's "authoritative" text.[26]

For those set on prosecuting Geoffrey on the charge of willfully misleading his readers, the prize exhibit in the case is a colorful and celebrated episode recounted in Gerald of Wales's revision of his *Journey Through Wales* in 1197. Gerald recounts the experiences of Meilyr of Caerleon, whose affliction by demons is cured by the touch of the Gospels, but made much more grievous when he touches the *DGB*. Gerald paints a lively and memorable scene which has been interpreted as an iconic proof of how Geoffrey's history was dismissed as a tissue of lies in the generations following its composition. But even here the evidence is less clear than it might appear. First, the passage appears as an addition to a single manuscript, suggesting that it might have been

23   It is a dilemma which leads Brynley Roberts to attempt to argue for both possibilities. See B.F. Roberts, "Geoffrey of Monmouth, *Historia regum Britanniae*, and *Brut y Brenhinedd*", in Bromwich et al. (eds.), *The Arthur of the Welsh*, pp. 97–116, at p. 108: "The Arthurian section is Geoffrey's literary creation and it owes nothing to a prior narrative, but elements here as throughout the book appear to be drawn from Welsh – or British – sources."

24   Hanning, *Vision*, p. 124.

25   N. Wright, "The Place of Henry of Huntingdon's *Epistola ad Warinum* in the Text-History of Geoffrey of Monmouth's *Historia regum Britanniae*: a Preliminary Investigation", in G. Jondorf and D.N. Dumville (eds.), *France and the British Isles in the Middle Ages and Renaissance: Essays by Members of Girton College, Cambridge, in Memory of Ruth Morgan*, Woodbridge, 1991, 71–113, text at p. 93, translation at p. 106: "Hoc tamen anno, cum Romam proficiscerer, apud Beccensem abbaciam, scripta rerum predictarum stupens inueni."

26   Wright, "The Place of Henry of Huntingdon's *Epistola ad Warinum*", pp. 88, 90–91.

added to meet the approval of a particular patron or audience.[27] Then, though Gerald is scarcely famed for the consistency of his judgements, it is worth noting that, throughout his career, he was, at the very least, inconsistent in his estimation of how much weight might be placed on Geoffrey as a supporting witness. Gerald did, on occasion, reuse material from Geoffrey, in particular in his two works on Wales, though, as Crick notes, such reliance was never acknowledged.[28] Moreover, he draws on some of the most sensitive areas of contention, such as Geoffrey's account of the Trojan origins of the Britons which are presented without skepticism. Similarly, the essential reliability of Geoffrey's account is presumed in Gerald's closing depiction of the Welsh:

> For the perpetual remembrance of their former greatness, the recollection of their Trojan descent, and the high and continued majesty of the kingdom of Britain, may draw forth many a latent spark of animosity, and encourage the daring spirit of rebellion.[29]

In this unresolved ambivalence, Gerald might be seen as no more and no less than a man of his time, pragmatic or cynical enough to be willing to make use of whatever might support his chosen causes (for example, the metropolitan status of St Davids) just as Richard I exploited the Arthurian myth of Excalibur/Caliburn, and the monks of Glastonbury cashed in on the "fortuitous" discovery of the grave of Arthur and Guinevere, an occasion chronicled and publicized by Gerald himself.[30] This pragmatism led Crick to question why "few commentators have stopped to question whether Gerald's hostility was

---

27   Dimock identifies three "editions" of the *Itinerary*. This passage is not found in the first edition of 1191. It does appear in what Dimock conjectures to be a second version of 1197, though it survives in a 16th-century witness, London, British Library, Harley 359: Gerald of Wales, *The Description of Wales*, ed. J.F. Dimock, *Giraldi Cambrensis Opera*, 8 vols., London, 1861–91, vol. 6, pp. 153–228, at pp. x–xxi.

28   J. Crick, "The British Past and the Welsh Future: Gerald of Wales, Geoffrey of Monmouth and Arthur of Britain", *Celtica* 23 (1999), 60–75, at pp. 64–65.

29   Gerald of Wales, *The Description of Wales* ii.10, ed. Dimock, p. 227: "Plurimam quippe animositatis scintillam exprimere, plurimam rebellionis audaciam imprimere potest continua pristinae nobilitatis memoria; et non solum Trojanae generositatis, verum etiam regni Britannici tantae et tam diuturnae regiae majestatis recordatio", translation in Gerald of Wales, *The Journey Through Wales* and *The Description of Wales*, trans. W.L. Williams, *The Itinerary Through Wales and the Description of Wales*, London, 1908, p. 205. See also J.P. Carley, "Arthur in English History", in W.R.J. Barron (ed.), *The Arthur of the English: The Arthurian Legend in Medieval English Life and Literature* (Arthurian Literature of the Middle Ages, 2), Cardiff, 1999, pp. 47–57.

30   Gerald recounts the discovery in the *Mirror of the Church* and *The Instruction of Princes*. See also Carley, "Arthur in English History", p. 44.

occasioned by anything more than his affronted historical sense".[31] Admittedly, in the *Description of Wales*, Gerald upbraided Geoffrey for error in terms which are a little ambiguous as to Geoffrey's intention to deceive, as opposed to mere ignorance: "The name of Wales was not derived from Wallo, a general, or Wandolena, the queen, as the fabulous history of Geoffrey Arthurius falsely maintains."[32] A characteristically Giraldian need to establish his superiority over Geoffrey's reliability seems to be signified in the prominent use of the passive voice in a (politically significant) Arthurian reference in the *Topography of Ireland*: "It can be read that Arthur, the fabled king of the Britons, received tribute from the kings of Ireland and that some of them attended his great court at Caerleon [the City of the Legions]."[33] But the much-repeated presumption of Gerald's hostility, or even contempt, for Geoffrey expressed in the tale of Meilyr cannot survive a more careful reading of the episode. It is striking that when the passage has been referred to by critics, it is generally presented in a heavily abridged form – it appears thus, for example, in Crick's article on Gerald's attitude to Geoffrey. In this abbreviated form it might appear that Gerald has "launched a devastating rhetorical attack on a compatriot and fellow writer".[34] When the passage is read in full, however, it becomes clearer that Geoffrey was not Gerald's primary inspiration or target in writing this scene. The passage presents an extended account of the difficulties and discomforts of consorting with demons which appear to have great powers to reveal deceit. Gerald is fascinated to consider the apparent paradox that, despite their ability to uncover human deception, demons are themselves unable to avoid error, or misleading their familiars:

31   Crick, "British Past", p. 60.
32   Gerald of Wales, *The Description of Wales* i.2, ed. Dimock, p. 179: "Wallia vero non a Walone duce, vel Wendoloena regina, sicut fabulosisa Galfridi Arthuri mentitur historia", Gerald of Wales, *The Journey Through Wales* and *The Description of Wales*, trans. Williams, p. 165. See also Ben Guy's contribution to this volume, pp. 31–66.
33   Gerald of Wales, *The Topography of Ireland* iii.8, ed. J.F. Dimock, *Giraldi Cambrensis Opera*, 8 vols., London, 1861–91, vol. 5, pp. 3–204, at p. 148: "'Legitur quoque famosum illum Britonum regem Arturum Hiberniae reges tributarios habuisse; et ad magnam etiam urbis Legonium curiam quosdam eorum accessisse." The effect is difficult to reproduce in English, so Wright, for example, loses the nuance: "we read also that Arthur, the famous king of the Britons, had the kings of Ireland tributary to him, and that some of them came to his court at the great city of Caerleon", Gerald of Wales, *The Journey Through Wales* and *The Description of Wales*, rev. T. Wright, trans. R.C. Hoare, *The Itinerary through Wales, and the Description of Wales, translated by Sir Richard Colt Hoare, Bart.*, London, 1863, p. 121.
34   Crick, "British Past", p. 60.

It is worthy of observation, that there lived in the neighborhood of this City of Legions, in our time, a Welshman named Melerius, who, under the following circumstances, acquired the knowledge of future and occult events. Having, on a certain night, namely that of Palm Sunday, met a damsel whom he had long loved, in a pleasant and convenient place, while he was indulging in her embraces, suddenly, instead of a beautiful girl, he found in his arms a hairy, rough, and hideous creature, the sight of which deprived him of his senses, and he became mad. After remaining many years in this condition, he was restored to health in the Church of St. David's, through the merits of its saints. But having always an extraordinary familiarity with unclean spirits, by seeing them, knowing them, talking with them, and calling each by his proper name, he was enabled, through their assistance, to foretell future events. He was, indeed, often deceived (as they are) with respect to circumstances at a great distance of time or place, but was less mistaken in affairs which were likely to happen nearer, or within the space of a year. The spirits appeared to him, usually on foot, equipped as hunters, with horns suspended from their necks, and truly as hunters, not of animals, but of souls. He particularly met them near monasteries and monastic cells; for where rebellion exists, there is the greatest need of armies and strength. He knew when any one spoke falsely in his presence, for he saw the devil, as it were, leaping and exulting upon the tongue of the liar. If he looked on a book faultily or falsely written, or containing a false passage, although wholly illiterate, he would point out the place with his finger. Being questioned how he could gain such knowledge, he said that he was directed by the demon's finger to the place. In the same manner, entering into the dormitory of a monastery, he indicated the bed of any monk not sincerely devoted to religion. He said, that the spirit of gluttony and surfeit was in every respect sordid; but that the spirit of luxury and lust was more beautiful than others in appearance, though in fact most foul. If the evil spirits oppressed him too much, the Gospel of St. John was placed on his bosom, when, like birds, they immediately vanished; but when that book was removed, and the History of the Britons, by Geoffrey Arthur, was substituted in its place, they instantly reappeared in greater numbers, and remained a longer time than usual on his body and on the book.[35]

---

35   Gerald of Wales, *The Journey Through Wales* i.5, ed. J.F. Dimock, *Giraldi Cambrensis Opera*, 8 vols., London, 1861–91, vol. 6, pp. 3–152, at pp. 57–58: "Notandum autem quod in his Urbis Legionum partibus fuit diebus nostris vir quidam Kambrensis, cui nomen Meilerius, futurorum pariter et occultorum scientiam habens; cui talis hanc eventus

Gerald's willingness to countenance the existence of magical or paranormal occurrences, and his unquestioning loyalty to the institutions of the church, render his judgements suspect. In this exemplum, Gerald's purpose is to contrast the limited and misleading powers of demons with the absolute authority of the church, in whose name the demons are obliged to flee. In context, it becomes clear that the reference to Geoffrey is merely tangential, rather than the primary purpose of the episode. The Gospel here functions simultaneously as a physical object, and as a figure of synecdoche, representing the full powers of the church, through hierarchy, liturgy, and sacrament. To infuse the scene with maximum power, Gerald needs an image, preferably a textual image, to contrast with the universal power of the Gospel, and it is perhaps a perverse compliment that he finds such an image in Geoffrey's text, chosen as the most popular and most influential Insular text in Latin known to Gerald. It is scarcely surprising that as ambitious and insecure a writer as Gerald could not resist a passing kick on the shins of a man who had so comprehensively laid claim to

---

scientiam dedit. Nocte quadam, scilicet Ramis palmarum, puellam diu ante adamatam, sicut forma praeferebat, obviam habens loco amoeno, et ut videbatur opportuno, desideratis amplexibus atque deliciis cum indulsisset, statim, loco puellae formosae, formam quamdam villosam, hispidam et hirsutam, adeoque enormiter deformem invenit, quod in ipso ejusdem aspectu dementire coepit et insanire. Cumque pluribus id annis ei durasset, tandem in ecclesia Menevensi, meritis sanctorum loci ejusdem, optatam sanitatem recuperavit. Semper tamen cum spiritibus immundis magnam et mirandam familiaritatem habens, eosdem videndo, cognoscendo, colloquendo, propriisque nominibus singulos nominando, ipsorum ministerio plerumque futura praedicebat. In longe vero futuris atque remotis, sicut et ipsi, frequentius fallebatur: in propinquioribus autem, et quasi infra annum futuris, minus falli consueverat. Videbat autem eos fere semper pedites et expeditos, et quasi sub forma venatorum, cornu a collo suspensum habentes, et vere venatores, non ferarum tamen nec animalium sed animarum. Circa monasteria quoque, et loca religiosa, magis eos et in multitudine majori videre solebat. Ibi nimirum exercitu, ibi numerosis opus est viribus, ubi rebellio. Quoties autem falsum coram ipso ab aliquo dicebatur, id statim agnoscebat: videbat enim super linguam mentientis daemonum quasi salientem et exultantem, Librum quoque mendosum, et vel falso scriptum, vel falsum etiam in se continentem inspiciens, statim, licet illiteratus omnino fuisset, ad locum mendacii digitum ponebat. Interrogatus autem, qualiter hoc nosset, dicebat daemonum ad locum eundem digitum suum primo porrigere. Similiter et dormitorium monasterii cujuslibet intrando, lectum monachi falsi, et religionem habitu non animo praeferentis, eisdem indiciis ostendebat. Dicebat autem spiritum gulositatis et crapulae supra et infra sordidum esse; spiritum vero libidinis et luxuriae pulchriorem aliis, sed foetidissimum. Contigit aliquando, spiritibus immundis nimis eidem insultantibus, ut Evangelium Johannis ejus in gremio poneretur: qui statim tanquam aves evolantes, omnes penitus evanuerunt. Quo sublato postmodum, et Historia Britonum a Galfrido Arthuro tractata, experiendi causa, loco ejusdem subrogata, non solum corpori ipsius toti, sed etiam libro superposito, longe solito crebrius et taediosius insederunt." Translation from Gerald of Wales, *The Journey Through Wales* and *The Description of Wales*, trans. Williams, pp. 52–53.

a body of literary material which he (and Walter Map) might otherwise have expected to claim as their own.

Gerald's balancing of Geoffrey against the Gospel reflects less a rejection of Geoffrey's historical method, and rather more a suspicion how far, in following the influence of classical writers, Geoffrey created a work which aspires to being, or could be characterized as, "secular". It is a term used by Hanning, interpreting Geoffrey's work as a development from the aesthetic of [pseudo] Nennius's *Historia Brittonum*.[36] A degree of caution is appropriate in using the term "secular", a term which requires nuanced differentiation of meaning in different historical contexts. But if, consciously or unconsciously, Gerald felt that, in comparison to the precedents set by Bede or Gildas, Geoffrey was engaged in a "systematic secularization of British history", then he would have found that direction of interpretation troubling, with its implicit challenge to the role of the church as the essential mediator of understanding.[37] The fear of secular or romance texts distracting monks and clerics from their vocation was frequently voiced in the Middle Ages.[38]

Whether or not Gerald feared an emerging secular hermeneutic revealed in Geoffrey's *DGB*, this would not have been his most pressing source of concern about Geoffrey's work.[39] The tale of Meilyr deals with the powers of demons to reveal the truth, and presumably the *DGB* was called into Gerald's mind due to the prominent role played by Merlin, whose prophetic powers were inherited from his demonic sire. If the *DGB* is, finally, ambivalent about the reliability of Merlin's gifts, the circulation of the *VM* seems to depend on the reliability of his prophecies. It is clear that Gerald did not reject the role of Merlin as being "fabulous" or "unhistorical" any more than Alan of Lille had. Typically, Gerald's

---

36   Hanning, *Vision*, p. 123.

37   Hanning, *Vision*, p. 23, n. 11.

38   It has generally been assumed that Ailred of Rievaulx's complaint on this topic contains a veiled reference to the *DGB*. See, for example, Loomis, *Arthurian Tradition*, p. 17: "In 1141–2 Ailred, then master of the novices at the Yorkshire abbey of Rievaulx, composed his *Speculum Caritatis*, in which he represents a novice as reproaching himself because, though in his past life he had frequently been moved to tears by fables which were invented and disseminated concerning an unknown Arthur (*fabulis quae vulgo de nescio quo finguntur Arcturo*), it was almost a miracle if he could extract a tear at a pious reading or discourse." The question whether the Arthur reference concerns Geoffrey's history or other, perhaps oral, circulating material has been considered by J. Tahkokallio, "Fables of King Arthur. Ailred of Rievaulx and Secular Pastimes", *Mirator* 9:1 (2008), 19–35.

39   J. Gillingham, "The Context and Purposes of Geoffrey of Monmouth's *History of the Kings of Britain*", *Anglo-Norman Studies* 13 (1990), 99–118 (repr. in id. (ed.), *The English in the Twelfth Century: Imperialism, National Identity and Political Values*, Woodbridge, 2000, pp. 19–39, at p. 21, n. 10): "That some readers were indeed disturbed by HRB's relatively secular and non-monastic tone is suggested by some early alterations to the text."

response to Merlin's prophecies is inconsistent. Southern notes Gerald's interest in the role of prophecy:

> [He] went further than anyone else in seeking unknown prophecies and
> trying to fit them into his contemporary histories. He seems to have had
> the idea of making a complete fusion between contemporary history and
> ancient Celtic prophecy, writing what he called a *Historia Vaticinalis*.[40]

On careful reading, Gerald's most vehement assault on Geoffrey proves to
be based not on a criticism of his historical accuracy but rather on whether
Geoffrey might have underestimated how far prophecies inspired by demons
were to be relied on.

Despite the inescapably memorable image of Meilyr beset by demons,
Gerald should not be considered the primary source of the vehemence with
which Geoffrey has been assaulted as a historian by 20th-century critics such
as Gransden or Loomis, who dubbed the DGB "one of the world's most brazen
and successful frauds".[41] Central to Loomis's interpretation is the attribution
to Geoffrey of a lack of belief in his own material which, it is then inferred,
must prove that Geoffrey consciously misrepresented the evidence available to
him in support of mendacious and misleading ideological objectives. In short,
Geoffrey has been arraigned for the unforgivable sin of being a historian in
bad faith.

It is both a more stringent and a more specific charge than Gerald's complaints about the *fabulosa* of Geoffrey's account, which might be the result of
exaggeration or excess credulity, and it is a complaint that unmistakably bears
the fingerprints of one writer who neither qualified nor concealed his scorn
for Geoffrey's work, William of Newburgh. In launching his own historical account, William felt obliged to pour scorn on a thicket of Galfridian alternatives.
He does so initially by criticizing the rigor of Geoffrey's literary procedure but,
when aiming what is designed as the *coup de grâce*, he chooses to denounce
Geoffrey's presumed political partiality:

> The venerable priest and monk Bede has composed a history of our race
> the English…. But in our own day a writer of the opposite tendency has
> emerged. To atone for these faults of the Britons he weaves a laughable
> web of fiction about them, with shameless vainglory extolling them far
> above the virtues of the Macedonians and the Romans. This man is called

---

40   R.W. Southern, *Medieval Humanism and Other Studies*, Oxford, 1970, p. 107.
41   Loomis, *Arthurian Tradition*, p. 17.

Geoffrey and bears the soubriquet Arthur, because he has taken up the stories about Arthur from the old fictitious accounts of the Britons, has added to them himself, and by embellishing them in the Latin tongue he has cloaked them with the honourable title of history. More audaciously still he has taken the most deceitful predictions of a certain Merlin which he has very greatly augmented on his own account, and in translating them into Latin he has published them as though they were authentic prophecies resting on unshakeable truth.[42]

However clumsily, in raising the question of Geoffrey's intentions, William draws attention to one of the most puzzling issues concerning Geoffrey's authorship. Modern critics have signally failed to determine what political agenda Geoffrey intended to promote, and there is little reason to suppose that his purposes would have seemed clearer in his own time. In so far as Geoffrey's history deviated from the "official" path of English self-aggrandizing history, it might seem obvious that the *DGB* would "please the Welsh". In fact, Welsh attitudes were, and have remained, ambivalent.[43] Geoffrey's importance was immediately recognized in the fulsome and continuing engagement with his works by Welsh commentators. For a few, Geoffrey's comments appeared supportive, a trend which reaches a highwater mark in Sir John Prise's *A Defense of the British History*, a mid-16th-century rejoinder to the skepticism of Polydore Vergil's *Anglica Historia*.[44]

---

42 Text and translation from William of Newburgh, *The History of English Affairs* Proemium §§2–3, ed. and trans. P.G. Walsh and M.J. Kennedy, *William of Newburgh: The History of English Affairs, Book I (Edited with Translation and Commentary)*, Warminster, 1988, pp. 28–29: "Historiam gentis nostrae, id est Anglorum, venerabilis presbyter et monachus Beda conscripsit.... At contra quidam nostris temporibus pro expiandis his Britonum maculis scriptor emersit ridicula de eisdem figmenta contexens, eosque longe supra virtutem Macedonum et Romanorum impudenti vanitate attollens. Gaufridus hic dictus est agnomen habens Arturi, pro eo quod fabulas de Arturo ex priscis Britonum figmentis sumptas et ex proprio auctas per superductum Latini sermonis colorem honesto historiae nomine palliavit: qui etiam majori ausu cujusdam Merlini divinationes quam authenticas et immobili veritate subnixas prophetias vulgavit."

43 For how slowly Galfridian influence can be detected in Welsh Arthurian literature, see O.J. Padel, *Arthur in Medieval Welsh Literature*, Cardiff, 2000, pp. 54–55: "There are several unexpected features of the Arthurian allusions in the twelfth-century court poetry. One of these is their small number. Arthur himself is named seven times in the poetry down to 1200, but hardly any of his warriors receives more than a single mention.... A further unexpected feature is that most of the Arthurian references are found in the work of only two poets."

44 John Prise, *Historiae Britannicae Defensio*, ed. and trans. C. Davies, *Historiae Britannicae Defensio. A Defense of the British History*, Oxford and Toronto, 2015.

Often, though, Welsh responses to Geoffrey seem colored with an insecurity that it was not Geoffrey's intention to laud the Welsh, a misgiving which has solidified into a conviction in the comments of modern Welsh critics. Characteristic is Brynley Roberts' judgement that "the later history of the Welsh ... was held in scant respect by him [Geoffrey]."[45] Furthermore, a key element of this Welsh ambivalence toward Geoffrey derives from the implications of the Arthurian section of the work, which might seem the most positive epoch of British history dealt with. Despite its high moral striving, the story of Arthur is one of (glorious) defeat, which offers limited precedent for hopes of Welsh disengagement from the English crown. The name of Arthur never became popular as a personal name in Wales, and it seems unlikely that the myth of Arthur's return was ever much consolation for Welsh setbacks.[46] There is no evidence of Welsh leaders invoking the spirit of a returning Arthur, for example, during the "anarchy" during the reign of King Stephen which coincided with the work's composition. Yet, as John Davies notes, some elements of the history could not fail to be of interest:

> His theme is Britain under Brythonic rule, and it was natural therefore that it should be of absorbing interest to the Welsh. It was frequently translated into Welsh; there are in existence about eighty manuscripts of *Brut y Brenhinedd* (The Chronicle of the Kings) – the name given to the Welsh version of Geoffrey's work – and *Brut y Tywysogion* was planned as its sequel.[47]

It was perhaps the opening account of the arrival of exiles from Troy which guaranteed Geoffrey's importance in Wales, leading to the regular appearance together of *Brut y Brenhinedd* ("History of the Kings") and *Brut y Tywysogyon* ("History of the Princes"), often accompanied by *Ystorya Dared*, a translation of Dares Phrygius's purported eyewitness account of the fall of Troy.[48] The exhaustive account of Welsh origins to be synthesized from these texts

---

45   Roberts, "Geoffrey of Monmouth, *Historia regum Britanniae*, and *Brut y Brenhinedd*", p. 98. Similarly, R.R. Davies concludes that "Geoffrey's *History* shows scant sympathy for the Welsh"; *Conquest, Coexistence and Change: Wales, 1063–1415*, Oxford, 1987, p. 106.

46   The idea of Arthur's possible return does not appear in the *DGB*, though it is mentioned in the *VM*. Admittedly, the tendency to circulate the two texts together would have tended to blur this important distinction.

47   J. Davies, *A History of Wales*, Harmondsworth, 2007, pp. 119–20.

48   H. Fulton, "Troy Story: The Medieval Welsh *Ystorya Dared* and the *Brut* Tradition of British History", in J. Dresvina and N. Sparks (eds.), *The Medieval Chronicle VII*, Amsterdam, 2011, pp. 137–50.

in close proximity is found, for example, in the Red Book of Hergest.[49] If the myth of Arthur as *Rex futurus* ever cheered the Welsh, it was not until after the Edwardian full annexation of *pura Wallia* redrew the relationship between Wales and England. In the 15th century, maybe some of the supporters of Owain Glyn Dŵr saw King Arthur as an inspiration, but it was Henry Tudor's supporters who promoted their man as the *mab darogan* – the son of prophecy – whose forces fought under the banner of the red dragon.[50]

It is clear that William of Newburgh protests too much. So why has William's display of petulance been treated with such respect for so long? There are two plausible explanations. The first is that his account offers welcome clarity in interpreting Geoffrey's purposes, even if it is a clarity that cannot withstand scrutiny.[51] A survey of more recent critics shows few convinced that Geoffrey's work favors, or was intended to favor, the Welsh. Generally, it has been assumed that Geoffrey's goal was to serve the ideological purposes of the ruling elite, that is, the Normans, enabling them to appropriate material from the British past to use as a cultural weapon to subjugate both the English and the British. It is a view clearly articulated by Helen Fulton:

> Geoffrey's method of seeking the origins of the present in the past worked very successfully to create an authentic British history for the Norman kings of his own time.... The myth of Arthur, then, supports the myths of Norman legitimacy in Britain. Carefully distinguished from the usurping and treacherous Saxons, the Normans are positioned by Geoffrey as the true heirs of Arthur's Britain – and his empire.[52]

Gransden, always an implacable critic of Geoffrey, imputes reluctance to his dealing with the topic at all:

> Undoubtedly ... Geoffrey chose to write about the ancient Britons because he wanted to demonstrate the cyclical view of history. However, he may also have chosen them by default, because, though wishing to provide the Anglo-Normans with glorious predecessors in Britain, he was

---

49   See Owain Wyn Jones's contribution to this volume, pp. 257–90.

50   See Maud Burnett McInerney's contribution to this volume, pp. 129–52.

51   In contrast, John Gillingham suggests that the *DGB* is "so full of material of different kinds that almost anyone who reads it with a particular interest in mind will be able to pick out passages which support their own interpretation"; "Context and Purposes", p. 19.

52   H. Fulton, "History and Myth: Geoffrey of Monmouth's *Historia Regum Britanniae*", in ead. (ed.), *A Companion to Arthurian Literature*, Chichester, 2008, pp. 44–57, at p. 48.

unable to extoll the Anglo-Saxons, *personae non gratae* with the ruling class of his day.[53]

Appearing to praise the "ancient" British seems to be the price to be paid for promoting the interests of the Anglo-Normans. It is perhaps surprising that Gillingham might seem to come closer to rehabilitating William of Newburgh's view: "Geoffrey was a Welshman whose object was to secure cultural respectability for his own nation."[54] But compared to William's vehemence, Gillingham proposes a much more qualified conclusion. He does not choose to deny that "HRB contains strains which would have struck a chord with the ruling elite" since this is not incompatible with his conclusion that Geoffrey did not write to praise the Welsh.[55] Rather, Gillingham presents Geoffrey as writing in rejoinder to a rising discourse, which dismisses the Welsh as *barbari*, "barbarians", and which he attributes to, or associates with, William of Malmesbury. Gillingham regards this characterization of the Welsh as being, in William of Malmesbury's work, "a relatively new point of view, one that is becoming fashionable and powerful" while "by the second half of the twelfth century this view had become the standard one".[56]

This changing, and increasingly contemptuous, attitude to the Welsh and Irish is widely rehearsed in Anglo-Norman written sources of the 12th century and it seems certain that it must have exerted an influence on Geoffrey's intention to write.[57] But it is harder to be sure of Geoffrey's place within this discourse. Gillingham contests Tatlock's famous claim that Geoffrey showed "contempt for the Welsh", but concedes that "this view is widely held, especially, interestingly enough, among the leading Welsh scholars of Welsh medieval history."[58] Nonetheless, it is still surprising to read Faletra's claim that,

---

53   A. Gransden, review of R.W. Hanning, *The Vision of History in Early Britain: From Gildas to Geoffrey of Monmouth*, *Catholic Historical Review* 55 (1969), 272–73.
54   Gillingham, "Context and Purposes", p. 20, quoting G. Barrow, "Wales and Scotland in the Middle Ages", *WHR* 10 (1980–81), 303–19, at p. 305.
55   Gillingham, "Contexts and Purposes", p. 21.
56   Gillingham, "Contexts and Purposes", p. 28, p. 27.
57   So, for example, John of Salisbury, discussed in S. Meecham-Jones, "Where Was Wales? The Erasure of Wales in Medieval English Culture", in R. Kennedy and S. Meecham-Jones (eds.), *Authority and Subjugation in Writing of Medieval Wales*, New York, 2008, pp. 27–55, at pp. 40–41.
58   Gillingham, "Context and Purposes", p. 24; Tatlock, *LHB*, p. 443; J.E. Lloyd, *A History of Wales from the Earliest Times to the Edwardian Conquest*, 2 vols., 3rd ed., London, 1939, vol. 2, p. 528; R.R. Davies, *Conquest*, p. 106; *Trioedd Ynys Prydein: The Triads of the Island of Britain*, ed. and trans. R. Bromwich, 4th ed., Cardiff, 2014, p. 399.

far from combatting the rise of anti-Welsh discourse in 12th-century Norman (or English) culture, Geoffrey's work is close to being the *fons et origo* of the discourse Gillingham describes:

> Geoffrey's *Historia Regum Britanniae*, one of the most popular and influential books of the European Middle Ages, almost single-handedly establishes the template with which Anglo-Norman and later English writers imagined and manipulated the relationship between England and its Welsh periphery.... Amid all (and, indeed, because of) its ambiguities and subterfuges, the *Historia* ultimately justifies the Normans and denigrates the Welsh.[59]

I have argued elsewhere that the developing anti-Welsh discourse of the 12th century was comprised of four major elements, which might be characterized as the discourse of Britishness, the discourse of peripherality, the discourse of authority, and the discourse of racial inferiority.[60] Unquestionably, the discourse of Britishness is central to the DGB and Geoffrey must be considered a significant and innovative promoter of what was to prove an influential weapon in the justification of English involvement in Wales.

But Faletra makes the far broader claim that in "Geoffrey's *Historia* [as] in no other text of Anglo-Latin or Anglo-Norman provenance ... all four ... colonial discourses reinforce each other so effectively".[61] An examination of the text makes this claim hard to substantiate. The discourse of peripherality is invoked from the beginning of the work, but it is the peripherality of Britain, rather than that of Wales, which is being asserted. Moreover, there is a certain defiance in Geoffrey's handling of the idea, paradoxically asserting the achievements of "peripheral" Britain, figured through repeated triumphs over

---

59 M.A. Faletra, *Wales and the Medieval Colonial Imagination: The Matters of Britain in the Twelfth Century*, New York, 2014, p. 16.

60 S. Meecham-Jones, "Introduction", in Kennedy and Meecham-Jones (eds.), *Authority and Subjugation*, pp. 1–11, at p. 2: "The cultural justification for the seizure of Wales was swiftly refined into four key concepts: the discourse of peripherality, the discourse of Britishness, the discourse of authority and discourse of racial inferiority. The discourse of peripherality drew attention to Wales's perceived status at the margins of European civilization. The discourse of Britishness proclaimed the 'natural' unity of the island(s) of Britain, inferring from physical continuity an inevitable political unity. The discourse of authority asserted the right of England to rule Wales by virtue of tradition, God's favor, and England's greater civilization. Allied to this myth was the myth of the racial inferiority of the Welsh (and Irish)."

61 Faletra, *Wales*, p. 34.

Rome, the city which, in its own estimation, represents the center of human civilization.

More contentious is Faletra's claim that the discourse of Welsh racial inferiority, an idea which Gillingham insists is a 12th-century development, is "fairly easy to detect throughout Geoffrey's *Historia Regum Britanniae*".[62] If that were true, William of Newburgh's counter-claim would seem absurd. In fact, Faletra's certainty rests on what he perceives as Geoffrey's portrayal of "the barbarity that marks the final transformation of Britons into Welshmen".[63] But even at the end of the *DGB*, Geoffrey's attention is barely involved by the Welsh. It is far from clear, also, that William would have recognized any suggested distinction between the Welsh and the Britons, since his claim for Geoffrey's partiality to the Welsh rests on his ascription of glory to the Britons, rather than its denial to their relict, the Welsh. Geoffrey's restricted engagement with the Welsh permits his text to function, not, as Faletra suggests, as a "vehicle for ideology", but rather as a plausible vehicle for wholly opposed ideologies.[64] Far more sensitive to the daring idiosyncrasy of Geoffrey's style and intention is Monika Otter's reading: "While the *Historia* is in many ways deeply and consciously political, and has a number of strong political points to make, it is not ... directly in the service of a single institution or faction."[65] She acknowledges that Geoffrey's carefully managed distancing of himself from ideological capture should be read not as evidence of his incapacity as a writer, but rather as evidence of his thoughtful and mature understanding of the form he is working with, and, perhaps, of the nature of his audience. Whether or not Flint is correct in the presumption that "it was found difficult to interpret as soon as it appeared", there is, and has presumably always been, a disjuncture between what Geoffrey's text attempts to achieve, and the expectations of much of its readership, which have caused it to be misunderstood.[66] For those interested in British cultural and political history, from Gerald and William of Newburgh to (from their different perspectives) Gransden and Faletra, the *DGB* has generally been read as a commentary on the exercise of power over the Britons and/or Welsh by the English.[67] In the hands of English kings, lawyers, and historians, the text has often served as a means of furthering that process.

---

62   Faletra, *Wales*, p. 36.

63   Faletra, *Wales*, p. 35.

64   Faletra, *Wales*, p. 34.

65   M. Otter, *Inventiones: Fiction and Referentiality in Twelfth-Century Historical Writing*, Chapel Hill, 1996, p. 75.

66   V.I.J. Flint, "The *Historia Regum Britanniae* of Geoffrey of Monmouth: Parody and Its Purpose. A Suggestion", *Speculum* 54:3 (1979), 447–68, at p. 447.

67   A. Gransden, *Historical Writing in England, c.550–c.1307*, London, 1974.

It would be wrong, though, to read the purpose of the work from the ways in which it has been used. William's fear of the text pleasing the Welsh reveals a fundamental misreading in its failure to recognize Geoffrey's reluctance to point the narrative with moralizing summaries (as Gerald, for example, would surely have done).

The Europe-wide popularity of the *DGB* reminds us that Geoffrey's work captured many different audiences. British critics and readers may have read the text as a commentary on the exercise of authority in Britain, but their concerns do not mark out the limits of Geoffrey's observation of the workings of history or the expressive potential of narrative. Furthermore, as the text traveled to readers in Spain, Germany, and Italy, specifically "British" references lost their immediacy and the centrality that William, like Gransden, presumed they demanded. Even in the work of Chrétien de Troyes, references to Wales or to place-names presumably derived from Welsh display no more engagement with Welsh topography than with the political condition of Wales and its people. There must have been great variation in the extent to which the *DGB* was read with any expectation of disinterest, a point obscured by William's comments. In considering the value of contemporary judgements of Geoffrey's style and his intended purpose it is important to recognize both that, from its composition, Geoffrey's text was often misunderstood, and that he must have anticipated that it would be. Less clear is how far he might have welcomed this interpretative distance between text and audience.

Such an idea seems to lie behind the theory, presented by Christopher Brooke and developed by Valerie Flint, of Geoffrey as an accomplished literary practitioner, taking a delight in writing against the expectations of his audience.[68] But Flint's admiration for Geoffrey as an "artist" lead her to two disappointingly limited conclusions – that Geoffrey is "a parodist of enormous skill" and that his "profound" purpose was to exaggerate "certain trends in historical writing ... to mock that literature and confound its authors" with the intention of "call[ing] into question the position held and hoped for in twelfth-century Anglo-Norman society by literate and celibate canons regular and monks".[69] There is a tension between Flint's belief that she has justified Geoffrey's status as a serious creative innovator – "The *Historia Regum Britanniae* emerged from this analysis as a heightened and artistic form of a developed historiographical

---

68   C.N.L. Brooke, "Geoffrey of Monmouth as a Historian", in C.N.L. Brooke, D. Luscombe, G. Martin, and D. Owen (eds.), *Church and Government in the Middle Ages: Essays Presented to C.R. Cheney on his 70th Birthday*, Cambridge, 1976, 77–91 (repr. in *The Church and the Welsh Border in the Central Middle Ages*, ed. D.N. Dumville (Studies in Celtic History, 8), Woodbridge, 1986, 95–107); Flint, "Parody and Purpose", pp. 448–50.

69   Flint, "Parody and Purpose", p. 449.

movement" – and the limitations inherent in the identification of his work as "parody".[70] There are several problems with what seems at first an ingenious rehabilitation of Geoffrey's work. The primary problem lies in Flint's choice of the word "parody", a word which has a longstanding history associated with satire and some deprecation of the text being parodied, and, in recent literary theory, a more restricted (but contested) meaning, initially derived from the Russian formalists, and developed by Jameson and others to describe postmodern practices of writing. This second meaning might be demonstrated by Hutcheon's attempt to distinguish parody from more ideologically charged forms of imitation:

> It will be clear by now that what I am calling parody here is not just that ridiculing imitation mentioned in the standard dictionary definitions.... Parody, therefore, is a form of imitation, but imitation characterized by ironic inversion, not always at the expense of the parodied text.[71]

The definition is not ideally clear, partly since it defines parody by what it may not always be – not always at the expense of the parodied text – but it is not clear how much such a definition would add to a description of a text we know to be influenced by prior texts. Nor does it add much to a description of how the *DGB* differs from its models.

Since Flint does not establish that she intends the more restricted meaning of parody, it seems sensible to see if applying the more general meaning sheds more light, but that also raises problems. It must be admitted that the first, or lasting, impression of the *DGB* is not that it reads as a comic or playful work. Admittedly, such a tone would have been difficult to sustain in a work that the readers know in advance will end in defeat and conquest, but it cannot be argued that comedy is one of Geoffrey's literary trademarks. Further, there is an irony in the disjunction between Flint's contention that "Geoffrey's desire to display his literary gifts is indeed the motive most in evidence in the *Historia*", albeit with the qualification that Geoffrey "did not use history purely in the service of parody", and her characterization of him as a parodist.[72] Implicit in this definition is the presumption that, for whatever literary purpose, Geoffrey presented a version of events which he knew or believed to be misleading or untrue. It is a conclusion that allies her with those she describes as being

---

70   Flint, "Parody and Purpose", p. 448.
71   L. Hutcheon, *A Theory of Parody: The Teachings of Twentieth-Century Art*, London, 1985, p. 5.
72   Flint, "Parody and Purpose", p. 449.

"inclined to be indulgent [who] saw Geoffrey's 'romanticism' as forgivable by reason of artistic license",[73] but in practice it does not mark out a great distance from Grandsen's charge that "Geoffrey was a romance writer masquerading as a historian",[74] or, indeed, William of Newburgh's attacks on Geoffrey as a liar. Flint's reading does not undermine, though it presumably intended to, the damaging tradition that Geoffrey is a writer, or certainly a historian, in "bad faith".[75]

Fortunately, William of Newburgh's other charges prove unexpectedly valuable in uncovering the sophistication and ambition of Geoffrey's work. William presents Geoffrey as dishonest partly because his account is not supported by the recognized authoritative source of Bede's *Ecclesiastical History*:

> Since these events accord with the historical truth as expounded by the Venerable Bede, it is clear that Geoffrey's entire narration about Arthur, his successors, and his predecessors after Vortigern, was invented partly by himself and partly by others. The motive was either an uncontrolled passion for lying, or secondly a desire to please the Britons, most of whom are ... said to be still awaiting the future coming of Arthur, being unwilling to entertain the fact of his death.[76]

William's argument underestimates the skill with which Geoffrey makes his way around this leviathan of authority, acknowledging Bede's status and not directly challenging his account, while at the same time presenting a great body of narrative which Bede must be presumed to have omitted, if not suppressed. But it is interesting to see how William accepts Bede's text, although it deals with history rather than theology *per se* as an absolute authority which cannot be challenged, almost as if it were holy writ. It is an argument accepted

---

73 Flint, "Parody and Purpose", p. 448.

74 Gransden, *Historical Writing*, p. 202.

75 Again, we might contrast Southern's more generous conclusion in *History and Historians*, p. 25: "It is highly likely that in his treatment of his sources, whether literary or traditional, he used the freedom of invention that the literary tradition of historical writing allowed. But we may also think that like other writers in this tradition he used his freedom in the interests of some larger truth."

76 Text and translation from William of Newburgh, *The History of English Affairs* Proemium §9, ed. and trans. Walsh and Kennedy, pp. 32–33: "Haec cum juxta historicam veritatem a venerabili Beda expositam constet esse rata, cuncta quae homo ille de Arturo et ejus vel successoribus vel post Vortigirnum praedecessoribus scribere curavit partim ab ipso, partim et ab aliis constat esse conficta, sive effrenata mentiendi libidine sive etiam gratia placendi Britonibus, quorum plurimi tam bruti esse feruntur ut adhuc Arturum tanquam venturum exspectate dicantur, eumque mortuum nec audire patiantur."

at face value by Peter Damian-Grint who similarly relies on the authority of Bede to describe William's account as "scrupulously scholarly":

> William's attack on Geoffrey, which is nothing if not vitriolic, is at the same time scrupulously scholarly; his arguments are based on contemporary concepts of *auctoritas*. Geoffrey is a liar because he contradicts or at least disagrees with Bede, the *auctor auctorum* of early British history ... The fact that Geoffrey has had the impudence to cover his lies with the veil of Latin merely makes matters worse, as he is perverting the language of authority to give an appearance of truth to his deceits.[77]

William's attack on Geoffrey's use of Latin is revealing, again showing his belief in the binding power of "authoritative" texts. In this we might see William as a characteristic figure of his time. Brian Stock has identified a crucial change in the understanding of textual culture this period:

> Before the year 1000 – an admittedly arbitrary point in time – there existed both oral and written traditions in medieval culture. But throughout the eleventh and twelfth centuries an important transformation began to take place. The written did not simply supersede the oral, although that happened in large measure: a new type of interdependence also arose between the two. In other words, oral discourse effectively began to function within a universe of communications governed by texts.[78]

Stock describes a developing expectation in which "texts ... emerged as a reference system both for everyday activities and for giving shape to many larger vehicles of explanation", and this process can be seen at work in William's reasoning.[79] Latin had always played an important part in Brythonic and then Welsh textual history, from its Romano-British days, and we should not be expected to believe that William was unaware of this.[80] Rather, it was a fact which disrupted William's sense of what was appropriate in the "sacred" language.

---

77   P. Damian-Grint, *The New Historians of the Twelfth-Century Renaissance: Inventing Vernacular Authority*, Woodbridge, 1999, p. 45.

78   B. Stock, *The Implications of Literacy: Written Language and Models of Interpretation in the Eleventh and Twelfth Centuries*, Princeton, 1983, p. 3.

79   Stock, *The Implications of Literacy*, p. 3.

80   The use of Latin in Welsh manuscripts is considered by Huws, *Medieval Welsh Manuscripts* and G. Henley, "From 'The Matter of Britain' to 'The Matter of Rome': Latin literary culture and the reception of Geoffrey of Monmouth in Wales", *AL* 33 (2016), 1–28.

We might draw a parallel with William's apparently surprising approval of the violation of sanctuary enacted by Hubert Walter, archbishop of Canterbury, who ordered the burning of the Church of St Mary Arches in London in 1193. In considering William's response, Gillingham begins by repeating the praise of modern critics for William's perceived "even-handedness", a reputation dependent in part on his assault on Geoffrey of Monmouth.[81] Having noted William's criticism of "Roger of Salisbury, Roger of Pont L'Eveque, archbishop of York, Hugh du Puiset, bishop of Durham, William Longchamp, bishop of Ely, Walter of Coutances, bishop of Lincoln and archbishop of Rouen, Geoffrey, archbishop of York and Robert, abbot of Caen",[82] Gillingham (perhaps with his tongue in his cheek) struggles to explain why William "wrote about Hubert Walter in extraordinarily positive terms",[83] leading him to the conclusion that:

> It can hardly be doubted that sources close to Philip of Poitou would have sympathized with the actions taken by Hubert Walter in April 1196, and it seems likely that it was from such government circles that William of Newburgh derived an interpretation of the events of that month so much at odds with his usual line on the morality of ecclesiastics meddling in secular politics. There can hardly be a better illustration of the efficiency with which Hubert Walter's administration dealt with protest than the way it used scandalous tales of sex and blasphemy in order to destroy an opponent's reputation and so persuade even as independent-minded and critical a historian as William of Newburgh.[84]

We could read William's willingness to excuse Hubert Walter's conduct as a symptom of his highly developed respect for hierarchical authority. The reassertion of this authority was to be a key struggle within the 12th century, and one which was caused in part by the changing understanding of the role of textual witnesses, in the transition between what Stock characterizes as "a nonliterate to a literate society".[85] Stock notes that, during such a process,

---

81   J. Gillingham, "The Historian as Judge: William of Newburgh and Hubert Walter", *EHR* 119:484 (2004), 1275–87, at pp. 1275–76.
82   Gillingham, "Historian as Judge", p. 1276.
83   Gillingham, "Historian as Judge", p. 1277. One might contrast this with Gerald of Wales, whose judgement of Hubert was so critical that he eventually felt obliged to write "*retractiones*" which acknowledge, though they do not wholly modify, the harshness of his criticism. Gerald of Wales, *Invectives* i.4, ed. W.S. Davies, "De Invectionibus", *Y Cymmrodor* 30 (1920), 1–248, at p. 97; Gerald of Wales, *Retractions*, ed. J.S. Brewer, *Giraldi Cambrensis Opera*, 8 vols., London, 1861–91, vol. 1, pp. 425–27, at pp. 426–27.
84   Gillingham, "Historian as Judge", pp. 1286–87.
85   Stock, *Implications of Literacy*, p. 9.

"as methods of interpretation were increasingly subjected to systematic scrutiny, the models employed to give meaning to otherwise unrelated disciplines more and more clustered around the concept of written language."[86] William's critique of Geoffrey might be seen as one exercise of systematic scrutiny.

Over time, the shift toward a text-based society would create a need for secular scribes, but in its early days, literacy was almost exclusively the preserve of the church, and this decisively influenced the nature of how ideas of the authority of the text developed. Clerical culture stressed the primacy of theology, and other disciplines were made subject to its predominance. This process involved not merely philosophy and rhetoric, but also history, a pattern of integration which is central to the design of Bede's *Ecclesiastical History*, but not to Geoffrey's.[87] In William's use of Bede's text as a measure to declare Geoffrey's text dishonest, we see an exposition of the view that literary authority is absolute, disqualifying all other possibilities. It is a claim which derives from, parallels, and supports the church's own claim to an absolute authority of understanding.

But William is a generation or more later than Geoffrey, and from a different regional tradition of the church in Britain. The 12th century saw the church set up increasingly systematic and harsh procedures to ensure that theological speculation did not overstep the bounds of propriety. These procedures were as much about maintaining hierarchical discipline as preventing the promulgation of error. As Peter Godman puts it, "authority rather than doctrine was the nub of the matter."[88]

In contrast, Geoffrey's work is infused with a skepticism about authority, for which he has been given insufficient credit. From his opening reference to the gaps in Bede's *Ecclesiastical History*, Geoffrey challenges the claim of literary authority to be absolute. Perhaps instinctively, or perhaps recognizing trends already gathering force in the church, Geoffrey seems to resist the ecclesiastical pressure to contain and censor what texts could be permitted to exist:

> In the ample embrace of Ecclesia, there was room for intellectuals. They earned it by knowing their place. Cautious not to trespass into territory that the hierarchy had declared beyond bounds, they were free to enjoy that measure of liberty defined by their acceptance of *auctoritas*.[89]

---

86   Stock, *Implications of Literacy*, p. 3.

87   Hanning cites the importance of Eusebius in annexing Roman history as an adjunct to the history of the church: *Vision*, pp. 20–28.

88   P. Godman, *The Silent Masters: Latin Literature and its Censors in the High Middle Ages*, Princeton, 2000, p. 12.

89   Godman, *Silent Masters*, p. 14.

Geoffrey's importance derives in large part from his refusal to "know his place". He may have been fortunate in the time he chose to write. Probably, the conflict between Stephen and Matilda caused some loosening of central supervision and authority in England. It is noticeable, also, that Geoffrey's text was composed and circulated a few years before the Council of Sens in 1141, which climaxed in the public denunciation and burning of Abelard's treatise on the Trinity.[90] Though not the first of its kind, the council proved a significant and much-noted proof of the church's concern to maintain full control of written culture. Abelard had been a very prominent teacher, fêted for his intellectual mastery, whereas Geoffrey's obscurity, in a province of the church regarded as isolated and obscure, might also have made it easier for Geoffrey to question the absolute nature of literary authority, but it seems William of Newburgh was perhaps the only commentator to have any recognition, however rudimentary, of the challenge Geoffrey was formulating.

In his *DGB*, Geoffrey expounded an alternative vision of literary authority, in which no one discourse could, by its presence, deny the possibility of other, perhaps not yet written, discourses. It was an idea which proved of central importance in the Europe-wide popularity of his work. At a time when the church was concerned to interpret the past through the overarching pattern of a universal history built on the foundations of Roman imperial history, Geoffrey declared both the possibility and the value of a myriad of national and local histories, not necessarily incompatible with, but certainly concealed by, this "authorized" structure. William had feared that Geoffrey was giving a voice to the Welsh, but his influence spread far wider than that, as Geoffrey implicitly licensed the preservation of previously untextualized histories in France, Germany, and beyond. Geoffrey set himself against the presumption that only the center of the "civilized" world (figured in his writings as "Rome") was worthy of textualization. His anti-hierarchical interpretation of literary authority provided a ledge for the obscured and the ignored to record their presence, even providing a narrative context for the Jews of central Europe to integrate their concerns within a resolutely European literary archetype.[91] The influence of Geoffrey's ideas can be seen, also, in the cumulative, rather than hierarchical, growth of Arthurian literature(s). Often, as in Chrétien's contribution, new strands of narrative were added which adapted the material to distinctive local

---

90   The dating of the council to 1141, rather than 1140, has been confirmed by C.J. Mews, "The Council of Sens 1141: Abelard, Bernard and the Fear of Social Upheaval", *Speculum* 79:2 (2002), 342–83.

91   *King Artus*, ed. C. Leviant, *King Artus. A Hebrew Arthurian Romance of 1279*, Syracuse, 2003; J.C. Frakes, *Early Yiddish Epics*, Syracuse, 2014.

requirements but which (generally) did not disrupt the foundational structure of the Arthurian story, even if the additions inflected the mood and perhaps the meaning of the story.

Geoffrey's name has endured in literary histories due to his seminal influence in making the Arthurian *topos* available to many centuries of later writers, in a variety of languages, but ideological concerns about his presentation of the Britons still seems to hamper an appreciation of the innovation and significance of his literary practice. Writing at a time when the transition from an oral to a text-based society encouraged fantasies of excluding from textual expression any ideas not promoted by those at the top of the clerical hope, Geoffrey deserves overdue praise, both as a literary theorist and as a much-imitated practitioner, as a crucial figure who resisted the closing of the shutters of literary speculation and expression in the name of literary authority.

CHAPTER 7

The Latin Reception of the *De gestis Britonum*

Siân Echard

Gerald of Wales famously skewered the veracity of Geoffrey of Monmouth's history in his story of Meilyr, an illiterate man who could spot falsehood, thanks to devils dancing on the offending tongues or pages. Meilyr's tormentors could be driven away by the Gospel of John, but when a copy of the *De gestis Britonum* was placed on his lap, the devils returned in ever greater numbers. Gerald's anecdote, written in his *Itinerary Through Wales* in the 1190s, is a witness to the incredible popularity of the *DGB* less than 50 years after Geoffrey's death, and that popularity would only grow, as the story was taken up in the vernacular translations discussed in Chapter Eight. Gerald's skepticism is of a piece with the reactions from other Latin authors dealt with in Chapter Six, but as the present chapter will show, the rise of Arthurian literature as a vernacular phenomenon, and the dismissal of Geoffrey's work (and Arthur's historicity) by some Anglo-Latin historians, give a potentially misleading impression about the importance that the *DGB* continued to have in the Latin tradition, well into the early modern period. First, while the centrality of the Arthuriad to the *DGB* cannot be overstated, Geoffrey is also responsible for promulgating several other highly popular and influential myths, of interest to both Latinate and vernacular readers in the Middle Ages and beyond; that is, Geoffrey's importance reaches beyond the Arthurian tradition. And second, while some Latin writers may have reacted negatively to Geoffrey's work, others set about commenting on it, supplementing it, and even writing their own Latin Arthurian narratives. This chapter will explore the many ways that the Latin tradition, both medieval and early modern, interacted with Geoffrey's myth-making through commentary, continuation, and outright creation.

1   Commentary

There are well over 200 surviving manuscripts of the *DGB*, ranging from small and modest, to large and elaborate.[1] In addition to the early manuscript

---

[1]   The bulk of the manuscripts are described in Crick, *SC*. There have been more manuscripts discovered since; see J. Crick, "Two Newly Located Manuscripts of Geoffrey of Monmouth's

tradition discussed in Chapter Five, there are many late medieval manuscripts that provide valuable evidence of how Geoffrey's work was being read, well into the 15th century. Some of the manuscripts, both early and late, have marginal notations added by contemporary and later readers, and in these clusters of annotation, we can see which of Geoffrey's stories were marked for attention. Attention can mean several things, of course. Many of the annotations discussed below are single words, and might serve as quick locators for particular parts of the text. Point of production glosses of this type can be understood as anticipating a particular readerly interest, even pre-constructing that interest. Later glosses show interest in action, as readers mark up a text according to their own focus, either creating an apparatus or supplementing an original one which in the end failed to anticipate their needs. There are also longer annotations, including original rubrics and later explanatory or responsive notes.[2] In all these kinds of activity, we can see traces of the reception of Geoffrey's text.

There is certainly interest, both anticipated and actual, in the Arthurian portion of the history. For example, even lightly-annotated manuscripts will often have a note on Arthur's conception and his death. Some of these notes were made at the time of production, as an integral part of the design. In London, British Library, Additional 15732, fol. 78r, for example, *De morte arturi*, "On the death of Arthur", appears in the margin next to the account of Arthur's death, in the same hand as the rest of the manuscript. This manuscript also has a manicule (the pointing hand that medieval and early modern readers often used to emphasize important passages) next to the story of Arthur's conception. Manicules can be difficult to date, but the manuscript in any case indicates that someone thought it important to pick out the beginning and the end of Arthur's story.

Arthur's weapons also attract annotation. London, British Library, Arundel 237 (Figure 7.1), a 13th-century manuscript, has notes beside the references to Arthur's shield and sword in the arming description, and also draws attention, on the same folio, to how many men he killed in a single day. This is a fairly heavily annotated manuscript, but Arthur's weapons may also be picked out in much more lightly-annotated copies. London, British Library, Arundel 319 (Figure 7.2), for example, has few glosses, but one is the marginal *Pridwen* (that is, the name of Arthur's shield) on fol. 89r, in the original scribe's hand, in red, next to the weapon description. This is a careful, clearly-planned original note, but more casual, after-the-fact additions in manuscripts show a similar

---

Historia regum Britanniae", *AL* 13 (1995), 151–56, and J. Tahkokallio, "Update to the List of Manuscripts of Geoffrey of Monmouth's *Historia regum Britanniae*", *AL* 32 (2015), 187–203.

2   Julia Crick offers an overview of the rubrics in Crick, *DR*, pp. 121–42.

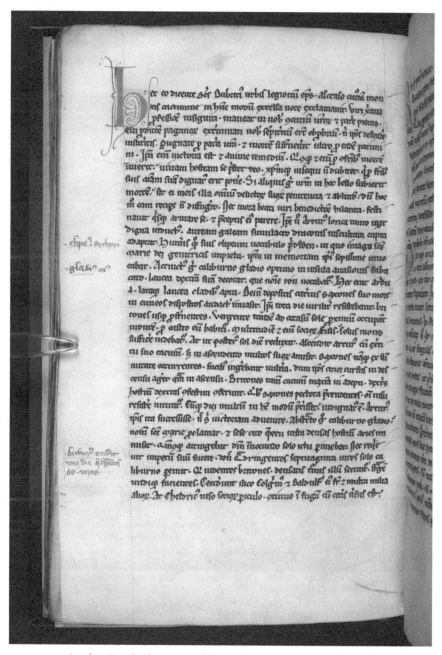

FIGURE 7.1 London, British Library, Arundel 237, fol. 47v

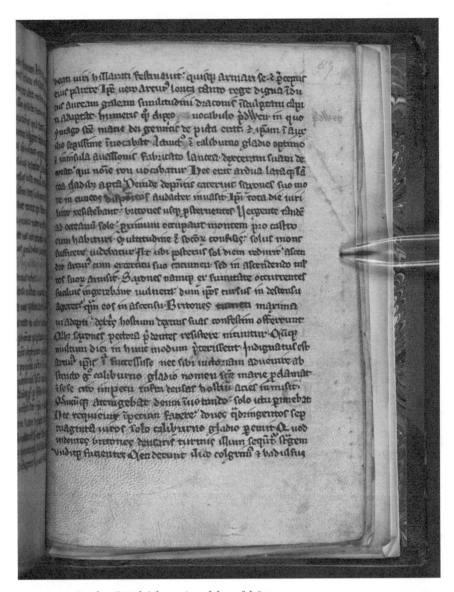

FIGURE 7.2 London, British Library, Arundel 319, fol. 89r
          © THE BRITISH LIBRARY BOARD

interest, one that is shared by medieval and early modern commentators alike.
London, Lambeth Palace, 503 has a medieval *Nota* mark, a manicule, and, in
an early modern hand, the gloss *Arthuri clipeus*, "Arthur's shield" (fol. 78v), next
to the description of Pridwen. London, Lambeth Palace, 454, a modest manuscript, has a doodle of a sword on fol. 94r, next to Arthur's accession, along with
underlining of the names Aurelius, Uther, Colgrin, and Arthur himself.

Drawings, like annotations, point us toward areas of readerly interest. London, British Library, Harley 4003 has a drawing of a castle, and the annotation *nota Tyndagel*, "take note of Tintagel", next to the story of Arthur's conception (fol. 120r). The same manuscript features a strange face and the label *Gogmagog* next to the story of Corineus and Gogmagog (fol. 86v), a reminder that readers turned to the *DGB* for more than the Arthuriad (Figure 7.3). The Gogmagog story was particularly popular; while in Harley 4003, the drawing and label are medieval, early modern annotators frequently comment on this section as well. London, British Library, Royal 13 A. iii has several 16th-century notes to this section, drawing attention both to the battle and to the derivation of Cornwall (fol. 13v). That etymological emphasis is typical in much of the early modern commentary on the *DGB*, and may account for some of the changes in frequency as well.

In some manuscripts, annotation or underlining picks up in the Arthurian section and then drops off, suggesting the pull of that part of the text. But in others, annotation patterns suggest something quite different. In London, British Library, Cotton Nero D. viii, for example, someone has underlined names and places almost constantly, right up until the Arthurian section. The underliner returns briefly for a few folios after Arthur's death, and then disappears entirely. This kind of variable attention is not uncommon in the manuscript tradition. Some readers perk up in the Roman section and lose interest thereafter. Others carefully annotate only the early, place-name etymologies in the opening chapters of the *DGB*. Many of these non-Arthurian reading patterns are associated particularly with early modern readers. London, British Library, Cotton Vespasian A. xxiii is a 13th-century manuscript that is heavily annotated in an early modern hand through Book VI. Thereafter, notes fall off precipitously, though the occasional later note in the same hand shows that the annotator was still reading. Some of this annotator's notes simply repeat names and places found in the text, as if the purpose were to make it easy to find certain passages. Others have a scholarly character, referring, for example, to other historical texts.

The etymological-geographical passages so popular with early modern readers, discussed further below, are less frequent in the Arthuriad, which might be one reason for the drop-off in annotation described thus far. Another reason might be growing concern over the historicity of Arthur, though more than one early modern antiquarian defended that historicity vehemently when Polydore Vergil questioned it.[3] Certainly other figures, who seem clearly legendary to us

---

3   For a discussion, see J.P. Carley, "Polydore Vergil and John Leland on King Arthur: The Battle of the Books", *Arthurian Interpretations* 15:2 (1984), 86–100 (repr. in E.D. Kennedy (ed.), *King Arthur: A Casebook*, New York, 1996, pp. 185–204).

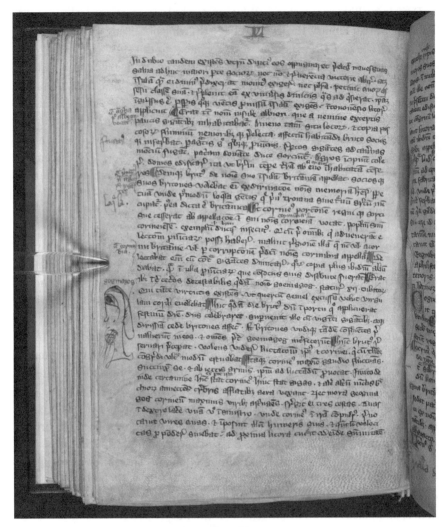

FIGURE 7.3   London, British Library, Harley 4003, fol. 86v
        © THE BRITISH LIBRARY BOARD

today, attracted the interest of later readers. For example, the Cotton Vespasian
A. xxiii reader devotes particular attention to Brutus. As the chapter after this
one notes, vernacular adaptations of the *DGB* were often called *Bruts*, from
the Brutus foundation myth. This was one of the most persistent and influential of Geoffrey's narratives in the Latin tradition as well. Both medieval
and early modern annotators show considerable interest in the Brutus story,
and in particular, in the account of his founding of Troia Nova, later known as
London. Both the foundation passage and the later account of Lud's additions

to the city can be the subject of notes by both medieval and early modern commentators.[4] Readers can also indicate (varying) interest through graphical means, as examples above of manicules, underlining, and marginal drawings indicate. And while manuscripts of the *DGB* are not normally illustrated, there is one manuscript that features elaborate marginal drawings of many of the cities mentioned. The drawings in Royal 13 A. iii date from the early 14th century, but these have also in some cases been annotated by an early modern reader. On fol. 14r, for example, which features an illustration of London in the bottom margin (labeled in both medieval and early modern hands), a marginal note records, in Latin in an early modern hand, that Nova Troia, also known as Troinovant, was built by Brutus, and later, called Kaerlud by Lud (Figure 7.4).

The interest of early modern readers in the place-names of the *DGB* aligns with the rise, in the same period, of chorography, the genre of geographical and historical description brought to its peak by William Camden in his *Britannia* (1586). One of the annotators of Lambeth 503 is William Lambarde (1536–1601), an antiquarian whose *Perambulation of Kent* is an early example of county history and a precursor to the work of Camden and other early modern chorographers. Lambarde picks out the place-names in the *DGB*, both before and after the Arthuriad. In the Arthurian portion of the text, he makes few notes, and these align with his general interest. For example, where a later medieval reader scrawls the note *Arturus letaliter vulneratus est*, "Arthur has been fatally wounded" (fol. 99r), next to Arthur's death, Lambarde writes, immediately below, *Aualonia insula*, "the island of Avalon", seeing the death through the lens of place (Figure 7.5). This focus on geography and etymology applies outside the Arthurian portion of the text as well. While we cannot know whether Lambarde drew the small picture of Stonehenge in the margin of fol. 69v of Lambeth 503, he did label it as *forma stonage*, "the shape of Stonehenge", noting as well that the passage describes the virtues of the stones. He manages, in this way, to note the fantastical elements of Geoffrey's story while also adhering to his interest in geographical description. Similarly, earlier in the manuscript, Lambarde's note to the story of Corineus and Gogmagog is again geographical, as he picks out Geoffrey's explanation for the place-name *Saltus goemagog*, "Gogmagog's Leap" (fol. 11r).

It might be the case that readers concentrate on such things as the etymologies beneath existing British places because the persistence of the place itself

---

4   I discuss the reception of this passage in "Palimpsests of Place and Time in Geoffrey of Monmouth's *Historia regum Britannie*", in G. Dinkova-Bruun and T. Major (eds.), *Teaching and Learning in Medieval Europe: Essays in Honour of Gernot R. Wieland*, Turnhout, 2017, pp. 43–59.

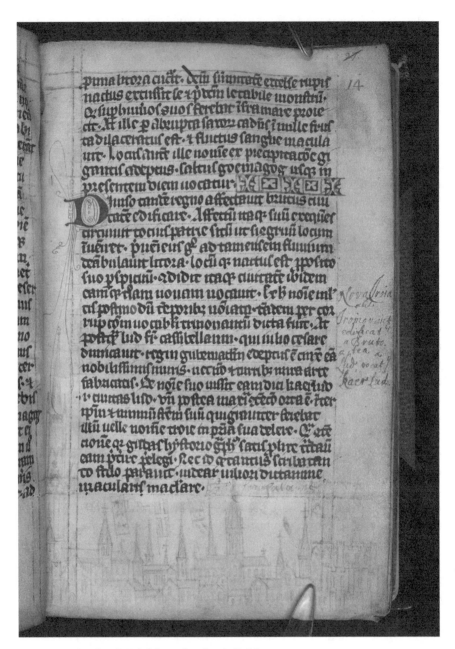

FIGURE 7.4 London, British Library, Royal 13 A. iii, fol. 14r

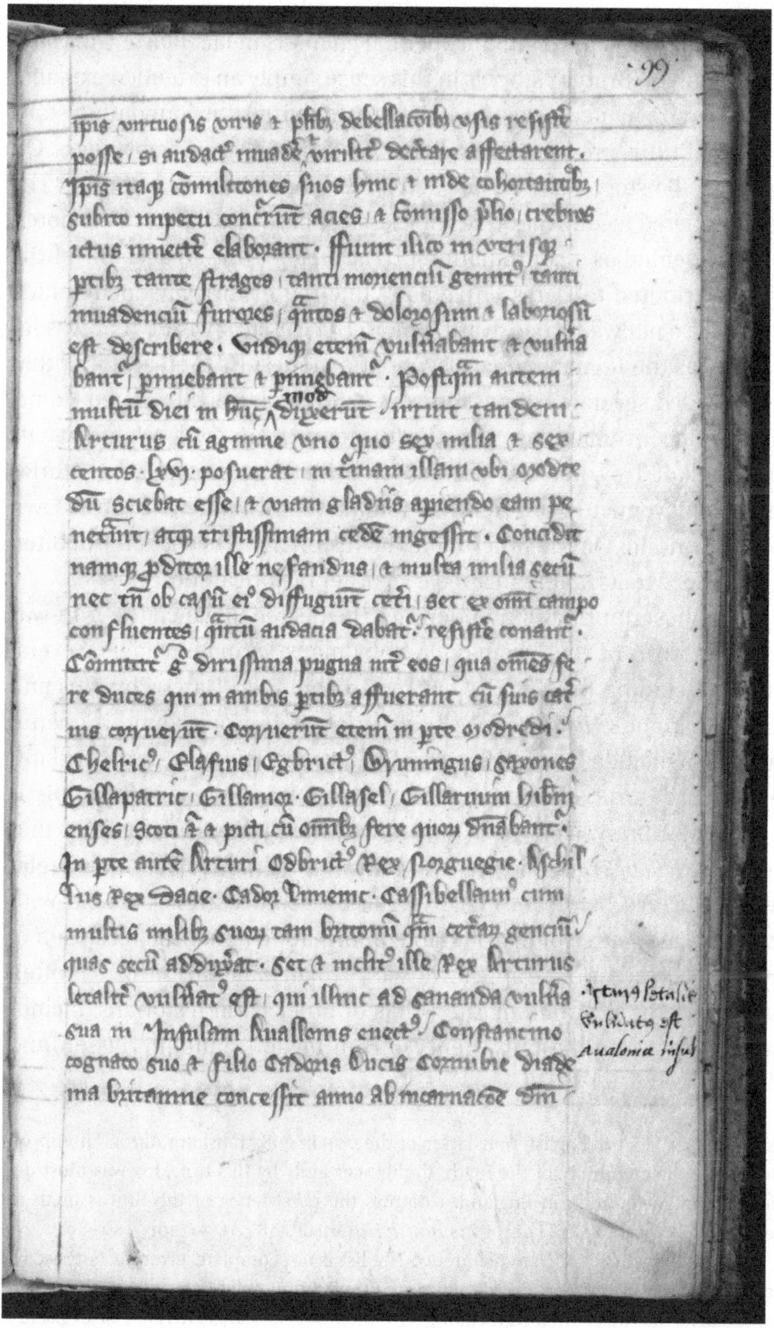

FIGURE 7.5 London, Lambeth Palace Library, 503, fol. 99r
BY PERMISSION OF LAMBETH PALACE LIBRARY

adds a certain plausibility to its foundation narrative, however fanciful. And Geoffrey's focus on etymology in the opening chapters in fact bolsters his larger foundation myth. Brutus's story is in this sense simply an extended explanation for the island's name; the name, in its turn, confirms the foundation story. As did Arthur, Brutus presented a problem to historically-minded readers. On the one hand, the story was very attractive, as its persistence suggests.[5] The Brutus story offered a connection to the classical past. As Chapter Two notes, the *DGB* is presented as a continuation of *The Fall of Troy*, an account of the fall of Troy attributed to Dares Phrygius. While the historically-documented Roman wars also allowed a backward look to the classical world, that was far more fraught, as the Roman story was one of conquest (it is no accident that Geoffrey provided several instances in which British kings conquered Rome, offsetting this inconvenient fact). The Brutus foundation myth might have its roots in the fall of Troy, but that fall was itself the beginning of other stories of imperial achievement, from Aeneas's foundation of Rome to Brutus's own settlement of Britain. On the other hand, its historicity was challenged, often through reference to its failure to appear in other historical sources.

Still, the manuscript tradition underlines the degree to which the *DGB* was understood in terms of the Trojan context by many Latinate readers. Several Trojan texts, including the *The Fall of Troy* attributed to Dares Phrygius and Guido delle Colonne's *History of the Destruction of Troy*, are found in manuscripts that also include Geoffrey's *DGB*.[6] Usually, the Trojan material will immediately precede *DGB*, effectively acting as an introduction. An example is Cardiff, Central Library, 2.611, a manuscript of the 13th or 14th century that opens with *The Fall of Troy*, followed by a genealogy of the Trojans and a prefatory poem to the *DGB*, before *DGB* itself begins. The co-occurrence of texts with the *DGB* is in fact a source of considerable information about the reception of Geoffrey's work. In addition to appearing with Trojan material, the *DGB* is often found in manuscripts containing the works of other Latin historians, including Bede, William of Malmesbury, Henry of Huntingdon, Ranulph Higden, and

---

5   As late as the first Modern English translation of the *DGB* in 1718, translator Aaron Thompson was defending the credibility of the myth, though certainly by this time, his was most definitively an outlier opinion in England. I discuss the persistence of the Brutus myth in "Remembering Brutus: Aaron Thompson's *British History* of 1718", *AL* 30 (2013), 141–69.

6   Crick, *DR*, pp. 19–77, lists associated contents. The list is not complete, given recent discoveries of more manuscripts than Crick knew at the time, but it still offers a very useful overview of the texts that most often travel along with the *DGB*. For Dares Phrygius, Crick lists 27 manuscripts that also contain the *DGB*, and for Guido delle Colonne, she lists five. She also notes that four manuscripts of the *DGB* include Trojan genealogies; see pp. 37–38, 47, and 43, respectively.

Martinus Polonus. Some of the compilers of these manuscripts copied these texts together at point of production; in Exeter, Cathedral Library, 3514, for example, the same hand copies *The Fall of Troy* and the DGB, one after another. Similarly, the *Historia Brittonum*, whose contents run parallel to some of the material in the DGB, precedes it in London, British Library, Additional 11702, and follows it in Cotton Nero D. viii. In both manuscripts the texts are copied in the same hand.[7] In other cases, later owners, either later in the Middle Ages or in the early modern period, have chosen to bind the DGB with other works. For instance, Cambridge, University Library, Ff.1.25 is a composite manuscript created by Matthew Parker (1504–75), archbishop of Canterbury, before he donated it to the University Library in 1574. It combines a medieval copy of William of Malmesbury's *History of the English Bishops* with 16th-century transcriptions of more of William's work; a 13th-century manuscript containing two Latin Crusades chronicles; and another 16th-century transcription, this one of the DGB.

In Matthew Parker's arrangement, Geoffrey's is one among several histories. The Crusades material suggests another popular emphasis in manuscripts containing the DGB, and that is material associated with places imagined to be exotic. Other Crusades texts found in manuscripts of the DGB include the pseudo-Turpin chronicles and Jacques de Vitry's *Oriental History* (*Historia orientalis*, or the *Historia hierosolimitana abbreuiata*).[8] One of the most popular companions to the DGB, the *Letter of Alexander to Aristotle*, might at first glance seem to align with the exotic elements found in the Crusades material: the *Letter* purports to be a letter from Alexander the Great to Aristotle, his tutor, recounting Alexander's adventures in India and the many marvels he encountered there. At the same time, the emphasis in the DGB on the deeds (and eventual deaths) of kings, particularly great ones like Brutus or Arthur, suggests a second thematic fit, the interest in the rise and fall of great rulers that would eventually give rise to the *On the Fates of Famous Men* tradition and to associated motifs such as the Nine Worthies, two of whom, of course, were Arthur and Alexander. Alexander material linked to manuscripts of the DGB also includes the *Deeds of Alexander* and Alexander's epitaph.[9] Some Latin historians criticized Geoffrey for suggesting Arthur was an equivalent to Alexander, but the Latin manuscript tradition routinely pairs the two rulers.

---

7 Crick, *DR*, p. 51, lists seven co-occurrences. The two texts are not always in direct sequence.
8 Crick, *DR*, pp. 54–55, lists four manuscripts containing the *Historia hierosolimitana abbreuiata* or *Historia Orientalis*, and ten with texts from the Pseudo-Turpin tradition, ibid., pp. 52–54.
9 Crick, *DR*, pp. 23–29, lists all the Alexander texts.

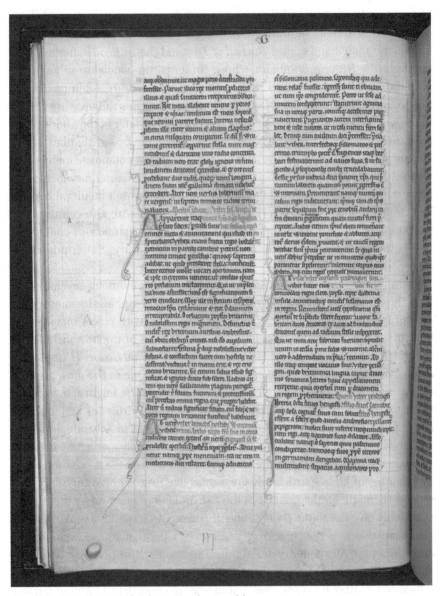

FIGURE 7.6   London, British Library, Royal 13 D. v, fol. 24v
© THE BRITISH LIBRARY BOARD

The *PM*, which had a manuscript tradition of its own (see Chapter Four), also often stands apart from the rest of the *DGB* in the manuscripts in which it is integral, partly because of variability in design (the degree to which the section is or is not highlighted by display capitals, rubrics, and so on), and partly because of the varying traces of readerly reaction. Sometimes, the prophecies are carefully and extensively annotated. Prophecy was of considerable interest to Latinate medieval readers, and its biblical roots gave it significant status. The *PM*, which attracted the praise of 12th-century readers like Orderic Vitalis and Abbot Suger of St Denis, rapidly became the subject of several Latin commentaries, and even inspired imitation like that of John of Cornwall.[10] Some manuscripts clearly show considerable readerly interest in this part of the *DGB*. Several different hands, of different periods, have made notes in the *PM* section of Arundel 237, a manuscript which also has a marginal note on Merlin's interpretation of the star forecasting Arthur's reign (fol. 42v). In another manuscript, London, British Library, Royal 13 D. v, there is a doodle of the star in the margin at this point (fol. 24v) (Figure 7.6). In other manuscripts, the annotating hand or hands pause during the *PM* and resume only once the narrative portion of the text does; an example of this practice is Cotton Nero D. viii whose underlining reader, as noted above, seems less interested in the Arthuriad than in other parts of the text. This reader leaves the prophecies almost completely unmarked, and with no underlining at all. London, College of Arms, Arundel 1 is a historical miscellany that includes a copy of the *DGB* that has been extensively annotated by John Dee (1527–1608), one of Elizabeth I's advisors and a noted mathematician and student of the occult. His notes include plot summary and source references, and show an interest in Geoffrey's synchronisms and etymologies. However, after providing a heading to the *PM* section, Dee stops annotating at all, picking up only when the narrative resumes, and continuing with his previous interests; he writes a long note, for example, on Stonehenge. Were the readers who suspended operations during the *PM* bewildered or disgusted by it? Were they simply not interested? (Dee also shows no interest in Arthur, as it happens). It is not possible to derive motives from the absence of commentary. What we do know is that while for some readers, Merlin was part of the outrageous falsehoods that led Meilyr's demons to settle on Geoffrey's pages, for others, the *PM* were among the most important parts of the *DGB*.

2   Continuation

Medieval history writing was in many ways an accretive and collaborative enterprise. Chronicle histories, for example, were often extended by their later

---

10   John of Cornwall's poem survives in only one manuscript, which is not a copy of the *DGB*. It clearly drew on Geoffrey's work but most of it, as Michael Curley has shown, cannot be directly traced to the *DGB*; see "A New Edition of John of Cornwall's *Prophetia Merlini*", *Speculum* 57:2 (1982), 217–49.

owners beyond the period covered by their original authors. Indeed, authors can be difficult to determine, precisely because so many texts were created as compilations, even pastiches, of other histories. Geoffrey is very insistent as to his own authorship, naming himself in two prefaces and making attempts to protect his content through his claim that only he possesses the very ancient book in the British tongue which he claims to be translating.[11] At the same time, his final colophon, leaving the deeds of those who came after the period he covers to other contemporary historians, also invites the participation of others in extending and promulgating the history he has begun.[12] While continuations of histories are often fairly staid affairs – an added list of kings, or a genealogy, are common features – two Latin texts offer more elaborate narrative extensions of Geoffrey's world.

As we have already seen, the story of Corineus and Gogmagog was popular with later readers of the *DGB*. It is not surprising, then, that some people asked what must have seemed an obvious question: where did the giants that the Trojans encountered in Britain come from? One answer was provided by *The Origin of Giants (De origine gigantum)*. This is a 14th-century Latin version of an Anglo-Norman poem that tells the story of Albina, eldest of 30 daughters of a Greek king, who leads her sisters in a plot to murder their husbands.[13] When one of the sisters reveals the plan (in another Anglo-Norman version, they actually succeed), the plotters are set adrift and land on an island which they name Albion, after Albina. The island is deserted; incubi visit it and copulate with the women, and a race of giants is born as a result. Versions of the Albina story often appear as prologues to Anglo-Norman, Latin, and Middle English *Bruts*.[14]

Ruth Evans has pointed out that the use of third-person prose narrative for the tale, when the original was in verse with a first-person narrator, gives the text a truthful cast, suggesting the world of chronicle history rather than romance.[15] Furthermore, Latin itself performs this particular alchemy. James Carley and

---

11   *DGB*, Prologus 3.9–12, 19; Prophetiae 110.21; xi.208.604–07.

12   *DGB*, xi.208.601–03, invites Caradog of Llancarfan, William of Malmesbury, and Henry of Huntingdon to continue the narrative of the Welsh and Saxon kings from the point where Geoffrey leaves off.

13   The Anglo-Norman original, *Des grantz geanz*, survives in two versions, one a shorter adaptation of the other. In their edition of *The Origin of Giants*, J.P. Carley and J. Crick write that the Latin translation derives from this abbreviated version; see "Constructing Albion's Past: An Annotated Edition of *De Origine Gigantum*", *AL* 13 (1995), 41–114, at p. 51.

14   For a discussion that focuses on the Middle English version of the story, see A. Bernau, "Beginning with Albina: Remembering the Nation", *Exemplaria* 21:3 (2009), 247–73.

15   R. Evans, "Gigantic Origins: An Annotated Translation of *De Origine Gigantum*", *AL* 16 (1998), 197–211, at p. 201.

Julia Crick point out that it was rare to translate from French into Latin, and that such translation "represented an elevation of the text".[16] That this elevation could be problematic is reflected by one of Geoffrey's harshest critics, William of Newburgh. He was particularly incensed that Geoffrey dressed up his fictions in Latin, the language of truth, writing that Geoffrey cloaked the "figments of the Britons" with "the honorable name of history by presenting them with the ornaments of the Latin tongue".[17] Casting the Albina story into the language and form of history, then, performs a significant reorientation of the text, making it acceptable for Latin readers. The manuscript history of *The Origin of Giants* suggests that the transmutation was successful. The text appears before the *DGB* in some manuscripts, and after it in others. Unrelated Latin versions of the story of Albina and her sisters also appear alongside the *DGB* in the manuscript tradition, one in two copies, and the other in four.[18]

Indeed, *The Origin of Giants* (and its Anglo-Norman source) pays attention to things that are not normally the purview of romance. It spends some of its short length detailing how Albina and her sisters found and prepared food on the island. The sisters first forage for fruits, and then turn to catching game (and not in the aristocratic form of the hunt as practiced in romance texts):

> Now indeed, because nutritious food was entirely lacking to them, nor did they have the capacity to capture wild animals and birds, through cunning invention they made twigs into snares, by means of which they could, by turns, seize and hold the wild beasts. They also fashioned cunning little devices from twigs to capture birds. And so, they disemboweled their captured game and, having coaxed fire from flint, cooked them in their hides and roasted the birds on the coals.[19]

---

16 Carley and Crick, "Constructing Albion's Past", p. 51.

17 William of Newburgh, *The History of English Affairs* Proemium §3, ed. and trans. P.G. Walsh and M.J. Kennedy, *William of Newburgh: The History of English Affairs, Book I (Edited with Translation and Commentary)*, Warminster, 1988, p. 28: "fabulas de Arturo ex priscis Britonum figmentis sumptas et ex proprio auctas per superductum Latini sermonis colorem honesto historiae nomine palliavit." My translation. I discuss the role of Latin in Arthurian history in "'Hic est Artur': Reading Latin and Reading Arthur", in A. Lupack (ed.), *New Directions in Arthurian Studies*, Cambridge, 2002, pp. 49–67.

18 Carley and Crick, "Constructing Albion's Past", p. 50.

19 Carley and Crick, "Constructing Albion's Past", pp. 107–09: "Iam uero quia cibus eis deerat nutritiuus nec habebant ingenia ad capiendas feras et aues excogitacione subtili fecerunt tendiculas uirgeas, quibus inuicem connodatis feras caperent et tenerent. Sed et ingeniola componebant ex uirgis pro auibus capiendis. Captam igitur uenacionem excoriarunt et extracto igne de silice coxerunt in coreiis et aues ad prunas torrebant." My translation.

The brief scene is similar to the interest in the forest life of Meriadoc and his protectors in *The Story of Meriadoc* (*Historia Meriadoci*), discussed below. The coexistence of incubi, monstrous progeny, and mundane details like snare-making and rabbit-skinning is not unique to the Latin translation – the French verse features similar details – but the shift to Latin prose underlines the prosaic nature of the description, and may contribute to the larger project of giving the foundation narrative what Anke Bernau, discussing the Albina tradition more generally, calls "plausibility"; that is, the story has familiar and acceptable outlines and, I would add, form.[20] Thus *The Origin of Giants* can function as a lead-in to the *DGB*, in the same way that the Trojan material discussed above often does.

These are different kinds of foundation narratives, however. Bernau points out the contrast between the female founders (Albina and her sisters) and the male (Brutus and the Trojans), noting that the men build cities, while the women seem to lead a hunter-gatherer existence.[21] Moreover, the women in *The Origin of Giants* are characterized by their appetites, quite literally; it is after they have gorged on the beasts they catch and kill that they become lustful. The combination of gluttony, lust, and women is a common trope in medieval anti-feminist literature, and while Geoffrey's *DGB* has plenty of examples of bad male behavior, his founder, Brutus, is exemplary, characterized by both wisdom and strength. The pairing of *The Origin of Giants* with the *DGB* might seem, then, to frame Geoffrey's text as a proper and corrective foundation narrative, as the Trojans cleanse the island of the monstrous race borne of female iniquity. The contrast is not a particularly Galfridian one, however. Geoffrey's queens, like his kings, act sometimes out of baser instincts, but many of them are also exemplary rulers, as Chapter Twelve in this collection notes.[22] Geoffrey left the pre-history of Albion unwritten; he might or might not have approved of the way the Albina narrative filled in that gap.

The Origin of Giants is clearly taken up by some readers as an appropriate prologue to the *DGB*. Another Latin text, *The True History of the Death of Arthur* (*Vera historia de morte Arthuri*), seems to function as an epilogue, though to the Arthuriad rather than to the *DGB* as a whole. This 12th-century Latin prose narrative tells its audience what happens after Arthur is wounded at

---

20   Bernau, "Beginning with Albina", pp. 256–57; Bernau is drawing here on Mary Carruthers' work on medieval memory in *The Book of Memory: A Study of Memory in Medieval Culture*, Cambridge, 1990.

21   Bernau, "Beginning with Albina", p. 271.

22   In addition to her contribution to this volume, Fiona Tolhurst has discussed Geoffrey's queens at length in *Geoffrey of Monmouth and the Translation of Female Kingship*, New York, 2013.

Camlan.[23] Geoffrey simply says that Arthur was taken to Avalon and that the crown passed to Constantinus. The long Arthurian pause in the relentless succession of kings that characterizes much of the *DGB* ends, and the text hurtles toward the final dominion of the Saxons. Arthur's death can seem particularly abrupt in the *DGB* precisely because we have spent so much time reading about him. *The True History* provides a much more colorful conclusion to the great king's life, showing us Arthur's fatal wounding by a mysterious youth wielding an elm spear dipped in adder's venom; Arthur's appropriately Christian death on a hair-shirt, after confession in the presence of the bishops of Bangor and Glamorgan; and a magical storm during his funeral rites, following which his body disappears, leaving his tomb behind, thus potentially preparing the ground for the messianic hope of Arthur's return, as no one knows where the king's body lies.[24] Yet as in the Albina story, the apparently fantastical coexists with the ordinary. There is no suggestion, for example, that Avalon is to be a place of miraculous restoration. Arthur seeks it out "because of the amenities of that delightful place (and for the sake of peace and for the easing of the pain of his wounds)", but "when he had come there, the doctors busied themselves with all the skill of their art over his wounds, but the king experienced no efficacious cure from their efforts."[25] Avalon is simply a pleasant place, home to skilled but clearly human doctors.

In two manuscripts containing the *DGB*, *The True History* is integrated with Geoffrey's own text. It is placed between chapters in Paris, Bibliothèque de l'Arsenal, 982, and, in Paris, Bibliothèque nationale de France, lat. 6401D, inserted after Arthur's death with an introductory note offering the account as that of "Geoffrey Arthur" himself.[26] This (partial) version of the text is presented throughout as if being quoted from Geoffrey's work. It is particularly notable that in this unusual manuscript, the *DGB* ends at this point, with Arthur's death and the appended material. Most undamaged manuscripts of the *DGB*,

---

23 For an edition, see *Vera Historia de Morte Arthuri*, ed. M. Lapidge, "An Edition of the *Vera Historia de Morte Arthuri*", *AL* 1 (1981), 79–93. The manuscripts are described in R. Barber, "The Manuscripts of the *Vera Historia de Morte Arthuri*", *AL* 6 (1986), 163–64, and in M. Lapidge, "Additional Manuscript Evidence for the *Vera Historia de Morte Arthuri*", *AL* 2 (1982), 163–68.

24 Lapidge, "An Edition of the *Vera Historia*", p. 90: "At deinde, cum caligo subducitur et serenitas restituitur, corporis regii nullas repperunt reliquias", "And finally, when the mist is gone and calm restored, they find no part of the royal body."

25 Lapidge, "An Edition of the *Vera Historia*", p. 86: "propter loci amenitatem perendinari proposuerat (et quietis gracia causaque uulnerum suorum mitigandi dolorem). Ad quam ubi peruentus est, medici pro sue artis industria pro regis sunt solliciti uulneribus; sed rex eorum sollicitudinibus nullam salubrem persensit efficaciam." My translation.

26 "Nunc uero ad Gualfredum Arturum reuertar stilo non mutato", fol. 74v.

of course, end where Geoffrey normally does,[27] but here too, we find later Latin writers (or compilers) effectively supplementing Geoffrey's history. Sometimes this supplementation is achieved simply by the addition of chronicle histories that extend Geoffrey's narrative beyond the period of the Saxon dominion. In addition to the works of the historians mentioned above, other texts used for this purpose include histories of the Normans and genealogies and lists of English kings up to the date of the manuscript's creation or emendation. In these manuscripts, the *DGB* is the prologue to more recent histories. In other manuscripts, a popular group of non-narrative additions takes the *DGB* in quite a different direction.

At the end of the *DGB*, attempting to interpret the angelic voice heard by Cadualadrus, Alanus gathers prophetic books, including those attributed to the Eagle of Shaftesbury, the Sibyl, and Merlin. As noted above and in Chapter Four, the *PM* had their own separate manuscript tradition, and often attracted annotation and commentary. In addition, other Latin prophetic texts, including the Sibylline prophecies and several versions of the Prophecy of the Eagle, can be found in manuscripts of the *DGB*. It is striking that Geoffrey refused to provide the Eagle's prophecy himself. He first mentions it at the end of his account of the building of Kaerguint (Winchester) by Rud Hudibras, but denies its credibility: "The Eagle spoke there while the wall was being built, whose words, if I judged them to be true, I would confidently set down with the rest."[28] Given what Geoffrey was willing to set down in Merlin's case, it seems reasonable to wonder if he is having a bit of fun with his audience here. If so, not everyone got the joke. The Welsh translation of the *DGB*, *Brut y Brenhinedd* ("History of the Kings"), inserts a set of prophecies at this point, translated from a Latin text of Merlinian prophecies,[29] and in over a dozen manuscripts of the *DGB*, a Latin Eagle prophecy appears. In several, it follows directly after the text.[30] Whether or not Geoffrey intended a sly joke in providing Merlin's prophecies but not the Eagle's, some later Latin readers were confronted with copies of the *DGB* whose design implied that the Eagle of Shaftesbury was, like Merlin, integral to the text – and, perhaps, equally reliable, whatever that might mean.

---

27   Though not always: BL Add. 11702 ends with the brief chapter that immediately follows
      Arthur's death, two-thirds of the way down the final page of the manuscript.

28   *DGB*, ii.29.120–22: "Ibi tunc aquila locuta est dum murus aedificaretur; cuius sermones si
      ueros esse arbitrarer sicut cetera memoriae dare non diffugerem." My translation.

29   See A.G. Rigg, *A History of Anglo-Latin Literature 1066–1422*, Cambridge, 1992, p. 47.

30   Crick lists the manuscripts in Crick, *DR*, pp. 65–66.

3   Creation

Both *The Origin of Giants* and *The True History* display some markers of history, and some of romance, underlining the fuzziness of the fact/fiction divide we are accustomed to making today. They could easily be considered in the final section of this essay, as they are clearly narratives with romance elements – creative works, to use anachronistic modern terms, though the creativity in *The Origin of Giants* is partly the Norman poet's, and not the Latin translator's. But they are also, as the manuscript tradition suggests, sometimes presented as expansions of Geoffrey's project, filling in the gaps he left. Similarly, while someone created the various Latin prophecies that often appear in conjunction with the *DGB* in the manuscript tradition, what is most striking is what I think of as creation by accretion; that is, all these texts are part of the packaging and categorizing of the *DGB*, as well as moves to supplement what later readers felt to be missing. The texts dealt with here, while they show Galfridian influence, are truly free-standing. Two of them, *The Story of Meriadoc* (*Historia Meriadoci*) and *The Rise of Gawain* (*De ortu Waluuanii*), are generally agreed to be by the same author, though disagreement as to their dating persists.[31] The third, *Arthur and Gorlagon*, is an engagement with anti-feminist tradition by means of a werewolf story in an Arthurian frame.[32] None had anything like the circulation or influence of the *DGB*. *The Rise of Gawain* and *Arthur and Gorlagon* (*Narratio de Arthuro Rege Britanniae et Rege Gorlagon lycanthropo*) each survive in single manuscripts only, and *The Story of Meriadoc* in two

---

31   The most recent editor of both texts, Mildred Leake Day, used details of armor, clothing, weaponry, and English law to argue for a 12th-century date for both works, and tentatively attributed them to Robert of Torigni, abbot of Mont-Saint-Michel, who showed Henry of Huntingdon a copy of the *DGB*, occasioning the latter's famous letter to Warin (see Robert of Torigny, *Chronicle*, ed. R. Howlett, *Chronicles of the Reigns of Stephen, Henry II and Richard I, Vol. IV*, London, 1889, p. 65, where Henry's letter uses the word *stupens*, "astonished, stupefied", to record his reaction upon reading Geoffrey's text). Day reviews and updates her arguments in *Latin Arthurian Literature*, Cambridge, 2005, which collects her earlier editions and translations, along with editions and translations of *Arthur and Gorlagon* and of the Arthurian portion of Etienne de Rouen's *Draco Normannicus*. There are also arguments for a 13th-century date (A. Galyon, "*De Ortu Walwanii* and the Theory of Illumination", *Neophilologus* 62:3 (1978), 335–41; H. Nicholson, "Following the Path of the Lionheart: The *De Ortu Walwanii* and the *Itinerarium Peregrinorum et Gesta Ricardi*", *Medium Ævum* 69:1 (2000), 21–33; and D. Porter, "The *Historia Meriadoci* and Magna Carta", *Neophilologus* 76:1 (1992), 136–46); and a 14th-century one (P. Larkin, who argues for Ranulph Higden as the author in "A Suggested Author for *De ortu Waluuanii* and *Historia Meriadoci*: Ranulph Higden", *JEGP* 103:2 (2004), 215–31).

32   See L. Brady, "Antifeminist Tradition in *Arthur and Gorlagon* and the Quest to Understand Women", *Notes and Queries* 59:2 (2012), 163–66, and "Feminine Desire and Conditional Misogyny in *Arthur and Gorlagon*", *Arthuriana* 24:3 (2014), 23–44.

(coming directly before *The Rise of Gawain* in one of these).[33] A.G. Rigg has suggested that the surprising paucity of Latin Galfridian romance might relate to an unwillingness to pair Latin with such subject matter; he writes that "the Latin language ... may have raised cultural expectations above the level of pure entertainment."[34] These three texts are all certainly entertaining, but they also wear their Latinity quite clearly.

The Story of Meriadoc and *The Rise of Gawain* both contain direct reflection on the process of composition. The opening of *The Story of Meriadoc* is reminiscent of Geoffrey's own remarks in his preface about praising deserving heroes while avoiding flowery language:

> I have thought it fitting to write down a story worthy of remembrance, whose text is decorated with records of such great prowess and attractiveness that, were I to run through each episode in turn, I would turn the sweetness of honey into disgust. Therefore, considering the benefit to my readers, I have set out to restrict it with a concise style, knowing that a brief oration with meaning is more worthy than a prolix, meaningless narration.[35]

The conclusion of *The Rise of Gawain*, on the other hand, suggests that the author's (Latin) style is worthier than the simple fare on offer from other story-tellers:

> Whoever wants to know what other virtuous exploits Gawain performs should ask them by request or payment from one who knows. Knowing that as it is more dangerous to take part in a battle than to report one, so is it more difficult to write down a history with eloquent style than to tell it in the words of common speech.[36]

---

33 *Arthur and Gorlagon* appears in Oxford, Bodleian Library, Rawlinson B. 149. The manuscript also includes *The Story of Meriadoc*. The second copy of *The Story of Meriadoc* is London, British Library, Cotton Faustina B. vi, where it is followed by the sole copy of *The Rise of Gawain*. The next text includes extracts from the *DGB*, ending with the introduction to the *PM* section.

34 Rigg, *Anglo-Latin Literature*, p. 48.

35 *The Story of Meriadoc, King of Cambria*, ed. M.L. Day, New York, 1988, p. 2: "Memoratu dignam dignum duxi exarare historiam, cuius textus tantarum probitatum tantique leporis decoratur titulis, ut, si singula seriatim percurrerem, favi dulcorem in fastidium verterem. Legencium igitur consulens utilitati illam compendioso perstringere stilo statui, sciens quod maioris sit precii brevis cum sensu oracio quam multiflua racione vanans locucio." My translation.

36 *The Rise of Gawain, Nephew of Arthur*, ed. M.L. Day, New York, 1984, p. 122: "Cetera que virtutum Waluuanii secuntur insignia qui scire desiderat a sciente prece vel precio exigat.

Of course, the references to plain language in the prologue to *The Story of Meriadoc* are a typical example of the modesty topos, something Geoffrey himself enjoyed playing with (his vocabulary in both examples of the topos from the *DGB* is in fact remarkably varied, given his claims to rhetorical inadequacy). The details of both romances seem designed similarly to straddle two worlds, offering plot elements and descriptions that manifest the interests and themes of Anglo-Latin historical writing alongside motifs and plot trajectories of a romance character.

Both *The Rise of Gawain* and *The Story of Meriadoc* have protagonists whose adventures suggest the Fair Unknown motif.[37] In *The Rise of Gawain*, Gawain is born as the illegitimate son of Arthur's sister Anna, who sends the infant away in the care of a group of merchants, to whom she also gives money and signs of Gawain's parentage. The merchants leave their boat and the child unattended, and the infant and treasure are taken by a poor man, Viamandus, who eventually makes his way with the child to Rome. After a series of adventures, including a trip to Arthur's court, Gawain proves his abilities, and his heritage is revealed to him by his uncle as the court welcomes its newest knight. In *The Story of Meriadoc*, Meriadoc and his sister are protected by faithful retainers from their murderous uncle, who has killed their royal father Caradoc of Cambria and seized the throne for himself. The servants raise the children in the forest until a series of mishaps separates them. Meriadoc experiences many adventures, some of them at Arthur's court, where he journeys in search of aid to defeat his uncle and regain the throne.

Despite the familiar plot arc, both of these Fair Unknown narratives have decidedly atypical features. In *The Rise of Gawain*, while Gawain's story begins and ends at the Arthurian court, his formative years are Roman. Geoffrey systematically subordinates the Romans to the Britons in the *DGB*. He minimizes the invasions; credits Britons rather than Romans for such innovations as roads and baths; creates marital linkages between the Romans and the Britons; and, of course, gives us an Arthur who conquers Rome.[38] The author of *The Rise of Gawain* takes a different approach in stressing his protagonist's Roman roots,

---

Sciens quod sicut discriminosius est bellum inire quam bellum referre, sic operosius sit composito eloquencie stilo historiam exarare quam vulgari propalare sermone." My translation.

37 Fair Unknown stories typically feature a young man who through his adventures discovers or proves his aristocratic origins, and in some cases reclaims a position or title that is rightfully his. For an overview of the motif in medieval romance, see J. Weldon, "Fair Unknown", in S. Echard and R. Rouse (eds.), *The Encyclopedia of Medieval Literature in Britain*, 4 vols., Chichester, 2017, vol. 2, pp. 783–87.

38 I discuss Geoffrey's treatment of Rome in "'Whyche thyng semeth not to agree with other histories ...': Rome in Geoffrey of Monmouth and his Early Modern Readers", *AL* 26 (2009), 109–29. It is possible that the story told in *The Rise of Gawain* might have been

but the effect – the integration of Roman and Briton, in a manner that suggests the recognizable excellence of the British protagonist – is the same. After Viamandus's death, Gawain becomes the protégé of the Emperor, and earns his nickname, the Knight of the Surcoat, from his admirers during his success at the *equirris*, the Roman military games. When he sails off with the goal of relieving the Christians in the Holy Land, he does so on a Roman fleet, in the company of a centurion who directs many of the battles. When on the way to Jerusalem Gawain is victorious over King Milocrates, described as *inimicus Romani populi*, "enemy of the people of Rome", the centurion enacts justice that is couched in Roman terms: "the leaders and magistrates, because they had aligned themselves with the enemy of the Roman people, were sawn into pieces."[39] In addition, the romance features many set-piece battles with careful descriptions of tactics, reminiscent of the attention Geoffrey pays to the deployment of troops in the Roman section of his history, in the account of Arthur's defeat of Lucius, and indeed throughout the *DGB*.

The lengthy digression on the manufacture of Greek fire, a real medieval weapon that Gawain and the centurion face in a naval battle with pirates, adds another unexpected element. While its details are clearly fantastical, it is not the fantasy of romance that is at play here, but rather, that of the *mirabilia* and travel narratives that, as noted above, sometimes accompany the *DGB* in the manuscripts. The ingredients of Greek fire are said to include poisonous toads, water snakes, a three-headed, fire-breathing asp, the gall bladder and testicles of a shape-shifting wolf, and a miraculous gemstone "brought forth from the ends of the earth".[40] Both the Roman coloring and the marvels and monsters of the Greek fire digression display the kind of reading and intellectual milieu which gave rise to the *DGB* and the kind of reception discussed above.

In *The Story of Meriadoc*, too, the romance and folkloric elements are accompanied by touches that suggest the world of Latin learning. At the beginning of the romance, Meriadoc's uncle, Griffin, is persuaded by evil counselors to murder his brother Caradoc. The counselors give a lengthy speech, carefully structured to manipulate Griffin into agreeing to the murder, alternating between praising him and asking questions designed to heighten his resentment and anger. The trope of the wicked counselors is a popular one in Latin court

---

suggested by a brief reference in the *DGB* to Gawain's having been placed in the service of Pope Sulpicius (*DGB*, ix.154.241–43).

39   *The Rise of Gawain*, ed. Day, p. 58: "principes et magistratus quod cum hoste Romani populi consensissent serratis carpentis transegit." My translation.

40   *The Rise of Gawain*, ed. Day, p. 70: "ligurius orbe in extremo repertus". My translation.

satire and princely advice literature popular throughout the Middle Ages.[41] The *DGB* is similarly full of scenes of counsel, and good kings are often revealed through their discernment and their willingness to listen to good advice. In *The Story of Meriadoc*, the interest in how kings behave suggested by the scene with the wicked counselors surfaces again when Meriadoc, having defeated his uncle with Arthur's help, chooses to continue his adventuring rather than immediately become king himself. Instead, he returns to Arthur's court where, in true romance fashion – (the author invokes the familiar motif of marvels occurring in Arthur's presence) – a mysterious Black Knight appears, claiming his rights, against Arthur, over the Black Forest. While the claim will eventually be settled by combat (with the Black Knight successively defeating 37 of Arthur's knights in single combat, until at last Meriadoc defeats him), both before and after this romance set-piece, the text concentrates on the legal details of the dispute, and on how those details reflect on Arthur's own rule. Witnesses testify that Arthur's father stocked the forest with black boars, thus proving his ownership. The Black Knight points out that his name is the Black Knight of the Black Forest, and that he is in himself black, both facts witnessing his ancestral rights. The lords of the court are called upon to settle the dispute, and it is at that point that the knight requests combat instead, because, he says, he cannot believe in the impartiality of the court. When Meriadoc has defeated the Black Knight, he then, surprisingly, rebukes Arthur for harming so many of his knights, and uses the verb *calumpnio* to characterize the claim Arthur pursued. The term is a legal one that can mean either simply to pursue a claim, or to make a false claim.[42] The concentration on the judicial details around the duel, along with a contemporary context that included frequent disputes between the crown and landowners around forest jurisdiction, suggests that the more pejorative sense could be at play here.

Like *The Rise of Gawain*, *The Story of Meriadoc* is stuffed full of marvels; indeed, it is the more extravagantly "romantic" of the two. The incident of the Black Knight of the Black Forest is followed by the arrival of two more knights, the Red Knight of the Red Forest, and the White Knight of the White Forest, who with the Black Knight become Meriadoc's companions through the rest of the story. The adventures encountered are a mixture of military campaigns against an Emperor whom Meriadoc first served and was then betrayed by, and mysterious encounters in strange castles in forests. The forest is the archetypal romance setting, and the forests in *The Story of Meriadoc* are stocked as

---

41   I discuss this context in *Arthurian Narrative in the Latin Tradition* (Cambridge Studies in Medieval Literature, 36), Cambridge, 1998.

42   *DMLBS*, s.v. *calumniare*, def. 1. "to accuse falsely, traduce".

expected with mysterious weather, a marvelous structure inhabited by a beautiful woman who claims to know all about Meriadoc (the goddess Fortuna, perhaps?), and an ominously-described castle which no one who enters may depart from without dishonor.[43] The forest at the beginning of the narrative, too, begins as a typical romance setting as Ivor and Morwen rescue the children from their would-be executioners, leading to a forest childhood for Meriadoc reminiscent of stories like Perceval/Peredur's. But here, too, another mode interacts with the apparatus of romance, as the narrative voice pauses to answer a question it would not normally occur to a romance audience to ask: "But perhaps it will be asked how they cooked their meat to eat, since they lacked both fire and vessels in which it could be boiled."[44] What follows is an elaborate description of how the fugitives used methods also used by forest outlaws, and so as with the disputes at Arthur's court, the romance locale becomes a site where the resources and interests of both vernacular and Latin worlds interact.

The final text to be dealt with in this chapter is perhaps the one that least clearly belongs in a discussion of Geoffrey's influence on the Latin tradition. There are clear echoes of the *DGB* in *The Rise of Gawain* and *The Story of Meriadoc*. Those romances also display an explicit and implicit reflection on what it means to write hybrid historical-fantastical narrative in the language of truth, that accords well with Geoffrey's own project. *Arthur and Gorlagon*, on the other hand, presents itself, at first, as a straightforward vernacular romance that just happens to be written in Latin. It opens with Arthur keeping the Pentecost feast at Caerleon. Guinevere, chastising him for kissing her exuberantly in public, tells him he does not truly understand women. Arthur vows never to eat again until he has learned what women truly think, and sets off on a quest to find his answer. Two kings, Gargol and Torleil, convince him to feast with them, despite his vow, only to confess on the morrow that they cannot answer his question. When he reaches the court of the third king, Gorlagon, Arthur has the sense to stay on his horse and refuse food until he has his answer. Gorlagon obliges with a story of a king whose unfaithful wife turns him into a wolf. The wolf eventually becomes the companion of another king, who himself turns out to have an unfaithful wife. When the wolf discovers the affair between the queen and the king's steward, he attacks the steward, and the queen, in retaliation, hides her infant child and claims that the wolf has eaten it. The wolf, however, succeeds, through its oddly human behavior, in

---

43   *Story of Meriadoc*, ed. Day, p. 130: "castellum ... neminem umquam illud intrasse qui sine dedecore exierit." My translation.

44   *Story of Meriadoc*, ed. Day, p. 40: "Set hic fortassis queritur quomodo sibi carnes ad esum paraverint, dum et ignis et vasa quibus elixari possent defuerint." My translation.

revealing the whole truth to the king, who executes the steward and his queen, and then helps the wolf, whom he is now convinced is a man, to regain his human shape and punish the deceitful wife who wrought the change in the first place. Gorlagon then reveals that he himself was the wolf, and Arthur gets off his horse, eats, and, as the text ends, "wondering greatly at the things he had heard, made his nine days' journey home".[45]

Unlike the two romances just discussed, there is no explicit reflection on writing practice in *Arthur and Gorlagon*. The plot has many obviously Welsh elements, so many, indeed, that its first editor, G.L. Kittredge, believed it to be a Latin translation of a Welsh original. It bears obvious similarities to later vernacular texts about the quest to understand women, such as *The Wife of Bath's Tale* or the story of Gawain and Ragnell. It is now generally understood as a Welsh Latin production, probably of the 12th century. Even the brief plot summary just provided makes clear that it is essentially an anti-feminist text in Arthurian dress, but the degree to which it engages carefully and specifically with the Latin anti-feminist tradition has only been recently recognized. Lindy Brady demonstrates "direct verbal parallels between the text of *Arthur and Gorlagon* and 'proverbial' antifeminist statements [in Latin] ... which were widely repeated throughout medieval works".[46] In a longer analysis that argues the text's main focus is not on feminine desire *tout court*, but rather on the improper, public display of that desire, she draws attention to the punishments that the guilty queens receive for their crimes, contrasting them to normal treatment in the English legal context of the period.[47] Indeed, there is a level of gleeful violence throughout that seems intent on grounding the fantasy in repeated bloodshed. The wolf-king – the innocent victim at the start of the narrative – seeking revenge on his wife, tears apart her two children by her lover and disembowels her two brothers. In retaliation, his own pups, conceived with a female wolf, are hanged. His grief at the loss leads him to a career of indiscriminate slaughter of both livestock and human beings, which ceases only when he meets the second king. When the affair between that king's queen and his steward are revealed, the steward is flayed alive and hanged, while the queen is torn apart by horses and burned. And at the end of the romance, the first wicked queen is revealed to be the woman sitting at Gorlagon's table with a bloodied head that she kisses repeatedly – a

---

45   *Arthur and Gorlagon*, ed. G.L. Kittredge, *Arthur and Gorlagon: Versions of the Werewolf's Tale*, New York, 1966, p. 162 (repr. from *Harvard Studies and Notes in Philology and Literature* 8 (1903), 149–275): "super hijs que audiuerat valde miratus, domum itinere dierum nouem redijt." My translation.

46   Brady, "Antifeminist Tradition", p. 163.

47   Brady, "Feminine Desire", pp. 32–34.

punishment that Brady reads as aligned with the text's concern about public and private sexuality.[48] An over-arching emphasis on action and retribution, some of it at the hands (or paws) of a fantastic creature and some of it explicitly couched in terms of royal, legal jurisdiction, presents us again with a blend of modes, some drawing on vernacular, and some on Latin textual worlds.

Geoffrey's *DGB* prompted a wide variety of responses in his Latinate readers. Some medieval and early modern annotators seem to have treated it as a source book, whether for historical information, interesting stories, or some combination of the two. Geoffrey's explicitly "British" brief, to tell the story of the kings of the Britons from before the Christian era through to the Saxon domination, had a clear appeal to later periods that were working through what British history might mean, as the annotations drawing attention to figures like Brutus, or Leir, or Arthur, suggest. The proliferation of prequels, insertions, and sequels steadily drew the *DGB* into an ever-growing web of associations, and suggest that the text retained its historical vitality long after its appearance in the 12th century. Whether through added regnal lists, explications of Merlin's prophecies to fit the events of the Wars of the Roses, or other kinds of interpolations and expansions, not to mention the frequent excerpting of Geoffrey's work in other Latin British histories, the *DGB* was kept alive for historical purposes well into the early modern period.

At the same time, those concerns or motifs found in texts like *The Origin of Giants* or *The True History of the Death of Arthur* that appear, through a retrospective critical gaze at least, to point toward romance, also remain firmly embedded in a Latin textual world. *The Story of Meriadoc* and *The Rise of Gawain* casually mix classical references with recognizable folk motifs, drawn perhaps from Welsh tradition, and in this practice their author mirrors Geoffrey's own approach. The anonymous author's explicit reflections on the writing practice shows us another British-Latin writer thinking through what it means to write *this* way, in *this* language. While the end of *The Rise of Gawain* draws an apparently negative comparison between the eloquent pen of the historian and the vulgar oral displays of paid storytellers, both his works find ample room for motifs and incidents that would be entirely at home in the vernacular, whether oral or written. And while the author of *Arthur and Gorlagon* does not directly reflect on either Geoffrey's work or his own process, his practice too reminds us that the *DGB* was not the only Latin text to combine the resources and interests of Latinate and vernacular culture. It was undoubtedly, however, the most popular, and was eagerly taken up itself in the vernacular context, as the next chapter illustrates.

---

48   Brady, "Feminine Desire", p. 37.

CHAPTER 8

Geoffrey of Monmouth's *De gestis Britonum* and Twelfth-Century Romance

Françoise Le Saux

Geoffrey of Monmouth's *De gestis Britonum* had a long and influential after-life. The work was exploited to endow Anglo-Norman Britain with a foundation myth on which to build a common (though not unproblematic) political identity, giving rise to a new historiographical tradition in Latin, French, and English. At the same time, the great deeds of past British kings form a treasure house of narratives, with the figure of King Arthur at the heart of a new literary phenomenon, the Arthurian romance.

The entertainment potential of the *DGB* is flagged up by Geoffrey of Monmouth himself in his prologue, where he sketches a context of oral tradition and popular story-telling "about Arthur and the many others who succeeded after the Incarnation" related "by many people as if they had been entertainingly and memorably written down".[1] The exact nature of this pre-existing narrative tradition is not specified, though the archivolt of the Porta della Peschiera of Modena Cathedral, depicting a scene where Arthur and his knights appear to be attacking a castle to free the captive Winlogee (Guinevere?), is proof of the popularity of tales of Arthur in western Europe by 1120–40.[2] The huge success of the *DGB* therefore reinforced and reshaped an already existing tradition, and as such was instrumental in the flowering of the courtly Arthurian romances of the latter 12th century. Geoffrey of Monmouth made King Arthur enter the Latinate cultural mainstream. His later *VM*, by contrast, failed to work the same magic for Merlin, its central character, and had no discernable impact on 12th-century romance.

An important contributory factor to the long-term success of the *DGB* was its rapid integration into the vernacular culture of medieval, francophone England. Geoffrey of Monmouth lived at a time of social and cultural ferment. The aftermath of the Norman Conquest had given rise to a network of baronial

---

1 *DGB*, Prologus 1.5–7: "de Arturo ceterisque compluribus qui post incarnationem successe-runt ... a multis populis quasi inscripta iocunde et memoriter".

2 See N.J. Lacy, "The Arthurian Legend Before Chrétien de Troyes", in N.J. Lacy and J.T. Grimbert (eds.), *A Companion to Chrétien de Troyes*, Cambridge, 2005, pp. 43–51.

courts that extended active patronage to writers in the French language and supported a wave of translations from the Latin of authoritative, learned works such as saints' lives, scientific texts, and histories.[3] This activity contributed to an increased confidence in the French vernacular as a means of literary expression. The extent to which the Anglo-Norman world was attuned to the potential of translation is apparent in Geoffrey of Monmouth's account of his obtaining of his source from Walter of Oxford.[4] The DGB is presented as a Latin translation of a vernacular authority in a Brittonic language – "a very old book in the British tongue".[5] This authoritative source is unfamiliar, in the sense that it does not belong to the Greco-Roman mainstream, while the extreme age of the *liber vetustissimus*, the "very old book", endows it with a validity within its own purview that implicitly trumps Latin histories. Geoffrey's audience would have had little difficulty in accepting such a scenario, as the Anglo-Normans were aware of the long-standing tradition of vernacular literacy in their new homeland, in Irish and English as well as in Welsh. Moreover, even though English had lost its status, the translation culture of pre-Conquest England offered intellectual and conceptual structures that eased the effort of making Latin texts available to a non-Latinate francophone audience. Geoffrey could rely on the willingness of his readers to accept the existence of authoritative texts written in a vernacular to an extent that might not have been quite as true in continental France at the same period.

A noteworthy aspect of the prologue of the DGB, along with its inversion of the direction of *translatio studii*, is its challenging of the presumption of aesthetic superiority of Latin over the vernacular. The supposedly "very old book" is written *perpulchris orationibus*, that is, with elegance and in the most beautiful style; this exquisite discourse (quite improbably) is itself placed *continue et ex ordine*, "in a continuous chronological order".[6] In other words, it

---

3   See M.D. Legge, *Anglo-Norman Literature and its Background*, Oxford, 1963; I. Short, "Patrons and Polyglots: French Literature in 12th-Century England", *Anglo-Norman Studies* 14 (1992), 229–49; and on Latin translation in early Anglo-Norman England, B. O'Brien, *Reversing Babel: Translation among the English during an Age of Conquests, c. 800 to c. 1200*, Lanham, MD and Newark, 2011. On the specifically socio-linguistic aspect, see also M. Banniard, "Du latin des illettrés au roman des lettrés. La question des niveaux de langue en France (VIIIe–XIIe siècle)", in P. Von Moos (ed.), *Entre Babel et Pentecôte, Différences linguistiques et communication orale avant la modernité (VIIIe–XVIe s.)*, Berlin, 2008, pp. 269–86.

4   DGB, Prologus 2.9–15: "Optulit Walterus Oxenefordensis archidiaconus, uir ... in exoticis hystoriis eruditus, quondam Britannici sermonis librum uetustissimum qui ... actus omnium continue et ex ordine perpulchris orationibus proponebat. Rogatu itaque illius ductus, ... codicem illum in Latinum sermonem transferre curaui."

5   DGB, Prologus 2.10.

6   DGB, Prologus 2.11–12.

has all the hallmarks of the Latin classics that formed the basis of medieval literacy – the works of a Lucan, a Sallust, a Virgil – without being indebted to them. Moreover, translation into Latin is not synonymous with improvement of any sort, but of loss. Geoffrey dismissively refers to his own, Latin style as rustic (*agresti ... stilo*), further underscoring the superiority of the Brittonic source.[7] This apparently very conventional use of the humility topos in the prologue is also an endorsement of the vernacular as an effective medium of authoritative discourse.

When the *DGB* was disseminated in the late 1100s, the Anglo-Norman world was already active in the production of didactic and scientific texts in the French language, with writers such as Philippe de Thaun composing his *Comput* (1113), a technical treatise on the calendar in hexasyllabic couplets, and *Bestiary* (between 1121 and 1139, in mixed verse form) under the patronage of the English court. Hagiography was also a popular choice for French adaptations, with Benedeit's *Voyage of St Brendan* (c.1118–21) being one of the earliest surviving saints' lives in French.[8] Geoffrey of Monmouth's stance in his prologue is thus in tune with the cultural mood of early 12th-century England; and while it would be an exaggeration to suggest that the prologue to the *DGB* contained an open invitation to further the chain of transmission through translation that Geoffrey purported to have initiated, it is unsurprising that his work was itself swiftly translated into French.

The first mention of a French vernacular history (*geste*) of the British people appears in Geffrei Gaimar's *Estoire des Engleis*, of which it may once have formed the first Book; a first redaction of this work, dated to 1137, was revised in 1141.[9] In his epilogue, Gaimar acknowledges the help of his patroness Constance fitz Gilbert in procuring the English, French, and Latin sources on which he based his account.[10] These sources unmistakably include a version of the *DGB*:

---

7   *DGB*, Prologus 2.13.
8   On hagiography in the Anglo-Norman domain, see F. Laurent, *Plaire et édifier: Les récits hagiographiques composés en Angleterre aux XIIᵉ et XIIIᵉ siècles*, Paris, 1998. For a concise contextual study of hagiography in the Middle Ages, see F. Laurent, L. Mathey-Maille, and M. Szkilnik, "L'hagiographie au service de l'histoire: enjeux et problématique", in F. Laurent, L. Mathey-Maille, and M. Szkilnik (eds.), *Des saints et des rois. L'hagiographie au service de l'histoire*, Paris, 2014, pp. 9–21.
9   See Geffrei Gaimar, *Estoire des Engleis*, ed. and trans. I. Short, *Estoire des Engleis / History of the English*, Oxford, 2009, pp. x–xii and xxii–xxxii.
10   Geffrei Gaimar, *Estoire*, ed. Short, pp. 348–50, ll. 6435–82.

Geoffrey Gaimar made a written copy of this book and added to it the supplementary material that the Welsh had omitted, for he had previously obtained, be it rightfully or wrongfully, the good book of Oxford that belonged to archdeacon Walter, and with this he made considerable improvements to his own book.[11]

It would appear from these lines that Gaimar had supplemented an already drafted history of the Britons with material from Geoffrey's work, misidentified as the *liber vetustissimus* itself, rather than having actually translated the entirety of the *DGB*, a reasonable conjecture considering the closeness of the dates of composition of the two texts.[12] As this work is now lost, the extent and nature of its indebtedness to Geoffrey's work cannot be known. However, Gaimar appears to have been in sympathy with Geoffrey's attractive way of depicting the past, and may have been directly influenced by it in his *Estoire des Engleis*.

Gaimar closes his narrative with a challenge to his rival David to continue his narrative with an account of the reign of Henry I, where he outlines what he himself would include in this sequel:

[Gaimar] could compose a verse account of the finest exploits, namely, the love affairs and the courting, the drinking and the hunting, the festivities and the pomp and ceremony, the acts of generosity and the displays of wealth, the entourage of noble and valiant knights that the king maintained, and the generous presents that he distributed. This is indeed the sort of material that should be celebrated in poetry, with nothing omitted and nothing passed over.[13]

The features highlighted by Gaimar in this passage are recognizably those that present-day scholarship associates with the romance. They are also prominent features in key episodes of the *DGB*, in particular in the Arthurian section.

---

11   Geffrei Gaimar, *Estoire*, ed. Short, p. 349, ll. 6459–66: "Geffrai Gaimar cel livre escri[s]t / [e] les transsa[n]dances i mist / Ke li Waleis ourent leissé / K[ë] il aveit ainz purchacé – / U fust a dreit u fust a tort – / Le bon livre dë Oxeford / Ki fust Walter l'arcedaien, / Sin amendat son livre bien."

12   See I. Short, "Gaimar's Epilogue and Geoffrey of Monmouth's *Liber vestustissimus*", *Speculum* 69:2 (1994), 323–43.

13   Geffrei Gaimar, *Estoire*, ed. Short, p. 352, ll. 6510–18: "Des plus bels faiz pot vers trover: / Ço est d'amur e dosnaier, / Del gaber e de boscheier, / E de festes e des noblesces, / Des largetez e des richesces / E del barnage k'il mena / Des larges dons k[ë] il dona: / D'iço cevreit hom bien chanter, / Nïent leissi[e]r ne trespasser."

Gaimar's epilogue points to an emerging set of expectations on the part of the audience of a historical text in French in the 12th century, which he strove to satisfy in his *Estoire*.

Gaimar's work exhibits a number of proto-romance features.[14] The *Estoire* adds three major interpolations to the main historical sources used, all three of which feature a striking female character: the wronged heiress Argentille, the wife of Buern Bucecarl, and King Edgar's scheming queen Ælfthryth. As Ian Short points out in his introduction to the *Estoire*, Gaimar's depiction of women is noticeably free of misogyny.[15] The image given of the young Ælfthryth in particular is that of a courtly lady of romance, beautiful, well-educated, wise, and gracious in her speech,[16] and generally so charming and well-bred "that no one could ever discover any discourtesy, jealousy or contempt in her, so discreet was she in her behavior".[17] Her beauty is such that the love-stricken Æthelwald is convinced she is a fairy rather than a human woman (p. 200, ll. 3661–62). Ælfthryth's luxurious apparel as she comes to court to marry King Edgar is described in detail, from the precious ring on her finger to the long train to her hooded gown under her miniver-lined cloak (p. 212, ll. 3882–91). This vignette culminates with the narrator exclaiming:

> "Hey!" – says Gaimar – "I have no wish to expatiate on her beauty and risk delaying [my narrative]. Were I to spend the whole day, from dawn to dusk, recounting the truth of the matter, I would not succeed in telling or describing even a small fraction of her beauty."[18]

Lavish descriptions of court life and state events also make an appearance in the reign of William Rufus, whose barons are presented in hyperbolic terms (pp. 316–20, ll. 5859–5908) while the king is described in terms evocative of King Arthur himself, attracting a huge number of retainers from overseas (p. 320, ll. 5909–16) and holding a sumptuous, grand crown-wearing ceremony at Whitsun, where he distributes great gifts (pp. 324–28, ll. 5975–6054). Gaimar

---

14   See, for example, A. Press, "The Precocious Courtesy of Geoffrey Gaimar", in G.S. Burgess (ed.), *Court and Poet: Selected Proceedings of the Third Congress of the International Courtly Literature Society*, Liverpool, 1981, pp. 267–76; see also Geffrei Gaimar, *Estoire*, ed. Short, pp. xli–xlii.

15   Geffrei Gaimar, *Estoire*, ed. Short, p. xli.

16   Geffrei Gaimar, *Estoire*, ed. Short, p. 204, ll. 3746–56.

17   Geffrei Gaimar, *Estoire*, ed. Short, p. 204, ll. 3757–60: "k'unches nul hom de nul'envie / ne d'eschar ne de vilainie / ne pout en lui rien trover / si ert sage de sei garder."

18   Geffrei Gaimar, *Estoire*, ed. Short, p. 212, ll. 3893–98: "'Ho!' feit Gaimar, 'ne rois parler / De sa bealté pur demurer. / Si jo disaie tut le veir / Dés le matin deskë al seir / N'avaraie dit ne aconté / La tierce part de sa bealté.'"

relates anecdotes of the king's generosity and sense of humor; his courtliness is illustrated by the story of the entire royal court cropping their hair in solidarity with Walter Giffard and his men, starting a new fashion (pp. 328–30, ll. 6077–6102). The Arthurian connotations to the account of William Rufus's Whitsun court of 1099 are inescapable.[19]

A number of French verse translations and adaptations of the *DGB*, known as *Bruts*, were made over the course of the 12th century. Using as their main source Geoffrey's vulgate version of the *DGB* or a Latin rewriting of it (especially the First Variant Version), most of these texts have only survived as fragments.[20] Only one of these verse translations has come down to us in its entirety: the *Roman de Brut*, by the Jersey-born cleric Wace (1155). Wace's *Roman de Brut* is a landmark in medieval French literature, and its success was such that other 12th-century translations into French of the *DGB* probably could not compete. The *Roman de Brut* has come down to us in over 30 manuscripts, 19 of which are complete or near-complete: a very large number for a non-religious work.[21] Despite the title by which it is now known, this is not a romance in the currently accepted generic sense of a work of fiction with a marked interest in the psychology of the central characters, but rather a *mise en romanz*, an adapted translation into the French language: within the poem, the work is referred to as the *geste des Bretuns*, "deeds of the Britons", a title echoing that of the vulgate version of Geoffrey of Monmouth's *De gestis Britonum*. Composed in octosyllabic couplets, it is 14,866 lines long, over 4000 of which recount the reign of King Arthur.

In the *Roman de Brut*, as in the *DGB*, Arthur is just one king in a long line. The focus is firmly on issues of dynastic succession and transmission of power, as may be seen from the importance granted by Wace to the rule of King Belin (who, with his brother Brennes, is said to have conquered Rome) and the

---

19   See Geffrei Gaimar, *Estoire*, ed. Short, p. xlvi. However, this parallel might not be entirely positive, as Arthur in the *Estoire* is responsible for the coming to power of the usurper of the throne of Haveloc's father; see G. Wheeler, "Kingship and the Transmission of Power in Geffrei Gaimar's *Estoire des Engleis*", unpublished PhD thesis, University of Sheffield, 2017.

20   On these fragments, see P. Damian-Grint, *The New Historians of the Twelfth-Century Renaissance: Inventing Vernacular Authority*, Woodbridge, 1999, pp. 61–65, and more recently, B. Barbieri, "La *Geste de Bretuns* en alexandrins (Harley *Brut*): Une traduction de l'*Historia* aux teintes épiques", in H. Tétrel and G. Veysseyre (eds.), *L'Historia regum Britannie et les "Bruts" en Europe, Tome I, Traductions, adaptations, réappropriations (XIIᵉ–XVIᵉ siècle)* (Rencontres 106, Civilisation médiévale, 12), Paris, 2015, pp. 141–55.

21   For a full list of surviving manuscripts and fragments of the *Roman de Brut*, see J. Blacker, with the collaboration of G.S. Burgess, *Wace: A Critical Bibliography*, St Helier, 2008, pp. 6–9.

passage of dominion to the English effected by the pagan invader Gurmund – episodes which all display varying amounts of expansion and elaboration of the poet's main sources.[22] The outlook is predominantly didactic with a bias toward religious history, a characteristic also of his main source, the First Variant Version of the *DGB*, on which much of the *Roman de Brut* is based. Wace clearly thought of his work as authoritative scholarship, not fiction, despite the use of amplificatory devices such as descriptions or direct speech and additions of material that the modern reader might more readily associate with romance.[23] In this, Wace was following the cue of Geoffrey of Monmouth himself, who in turn was ostensibly following the conventions of classical Latin historiography, which also include descriptions and set speeches.

The Norman poet consistently recognizes the entertainment value of the material, while its political implications are underplayed. The *PM*, touching on sensitive issues for the Anglo-Norman kings, is thus omitted entirely. The reason given by Wace for this decision is ostensibly of a scholarly nature: *Ne vuil sun livre translater / Quant jo nel sai interpreter; / Nule rien dire nen vuldreie / Que si ne fust cum jo dirreie* (pp. 399–400, ll. 7539–42).[24] The literal translation of this extract is: "I do not wish to translate his book because I do not know how to interpret it; I would not want to say something about it that might not be as I said." Rather than transmit potentially faulty information to his reader, Wace excised the entire Book. This decision results in the loss of an important dimension of Geoffrey's work. Where, in the *DGB*, the *PM* creates a bridge between the past, present, and future of a beloved homeland, the focus of Wace's *Roman de Brut* is now the faded past of an alien culture. The poet's emotional distance toward the ancient British people whose history he recounts is further expressed in his dismissal of the Welsh (p. 778, ll. 14851–54) as degenerate and unworthy descendants of their great ancestors, adding moral condemnation to Geoffrey's picture of political decline.[25]

The exotic aura of Wace's Britain is enhanced by his adding to Geoffrey's already wondrous account of the reign of King Arthur the mention of the Round Table: because of rivalry between his noble barons, "Arthur made the Round Table, about which the Bretons tell many tales."[26] In this first attested reference to Arthur's Round Table, Wace takes pains to dismiss these tales as fables,

---

22   See F. Le Saux, *A Companion to Wace*, Cambridge, 2005, pp. 94–102.

23   See Damian-Grint, *The New Historians*, esp. pp. 85–142.

24   All quotes of the *Roman de Brut* are from Wace, *Roman de Brut*, ed. I.D.O. Arnold, *Le Roman de Brut de Wace*, 2 vols., Paris, 1938–40.

25   *DGB*, xi.207.587–600.

26   Wace, *Roman de Brut*, ed. Arnold, vol. 2, p. 460, ll. 9751–52: "Fist Artur la Runde Table / Dunt Bretuns font mainte fable."

and therefore inferior to his own work; yet he also recognizes in them a kernel of truth that he, as a historian, can identify. The creation of the Round Table and the stories attached to it are thus explicitly dated to a twelve-year window within Arthur's rule, when the great conqueror enjoyed an extended period of peace after having regained control over Britain and subdued Scotland and Scandinavia. These stories of *merveilles pruvees*, "marvels" (p. 515, l. 9789), and adventure (p. 515, l. 9790) are thus based in fact, even though they have been retold so often that they have become legendary. The existence of a factual core at the heart of these tales is stressed by Wace, who insists that they are "neither all lies nor all truth, neither all frivolous nor all wise".[27] This is not a wholesale debunking of such stories; they certainly exaggerate what actually happened, but they nevertheless relate to "real" events that took place at a very specific point of the reign of a supposedly real king. Arthur thus becomes comparable with an Alexander the Great or a Charlemagne, making his tales worthy of written transmission.

Geoffrey's narrative offers tales of chivalry, conquest, and giant-killing; to this, Wace adds the influence of women in periods of peace. When the warlike Cador expresses his joy at the thought of going to war with Rome, Gawain counters with the praise of peace: "Peace is good after war, the land is more beautiful and the better for it; it's very good to have fun, and love affairs are good. For love and for their beloved, knights perform deeds of chivalry."[28] The link between *drueries*, "love", and *chevaleries*, "chivalry", gives this passage a courtly coloring that fits well with the reputation of Gawain as a seducer of ladies in the later romance tradition.[29] The main point here, however, is that peace is both transient and desirable. Love is just one of a number of benefits of peacetime, mentioned after the land's increased prosperity (p. 563, l. 10768) and the joys of *gaberies*, "light-hearted leisure". Moreover, within the cycle of war, love provides the motivation for knights to keep up with their military

27   Wace, *Roman de Brut*, ed. Arnold, vol. 2, p. 515, ll. 9793–94: "Ne tut mençonge, ne tut veir, / Ne tut folie ne tut saveir".

28   Wace, *Roman de Brut*, ed. Arnold, vol. 2, pp. 563–64, ll. 10767–72: "Bone est la pais emprès la guerre / Plus bele et mieldre en est la terre; / Mult sunt bones les gaberies / E bones sunt les drueries. / Pur amistié e pur amies / Funt chevaliers chevaleries."

29   For different readings of this very rich passage, see A. Putter, "Arthurian Literature and the Rhetoric of Effeminacy", in F. Wolfzettel (ed.), *Arthurian Romance and Gender: Masculin/féminine dans le roman arthurien medieval*, Amsterdam and Atlanta, 1995, pp. 34–49, esp. p. 44; and M.B. Schichtman, "Gawain in Wace and Layamon: A Case of Metahistorical Evolution", in L.A. Finke and M.B. Schichtman (eds.), *Medieval Texts and Contemporary Readers*, Ithaca, NY and London, 1987, pp. 103–19.

training, in anticipation of the next military campaign.[30] The *chevaleries* of the knights are not just gratuitous display or mere tokens of affection.

Though Wace is at ease depicting female characters, his treatment of them is not noticeably influenced by the *fin'amor* of Old Provençal lyrical poetry, neither do we find in his work a celebration of female beauty comparable to Gaimar's description of Ælfthryth. There is little evidence of idealization; instead, one can discern a tendency toward what the present-day reader might see as a form of realism that can be traced back to Wace's hagiographical works. In Wace's *Life of St Margaret of Antioch*, the effects of the torture inflicted on the saint are thus described without restraint, from the blood flowing from her wounds (pp. 196–97, ll. 188–92) to the exposed entrails hanging out of her martyred body (pp. 200–01, ll. 274–78).[31] A comparable bluntness can be observed in the *Roman de Brut* in the depiction of Tonwenne, the elderly mother of Belin and Brennes, who interposes herself between the two warring brothers, pointing to the breasts that had once fed them. The queen mother is not merely described as being old, we are told that her breasts are "withered and hairy with age".[32] The beauty of younger women, on the other hand, is referred to in a perfunctory and vague manner, and love intrigues only appear where they are also found in Wace's sources. The occasional mention in the French poem of a bride's high lineage says more about the political value of the match than about the lady herself, and the feelings of the characters remain unexplored.[33]

The *Roman de Brut* cannot therefore be considered a courtly romance. In this respect, Wace is simply following his source material. The DGB is predominantly a narrative of power struggles, punctuated by conflict, battles, and warfare, with a religious dimension provided by regular synchronisms of the British past with biblical events. After the conversion to Christianity of the British people, the defense of their faith against pagan enemies is a recurrent theme: Wace, who had a distinguished record as a hagiographer, would doubtless have been particularly sensitive to this aspect of his source. It is significant

---

30   On the cycle of war and peace in the DGB and its translations and adaptations, see A. Lynch, "'Peace is good after war': The Narrative Seasons of English Arthurian Tradition", in C. Saunders, F. Le Saux, and N. Thomas (eds.), *Writing War: Medieval Literary Responses to Warfare*, Cambridge, 2004, pp. 127–46.

31   Wace, *Conception Nostre Dame*, trans. J. Blacker, G.S. Burgess, and A.V. Ogden, *Wace, The Hagiographical Works: The 'Conception Nostre Dame' and the Lives of St Margaret and St Nicholas* (Studies in Medieval and Reformation Traditions, 169 / Texts and Sources, 3), Leiden, 2013, pp. 196–97 and 200–01.

32   Wace, *Roman de Brut*, ed. Arnold, vol. 2, p. 148, l. 2724: "flaistres de vieillesce e pelues".

33   See G.S. Burgess, "Women in the Works of Wace", in G.S. Burgess and J. Weiss (eds.), *Maistre Wace. A Celebration: Proceedings of the International Colloquium held in Jersey, 10–12 September 2004*, St Helier, 2006, pp. 91–106, at pp. 94–98.

that outside of the Arthurian section, the major additions in the *Roman de Brut*
relate to what might be termed the spiritual history of the land: the prophecy
of Teleusin announcing the birth of Christ (p. 260, ll. 4855–76); the destruction of the town of Cirencester by the pagan Gurmund, emblematic of his
destruction of Christianity (pp. 707–13, ll. 13529–632); or anecdotes of the mission of St Augustine of Canterbury, such as the punishment of the people of
Dorchester, who had mocked the saint by hanging fish tails on his clothes, and
thereafter bore tails themselves (pp. 718–19, ll. 13713–44).[34] Wace's sensitivity
to theological and doctrinal aspects is also perceptible in his reshaping of the
prayer of St Oswald before the battle of Heavenfield (pp. 756–57, ll. 144459–71),
foregrounding repentance rather than asking for protection in battle.[35]

The prevalence of military episodes in the material of the *Roman de Brut*
would lead one to expect the poem to draw upon the phraseology and conventions of the Old French epic, the *chanson de geste*, of which the *Song of Roland*
is the most celebrated example. While Wace certainly was familiar with the
genre, there is little evidence that he made use of it in composing his work.
Stylistically, the *chanson de geste* is typically composed in stanzas (*laisses*) of
a varying number of lines, usually of ten syllables, linked by the one rhyme,
whereas the *Roman de Brut* is composed in rhyming octosyllabic couplets.
The battle scenes do share with the *chanson de geste* a number of motifs and
formulae, but these could equally be attributed to Geoffrey's own use of epic
motifs in these passages. In addition, the *Roman de Brut* distinguishes itself
from both the Galfridian narrative and the *chanson de geste* by the emotional
distance of the narrator, who recounts events in a relatively impartial manner.
This contrasts sharply with the openly partisan stance of the narrator in the
DGB, where there is no doubt as to where sympathies should lie.[36]

Wace appears to have been consciously creating his own poetic and narrative idiom when adapting his source material, with a predominantly didactic and scholarly intent designed to enhance its authority. He thus transmits
Geoffrey of Monmouth's work to the French-speaking world as "serious" yet
entertaining history, while the apparently dismissive passage in the *Roman de
Brut* mentioning the popular tales of Arthur also contains a vindication of these

34 Wace, *Roman de Brut*, ed. Arnold, vol. 2, pp. 718–19, ll. 13715–43. On this episode, see Le Saux,
    A Companion to Wace, pp. 98–99, 116–20, and 145; see also ead., "Wace as Hagiographer", in
    Burgess and Weiss (eds.), *Maistre Wace. A Celebration*, pp. 139–48.
35 Oswald's prayer is very much focused on protection from a cruel enemy in both the *DGB*,
    xi.199.448–51, and the *First Variant Version*, ed. Wright, p. 185, §199.
36 These points are made in *L'Estoire de Brutus. La plus ancienne traduction en prose fran-
    çaise de l'Historia Regum Britannie de Geoffroy de Monmouth*, ed. G. Veysseyre (Textes lit-
    téraires du Moyen Age, 33), Paris, 2014, pp. 103–08.

narratives. The legitimacy of the Matter of Britain for those Anglo-Norman and French writers exploring the emerging genre of courtly romance had been established. By the end of the century, Jehan Bodel, in his *Chanson des Saisnes*, counts the Matter of Britain among the three narrative *matières* appropriate for literary development, alongside the Matter of France and the Matter of "*Rome la Grant*".[37]

The mid 1150s, when the *Roman de Brut* was being composed, was a period of literary innovation. The figure of Alexander the Great was inspiring vernacular literary production from the first third of the 12th century already,[38] and narrative poems in French, on non-religious themes, were being commissioned by the Anglo-Norman royal court. The oldest surviving romances are a trilogy of *romans d'antiquité*: *Roman de Thèbes* (c.1150), *Roman d'Enéas* (1155–60) and *Roman de Troie* (1160–65).[39] The subject matter of these three romances is recognizably drawn from Greco-Roman narratives: the *Roman de Thèbes* is an adaptation of Statius's *Thebaid*, by an anonymous author from Poitou; the *Éneas*, composed by an anonymous Norman cleric, is loosely based on Virgil's *Aeneid*; while the *Roman de Troie*, by Benoît de Sainte-Maure, uses the accounts of two supposed eyewitnesses of the war of Troy, *The Fall of Troy*, attributed to Dares Phrygius, and *A Record of the Trojan War* (*Ephemeris belli Troianni*), attributed to Dictys Cretensis. This material is therefore scholarly and of high status, a fact stressed by the author/narrator of the *Roman de Thèbes*, who projects himself as heir to Homer, Plato, Virgil, and Cicero.[40] These texts have in common with Wace's *Roman de Brut* their historical subject matter, but display a heightened degree of rhetorical and stylistic adornment, with a fondness for the device of ekphrasis, the elaborate verbal description of visual objects, such as paintings or embroideries. The description of the tent of King Adraste of Argos in the *Roman de Thèbes* (pp. 294–300, ll. 4300–85) is a good example of this feature. Made out of blue and red silk covered with floral embroidery,

---

37   Jehan Bodel, *La chanson des Saisnes*, ed. A. Brasseur, *La chanson des Saisnes* (Textes littéraires français, 369), 2 vols., Geneva, 1989, vol. 1, p. 3, ll. 6–11.

38   The first of these texts to have come down to us, in monorhymed octosyllabic *laisses*, was written in the south of France by Alberic of Pisançon; only 105 lines of this work, which deal with Alexander's early deeds, survive. Alberic's work was recast in decasyllabic *laisses* around 1160, and then in the 1170s gave rise to three further poems which were combined around 1180 into a complete romance in dodecasyllabic lines by Alexandre de Paris: *Le Roman d'Alexandre*. On these texts, see *Les Romans d'Alexandre: aux frontiers de l'épique et du romanesque*, ed. C. Gaullier-Bougassas (Nouvelle bibliothèque du Moyen Age, 42), Paris, 1998.

39   On these texts and their place in the development of the romance genre, see F. Mora-Lebrun, *L'Énéide mediévale et la naissance du roman*, Paris, 1994.

40   *Le Roman de Thèbes*, ed. and trans. F. Mora-Lebrun, Paris, 1995, p. 44, ll. 5–6.

the tent's panels are decorated with paintings: on one panel, a *mapamunde*, a pictorial representation of the earth, lavishly embellished with gold and precious stones, comprising the five climatic zones and all the cities, kingdoms, and sovereigns within them; on another, the seasons and the twelve months of the year, alongside the laws upheld by the king's ancestors; and on a curtain, pictures of leopards, bears, and lions. Such instances of ekphrasis are ornamental, but also function as an indirect means of characterization:[41] the wondrous tent of King Adraste reflects the quasi-universal ambit of his authority and his duties as upholder of the laws established by his ancestors, as much as it is evidence of his wealth as king of Argos.

An important novelty in the *romans d'antiquité* is the influence of the Latin writer Ovid. Descriptive passages such as Adraste's tent draw upon models found in the *Metamorphoses*, while Ovid's *Art of Love* provides the inspiration for what will become the hallmark of the courtly romance: an interest in, and careful exploration of, the feelings of the protagonists.[42] The heroes of these narratives remain warriors whose deeds take place on the battlefield, yet a prominent role is now given to their relations with female characters, who are depicted in an idealized manner. In sharp contrast to Wace's decrepit Tonwenne, the elderly queen Jocaste is depicted in the *Roman de Thèbes* as a dignified and statesmanlike sovereign. The same *Roman de Thèbes* adds to its main source, Statius's *Thebaid*, a whole new love affair, between Antigone and Parthénopée. The foregrounding of the heroes' sentiments is particularly in evidence in the final section of the *Roman d'Enéas* (p. 496, ll. 8109–10335), where the nascent love of Eneas and Lavinia overshadows chivalric deeds.

The 12th-century Arthurian romances all have Geoffrey of Monmouth's DGB as an implicit sub-text, but they rarely draw directly upon the work. The Arthur of the 12th-century romances has little in common with the great conqueror of Geoffrey's narrative. The focus, as hinted by Wace in his reference to the fables of the Round Table, is on the adventures of Arthur's knights; the king is above all an observer and an enabler, whose court is a largely ceremonial locus.[43] Such is also the case in what might be the first Arthurian stories to have come down to us in the French language, in Marie de France's *Lais*.[44] This collection of twelve

---

41 On medieval ekphrasis, see V. Allen, "Ekphrasis and the Object", in A.J. Johnston, E. Knapp, and M. Rouse (eds.), *The Art of Vision. Ekphrasis in Medieval Literature and Culture*, Columbus, 2015, pp. 17–35.

42 R. Jones, *The Theme of Love in the Romans d'Antiquité*, London, 1972, esp. pp. 30–42.

43 D. Maddox and S. Sturm-Maddox, "*Erec et Enide*: The First Arthurian Romance", in Lacy and Grimbert (eds.), *A Companion to Chrétien de Troyes*, pp. 103–19, at p. 103.

44 Quotes are from Marie de France, *Lais*, ed. K. Warnke and trans. L. Harf-Lancner, *Lais de Marie de France*, Paris, 1990.

short narratives in octosyllabic couplets, probably composed in the 1160s, is presented by the narrator/poet as being adaptations from tales sung by the "Bretons". One of these *lais*, "Lanval", is located at Arthur's court, while another, "Chievrefueil", features the star-crossed lovers Tristan and Yseut, whose adventures were absorbed by an early date into the Arthurian Matter of Britain.[45] In "Chievrefueil", the Arthurian backdrop would only have been grasped by readers already familiar with the Tristan legend as a whole, as the tale does not take place at Arthur's court or involve the king in any way. In "Lanval", which is set at Arthur's court and features a judicial hearing presided over by the king, the Arthurian world is a far cry from the glory depicted by Geoffrey of Monmouth or Wace. Arthur in "Lanval" comes over as distant and unjust, neglecting to reward a young retainer and easily manipulated by a faithless queen. In this *lai*, the feudal bond is secondary to issues of appropriate behavior in a courtly society and in affairs of the heart. Lanval, a foreigner, does not mix well and does not spend his money wisely, ending up destitute. His problems are solved by a fairy mistress who magically provides him with all his financial and emotional needs, on condition that her existence remain a secret. Guinevere takes on the role of a temptress, who, when spurned, accuses Lanval of having slighted her by claiming that the plainest of his beloved's handmaidens was more beautiful than she. Lanval, called upon to justify himself in front of Arthur's tribunal, is saved at the last moment by the arrival of the fairy mistress who vindicates him and takes him away to her fairy realm. The powerful character in this story is unmistakably the fairy lover, not the king.

Fairy magic was clearly an important feature of the tales of Arthur circulating in 12th-century Europe. Wace's parenthesis in his *Roman de Rou*, a history of the dukes of Normandy composed between 1160 and the early 1170s,[46] gives us an insight into these fables. In an aside to a list of William the Conqueror's allies, some of whom are said to come from the area of Brocéliande, Wace admits to having been bitterly disappointed when he visited the fountain of Barenton in the fabulous forest of Brocéliande, the setting of many a Breton tale (vol. 2, p. 121, ll. 6374) and home to fairies and wonders. The supposed qualities of this fountain were such that when hunters wished to refresh themselves in summer, they would pour water on the stone next to the spring. This would cause it to rain over the forest (vol. 2, p. 122, ll. 6377–89). Needless to say, Wace failed

---

45   T. Hunt and G. Bromiley, "The Tristan Legend in Old French Verse", in G.S. Burgess and
      K. Pratt (eds.), *The Arthur of the French. The Arthurian Legend in Medieval French and
      Occitan Literature* (Arthurian Literature in the Middle Ages, 4), Cardiff, 2006, pp. 112–34.
46   All references are from Wace, *Roman de Rou*, ed. A.J. Holden, *Le Roman de Rou de Wace*,
      2 vols., Paris, 1973.

to make it rain, nor did he find any fairies or marvels; he witheringly states, "I went there a fool, a fool I returned."[47] The marvel of the fountain which causes rain to fall if its stone slab is splashed with water reappears in a very similar form in the Arthurian romance of *Yvain* (c.1177), composed by Chrétien de Troyes, the poet who is credited with having invented the genre.[48]

The romance of *Yvain* can be seen as paradigmatic of the Arthurian romance.[49] It opens on the Whitsun festivities at Arthur's court. The knight Calogrenant relates his shameful defeat at the hands of the defender of a wondrous fountain in the forest of Brocéliande. His cousin Yvain vows to avenge him and sets out to seek the fountain, where he pours a whole basinful of water on the stone slab (*Versa seur le perron de plain / De l'yaue le bachin tout plain*, p. 112, ll. 800–01). The ensuing storm of wind and rain summons the protector of this *fontaine perillouse*, "perilous fountain" (p. 112, l. 808); Yvain kills him in the ensuing fight and marries his beautiful widow.

While a fund of motifs in the Arthurian romances are thus clearly borrowed from these marvelous tales, the narratives themselves are informed by the conventions established by the *romans d'antiquité*. Even Marie de France's *Lais*, which arguably remain structurally closer to the oral tales they rework than do Chrétien's romances, show evidence of cultural hybridity, both in the nature of the marvels featured in them and in the stylistic devices used.[50] The cross-cultural approach of Marie de France is explicitly flagged up in certain *lais*, which are given alternative titles in French, a Brittonic language, and even English. Her tale of the nightingale taken as excuse by a lady for rising in the middle of the night to talk with her lover, and consequently killed by her irate husband, is, we are told, called *L'Aüstic* by the Breton/British, *russignol* in French, and *nihtegale* in English (p. 210, ll. 1–6). These vernacular roots are moreover refracted through the prism of Latinate culture. The first of the collection of *lais*, "Guigemar", thus has a hero with a Brittonic-sounding name who embarks on a magical ship to be cured from a hunting wound, but the description of the bed within the ship, with its carved golden ornamentation *a l'uevre*

47   Wace, *Roman de Rou*, ed. Holden, vol. 2, p. 122, l. 6396: "fol m'en revinc, fol i alai."
48   References to *Yvain* are from Chrétien de Troyes, *Yvain*, ed. and trans. D.F. Hult, *Le Chevalier au lion ou Le Roman d'Yvain. Édition critique d'après le manuscript B.N. fr 1433*, Paris, 1994. On Chrétien de Troyes, see D. Kelly, "Chrétien de Troyes", in Burgess and Pratt (eds.), *The Arthur of the French*, pp. 135–85, esp. pp. 135–37.
49   This aspect is analysed by L. Spetia, *Li conte de Bretaigne sont si vain et plaisant. Studi sull'Yvain e sul Jaufre*, Soveria Mannelli, 2012, pp. 11–119.
50   On Marie de France and her Arthurian *lais*, see M.T. Bruckner and G.S. Burgess, "Arthur in the Narrative Lay", in Burgess and Pratt (eds.), *The Arthur of the French*, pp. 186–214, esp. pp. 186–98.

Salemun (p. 34, l. 171), is both technical and evocative of the *roman d'antiquité*.[51] The journey is made necessary by a curse laid on the hero (a common theme in medieval Celtic literature), but the lady he falls in love with is imprisoned in a tower decorated with a painting representing Venus burning *le livre Ovide*, "the book of Ovid" (p. 38, l. 239) – probably Ovid's *Remedies of Love* – and the two lovers explore their nascent feelings in the Ovidian tradition.

Chrétien de Troyes' *Erec and Enide*, composed c.1170 and therefore the oldest Arthurian romance to have come down to us,[52] also bears the mark of stylistic cross-fertilization. In particular, magical wonders are partly rationalized. Erec's coronation robes, described in great detail over some 70 lines (pp. 508–12, ll. 6729–6801), thus features depictions of Geometry, Mathematics, Music, and Astronomy, the four areas of the *quadrivium*, encompassing the knowledge of the natural world. Macrobius is twice mentioned as an authority vouching for the accuracy of description, yet the robe itself is the work of four *fees*, created "with great skill and mastery".[53] The de-eroticization and attendant rationalizing of the fairy figure as a craftsperson may suggest a degree of discomfort on Chrétien's part with his material, which he will implicitly disavow in his *Lancelot or Le Chevalier de la charrette* (c.1177), recounting the efforts of the Round Table (in particular Lancelot) to free the captive Guinevere from her abductor Méléagant. This story-line, which recalls the scene depicted on the Arthurian archivolt of Modena Cathedral and has as its hero the archetypical courtly lover, was apparently imposed on the poet by his patroness Marie of Champagne.[54] Chrétien left it unfinished, entrusting its completion to Godefroi de Leigni (p. 466, ll. 7102–12).[55]

---

51 On the precise nature of the engraving technique thus referred to, see G.D. West, "L'uevre Salomon", *Modern Language Review* 49 (1954), 176–82.

52 Maddox and Sturm-Maddox, "*Erec et Enide*", pp. 103–19.

53 Maddox and Sturm-Maddox, "*Erec et Enide*", p. 508, ll. 6736–37: "Par grant sens et par grant maistrie".

54 Chrétien de Troyes, *Le Chevalier de la charrette*, ed. and trans. C. Méla, *Le Chevalier de la charrette ou le Roman de Lancelot*, Paris, 1992, p. 46, ll. 24–29. How exactly to read this prologue is a matter of debate. See M.T. Bruckner, "*Le Chevalier de la Charrette*: That Obscure Object of Desire, Lancelot", in Lacy and Grimbert (eds.), *A Companion to Chrétien de Troyes*, pp. 137–55, at pp. 140–42.

55 This is also the case of Chrétien's *Perceval ou le Conte du graal* which, if the Middle Welsh analogue *Peredur* is anything to go by, was based on a tale that could only be transposed into the courtly idiom with some difficulty; see I. Lovecy, "*Historia Peredur ab Efrawg*", in R. Bromwich, A.O.H. Jarman, and B.F. Roberts (eds.), *The Arthur of the Welsh: The Arthurian Legend in Medieval Welsh Literature* (Arthurian Literature in the Middle Ages, 1), Cardiff, 1991, pp. 171–82. It is however also possible that *Perceval* was interrupted by the death of the poet.

Ultimately, the romances have little in common with the Arthurian world portrayed by Geoffrey of Monmouth. Arthur's Whitsun court is a ritual meeting-place, providing a framework around which to weave the adventures of his knights, but the king himself remains a shadowy character. When Calogrenant tells his tale to Yvain and the court in *Erec and Enide*, Arthur is actually fast asleep. The matter of the Arthurian romance focuses on the Round Table and the ability of its knights to seek out and resolve crises of a military, political, and sentimental nature. Hence Jehan Bodel's description in *Chanson des Saisnes* of the Matter of Britain as *vain et plaisant*, "pleasant froth" (p. 3, l. 9), as opposed to the worthy didacticism of the *sage et de san aprenant*, "wise and teaching of wisdom" (p. 3, l. 10), Matter of Rome or the truth-bearing Matter of France (p. 3, l. 11).

The Arthurian romances of the 12th century are in constant dialogue with the clerical tradition informing the *roman d'antiquité* and narratives of the marvels of the East, which they supplement with a magical twist: an aspect in evidence in Chrétien de Troyes' *Cligès*, where the Byzantine East is made to meet the Arthurian West in the person of the Greek prince Alexander, who goes to serve at Arthur's court where he meets his wife. Their son eventually becomes emperor of Constantinople. These fashionable literary developments also influenced the way Geoffrey's material was treated by translators and adaptors. Fragments, some of them substantial, of verse translations other than by Wace are evidence that Geoffrey's gallery of villains and heroes was viewed to some extent through the lens of epic and romance even by scholars. Most of the surviving fragments or partial redactions are versions of the *PM*, composed to fill the gap left by Wace, but five important remnants of broader narratives have also come down to us, from the late 12th and early 13th centuries:[56] the Bekker fragment, in alexandrines, recounting the story of Stonehenge;[57] the Harley *Brut* (five fragments, London, British Library, Harley 1605), also in alexandrines, which include the story of Stonehenge and the *PM*;[58] London, British Library, Harley 4733 (254 lines in octosyllabic couplets) which tells of

---

56   See P. Damian-Grint, "Arthur in the *Brut* tradition", in Burgess and Pratt (eds.), *The Arthur of the French*, pp. 101–11, at pp. 101–04.

57   Edited in "Le fragment Bekker et les anciennes versions françaises de *l'Historia Regum Britanniae*", ed. S. Lefèvre, *Romania* 109 (1988), 225–46.

58   Fragments 1–4 are transcribed by P. Damian-Grint, "Vernacular History in the Making: Anglo-Norman Verse Historiography in the Twelfth Century", unpublished PhD thesis, University of London, 1994; Fragment 5 is edited in "The Harley *Brut*: An Early French Translation of Geoffrey of Monmouth's *Historia Regum Britanniae*", ed. B. Blakey, *Romania* 82 (1961), 44–70. See also B. Barbieri, "'Una traduzione anglo-normanna dell'*Historia Regum Britannia*': la *geste des Bretuns* in alessandrini (*Harley Brut*)", *Studi mediolatini e volgari* 57 (2011), 163–76.

Arthur's campaign against Colgrim and the Saxon return after their defeat at Lincoln;[59] the Royal *Brut* (6,237 lines in octosyllabic couplets; London, British Library, Royal 13 A. xxi),[60] covering the narrative from the beginning up to the conception of Arthur, at which point it switches to Wace's text; and the Munich *Brut* (4,180 lines in octosyllabic couplets; Munich, Bayerische Staatsbibliothek, Gall. 29), from the founding of Britain and the early kings, up to the foundation of Rome, which is the object of a lengthy interpolation.[61] These fragments display marked variations, both stylistically and in their approach to their material.

The Harley *Brut* has an experimental flavor, with a quasi-epic meter: alexandrine lines, grouped in rhyming *laisses* of varying lengths evocative of the *chanson de geste*; however, it also features a remarkable instance of ekphrasis, a feature more commonly associated with romance, as we have seen. Some 116 lines (six *laisses*) are devoted to an elaborate description of Arthur's tent, which has detailed scenes painted on each of its panels.[62] The first panel (*laisses* CLXII and CLXIII) shows Moses leading the children of Israel out of Egypt through the Red Sea; his receiving of the Tables of the Law on Mount Sinai; his anger when discovering that his people were worshipping the golden calf; his shattering of the Tables of the Law and subsequent prayer for mercy for his errant people. The narrator stresses the completeness of this pictorial narrative, which, we are told, omits none of the adventures or hardships experienced by the Israelites in the desert (p. 51, ll. 2735–37). The scene of Moses's anger ends on a reassuring apostrophe to the audience before showing the wrongdoers being consumed by the ground beneath them. The second panel (*laisse* CLXIV) depicts the anointing of David by Samuel and the slaying of Goliath; on the third panel (*laisse* CLXV) is an episode from the history of *Troie la cité*, "the city of Troy" (p. 52, l. 2780), the story of Ulysses and the enchantress Circe, whose potions turned men into animals (p. 53, l. 2800); the fourth panel (*laisse* CLXVI) tells the story of Judith and Holofernes, culminating in the decapitation of the king. The visual narrative of these panels is clarified for the viewer

59   Edited in "A 12th-century Anglo-Norman *Brut* Fragment (MS BL Harley 4733, f. 128)", ed. P. Damian-Grint, in I. Short (ed.), *Anglo-Norman Anniversary Essays* (Anglo-Norman Text Society Occasional Publications Series, 2), London, 1993, pp. 87–104.

60   Edited in *An Anglo-Norman Brut (Royal 13.A.xxi)*, ed. A. Bell (Anglo-Norman Text Society, 21–22), Oxford, 1969.

61   *Der Münchener Brut*, ed. K. Hofmann and K. Vollmöller, *Der Münchener Brut, Gottfried von Monmouth in französischen Versen des xii. Jahrhunderts*, Halle, 1877. For a more recent edition, see also "An Edition of the Munich *Brut*", ed. P.B. Grout, unpublished PhD thesis, University of London, 1980.

62   All quotes from Fragment 5 are drawn from "The Harley *Brut*", ed. Blakey (pp. 48–50) convincingly situates this passage within the context of Arthur's French campaign.

by inscriptions above the scenes depicted, a detail stressed by the narrator: the names of different figures in the first panel are inscribed above them: "Above them the text was written, giving the name and appearance of each character"; the events of the second panel are written in engraved golden letters highlighted in black: "All this is shown by the letters carved with a chisel, the gold then filled in with black";[63] while the scenes of the third and fourth panel are explained to the viewer by a text above the image (*lettre surescrite*, p. 53, ll. 2800 and 2825).

These panels contain a double narrative strand, combining biblical references and classical tradition. The first three panels provide a symbolic summary of the strengths of the good king, of which Arthur may be seen as an example: a law-giver, like Moses, who guides his people with justice yet mercy; the Lord's anointed, fighting for a just cause, and therefore favored by divine providence against overwhelming odds, like David; and a wise man like Ulysses, able to discern evil and resist the temptation of self-indulgence. The fourth panel may be read as a warning, illustrating the fate of the king lacking in these qualities: an inglorious death, like that of Holofernes at the hand of a woman. Such a program is conventional in its didacticism, while the story of Ulysses, presented as a tale from the fall of Troy, is an indirect homage to the supposed Trojan origins of the British – and thus of the owner of the tent, King Arthur himself.

The depiction of the door of the tent which follows contrasts sharply with the heavily didactic pictorial program contained on its panels. The door is openly magical in properties – it denies access to anyone with bad intentions – and is described in terms that evoke both the luxurious wonders of the East and the Arthurian "*merveilleux*": adorned with 1000 precious stones encased in solid gold, and set with an immensely valuable wondrous mirror by fairies (p. 54, ll. 2835–36). This unexpected intrusion of romance motifs into a passage that is otherwise epic, in its outlook as well as its verse form, brings an element of tension to the avowed program of the tent as a whole, if only because fairy attributes and evil are very much equated on the third panel, in the person of the enchantress Circe. Circe is described as possessing the extreme physical beauty associated with fairies: "She was the daughter of the sun, a woman of great beauty. There was no woman as beautiful as she in the whole realm", while practicing black magic: "She had total mastery of necromancy."[64] The

---

63   "The Harley *Brut*", ed. Blakey, p. 51, ll. 2738–39: "Par desus esteit fait la lettre de l'Escriture / Ki rendeit a chascun sun nom et sa figure"; p. 52, ll. 2776–77: "Tot ço mustre la lettre entaillé a cisel, / E après entraite enz en l'or a nüel."

64   "The Harley *Brut*", ed. Blakey, p. 52, ll. 2785–86: "fille esteit del soleil, femme de grant bealté / N'aveit si bele femme en trestut le regné"; p. 52, l. 2790: "sout de nigromance tot a sa volenté".

possession of magical fairy artifacts thus does not sit well with the stern moral and religious message of the tent panels: the description of Arthur's tent in the Harley *Brut* blends two very different types of motifs.

The Harley fragments are unusual in that the surviving early French translations of the *DGB* tend to switch to Wace's version of the Arthurian episode.[65] This is significant, as the pre-Arthurian section of the *DGB* does not offer a comparable scope for translators to amplify their source narrative with romance-inspired features. The reign of King Leir, with its psychological exploration and scenes of court ceremonial as well as of conflict and warfare, certainly offered potential for imaginative expansion in the romance idiom, but this did not happen to any significant extent.[66] A striking exception to this general observation, however, is offered by the so-called Munich *Brut*.

The Munich *Brut* makes a number of important additions and modifications to Geoffrey's account of the founding of Britain that are evidence of a didactic intent. The work opens with a prologue describing the island of Britain (pp. 1–3, ll. 1–90). The aftermath of the fall of Troy and Eneas's union with Lavine is then expanded with material from accepted authorities, named as Virgil, Cato, and Isidore.[67] A spirited refutation of Virgil's account of the outcome of the battle between Eneas and Turnus (p. 6, ll. 195–214) signals to the reader that the poet is well-informed and critical of his authorities, while adept at interpreting his sources. Virgil, we are told, lied *selunc la letre*, "in the literal sense" (p. 6, l. 211), because he wanted to flatter Caesar Augustus, but his work is still truth-bearing in its own way, as it is philosophical rather than informative in nature: "It must be given a different meaning, for his books are all about philosophy."[68] The Munich *Brut*'s interest in Roman history is again evidenced in a lengthy interpolation (pp. 96–108, ll. 3711–4178) repeating some of the Eneas material in order to anchor the story of the birth of Romulus and Remus and the foundation of Rome to the chronology of Britain. This is the work of a scholar, or someone who wishes to be perceived as such. Matrimonial policy is in evidence, with an effort to enhance the dignity of the noble brides, and

---

65   The other exception to this observation is London, British Library, Harley 4733, fol. 128, which recounts Arthur's coming to power and first campaign against the Saxons. See "A 12th-century Anglo-Norman *Brut* Fragment", ed. Damian-Grint.

66   Rewriting in this episode tends to be focused on speeches. For an edition and contemporary French translation of the Leir episode in Geoffrey of Monmouth, Wace, Laȝamon, the Munich *Brut*, and the Royal *Brut*, see *Le Roi Leïr. Versions des XIIe et XIIIe siècles*, ed. F. Zufferey and trans. G. Nussbaumer, Paris, 2015.

67   *Der Münchener Brut*, ed. Hofmann and Vollmöller, pp. 6–7, ll. 195, 216, 261, 262.

68   *Der Münchener Brut*, ed. Hofmann and Vollmöller, p. 6, ll. 212–14: "altre sens i covient metre / Quar cho est tot philosophie, / Quantque ses livres sinefie."

therefore, indirectly, of their spouses; Eneas's powerful rival Turnus is strikingly dismissed in the prophecy of Latinus's soothsayer as a mere local man, a *païsant de la contree* (p. 4, l. 128).

However, more space is devoted to psychological analysis than might have been expected. The quandary in which the captured Anacletus finds himself, having to choose between betrayal or death, is presented with some understanding by the narrator (pp. 19–20, ll. 730–43), while Brutus's blandishments of Ignogen on the ship taking her away from her homeland are motivated by the fact that he wishes to secure her affections (*de li ameir vuelt avoir gratie*, p. 29, l. 1120). A glimpse into the more mundane aspects of life is afforded by the mention that before arming himself to go to battle with King Gaiffiers of Poitou, Brutus has a bite to eat (*dinne se un poi*, p. 44, l. 1694). The space afforded to the private thoughts and actions of the characters is not the only evidence of the influence of the aesthetic of the romance. The description of the captive Estrild and her effect on Locrin is inescapably in the courtly idiom. The girl is the daughter of a king, and her incomparable beauty is described in terms that are evocative of the courtly lyric: whiter than ivory, snow, or the lily flower (p. 57, ll. 2205–07). Locrin's response is that of the typical Ovidian lover, sighing, besotted, and in thrall to Venus. His symptoms, described over 12 lines, end with a reference to the god of love wounding the hero with his arrow – "The god of love has dealt roughly with him, with his arrow he has wounded him" – that would not be out of place in a *lai* or a courtly romance.[69]

The attraction of the romance is perhaps even more in evidence in the *locus amoenus* where Rea Sylvia falls asleep in a state of partial undress, in the interpolation recounting the birth of Romulus and Remus at the end of the Munich *Brut* (p. 101, ll. 3907–22). If this passage had been transmitted as an isolated fragment, it is unlikely the reader would have associated it with a *Brut*. Much of it is conventional: *lo riu cleir de la fontaine*, "the clear waters of a fountain" (p. 101, l. 3911), the abundance of grass and flowers (p. 101, ll. 3914–15), the protective shade offered by the trees (p. 101, l. 3917), and sweet birdsong, in particular that of the nightingale and the parrot (p. 101, ll. 3921–22). The nightingale, associated with both love and brutal rape, is particularly appropriate, as Mars will rape the girl in her sleep and sire on her the twins Romulus and Remus. The singing parrot, however, is a touch of exotic extravagance betraying the extent of the stylistic attraction of romance on the redactor at this point.

The *Brut* fragments show that the influence of romance themes and motifs on 12th-century translators and adapters of the DGB was strong, but not

---

69   *Der Münchener Brut*, ed. Hofmann and Vollmöller, p. 58, ll. 2219–20: "Li deus d'amor l'ot mal menei, / De sa sajete el cors nafrei."

consistent or pervasive. Amplification tends to occur at points of contact with other narrative traditions: classical accounts of the foundation of Rome in the early history of Britain, and the Arthurian romance in the account of the reign of Arthur. Something that is missing in these fragments, and which would have offered a valuable point of reference to assess this phenomenon, is the end of Arthur's reign. Arthur's journey to Avalon to be cured of his wounds and the promise of his return must have been an important feature of the stories hinted at by Geoffrey of Monmouth in his prologue. Where the *DGB* merely states that Arthur was taken to the island of Avalon to have his mortal wounds tended (xi.178.81–82), Wace explicitly mentions in his *Roman de Brut* (p. 693, ll. 13279–81) the belief of the "Bretun" that Arthur will return from Avalon, which he treats with cautious skepticism. Wace's English translator, Laȝamon, in the early 13th century, further fills in the picture with the fairy healer Argante, who will cure the wounded king in Avalon.[70] That the legend was strongly implanted and carried genuine political resonances may also be deduced from the publicity around the exhumation of Arthur's supposed remains in Glastonbury in 1191.[71]

The apparent lack of interest of 12th-century romances for the life and death of Arthur cannot therefore be attributed to the absence of narrative material, as much as to the fact that the Arthurian romance of this period is not truly about Arthur at all. As noted by Kelly, "all twelfth and thirteenth-century Arthurian verse romances seem to take Chrétien's romances as models to emulate, rewrite or correct":[72] and as we have seen, the king at the head of the Round Table in the romances of Chrétien de Troyes has only tenuous links with Geoffrey's Arthur. We have to wait for the beginning of the 13th century to see the emergence of narratives of Arthur the heroic warrior-king, within narrative cycles roughly structured on a chronological principle.[73] Arthur's twelve years of peace – and, crucially, his involvement in the Quest for the Holy Grail, an

70 Laȝamon, *Brut*, ed. G.L. Brook and R.F. Leslie, *Layamon: Brut. Edited from British Museum MS Cotton Caligula A ix and British Museum MS Otho C xiii*, 2 vols., London, 1963–78, vol. 2, p. 750, ll. 14277–82, and 14288–97, where, contrary to Wace, the English poet appears to be validating the belief in Arthur's return. Laȝamon's newborn Arthur is also said to be magically endowed by elves with the gifts of power, long life, and generosity (ll. 9607–15).

71 See J.P. Carley, "Arthur in English History", in W.R.J. Barron (ed.), *The Arthur of the English. The Arthurian Legend in Medieval English Life and Literature* (Arthurian Literature of the Middle Ages, 2), Cardiff, 1999, pp. 47–57, esp. pp. 48–50.

72 Kelly, "Chrétien de Troyes", p. 393.

73 See F. Bogdanow and R. Trachsler, "Rewriting Prose Romance: The post-vulgate *Roman du Graal* and related texts", in Burgess and Pratt (eds.), *The Arthur of the French*, pp. 342–92.

invention of the continuators of Chrétien de Troyes' *Perceval*[74] – are replaced within the context of his entire lifespan, a moment of glory that makes the tragedy of his death even more acute.

Around the same time that Geoffrey of Monmouth's Arthur is adopted as a fully-fledged, complex literary character, so do adaptations and continuations of the *DGB* start to distance themselves from the stylistic approach evidenced in the verse *Brut* fragments. The Prose *Bruts*, whether in French or in English, increasingly underplay the *mirabilia* contained in the *DGB*; from the 13th century onwards, the cultural dimension to Geoffrey's vision of the past is pruned down and replaced with a predominantly political outlook, with very little allowance for flights of fancy.[75] The careful blend of legend and history created by Geoffrey of Monmouth in the *DGB* has been unpicked and reshaped for a new age.

---

74   See R.T. Pickens, K. Busby, and A.M.L. Williams, "Perceval and the Grail: The Continuations, Robert de Boron and *Perlesvaus*", in Burgess and Pratt (eds.), *The Arthur of the French*, pp. 213–73.

75   See F. Le Saux, "La Grande Bretagne, patrie des sciences? La représentation des technologies scientifiques dans Geoffroy de Monmouth et Layamon", in Tétrel and Veysseyre (eds.), *L'Historia regum Britannie*, pp. 157–75, esp. pp. 174–75.

CHAPTER 9

The Most Excellent Princes: Geoffrey of Monmouth and Medieval Welsh Historical Writing

Owain Wyn Jones

A late 14th-century manuscript of *Brut y Brenhinedd* ("History of the Kings"), the Welsh translation of Geoffrey of Monmouth's *De gestis Britonum*, closes with a colophon by the scribe, Hywel Fychan,

> Hywel Fychan ap Hywel Goch of Buellt wrote this entire manuscript lest word or letter be forgotten, on the request and command of his master, none other than Hopcyn son of Tomos son of Einion ... And in their opinion, the least praiseworthy of those princes who ruled above are Gwrtheyrn and Medrawd [Vortigern and Mordred]. Since because of their treachery and deceit and counsel the most excellent princes were ruined, men whose descendants have lamented after them from that day until this. Those who suffer pain and subjection and exile in their native land.[1]

These words indicate the central role Geoffrey's narrative had by this point assumed not only in vernacular historical writing, but also in the way the Welsh conceived of their past and explained their present. Hywel was writing around the time of the outbreak of Owain Glyn Dŵr's revolt, and the ethnic and colonial grievances which led to that war are here articulated with reference to the coming of the Saxons and the fall of Arthur.[2] During the revolt itself, Glyn Dŵr's supporters justified his cause with reference to the Galfridian past, for

---

1   Philadelphia, Library Company of Philadelphia, 8680.O, at fol. 68v: "Y llyuyr h6nn a yscri-uenn6ys Howel Vychan uab Howel Goch o Uuellt yn ll6yr onys g6naeth agkof a da6 geir neu lythyren, o arch a gorchymun y vaester, nyt amgen Hopkyn uab Thomas uab Eina6n ... Ac o'e barn 6ynt, anuolyannussaf o'r ty6yssogyon uchot y llywyassant, G6rtheyrn a Medra6t. Kanys oc eu brat 6ynt a'e t6yll ac eu kyghor uynt y distry6yt y tywyssogyon arbennickaf, yr hynn a g6yna6d eu hetiuedyon g6edy 6ynt yr hynny hyd hedi6. Y rei yssyd yn godef poen ac achenoc-tit ac alltuded yn eu ganedic dayar." My transcription and translation.

2   For Hopcyn and the manuscript, see B.F. Roberts, "Un o Lawysgrifau Hopcyn ap Tomas o Ynys Dawe" [One of the manuscripts of Hopcyn ap Tomas of Ynys Dawe], *BBCS* 22 (1966–68), 223–28, and more recently B. Guy, "A Welsh Manuscript in America: Library Company of Philadelphia, 8680.O", *National Library of Wales Journal* 36 (2014), 1–26.

example, in Glyn Dŵr's letter to the king of Scotland, where the opposition
of both the Scots and the Welsh to the English was contextualized as deriving
from the Saxon invasion. Here, Glyn Dŵr as Prince of Wales was portrayed as
the heir of Camber and Cadwaladr, with Robert of Scotland depicted as the
descendant of Albanactus.[3] On campaign in 1403, Glyn Dŵr himself consulted
with Hopcyn ap Tomos, Hywel Fychan's patron and the owner of the manuscript quoted above, because of his reputation as a master of *brut*, that is,
history and prophecy.[4] More than 100 years before, in the last days of an independent Gwynedd, Galfridian history was also put to political use in the reply
of Prince Llywelyn ap Gruffudd's royal counselors to the peace proposals of
Archbishop Peckham, which justified Llywelyn's position, and that of Wales in
relation to the English king, with reference to the division of Britain between
Locrinus, Camber, and Albanactus after the death of Brutus in Geoffrey's history, maintaining that Snowdonia had belonged to the prince of Wales since the
time of Brutus.[5] Contemporary English chronicles also claim that Llywelyn's
fellow countrymen spurred him on with Merlin's prophecies and predictions
that he would wear the diadem of Brutus.[6]

These are some of the clearest examples of the use of Geoffrey's history
for political ends in medieval Wales, and indicate the pervasive influence of
Geoffrey's work on Welsh historical culture and on ideas of Welsh nationality. Between the late 12th and the 14th century his work had become accepted
as the foundational narrative of Welsh history, and it is this process which is
the primary concern of this chapter. Geoffrey described himself as a Briton
and a man of Monmouth, and he can be considered a Welsh author in the
sense that his origins lay in Wales and his historical writing drew on and developed pre-existing themes in Welsh ideas of the past. The central themes of
Geoffrey's history were not his own invention, and are clearly seen in one of his

3 Adam Usk, *Chronicle*, ed. C. Given-Wilson, *The Chronicle of Adam Usk*, Oxford, 1997,
   pp. 148–50.
4 R.R. Davies, *The Revolt of Owain Glyn Dŵr*, Oxford, 1995, pp. 159–60; G.J. Williams, *Traddodiad
   Llenyddol Morgannwg* [The literary tradition of Morgannwg], Cardiff, 1948, p. 11; *Original
   Letters Illustrative of English History*, ed. H.F. Ellis, second series, 4 vols., London, 1827, vol. 1,
   pp. 21–23.
5 *The Acts of Welsh Rulers, 1120–1283*, ed. H. Pryce, Cardiff, 2005, no. 431; J. Beverley Smith,
   Llywelyn ap Gruffudd, Prince of Wales, Cardiff, 1998, pp. 326, 542–45; id., *Yr Ymwybod â Hanes
   yng Nghymru yn yr Oesoedd Canol: Darlith Agoriadol/The Sense of History in Medieval Wales:
   an Inaugural Lecture*, Aberystwyth, 1989, pp. 14–15.
6 *Flores Historiarum*, ed. H.R. Luard, 3 vols., London, 1890, vol. 3, p. 57; "Annales Londonienses",
   ed. W. Stubbs, *Chronicles of the Reigns of Edward I and Edward II*, 2 vols., London, 1882–83,
   vol. 1, pp. 1–251, at p. 90.

most important sources, *Historia Brittonum*.[7] The importance of these themes, such as the relationship between the Britons and the Romans, the status of the Britons as the rightful owners of the island of Britain and their loss of dominance through sin, the unity of the island of Britain, and the central role of figures such as Vortigern and Arthur, were important in earlier Welsh writing. Geoffrey, however, drew these together into an epic account of the past and the future, and the popularity and sheer coherence of his work had a profound effect in giving permanent shape to these earlier ideas.[8]

Geoffrey wrote in a period when political developments across Britain required urgent redefinitions of Welsh identities, and his history, both in its Latin form and in translation, became a point of reference in defining the Welsh, both in their own eyes and through those of their enemies. The history influenced the chronicles compiled at monasteries in Wales, particularly the Cistercian daughter houses of Whitland, which formed a network across native Wales. The influence of his writing can be detected in the poetry of the *Gogynfeirdd*, "not-so-early poets", the court poets of the Welsh princes, from the turn of the 13th century, and is also apparent in definitive texts of native Welsh historical lore such as *Trioedd Ynys Prydein* ("Triads of the Island of Britain"), genealogical collections, and prose tales. It was the subject of editing and interpretation in Latin by Madog of Edeirnion, as well as being translated and reformulated in Welsh numerous times. By defining so coherently the scope of pre-medieval Welsh history, as well as forcing reaction and redefinition of existing ideas and texts, it also exerted a fossilizing influence on ideas of the Welsh past. The definitive combination of *Ystorya Dared*, *Brut y Brenhinedd*, and *Brut y Tywysogyon* ("History of the Princes"), in which the Welsh translation of Geoffrey's history assumes a central place, became the most important account of the Welsh past and left little room for any re-interpretation of a national narrative in the early modern period.[9]

---

7 See Ben Guy's chapter in this volume.

8 B.F. Roberts, "Sylwadau ar Sieffre o Fynwy a'r *Historia Regum Britanniae*" [Remarks on Geoffrey of Monmouth and the *Historia Regum Britanniae*], *Llên Cymru* 12 (1972–73), 127–45, at pp. 139–45. Roberts notes three pervasive themes indicative of Welsh historical writing that Geoffrey correctly expresses: the unity of the island of Britain expressed through one crown; an awareness of the fall and loss of this lordship; and the hope for its restoration promised through prophecy. Roberts also argues for the centrality of the theme of the relationship between the Britons and the Romans, as well as the importance of considering the prophesied restoration of British overlordship over the island in any assessment of Geoffrey's national sympathies. See also B.F. Roberts, "Geoffrey of Monmouth and Welsh Historical Tradition", *Nottingham Medieval Studies* 20 (1976), 29–40.

9 *Ystorya Dared* is a Welsh translation of the Trojan history of pseudo-Dares, discussed most fully by B.G. Owens, "Y Fersiynau Cymraeg o Dares Phrygius (Ystorya Dared): eu Tarddiad, eu

1   Geoffrey's Welsh Context

This chapter discusses Geoffrey's influence on Wales, but in doing so, consideration must be given to Geoffrey's own relationship with the country. Another chapter in this volume has discussed Geoffrey's use of Welsh sources in detail, but it will be necessary to briefly reconsider these issues in order to establish Geoffrey in his context.[10] It is clear that Geoffrey cannot be placed in the main stream of existing Welsh historical thought, just as he was, in certain ways, not in the main stream of Anglo-Norman historiography.[11] Nevertheless, he understood and manipulated the essential themes of existing Welsh historical texts, and was well acquainted with them.

The known sources of Geoffrey's work include some of the most important early medieval accounts of the British past: Gildas's *The Ruin of Britain*, the *Historia Brittonum* of Nennius, and Bede's *Ecclesiastical History*. These, along with his mentions of William of Malmesbury and Henry of Huntingdon in his history's final chapter, indicate clearly that Geoffrey was writing in an Insular Latinate tradition, and one which was revivified and redefined in the decades after the Norman Conquest.[12] He used and expanded upon these earlier accounts, but his work was also one of subversion and distortion. He was deliberately superseding and undermining the work of Bede and his Anglo-Norman successors, putting his Britons at the forefront of a narrative that went far beyond these Anglocentric accounts in its chronological scope.[13]

Nodweddion a'u Cydberthynas" [The Welsh versions of Dares Phrygius (Ystorya Dared): their origin, their attributes, and their interrelationships], unpublished MA thesis, University of Wales, 1951, and most recently by H. Fulton, "Troy Story: The Medieval Welsh *Ystorya Dared* and the *Brut* Tradition of British History", in J. Dresvina and N. Sparks (eds.), *The Medieval Chronicle VII*, Amsterdam, 2011, pp. 137–50. *Brut y Brenhinedd* is the collective term used for Welsh translations of the *DGB*, and *Brut y Tywysogyon* is a family of Welsh vernacular chronicles covering the history of Wales from the late 7th century to the late 13th. These last two are discussed in more detail below.

10   See Ben Guy's chapter in this volume.
11   See Georgia Henley and Rebecca Thomas's chapters in this volume.
12   For the impact of the conquest on historical writing in England, see R.W. Southern, "Aspects of the European Tradition of Historical Writing, 4: The Sense of the Past", *Transactions of the Royal Historical Society*, fifth series, 23 (1973), 243–63, at pp. 246–56, although Southern maintains a distinction between this historical revival and Geoffrey: id., "Aspects of the European Tradition of Historical Writing, 1: The Classical Tradition from Einhard to Geoffrey of Monmouth", *Transactions of the Royal Historical Society*, fifth series, 20 (1970), 173–96, at pp. 193–95.
13   R.W. Leckie, Jr., *The Passage of Dominion: Geoffrey of Monmouth and the Periodization of Insular History in the Twelfth Century*, Toronto, 1981, pp. 11–21, 54, 57, 66–68; K. Jankulak, *Geoffrey of Monmouth*, Cardiff, 2010, p. 20.

In so doing it can be argued that he had a comparable agenda to one of his main sources, Nennius's *Historia Brittonum*. Geoffrey transformed elements of the more patchwork *Historia Brittonum* into some of the key set-pieces of his grand narrative history, and the two texts are very different. Nevertheless both are pseudo-histories with similar preoccupations, with *Historia Brittonum* reading "almost like a reply to Bede".[14] One of its preoccupations was to present an alternative view of the Britons to the unflattering one provided by Bede, and to establish them as a providential people.[15] For example, Nennius's mention of Rhun ab Urien's conversion of Edwin of Northumbria specifically contradicts Bede's account of the conversion of this first Christian king of Northumbria by the Roman missionary Paulinus, and more broadly contradicts Bede's claim that the Britons never preached the word of God to the English.[16]

Similarly, Geoffrey pulls the rug from under Bede and his successors in innumerable ways, most notably in his portrayal of the maintenance of British rule over Britain between the Romans and the 7th century. In undermining and challenging the Bedan account of British history, Geoffrey was writing within a Welsh Latinate tradition. While the *DGB* clearly fits into the context of 12th-century Anglo-Norman historical writing, and is intended for an Anglo-Norman audience, it also fits into the Welsh tradition of its immediate sources. It took from *Historia Brittonum* the most essential elements of its narrative, including the Trojan origins of the Britons, but they were transformed and developed by Geoffrey.

While his direct links with earlier, well-attested Latinate sources are reasonably straightforward, the same cannot be said for Geoffrey's dependence on Welsh vernacular sources, which indicate a process of independent development, imitation, and cross-fertilization appreciable from a distance, but rarely traceable in detail. Although there were certainly vernacular manuscripts long before this point, the earliest surviving manuscripts postdate the publication of the *DGB* by about a century, and indeed are later than the time at which Geoffrey's work is estimated to have been translated into Welsh.[17] It is therefore only with some difficulty that we can appreciate the form of vernacular ideas of the Welsh past before Geoffrey's influence was felt. Certain texts are certainly older than Geoffrey, some show no influence from his work, and others

---

14   P. Sims-Williams, "Some Functions of Origin Stories in Early Medieval Wales", in T. Nyberg (ed.), *History and Heroic Tale: a Symposium*, Odense, 1985, pp. 97–131, at p. 117.

15   N.J. Higham, *King Arthur: Myth-Making and History*, London, 2002, pp. 116–66.

16   Bede, *Ecclesiastical History* i.22, ii.9, ii.13, ed. and trans. B. Colgrave and R.A.B. Mynors, *Bede's Ecclesiastical History of the English People*, Oxford, 1969, pp. 66–68, 162–66, 182–86; *Historia Brittonum*, ed. Faral, *LLA*, pp. 2–62, at pp. 40, 43, 46.

17   D. Huws, *Medieval Welsh Manuscripts*, Aberystwyth, 2000, pp. 36–41.

in their different and developing versions betray the gradual intensification of the hold of Geoffrey's work on the Welsh historical imagination.

Geoffrey claimed a debt to vernacular writing, as is clear from his references to the *liber vetustissimus*, "very ancient book".[18] This claim is basically spurious, but it is indicative of a broader truth, as suggested by parallels between his work and vernacular texts. The small number of inconsistencies between it and independent Welsh accounts of the past, often noted or subtly avoided by Welsh scribes and translators, indicates the broader consistency between Galfridian history and earlier Welsh ideas. Some aspects of the *DGB* are appreciable in *Historia Brittonum*, but its wider themes and many of the historical and pseudo-historical characters are also apparent in vernacular Welsh texts. The most comprehensive of these in historical terms is *Trioedd Ynys Prydein*, a collection of historical and legendary triads which represent one of the key authorities on native Welsh history available to medieval poets.[19] The date of composition of these triads is difficult to determine, since information in triadic form is likely to have circulated before the collection of the *Trioedd* in their current form. The earliest surviving version of *Trioedd Ynys Prydein* cannot be earlier than the early 12th century, and was perhaps compiled around the middle of that century.[20]

The compilation of the earliest version of *Trioedd Ynys Prydein* may therefore have been roughly contemporary with Geoffrey's writing, although its method of codifying the past is strikingly different. A triad, at its simplest, is a list of three items grouped thematically. In Wales, triads were used for legal codes and poetic technique as well as for cataloguing legendary figures. The legendary triads in *Trioedd Ynys Prydein* usually consist of a title, such as "The Three Battle-Rulers of the Island of Britain", and then a list of three figures or events. Some triads are much fuller, relating many details of the stories connected with these figures, but for the most part the references are either to characters known from elsewhere in medieval Welsh literature and history, or to figures whose stories have not survived.

---

18   *DGB*, Prologus 2.10.

19   *Trioedd Ynys Prydein: The Triads of the Island of Britain*, ed. and trans. R. Bromwich, 4th ed., Cardiff, 2014.

20   The earliest version occurs in Aberystwyth, National Library of Wales, Peniarth 16.iv (s. xiii²). The rationale for this dating includes references to the *Trioedd* by poets such as Cynddelw (*fl.*1155–95); an indication of interest in the earliest version of *Trioedd Ynys Prydein* in the controversy over St Davids' archiepiscopal status; and the occurrence in this same version of references to Gilbert mab Catgyffro, probably Gilbert fitz Richard de Clare (d. 1114), and Alan Fergant (d. 1119). Huws, *Medieval Welsh Manuscripts*, p. 60; *Trioedd*, ed. and trans. Bromwich, pp. xvi, lxxxvi, xc–xciii, 1, 46, 66.

The characters and subject-matter of the earliest version of *Trioedd Ynys Prydein* show a considerable overlap with Geoffrey but also some important differences. For instance, the first triad in the collection speaks of the *Teir Lleithicl6yth*, "three tribal thrones", of the island of Britain, echoing Geoffrey's tripartite division of the island. But although Arthur is thrice named in this triad, the divisions of the island do not reflect Geoffrey's history and the details of the triad are clearly independent of his work.[21] In some few instances, such as the idea of Edwin of Northumbria's fosterage in Gwynedd and the exile of Cadwallon in Ireland, it seems that Geoffrey was independently drawing on historical information which was also contained in the *Trioedd*.[22] It is also apparent that in later versions of the *Trioedd* there is an increasing influence from Geoffrey's work. For example, the first triad in the collection names Arthur's chief courts as Mynyw (St Davids), Celliwig, and Pen Rhionydd, but in later versions the first of these is changed to Caerleon in deference to Geoffrey.[23]

Rachel Bromwich's discussion and edition of the *Trioedd* and their use by court poets reveals a busy and engaging historical tradition that was informed of Geoffrey's work, but by no means dominated by it. She also argues that *Trioedd Ynys Prydein* represented a "safeguarded bardic learning" to which Geoffrey did not have access.[24] This reveals something of the ambiguity of Geoffrey's place in Welsh tradition – he is in some ways both an outsider and an insider, the writer of a confected history which confounded and then convinced not only his Anglo-Norman audience, but also the native Welsh intellectual elite. This elite can be conceived of as primarily dependent on the Welsh princely courts, and formed of *cyfarwyddiaid*, "court poets and storytellers", whose works, though essentially oral and performative, were increasingly recorded in writing from the mid-13th century onwards and defined contemporary ideas of the Welsh past.[25]

The *Trioedd* themselves also suggest a reason for both the popularity and the novelty of Geoffrey's narrative in Wales, as well as the dominant position his account achieved. The *Trioedd* are a very different way of recording and

---

21   *Trioedd*, ed. and trans. Bromwich, pp. 1–4.
22   *Trioedd*, ed. and trans. Bromwich, p. lxxx.
23   For a discussion of the different versions of the *Trioedd* with particular attention given to the importance of Arthur and the increasing influence of Geoffrey, see R. Shercliff, "Arthur in *Trioedd Ynys Prydain*", in C. Lloyd-Morgan and E. Poppe (eds.), *Arthur in the Celtic Languages: The Arthurian Legend in Celtic Literatures and Traditions* (Arthurian Literature in the Middle Ages, 9), Cardiff, 2019, 173–86.
24   *Trioedd*, ed. and trans. Bromwich, p. lxxx.
25   Sims-Williams, "Some Functions of Origin Stories", pp. 101–02.

understanding the past, in that they do not present a coherent sequential narrative, but rather group events by association – the past is catalogued in terms of the similarity of one event to the other, rather than the chronological relationship between events. Geoffrey, however, presented a grand and compelling chronological narrative into which it was possible to fit earlier traditions, but in doing so changed the framework of those traditions – in later versions of the *Trioedd*, the formula *tri x Ynys Prydein*, "the three x of the Island of Britain", is replaced by *tri x Llys Arthur*, "the three x of Arthur's Court".[26]

There are other indications of Welsh ideas of the past which were close to Geoffrey's version, but independent of it. In the case of the Welsh laws, *Cyfraith Hywel* ("The Law of Hywel"), details relating to the establishment of laws, the setting of measurements, and the building of roads by Dyfnwal Moelmut correspond in some ways with Geoffrey's own account of Dunuallo Molmutius. Although the laws in their current form post-date Geoffrey's work, there are differences between the two accounts which suggest that the account of Dyfnwal in *Cyfraith Hywel* is not derived solely from Geoffrey, but may draw on an independent account which also saw Dyfnwal as a law-giver with an interest in roads.[27] We see here then an indication that Geoffrey was able to draw on some older ideas about the British past and give them a concrete and coherent, though changed form in his history. But some texts indicate considerable difference, such as *Enweu Ynys Prydein* ("The Names of the Island of Britain"), which first occurs in 14th-century manuscripts. This short text embodies ideas of the Welsh past independent of Geoffrey's work, to the extent that it contains a different account of the settlement and conquest of Britain. It has been said to represent "a pseudo-learned Welsh tradition which is long anterior to the time of Geoffrey of Monmouth".[28] Its antiquity is difficult to establish, though its difference cannot be doubted.

The themes and preoccupations of Geoffrey's work were also articulated in contemporary Welsh Latinate chronicling. I have elsewhere suggested parallels

---

26   While the compilation of the earliest version of *Trioedd Ynys Prydein* is perhaps roughly contemporary with Geoffrey, the antiquity of the triadic form as a way of cataloguing history is apparent from earlier sources such as the Gododdin: *Trioedd*, ed. and trans. Bromwich, pp. liii–xcix.

27   *Llyfr Colan: y Gyfraith Gymraeg yn ôl Hanner Cyntaf Llawysgrif Peniarth 30* [The *Llyfr Colan*: Welsh law according to the first half of manuscript Peniarth 30], ed. D. Jenkins, Cardiff, 1963, pp. 38–39, 159; *The Laws of Hywel Dda: Law Texts from Medieval Wales*, ed. D. Jenkins, Llandysul, 1986, pp. 120, 268; *DGB*, ii.34.305–37; Jankulak, *Geoffrey of Monmouth*, pp. 16–17; M.E. Owen, "Royal Propaganda: Stories from the Law-Texts", in T.M. Charles-Edwards, M.E. Owen, and P. Russell (eds.), *The Welsh King and His Court*, Cardiff, 2000, pp. 224–54, at pp. 229–32, 250–51.

28   *Trioedd*, ed. and trans. Bromwich, pp. c–civ, 246–55.

between Geoffrey's approach to historical writing and that of the author of the "Llanbadarn History", a section of the chronicle *Brut y Tywysogyon* probably written sometime before 1127.[29] Specifically, the theme of a loss of kingship among the Welsh through the judgement of God and the use of rhetorical speeches to expound this theme are present in both texts. The author, though undoubtedly Welsh, also shows a political ambiguity toward his countrymen reminiscent of Geoffrey. Geoffrey's connections with men such as Caradog of Llancarfan, his contemporary, and Rhygyfarch ap Sulien from the generation before, place him in the same cultural milieu as the author of this "Llanbadarn History", and their similarity in historiographical ideas is a further illustration of this.[30]

Geoffrey's use of the genealogical corpus, as discussed in another chapter, reveals a keen historical understanding combined with the cavalier attitude which is so characteristic of his use of sources. His plundering of the Harleian genealogies for the list of attendees at Arthur's court could be characterized as showing scant regard for Welsh historical convention, but it is entirely in keeping with the approach of vernacular texts. The prose tale *Culhwch and Olwen* cannot be proven to predate the *DGB*, but it is certainly independent of its influence in terms of content. It contains a similar, though more extensive, list which shows a comparable willingness to plunder disparate source material for the purpose of filling Arthur's court, and a comparable disregard for the earlier historical context of these names.[31]

Links between Geoffrey's work and earlier vernacular poetry can be established with some confidence. As already noted in a previous chapter, he shows a clear acquaintance with the 10th-century prophetic poem *Armes Prydein Vawr*, and the *VM* shows a wider familiarity with poetry surrounding Myrddin. The matter of the *VM*'s relationship with Welsh vernacular texts encapsulates many of the issues which confront us when trying to disentangle Geoffrey's Welsh sources from those influenced by him. The Welsh literary material relating to Myrddin, most notably the poems contained in *Llyfr Du Caerfyrddin* ("The Black Book of Carmarthen"), present a picture which is comparable to that of

---

29 O.W. Jones, "*Brut y Tywysogion*: the History of the Princes and Twelfth-Century Cambro-Latin Historical Writing", *Haskins Society Journal* 26 (2014), 209–27, at pp. 222–27.

30 Geoffrey was probably familiar with Rhygyfarch's *Life of St David*. See N. Wright, "Geoffrey of Monmouth and Gildas Revisited", *AL* 5 (1985), 155–63, at p. 156; see also Ben Guy's chapter in this volume, p. 59.

31 *Culhwch and Olwen*, ed. R. Bromwich and D.S. Evans, *Culhwch ac Olwen: an Edition and Study of the Oldest Arthurian Tale*, Cardiff, 1992, pp. 7–15, 68–112.

the *VM*.[32] The classic view of the relationship of these texts is A.O.H. Jarman's, who argued that after the publication of the *DGB*, Geoffrey became acquainted with earlier Welsh material which placed Myrddin in the context of the battle of Arfderydd, known from earlier Cambro-Latin annals and the *Trioedd Ynys Prydein*. He adapted this in his later work, the *VM*, which took many of these themes and developed them into polished, literary, and Latinate form.[33] An issue here is again the later date of our earliest versions of these Welsh texts, which all post-date Geoffrey: *Llyfr Du Caerfyrddin* is a manuscript of *c.*1250, therefore roughly contemporary with our earliest manuscripts containing vernacular translations of the *DGB*. This has led to more recent reassessments which suggest that the Welsh material betrays considerable influence from Geoffrey's own work rather than vice-versa.[34]

What is undoubtedly true is that the exact relationship between these Welsh sources and Geoffrey's work could, like the *VM* itself, benefit from considerable further study.[35] The relatively limited distribution of the *VM* in its Latin form, and the nature of the Welsh references to Myrddin, leads the current author to suspect that Geoffrey did draw to a considerable degree on earlier Welsh sources in creating the Myrddin of the *VM*.[36] The parallels between the Welsh and Galfridian material are rarely exact, particularly compared to the relatively faithful translations of the *DGB*, and this in itself suggests a process of reformulation and creative recasting on Geoffrey's part of a fairly wide range

---

32   *Llyfr Du Caerfyrddin: gyda Rhagymadrodd, Nodiadau Testunol, a Geirfa* [The Black Book of Carmarthen: with introduction, textual notes, and vocabulary], ed. A.O.H. Jarman, Cardiff, 1982, pp. 1–2, 26–35; an additional relevant poem is *Cyfoesi Myrddin a Gwenddydd ei Chwaer* ("The Prophecy of Myrddin and Gwenddydd his Sister"), which first occurs in a manuscript of *c.*1330; see M.B. Jenkins, "Aspects of the Welsh Prophetic Verse Tradition: Incorporating Textual Studies of the Poetry from 'Llyfr Coch Hergest' (Oxford, Jesus College, MS cxi) and 'Y Cwta Cyfarwydd' (Aberystwyth, National Library of Wales, MS Peniarth 50)", unpublished PhD thesis, University of Cambridge, 1990, pp. 80–83. English translations of these items are in J.K. Bollard, "Myrddin in the Early Welsh Tradition", in P. Goodrich (ed.), *The Romance of Merlin: An Anthology*, New York, 1990, pp. 13–54; *VM*.

33   A.O.H. Jarman, "The Welsh Myrddin Poems", in R.S. Loomis (ed.), *Arthurian Literature in the Middle Ages*, Oxford, 1959, pp. 20–30; id., *The Legend of Merlin*, Cardiff, 1960; id., "The Merlin Legend and the Welsh Tradition of Prophecy", in R. Bromwich, A.O.H. Jarman, and B.F. Roberts (eds.), *The Arthur of the Welsh: The Arthurian Legend in Medieval Welsh Literature* (Arthurian Literature in the Middle Ages, 1), Cardiff, 1991, 117–45. Jarman's views are well summarized in O.J. Padel, "Geoffrey of Monmouth and the Development of the Merlin Legend", *CMCS* 51 (2006), 37–65, at pp. 37–39.

34   Padel, "Geoffrey of Monmouth and the Development of the Merlin Legend".

35   Initial steps are made by Ben Guy elsewhere in this volume.

36   This is broadly the conclusion of Nikolai Tolstoy's reassessment in light of Padel's argument, "Geoffrey of Monmouth and the Merlin Legend", *AL* 25 (2008), 1–42, and of Ben Guy in this volume. For the manuscripts, see *VM*, pp. 43–45.

of Welsh texts, a process already familiar from the *DGB*. As noted by Ben Guy elsewhere in this volume, the closest direct parallels between Geoffrey's work and definitely earlier Welsh poetry are between the *VM* and *Armes Prydein*. Overall, the *VM* suggests Geoffrey's familiarity with and creative recasting of vernacular Welsh texts.

Whereas Geoffrey owed a debt to Welsh poetry himself, it is also possible, through the easily-datable corpus of court poetry from the early 12th century onwards, to appreciate the growing influence of his work on the bards' own ideas of the past. The poetry of the *Gogynfeirdd* is preserved relatively consistently from the early 12th century to the late 13th, and some of the earliest poems in this corpus demonstrate Geoffrey's fundamental agreement with earlier Welsh tradition. The anonymous praise poem to Hywel ap Goronwy, a southern Welsh ruler who died in 1106, refers to the tripartite division of Britain, suggests the importance of the crown of London, and mentions a figure used by Geoffrey, Urien (*Urianus*).[37] Poems such as this demonstrate thematic closeness but not direct influence.

The poetry of Cynddelw (active 1155–95), one of the greatest of the court poets in both the quality and volume of his poetry, shows little indication of Galfridian influence. In general, Cynddelw's poetry is a repository of antiquarian and traditional references, sometimes to figures which are no more than names in our surviving material.[38] His few Arthurian references indicate a familiarity with *Culhwch and Olwen*, a text which shows no Galfridian influence.[39] Later poets, however, reveal the increasing influence of Geoffrey, perhaps through the vernacular translations of his work. Whereas Cynddelw only mentions Arthur twice, Llywarch ap Llywelyn (active 1174/75–1220) mentions

---

37 "Mawl Hywel ap Goronwy" [In praise of Hywel ap Goronwy], ed. R.G. Gruffydd, *Gwaith Meilyr Brydydd a'i Ddisgynyddion* [The work of Meilyr Brydydd and his descendants] (Cyfres Beirdd y Tywysogion, 1), ed. J.E.C. Williams, P. Lynch, and R.G. Gruffydd, Cardiff, 1994, pp. 1–21, ll. 20, 36, 40.

38 Cynddelw Brydydd Mawr, *Opus*, ed. N.A. Jones and A.P. Owen, *Gwaith Cynddelw Brydydd Mawr I–II* [The work of Cynddelw Brydydd Mawr I–II] (Cyfres Beirdd y Tywysogion, 3–4), 2 vols., Cardiff, 1991, vol. 1, pp. xli–xlii; A.P. Owen, "Cynddelw Brydydd Mawr a'i Grefft" [Cynddelw Brydydd Mawr and his craft], in M.E. Owen and B.F. Roberts (eds.), *Beirdd a Thywysogion: Barddoniaeth Llys yng Nghymru, Iwerddon a'r Alban* [Poets and princes: court poetry in Wales, Ireland, and Scotland], Cardiff, 1996, pp. 143–65, at pp. 151–53, 163.

39 R. Bromwich, "Cyfeiriadau Traddodiadol a Chwedlonol y Gogynfeirdd" [Traditional and mythological references in the work of the Gogynfeirdd], in Owen and Roberts (eds.), *Beirdd a Thywysogion*, pp. 202–18, at pp. 202–03. For references to Arthur, the *Twrch Trwyth*, and Celli Wig, see Cynddelw Brydydd Mawr, *Opus*, ed. Jones and Owen, vol. 2, pp. 52, 79, 122, 148, 305, 320.

him six times in fewer poems.[40] After the turn of the 13th century, there are a much greater number of unambiguous references to characters derived from Geoffrey's work or influenced by it, and Llywarch ap Llywelyn stands on the brink of this change.[41]

The place of Geoffrey within earlier Welsh traditions of historical writing appears from the brief sketch above to be a relatively close one, although somewhat conflicted. He is consistent with the native Latinate tradition of historical writing apparent in one of his main sources, *Historia Brittonum*. He also has a close relationship with vernacular learning, although here he appears to be more of an outsider. If the earliest version of *Trioedd Ynys Prydein* was compiled around the mid-12th century, it demonstrates an impulse of historical collection, definition, and cataloguing which is strikingly similar to Geoffrey's in date and in its definition of the British past, although strikingly different in form and execution. The triads defined and codified the historical understanding of the court poets, but it was Geoffrey's history which was to have a more fundamental effect on Welsh ideas of the past.

The question of Geoffrey's ethnic origins is of course relevant when considering his place in an earlier Welsh historical tradition. It is discussed in more detail elsewhere in this volume, but the current author is largely in agreement with the editor's introduction.[42] The longstanding idea that he was of Breton origin and that his sympathies lay with the Bretons rather than the Welsh, and more broadly with the Anglo-Norman elite, derive from a particular reading of his history.[43] While the close of the *DGB* could make depressing reading for a 12th-century Welshman, the larger prophetic structure of the work promises redemption and restoration. His ambiguity toward the Welsh of his own day is an attitude replicated by other Welsh authors of the same period.[44] Welsh responses to his work, such as that of Madog of Edeirnion, chime better with John Gillingham's understanding of the history as a circular narrative promising redemption and restoration rather than Michael Faletra's more linear

---

40   Llywarch ap Llywelyn, *Opus*, ed. E.M. Jones and N.A. Jones, *Gwaith Llywarch ap Llywelyn, 'Prydydd y Moch'* [The work of Llywarch ap Llywelyn, 'Prydydd y Moch'] (Cyfres Beirdd y Tywysogion, 5), Cardiff, 1991, poem and line numbers: 5.12, 11.53, 12.8, 20.5, 23.64, 26.96.

41   Bromwich, "Cyfeiriadau Traddodiadol", pp. 203–04.

42   See Joshua Byron Smith's Introduction, pp. 11–21.

43   Tatlock, *LHB*, pp. 414, 443.

44   For example, Rhygyfarch ap Sulien, whose *Planctus* denounces the servile and cowardly nature of the Welsh, and the author of the "Llanbadarn History": Rhygyfarch ap Sulien, *Planctus*, ed. M. Lapidge, "The Welsh-Latin Poetry of Sulien's Family", *Studia Celtica* 8/9 (1973–74), 68–106, at pp. 88–93; O.W. Jones, "*Brut y Tywysogion*", pp. 224–26.

reading, which emphasizes the fallen status of the Welsh as a legitimation of Anglo-Norman power.[45]

What must be emphasized is Geoffrey's articulation of an ancient British identity within which he places himself, both in ethnic terms and as a historian. He considered himself one of the Britons, and this, his command of the British language, and the authority of his ancient book established his credentials as their historian. He created a coherent and attractive past for the ancient inhabitants of Britain from whom the Welsh, Cornish, and Bretons claimed descent. He must in some sense be considered a Welsh author, not only in terms of his source material but also his origin in Monmouth, and his regard for Caerleon which shows his close connection with Gwent. Considering his interests and his origin in Welsh-speaking Gwent/Ergyng, it would be strange if he was not proficient in Welsh, and the available evidence suggests that he was.[46] A feature of William fitz Osbern's conquest of Gwent was considerable institutional continuity on the part of the Welsh administrative class of the region.[47] An origin among such a Welsh family that benefitted from the Norman settlement in Wales could explain his sympathies just as well as a Breton descent, if indeed we need to invoke ethnic origins to explain political sympathies.

Geoffrey is a Welsh author in terms of his environment and source material, but there is a deliberate ambiguity in his identity. His description of the *Britannici sermonis liber*, "book in the British language", which came *ex Britannia*, "from Britain", might be read as a source from Brittany, given the fact that he excludes the Welsh from the name "British" at the end of his history, and he consistently uses *Kambria* for Wales. However at all other points

45 I owe this insight to J. Byron Smith, "Feasting on the Past: Madog of Edeirnion's Version of the *Historia Regum Britanniae*", unpublished paper delivered at the Celtic Studies Association of North America annual meeting, St Francis Xavier University, Antigonish, Nova Scotia, 5 May 2016; J. Gillingham, "The Context and Purposes of Geoffrey of Monmouth's *History of the Kings of Britain*", Anglo-Norman Studies 13 (1990), 99–118 (repr. in id. (ed.), *The English in the Twelfth Century: Imperialism, National Identity and Political Values*, Woodbridge, 2000, pp. 19–39, at p. 31); M.A. Faletra, "Narrating the Matter of Britain: Geoffrey of Monmouth and the Norman Colonization of Wales", *The Chaucer Review* 35:1 (2000), 60–85, at pp. 67–69.

46 For Ergyng, which bordered Gwent and from which Monmouth was later separated, see B.G. Charles, "The Welsh, their Language and Place-Names in Archenfield and Oswestry", in *Angles and Britons: O'Donnell Lectures*, Cardiff, 1963, pp. 85–110; D.F. Evans, "Talm o Wentoedd: the Welsh Language and its Literature c.1070–c.1530", in R.A. Griffiths, T. Hopkins, and R. Howell (eds.), *The Gwent County History vol. 2: the Age of the Marcher Lords, c.1070–1536*, Cardiff, 2008, pp. 280–308, at pp. 281–83; T.D. Crawford, "On the Linguistic Competence of Geoffrey of Monmouth", *Medium Ævum* 51 (1982), 152–62.

47 D. Crouch, "The Transformation of Medieval Gwent", in Griffiths, Hopkins, and Howell (eds.), *Gwent County History*, vol. 2, pp. 1–45, at pp. 4–6, 14–16.

in the *DGB* where Brittany is meant, it is qualified as *Armoricana Britannia*, "Armorican Britain", *altera Britannia*, "the other Britain", or *minor Britannia*, "lesser/smaller Britain".[48] Had Geoffrey intended clarity, he would have made this clearer. Rather, Geoffrey is preserving and using the ambiguity of British terminology to establish his own intimate link to the ancient Britons he had gone to such lengths to define. The British language was that of the ancient Britons, and *Britannia* could be taken to mean Brittany or his island of Britain in the distant past.

Geoffrey's career was spent in England, probably as a secular canon of the collegiate church of St George in Oxford.[49] He had a close relationship with Welsh source material, but his apparent lack of knowledge of sources such as Welsh triads suggests that he was an outsider in relation to the vernacular tradition of the Welsh poets. The subversiveness of his history with regard to the conventional, Bedan narrative of English/British history also shows him as an outsider in an Anglo-Norman context. A process of mimicry and subversion is apparent in his work, both in relation to its undermining of accepted ideas of English/British history and its ambiguous relationship with existing Welsh ideas of the past.[50] Geoffrey wrote in a tradition of Welsh pseudo-history and of Anglo-Norman historical writing, but as an outsider he redefined and transformed both.[51]

2   The Reception of Geoffrey's Work in Wales

Regardless of Geoffrey's strong links with Wales, the *DGB* was a work written in England for Anglo-Norman patrons, and while the stir it caused on its publication is apparent from Henry of Huntingdon's response in 1139, we have

---

48   *DGB*, v.84.311, v.84.325, v.86.354, v.88.411, vi.92.88, vi.96.235, vi.97.245, viii.120.63, xi.186.166, xi.194.332. In the last case, the *meae Britanniae* of King Salomon is distinguished from *uestra Britanniae*.

49   H.E. Salter, "Geoffrey of Monmouth and Oxford", *EHR* 34 (1919), 382–85.

50   I use the term mimicry as defined by Homi Bhabha. Mimicry entails the adoption of elements of the culture of the colonizers by the colonized in order to elevate their status in terms of the dominant, colonial discourse. There can be a subversive element to this mimicry, since the mimicry of the colonizer by the colonized changes and undermines those same elements of culture. The transformed image of the colonizer produced can be a threat to his authority. H.K. Bhabha, *The Location of Culture*, London and New York, 1994, pp. 85–92.

51   For an excellent discussion of his relationship to both traditions, see Jankulak, *Geoffrey of Monmouth*, esp. pp. 22–28, 94.

no indication of the nature of the initial response within Wales.[52] Our main evidence for the initial reception of Geoffrey's work in Wales consists of early manuscripts, Gerald of Wales's response to Geoffrey's work, and the influence of the history on vernacular literature, more noticeable from around 1200. These will be taken in turn.

Few of the over 200 manuscripts of the *DGB* can be said with certainty to be of Welsh provenance. Nevertheless one early manuscript of the 12th century with Welsh connections deserves consideration here. This is London, British Library, Royal 13 D. ii, which two *ex libris* inscriptions mark as having been the property of Margam Abbey in Glamorgan. It contains a copy of the vulgate version of the *DGB* with the dedication to Robert of Gloucester, and can be dated to the late 12th century.[53]

While there is no certainty that the manuscript was itself compiled at Margam, the connections of that monastery with Geoffrey's work suggest a possible route for the dissemination of Geoffrey's history in Wales. Robert was not only a dedicatee of Geoffrey's work but also the patron of Margam, and there is at least a possibility that the monastery acquired a copy from Robert himself: Walter Espec is known to have acquired a copy of the history from him before lending it to Ralf fitz Gilbert, husband of Gaimar's patroness, Lady Constance.[54] The text of the *DGB* in this manuscript is derived from one of the earliest available versions, and indicates that the monastery may have received a copy soon after publication.[55] An interest in the work here is hardly surprising given that Margam itself is one of the few specific places in Wales named in Geoffrey's narrative.[56] There are therefore reasons to suspect that this house may have played a role in the initial popularization of Geoffrey's work within Wales. This is interesting given that Margam can be seen as the Marcher Cistercian house with the strongest connections to native Wales, and the only

---

52   N. Wright, "The Place of Henry of Huntingdon's *Epistola ad Warinum* in the Text-History of Geoffrey of Monmouth's *Historia regum Britanniae*: a Preliminary Investigation", in G. Jondorf and D.N. Dumville (eds.), *France and the British Isles in the Middle Ages and Renaissance: Essays by Members of Girton College, Cambridge, in Memory of Ruth Morgan*, Woodbridge, 1991, 71–113.

53   Crick, *SC*, no. 112.

54   Geffrei Gaimar, *Estoire des Engleis*, ed. and trans. I. Short, *Estoire des Engleis / History of the English*, Oxford, 2009, p. 348; see also Jaakko Tahkokallio's chapter on early manuscript dissemination in this volume.

55   See Jaakko Tahkokallio's discussion of the manuscript elsewhere in this volume.

56   *DGB*, ii.32.280–82.

one where an attempt may have been made to found a daughter-house under native patronage, the failed foundation of Pendar.[57]

It is worth noting briefly that one of the figures linked with Pendar in charters, Meilyr *awenydd*, is associated with Geoffrey of Monmouth's work by Gerald of Wales.[58] Gerald describes how the demons who tormented Meilyr, though put to flight when St John's gospel was placed on his lap, would return in full force and with greater severity when a copy of the *"Historia Britonum"* of Galfridus Arturus was put in its place.[59] Although Gerald states that Meilyr was completely illiterate (which perhaps indicates his disapproval of Meilyr's activities rather than being strictly true), his account is good evidence for the spread of Geoffrey's influence in Wales by the later 12th century. Meilyr appears to have been an important intermediary between earlier Welsh religious traditions and the expanding, reforming monastic orders of the 12th century. This, at least, is the impression gained from his role in the Pendar charters together with Gerald's account. He appears as a key figure in the foundation of Pendar, receiving land from the native rulers of Morgannwg and confirmation from Earl William of Gloucester, and was an intermediary in the granting of lands from the native rulers of Morgannwg to Margam.[60] Gerald's fantastical account relates that Meilyr spent time at St Davids and advised or criticized the abbots of Strata Marcella and Whitland.[61]

Gerald of Wales himself provides the clearest example of a Latinate response to Geoffrey's work in Wales. Gerald's knowledge of Geoffrey may have had more to do with his Norman background than his Welsh. The *PM* in particular was popular at the court of Henry II, although the Welsh background of this material was apparent to Gerald from his own experiences, particularly his

57   F.G. Cowley, *The Monastic Order in South Wales 1066–1349* (Studies in Welsh History, 1), Cardiff, 1977, pp. 23–24.

58   *Awenydd* signifies "inspired person" or "soothsayer". *Acts*, ed. Pryce, no. 616.

59   Gerald of Wales, *The Journey Through Wales* i.5, ed. J.F. Dimock, *Giraldi Cambrensis Opera*, 8 vols., London, 1861–91, vol. 6, pp. 3–152, at pp. 57–58. The name Galfridus Arturus is also given to Geoffrey in contemporary charters, and both Robert of Torigni and Henry of Huntingdon refer to Geoffrey in this way. *Bern*, ed. Wright, p. ix.

60   *Cartae et alia munimenta quae ad dominium de Glamorgancia pertinent*, ed. G.T. Clark, 6 vols., 2nd ed., Cardiff, 1910, nos. CXXX, CLXIX.

61   B. Golding, "Gerald of Wales and the Cistercians", *Reading Medieval Studies* 21 (1995), 5–30, at p. 12. For more recent work on Meilyr and Pendar, see P.A. Watkins, "The Problem of Pendar: a Lost Abbey in Medieval Senghenydd and the Transformation of the Church in South Wales", unpublished MPhil thesis, University of Wales, Lampeter, 2015, available at <http://repository.uwtsd.ac.uk/647/1/Paul%20Anthony%20Watkins%20MPhil%20FINAL%20Thesis%20%281%29.pdf> (accessed 25 September 2017).

discovery of a book of prophecies attributed to Myrddin in Nefyn.[62] Gerald's interest in the work may have contributed to the popularization of Geoffrey in Wales, particularly Gerald's acquaintance with churchmen across Wales. It has been suggested that Gerald's use of "Cambrian" terminology may derive from Geoffrey, since *Cambria* as a Latinization of Welsh *Cymry/Cymru* seems to originate with Geoffrey. The popularity of this terminology in texts associated with St Davids would seem to indicate the popularity of Geoffrey's history at St Davids by the later 12th century.[63] It is clear that Geoffrey's popularity in Wales grew during Gerald's lifetime, and the nature of Gerald's use of Geoffrey is instructive. While he several times casts doubt on the veracity of the work, he nevertheless uses it as a basis for many parts of his account of Welsh history.[64]

Although an unreliable and suspect source, the coherence of the DGB with regard to earlier Welsh historical themes, as well as its all-encompassing nature, meant it was already unavoidable as a source. That this was also the case with more native Latinate writing is apparent from the *Life of Gruffudd ap Cynan*. This biography of King Gruffudd ap Cynan of Gwynedd was written at some point between 1137 and 1170. Not only does it use "Cambrian" terminology derived ultimately from Geoffrey, an argument among other features for its possible composition at St Davids, but the genealogies of Gruffudd which introduce the history also show the influence of the DGB.[65]

It has been noted above that references within court poetry indicate the influence of Geoffrey's work from around the turn of the 13th century. The earliest surviving manuscripts of Welsh translations of the DGB, usually referred to under the collective title *Brut y Brenhinedd*, date from the mid-13th century and are among the earliest surviving vernacular manuscripts. There were several translations, re-translations, and combinations of previously existing versions throughout the Middle Ages, which created a complex relationship between the different vernacular versions of Geoffrey's history. Overall they show a great degree of faithfulness to the Latin text, but also a willingness

---

62   J. Crick, "Geoffrey and the Prophetic Tradition", in S. Echard (ed.), *The Arthur of Medieval Latin Literature: The Development and Dissemination of the Arthurian Legend in Medieval Latin* (Arthurian Literature of the Middle Ages, 6), Cardiff, 2011, pp. 67–82, at p. 69; Gerald of Wales, *The Journey through Wales* ii.6, ed. Dimock, p. 124.

63   H. Pryce, "British or Welsh? National Identity in Twelfth-Century Wales", *EHR* 116 (2001), 775–801, at pp. 797–98.

64   J. Crick, "The British Past and the Welsh Future: Gerald of Wales, Geoffrey of Monmouth and Arthur of Britain", *Celtica* 23 (1999), 60–75, at pp. 61, 65, 74–75.

65   *Life of Gruffudd ap Cynan*, ed. P. Russell, *Vita Griffini Filii Conani. The Medieval Latin Life of Gruffudd ap Cynan*, Cardiff, 2005, pp. 52–55; D. Thornton, "The Genealogy of Gruffudd ap Cynan", in K.L. Maund (ed.), *Gruffudd ap Cynan: A Collaborative Biography*, Woodbridge, 1996, pp. 79–108, at pp. 82, 86–87.

to occasionally insert new material or to comment on alternative accounts known to the scribe or translator.

Four of these versions first appear in the 13th century. These are the "Peniarth 44", "Llanstephan 1", "Dingestow", and "Peniarth 21/Peniarth 23" versions. The first manuscripts of the "Cotton Cleopatra" and "Red Book of Hergest" versions belong to the 14th century, and the 15th century sees the first manuscript of the "Peniarth 24" version.[66] The groundwork for the study of these texts was laid by John Jay Parry and considerably developed by Brynley F. Roberts in a number of important studies.[67] More recent work by Patrick Sims-Williams has outlined a new approach to understanding the complex and incestuous relationship between these texts.[68] It is now difficult to see the different versions as entirely independent translations. More than one act

66   These are edited, wholly or partially, in the following: *Brut Dingestow*, ed. H. Lewis, Llandysul, 1942; B.F. Roberts, "Astudiaeth Destunol o'r Tri Cyfieithiad Cymraeg Cynharaf o *Historia regum Britanniae* Sieffre o Fynwy, Yngyd ag 'Argraffiad' Beirniadol o Destun Peniarth 44" [A textual study of the three earliest Welsh translations of Geoffrey of Monmouth's *Historia regum Britanniae*, together with a critical edition of the Peniarth 44 text], unpublished PhD thesis, University of Wales, 1969; *Brut y Brenhinedd: Cotton Cleopatra Version*, ed. and trans. J.J. Parry, Cambridge, MA, 1937; *Text of the Bruts from the Red Book of Hergest*, ed. J. Rhŷs and J.G. Evans, Oxford, 1890. Most of the relevant manuscripts are also available from <http://cadair.aber.ac.uk/dspace/handle/2160/5811> and *Rhyddiaith Gymraeg 1300–1425* [Welsh prose 1300–1425], ed. D. Luft, P.W. Thomas, and D.M. Smith, Cardiff, 2007–13, <http://www.rhyddiaithganoloesol.caerdydd.ac.uk/> (accessed 3 August 2017).

67   J.J. Parry, "The Welsh Texts of Geoffrey of Monmouth's *Historia*", *Speculum* 5:4 (1930), 424–31; E. Reiss, "The Welsh Versions of Geoffrey of Monmouth's *Historia*", *WHR* 4 (1968/9), 97–127; Roberts, "Astudiaeth Destunol"; *Brut y Brenhinedd: Llanstephan MS. 1 Version*, ed. B.F. Roberts (Mediaeval and Modern Welsh Series, 5), Dublin, 1971; id., "Ymagweddau at *Brut y Brenhinedd* hyd 1890" [Attitudes toward *Brut y Brenhinedd* until 1890], *BBCS* 24 (1971), 122–38; id., "The Treatment of Personal Names in the Early Welsh Versions of *Historia Regum Britanniae*", *BBCS* 25 (1973), 274–89; id., "Fersiwn Dingestow o *Brut y Brenhinedd*" [The Dingestow version of *Brut y Brenhinedd*], *BBCS* 27 (1976–78), 331–61; id., "The Red Book of Hergest Version of *Brut y Brenhinedd*", *Studia Celtica* 12/13 (1977–78), 147–86; id., "Geoffrey of Monmouth, *Historia regum Britanniae*, and *Brut y Brenhinedd*", in Bromwich et al. (eds.), *The Arthur of the Welsh*, pp. 97–116; id., "*Ystoriaeu Brenhinedd Ynys Brydeyn*: a fourteenth-century Welsh Brut", in J.F. Eska (ed.), *Narrative in Celtic Tradition: Essays in Honor of Edgar M. Slotkin* (CSANA Yearbook, 8–9), Hamilton, NY, 2011, pp. 215–27.

68   P. Sims-Williams, *Rhai Addasiadau Cymraeg Canol o Sieffre o Fynwy* [Some Middle Welsh adaptations of Geoffrey of Monmouth], Aberystwyth, 2011; id., "The Welsh Versions of Geoffrey of Monmouth's 'History of the Kings of Britain'", in A. Harlos and N. Harlos (eds.), *Adapting Texts and Styles in a Celtic Context: Interdisciplinary Perspectives on Processes of Literary Transfer in the Middle Ages. Studies in Honour of Erich Poppe*, Münster, 2016, pp. 53–74.

of translation is certainly represented within this family of texts, but there was also the combination of existing translations, the adaptation of existing translations with an awareness of the original Latin text, and the addition of other material. Sims-Williams has shown how much work remains to be done on the relationship of these versions to each other and to the Latin manuscripts of the *DGB*, especially in light of our increased understanding of the latter since the work of Julia Crick and Neil Wright.[69]

It can nevertheless be said with certainty that these different Welsh versions of Geoffrey's history demonstrate a keen and lively intellectual interest in his work, which exerted a dominant influence on Welsh ideas of the past. The translations differ in their literary character and overall feel, but all exhibit a conscientious respect for the authority of their Latin source. The Llanstephan 1 *Brut* shows a cautious and conscientious closeness to the original Latin, but this often results in wooden constructions and literal translations that misrepresent the true sense of the original text. The Dingestow *Brut* has more of a tendency to condense and shorten the narrative, but it does so effectively and infuses the work with color and liveliness. Peniarth 44 is a more natural translation than Llanstephan 1, but is more direct and less literary than Dingestow, and shows a tendency to condense the narrative which becomes more pronounced as it progresses.[70] The later versions are also distinctive, with the literary and engaging Cotton Cleopatra version utilizing a wide range of historical texts in an attempt to harmonize Geoffrey's history with native traditions and world history.[71]

There are indications that the Cistercian monasteries of native Wales were important in the production of these texts. The spread of Cistercian monasteries in 12th-century Welsh kingdoms was remarkable. Welsh patronage of these monasteries began in earnest with the assumption of patronage over Strata Florida in Ceredigion by the Lord Rhys in 1165, and the following half-century saw the enthusiastic adoption of the Cistercian order by the other Welsh princes – by the turn of the 13th century every Welsh kingdom contained a

---

69   N. Wright (ed.) and J. Crick, *The Historia regum Britannie of Geoffrey of Monmouth*, 5 vols.,
       Cambridge, 1985–91. See also Jaakko Tahkokallio's chapter in this volume.

70   Roberts, "Astudiaeth Destunol", pp. lxxxii–lxxxv, clxvii–clxix, cxc–cxcvii. This tendency
       to condense is also apparent in the First and Second Variant Versions of the *DGB*, as dis-
       cussed in Tahkokallio's chapter in this volume. This parallel is interesting given both the
       association of First Variant manuscripts with Wales, and the fact that Welsh translations
       could depend both on the Vulgate and First Variant Versions of the *DGB* – especially
       Llanstephan 1, which seems to be based on a conflation of both those versions. Roberts,
       "Geoffrey of Monmouth, *Historia regum Britanniae*, and *Brut y Brenhinedd*", p. 111; *Brut y
       Brenhinedd*, ed. Roberts, pp. xxxiv–xxxvi.

71   *Brut y Brenhinedd*, ed. Parry; Roberts, "*Ystoriaeu Brenhinedd*", pp. 223–26.

Cistercian monastery.[72] They often assumed a cultural and political role that made them the successors of older monasteries, and the princes encouraged them in this superseding of earlier institutions.[73] This gave the order a strong influence on intellectual life in this period: the majority of Welsh vernacular manuscripts between 1250 and 1350 seem to be Cistercian productions.[74] In these monasteries there was a close connection between Welsh cultural and political concerns and a wider Latin learning which made them likely centers of translation. The involvement of the Cistercians with the politics of their princely patrons suggest that the audience for these translations may have been the lay elite of native Wales, although an interest within the monasteries themselves should not be discounted.

While there are no deliberate, explicit contemporary assessments of Geoffrey's work in the vernacular, the editorial comments, additions, and marginalia present in the Welsh translations reveal something of this. In the Dingestow *Brut*, for example, the deliberate ambiguity of Geoffrey's account of Arthur's final fate elicits the curt aside "the book says nothing further or clearer about him than that."[75] Certainty rather than elusiveness would have been more to the translator's taste. A response similarly concerned with the accuracy and believability of this important historical narrative may be apparent

72 H. Pryce, "Yr Eglwys yn Oes yr Arglwydd Rhys" [The church in the age of the Lord Rhys], in
    N.A. Jones and H. Pryce (eds.), *Yr Arglwydd Rhys* [The Lord Rhys], Cardiff, 1996, pp. 145–77,
    at pp. 155–67.

73 J. Bezant, "The Medieval Grants to Strata Florida Abbey: Mapping the Agency of Lordship",
    in J. Burton and K. Stöber (eds.), *Monastic Wales: New Approaches*, Cardiff, 2013, pp. 73–87,
    at pp. 73–75; D.H. Williams, *The Welsh Cistercians: written to commemorate the centenary
    of the death of Stephen William Williams (1837–1899)* (*The father of Cistercian archaeology
    in Wales*), Leominster, 2001, pp. 272–75. The eclipse of the important *clas* of Llanbadarn
    Fawr by the nearby monastery of Strata Florida, and the transfer of the older monas-
    tery's chronicle to the newer, is also indicative. Cowley, *Monastic Order*, pp. 140–41; *Brut y
    Tywysogyon, Peniarth MS. 20*, ed. T. Jones (History and Law Series, 6), Cardiff, 1941, p. 154;
    id., *Brut y Tywysogyon: or, The Chronicle of the Princes. Peniarth MS. 20 Version*, trans.
    T. Jones (History and Law Series, 11), Cardiff, 1952, p. xli; J.E. Lloyd, *The Welsh Chronicles*,
    The Sir John Rhys Memorial Lecture, British Academy, London, 1928, also printed in
    Proceedings of the British Academy 14 (1928), 369–91. Pictures derived from Evangelist
    symbols characteristic of early Insular gospel books in the margins of London, British
    Library, Cotton Caligula A. iii, a manuscript of the Welsh laws produced at Valle Crucis
    Abbey, may indicate the inheritance of earlier scribal practices at the monastery. Huws,
    Medieval Welsh Manuscripts, p. 184.

74 Huws, *Medieval Welsh Manuscripts*, pp. 52–53.

75 *Brut Dingestow*, ed. Lewis, p. 185: "Na dyweit y llyuyr amdanav a uo diheuach na hyspys-
    sach na hynny"; B.F. Roberts, "Testunau Hanes Cymraeg Canol" [Middle Welsh historical
    texts], in G. Bowen (ed.), *Y Traddodiad Rhyddiaith yn yr Oesau Canol* [The prose tradition
    in the Middle Ages], Llandysul, 1974, pp. 274–302, at p. 290.

in the Peniarth 44 translator's decision to omit the *PM*. In so doing he changes the *DGB*'s comment that Merlin's words reduced the bystanders to amazement to say that he spoke words "difficult for men to believe".[76] It is tempting to associate this sobriety of approach with translation in a reformed monastery. In another context, such as that of the court poets, it is doubtful whether a prophecy so evocative of earlier Welsh vaticinatory verse would have elicited skepticism.

There were few occasions when Geoffrey's account was in direct conflict with existing tradition, but when there were clear differences, they could be pointed out, as in the case of the parentage of Gwalchmai/Walwanus. Geoffrey's Walwanus is said to be the son of Anna, Arthur's sister, but in Welsh tradition his equivalent Gwalchmai was given the matronymic epithet *fab Gwyar*, "son of Gwyar". This conflict was resolved in several ways in the Welsh translations. Llanstephan 1 seems to be signaling uncertainty when it relates that Gwalchmai's mother was Anna "according to the truth of the Historia".[77] Peniarth 44 neatly solves the problem by noting that Anna was also called Gwyar, whereas Dingestow keeps Geoffrey's account of Walwanus's parentage but on subsequent mentions calls the character Gwalchmai fab Gwyar, creating in effect two characters.[78] These issues arose in Latin as well as in Welsh. Dublin, Trinity College, 515 (E.5.12) is a manuscript from around 1300 containing the Trojan history of pseudo-Dares followed by the *DGB*, with marginal notes on the latter in Welsh. It was probably produced at a Welsh Cistercian monastery. The marginal comments relate to the parentage of Walwanus, giving his mother as Goear, as well as a note on Severus's wall also derived from *Brut y Brenhinedd*.[79] These notes demonstrate the close interplay between Latin and vernacular responses to Geoffrey's work in medieval Wales.

Another Latin manuscript which also indicates a Latinate Welsh response to Geoffrey's history is Cardiff, Central Library, 2.611, dating from around the turn of the 14th century and containing a distinct combination of the vulgate and First Variant versions.[80] The compiler of this manuscript completed a partial

---

76 Roberts, "Testunau Hanes", p. 290: "anhavd kan dynyadon ev credv"; *DGB*, vii.118.1–2.

77 Cardiff, Central Library, 1.363, fol. 140r: "herwyd gwyryoned er hystorya". This part of the "Llanstephan 1" version survives in Cardiff 1.363. For a transcription, see *Rhyddiaith Gymraeg 1300–1425*, ed. Luft et al., <http://www.rhyddiaithganoloesol.caerdydd.ac.uk/cy/ms-page.php?ms=Crd1363&page=140r> (accessed 14 July 2017).

78 Roberts, "Geoffrey of Monmouth, *Historia regum Britanniae*, and *Brut y Brenhinedd*", p. 113.

79 First Variant Version, ed. Wright, p. lxxxii; B.F. Roberts, "Glosau Cymraeg *Historia Regum Britanniae* Dulyn, Coleg y Drindod, llsgr. 515 (E.5.12)" [Welsh glosses on the *Historia Regum Britanniae* in Dublin, Trinity College, manuscript 515 (E.5.12)], *Studia Celtica* 37 (2003), 75–80.

80 Geoffrey of Monmouth, *De gestis Britonum*, ed. J. Hammer, *Geoffrey of Monmouth. Historia regum Britanniae. A variant version edited from manuscripts*, Cambridge, MA, 1951, pp. 8,

copy of the vulgate version of the *DGB* using another, more distinctive version
of the history which was itself a conflation of the First Variant and the vulgate.
This latter version was produced by one brother Madog of Edeirnion, his authorship stated in 26 lines of Latin verse which precede the text.[81] This poem
combines praise of the deeds of the Britons with admiring words for Geoffrey
of Monmouth. The response of Madog of Edeirnion to this history was one
of creative compilation and verse composition. He saw Geoffrey as an author
whose account celebrated the glorious history of the Welsh race. In the 13th
century, Madog's response indicates the acceptance of the *DGB* as an account
of the Welsh past which is to be celebrated and popularized, and in which he
emphasized the martial prowess of the Britons rather than the centrality of figures such as Arthur. For Madog, at least, the *DGB* made unproblematic reading
for a contemporary Welsh audience.[82]

It has been suggested that *Frater Madocus Edeirnianensis* is to be identified
with Madog ap Gwallter, the author of three Middle Welsh religious poems
who probably flourished around 1250.[83] The reasons for connecting the two
are a perceived similarity in date, since Madog of Edeirnion compiled his
version of Geoffrey's history at some point between *c*.1200 and *c*.1300, and
Madog ap Gwallter's supposed birthplace of Llanfihangel Glyn Myfyr, which,
though actually in Dinmael, was often misrepresented as being in neighboring
Edeirnion.[84] The link between Madog ap Gwallter and Madog of Edeirnion is a
weak one, and the question of the latter's identity is best dealt with separately.

Given Madog of Edeirnion's active and lively engagement with Galfridian
material, it may be that he belonged to the Cistercian order which was so prominent in the production of manuscripts of Geoffrey's work both in Latin and
the vernacular. Valle Crucis is the closest Cistercian house to Edeirnion, in the
neighboring *cwmwd* of Iâl, and this is also the house whose patrons were the

---

    12–19; D.N. Dumville, "The Origin of the C-Text of the Variant Version of the *Historia regum Britannie*", *BBCS* 26 (1974–76), 315–22; First Variant Version, ed. Wright, pp. lxxix–lxxx.

81   First Variant Version, ed. Wright, p. lxxx.

82   J. Byron Smith, "Feasting on the Past".

83   The only direct indication of date is a later note by John Davies of Mallwyd, which gives him a *floruit* of *c*.1250; I. Williams, "Cyfeiriad at y Brawd Fadawg ap Gwallter?" [A refer-ence to Brother Madog ap Gwallter?], *BBCS* 4 (1928), 133–34; Madog ap Gwallter, *Opus*, ed. R.M. Andrews, "Gwaith Madog ap Gwallter" [The work of Madog ap Gwallter], in R.M. Andrews et al. (eds.), *Gwaith Bleddyn Fardd a Beirdd Eraill Ail Hanner y Drydedd Ganrif ar Ddeg* [The work of Bleddyn Fardd and other poets of the second half of the 13th century] (Cyfres Beirdd y Tywysogion, 7), Cardiff, 1996, pp. 345–92.

84   D.M. Lloyd, "Madog ap Gwallter", in J.E. Lloyd, R.T. Jenkins, and W.L. Davies (eds.), *Y Bywgraffiadur Cymreig Hyd 1940* [Welsh biography up to 1940], London, 1953, pp. 571–72. There are numerous Llanfihangels in Wales, none of them actually within Edeirnion.

rulers of Powys Fadog, in which Edeirnion lay. This monastery was active in the production of vernacular historical manuscripts, with two of the three earliest manuscripts of *Brut y Brenhinedd* probably produced there in the 13th century. The earliest manuscript of the Cotton Cleopatra version of *Brut y Brenhinedd* was also produced there around 1330.[85] There is a variant reading in Madog's Latin text which is also present in several versions of *Brut y Brenhinedd*, including the Cotton Cleopatra version.[86] Valle Crucis would therefore appear a likely contender for Madog's place of writing. Two monks of Valle Crucis are known to have been called Madog. One was abbot between 1276–84, and another is noted as prior in 1234 and as abbot in 1254.[87] Regardless of whether either is identical to Madog of Edeirnion, the importance of this monastery as a center of historical production as well as its proximity to Edeirnion makes it possible that he is to be associated with Valle Crucis.

Madog of Edeirnion's response to the history demonstrates its acceptance as a key element of the Welsh past. There are numerous features in the vernacular translations which also demonstrate a willingness to relate Galfridian history to wider historical traditions as well as a cautious acceptance of this account as a key part of that tradition. For example, the Llanstephan 1 version of *Brut y Brenhinedd* contains numerous small additions which show an attempt to harmonize parts of the history with other texts. These include one reference to a triad and the quotation of another triad.[88] The content if not the exact narrative of Geoffrey's history could be harmonized with existing traditions fairly easily. For example, it was a natural step for a translator, seeing Geoffrey's Urianus of Mureif, to equate him with the historical/legendary northern hero Urien Rheged and subsequently to equate Geoffrey's Mureif with the kingdom of Rheged.[89] Geoffrey clearly knew enough of Urien's place in Welsh tradition to give him a northern location and have him succeeded by his son Owain, and the Welsh translators could naturally expand on these details by correcting the name of his kingdom to Rheged and by naming Urien's own father as Cynfarch, as attested in Welsh sources.[90]

The most notable and substantial addition to the vernacular translations of Geoffrey is the prose tale *Lludd and Llefelys*. This addition first appears in the Llanstephan 1 version but is also present in most subsequent versions. Into

---

85   Roberts, "*Ystoriaeu Brenhinedd*", p. 222.

86   J. Byron Smith, "Feasting on the Past".

87   D.H. Williams, "Fasti Cistercienses Cambrenses", *BBCS* 24 (1971), 181–229, at p. 206.

88   *Brut y Brenhinedd*, ed. Roberts, p. xxxiii; *Trioedd*, ed. and trans. Bromwich, pp. 81–89, 153–55.

89   *DGB*, ix.152.201–08, ix.156.329; *Brut Dingestow*, ed. Lewis, pp. 152–53, 158; *Trioedd*, ed. and trans. Bromwich, pp. 508–12.

90   *DGB*, xi.177.24.

Geoffrey's account of Lud son of Heli, the translator inserts the story of Lludd fab Beli and his brother Llefelys, the latter having no Latin equivalent. It is a story of supernatural oppressions or *gormesoedd*, which partially provides a back-story to the discovery of dragons by Merlin and Vortigern later in the history. The story seems to be independent of the *DGB*, with the brothers mentioned in a poem of Llywelyn Fardd which may date to the third quarter of the 12th century.[91] It has been said that the tale "belongs, in origin, to the same pseudo-historical traditions as [the] Triads", and what is again apparent here is the reconciliation of Geoffrey's account with historical traditions with which it was thematically broadly consistent but which differed in many details.[92]

The nature of the interaction between more traditional learning and the new influence of Geoffrey's history is indicated in the way the translator introduces the subject of Llefelys. He narrates the Galfridian account of Beli's three sons, then adds, "as some of the *cyfarwyddiaid* say, he had a fourth son, Llefelys", with *cyfarwyddiaid* here referring to a class of professional storyteller.[93] Brynley Roberts notes that, although *Lludd and Llefelys* derives from such tales, its written style is entirely consistent with the translated, historical

---

91   A difficulty in dating this poem lies in the fact that the date range of poems ascribed to a Llywelyn Fardd means there must have been at least two poets of this name, perhaps three. The poem in question, written in praise of Llywelyn ab Iorwerth (active career 1187–1240), could be ascribed either to an earlier or a later Llywelyn Fardd or, as Nerys Ann Jones suggests, the second of three similarly-named bards. Brynley Roberts ascribes it to an elder Llywelyn Fardd, and therefore to around 1187–1200, whereas the editors of *Cyfres Beirdd y Tywysogion* ascribe it to the younger poet. In the latter case, Catherine McKenna suggests a date of around 1216 for the poem to Llywelyn ab Iorwerth, which may mean that the reference in this poem to Lludd and Llefelys post-dates the inclusion of the tale in the Welsh *Brut* translations of Geoffrey's work. She also, however, acknowledges a reasonable alternative date of c.1187, which would imply authorship by the elder Llywelyn Fardd. I prefer to read the poem as one sung for Llywelyn ab Iorwerth very early in his career, as suggested by Nerys Ann Jones. *Cyfranc Lludd and Llefelys*, ed. B.F. Roberts (Mediaeval and Modern Welsh Series, 7), Dublin, 1975, p. xx; Llywelyn Fardd I, *Opus*, ed. C. McKenna, "Gwaith Llywelyn Fardd I" [The work of Llywelyn Fardd I], in M.E. Owens et al. (eds.), *Gwaith Llywelyn Fardd I ac Eraill o Feirdd y Ddeuddegfed Ganrif* [The work of Llywelyn Fardd I and other poets of the 12th century] (Cyfres Beirdd y Tywysogion, 2), Cardiff, 1994, pp. 1–100, at p. 3; Llywelyn Fardd II, *Opus*, ed. C. McKenna, "Gwaith Llywelyn Fardd II" [The work of Llywelyn Fardd II], in N.G. Costigan et al. (eds.), *Gwaith Dafydd Benfras ac Eraill o Feirdd Hanner Cyntaf y Drydedd Ganrif ar Ddeg* [The work of Dafydd Benfras and other poets of the first half of the 13th century] (Cyfres Beirdd y Tywysogion, 6), Cardiff, 1995, pp. 99–157, at pp. 106–13; N.A. Jones, "Llywelyn Fardd I, II, III?" *Llên Cymru* 29 (2006), 1–12, esp. pp. 7, 10–11.
92   *Lludd and Llefelys*, ed. Roberts, pp. xvii, xx.
93   Cardiff 1.363, fol. 46r: "megys y dyweyt rey o'r kyuarwydyeyt, petweryd mab a wu ydaw Llevelys." See *Lludd and Llefelys*, ed. Roberts, p. xv.

style of the rest of *Brut y Brenhinedd*. The author was not, therefore, writing in
the style of the *cyfarwyddiaid*, but rather adopting a story from that tradition
and adapting it to suit the style of the translations of the DGB. He is more likely
to have been an ecclesiastic with a learned Latin background, similar perhaps
to Madog of Edeirnion, rather than a court poet or one of the *cyfarwyddiaid*.[94]
Lludd and Llefelys indicates a dynamic interplay between texts, languages,
and genres which characterizes the response to Geoffrey in Wales. The DGB is
changed by translation and by the addition of a native prose tale, but the style
of this *cyfarwyddyd* itself is changed to the sparer, translated Welsh prose of
Brut y Brenhinedd.

The dialogue between Galfridian and other native traditions is apparent in
other sources. When the Peniarth 44 translator noted of Severus's wall *hvnnv
a eylw e beyrd gweyth Escavl Vynyd*, "this the poets call the work (*gweyth*) of
Escawl Mountain", he was misunderstanding poetic traditions concerning the
7th-century king Cadwallon's battle of *Gweyth Canyscawl*, with *gweyth* here
signifying "battle".[95] This same mistake was made by the author of the Welsh
marginalia in TCD 515.[96] This dialogue is apparent beyond the texts and translations of Geoffrey, as in the genealogy of Llywelyn ap Gruffudd in Aberystwyth,
National Library of Wales, 3036B, previously known as Mostyn 117. Here, a
discrepancy in the parentage of the grandson of Maelgwn Gwynedd is noted,
with one account being *herwyd dull y beird*, "according to the way of the poets".
The other option is given *herwyd yr Istoria*, "according to the *Historia*", with
Maelgwn further described as the fourth king over the island of Britain after
Arthur.[97] We know from Gerald of Wales that the Welsh poets kept their own
written genealogies, and this genealogy gives a further indication that in
Gwynedd by the second half of the 13th century, the discrepancies between
these accounts and Galfridian pseudo-history were being acknowledged and
reconciled. That this should have happened in the genealogy of Llywelyn ap
Gruffudd of Gwynedd, who had come to dominate native Wales, indicates the
political significance of this history. Llywelyn's attempts to transform his hegemony over the other Welsh princes into a more consistent and lasting authority
depended on the English king recognizing him as Prince of Wales, who exerted
authority over the other native princes despite himself paying homage and fealty to the king of England.[98] In this respect, it is probably significant that by

---

94   *Lludd and Llefelys*, ed. Roberts, p. xxviii.
95   For the references to this battle in *Historia Brittonum* and *Annales Cambriae*, see Faral,
      LLA, vol. 3, pp. 43, 46.
96   Roberts, "Testunau Hanes", pp. 291–92; First Variant Version, ed. Wright, p. lxxxii.
97   *Early Welsh Genealogical Tracts*, ed. P.C. Bartrum, Cardiff, 1966, pp. 38–39.
98   J. Beverley Smith, *Llywelyn ap Gruffudd*, pp. 20–27, 335–37.

this point Llywelyn's genealogy is traced through Camber, son of Brutus, rather than Locrinus, as was the case in the Galfridian-influenced Gwynedd genealogies in the *Life of Gruffudd ap Cynan*.[99] Claiming descent from Locrinus made Llywelyn a descendant of the kings of Britain, who lost their authority after the death of Cadwallon. Claiming descent from Camber, however, offered a model of independent rule subject to the crown of London which was supported by the authority of a history accepted both in Wales and in England.[100]

The Welsh and Latin versions of Geoffrey's history produced in Wales demonstrate a remarkable closeness in their response, as well as indicating that the class of men who were involved in this translation and copying were not lay poets and *cyfarwyddiaid* but rather monks and ecclesiastics. The historical work undertaken at the monasteries of native Wales, particularly the Cistercian monasteries affiliated to Whitland, had a strong role in the ultimate assimilation of Geoffrey's work into Welsh historical tradition and its acceptance as one of the central texts of the Welsh past. This came about through the copying and translation of Geoffrey's work and its reconciliation with existing traditions, but also through the association of the Galfridian past with the pre-existing and independent compilation of monastic chronicles in Latin.

The chronicles of native Wales can be divided into vernacular and Latin annals, but again, as with Galfridian texts, the linguistic division exposes a fundamental similarity, with both being different reflexes of the same activity. Latin annals had been kept at Welsh monasteries since at least the mid-8th century, most notably at St Davids.[101] The new monasteries of 12th-century Wales began to keep chronicles fairly soon after their foundation, and in some cases incorporated the annals of older churches, most notably those of St Davids and Llanbadarn Fawr, in their own chronicles.[102] Our first examples of vernacular chronicles occur in 14th-century manuscripts, but they may have been

---

99   D.E. Thornton, "A Neglected Genealogy of Llywelyn ap Gruffudd", *CMCS* 23 (1992), 9–23, at pp. 18–20.

100   My thanks to Ben Guy for discussing this genealogy and indicating the significance of its use of Geoffrey's history in a conference paper and personal correspondence; B. Guy, "'O herwyd yr Istoria': The Appropriation of Geoffrey of Monmouth's British History in Medieval Welsh Genealogy", unpublished paper delivered at the International Medieval Congress, University of Leeds, 8 July 2015.

101   K. Hughes, *Celtic Britain in the Early Middle Ages, Studies in Scottish and Welsh Sources*, ed. D.N. Dumville (Studies in Celtic History, 2), Woodbridge, 1980, pp. 68–69, 85–88, 100; B. Guy, "The Origins of the Compilation of Welsh Historical Texts in Harley 3859", *Studia Celtica* 49 (2015), 21–56, at pp. 25–45.

102   Hughes, *Celtic Britain*, pp. 73–85, especially the summary on p. 85; O.W. Jones, *"Brut y Tywysogion"*, pp. 215–16.

translated earlier, in the 13th century.[103] They are almost all derived from Latin originals, and their translation was closely bound with the translation and compilation of the vernacular versions of Geoffrey's history. Much of their material derives from the chronicle of the Cistercian monastery of Strata Florida, a chronicle which also influenced some of the surviving Latin chronicles but which does not survive in an untranslated or unabridged guise.[104]

The influence of Galfridian historical ideas on these chronicles is great in terms of their framing and presentation, but far less so in the case of their actual narrative content. For example, both the Breviate and Cottonian chronicles, two of the Latin annals commonly referred to as *Annales Cambriae*, place their narratives in a framework of world-history which derives substantial material from the *DGB*.[105] The vernacular chronicles, collectively termed *Brut y Tywysogyon*, themselves begin with the death of King Cadwaladr, and from their openings are quite clearly conceived of as continuations of a British/Welsh narrative in which Geoffrey's history had assumed a central part.[106] However, the influence of Geoffrey's work, and the frequency of Galfridian references, in the body of the narrative of both the Welsh and Latin chronicles is

---

103 The earliest Welsh vernacular chronicle seems to be the short text *O Oes Gwrtheyrn*, for which see O.W. Jones, "O Oes Gwrtheyrn: a Medieval Welsh Chronicle", in B. Guy, G. Henley, O.W. Jones, and R.L. Thomas (eds.), *The Chronicles of Medieval Wales and the March: New Contexts, Studies and Texts* (Medieval Texts and Cultures of Northern Europe), Turnhout, forthcoming.

104 The different chronicles and editions are as follows. Latin: Harleian chronicle (A-text), ed. Faral, *LLA*, vol. 3, pp. 44–50; Breviate chronicle (B-text), ed. H. Gough-Cooper, *Annales Cambriae: A, B and C in Parallel, from St Patrick to AD 954*, 2016, <http://croniclau.bangor.ac.uk/editions.php.en> (accessed 4 August 2017); Cottonian chronicle (C-text), ed. H. Gough-Cooper, *Annales Cambriae: A, B and C in Parallel, from St Patrick to AD 954*, 2016, <http://croniclau.bangor.ac.uk/editions.php.en> (accessed 4 August 2017); *Cronica de Wallia*, ed. T. Jones, "'Cronica de Wallia' and other documents from Exeter Cathedral Library MS. 3514", *BBCS* 12 (1946), 27–44. Welsh-language: *Brut y Tywysogyon, Peniarth MS. 20*, ed. Jones; *Brut y Tywysogyon: or, The Chronicle of the Princes. Peniarth MS. 20*, trans. Jones; *Brut y Tywysogyon: or, The Chronicle of the Princes. Red Book of Hergest Version*, ed. and trans. T. Jones (History and Law Series, 16), Cardiff, 1955; *Brenhinedd y Saesson: or, The Kings of the Saxons: BM Cotton MS. Cleopatra B v and the Black Book of Basingwerk, NLW MS. 7006*, ed. and trans. T. Jones (History and Law Series, 25), Cardiff, 1971. For the Latin chronicles, the terminology "Breviate" and "Cottonian" chronicles is to be preferred to the more established terminology which describes them as the "B" and "C" versions of *Annales Cambriae*, since it clarifies the fact that these two are very different chronicles.

105 C. Brett, "The Prefaces of Two Late Thirteenth-Century Welsh Latin Chronicles", *BBCS* 35 (1988), 63–73.

106 *Brut y Tywysogyon: or, The Chronicle of the Princes, Peniarth MS. 20*, trans. Jones, pp. xxxviii–xxxix.

negligible, more often derived from an intermediary source than inserted as part the chronicler's historiographical vision.

For example, a reference to the prophecies of Myrddin present in all three versions of the Welsh chronicles *Brut y Tywysogyon/Brenhinedd y Saesson* for 1279 seems to be due to the influence of English chronicling, being noted in the chronicle of William Rishanger.[107] An earlier instance of a similar reference to the *PM* can be found in the Latin Breviate chronicle's entry for 1214, again with reference to English affairs.[108] Whereas the vernacular Peniarth 20 *Brut y Tywysogyon* mentions Camber, Locrinus, and Albanactus at the death of the Lord Rhys of Deheubarth in 1197, it does so in quoting a contemporary Latin poem lamenting his death.[109] While the figures of Galfridian history were by this point appropriate figures of comparison for a rhetorical lament, as they had become in the case of vernacular court poetry, they had no real place in the main body of these monastic chronicles.

In fact, when allusions are present in the chronicles they place them in the wider framework of Christian history rather than showing a debt to Geoffrey's work. References to the books of Maccabees provide such an example. The first book is frequently referred to in the Latin *Life of Gruffudd ap Cynan*, where the characterization of Gruffudd as equivalent to Judas Maccabaeus and Hugh of Chester as Antiochus is sustained throughout much of the text.[110] Twice in the Breviate chronicle the Welsh are compared to the Maccabees, both times in the context of resistance to English armies.[111] The high adventure and war-like character of the account of the revolt of the Maccabees made it popular in general in the Middle Ages as a model for martial prowess, but in a Welsh context there were more specific parallels.[112] The revolt was against a powerful kingdom to free a nation from foreign domination, the resurgent rebels having

---

107   William Rishanger was a monk of St Albans and a continuator of Matthew Paris's *Chronica majora* from 1259 to 1307. A. Gransden, *Historical Writing in England, II: c. 1307 to the Early Sixteenth Century*, London, 1982, pp. 4–5; *Brut y Tywysogyon, Peniarth MS. 20*, ed. Jones, p. 226; *Brut y Tywysogyon: or, The Chronicle of the Princes. Red Book of Hergest Version*, ed. and trans. Jones, p. 268; *Brenhinedd y Saesson*, ed. and trans. Jones, p. 256; L. Keeler, *Geoffrey of Monmouth and the Late Latin Chroniclers, 1300–1500*, Berkeley, 1946, pp. 50, 102; William Rishanger, *Chronicle*, ed. H.T. Riley, *Willelmi Rishanger, quondam monachi S. Albani, et quorundam anonymorum, chronica et annales, regnantibus Henrico tertio et Edwardo primo*, London, 1865, pp. 1–230, at p. 94.

108   Breviate chronicle, ed. Gough-Cooper, s.a. 1236=1214.

109   *Brut y Tywysogyon, Peniarth MS. 20*, ed. Jones, p. 140.

110   *Life of Gruffudd*, ed. Russell, pp. 48, 219.

111   Breviate chronicle, ed. Gough-Cooper, s.a. 1267=1246, 1277=1256; J. Beverley Smith, *Ymwybod â Hanes yng Nghymru*, p. 8.

112   M. Keen, *Chivalry*, Bath, 1984, pp. 119–22.

to cope with internal betrayal as well as overwhelming odds on the side of the aggressors.[113] For monastic chroniclers intimately involved in the struggle for Welsh independence, this may have been a more illuminating and inspiring allusion than Geoffrey's story of British loss and decline, albeit with a promise of eventual redemption.

Galfridian influence on the structure and setting of chronicles increased during the course of the 13th century. By the turn of this century the authority of Geoffrey's work was accepted in principle by Gerald of Wales, and its influence on vernacular poetry is perceptible from around 1200. The setting of the Latin Breviate and Cottonian chronicles within a framework of world-history under considerable Galfridian influence must be dated after 1202. The world-history material they both draw on was from St Davids, but whereas the Cottonian chronicle was combined with this material at St Davids itself, in the case of the Breviate this was probably undertaken at a Welsh Cistercian monastery. That both chronicles were joined to this material independently is indicative of a broader impulse for the acceptance of the Galfridian past.[114] In the vernacular, the short chronicle *O Oes Gwrtheyrn* ("From the Age of Vortigern") was also framed in Galfridian terms around 1212.[115] A grander example of such an impulse is Exeter, Cathedral Library, 3514, a manuscript of the late 13th century containing a constructed composite history consisting of Dares Phrygius, the First Variant version of Geoffrey's history, and Henry of Huntingdon's *History of the English*.[116] After these texts the manuscript contains the *Cronica de Wallia*, a Latin chronicle focused on the affairs of the princes of Deheubarth, which indicates that the Exeter manuscript is probably a product of the Cistercian monastery of Whitland.[117] The manuscript illustrates the role of Geoffrey's work in placing Welsh history in a wider chronological and historiographical tradition – it is how the Welsh material is placed in both a British and an English context.[118] In the 13th century, when conflict between Welsh

---

113   *Life of Gruffudd*, ed. Russell, p. 48. For a comparable case of Maccabees being seen as a parallel for contemporary military conflict on the 10th-century German frontier, see J. Dunbabin, "The Maccabees as Exemplars in the Tenth and Eleventh Centuries", in K. Walsh and D. Greenway (eds.), *The Bible in the Medieval World: Essays in Memory of Beryl Smalley* (Studies in Church History, Subsidia 4), Oxford, 1985, pp. 31–41.

114   Brett, "The Prefaces", pp. 70, 72.

115   O.W. Jones, "O Oes Gwrtheyrn", forthcoming.

116   Crick, *SC*, no. 70.

117   J. Beverley Smith, "The 'Cronica de Wallia' and the Dynasty of Dinefwr: a Textual and Historical Study", *BBCS* 20 (1962–64), 261–82, at pp. 279–82.

118   J. Crick, "The Power and the Glory: Conquest and Cosmology in Edwardian Wales (Exeter, Cathedral Library, 3514)", in O. Da Rold and E. Treharne (eds.), *Textual Cultures: Cultural Texts*, Cambridge, 2010, pp. 21–42, at pp. 21–25, 30–36.

rulers and the English crown produced increasing political and cultural polarization, Geoffrey's ambiguous history had come to form part of the historiographical background of Wales. But rather than being a wholesale acceptance of Anglo-Norman historiographical norms, this history was accepted in Wales with careful consideration of existing ideas of the past, and this acceptance was the product of a society divided by imperfect conquest. It was achieved with essentially the same texts but independently at St Davids and Whitland, on the one hand an episcopal seat which became increasingly Anglicized in the 13th century, and on the other a Welsh Cistercian house which assumed a position of authority over the other monasteries of native Wales.

The conception and manuscript setting of the vernacular chronicles are closely related to the situation apparent in Latin manuscripts. In an indirect way, the Exeter manuscript can be seen as a precursor to the vernacular manuscripts of the 14th century which contain Welsh versions of Dares Phrygius (*Ystorya Dared*) and the *DGB* (*Brut y Brenhinedd*), as well as *Brut y Tywysogyon*. The effect of combining these three works in sequence was to create a continuous historical narrative which related first the Trojan War, then the foundation of Britain by Trojan exiles followed by their loss of sovereignty over the island, and then the subsequent history of these Britons as the Welsh from the 7th century to the 13th.

The earliest full manuscript of this "Welsh Historical Continuum" (Aberystwyth, National Library of Wales, 3035B, previously known as Mostyn 116) dates to the second half of the 14th century. The works contained in this triad of texts can be associated with different parts of Wales. *Brut y Tywysogyon* in its 13th-century form is a product of Strata Florida in Ceredigion. The "Red Book" version of *Brut y Brenhinedd* present here was compiled from two 12th-century versions, one of which first survives in a manuscript (Aberystwyth, National Library of Wales, Llanstephan 1) that was probably produced at another Cistercian house, Valle Crucis in northern Powys, the other of which occurs in manuscripts which can be associated with North Wales (Aberystwyth, National Library of Wales, 5266B, "*Brut Dingestow*"; Aberystwyth, National Library of Wales, 3036B, previously known as Mostyn 117).[119] However, most of the manuscripts of this version of the complete continuum have a South Welsh provenance. What is clear is that the Welsh Historical Continuum found

---

119 Huws, *Medieval Welsh Manuscripts*, pp. 53, 179; id., "The Manuscripts", in T.M. Charles-Edwards, M.E. Owen, and D.B. Walters (eds.), *Lawyers and Laymen: Studies in the History of Law Presented to Professor Dafydd Jenkins on his Seventy-Fifth Birthday, Gŵyl Ddewi 1986*, Cardiff, 1986, pp. 119–36, at pp. 127–30; id., *A Repertory of Welsh Manuscripts and Scribes*, forthcoming; NLW 5266B (*Brut Dingestow*), NLW 3036B (Mostyn 117), Llanstephan 1.

in NLW 3035B/Mostyn 116 was the end result of several axes of transmission of historical material which crossed Wales. These were undoubtedly dependent on links between Welsh Cistercian houses, given the fact that most of these manuscripts themselves seem to be products of Cistercian monasteries. In the late 14th century and into the 15th, manuscripts of the Red Book version are apparent both in North and South Wales, underlining the importance of these networks in the spread of historical material as well as its composition.

By this point the princes who had founded and patronized these monasteries, and who used their abbots as officials and ambassadors, had vanished as a result of the Edwardian conquest of the late 13th century. The court poets, who had formed one of the intellectual elites of native Wales, had lost their most important sponsors with the disappearance of the princely court as an institution. Welsh poetry nevertheless survived under the patronage of the *uchelwyr*, the native gentry, and these men were also important as the audience for the Welsh Historical Continuum which established Geoffrey's account as the central narrative of the Welsh past. It is in this context that Hopcyn ap Thomas and his scribe, Hywel Fychan, with whom this chapter opened, read the Philadelphia manuscript and decided that the current conquered state of the Welsh had roots far further back than the 13th-century conquest.

Geoffrey's account was written in the 12th century, when the ambitions and interests of the Anglo-Norman elite and their expansion in Wales created a ready audience for an account of the British past. In the course of the 13th century it became accepted as an essential part of Welsh history, and in the context of a struggle for the maintenance of Welsh political autonomy, it sometimes assumed a political role, whether in Llywelyn ap Gruffudd's claims to descent from Camber or in Edward I's conscious appropriation of these ideas in the wake of his conquest of Gwynedd. Edward's purported discovery of the body of Magnus Maximus at Caernarfon in 1283, and indeed the entire structure of the castle at Caernarfon, with its imperial eagles and banded masonry evocative of Roman construction, was intended to echo and to appropriate the inheritance that the Welsh claimed, under the influence of Geoffrey, as historical equals of the Romans.[120] This appropriation went hand in hand with

---

120   R.R. Davies, *Conquest, Coexistence and Change: Wales, 1063–1415*, Oxford, 1987, p. 360; A.J. Taylor, *Welsh Castles of Edward I*, Bristol, 1986, pp. 77–79; A. Wheatley, "Caernarfon Castle and its Mythology", in D.M. Williams and J.R. Kenyon (eds.), *The Impact of the Edwardian Castles in Wales: the Proceedings of a Conference Held at Bangor University, 7–9 September 2007*, Oxford, 2010, pp. 129–39; *Flores Historiarum*, ed. Luard, vol. 3, p. 59. *Flores Historiarum* relates the discovery of the grave of Maximus, father of the noble Constantine. *Historia Brittonum* had earlier referred to a tomb of Constantine there; *Historia Brittonum*, ed. Faral, LLA, vol. 3, p. 19.

discouragement, as in June 1284 when Archbishop Peckham issued injunctions for the clergy of the diocese of St Asaph reminding them of their responsibility to reconcile Welsh and English, and specifically warned against Welsh tales of their glorious descent from the Trojans.[121]

3   Conclusion

The narrative formulated by Geoffrey of Monmouth was given historical and political authority in a Wales where claims of authority were articulated and disputed frequently. Wales itself was a deeply divided country throughout the 12th and 13th centuries, and many of these divisions are apparent in the processes of historiographical dialogue, acceptance, and translation outlined above. Geoffrey, elusive and ambiguous though he is as an author, was himself divided between the Anglo-Norman world for which he wrote, and the Welsh world which provided most of the source material and thematic preoccupations of his history. The response to the *DGB* in Wales shows the reconciliation and fusion of older Welsh ideas of history to Geoffrey's reformulation of these same ideas.

This response itself indicates both divisions and connections. The production of vernacular court poetry, and closely-related vernacular texts such as *Trioedd Ynys Prydein*, depended on the context of the Welsh princely courts. The articulation of the Welsh past was here dependent on the patronage of Welsh rulers, their families, officials, and of the wider court, a place of central importance in the articulation of prophecy, lore, history, and "cultural orientation".[122] The peripatetic nature of the court itself and of the court poets and *cyfarwyddiaid* who were associated with it extended the influence of their articulation of the past. The acceptance of Geoffrey's history in this context is apparent from the turn of the 13th century in the court poetry, but it is never dominant – rather it simply emerges in such poetry as one of many sources of reference and allusion, one of many ways in which the Welsh past could be viewed.

The Latin evidence indicates a slightly earlier acceptance of Geoffrey's account. The Latin *Life of Gruffudd ap Cynan* and Gerald of Wales show Geoffrey's influence by the second half of the 12th century. The response of

---

121   G. Williams, *The Welsh Church from Conquest to Reformation*, 2nd ed., Cardiff, 1976, p. 41; John Peckham, *Epistles*, ed. C.T. Martin, *Registrum Epistolarum Fratris Johannis Peckham, Archiepiscopi Cantuariensis*, 3 vols., London, 1882–85, vol. 2, pp. 737–43.

122   Sims-Williams, "Some Functions of Origin Stories", pp. 101–02.

Brother Madog of Edeirnion in the 13th century illustrates his importance by that point, and, along with other manuscript evidence from Cistercian monasteries, shows the key role of reformed monasteries in the articulation of the Welsh past in Galfridian terms. The Cistercian monasteries of native Wales were also important in the establishment of a sequential relationship between Geoffrey's narrative and the chronicle writing undertaken at these institutions, apparent in Latin and later in vernacular manuscripts.

The significant division in terms of the Welsh response to Geoffrey is not a linguistic one, but rather one of genre, as well as of institutions. The Welsh translations of Geoffrey are similar to Welsh Latin manuscripts in terms of their preoccupations and marginal additions, and were probably also the work of monks rather than *cyfarwyddiaid*. Whereas vernacular court poetry refers to figures of Geoffrey's from around 1200, the same can be said for the Latin lament for Rhys ap Gruffudd which dates to around 1197, similar to vernacular court poetry in terms of genre.[123] In institutional terms, we should perhaps ascribe a more important role in the popularization of Galfridian history to Cistercian monasteries rather than to the *cyfarwyddiaid* and court poets, although the acceptance of Geoffrey's account by the latter two is clear in the course of the 13th century.

The role Galfridian history played in the closing years of the struggle between the princes of Gwynedd and the English crown was discussed above. This struggle was the dominant political process of the 13th century in Wales, and resulted in the disappearance of the Welsh princely court as an institution. Whereas the evidence for the 13th century indicates a dynamic process of response, reformulation, and acceptance, it is arguable that the 14th century saw the assumption by Geoffrey's history of a role as the central authority on the Welsh past, best articulated in the "Welsh Historical Continuum" of some vernacular manuscripts. This importance was the product of the historiographical activity of the 13th century, but also perhaps of the disappearance of the Welsh court which provided an alternative center of cultural orientation to the reformed monasteries. The assumption of a leading cultural role by Cistercian monasteries in the wake of the disappearance of the princely courts is perhaps best exemplified by the production of the Hendregadredd manuscript, a comprehensive collection of vernacular court poetry, at Strata Florida in the

---

123   For the Latin poetry to the Lord Rhys, see "Y Canu Lladin er Cof am yr Arglwydd Rhys" [The Latin poetry commemorating the Lord Rhys], ed. H. Pryce, in Jones and Pryce (eds.), *Yr Arglwydd Rhys*, pp. 212–23. For a recent discussion noting the similarity between this and vernacular poetry, see P. Russell, "'Go and Look in the Latin Books': Latin and the Vernacular in Medieval Wales", in R. Ashdowne and C. White (eds.), *Latin in Medieval Britain* (Proceedings of the British Academy, 206), London, 2017, pp. 213–46.

years after 1282.[124] These abbeys were culturally and politically important before the conquest, but whereas the loss of the princes and their court at the conquest decreased their political importance, they increased their centrality in cultural terms. They did so in association with a lay elite who had survived the conquest and who were now the chief sponsors of the Welsh poets. Their association with Cistercian monasteries is clear from instances such as the ties between Strata Florida and the family of Parcrhydderch, and the rich corpus of inscribed gravestones which commemorates the attachment of such families to Valle Crucis in the first half of the 14th century.[125]

By the time of Hywel Fychan's scribal colophon, Galfridian history was part of an authoritative narrative of Welsh history which provided ideological justification for Glyn Dŵr's revolt. Even with the failure of this revolt, Geoffrey's legacy maintained this role. Indeed, its emphasis on the British dimension of the Welsh past, though founded on impeccable native tradition, was useful in a situation when the Welsh now needed to reconcile themselves to operating within an English dimension. It was especially useful, and especially misleading, in interpreting the victory of Henry VII in 1485 as a return of British sovereignty to the island, giving the Welsh elite historical and political justification for their role in the Tudor state.[126] The debate over the veracity of Geoffrey's history in the 16th century exposes the continuing importance of this narrative to national self-definition.[127] And whereas Geoffrey was largely no longer considered a reliable historical source in England by 1600, in Wales the debate went on, so tied was the work to ideas of national pride. This debate continued into the 19th century, and it was only then that the hold of Galfridian history over the Welsh historical consciousness, along with the manuscript tradition of copying and recopying the Welsh translations, was broken.[128]

---

124 *Llawysgrif Hendregadredd* [The Hendregadredd manuscript], ed. J. Morris-Jones and
      T.H. Parry-Williams, Cardiff, 1933; Huws, *Medieval Welsh Manuscripts*, pp. 193–226.

125 Huws, *Medieval Welsh Manuscripts*, pp. 247–54; C.A. Gresham, *Medieval Stone Carving in
      North Wales*, Cardiff, 1968, pp. 79–84, 89, 94–96, 113–16, 137–41, 182–88.

126 Sims-Williams, "Some Functions of Origin Stories", pp. 110–11.

127 See for example David Powel's careful distinction between the activities of Welsh kings
      and princes in the past and the contented situation of Wales in the present under the
      Tudor monarchs, in his edition of Humphrey Lhuyd's *Cronica Walliae*. A.O.H. Jarman, "Y
      Ddadl Ynghylch Sieffre o Fynwy" [The debate surrounding Geoffrey of Monmouth], *Llên
      Cymru* 2 (1952), 1–18, at pp. 11, 13–14; *The historie of Cambria, now called Wales*, ed. D. Powel,
      London, 1584.

128 Roberts, "Ymagweddau", pp. 123, 126, 135–38. I wish to thank Huw Pryce, Ben Guy, Georgia
      Henley, and Joshua Byron Smith for wise and valuable comments on drafts of this chapter.

CHAPTER 10

Geoffrey of Monmouth and the Conventions of History Writing in Early 12th-Century England

Georgia Henley

Modern critics of Insular 12th-century history have tended to view Geoffrey of Monmouth's historiographical project in terms of its differences from the other Latin works of Insular history of his time (particularly William of Malmesbury, Henry of Huntingdon, Orderic Vitalis, and John of Worcester), reading him as an outlier departing from the conventions of his contemporaries by penning something previously unknown, outside the historical mode, and likely spurious. Yet when viewed in tandem, the works of Geoffrey and his contemporaries are in fact united by key similarities in form, structure, classical allusion, and scope, even as they are separated by treatment of sources, content and focus, and reception. In this chapter, I situate Geoffrey's *De gestis Britonum* in the context of the longform histories of his contemporaries, particularly William of Malmesbury's *Deeds of the English Kings* (*Gesta regum Anglorum*) and Henry of Huntingdon's *History of the English* (*Historia Anglorum*), establishing their shared adherence to the conventions of history writing and its attendant rhetorical strategies, and noting where Geoffrey departs – perhaps subversively – from such conventions. Though Caradog of Llancarfan seems to have been an important contemporary of Geoffrey as well, given that Geoffrey mentions him by name, I do not compare Geoffrey's work to Caradog's saints' lives, focusing instead on longform narrative history; nor do I discuss other contemporaries due to constraints of space. Following an assessment of the conventions of the genre and how they are satisfied by each of the three authors, I examine the three works according to the unifying theme of conquest, demonstrating that Geoffrey's departure from his contemporaries lies primarily in his treatment of sources and his focus on the Britons, not on the flagrant departure from history conventions as is sometimes claimed. These key differences have nevertheless resulted in a vastly different reception history for his work, including modern critical reception, compared to William and Henry. I conclude by offering an interpretation of Geoffrey's motives for writing in light of this comparison.

1   Conventions of Historical Writing

I begin by considering the ways in which the three works are united by purpose and history conventions. The three historians were working in the second generation after the Norman Conquest of England: the earliest version of
William's *Deeds of the English Kings* was written by c.1125, Geoffrey's *DGB* was in
circulation before January 1139, and Henry's *History of the English* circulated by
c.1130 with a series of expanded versions issued until c.1154.[1] They are dedicated to patrons within the same milieu, including Alexander, bishop of Lincoln,
and Robert, earl of Gloucester, indicating similar audiences and aspirations
for the three works.[2] The works were also considered together by contemporary readers: the *DGB* is paired with William's *Deeds of the English Kings* in six

---

1   I am grateful to Joshua Byron Smith, Thomas O'Donnell, and anonymous reviewers for
comments on this chapter. For background on William of Malmesbury, see D.H. Farmer,
"William of Malmesbury's Life and Works", *Journal of Ecclesiastical History* 13 (1962), 39–54
and R.M. Thomson, *William of Malmesbury*, Woodbridge, 2003; for background on Henry
of Huntingdon, see D. Greenway, "Henry (c. 1088–c. 1157), Historian and Poet", *Oxford
Dictionary of National Biography*, <https://doi.org/10.1093/ref:odnb/12970> (accessed
18 May 2019); J. Gillingham, "Henry of Huntingdon and the Twelfth-Century Revival of the
English Nation", in S. Forde, L. Johnson, and A. Murray (eds.), *Concepts of National Identity in
the Middle Ages*, Leeds, 1995, pp. 75–101 (repr. in id. (ed.), *The English in the Twelfth Century:
Imperialism, National Identity and Political Values*, Woodbridge, 2000, pp. 123–44); and id.,
"Henry of Huntingdon in His Time (1135) and Place (between Lincoln and the Royal Court)",
in K. Stopka (ed.), *Gallus Anonymous and His Chronicle in the Context of Twelfth-Century
Historiography from the Perspective of the Latest Research*, Krakow, 2010, pp. 157–72.
2   Geoffrey dedicates the *DGB* to Robert, earl of Gloucester, with some versions dedicat-
ing the work jointly to Robert and Waleran, count of Meulan. One manuscript (Bern,
Burgerbibliothek, 568) contains a joint dedication to Robert, earl of Gloucester and King
Stephen. The *PM*, which circulated independently prior to the issuing of the *DGB*, was report-
edly commissioned by Alexander, bishop of Lincoln, and the *VM* is addressed to Robert de
Chesney, bishop of Lincoln. Henry of Huntingdon says the *History of the English* was com-
missioned by Alexander, bishop of Lincoln, the same bishop who requested the prophecies
from Geoffrey; a later (5th) version is dedicated to Robert de Chesney, the next bishop of
Lincoln; to whom Geoffrey's *VM* is addressed. William dedicates version T of *Deeds of the
English Kings* to Empress Matilda, whose mother commissioned it, and versions A, B, C, and
D to Robert, earl of Gloucester, the same dedicatee as Geoffrey's *DGB*. (William also writes a
letter to David, king of Scotland and brother of Queen Matilda, asking him to authorize the
work and give it to Empress Matilda). These overlaps in dedicatees indicate that the three authors ran in the same literary circles. For discussion of these dedicatees, how dedication was
a targeted attempt at wide distribution and career advancement, as well as the publishing
history of the three works, see J. Tahkokallio, *The Anglo-Norman Historical Canon: Publishing
and Manuscript Culture* (Cambridge Elements in Publishing and Book Culture), Cambridge,
2019, pp. 9–12, 18–31, 35–70.

manuscripts,[3] William's *Contemporary History* in four manuscripts,[4] William's *Deeds of the Bishops of the English* in two manuscripts,[5] Henry of Huntingdon's *History of the English* in five manuscripts,[6] and Henry's description of Britain in four manuscripts.[7] These groupings suggest common interest in Insular history on the part of medieval and early modern readership. Furthermore, Henry himself was interested in the content of the DGB: after seeing a copy of the text at Le Bec in January 1139, he wrote a letter to one Warin the Breton describing the work.[8] While Henry did not see fit to add it to his own history, perhaps because, as Wright argues, it did not accord with Bede (the Trojan narrative of *History of the English* §9 is from *Historia Brittonum*), the letter indicates interest in the Britons that is borne out in Henry's representation of the *aduentus Saxonum*, discussed in further detail below.[9]

The works are united by similarities. All three authors recognize a need to draw together a range of authoritative sources for Insular history (particularly Bede, Gildas, and *Historia Brittonum*, though each uses additional sources) to

3 Cambridge, Trinity College, R.5.34; London, British Library, Royal 13 D. ii and Royal 13 D. v; Oxford, All Souls College, 35; Philadelphia, The Free Library, E.247; Valenciennes, Bibliothèque Municipale, 792; information from Crick, *SC*. BL Royal 13 D. ii, containing the DGB, William's *Deeds of the English Kings* and *The Contemporary History*, is particularly interesting because of its associations with Robert, earl of Gloucester, including the fact that it was at Margam Abbey, a foundation of Robert's, by the early 13th century. Tahkokallio, *Anglo-Norman Historical Canon*, pp. 25–26 argues that its exemplars may have been presentation copies given to Robert by the authors.

4 TCC R.5.34; BL Royal 13 D. ii and Royal 13 D. v; All Souls' College, 35.

5 TCC R.5.34, BL Royal 13 D. v.

6 Brussels, Bibliothèque royal, 8495–8505 (just Book 9); Cambridge, St John's College, G.16; Exeter, Cathedral Library, 3514; Rouen, Bibliothèque municipal, U.74 (1177); Ushaw, Ushaw College, 6.

7 Cambridge, Gonville and Caius College, 103/55; Cambridge, University Library, Mm.5.29; Lincoln, Cathedral Library, 98; and BL Royal 13 D. v. Compare all of this to Orderic Vitalis's *Ecclesiastical History*, which travels with the DGB in just one manuscript (Leiden, Universiteitsbibliotheek, B.P.L. 20). For further details, see Crick, *SC*.

8 Henry of Huntingdon, *History of the English* Letter to Warin, ed. and trans. D. Greenway, *Henry, Archdeacon of Huntingdon: Historia Anglorum. The History of the English People*, Oxford, 1996, pp. 558–83. For further discussion, see N. Wright, "The Place of Henry of Huntingdon's *Epistola ad Warinum* in the Text-History of Geoffrey of Monmouth's *Historia regum Britanniae*: a Preliminary Investigation", in G. Jondorf and D.N. Dumville (eds.), *France and the British Isles in the Middle Ages and Renaissance: Essays by Members of Girton College, Cambridge, in Memory of Ruth Morgan*, Woodbridge, 1991, pp. 71–113. For the manuscript Henry might have seen at Le Bec Abbey, see Jaakko Tahkokallio's chapter in this volume.

9 Tatlock, *LHB*, p. 49, suggests that Henry borrows the name *Kaerperis* for Porchester from Geoffrey. In turn, Geoffrey seems to have used Henry's *History of the English* as a source for information about Constantine, Coel, Helena, and Maximus, as well as for information about the four paved Roman roads (see Tatlock, *LHB*, pp. 34, 121, 281).

produce a unified survey of the history of the island on a massive scale. While Geoffrey focuses on the history of the Britons from the end of the Trojan war to the passage of dominion over the island to the English, and William and Henry focus on the history of the English from their arrival in Britain down to their own time, all three works are inflected by the political events of the times in which they wrote, particularly the struggle for succession between Matilda and Stephen. This results in a keen focus throughout each of the histories on the peaceful transfer of power, dynastic continuity and stability, and the dangers of civil war. In other words, quotations of Lucan are at the tips of their pens.[10] The dedications to secular rulers and power brokers of the day indicate that the intended audiences included secular readers rather than monastic/scholarly readers alone (unlike some other chronicles written in that era).[11] The structure is longform narrative rather than annalistic, with attention to moral lessons, particularly the virtues of good rulers and the counterexamples of bad ones, as well as courtly entertainment, miracles and marvels, and concordance with international events.

Rhetorical similarities in all the prologues indicate high levels of education and Latin literacy and an awareness of the commonplaces of history according to the norms of the time. All three identify silences in the historical record that they desire to fill, presenting their histories as participating in the recovery of valuable, lost information. For Geoffrey, this is a gap that would have seemed larger and more pressing to him after reading the histories by William of Malmesbury and Henry of Huntingdon, and he opens his history with this very problem:

> I was surprised that, among the references to [the kings of Britain] in the fine works of Gildas and Bede, I had found nothing concerning the kings who lived here before Christ's Incarnation, and nothing about Arthur and the many others who succeeded after it, even though their deeds were worthy of eternal praise and are proclaimed by many people as if they had been entertainingly and memorably written down.[12]

---

10   For Geoffrey and civil war, see P. Dalton, "The Topical Concerns of Geoffrey of Monmouth's *Historia Regum Britannie*: History, Prophecy, Peacemaking, and English Identity in the Twelfth Century", *Journey of British Studies* 44:4 (2005), 688–712; for Henry, civil war, and Lucan, see C.A.M. Clarke, "Writing Civil War in Henry of Huntingdon's *Historia Anglorum*", *Proceedings of the Battle Conference on Anglo Norman Studies* 30 (2009), 31–48.

11   Though see Tahkokallio's chapter in this volume for the monastic reception of the DGB.

12   DGB, Prologus 1.2–7: "in mirum contuli quod infra mentionem quam de eis Gildas et Beda luculento tractatu fecerant nichil de regibus qui ante incarnationem Christi inhabitauerant, nichil etiam de Arturo ceterisque compluribus qui post incarnationem successerunt

With this statement, Geoffrey sets up the timely discovery of Walter's ancient book in the British tongue that conveniently fills the observed gap.[13] At the same time, he positions himself as the authoritative interlocutor of the book because he has already heard stories about Arthur from the many (presumably Brittonic-language-speaking) people who have them memorized, a medium inaccessible to his Anglo-Norman audience.

In the same vein, in his opening letter to Empress Matilda, William says that his work was prompted by her mother Queen Matilda's desire to know more about Aldhelm and her West Saxon predecessors, which he fulfilled first with a list of the English kings, and then, when the list provoked further interest, a fully fleshed-out narrative of the queen's royal predecessors.[14] That the queen would not know her family's history and would need to consult an expert to uncover it for her places William in a position of historical authority which he modulates with appropriate humility. When William's grief over the queen's death causes him to put the work aside, he is persuaded by his friends, and by the importance of the work itself, to take it up again, "for it both seemed and was quite wrong that the memory of those great men should remain buried and their deeds die with them."[15] His history recuperates the deeds of the great English kings both in honor of their memory and for the benefit of their descendants, in this case, Empress Matilda and her half-brother Robert of Gloucester. Another of his motivations for writing is "to bring forcibly into the light things lost in the rubbish-heap of the past".[16]

Henry of Huntingdon, though he does not write specifically of recovery and recuperating historical gaps as William and Geoffrey do, raises the stakes of history in his dedication to Bishop Alexander by presenting history as the line dividing men from brutes:

> The knowledge of past events has further virtues, especially in that it distinguishes rational creatures from brutes, for brutes, whether men or

---

repperissem, cum et gesta eorum digna aeternitate laudis constarent et a multis populis quasi inscripta iocunde et memoriter praedicentur."

13   *DGB*, Prologus 2.10.

14   William of Malmesbury, *Deeds of the English Kings* Letter II, 5, ed. and trans. R.A.B. Mynors, completed by R.M. Thomson and M. Winterbottom, *William of Malmesbury: Gesta Regum Anglorum, The History of the English Kings*, 2 vols., Oxford, 1998–99, vol. 1, pp. 8–9.

15   William of Malmesbury, *Deeds of the English Kings* Letter II, 6, ed. and trans. Mynors, vol. 1, pp. 8–9: "quia uidebatur et erat indignum ut tantorum uirorum sepeliretur memoria, immorerentur gesta."

16   William of Malmesbury, *Deeds of the English Kings* Prologue to Book II, 2, ed. and trans. Mynors, vol. 1, pp. 150–51: "ut res absconditas, quae in strue uetustatis latebant, conuellerem in lucem".

beasts, do not know – nor, indeed, do they wish to know – about their origins, their race and the events and happenings in their native land ... now we must pass over those whose life and death are to be consigned to perpetual silence.[17]

For Henry, awareness of the past, and even more importantly, learning lessons from past deeds, has a moral imperative, separating men from the mindless presentism that characterizes animals and "brutish" men. In doing so, he places the history of the English in the sacred history of salvation, elevating it above the narratives of the classical poets like Homer. While he cites Homer as precedent, his history – and the English people themselves – exceeds classical precedent by striving not for worldly glory and fame alone, but for eternal life.[18]

Throughout his first prologue, Henry emphasizes the didactic function of history, contextualizing the deeds of the English kings in the models of Homer and the Old Testament.[19] He takes Homer as precedent for recording, better than the moral philosophers, the virtues of great men like Ulysses, Agamemnon, Nestor, and Menelaus, and the negative examples of Ajax, Priam, Achilles, and Paris; he also cites the Old Testament models of Abraham, Moses, Jacob, Joseph, Ahab, and others for moral instruction.[20] Several times he professes the edifying, moral function of the genre in language like the following:

> In the recorded deeds of all peoples and nations, which are the very judgements of God, clemency, generosity, honesty, caution and the like, and their opposites, not only provoke men of the spirit to what is good and deter them from evil, but even encourage worldly men to good deeds and reduce their wickedness ... In this work the attentive reader will find what to imitate and what to reject, and if, by God's help, he becomes a

---

17   Henry of Huntingdon, *History of the English* Prologue, ed. and trans. Greenway, pp. 4–5: "Habet quidem et preter hec illustres transactorum noticia dotes, quod ipsa maxime distinguat a brutis rationabiles. Bruti namque homines et animalia unde sint nesciunt, genus suum nesciunt, patrie sue casus et gesta nesciunt, immo nec scire uolunt."

18   For discussion of Henry of Huntingdon's focus on the theme of *contemptus mundi*, see N.F. Partner, *Serious Entertainments: The Writing of History in Twelfth-Century England*, Chicago and London, 1977, pp. 33–39.

19   For discussion of a shift away from didactic function in history writing of the late 12th century, see M. Staunton, "Did the Purpose of History Change in England in the Twelfth Century?" in L. Cleaver and A. Worm, *Writing History in the Anglo-Norman World. Manuscripts, Makers, and Readers, c.1066–c.1250*, Woodbridge, 2018, pp. 7–28.

20   Henry of Huntingdon, *History of the English* Prologue, ed. and trans. Greenway, pp. 2–5.

better person for this emulation and avoidance, that will be for me the reward I most desire.[21]

His justification for writing *History of the English* articulates one of the essential functions of medieval history writing: to provide moral examples *digna memoria*, "worthy of memory", for readers to follow and to learn from, in the same way that they might benefit from reading hagiography or the Bible.

In his study of the conventions of medieval historiography, which did not see historical truth in the same way we see it in today, Ray cites Funkenstein who "has of late contended that in the Middle Ages the basic materials of history were not our facts but *digna memoria*, things made worthy of memory by their pertinence to a Christian conduct of life. A medieval 'fact' was therefore proper to moral experience and so had about it certain ideal associations", rather than the literal factual accuracy we anticipate from history today.[22] This idea of history as a teacher precedes the medieval period, with roots in the writings of Cicero, Livy, and St Paul; it is also expressed by contemporaries John of Salisbury, Gervase of Canterbury, and Robert of Torigni.[23]

The didactic purpose of history is a function of medieval writers' conceptions of historical truth. Medieval writers of history took a providential view of history that is different from modern conventions. For medieval writers, the truth quality of history was not a matter of facts, as we would see them today, but of theology.[24] Bede, for example, is not interested in causality or how human affairs might unfold naturally "by a standard of factual truth", but rather in how events occur according to God's power.[25] In the providential view, God's judgement is not something we wait for but something that is carried out piecemeal, prefiguring the last judgement.[26]

---

21   Henry of Huntingdon, *History of the English* Prologue, ed. and trans. Greenway, pp. 4–5, 6–7: "Sic etiam in rebus gestis omnium gentium et nationum, que utique Dei iudicia sunt, benignitas, munificentia, probitas, cautela et his similia, et contraria, non solum spirituales ad bonum accendunt et a malo repellunt, sed etiam seculares ad bona sollicitant et in malis minuunt ... In quo scilicet opere sequenda et fugienda lector diligens dum inuenerit, ex eorum imitatione et euitatione Deo cooperante melioratus, michi fructum afferet exoptabilem."

22   R.D. Ray, "Medieval Historiography Through the Twelfth Century", *Viator* 5 (1974), 33–59, at p. 47; A. Funkenstein, *Heilsplan und natürliche Entwicklung: Formen der Gegenartsbestimmung im Geschichtsdenken des hohen Mittelalters*, Sammlung Dialog 5, Munich, 1965.

23   Staunton, "Did the Purpose of History Change", pp. 10–11, 18.

24   Ray, "Medieval Historiography", p. 46.

25   Ray, "Medieval Historiography", pp. 43–44.

26   Ray, "Medieval Historiography", p. 45.

William of Malmesbury, too, sees his work as performing the didactic function, following the precedent set by authors in the "old days" (*antiquitus*):

> It is true that in the old days books of this kind were written for kings or
> queens in order to provide them with a sort of pattern for their own lives,
> from which they could learn to follow some men's successes, while avoid-
> ing the misfortunes of others, to imitate the wisdom of some and to look
> down on the foolishness of others.[27]

This didactic value, William writes, is what motivates Matilda's interest in history and his interest in writing it. History, he writes, "adds flavor to moral instruction by imparting a pleasurable knowledge of past events".[28] To William,
history is an enjoyable way to absorb moral instruction. He follows through
on this idea throughout his work, commenting on the moral virtues and vices
of England's kings, overall promoting wisdom, learning, piety, pilgrimage to
Rome, and lawfulness, and maligning bad decision-making, treachery, adultery, conspiracy, and tyranny. It is clear that he is urging his intended aristocratic audience to follow the good examples of English saints, like Æthelthryth,
Edmund, and Cuthbert, and peaceful, just Christian kings like Æthelberht,
Cenwulf, Oswald, Alfred, and Æthelstan over violent, cowardly kings who de-
grade learning like Ceolred, Osred, and Æthelred. By contrast, the moral imperative of history is not explicit in Geoffrey's prologue to the DGB, nor in the
VM. The lessons of history are instead implicit, both in Geoffrey's character
descriptions, which provide the occasional positive example for kings to follow, with particular emphasis on generosity, martial prowess, wisdom, and the
building of civic works during peacetime.[29]

In contrast to William and Henry, who are building a precedent for peacetime stability and piety for their intended readers, Geoffrey offers far more
negative examples of rulership than positive ones. The picture he paints of
early Britain is one of constant treachery, power struggle, jealousy, and vin-
dictiveness, resulting in constant instability and an overall downward arc of
history. Unlike Henry and William, Geoffrey uses negative examples of morally

---

27   William of Malmesbury, *Deeds of the English Kings* Letter II, 4, ed. and trans. Mynors,
      vol. 1, pp. 6–7: "Solebant sane huiusmodi libri regibus siue reginis antiquitus scribi, ut
      quasi ad uitae suae exemplum eis instruerentur aliorum prosequi triumphos, aliorum
      uitare miserias, aliorum imitari sapientiam, aliorum contempnere stultitiam."

28   William of Malmesbury, *Deeds of the English Kings* Prologue to Book II, 1, ed. and trans.
      Mynors, vol. 1, pp. 150–51: "iocunda quadam gestorum notitia mores condiens, ad bona
      sequenda uel mala cauenda legentes exemplis irritat".

29   Brutus, for example, is generous, wise, and aggressive in battle (DGB, i.7); Riuallo is peace-
      ful and fortunate (DGB, ii.33).

deficient, treacherous ruling families to argue for present-day stability and the assurance of peace afforded by dynastic continuity. This is still a providential view of history with didactic meaning.[30]

With the didactic function of history in mind, each of the three authors make the decision to attach morality to rightful rule over the island of Britain, bringing Insular history in line with sacred history. Taking inspiration from Gildas and from the punishments inflicted by God on the Israelites when they broke the commandments, they associate bad rulers with moral decline, especially with reference to the Britons.[31] For Henry and William, the theme of divine punishment positions the Britons as a negative example that the English should be careful not to follow. For Geoffrey, the theme provides explanation for the Britons' decline and loss of their independent kingdom, and he describes the Britons' decline and consequent loss of the island of Britain in moral terms. Following a description of Gormundus and his Saxon allies pushing Kareticus into Wales and laying waste to the whole island, he addresses the readers in the language of lamentation:

> Why, you slothful race, weighed down by your terrible sins, why with your continual thirst for civil war have you weakened yourself so much by internal strife? ... Your kingdom is divided against itself, lust for civil strife and a cloud of envy has blunted your mind, your pride has prevented you from obeying a single king, and so your country has been laid waste before your eyes by most wicked barbarians ...[32]

Here Geoffrey is at his most direct in blaming British vices for the triumph of the pagan Saxons, whose arrival occurs during the disastrous rule of the cunning and jealous Vortigern.[33] A similar explanation is given later in the voice of Caduallo. Having fled into exile in Brittany, Caduallo, who knows his Gildas,

---

30   For further discussion of Geoffrey's participation in providential history, which goes against some critical views of him as a secular writer in the extreme, see Barry Lewis's contribution to this volume.

31   For discussion see Henry of Huntingdon, *History of the English*, ed. and trans. Greenway, p. lix; Lev. 26, Jer. 14, Isaiah 24; for Geoffrey's biblical quotations and allusions, see Paul Russell's chapter in this volume.

32   *DGB*, xi.185.141–43, 147–50: "Quid, ociosa gens pondere inmanium scelerum oppressa, quid semper ciuilia proelia siciens tete domesticis in tantum debilitasti motibus ... Quia ergo regnum tuum in se diuisum fuit, quia furor ciuilis discordiae et liuoris fumus mentem tuam hebetauit, quia superbia tua uni regi oboedientiam ferre non permisit, cernis iccirco patriam tuam ab impiissimis paganis desolatam ..."

33   *DGB*, vi.98.248–50. In Geoffrey's version of events, Vortigern does not invite Hengist and Horsa to Britain to help defend its people; they arrive on their own, and Vortigern makes a deal with them.

attributes the loss of his kingdom to his unworthy ancestors, who were proud, immoral, and filled with greed. The moral judgement is explicit:

> As the historian Gildas bears witness, they harbored not just this sin, but all sins to which mankind is prey, and above all, those which suppress all virtue, namely hatred of truth and those who maintain it, love of lies and those who weave them, preference for evil in the place of good, respect for wickedness in the place of kindness ...[34]

For this reason, God has sent the Saxons to dispossess them of their land. A similar sentiment is expressed in the *VM* in the voice of Merlin, uttering a prophecy to his sister, Ganieda, in King Rodarch's hall: "O the madness of the Britons! Their universal affluence leads them to excess. They are not satisfied with peace. A Fury goads them on. They engage in civil war and family feuds. They allow the churches of the Lord to go to ruin, and drive the holy bishops out into distant lands."[35] Merlin predicts the successive conquests of the Saxons, Danes, and Normans. In this, Geoffrey provides an explanation for the Britons' loss of sovereignty, placing blame on the Britons themselves and implicitly informing his contemporary audience of aristocratic rulers of the dangers of straying off the moral path.

William and Henry, too, associate bad rulership with moral decay. William frequently promotes piety and learning and opposes bad behavior through the examples of England's early rulers. Eadbald, for example, begins his reign by reverting to paganism and sexually assaulting his stepmother, though later he repents, converts, and gives gifts to the monastery outside Canterbury, which is to be praised.[36] There are many examples of this sort of royal conversion narrative in *Deeds of the English Kings*. Boniface's letter to Æthelbald, recorded by William, admonishes Æthelbald for abolishing the privileges of various monasteries and for the widespread sin of adultery, which will corrupt his race:

---

34 *DGB*, xi.195.355–59: "ut Gildas historicus testatur, non solum hoc uitium sed omnia quae humanae naturae accidere solent et praecipue, quod tocius boni euertit statum, odium ueritatis cum assertoribus suis amorque mendacii cum fabricatoribus suis, susceptio mali pro bono, ueneratio nequitiae pro benignitate ..."

35 *VM*, ll. 580–85: "O rabiem Britonum, quos copia diviciarum / usque superveniens ultra quam debeat effert! / Nolunt pace frui, stimulis agitantur Herenis. / Civiles acies cognataque prelia miscent. / Ecclesias Domini paciuntur habere ruinam pontificesque sacros ad regna remota repellunt."

36 William of Malmesbury, *Deeds of the English Kings* i.10.2–4, ed. and trans. Mynors, vol. 1, pp. 30–31.

> If the English nation does as we are accused of doing in France and Italy and by the very heathen themselves, and spurning lawful wedlock becomes rotten with adultery, there will arise from such mingled unions a coward race, despising God, whose corrupt behavior will be the ruin of their country ...[37]

Eventually, the Mercian line withers due to weakness.[38] By implication, repeated sins and poor rulership corrupt the royal line and cause it to fail, both in body and in rule over England.

Like Geoffrey, a Gildasian view of history is present in William's narrative. Following the death of Bede, William laments the loss of letters and the increase of evil in the kingdom of Northumbria, quoting a letter from Alcuin to Æthelheard, archbishop of Canterbury:

> It is written in the book of Gildas, wisest of the Britons, that it was through the avarice and rapine of their princes, through the iniquity and injustice of their judges, because their bishops would not preach and their people were wanton and corrupted, that those same Britons lost their country. Let us beware that the self-same vices do not re-establish themselves in our own day ...[39]

An explicit connection is made between vice and the right to rule a kingdom, determined by God and punishment. Peoples who have polluted their line with sin are not fit to rule. Vortigern is "unready and unwise, devoted to carnal pleasures and the servant of almost every vice", including incest.[40] When William mentions descendants of the Britons in his day, it is in the language of

---

37 William of Malmesbury, *Deeds of the English Kings* i.80.4, ed. and trans. Mynors, vol. 1, pp. 116–17: "quod si gens Anglorum, sicut in Frantia et Italia et ab ipsis paganis nobis improperatur, spretis legitimis matrimoniis per adulteria defluit, nascitura ex tali commixtione sit gens ignaua et Dei contemptrix, quae perditis moribus patriam pessumdet ..."

38 William of Malmesbury, *Deeds of the English Kings* i.96, ed. and trans. Mynors, vol. 1, pp. 140–41.

39 William of Malmesbury, *Deeds of the English Kings* i.70.4, ed. and trans. Mynors, vol. 1, pp. 104–05: "Legitur in libro Gildae, sapientissimi Britonum, quod idem Britones propter auaritiam et rapinam principum, propter iniquitatem et iniustitiam iudicum, propter desidiam predicationis episcoporum, propter luxuriam et malos mores populi patriam perdidere. Caueamus haec eadem uitia nostris temporibus inolescere ..."

40 William of Malmesbury, *Deeds of the English Kings* i.4.1, ed. and trans. Mynors, vol. 1, pp. 20–21: "nec manu promptus nec consilio bonus, immo ad illecebras carnis pronus omniumque fere uitiorum mancipium ..."

corruption: Æthelstan sweeps the Western Britons, or Cornish, out of Exeter, ridding the city of a *contamina gens*, "infected race".[41]

Henry of Huntingdon, too, uses the Britons as a didactic lesson, warning his own noble readers against following in their path. At the conclusion to Book I, which sets out a Roman imperial past for early Britain, Henry writes that God sends prosperity to the Britons to test them. They respond to the time of plenty by falling into crime, cruelty, and wickedness. God punishes them with a plague, but this does not stop them, so he sends a worse punishment: invasions by Scots and Picts and, eventually, the Saxons. The link between the Britons' sin and punishment is explicit.[42] At the beginning of Book II, on the coming of the English to Britain, Henry transforms the pagan wish for worldly glory and fame into a Christian trust in God:

> We shall have true glory, fame, and honour if we rely, with cheerfulness and joy, on Him who is the only true one, if we put all our hope and trust in God, not in the sons of men, as did the Britons, who, deserting God and the grandeur of His fear, sought aid from pagans [i.e. Hengist and Horsa], and gained their just deserts.[43]

Their punishments, Henry writes, include the loss of glory on earth and the posthumous treatment of their deeds as *amara, tedii scilicet et odii generatrix*, "distasteful, a cause for loathing and disgust".[44] All three authors thus attach moral virtue to rightful rule over the island of Britain, and use the Britons as a negative example for their contemporary readers. Sin and vice lead to the withering of the royal line, pollution and disgust, the loss of learning and letters, and the failure of whole kingdoms. The didactic function of history is a backdrop to all they depict.

---

41 William of Malmesbury, *Deeds of the English Kings* ii.134.6, ed. and trans. Mynors, vol. 1, pp. 216–17. For William, the Welsh descendants of the Britons are reduced to two general uses in his narrative: they turn up occasionally to demonstrate the antiquity and primacy of Glastonbury, and they are a foil to the victorious English kings, who often demonstrate emergent martial and imperial prowess by putting down Welsh rebellions.

42 Henry of Huntingdon, *History of the English* i.47, ed. and trans. Greenway, pp. 74–77.

43 Henry of Huntingdon, *History of the English* ii.1, ed. and trans. Greenway, pp. 78–79: "Veram autem gloriam et famam et honorem habebimus, si ei qui solus uerus est cum iocunditate et leticia innitamur, si spem nostram et fiduciam omnem in Deo ponamus, non in filiis hominum, sicut Britanni, qui Deo abiecto et magnificentia timoris eius auxilium pecierunt a paganis, habueruntque sed quale decebat." For discussion of this passage, see Henry of Huntingdon, *History of the English*, ed. and trans. Greenway, p. lxii, who notes its thematic debt to Psalms 57:8.

44 Henry of Huntingdon, *History of the English* ii.1, ed. and trans. Greenway, pp. 78–79.

A number of additional conventions are shared by the three authors, including an episodic structure fit for short, digestible bits of reading (typically divided neatly by successions of kings); gestures toward writing in a "humble" style punctuated by moments of elevation that show off learning; and commonplace tools to portray characters' personalities, including direct discourse and physical description.[45] Geoffrey, Henry, and William use direct discourse most often in battle preparation, in which kings rouse their men with inspired speeches, a commonplace in history writing probably modeled after Sallust. Other than pre-battle speeches and the *PM* in the voice of Merlin, Geoffrey does not depart from the authorial voice he uses to narrate the *DGB* throughout. By contrast, William and Henry include a number of written sources in their histories that disrupt their own authorial voices with the insertion of other authorities relevant to early English history, including letters by Alcuin, Gregory, and Boniface that they have gotten from Bede. William, for example, often includes grants from kings to various monasteries, with particular focus on Glastonbury in order to inscribe these royal gifts into perpetuity. These digressions add international scope, relevance, and legitimacy to William's narrative. In other words, Geoffrey's contemporaries include the voices of other authors in their histories. It is not in their interest to disguise written sources; rather, it adds to their authority.

It is through the elision of sources and the establishment of authority that Geoffrey departs the most from the commonplace tools of history writing exemplified by his two contemporaries. The entire *DGB* is written in his voice, with no departure or digression from the main narrative other than the deliberately marked departure of the *PM*, and little discussion of sources. While this results in a cohesive narrative structure, it has not won Geoffrey any favors in the reception of his work, contemporary or modern. The *DGB* is widely regarded as a work of imagination rather than history, and the lack of survival of Welsh written sources does not help.[46]

The establishment of authority by the historian through proper handling of evidence was particularly important "in a world of slow and often unverifiable communications".[47] For this reason, historians typically spent some time proving the quality of their interpretive faculties by discussing education level, research methods, and ability to assess evidence carefully.[48] William and

---

45   Ray, "Medieval Historiography", p. 56. Joshua Byron Smith reminds me that the redactor of the First Variant mostly rids the text of speeches.
46   For similar discussion, see Simon Meecham-Jones's contribution to this volume.
47   C. Given-Wilson, *Chronicles: The Writing of History in Medieval England*, London and New York, 2004, p. 6.
48   Given-Wilson, *Chronicles*, pp. 6–10.

Henry follow these rules well, establishing their authority and claim to truth by discussing their sources explicitly, which they have painstakingly gathered and analyzed. Henry says, "I have followed the Venerable Bede's *Ecclesiastical History* where I could, selecting material also from other authors and borrowing from chronicles preserved in ancient libraries, and I have described past events down to the time of our own knowledge and observation", while William says he expands upon Bede and Eadmer with the addition of recent, eyewitness sources: "Whatsoever I have added out of recent history, I have either seen myself or heard from men who can be trusted."[49] William, in particular, frequently mentions where he found his written sources, why he is including them, and whether they are truthful. Sometimes he risks potentially disreputable sources, asking his reader to judge for themselves; other times he vouches for their accuracy. As mentioned above, he includes letters, charters, and other documents in his text, which results in a sometimes digressive narrative that loops back to pick up dropped threads, but has the end result of establishing unimpeachable authority and trustworthiness. Henry refers to historians from whom he has gotten information and, following Bede, includes correspondence from the popes directing the conversion of the English. In both texts, written (and eyewitness) sources are undisguised, leaving the impression that they have not been tampered with.

Henry and William also do a good job of describing (some might say flaunting) their education. William, for example, communicates his authority by describing himself as a lifelong, learned reader, educated in the traditional disciplines:

> I studied many kinds of literature, though in different degrees. To Logic, the armourer of speech, I no more than lent an ear. Physic, which cures the sick body, I went deeper into. As for Ethics, I explored parts in depth, revering its high status as a subject inherently accessible to the student and able to form good character; in particular I studied History, which adds flavour to moral instruction by imparting a pleasurable knowledge of past events, spurring the reader by the accumulation of examples to follow the good and shun the bad.[50]

---

49   Henry of Huntingdon, *History of the English* Prologue, ed. and trans. Greenway, pp. 6–7: "Bede uenerabilis ecclesiasticam qua potui secutus historiam, nonnulla etiam ex aliis excerpens auctoribus, inde cronica in antiquis reseruata librariis compilans, usque nostrum ad auditum et uisum preterita representaui"; William of Malmesbury, *Deeds of the English Kings* Prologue to Book I, 8, ed. and trans. Mynors, vol. 1, pp. 16–17: "Quicquid uero de recentioribus aetatibus apposui, uel ipse uidi uel a uiris fide dignis audiui."

50   William of Malmesbury, *Deeds of the English Kings* Prologue to Book II, 2, ed. and trans. Mynors, vol. 1, pp. 150–51: "Et multis quidem litteris impendi operam, sed aliis aliam.

The degree of agency he gives himself in this description of his educational credentials feeds directly into his self-fashioning as a skilled historian: curious, highly self-motivated, and dogged in gathering information. Henry, too, flashes his educational credentials at the very beginning of *History of the English*, quoting Horace in a proclamation that the best relief from suffering and affliction in the world comes from studying literature.[51] He follows this statement with a proliferation of classical and biblical references that reinforce this professed learned background.

Geoffrey, in contrast, has polished his sources to such a sheen as to be unrecognizable, and he does not spend time explicitly discussing his educational credentials.[52] His knowledge of classical authors must be discerned by the equally-educated reader. He attributes his work to a book in the British tongue brought to him by Walter, archdeacon of Oxford, which he himself has translated into Latin.[53] The authority of his work rests on these three details: it is ancient, it is in the British tongue, and Geoffrey has translated it faithfully. Geoffrey does not spend time in his prologue nor elsewhere establishing other kinds of credibility as a historian; he does not brag of his book learning, as Henry does, nor include letters and other documents. He does not perform his ability to gather and judge evidence. His departure from the conventions of historical writing in this way – which stands in particularly stark contrast to William and Henry's successful adherence to source study as establishing authority – perhaps explains the modern critical judgements about the success of the *DGB* as credible history. William and Henry are available for modern historians' research; Geoffrey is not.[54]

This key difference has set Geoffrey on a fundamentally different reception trajectory than his contemporaries. Henry is remembered for his good judgement and rationality: for example, Elisabeth van Houts calls him a "pragmatic historian and an annalist" whose account of the Norman Conquest is "down to earth and rational".[55] William, according to Antonia Gransden, is

---

Logicam enim, quae armat eloquium, solo libaui auditu; phisicam, quae medetur ualitudini corporum, aliquanto pressius concepi; iam uero ethicae partes medullitus rimatus, illius maiestati assurgo, quod per se studentibus pateat et animos ad bene uiuendum componat; historiam precipue, quae iocunda quadam gestorum notitia mores condiens, ad bona sequenda uel mala cauenda legentes exemplis irritat."

51 Henry of Huntingdon, *History of the English* Prologue, ed. and trans. Greenway, pp. 6–7; Horace, *Carmina* i.32.14, *Epistles* i.2.3–4.
52 For Geoffrey's demonstrable use of Welsh, classical, and biblical sources, see chapters in this volume by Ben Guy and Paul Russell.
53 *DGB*, Prologus 2.10.
54 Ray, "Medieval Historiography", p. 33.
55 E. van Houts, "Historical Writing", in C. Harper-Bill and E. van Houts (eds.), *A Companion to the Anglo-Norman World*, Woodbridge, 2003, pp. 103–22, at pp. 114, 113.

"conscientious", "highly intelligent", showing "considerable critical acumen" and, happily, "circumspect about Arthurian legends and oral tradition".[56] He is commended by Rodney Thomson for "set[ting] an example of intelligent and imaginative judgement, of elegant expression and lucid planning, which are the hallmarks of the great historian".[57] William's methods of research and his scrupulous attention to sources appeal to modern critics because they align so closely with our own expectations of historical accuracy. Sigbjørn Sønneysn writes, "it has been taken for granted that William in his capacity as a historian pursued the same ends as those pursued by modern-day historians."[58] This reputation has probably also protected William's marvel stories and prophecies from the criticisms that Gerald of Wales and Geoffrey of Monmouth receive for the same sort of material. By contrast, C.N.L. Brooke declares that "there has scarcely, if ever, been a historian more mendacious than Geoffrey of Monmouth", while Alan Cobban labels him a "romance writer and historical poseur".[59] Francis Ingledew calls the *DGB* "a massive piece of fiction making", while Elisabeth van Houts styles it "bizarre", a "historical novel", a piece of "escapist historical writing".[60] More criticisms of this sort could be furnished, but suffice it to say, critics take objection to how Geoffrey spurns the conventions of transparency of source material and treatment of evidence.[61] And yet he shares many other conventions and features with his contemporaries – it is the use of evidence, inflected by the wide reception of the *DGB* in the genre of romance, that fundamentally divides them.[62]

---

56   A. Gransden, *Historical Writing in England, c.550–c.1307*, London, 1974, pp. 168, 175.

57   R.M. Thomson, "William of Malmesbury: Life and Works", in id. in collaboration with M. Winterbottom, *William of Malmesbury: Gesta Regum Anglorum, The History of the English Kings, Volume II. General Introduction and Commentary*, Oxford, 1999, pp. xxxv–xlv.

58   S.O. Sønnesyn, *William of Malmesbury and the Ethics of History*, Woodbridge, 2012, p. 2.

59   A.B. Cobban, *The Medieval English Universities: Oxford and Cambridge to c.1500*, Berkeley, 1988, p. 38; C.N.L. Brooke, "Geoffrey of Monmouth as a Historian", in C.N.L. Brooke, D. Luscombe, G. Martin, and D. Owen (eds.), *Church and Government in the Middle Ages: Essays Presented to C.R. Cheney on his 70th Birthday*, Cambridge, 1976, pp. 77–91, at p. 78.

60   F. Ingledew, "The Book of Troy and the Genealogical Construction of History: The Case of Geoffrey of Monmouth's *Historia regum Britanniae*", *Speculum* 69:3 (1994), 665–704, at p. 670; van Houts, "Historical Writing", pp. 114, n. 59, pp. 114–15.

61   For discussion see J. Blacker, *The Faces of Time: Portrayal of the Past in Old French and Latin Historical Narrative of the Anglo-Norman Regnum*, Austin, 1994, pp. 1–52; Partner, *Serious Entertainments*, pp. 183–230; R. Ray, "Historiography", in F.A.C. Mantello and A.G. Rigg (eds.), *Medieval Latin: An Introduction and Bibliographical Guide*, Washington, 1996, pp. 639–49.

62   For Geoffrey as a writer of romance, see R.M. Stein, *Reality Fictions: Romance, History, and Governmental Authority, 1025–1180*, Notre Dame, 2006, pp. 108–20.

2   Thematic Considerations

In addition to the shared historical conventions (with the exception of treat-ment of sources) discussed above, the three large-scale surveys of the history of Britain share additional structural and thematic characteristics. Each is in-debted to Bede's *Ecclesiastical History*, William and Henry quite closely, and Geoffrey less faithfully.[63] Each uses an episodic structure, without annalis-tic dating, punctuated by the rise and fall of lines of kings, whether one line (in the case of Geoffrey), or five replaced by one (in the case of William and Henry). Their successes and failures are predicated upon a capricious mixture of Fortuna, God, and free will, each providing lessons to the intended aristo-cratic audience of royals and bishops. The histories are violent, bloody, and full of battles and treacherous acts, punctuated by moments of religious piety and peaceful governance, with cities settled and gifts made to churches. Each is substantively an origin legend, depicting the arrival of people by ship to the island of Britain and their conquest of the people who are already there. Conquest narratives from the perspective of the conqueror implicitly require justification of the act, and each author justifies the validity of conquest by explaining why the previous people deserved to lose control. This may be be-cause they have sinned egregiously and are being punished by God, in the case of the Britons, or because they are monstrous, racialized giants without in-terest in governing nor indeed the ability to do so, in the case of Geoffrey's account of the arrival of Brutus and his people, or because they are weak, ill-advised, and fail to produce heirs, in the case of the Norman Conquest of the English. In addition, each of the histories is interested in themes of conquest, divine punishment, sainthood, kingship, and national governance. The key dif-ference in the texts is not form or structure, but content.

Having discussed how each of the works follow or subvert the conventions of their genre, the remainder of the chapter is interested in how each of the works treats the shared theme of conquest and the attendant treatment and portrayal of the Britons. Their interpretations of the *aduentus Saxonum*, which

---

63   For Geoffrey's reworking of Bede, see Rebecca Thomas's chapter in this volume and N. Wright, "Geoffrey of Monmouth and Bede", *AL* 6 (1986), 27–59. For William's debt to Bede, see E.J. Ward, "Verax historicus Beda: William of Malmesbury, Bede and Historia", in R.M. Thomson, E. Dolmans, and E.A. Winkler (eds.), *Discovering William of Malmesbury*, Woodbridge, 2017, pp. 175–87; Sønnesyn, *William of Malmesbury*, pp. 125–27; for Henry's, see Henry of Huntingdon, *History of the English*, ed. and trans. Greenway, pp. lxxxvi–lxxxix; ead., "Authority, Convention and Observation in Henry of Huntingdon's *Historia Anglorum*", *Anglo-Norman Studies* 18 (1995), 105–21.

is the main event shared by all three of the histories, shows the difference in perspectives of the authors.

William, writing first (in and before c.1125), dedicates the first several sections of his history (§§1–8) to a succinct narrative of the arrival of the Angles, Saxons, and Jutes, taken mostly from Bede. The brief image of the pre-Saxon past of Britain that he projects in §§1–2 is one of discord and struggle. Britain is exposed to greatness under the Romans, with the great princes Severus and Constantine buried on the island. But, following Maximus's disastrous campaign in Gaul and the flight of all the good Britons to a colony on the western coast of Gaul, the island is left *conterminarum gentium inhiationi ... obnoxia*, "exposed to the greed of neighbouring peoples".[64] Enter the Picts and Scots, who harry the remaining Britons even after they convince the Romans to help them build a defensive wall. The Britons beg for aid from King Vortigern, who invites the Angles and Saxons from Germany to help defeat the Scots. Vortigern, as discussed above, is depraved and ill-prepared for this alliance, focused instead on violating his own daughter and other sins. The arrival of the three Germanic peoples to the island is depicted positively from their point of view; their ships are spurred on by joy, prayers, and favorable winds; they are led by Hengist and Horsa of venerable lineage; they are received joyfully by the people of Britain.[65] In short, they are depicted as saviors. The English quickly dispatch the Scots and settle the kingdoms of Kent and Northumbria in a marriage deal between Hengist's daughter and the lustful Vortigern. Concerning the transfer of power from the Britons to the English, William writes of the death of Vortigern's son, Vortimer: "with his decease the Britons' strength withered away, and their hopes dwindled and ebbed".[66] A brief resurgence by Ambrosius "the sole surviving Roman" with the help of Arthur is dashed by the treachery of the long knives.[67] Following the death of Hengist, William dives into an account of the succession of the kings of Northumbria: Eisc, Ohta, Eormenric, Æthelberht. He does not discuss the fate of the Britons; they disappear altogether from the narrative, cropping up only occasionally in the deeds of future English kings who must battle them at various points. The Roman and British past merely sets the stage for his careful, lengthy histories of each of the English kingdoms.

---

64   William of Malmesbury, *Deeds of the English Kings* i.2, ed. and trans. Mynors, vol. 1, pp. 18–19.

65   William of Malmesbury, *Deeds of the English Kings* i.5–6, ed. and trans. Mynors, vol. 1, pp. 22–23.

66   William of Malmesbury, *Deeds of the English Kings* i.8.2, ed. and trans. Mynors, vol. 1, pp. 26–27: "Sed eo extincto Britonum robur emarcuit, spes imminutae retro fluxere".

67   William of Malmesbury, *Deeds of the English Kings* i.8.2, ed. and trans. Mynors, vol. 1, pp. 26–27: "solus Romanorum superstes".

While the English kings are certainly not always depicted in a positive light, the overall depiction William aims for is one of steadily increasing Christianity, learning, lawfulness, civic organization, and peace. For William, the conquest of Britain by the English is ordained and logical, a necessary blip before turning to the matter of the progressive development of the English kingdoms.[68]

By contrast, Henry's narrative of the *aduentus Saxonum* is much longer and much more interested in the Britons. He prefaces the event with a lengthy description of the island from Bede, a list of the cities of Britain and the Saxon shires of the current day, the island's weather, highways, and languages, and the Trojan origin of its founder, Bruto, taken from *Historia Brittonum*. In later versions of the history he includes a long succession of *laudes* for Roman emperors, taken from the *Historia Romana*. These men rule the Roman empire which, he takes pains to note, included Britain at that time. Britain's imperial Roman past is important to Henry, with particular interest in the emperor Constantine who marries Helena, daughter of Cole, the British king of Colchester. Following the *aduentus Saxonum*, which largely follows the William/Bede narrative outlined above with some minor variations, Hengist and his son Æsc violently expel the Britons and establish the kingdom of Kent.

Notably, unlike William, Henry does not exclude the Britons from his story of the rise of the English kingdoms. The death of Vortimer and the last battle with Ambrosius Aurelianus is not the final word on the subject. Hengist and his descendants fight dozens of bloody battles against Briton armies for several generations following their arrival (§§4–9), as do the rulers of Sussex (§§10–15), Wessex (§§16–18), Northumbria (§22), East Anglia (§25), and Mercia (§§27–29). The Britons in these battles are favorably portrayed, even if they lose. Fighting Hengist and Æsc, they are "splendidly arrayed" in twelve organized phalanges; in Ælle's siege of the city of *Andredecester* (Pevensey) they "swarm like bees" with "superior speed" and battle tactics; in a battle against Cerdic's nephews recently arrived from Germany the British leaders "drew up their battle lines against them most excellently according to the rules of warfare".[69] They are organized, disciplined, and frightening. In the battle with Cerdic's nephews, Stuf and Wihtgar, the gilded shields of the Britons are illuminated by the light of the sun, reflecting it off the hills as they approach

---

68   For William's history as a progression from barbarism to civilization, see J. Gillingham, "The Context and Purposes of Geoffrey of Monmouth's *History of the Kings of Britain*", *Anglo-Norman Studies* 13 (1990), 99–118 (repr. in id. (ed.), *The English in the Twelfth Century*, pp. 19–39, at pp. 28–29).

69   Henry of Huntingdon, *History of the English* ii.7, ed. and trans. Greenway, pp. 88–89: "nobiliter ordinatas", pp. 92–93: "quasi apes ... celeritate prestantiores"; pp. 96–97: "acies in eos secundum belli leges pulcherrime construxerunt."

the Saxon army, terrifying them. Even if only to emphasize the significance of
the English peoples' eventual dominance over the Britons, this editorializing of
material taken from the *Anglo-Saxon Chronicle* links the Britons' battle strategies to their Roman imperial past, which Henry describes at length prior to the
English arrival. Their fierceness in battle also recalls their pre-Roman ancestors
who were able to hold off Julius Caesar for some time.[70] Overall, for Henry,
the suppression of the Britons is a piecemeal process, not assured, requiring
immense planning, battle tactics, bravery, and perseverance over several generations of leaders and across a large geographical space. Eventually they win
because of numbers, with more ships constantly arriving, and because God has
rejected the Britons.[71]

Conquest is a thematic interest for each of the authors and each of them
treat it slightly differently. Overall, Henry sees history as a series of successive conquests, plagues sent by God as punishment. The English conquest of
Britain is one of many, with the Norman Conquest the most recent:

> From the very beginning down to the present time, the divine vengeance
> has sent five plagues into Britain, punishing the faithful as well as un-
> believers. The first was through the Romans, who overcame Britain but
> later withdrew. The second was through the Picts and Scots, who griev-
> ously beleaguered the land with battles but did not conquer it. The third
> was through the English, who overcame and occupy it. The fourth was
> through the Danes, who conquered it by warfare, but afterwards they per-
> ished. The fifth was through the Normans, who conquered it and have
> dominion over the English people at the present time.[72]

For Henry, the English conquest of Britain is paralleled by the more recent
Norman Conquest, happening for the same reason (sent by God as punishment) and with the same results (a transfer of power to the new people).
Incidentally, Henry does not see Brutus's arrival following a period of wandering from Italy, discussed several sections later, as one of the plagues. For Henry,

---

70   Henry of Huntingdon, *History of the English* i.12, ed. and trans. Greenway, pp. 31–33.

71   Henry of Huntingdon, *History of the English* ii.14, ii.18, ed. and trans. Greenway, pp. 96–97,
      100–01.

72   Henry of Huntingdon, *History of the English* i.4, ed. and trans. Greenway, pp. 14–15:
      "Quinque autem plagas ab exordio usque ad presens immisit diuina ultio Britannie,
      que non solum uisitat fideles, sed etiam diiudicat infideles. Primam per Romanos, qui
      Britanniam expugnauerunt sed postea recesserunt. Secundam per Pictos et Scotos, qui
      grauissime eam bellis uexauerunt, nec tamen optinuerunt. Terciam per Anglicos, qui eam
      debellauerunt et optinent. Quartam per Dacos, qui eam bellis optinuerunt, sed postea
      deperierunt. Quintam per Normannos, qui eam deuicerunt et Anglis inpresentiarum
      dominatur."

the meaning that can be drawn from conquest is the theme of *contemptus mundi*, "contempt of the world": worldly power is temporary, and we should turn the eternal kingdom instead.[73]

Geoffrey's *DGB*, also interested in conquest throughout, is bookended by two conquests: first, Brutus's establishment of the kingdom of Britain following his ancestors' flight from Troy, a period of wandering, and the driving away of the giants who inhabited the island, and second, the arrival and rise of the Saxons, who take over from the Britons as divine punishment for their sins. In the middle of the *DGB* is a protracted struggle against conquest by the Romans.

In Book i, the giants do nothing more than position Brutus and his friend Corineus as rightful conquerors of the island, for they had not occupied the land in a civilized manner.[74] Brutus and his people gain ownership over the land more by divine right than by a series of violent battles. By contrast, Constantinus's conquest of Rome, and Arthur's conquest of much of Gaul, Scandinavia, and the islands neighboring Britain, plus his attempt to conquer Rome, position the Britons as an imperial power, in the same vein as Henry of Huntingdon.[75] Hoelus, king of the Armoricans, addresses Arthur as follows: "for a third time one born of British blood will rule the Roman state. [The Sibyl's] prophecies have come true for two men already, since it is clear, as you said, that the noble princes Beli and Constantine have worn the crown of Rome."[76] The Roman associations of Britain's kings are necessary for understanding Geoffrey's depiction of the *aduentus Saxonum*. For Geoffrey, the story of Vortigern and Vortimer is simply a prelude to the extended story of

---

73   Henry of Huntingdon, *History of the English* ii.40, ed. and trans. Greenway, pp. 136–37. For discussion of this theme in Geoffrey's *VM*, see Barry Lewis's chapter in this volume.

74   *DGB*, i.21.456–59: "Peragratis ergo quibusque prouinciis, repertos gigantes ad cauernas montium fugant, patriam donante duce sorciuntur, agros incipiunt colere, domos aedificare, ita ut in breui tempore terram ab aeuo inhabitatem censeres", "After exploring its various territories and driving off to mountain caves any giants they came upon, they portioned out the land, at their leader's invitation, and began to till the fields and build homes so that, in a short time, the country appeared to have been occupied for many years." For further discussion of the giants and the rhetoric of conquest and colonization, see Coral Lumbley and Michael Faletra's chapters in this volume.

75   Stein, *Reality Fictions*, p. 112 notes that Arthur's territorial holdings are roughly equivalent to what was controlled by the Anglo-Norman elite in the early 12th century if one includes Cnut's overseas lands. For doubt about whether Geoffrey's Arthur would have recognizably served Anglo-Norman interests at the time, see Gillingham, "Context and Purposes", pp. 21–23.

76   *DGB*, ix.160.492–96: "ex Britannico genere tercio nasciturum qui Romanum optinebit imperium. De duobus autem adimpleta sunt ipsius oracula, cum manifestum sit praeclaros ut dixisti principes Beli atque Constantinum imperii Romani gessisse insignia."

Arthur as an imperial figure.[77] In the *DGB*, Arthur is not a final, brief stand against the Saxons before they take over, but an extension of a continuous imperial project. Arthur is not satisfied with simply defeating and expelling the Saxons; he conquers Europe and attempts to become the third British king to rule Rome as well. It is not until Arthur dies that a succession of rulers, riven by weakness, sodomy, and love of civil strife, allow the Saxons to take over Loegria.[78] The remainder of the Britons flee to Cornwall and Wales, and the last king, Cadualadrus, is exiled to Brittany.[79] For Geoffrey, the "passage of dominion" is a long, drawn-out process, compounding many mistakes and failures to unite, that also explains how the descendants of the Britons ended up in Wales, Cornwall, and Brittany. Geoffrey leaves the subsequent history of the Welsh kings to his contemporary Caradog of Llancarfan and the history of the English kings to William and Henry, refusing the continuity between British and English rule that so interests his contemporaries.[80] Instead, he looks forward to such time as the British can return with the help of their messianic figure.

Because Geoffrey ends his history in 682 and does not bring it up to the present day, the parallels between earlier conquests and the Norman Conquest are less explicit. He does not see the history of the island as beset by a succession of plagues of conquest as Henry does. The Norman Conquest would have been present in the minds of all three authors (and their patrons) since it was so recent, and their interest in conquest can be read in that light. In the case of the Britons, each author sets up the failure of the Britons in moral terms, as discussed above, and in terms of the desertion of the Britons by all its greatest leaders and men: according to Geoffrey and Henry, the British people are left exposed to attack by the Picts and Scots because the best of the Britons have escaped to Brittany, leaving a power vacuum filled by the disastrous Vortigern; according to William, the disastrous reigns of Maximus and the second

---

77   For Geoffrey's departure from the standard story of Vortigern, Hengist, and Horsa, see Rebecca Thomas's chapter in this volume. Key differences are as follows: Vortigern does not invite the Saxons to Britain; they arrive on their own and then he makes a deal with them. Influenced by Satan, Vortigern is blinded by love for Hengist's daughter Ronwein, and it is the people of Britain who object to the pagan Saxons' presence in Britain because they recognize that they should not mix with pagans. Instead, they nominate Vortimer as their legitimate king. He is a great king, but he is killed, poisoned by his stepmother, Ronwein. For Geoffrey's portrayal of the Britons' resistance of the pagan Saxons as religious war, see Barry Lewis's chapter in this volume.

78   *DGB*, xi.180–87.

79   *DGB*, xi.186.157–60. Stein, *Reality Fictions*, p. 119, n. 18 notices that the Saxons assuming ownership by building houses echoes the language of the Britons' arrival at the beginning of the *DGB*.

80   *DGB*, xi.208.601–03.

Constantinus leave Britain exposed to neighboring peoples. Vice, misrule, and lack of leadership account for the shift in power.

Parallels are discernible in Henry's and William's accounts of the Norman Conquest, precipitated by the misrule of Æthelred, which prompts the remaining powerful men of England to look to Duke William for direction. Geoffrey implies that the Germans lose rule of the island as retribution for treason,[81] while Henry writes, "For the Lord Almighty had planned a double affliction for the English people, which He had decided to exterminate for their compelling crimes, just as the Britons were humbled when their sins accused them."[82] Through a combination of Fortuna (which William favors as explanation for events), sin, misrule, divine punishment, and the individual choices of the island's rulers, a practical and providential explanation for conquest can be found, undergirding the Norman Conquest and the continued punishment of the descendants of the Britons.

3   Conclusion

These three authors are united by several common elements: they sought explanation for present-day conditions, with a focus on the conquests the Insular peoples experienced; they were interested in themes of unity, divine punishment, kingship, piety, and the importance of peaceful rulership; they cultivated the same group of patrons; and they constructed their histories according to the conventions of their genre, including the rhetorical flourishes expected of a good prologue: praise of a noble patron, the humility topos, and gestures toward writing in a humble style. Where Geoffrey and his contemporaries depart is in choice of subject matter and the treatment of sources.

In choosing to write a history of the Britons rather than of the English (reflected in the title, *De gestis Britonum*), Geoffrey must have recognized the value of the subject for his own career advancement as well as for the understanding of history in his day. Because he was raised in Monmouthshire, knew Brittonic language(s) (for he would not claim to have translated the British

---

81   *DGB*, Prophetiae 113.69–71: "Vix obtinebit cauernas suas Germanicus draco, quia ultio prodicionis eius superueniet. Vigebit tandem paulisper, sed decimatio Neustriae nocebit", "The German dragon will be hard put to keep possession of its caves, since retribution will be visited on its treason. Then it will prosper for a time, but Normandy's tithe will injure it."

82   Henry of Huntingdon, *History of the English* vi.1, ed. and trans. Greenway, pp. 338–39: "Genti enim Anglorum, quam sceleribus suis exigentibus disterminare proposuerat, sicut et ipsi Britones peccatis accusantibus humiliauerant, Dominus omnipotens dupplicem contricionem proposuit et quasi militares insidias adhibuit."

book for his contemporaries had it not seemed credible to them) and was able to find written Welsh and probably Breton sources on the topic, the British past was something he could tackle.[83] The "gap" he observes in his prologue is therefore not just a trope, but a real gap he identified, recognized, and knew he could best occupy among his contemporaries.[84] To Geoffrey, the British past was something that he could use to communicate universal truth, to instruct, and to fill a gap in the historical record. He found history to be a suitable form through which to communicate these truths, the *gesta*, "deeds", of the Britons, which would provide instruction about royal virtue and the dangers of civil war and treachery for the rulers of his own time. This does not necessarily mean he was "pro-Norman" or sought an agenda of Welsh colonization, but that he was using the expertise *he* had to offer to gain patronage and favor and, through the didactic lessons offered in the DGB, to help clean up the mess being wrought by the civil war.

The close attention to written sources and eyewitness testimony is a convention of history writing that Geoffrey deliberately elides throughout the work. Rather than referencing sources throughout his narrative, he references two sources directly, Merlin's prophecies and Walter's ancient book, in what may be a classicizing trope and/or an echo of the Prologue to Dares Phrygius's *The Fall of Troy* (as well as others in the form of allusion and indirect quotation).[85] Without extensive references to his sources, his work has not made sense as serious history to modern historians. Instead, it shows a different kind of learning that is just as perceptive and current. The wide reception of the DGB shows that the conventions of eyewitness testimony, evidence gathering, and discernment, while helpful for establishing a work's authority, were not necessary for the success of a historical work in the medieval period. Geoffrey may have sacrificed authority in the eyes of some critics, but he was rewarded richly for providing a compelling, entertaining narrative that filled a much-lamented gap: a reception history that communicated his ideas to a wider audience than he could have imagined.

---

83   See T.D. Crawford, "On the Linguistic Competence of Geoffrey of Monmouth", *Medium Ævum* 51 (1982), 152–62.

84   This is not to minimize the very real *political* implications of much of the material he offers in the DGB, some of which seems quite pro-Norman, though not uncritical of Stephen and Matilda, while elsewhere particularly pro-Breton. Breton and Norman concerns would not in fact have been incompatible at the time, given that Breton nobles were part of the Anglo-Norman ruling class of the day, their ancestors having helped William the Conqueror gain England.

85   See Paul Russell's chapter and the Introduction to this volume for discussion of these points.

PART 3

Approaches

∴

CHAPTER 11

Colonial Preoccupations in Geoffrey of Monmouth's *De gestis Britonum*

Michael Faletra

Nearly three quarters of the way through the sweep of legendary history that constitutes Geoffrey of Monmouth's *De gestis Britonum*, the narrative grinds almost to a halt. Whereas parts of the history had glossed over dozens of kings and hundreds of years, sometimes in a page or two, the pace of events leading up to the reign of King Arthur had steadily slowed, only to arrive at a near standstill in Geoffrey's description of Arthur's Plenary Court. It is a moment of great political importance, the celebration of the king's victory both over the Saxons who had plagued the realm for a generation and over much of what is now France: like several of his more successful predecessors on the British throne, Arthur returns to Britain a conqueror. The Plenary Court held to stage Arthur's coronation and to celebrate his glorious new order takes place on Pentecost in the Welsh city of Caerleon: "Located in Glamorgan on the River Usk at a lovely site not far from where the Severn empties into the sea, it had an abundance of riches greater than that of any other city and was thus an excellent place to hold a high feast."[1] No expense is spared, Geoffrey reminds his Anglo-Norman readers, and he treats them to lavish descriptions of the coronation processions, the splendid regalia, the celebratory games, and the feasting for many hundreds of guests – all of which seem calculated to drive home the fact that ancient Britain had attained a cultural pinnacle: "Britain had at that point acquired such a state of dignity that it surpassed all other kingdoms in its courtliness, in the extravagance of its fineries, and in the polished manners of its citizens."[2] In their enjoyment of the trappings of a cultural modernity characterized by courtly behavior and fine clothing (and later by Europe's first literary description of a tournament), the ancient Britons under King Arthur revel in a Caerleon that stands as the metropole of expansive

---

1   *DGB*, ix.156.312–14: "In Glamorgantia etenim super Oscam fluuium non longe a Sabrino mari amoeno situ locata, prae ceteris ciuitatibus diuitiarum copiis abundans tantae sollempnitati apta erat." All translations are my own.

2   *DGB*, ix.157.385–87: "Ad tantum etenim statum dignitatis Britannia tunc reducta erat quod copia diuitiarum, luxu ornamentorum, facetia incolarum cetera regna excellebat."

empire. The Arthurian moment is an imperial moment, and it reveals Geoffrey of Monmouth's preoccupation throughout his writings with the dynamics of colonization and conquest.

Among the many guests at this coronation are the subject-kings of Arthur's newly-won and far-flung empire: the kings of Iceland, Denmark, Norway, Gotland, and the Orkneys all pay their obeisance. But the most prominent under-kings are the ones who lead Arthur's coronation procession, namely the kings of Scotland, Moray, Cornwall, North Wales, and South Wales. The presence of these kings passes without comment, and Geoffrey tellingly never mentions Arthur as having subdued any of these areas. This silence, however, paradoxically reveals one of the most important of the ideological underpinnings of the *DGB*, a phenomenon that Simon Meecham-Jones calls the "discourse of Britishness", or what we might more broadly call the "myth" of Insular British unity, an idea that had assumed textual form as early as Gildas's 6th-century *The Ruin of Britain*.[3] As Meecham-Jones sees it, "the discourse of Britishness proclaimed the 'natural' unity of the island(s) of Britain, inferring from physical continuity an inevitable political unity."[4] The ready submission of the kings of Scotland, Wales, and Cornwall to King Arthur ratifies Meecham-Jones's insight, and it allows us to see more clearly that the concept of "Britain" itself is for Geoffrey hardly an apolitical one, suggesting that the island's various ethnic or political entities are rightly or naturally subordinated to a greater whole. The very concept of Britain being named after its single founder – the Trojan exile Brutus – reinforces the concept of a primal British unity, a unity standing in contrast to the more piecemeal ethnic, linguistic, and political subdivisions of the island in Geoffrey of Monmouth's own day.

Geoffrey's account of the initial division of the island into subsidiary realms brings to the fore some of the colonialist and imperialist impulses motivating his work. The second book of the *DGB* opens with what almost amounts to a second origin myth, the partition of the island after the death of its first king, Brutus, among his three sons Locrinus, Albanactus, and Kamber:

> Locrinus, the eldest, possessed that part of the island that was later called
> Loegria after him. Kamber received the area that lies beyond the River
> Severn and which is now called Wales, but which was called for a long
> time Kambria after him, which is why the people of that land who speak

---

3   See Gildas, *The Ruin of Britain*, ed. and trans. M. Winterbottom, *Gildas: The Ruin of Britain and Other Works* (Arthurian Period Sources, 7), Chichester, 1978.

4   S. Meecham-Jones, "Introduction", in R. Kennedy and S. Meecham-Jones (eds.), *Authority and Subjugation in Writing of Medieval Wales*, New York, 2008, pp. 1–11, at p. 2.

the British tongue still call themselves the *Cymry*. And Albanactus, the youngest, ruled over that land which is now called Scotland but which he named *Alban* after himself.[5]

Almost from its inception, then, the island of Britain fosters a plurality of realms, which Geoffrey frequently naturalizes through references to the rivers Humber and Severn as providing intuitive ways of subdividing the island. Yet two observations should be made about this second foundation myth. First, by its very references to dividing what was once whole – and by its showcasing the patrimony of Brutus, the eponymous founder himself – Geoffrey's account of the origins of Scotland, Wales, and Loegria (the area that his readers would easily recognize as "England") paradoxically reaffirms the preexistence and conceptual preeminence of the whole; England, Scotland, and Wales are inescapably, for Geoffrey, parts of a larger, geopolitically organic whole. Secondly, the story of the partition of the island among Brutus's three sons highlights the privilege given to the eldest. Locrinus receives what is geographically (and certainly economically) the lion's share of the island, the fertile lowlands of Loegria, which is also the site of most of the action of Geoffrey's history as a whole. In contrast, Kamber and Albanactus, the younger sons, receive the more peripheral portions of the realm.[6] And while Albanactus, as Geoffrey relates, swiftly falls before incursions of Huns, thus delegitimizing from the outset the parity of Scotland with the other portions of Britain, Kamber assumes a quietly subordinate role to his brother Locrinus. It is, notably, the tale of Locrinus's descendants that Geoffrey follows through the *DGB*; the rulers of Wales – the petty kings of Demetia (Dyfed) and Venedotia (Gwynedd) who serve King Arthur at his Plenary Court – are in contrast a decidedly cadet branch of the royal line of Brutus.

Geoffrey's myth of this primitive (and distinctly hierarchical) partition of the island of Britain is not innocent of many of the power dynamics that animated the Anglo-Norman ruling classes in England during the 12th century. Monika Otter has written of the prevalence of the trope of *gaainable tere* – the idea of (new) territory that can be captured, settled, and cultivated – across a

---

5   *DGB*, ii.23.5–11: "Locrinus, qui primogenitus fuerat, possedit mediam partem insulae, quae postea de nomine suo appellata est Loegria; Kamber autem partem illam quae est ultra Sabrinum flumen, quae nunc Gualia uocatur, quae de nomine ipsius postmodum Kambria multo tempore dicta fuit, unde adhuc gens patriae lingua Britannica sese Kambro appellat; at Albanactus iunior possedit patriam quae lingua nostra his temporibus appellatur Scotia et nomen ei ex nomine suo Albania dedit."

6   For a fuller version of this argument, see M.A. Faletra, *Wales and the Medieval Colonial Imagination: The Matters of Britain in the Twelfth Century*, New York, 2014, pp. 28–36.

variety of Anglo-Latin and Anglo-Norman fictions in the mid-12th century, and she credits the inception of this trope to Geoffrey of Monmouth.[7] In the generations following the Norman Conquest of England in 1066, Anglo-Norman elites engaged in a series of expansionist, essentially colonialist, campaigns that were both discursive and ideological and also sometimes openly employed diplomacy and military force in a bid to dominate the island of Britain beyond England itself. William the Conqueror, for instance, led an armed "pilgrimage" to St Davids in Wales in 1081, a harbinger of the Anglo-Norman Marcher barons who would follow in his wake, and both William Rufus and Henry I meddled seriously in Scottish politics.[8] And all the Norman kings maintained a complicated arrangement of Marcher fiefdoms and colonies in Wales and along the ever-shifting Anglo-Welsh and Anglo-Scottish borders. Welsh poets and chroniclers felt the incipient loss of their lands most acutely. As the poet-priest Rhygyfarch ap Sulien puts it, "Now the labors of earlier days lie despised; the people and the priest are despised by word, heart, and work of the Normans. For they increase our taxes and burn our properties."[9]

With a perhaps very canny understanding of his Anglo-Norman audiences, Geoffrey of Monmouth constructs in his King Arthur not only an embodiment of some amalgam of "courtly" values, and not only a fitting representative of the restored unity of ancient Britain, but also a victorious conqueror. Arthur's coronation at Caerleon follows both his eradication of all the Saxon invaders and especially his conquest of Gaul. But just as the wheels of history might seem to slow to a halt at this moment, the action (and narrative pace) begins again with the arrival of an embassy of Romans to the newly-crowned Arthur's court. The Romans' haughty insistence that Britain pay its long overdue tribute is met with a swift military response from Arthur and his advisors, who mobilize the realm for war with Rome. Geoffrey thus supplies Anglo-Norman audiences with an eye to conquest and territorial expansion the greatest spectacle of all as he stages King Arthur's war upon – and decisive defeat of – the Roman empire. For later readers such as the 16th-century humanist Polydore Vergil,

---

7 M. Otter, *Inventiones: Fiction and Referentiality in Twelfth-Century English Historical Writing*, Chapel Hill, 1996, pp. 69–73, esp. p. 76.

8 For an authoritative examination of the Norman colonization of Wales, see R.R. Davies, *The Age of Conquest: Wales, 1063–1415*, Oxford, 2000; for a full discussion of Anglo-Norman policies concerning Scotland, see R. Bartlett, *England Under the Norman and Angevin Kings, 1075–1225*, Oxford, 2000, pp. 77–85.

9 Rhygyfarch ap Sulien, *Planctus*, ed. M. Lapidge, "The Welsh-Latin Poetry of Sulien's Family", *Studia Celtica* 8/9 (1973–74), 68–106, at pp. 90–91, ll. 15–18: "Nunc dispecta iacent ardua quondam; / dispicitur populus atque sacerdos / uerbo, corde, opere Francigenarum, / namque tributa grauant, propria perurunt."

Arthur's continental conquests were a little difficult to swallow, and Vergil takes advantage of their implausibility (including the absence of Arthur in any reliable corroborating sources) to unravel the entire skein of the Galfridian history of Britain. However, to judge by the enthusiasm with which Geoffrey's account of Arthur's conquests of Rome made it into the Anglo-Norman and Middle English chronicle and romance traditions, Geoffrey's English audiences seemed to have regarded this conquering Arthur with admiring eyes. (Even Malory's cycle of Arthurian romances, *Le Morte D'Arthur*, does not omit the Roman campaign). Despite Arthur's eventual fall at the hands of his nephew Mordred, the king long remained a vital repository of English imperialist ambitions.

Modern scholarship has on the whole remained agnostic about Geoffrey's intentions behind his expansionist, conquering King Arthur, a depiction not appearing in any of the text's known extant sources, although the epithet *amherawdur*, "emperor", appears in some of the early Welsh analogues.[10] Robert Hanning considered Geoffrey's entire narrative, and King Arthur in particular, as a rather abstract meditation on the futility of the writing of history as a secular practice; Valerie Flint took this a step farther, in what remains perhaps one of the best pieces ever written on Geoffrey of Monmouth, arguing for the *DGB* as a historiographic "parody" enabled by the author's status as a secular canon.[11] For such critics, Arthur's continental conquests are not to be taken seriously: they either reveal the aimlessness of history or revel in that very aimlessness. Susan M. Shwartz, in contrast, reads Geoffrey's history of Arthur in a more Augustinian and penitential mode, seeing the king's failure to solidify his continental empire, and especially the poignant fact of his not being able to enter Rome itself, as a check on the very idea of imperial ambition.[12]

Against such claims that Arthur's continental exploits fuel an essentially anti-imperialist, anti-expansionist agenda, we might consider the campaign against Rome in tandem with some of the larger narrative patterns of the *DGB*. While Siân Echard has noted the tension between Arthur's apparent "superexcellence" and the fact that he is just one among a long, long series of Insular

10 P. Sims-Williams, "The Early Welsh Arthurian Poems", in R. Bromwich, A.O.H. Jarman, and B.F. Roberts (eds.), *The Arthur of the Welsh: The Arthurian Legend in Medieval Welsh Literature* (Arthurian Literature in the Middle Ages, 1), Cardiff, 1991, p. 48.

11 R.W. Hanning, *The Vision of History in Early Britain: From Gildas to Geoffrey of Monmouth*, New York, 1966, pp. 121–72; V.I.J. Flint, "The *Historia Regum Britanniae* of Geoffrey of Monmouth: Parody and Its Purpose. A Suggestion", *Speculum* 54:3 (1979), 447–68.

12 S. Shwartz, "The Founding and Self-Betrayal of Britain: An Augustinian Approach to Geoffrey of Monmouth's *Historia Regum Britanniae*", *Medievalia et Humanistica* 10 (1981), 33–58.

monarchs, consideration of Arthur's conquests as themselves part of a long tradition – almost a royal prerogative of strong British kings – helps to resolve such ambiguities.[13] As Arthur himself puts it:

> For if [Rome] declares that tribute now be rendered merely because Julius Caesar and the other Roman rulers once subjugated Britain, then I believe that the Romans should now pay tribute to me, since my ancestors captured Rome in ancient times. The most noble Beli, with the aid of his brother Brennius, duke of the Allobroges, captured Rome and hanged twenty noble Romans in the middle of the Forum. He held the city for many years. And let us not forget Constantine, the son of Helen, or Maximianus, both my near kinsmen: they were both kings of Britain who also ascended to the throne of the Roman Empire.[14]

Arthur's references to the earlier kings here are far from coincidental. These kings were not only conquerors of Rome but also unifiers of the island of Britain, men who renewed the peace of the kingdom. Constantinus, for instance, "diminished the rapacity of thieves, trampled down the savagery of tyrants, and strove to restore peace everywhere".[15] The reference to the story of Beli and Brennius is even more powerful. These two brothers had co-inherited the throne of Britain, which led to a bloody civil war. However, once they had made peace and united, they were able to conquer Rome itself. The historical episode thus serves as an object lesson: maintaining the integrity of the kingdom – that is, of the island of Britain as a cohesive geopolitical whole – leads almost inexorably to the desire to expand its frontiers.

King Arthur as both a unifying force and as an index of expansionist power may have been a particularly poignant figure for Geoffrey's initial audiences. The England in which Geoffrey composed the *DGB* in the years between 1136 and 1138 was a country riven by civil dissension. The death of Henry I and the

---

13   S. Echard, *Arthurian Narrative in the Latin Tradition* (Cambridge Studies in Medieval Literature, 36), Cambridge, 1998, p. 55.

14   *DGB*, ix.159.466–74: "Nam si quia Iulius Caesar ceterique Romani reges Britanniam olim subiugauerunt uectigal nunc debere sibi ex illa reddi decernit, similiter ego censeo quod Roma michi tributum dare debet, quia antecessores mei eam antiquitus optinuerunt. Beli etenim, serenissimus ille rex Britonum, auxilio fratris sui usus, Brennii uidelicet ducis Allobrogum, suspensis in medio foro uiginti nobilioribus Romanis urbem ceperunt captamque multis temporibus possederunt. Constantinus etiam Helenae filius nec non Maximianus, uterque michi cognatione propinquus, alter post alterum diademate Britanniae insignitus, thronum Romani imperii adeptus est."

15   *DGB*, v.79.147–48: "Latronum rapacitatem hebetabat, tyrannorum saeuitiam conculcabat, pacem ubique renouare studebat."

naming of his daughter Matilda as his heir, and the subsequent contestation
of the throne by Henry's nephew Stephen, split the Anglo-Norman aristocracy
and weakened the realm. At the same time, it also undercut efforts at expanding the territorial base of the Anglo-Norman barons beyond England proper. In
particular, Anglo-Norman power in Wales was significantly checked. The years
1136–37 saw the commencement of what can only be called a native Welsh resurgence as Welsh chieftains captured or destroyed numerous English strong-
holds throughout their country.[16] Indeed, the English would not regain control
of many of these lost territories until the Edwardian conquest of Wales in the
1280s. Certainly the events of 1136–37 more or less set the political map of Wales
for the rest of the 12th century, and Geoffrey of Monmouth cannily recognized
the ways in which the history he was in the process of composing might resonate with the new colonial situation. The figure of a triumphalist King Arthur
who could unify the country, exert suzerainty over Wales and Scotland, and
even extend British influence beyond its merely Insular sphere proved an in-
valuable imaginative touchstone for writers and readers throughout the 12th
century and well beyond it. Certainly, as Amaury Chauou has argued, and as
the manuscript tradition suggests, Geoffrey's model of an expansive Britain
remained popular during the heyday of Henry II's "Angevin Empire".[17]

Nevertheless, many of the finer-grain political concerns of the *DGB* have
proven difficult for readers to detect, and Rees Davies has accused Geoffrey
of being "a deliberate trader in multiple ambiguities".[18] In terms of Geoffrey's
interest in the intersection between the writing of history and the vexed issues
of territorial acquisition both within and without Britain, Francis Ingledew
probably best captures the critical ambivalence about the larger political and
philosophical meanings of Geoffrey's project, writing that it is "especially as-
tonishing" that Geoffrey should devise such an imperialist history for the ancient Britons.[19] Ingledew here identifies a critical, and probably deliberate,
confusion that Geoffrey perpetrates: the ancient Britons whose long history
he narrates, whose kings he (more often than not) extols, and whose troubles
he sometimes bewails – in short, the very Britons whose name is showcased
in what Michael Reeve has now surmised was Geoffrey's original title for his

16   R.R. Davies, *Age of Conquest*, pp. 45–49.
17   A. Chauou, *L'Idéologie Plantagenêt: Royauté arthurienne et monarchie politique dans l'espace Plantagenêt (XIIe–XIIIe siècles)*, Rennes, 2001, pp. 37–39.
18   R.R. Davies, *The Matter of Britain and the Matter of England: An Inaugural Lecture Delivered Before the University of Oxford on 29 February 1996*, Oxford, 1996, p. 6.
19   F. Ingledew, "The Book of Troy and the Genealogical Construction of History: The Case of Geoffrey of Monmouth's *Historia regum Britanniae*", *Speculum* 69:3 (1994), 665–704, at p. 677.

work, the *DGB* – are in many real ways continuous with, and identifiable with, the contemporary 12th-century Welsh. Geoffrey's book attempts to have it both ways: it offers praise for the glories of the ancient Britons while also emphasizing the degeneracy of their Welsh descendants from precisely that former glory.

Some earlier scholars, especially those whose focus was more on historiography than politics, saw little contradiction here. For Robert Hanning, "the 'meaning' of British history for Geoffrey … is simply that Britain, like other nations, rises, flourishes, and falls."[20] And "the *Historia regum Britanniae*", William Leckie writes, simply "chronicles the deeds of a flawed people, in whom the potential for greatness was matched and often surpassed by the capacity for folly".[21] Still, there is little denying that the narrative arc of the *DGB* concludes with a fairly unequivocal account of a *translatio imperii*, as the Saxons wrest control of the island from the native Britons, who subsequently are transformed into the first modern Welshmen:

> Britain, having lost its entire population, except a few whom death had spared in the region of Wales, was hateful to the Britons for eleven years … On receiving the news, that wicked people [the Saxons] assembled a vast crowd of men and women, landed in the region of Northumbria and filled the empty tracts of land from Scotland to Cornwall. There were no natives to stop them, save a few remaining Britons in the remote forests of Wales. This marked the end of British power in the island and the beginning of English rule.[22]

The English occupation of Britain is thus less a conquest than the resettlement of an uninhabited territory (itself a sort of fantasy of colonial acquisition that would survive well into the early modern colonization of the New World). The Britons, weakened at this stage by wars, plagues, famines, and internal dissension, do nothing to contest the claims of the new settlers. Geoffrey

---

20   Hanning, *Vision*, p. 171.

21   R.W. Leckie, Jr., *The Passage of Dominion: Geoffrey of Monmouth and the Periodization of Insular History in the Twelfth Century*, Toronto, 1981, p. 3.

22   *DGB*, xi.204.547–48, 53–58: "Britannia ergo, cunctis ciuibus, exceptis paucis quibus in Gualiarum partibus mors pepercerat, desolata, per .xi. annos Britonibus horrenda fuit…. Quod cum ipsis indicatum fuisset, nefandus populus ille, collecta innumerabili multitudine uirorum et mulierum, applicuit in partibus Northamhimbriae et desolatas prouincias ab Albania usque ad Cornubiam inhabitauit. Non enim habitator qui prohiberet praeter pauperculas Britonum reliquias quae superfuerant, quae infra abdita nemorum in Gualiis commanebant. Ab illo tempore potestas Britonum in insula cessauit et Angli regnare coeperunt."

reinforces the justness of the advent of the Saxons – an act that amounts, essentially, to the legitimation of the transformation of British "Loegria" into Saxon "England" – by also suggesting that the concurrent transformation of the remaining Britons into the Welsh marks a descent into barbarity: "Resolute in their barbarous ways, they were no longer called Britons, but Welsh, a term derived either from their leader Gualo, or from queen Galaes or else from their very barbarity."[23] Geoffrey adds that these barbarous Welsh-Britons foolishly engaged in foreign wars and civil strife, further hamstringing any attempts at future resurgence.

Geoffrey's fairly undiluted emphasis on Welsh barbarity on the closing page of the *DGB* might imply, as a point of contrast, a strong sense of English/Anglo-Norman cultural superiority, thus suggesting possible cultural justifications for the annexation of Welsh territories. Nonetheless, critical understandings of Geoffrey's precise political message have been quite diverse, with views ranging from seeing Geoffrey as a ruthless apologist for Anglo-Norman hegemony in Wales to Geoffrey as a proponent of Welsh proto-nationalism or as a postcolonial subaltern speaking back to empire. Many scholars in the earlier part of the 20th century, in fact, tended to view Geoffrey fairly unproblematically as a Welshman, taking his toponymic "of Monmouth" as an index of ethnic origin and thus ethnic loyalty; this opinion still occasionally garners modern proponents.[24] Under such an understanding, Geoffrey's narration of the (mostly glorious) deeds of the ancient Britons was seen as a way in which the historian celebrated his own ancestry, for the benefit of Latin-speaking audiences in his homeland and beyond. J.S.P. Tatlock's landmark 1950 volume *The Legendary History of Britain* endorsed a rather different paradigm, one first proposed by J.E. Lloyd in 1911 and one that opened up ways of making sense of Geoffrey's well-documented sense of ambiguity.[25] Tatlock, following Lloyd, conjectured that either Geoffrey or one of his immediate ancestors was among the contingent of continental Bretons who had occupied Monmouth in the wake of the Norman Conquest, quite possibly a relative of the Breton baron Wihenoc, an early Norman lord of Monmouth.[26] The Breton solution – which

---

23   *DGB*, xi.207.592–94: "Barbarie etiam irrepente, iam non uocabantur Britones sed Gualenses, uocabulum siue a Gualone duce eorum siue a Galaes regina siue a barbarie trahentes."

24   See, for instance, B.F. Roberts, "Geoffrey of Monmouth and Welsh Historical Tradition", *Nottingham Mediaeval Studies* 20 (1976), 29–40; and, most recently, K. Jankulak, *Geoffrey of Monmouth*, Cardiff, 2010, pp. 3–4.

25   J.E. Lloyd, *A History of Wales from the Earliest Times to the Edwardian Conquest*, 2nd ed., London, 1912, pp. 523–24; id. "Geoffrey of Monmouth", *EHR* 57 (1942), 460–68, at pp. 467–68.

26   Tatlock, *LHB*, pp. 440–43.

is, incidentally, still a tenable position – has the advantage of making sense out of what is, for some, Geoffrey's otherwise rather inexplicable denigration of the Welsh Britons. For Geoffrey, Tatlock suggests, the Bretons of northwestern Gaul were the only legitimate descendants of the ancient Britons, and so the account of the degeneration of the Welsh at the end of the history is concomitantly an affirmation of Breton legitimacy.[27] The supposition that Geoffrey was of Breton extraction also allows one to make sense of the curiously positive role played by Brittany throughout the *DGB*, and, in a broader way, it enables readers to come to terms with some of Geoffrey's more ambivalent attitudes toward the Britons in general. It was on this basis that John Gillingham argued for a Geoffrey of Monmouth who, as a fellow Cambro-Norman, appreciated the noble ancestry of the Welsh and could thus compose the *DGB* as a piece of propaganda to encourage his Anglo-Norman patrons to enlist Welsh aid during the English civil wars of the 1130s and 1140s.[28]

In the wake of the fuller understanding of the manuscript and textual traditions behind the *DGB* provided by the prodigious work of Neil Wright and Julia Crick in the 1980s and 1990s and culminating in the Michael Reeve and Neil Wright edition of 2007, more recent scholars have been inclined to emphasize the importance of Geoffrey of Monmouth's ties to his English patrons, regardless of his ethnic origins.[29] Geoffrey was, to be sure, a protégé of Bishop Alexander of Lincoln; he was a secular canon at St George's collegiate church in Oxford (which received royal patronage), and seems to have been closely associated with several of the major players in the civil wars, even standing as a witness to the historic Treaty of Westminster in 1153. His appointment to the vacant bishopric of St Asaph in North Wales in 1152, a post he never occupied

---

27   Tatlock, *LHB*, pp. 396–402.

28   J. Gillingham, "The Context and Purposes of Geoffrey of Monmouth's *History of the Kings of Britain*", *Anglo-Norman Studies* 13 (1990), 99–118 (repr. in id. (ed.), *The English in the Twelfth Century: Imperialism, National Identity and Political Values*, Woodbridge, 2000, 19–39).

29   See, for example, K. Robertson, "Geoffrey of Monmouth and the Translation of Insular Historiography", *Arthuriana* 8:4 (1998), 42–57; Otter, *Inventiones*; Echard, *Arthurian Narrative*; J. Blacker, *The Faces of Time: Portrayal of the Past in Old French and Latin Historical Narrative of the Anglo-Norman Regnum*, Austin, 1994; M.A. Faletra, "Narrating the Matter of Britain: Geoffrey of Monmouth and the Norman Colonization of Wales", *The Chaucer Review* 35:1 (2000), 60–85; P.C. Ingham, *Sovereign Fantasies: Arthurian Romance and the Making of Britain*, Philadelphia, 2001, pp. 21–50; P. Dalton, "The Topical Concerns of Geoffrey of Monmouth's *Historia Regum Britannie*: History, Prophecy, Peacemaking, and English Identity in the Twelfth Century", *Journal of British Studies* 44:4 (2005), 688–712; and F. Tolhurst, *Geoffrey of Monmouth and the Feminist Origins of the Arthurian Legend*, New York, 2012.

due to Welsh unrest in the region, is a further sign of his implication within Anglo-Norman elite power structures. Should he have taken up his seat at St Asaph, Geoffrey – whatever his ultimate political loyalties – would have had to acknowledge both the king of England and the archbishop of Canterbury as his functional overlords and would have surely been in the position of having to facilitate, or at least not actively resist, English colonial expansion into northern Wales.

Michelle Warren, perhaps seeing speculation about Geoffrey's political and/ or ethnic loyalties as fruitless, applies the lens of postcolonial literary theory to bear on the historian, painting a convincing picture of Geoffrey as a "border writer" whose upbringing in Monmouth and whose learned perspectives would have encompassed both Welsh and English modes of perceiving and inflecting power.[30] What earlier scholars such as Valerie Flint or John Gillingham might view as Geoffrey's wry ambiguity or studied ambivalence Warren views as a series of "subtle negotiations" of power: "By alternately claiming and disavowing his textual authority Geoffrey unsettles paradigms of domination."[31] As a result, Warren writes, the *DGB* "thus equivocates between admiration and condemnation of conquering history; it mediates between colonial and postcolonial imaginations".[32] In a similar vein, and through a similar application of postcolonial theory, Jeffrey Jerome Cohen sees Geoffrey as offering "an alternative account of Britain that could challenge the Anglo-centric version originated by Bede and reinvigorated by William [of Malmesbury]".[33] While such perspectives built upon postcolonial cultural theory certainly help to make sense of the many contradictions and often frustrating ambiguities of Geoffrey's work, and while they also draw many fruitful parallels with many more recent contestations of colonial power in the 19th and 20th centuries, the reader must tread carefully in applying postcolonial critiques unreflectively or ahistorically. As any student of literature understands, the assignment of intention to an author (or "meaning" to a text) is no easy matter and necessarily rests upon detailed and historicized understanding of the background, narrative structures, and systems of imagery of a given text.

Geoffrey, for his part, was happy to defer questions about the ultimate meaning of his text to his putative source, "a certain very ancient book in the

---

30   M.R. Warren, *History on the Edge: Excalibur and the Borders of Britain, 1100–1300* (Medieval Cultures, 22), Minneapolis, 2000, pp. 25–59.

31   Warren, *History on the Edge*, p. 27.

32   Warren, *History on the Edge*, p. 25.

33   J.J. Cohen, *Hybridity, Identity, and Monstrosity in Medieval Britain: On Difficult Middles*, New York, 2006, p. 7.

British tongue".[34] Naturally, the precise identity, qualities, and content of this ancient book – if it even ever existed, which it likely never did – have been the subject of considerable critical scrutiny and have had an important bearing on questions about Geoffrey's political alignment and especially his attitudes regarding English colonialism in Wales. In general, the assumption that Geoffrey was indeed working with a legitimate source *in the British language* correlates with the notion that his attitudes toward Wales and the Welsh were largely sympathetic: he can thus be taken at face value as wishing to resuscitate for modern audiences the (mostly) glorious deeds of the ancient British kings, and perhaps especially of King Arthur.[35] And certainly some earlier scholarship viewed Geoffrey and his source in this light. Acton Griscom's magisterial 1929 edition of the *DGB* was so confident of Geoffrey's reliance on a genuine Welsh source (or perhaps an amalgam of various "British" sources) that he printed a later Welsh translation of the text beneath his edited Latin version.[36] Griscom's underlying assumption is that Geoffrey's text, being the real translation of an actual British or Welsh history, represents a legitimate and broadly accurate account of the pre-Saxon Insular past.

Conversely, skepticism about Geoffrey's claims to be translating an actual British book given to him by Walter, the archdeacon of Oxford, often correlates with a skepticism about the historian's Welsh sympathies and with an understanding of him as a sophisticated, canny, and maybe even playful ally of the English intelligentsia. Certainly whatever patchwork of sources that Geoffrey cobbled together included Welsh materials, as Ben Guy argues in this volume, and probably also sources in Cornish and even Breton, but the idea that the "very ancient book in the British tongue" ever existed as an integral whole seems difficult to maintain, thus weakening the claims that Geoffrey, in transmitting the deeds of the British kings to future generations, was thereby necessarily advancing the cause of Welsh proto-national sovereignty.

Viewing Geoffrey of Monmouth as a fabricator rather than a faithful copyist of the history he narrates allows one to perceive more clearly some of the power dynamics underlying the work as a whole. Monika Otter perhaps puts

---

34   *DGB*, Prologus 2.10: "quendam ... Britannici sermonis librum uetustissimum".
35   This is how one might regard Geoffrey's desire to "set out in excellent style a continuous narrative of all their [the kings'] deeds", "actus omnium [regum] continue et ex ordine perpulcris orationibus proponebat", *DGB*, Prologus 2.11–12 (trans. Wright). And see Gillingham, "Context and Purposes", p. 100.
36   See Geoffrey of Monmouth, *De gestis Britonum*, ed. A. Griscom, *The Historia Regum Britanniae of Geoffrey of Monmouth with Contributions to the Study of its Place in early British History with a Literal Translation of the Welsh Manuscript No. LXI of Jesus College Oxford*, London, 1929.

it best when she claims that "[t]he historian is a pioneer, but the land is not entirely pristine; appropriating a space of one's own involves both exploitation and denial of what came before."[37] Otter shrewdly observes that every act of writing history is necessarily a sort of colonization, an imposition of ideas of causation, of points of thematic emphasis, and of narrative structures upon the past. And certainly, one of Geoffrey's most evident and consistent narrative interests lies in the theme of *translatio imperii* or what Leckie has called "the passage of dominion".[38] An examination of the ways in which sovereignty over the island of Britain changes hands throughout the *DGB* allows one to better gauge the vexed assessment of the history as a colonial or even a postcolonial text. Through his creation of a new myth of British origins, through his strategic use of prophecies – especially the prophecies of Merlin – and through his narration of the "end" of Insular British history, Geoffrey reveals the contours of his thought about the status of Wales and the Welsh and about the persistent Anglo-Norman colonial interest in Wales in particular and throughout Britain as a whole.

Geoffrey in fact seems preoccupied with the interrelated ideas of conquest, colonization, and settlement. Indeed, "pre-occupation" may be the operative term here, as his foundation myth for the island of Britain demonstrates. On the face of it, Geoffrey's account of the foundation of Britain is hardly surprising. Like many historians throughout the Middle Ages, Geoffrey traces the origins of the ancient Britons to Troy, the great city of Homeric and Virgilian epic whose "fortunate fall" spawned foundation legends for many a medieval polity. As Ingledew points out, the myth of Trojan origin provided nascent medieval states with a secular origin story that could stand in contrast to the more Augustinian historiographies of the earlier Middle Ages.[39] In the case of the *DGB*, Geoffrey found a ready-made tale in (pseudo-)Nennius's 9th-century *Historia Brittonum*. For Nennius and Geoffrey both, Britain was founded by Brutus (the name is Britto in the earlier text), a descendant of Aeneas and thus a member of the same Trojan family that had founded Rome. Exiled from Italy because of accidental parricide, Brutus eventually makes his way to the isle of Albion, which he renames Britain after himself. The Nennian account rounds the story off neatly, stating merely that "[Britto] came afterward to this island, which is named after him – that is, Britain – and he populated it with his kindred and dwelt there. Thus Britain has been inhabited from that very

---

37   Otter, *Inventiones*, p. 83.
38   Leckie, *Passage of Dominion*.
39   Ingledew, "Book of Troy", p. 671.

day until this very day."[40] Geoffrey later reinforces this myth of Trojan origins by noting that the ancient, original name of London was *Trinovantum* (derived from *Troia Nova*: "New Troy") and that, many centuries later, in the days of King Arthur, certain Trojan courtly customs were still maintained.[41] The link to Troy remained for Geoffrey a vibrant thematic thread throughout his history.[42]

Although his Nennian source thus provides a simple and solid outline of the foundation, naming, and initial populating of Britain, Geoffrey adds considerable complications to the story as he adapts it in the *DGB*. In Geoffrey's version, the land in which Brutus and his band of Trojan exiles arrive is, unexpectedly and unmistakably, already inhabited:

> In those days, the island was called Albion, and was uninhabited except for a few giants. It was a beautiful place, filled with forests and with rivers that teemed with fish. It inspired Brutus and his companions with a great desire to settle there. As they explored the various regions of the island, the Trojans discovered giants who had fled to caves in the mountains. With the approval of their leader, the Trojans then partitioned the land among themselves and began to cultivate the fields and construct buildings so that, after a short space of time, you would think that they had lived there forever.[43]

On the one hand, Geoffrey deftly relegates his mention of the giants here almost to an aside in the narrative, a historical footnote. But in a larger sense, the vestigial presence of even "a few giants" seriously undermines the idea of a pristine Britain, ripe for colonization, calling into question the very force of the idea of foundation. The text's juxtaposing of the presence of these few giants with the mention of the island's original name of Albion (a name absent in the Nennian account) suggests a longer, earlier, and unexplored past looming – if

---

40   *Historia Brittonum*, ed. and trans. J. Morris, *Nennius: British History and the Welsh Annals* (Arthurian Period Sources, 8), London, 1980, p. 60: "postea ad istam pervenit insulam, quae a nomine suo accepit nomen, id est Brittanniam, et inplevit eam cum suo genere, et habitavit ibi. Ab illo autem die habitat est Brittannia usque in hodiernum diem."

41   *DGB*, ix.157.375–77.

42   On this topic, see esp. Ingledew, "Book of Troy"; and S. Federico, *New Troy: Fantasies of Empire in the Late Middle Ages*, Minneapolis, 2003, pp. ix–xxiv.

43   *DGB*, i.21.453–59: "Erat tunc nomen insulae Albion; quae a nemine, exceptis paucis gigantibus, inhabitabatur. Amoeno tamen situ locorum et copia piscosorum fluminum nemoribusque praeelecta, affectum habitandi Bruto sociisque inferebat. Peragratis ergo quibusque prouinciis, repertos gigantes ad cauernas montium fugant, patriam donante duce sorciuntur, agros incipiunt colere, domos aedificare, ita ut in breui tempore terram ab aeuo inhabitatam censeres."

only fleetingly – before the reader: Was Albion the giants' name for their own land? Were they autochthonous? How long had they lived there, and in what numbers? How did it come about that their numbers had now so drastically dwindled? One might say that the presence of the giants in fact haunts the entire subsequent description of the Trojan's initial exploration and cultivation of Britain.

Geoffrey's Britain is thus always already inhabited. For Jeffrey Jerome Cohen, the presence of the giants is an example of what he calls *extimité*, a figure for the excess of the Lacanian Real that surpasses any narrative, logical, or ideological attempts to impose authoritative orders on the world.[44] While Cohen admits that "Geoffrey of Monmouth is the true father of 'Britain' as an imagined community", he also emphasizes that the presence of the aboriginal giants is a function of the violence of foundation (and, implicitly, colonization), a reminder that the repressed will return.[45] And return they do. Not long after the Trojans solidify their initial settlements, they are faced with an uprising of Albion's gigantic aboriginals:

> There was among them a certain loathsome one named Goemagog who stood some twelve cubits tall. This Goemagog was so strong that he once uprooted an oak tree as if it were a hazel-shoot. One day, when Brutus was celebrating a feast to the gods at the place where the Trojans had first landed, Goemagog came with twenty other giants and caused great slaughter among the Britons.[46]

Although the band of giants is summarily dispatched, they nonetheless leave an indelible trace on the otherwise pristine British topography. Goemagog himself meets his death by being wrestled to the death by Brutus's Herculean wingman, Corineus, and is cast off a precipice which, Geoffrey notes, bears his name "up to the present day".[47] The giant himself is literally expelled from the landmass of Britain, but his name remains. And lurking behind his name lie the enigmatic, biblical Gog and Magog, a confederacy of Japethic tribes

---

44   J.J. Cohen, *Of Giants: Sex, Monsters, and the Middle Ages* (Medieval Cultures, 17), Minneapolis, 1999, pp. xii–xiii.

45   Cohen, *Of Giants*, p. 40; see also Cohen's seminal essay "Monster Culture: Seven Theses", in id. (ed.), *Monster Theory: Reading Culture*, Minneapolis, 1996, pp. 3–25, esp. pp. 4–7.

46   *DGB*, i.21.469–74: "Erat ibi inter ceteros detestabilis quidam nomine Goemagog, staturae duodecim cubitorum, qui tantae uirtutis existens quercum semel excussam uelut uirgulam corili euellebat. Hic quadam die, dum Brutus in portu quo applicuerat festiuum diem deis celebraret, superuenit cum uiginti gigantibus atque dirissima caede Britones affecit."

47   *DGB*, i.21.487–89: "usque in praesentem diem".

inimical to God's Chosen People whose return, as Geoffrey knew well from the biblical books of Ezekiel and Revelation, was an omen of the end of the world.[48]

Geoffrey's devising of Goemagog's name, then, was hardly accidental: he well understood the power of apocalyptic imagery to unsettle the reader and to lend an episode a sense of historic import. Nowhere is this so evident than in his presentation of the prophecies of Merlin, which, because they stand almost as a metatext that comments on the unfolding of British history as a whole, have a significant bearing on our understanding of Geoffrey's colonial preoccupations.[49] The *PM* originally circulated independently, and Geoffrey's composition of it around the year 1135 earned him some small literary fame even before the completion of the *DGB* a few years later; around 1150 he revisited the genre of Merlinic prophecy with a new book, the *VM*, which would feature an extended dialogue between Merlin and the legendary Welsh figure of Taliesin.[50] As it stands integrated into the larger history, Geoffrey's rendition of the prophetic utterances of the boy-prophet Merlin to King Vortigern function, as Michael Curley has argued, as a sort of pivot point in the text: located at almost the center of the narrative of the *DGB*, the prophecies provide a symbolic counterpoint to the text's introduction of the Saxons, who figure both as the villainous allies of the nefarious Vortigern and as a foreign people who threaten to precipitate a new passage of dominion (*translatio imperii*) upon the island of Britain.[51] The prophecies are thus hardly innocent of the dynamics of power and a concern with the relationships between the ancient Britons and later colonists of the island.

The core of Geoffrey's *PM* derives from an episode in the *Historia Brittonum*, where the boy-prophet Ambrosius, gifted with uncanny powers, explains to Vortigern why the tower he had been attempting to build keeps collapsing. The *Historia Brittonum*'s Ambrosius (and later the *DGB*'s Merlin) instructs the king to excavate beneath the foundations of the tower, an action that reveals and releases two "dragons" (*vermes* in the *Historia Brittonum*, *dracones* in the *DGB*), one red and one white. The initial interpretation that Geoffrey's Merlin offers of this strange omen is fairly straightforward:

---

48   See Ezekiel 38–39 and Revelation 20:7–10.

49   For a full discussion of the *PM*, see especially Maud Burnett McInerney's contribution to the present volume.

50   M.J. Curley, *Geoffrey of Monmouth* (Twayne's English Authors Series, 509), New York, 1994, pp. 48–49. For a more general overview of the dynamics of the Merlinic prophecies in Geoffrey's work, see J. Crick, "Geoffrey of Monmouth, Prophecy and History", *Journal of Medieval History* 18:4 (1992), 357–71. And see *VM*.

51   Curley, *Geoffrey of Monmouth*, p. 48.

Woe to the Red Dragon, for its end hastens! The White Dragon, which refers to the Saxons whom you have invited here, will occupy its caves. The Red Dragon stands for the people of Britain who shall be oppressed by the White Dragon.[52]

The fact that Merlin so explicitly interprets this first prophecy is significant: it establishes as clearly as one can in the genre of prophetic interpretation that the ancient Britons will suffer defeat, displacement ("the white dragon will occupy its caves"), and extermination by foreign invaders of the island of Britain.[53] If the *PM* thus begins with the idea of British defeat (and the subsequent colonization of Britain by other peoples), it does little to reverse or even to mitigate the idea. Many, many prophecies follow – 15 pages of prose in the most recent edition of the Latin[54] – but they provide few rallying cries for the Britons. At one point not far from the beginning of the *PM*, Geoffrey might seem to offer, however cryptically, a gleam of hope:

At that time there will be slaughter of the foreigners, and the rivers shall run with blood, and the mountains of Armorica will crumble, and they will don the crown of Brutus. Wales shall be filled with gladness, and the oaks of Cornwall will flourish. The island will be called by the name of Brutus and its foreign name will perish.[55]

This prophecy would promise a sort of "Celtic revival" involving Brittany, Cornwall, and Wales – all Brittonic nations – in the general resurgence, but, once one attempts to coordinate Merlin's prophecies with historical events, the difficulty in pinpointing exactly what series of events are being referenced here proves insurmountable. If one looks within the pages of Geoffrey's own history (and thus to the character Merlin's own future), the only possible moment of such native resurgence would be the reign of King Arthur, who did indeed extirpate the Saxons and restore legitimate British rule. Looking beyond the pages of the *DGB* itself and up to the time of Geoffrey's writing, one again

---

52 *DGB*, Prophetiae 112.34–36: "Vae rubeo draconi; nam exterminatio eius festinat. Cauernas ipsius occupabit albus draco, qui Saxones quos inuitasti significant. Rubeus uero gentem designat Britanniae, quae ab albo opprimetur."
53 *DGB*, Prophetiae 112.34–35: "cauernas ipsius occupabit albus draco."
54 *DGB*, Prophetiae 112–17.
55 *DGB*, Prophetiae 115.111–14: "Tunc erit strages alienigenarum, tunc flumina sanguine manabunt, tunc erumpent Armorici montes et diademate Bruti coronabuntur. Replebitur Kambria laeticia, et robora Cornubiae uirescent. Nomine Bruti uocabitur insula, et nuncupatio extraneorum peribit."

searches in vain for such a moment; even if Geoffrey is obliquely referencing here the Welsh rebellion of the 1130s, the *PM* disallows anything like an authoritative interpretation. Significantly, this brief prophecy of British resurgence is swiftly followed by many more vertiginous pages of even more covertly symbolic prophecies, culminating in the end not in the promise of a renewal of British fortunes but in a maelstrom of apocalyptic imagery drawn largely from the biblical books of Ezekiel, Isaiah, and Revelation.

Geoffrey of Monmouth acknowledged the popularity of his Merlinic prophecies, and he readily capitalized on this fame (or notoriety) in his composition in Latin hexameter verse of the *VM* later in his career. Whereas the *DGB* had featured Merlin as a boy speaking truth to power, a sort of Samuel to Vortigern's Saul, the *VM* depicts him as an older, sadder, and perhaps wiser man. Driven temporarily insane by the outcome of a disastrous battle and estranged from his wife Guendolena, Merlin retreats to the depths of the forest of Calidon, seeking there a life of pastoral simplicity and astronomical study and all the while continuing to prophesy. He is eventually joined there by Taliesin, a figure (originally a historic 6th-century Welsh bard) about whom much disparate Welsh lore had aggregated and through whom Geoffrey stages a lengthy exposition of natural philosophy; by the madman Maeldinus, whom Merlin is able to restore to his right mind; and by Merlin's own sister Ganieda, to whom he passes his prophetic gift at the end of the poem. In the course of the poem, Merlin rehearses much of the narrative historical material found in books eight through ten of the *DGB*. In particular, Merlin provides further details of King Arthur's enigmatic death. Cognizant of the potential of Arthur both as a rallying-point for Welsh resistance to foreign rule and also as a paradigm of an expansionist Britain centered around Loegria (England), the *VM* keeps Arthur handily alive: the wounded king was rescued from the fateful Battle of Camlan and taken to the *Insula Pomorum* ("the Island of Apples" – certainly a gloss on the *DGB*'s Avalon) to be healed of his wounds by the mysterious Morgen, the forerunner of the Morgan le Fay of the later Arthurian romances. Geoffrey has Merlin carefully emphasize that Arthur will have to remain with Morgen for a long but unspecified duration of time.[56]

The king's uncertain future mirrors in a way the uncertainty of the prophecies as a whole. By and large, the prophecies uttered by Merlin and Taliesin in the *VM* do little to elucidate any of the specific predictions in the *PM*, and Geoffrey in fact employs many of the same rhetorical tricks: animal symbolism, astrological omens, and an often pointedly biblical diction. The Boar of Cornwall, the Sea Wolf, the Lion of Justice – all figures familiar from the *DGB*'s

56   *VM*, ll. 929–38.

version of the prophecies – return in the *VM*, and yet their referents are hardly made clearer, even if the *VM* is somewhat more explicit about mentioning specific groups of peoples, such as the Gewissei, the Armoricans, and the Danes. However, if Galfridian prophecy in general aims at a studied ambiguity, the one moment where it departs from this mode is Ganieda's prophecy at the end of the *VM*. Her words are clear and difficult to misinterpret:

> Leave, Normans, and stop your wanton armies from bearing their weapons through our homeland. There is nothing left now worth feeding your greed, for you have gobbled up everything that Mother Nature has long produced here in her marvelous fertility. Christ, aid Your people! Hold the Lions back! Restore the realm's tranquility and freedom from wars.[57]

On the one hand, such a passage, narrated as it is at the dramatic moment of Ganieda's assumption of the prophetic gift from her brother, articulates a clearly anti-Norman political message. And yet, couched as it is at the end of a series of dark and difficult prophetic utterances, and addressed as the *VM* is to a patron (the bishop of Lincoln) thoroughly implicated in Norman power structures, one wonders whether Ganieda's, or Geoffrey's, speech-act can be held to be efficacious. The question – as Geoffrey no doubt intended – remains an open one.

It has thus become a critical commonplace to emphasize that the specific predictions in both the *PM* and the *VM* are obscure, probably deliberately so.[58] While Merlin does interpret the omen of the two dragons for Vortigern (and for Geoffrey's readers) in the *DGB*, no key is given for any of the other prophecies; indeed, their sheer length alone would confound most attempts at systematic interpretation. For Echard, the increasing hermeneutic difficulty of the *PM*, taken in conjunction with its centrality to the narrative of the *DGB* as a whole, reflects Geoffrey's sense of the fundamental directionlessness and unpredictability of history.[59] Perhaps. But comparison with the analogues and potential sources of the *PM* also reveals Geoffrey's preoccupation with the ways in which prophecy can make meaning of history and even make contemporary actions in the present meaningful.

---

57 *VM*, ll. 1511–17: "Iteque Neustrenses, cessate diutius arma / ferre per ingenuum violente milite regnum! / Non est unde gulam valeatis pascere vestram. / Consumpsistis enim quicquid natura creatrix / fertilitate bona dudum produxit in illa. / Christe, tuo populo fer opem, compesce leones, / da regno placidam bello cessante quietem!" (translation mine).

58 Faletra, "Narrating the Matter of Britain", p. 75.

59 Echard, *Arthurian Narrative*, p. 59.

Although no exact source has ever been identified for Geoffrey's version
of the prophecies in either the *PM* or the *VM*, it is clear that he was familiar
with some of the Welsh traditions of political prophecy – a genre that dates
back to at least the 10th-century Welsh poem *Armes Prydein Vawr* ("The Great
Prophecy of Britain") and that often employed the voice of the fictionalized
poet-prophet Myrddin (whose name Geoffrey Latinized as *Merlinus*).[60] These
Welsh Merlinic prophecies were virulently anti-Saxon and, as the tradition developed, also anti-Norman: the *VM*'s dramatic gesturing about casting off the
Norman yoke likely derives from the same or similar traditions. Although the
Welsh prophecies do traffic in some difficult imagery (as well as in topical references we will likely never reconstruct), their overall political thrust was quite
clear: they articulated an anti-colonialist fantasy in which the Welsh would rise
up, slaughter all the foreigners in the land, and reconquer the entirety of the island of Britain for themselves. Any reader familiar with such prophecies would
immediately recognize how different Geoffrey's are. In Geoffrey's version, the
symbolism seems quite deliberately obscurantist, the political intent deeply
unclear, and the only prophecy whose images seem even vaguely redolent
of a resurgence by the ancient Britons (or the more contemporary Welsh or
Bretons) is buried in the middle of a long series of other prophecies predicting
a general period of civic unrest. In presenting his own version of the Merlinic
prophecies, Geoffrey of Monmouth thus defuses much of the genre's anti-
colonial content while co-opting its rhetorical force to create what might well
be, judging from the reception history of the *PM*, an elaborate parlor game for
the Anglo-Norman intelligentsia.[61] The *VM* likewise affords the curious reader
with little purchase in decoding its patterns of symbolism, even if it makes a
few clearer references to the Arthurian and post-Arthurian worlds. In other
words, Geoffrey himself might be said to be colonizing the Merlinic prophecy
in the act of purporting to translate it and incorporating it into his own work.

The work of a contemporary Anglo-Latin writer, John of Cornwall (*fl.*1155–
76), brings the extent of Geoffrey's use of the native anti-English prophetic
tradition into relief.[62] John composed his own Latin translation of a set of

---

60   For an overview of the early Welsh prophetic tradition, see A.O.H. Jarman, "The Merlin
      Legend and the Welsh Tradition of Prophecy", in R. Bromwich, A.O.H. Jarman, and
      B.F. Roberts (eds.), *The Arthur of the Welsh: The Arthurian Legend in Medieval Welsh
      Literature* (Arthurian Literature in the Middle Ages, 1), Cardiff, 1991, pp. 117–46; and see
      also *Armes Prydein Vawr*, ed. and trans I. Williams and R. Bromwich, *Armes Prydein: The
      Prophecy of Britain from the Book of Taliesin*, Dublin, 1972.

61   Faletra, "Narrating the Matter of Britain", pp. 77 and 84, n. 63.

62   For the text of John of Cornwall's *Prophetia Merlini*, see M.J. Curley, "A New Edition of
      John of Cornwall's *Prophetia Merlini*", *Speculum* 57:2 (1982), 217–49. For a full discussion of

Merlin's prophecies around 1150–52, most likely in response to the popularity of Geoffrey's version of the prophecies in the *DGB*. John's *Prophecy of Merlin* (*Prophetia Merlini*) is far briefer than Geoffrey's version, and far more to the point: John in fact provides it with a series of clarifying glosses. Indeed, even a cursory comparison demonstrates that, while John's prophecy shares many details of image and wording with Geoffrey's, its overall tone is closer to the political vehemence of the Welsh political poetry; John even evinces details drawn from that tradition – or, quite possibly, from a parallel tradition of political prophecy in Cornish. Most importantly, John of Cornwall does not dilute, delete, or obscure this political content but instead showcases it right up until his final line. The explanatory glosses he provides to his *Prophecy*, moreover, enable less erudite readers (and one wonders if there were ever any readers erudite enough to follow Geoffrey's *PM*) to make more authoritative connections with real-world events, through to the 12th century. In contrast, the widely varying commentaries on Geoffrey's version of the prophecies expose a fundamental hermeneutic confusion. John of Cornwall, in other words, may well supply some of the same elite Anglo-Latin audiences with the authoritative, relatively clear, and resolutely anti-colonialist Merlinic prophecy that Geoffrey did (and could) not.

If Geoffrey's *PM* seems calculated to disable any easy or authoritative interpretation, the third and final prophetic moment in the *DGB* offers a much more transparent stance on the meaning of British history and the place of the peoples of Britain therein. This third prophecy is directed to Cadualadrus, the unsuspecting last king of the Britons, by an angelic voice (*uox angelica*) – in contrast to the two earlier prophecies which were uttered by the pagan goddess Diana and the half-daemonic Merlin (son of an incubus and a nun), respectively – thus immediately lending it a far greater authority. The injunctions of this angelic voice are crystal clear:

> While [King Cadualadrus] was preparing the fleet, the Angelic Voice rang out and commanded him to stop his undertaking. God did not want the Britons to rule in the island of Britain any longer, not until the time came that Merlin had prophesied to Arthur. The Voice commanded him to go to Pope Sergius in Rome to do penance and be counted among the blessed. It said that the Britons might once again win back the island on the merit of their faith when the destined day arrived; but that would not

---

the complex relationship between John of Cornwall and Geoffrey of Monmouth's respective versions of the *PM*, see M.A. Faletra, "Merlin in Cornwall: The Source and Contexts of John of Cornwall's *Prophetia Merlini*", *JEGP* 111:3 (2012), 303–38.

happen until the Britons had brought Cadwallader's body back to Britain from Rome. Then, at long last, after the recovery of the relics of all the other saints as well, which they had hidden in the face of pagan invasion, they would regain their lost kingdom.[63]

The angel's voice is both a prophecy and not a prophecy: it issues statements about the future, it renders commands for the present, and it outlines conditions that need to be fulfilled. It claims both that the Britons will lose Britain (presumably to the Angles and Saxons who will rule the island for hundreds of years, as Geoffrey well knew), and that they might regain it one day. Like the previous two prophecies, this third one is also explicitly about the passage of dominion – about the transferal of Insular sovereignty – and thus also intimately linked with the colonial relations between the peoples of Britain (Welsh, Scots, Normans) in Geoffrey's own day. On the other hand, the angelic prophecy, despite its divine origin, is also surprisingly opaque, and it would seem to undercut any real use of it as a focal point for, say, a Welsh or pan-Brittonic insurgency against the 12th-century English. The Voice refers, for instance, to an alleged prophecy of Merlin to Arthur, an event that Geoffrey never narrates in the *DGB*, where, in fact, Merlin exits the stage after Arthur's conception. Moreover, the conditions tied to the recovery of all the lost saints' relics seem to be setting up a Herculean task, perhaps an impossible one. Add to this the fact that Geoffrey probably knew from at least some of his sources that King Cadwaladr actually died in Britain of the plague and not in Rome – and that at least some of his readers may have known this story too – and it seems rather more likely that, in many aspects, the angel's prophecy of British restoration may be Geoffrey's way of saying "when Hell freezes over". Geoffrey, in other words, offers a prophecy of a native British insurgence against the island's foreign occupiers, who would certainly include his elite Anglo-Norman audiences, only to foreclose, or indefinitely forestall, the likelihood of its ever coming to fruition.

---

63   *DGB*, xi.205.563–73: "intonuit ei uox angelica dum classem pararet ut coeptis suis desisteret. Nolebat enim Deus Britones in insulam Britanniae diutius regnare antequam tempus illud uenisset quod Merlinus Arturo prophetauerat. Praecepit etiam illi ut Romam ad Sergium papam iret, ubi peracta paenitentia inter beatos annumeraretur. Dicebat etiam populum Britonum per meritum suae fidei insulam in futuro adepturum postquam fatale tempus superueniret; nec id tamen prius futurum quam Britones, reliquiis eius potiti, illas ex Roma in Britanniam asportarent; tunc demum, reuelatis etiam ceterorum sanctorum reliquiis quae propter paganorum inuasionem absconditae fuerant, amissum regnum recuperarent."

Still, even in the end, Geoffrey prefers to hedge his bets, and both the *DGB* and the *VM* remain ambivalent at best, and sometimes even contradictory, in their thinking about colonizers and colonized, about a divinely-ordained *translatio imperii*, and about the claims of any people to Insular sovereignty. Geoffrey ends his book by showing the British fall into barbarity, and yet he also enables a possible future, however improbable and however distant, that would restore native control of Britain. He narrates a robust myth of Trojan origins for the ancient Britons and then undercuts it by positing a race of giants as Albion's *real* aboriginals. He glorifies the Welsh folk-hero Arthur and gives him an empire while also showing how this empire too crumbles to dust in the end. And in the *VM* he revives his hallmark character only to have him cede his prophetic authority in the end to his equally enigmatic sister. All in all, we might say that Geoffrey is committed to expressing the playfulness, as Valerie Flint puts it, and the directionlessness, as Siân Echard puts it, of history itself.

And yet, despite the ludic energies bristling beneath the surface of the *DGB*, Geoffrey's work as a whole presents itself as a history, and was certainly understood as such, despite the occasional skeptic, for hundreds of years. Given the energy that the *DGB* exerts in thinking through issues of colonization and native sovereignty, however, it seems that the text is hardly innocent of the realities of power in 12th-century Britain, a dynamic that Michelle Warren characterizes well:

> When Geoffrey of Monmouth provided the master narrative of the Britons' imperial past, he gave them a history and thus an identity for the future. The gift (identity through history), however, remained the property of others and therefore contested territory. The writing and rewriting of Briton history thus creates and retrenches the boundary between those with and without their own past.[64]

The historiographical traditions that emerge from Geoffrey's *DGB* bear witness to the text's rich capacity to serve as an instrument of power for both colonizers and colonized. Translated into both French (Wace, Gaimar) and Middle English (Laȝamon), the contents of the *DGB* passed rapidly into mainstream English chronicle tradition, engendering a host of Prose *Bruts* and even being taken up by such serious later historians as Matthew Paris and Ranulph Higden. Typically, the medieval English regarded Geoffrey's account of the British past valuable primarily because it provided a pre-history that seemed in the main to smooth the way to a comfortable English hegemony and because it supplied

---

64   Warren, *History on the Edge*, p. 11.

several exemplary figures – conveniently sanitized of any ethnic (i.e. Welsh) origins – to claim as part of their own past, especially King Arthur. On the other hand, Geoffrey's history also found its way to Wales, where it was quickly adapted to Welsh political concerns in the robust Welsh chronicle traditions of *Brut y Brenhinedd* ("History of the Kings") and *Brut y Tywysogyon* ("History of the Princes"), the former a loose translation of the *DGB* and the latter explicitly conceived as a continuation of Galfridian history in the present. Indeed, the First Variant Version of the *DGB* was plausibly composed in Wales, and it interestingly mitigates much of Geoffrey's more objectionable content, such as his discussion of Welsh barbarity. The variety of responses to Geoffrey's project may well bear witness to the pseudo-history's success at not overcommitting itself to any particular political position, but it also demonstrates the lasting appeal of Geoffrey's preoccupation with the way colonization and conquest form a vital element of the weft and warp of any account of the past, even a largely fictitious one.

CHAPTER 12

Geoffrey and Gender: the Works of Geoffrey of Monmouth as Medieval "Feminism"

Fiona Tolhurst

1   Geoffrey and Gender

Readers of the extant works of Geoffrey of Monmouth will not be surprised to find a chapter on Geoffrey and gender issues in this volume, for the work in feminist theory produced during the 1980s and 1990s made such a strong case for the relevance and usefulness of feminist approaches to medieval texts that feminist interpretations are now part of the critical mainstream in medieval studies.[1] However, postcolonialist work on Geoffrey's oeuvre has tended to overshadow feminist work on it.[2] A possible explanation of this pattern is

---

1   See, for example, J.M. Bennett, *Ale, Beer, and Brewsters in England: Women's Work in a Changing World, 1300–1600*, Oxford, 1996; E.J. Burns, *Bodytalk: When Women Speak in Old French Literature*, Philadelphia, 1993; C.W. Bynum, *Jesus as Mother: Studies in the Spirituality of the High Middle Ages*, Berkeley, 1982; S. Delany, "'Mothers to Think Back Through': Who Are They? The Ambiguous Example of Christine de Pizan", in L.A. Finke and M.B. Shichtman (eds.), *Medieval Texts & Contemporary Readers*, Ithaca, 1987, pp. 177–97; C. Dinshaw, *Chaucer's Sexual Poetics*, Madison, 1989; L. Finke, "The Rhetoric of Marginality: Why I Do Feminist Theory", *Tulsa Studies in Women's Literature* 5:2 (1986), 251–72; B.A. Hanawalt, *"Of Good and Ill Repute": Gender and Social Control in Medieval England*, Oxford, 1998; R.L. Krueger, *Women Readers and the Ideology of Gender in Old French Verse Romance*, Cambridge, 1993; K. Lochrie, *Margery Kempe and Translations of the Flesh*, Philadelphia, 1991; and L. Lomperis and S. Stanbury (eds.), *Feminist Approaches to the Body in Medieval Literature*, Philadelphia, 1993. For retrospectives on feminist work in medieval studies, see J.M. Bennett, "Medievalism and Feminism", *Speculum* 68:2 (1993), 309–31; C. Dinshaw, "Medieval Feminist Criticism", in G. Plain and S. Sellers (eds.), *A History of Feminist Literary Criticism*, Cambridge, 2007, pp. 11–26; E. Robertson, "Medieval Feminism in Middle English Studies: A Retrospective", *Tulsa Studies in Women's Literature* 26:1 (2007), 67–79; and N.N. Sidhu, "Love in a Cold Climate: The Future of Feminism and Gender Studies in Middle English Scholarship", *Literature Compass* 6:4 (2009), 864–85.

2   Postcolonialist interpretations of Geoffrey's works include C. Chism, "'Ain't gonna study war no more': Geoffrey of Monmouth's *Historia regum Britanniae* and *Vita Merlini*", *The Chaucer Review* 48:4 (2014), 458–79; J.J. Cohen, *Of Giants: Sex, Monsters, and the Middle Ages* (Medieval Cultures, 17), Minneapolis, 1999, pp. 29–61; M.A. Faletra, *Wales and the Medieval Colonial Imagination: The Matters of Britain in the Twelfth Century*, New York, 2014, pp. 19–54; L.A. Finke & M.B. Shichtman, *King Arthur and the Myth of History*, Gainesville, 2004,

that much of the best work in Galfridian studies has combined postcolonial-ist and feminist methodologies.[3] The only book-length studies to focus solely on Geoffrey's unusually flexible conception of gender roles in his *Prophetiae Merlini*, *De gestis Britonum*, and *Vita Merlini* are my own.[4] Nevertheless, a historicist-feminist approach provides a useful vantage point from which to analyze Geoffrey's extant works because he completed his history in late 1138 – the historical moment at which Empress Matilda was preparing for her September 1139 military campaign to take the English throne from her usurping cousin Stephen of Blois.[5] Historicist-feminist analysis confirms what J.S.P. Tatlock asserted in 1938: that Geoffrey's creation of several female rulers of early Britain in the *DGB* constituted support for Empress Matilda's claim to the English throne, a claim based on hereditary right through her father King Henry I.[6]

However, this type of analysis also reveals that Geoffrey's extant works re-quire two modifications to Maureen Fries' categories for female characters in the Arthurian tradition: female counter-heroes, heroines, and female heroes.[7] Although the categories of female counter-hero (a character who often acts out of self-interest and rejects traditional female roles that support male en-deavors) and heroine (a passive figure who inspires and rewards the actions of knights) are useful, Fries' definition of the female hero as deliberately playing female roles to transform her "male-dominant world" while always benefitting knights does not encompass the variety of heroisms that Galfridian females embody.[8] Therefore, scholars must broaden Fries' definition to include females

pp. 35–70; P.C. Ingham, *Sovereign Fantasies: Arthurian Romance and the Making of Britain*, Philadelphia, 2001, pp. 21–50; and M.R. Warren, *History on the Edge: Excalibur and the Borders of Britain, 1100–1300* (Medieval Cultures, 22), Minneapolis, 2000, pp. 25–59.

3   Interpretations of Geoffrey's works that combine postcolonialist and feminist methodologies include Chism, "'Ain't gonna study war no more'", pp. 458–79; Cohen, *Of Giants*, pp. 29–61; Finke and Shichtman, *Myth of History*, pp. 35–70; and Warren, *History on the Edge*, pp. 25–59.

4   F. Tolhurst, *Geoffrey of Monmouth and the Feminist Origins of the Arthurian Legend*, New York, 2012; ead., *Geoffrey of Monmouth and the Translation of Female Kingship*, New York, 2013.

5   Geoffrey's history was completed by January 1139 when fellow historian Henry of Huntingdon learned of its existence, and both historian Neil Wright and editor of the *DGB* Michael Reeve argue for a date shortly before January 1139 – making late 1138 the most accurate estimate. *Bern*, ed. Wright, p. xvi; M.D. Reeve, "The Transmission of the *Historia regum Britanniae*", *Journal of Medieval Latin* 1 (1991), 73–117, at p. 73.

6   J.S.P. Tatlock, "Geoffrey of Monmouth's Motives for Writing His *Historia*", *Proceedings of the American Philosophical Society* 79:4 (1938), 695–703, at pp. 695 and 701–02.

7   M. Fries, "Female Heroes, Heroines and Counter-Heroes: Images of Women in Arthurian Tradition", in S.K. Slocum (ed.), *Popular Arthurian Traditions*, Bowling Green, OH, 1992, pp. 5–17.

8   Fries, "Female Heroes", p. 15.

who take on at least some of the characteristics of a male hero, such as protecting another, weaker character. Scholars must also add the category of female king: a woman who, unlike a queen consort, wields political power independent of male influence.

The varied, complex, and predominantly positive images of women Geoffrey creates in all three of his extant works distinguish him from most male authors of the Middle Ages and support the claim that he is a "feminist" for his time, if readers define "feminist" in a period-specific sense: his works depart from, and implicitly reject, the antifeminist tradition of the Middle Ages. Admittedly, this definition of "feminist" is limited (even conservative by modern standards), yet it is appropriate within a 12th-century cultural context: neither Geoffrey of Monmouth – a man embedded in and trying to benefit from the male-dominated power structures of the Anglo-Normans – nor his fellow 12th-century clerics seeking the patronage of powerful nobles would have had any reason to call for fundamental changes to those power structures. Nevertheless, as L.A. Finke and M.B. Shichtman have noted, Geoffrey's work differs from that of other medieval historians in its "feminist" inclusiveness: "Geoffrey's *Historia* seems unable *not* to mention women. It is populated by all sorts of women, whose stories weave their way through the battles, trades, and negotiations" (my emphasis).[9] As I have argued elsewhere, Geoffrey's choice to include in his history women who play roles other than those of saint, loyal wife, nurturing mother, and temptress sets him apart from his predecessors, contemporaries, and successors in Insular historiography, but his choice to do so in all three of his extant works makes him worthy of the title of "feminist" in the sense of working against the antifeminist mainstream of medieval historiography.[10] In Geoffrey's *PM*, *DGB*, and *VM*, female figures not only play pivotal roles but also perform actions that do the "feminist" work of providing implicit critiques of the brutality, warmongering, moral weakness, and immorality that tend to characterize powerful males in the Galfridian world.

2   The *Prophetiae Merlini*: Images of Female Rule and Female Healing

Geoffrey of Monmouth's *PM* circulated separately from his history and had significant cultural power, both as a sacred text among scholars who redacted it in Latin and translated it into French, and as a literary text that might have

---

9   Finke and Shichtman, *Myth of History*, p. 55.
10   Tolhurst, *Translation of Female Kingship*, pp. 73–81, 133–259; ead., *Feminist Origins*, pp. 113–40.

been responsible for popularizing prophetic literature in England.[11] Within the
DGB, however, these prophecies appear at the midpoint of Geoffrey's history
and constitute a lengthy digression from his account of the reigns of more than
100 rulers of early Britain. This digression's position in the history invites readers to link it to both other sections of the book and events in Anglo-Norman
history. Because Geoffrey's prophecies are expressed in obscure language and
become increasingly opaque as the *PM* section moves toward its conclusion,
scholarly speculation about what the various animals might represent tends to
overshadow examination of how the text presents two intriguing departures
from traditional gender roles: Empress Matilda as rightful heir to the English
throne, and two unnamed female figures as healers of harms that males have
either failed to remove or somehow caused.

The *PM* section injects the fantastic into a narrative dominated by military
struggles for political power, yet it is like the rest of the non-Arthurian material in Geoffrey's history in agenda: it invokes Anglo-Norman anxieties about
the issue of succession to the English throne, while presenting female figures
as much-needed correctives to the foolish and destructive actions of males.
Although readers today find Geoffrey's prophecies both vague and difficult to
understand, it is likely that his contemporaries in the political know would
have had the cultural context necessary to understand his use of various figures
and events as coded references to the conflict between Empress Matilda and
King Stephen, a conflict that would erupt into civil war in September of 1139.
Within the context of the *PM*'s opening passage that contrasts the red dragon representing the Britons with the white dragon representing the Saxons,
and Geoffrey's anti-civil-war diatribe that mentions a lioness and her cubs,
Anglo-Norman readers might well have interpreted this statement as referring
to the Empress: "The white dragon will rise in revolt again and summon/invite
the daughter of Germany."[12] Certainly, readers today might wonder whether
"the daughter of Germany" might refer to a people or an army rather than a female person; however, the *PM*'s references to sons and daughters seem to refer
to gendered people, so there is no reason not to assume that this "daughter"

---

11   *DGB*, vii.109.1–7 and Reeve, "Transmission", pp. 94–97; J. Crick, "Geoffrey of Monmouth,
      Prophecy and History", *Journal of Medieval History* 18:4 (1992), 357–71, at p. 360, n. 13;
      "Anglo-Norman Verse Prophecies of Merlin", ed. and trans. J. Blacker, *Arthuriana* 15:1
      (2005), 1–125, at p. 10; A.F. Sutton and L. Visser-Fuchs, "The Dark Dragon of the Normans:
      A Creation of Geoffrey of Monmouth, Stephen of Rouen, and Merlin Silvester", *Quondam
      et Futurus: A Journal of Arthurian Interpretations* 2:2 (1992), 1–19, at p. 2.

12   *DGB*, vii.112.34–38, xi.185.141–186.154, vii.112.63: "Exurget iterum albus draco et filiam
      Germaniae inuitabit." Translations from Geoffrey's *DGB* and *VM* are my own. For more on
      the *PM*, see Maud Burnett McInerney's contribution to this volume.

refers to a female person – although which female person is open to debate. Furthermore, an Anglo-Norman audience familiar with King Henry I's attempt to ensure that his daughter Matilda would succeed him by requiring his barons to swear fealty to her at two public oathtakings likely saw in this prophecy a suggestion about Matilda: that she was invited, even summoned, by "the white dragon" to leave her home in the German-speaking Holy Roman Empire and rule the disordered island of Britain.[13] Despite the fact that no historiographical text with which I am familiar labels either the Norman or the Frankish ancestors of Matilda and her cousin Stephen as "Germanici", the referent for the white dragon, that in the opening lines of the *PM* is the Saxons, suddenly seems to become the Anglo-Normans. A possible explanation for this odd shift in referent is Geoffrey's desire to produce for the Anglo-Normans "a history that elided, as much as possible, the conflicted relationships among the five *populis*" in Britain (the Normans, Britons, Saxons, Scots, and Picts).[14] This desire might have caused Geoffrey to conflate one Germanic bloodline (the Saxon) with other ones connected with Empress Matilda: she was born to a mother of English lineage and a father of Frankish lineage, and she became the wife of the German-speaking Emperor Henry V. If Geoffrey's Anglo-Norman audience did connect Merlin's prophecy about "Germans" with their own present, then Empress Matilda would have emerged for them as a better king-candidate than Stephen. The prophet says first that "the German worm will be crowned" and then that "the German dragon will barely maintain his caves because vengeance will be visited upon treason."[15] Geoffrey's contemporaries would have found it easy to interpret these statements as applying to King Stephen, for he had committed treason – in "worm"-like fashion – by failing to honor his oath of fealty to his cousin, and then suffered what they might have construed as God's vengeance: Stephen struggled to retain the throne he had usurped. The contrast between dragon and worm could even be Geoffrey's playful way of encoding Stephen's dishonesty and moral weakness. Orderic Vitalis's often-cited identification of the *leo iusticiae*, "lion of justice", of Merlin's prophecies

---

13   William of Malmesbury, *The Contemporary History* i.2, i.8, ed. E. King, trans. K.R. Potter, *William of Malmesbury. Historia novella: The Contemporary History*, Oxford, 1998, pp. 6–7, 18–21; C. Beem, *The Lioness Roared: The Problems of Female Rule in English History*, New York, 2006, p. 26. Although the "Holy" part of the term *Sacrum Romanum Imperium*, "Holy Roman Empire", did not come into use until 1157 and is not attested until 1254, I follow the convention of using the term "Holy Roman Empire" to refer to the medieval Roman empire from the time of Otto I in 962 until that of Francis II in 1806.

14   *DGB* i.5.42–44; Finke and Shichtman, *Myth of History*, p. 54.

15   *DGB*, vii.112.65, vii.113.69–71: "coronabitur Germanicus uermis", "Vix obtinebit cauernas suas Germanicus draco, quia ultio prodicionis eius superueniet."

with Henry I not only sharpens the contrast between the morally questionable Stephen and the admirable figures of Empress Matilda and her father but also causes other references in the *PM* to take on political meaning.[16]

Having referenced the 1120 drowning of three of King Henry I's children (the event that made Matilda her father's only surviving legitimate heir) by noting that "[t]he cubs of the lion were transformed into fish of the ocean", Merlin makes two comments about an eagle that, for Anglo-Norman elites, could have functioned as coded references to the Empress.[17] The first eagle reference is gendered feminine, both by virtue of the feminine noun *aquila*, "eagle", and by the bird's activity of nesting that Anglo-Norman readers would likely have associated with a mother bird's caring for her young within the nest. Because this reference immediately follows the mention of the cubs' transformation into fish, it suggests that the dead King Henry's wishes will triumph: "and his eagle will build a nest on Mount Aravius."[18] Anglo-Norman readers who identified this mount with Snowdon in Wales might have viewed the nest as signifying Matilda's potential base of military operations in Wales – where her half-brother Robert of Gloucester, who later led Matilda's troops, held Glamorgan.[19] Amid references to tears soaking the island nightly, Stephen's and Matilda's factions behaving badly, and Scotland rising up in anger, the second reference to the eagle seems to flatter Matilda: "The eagle of the broken pact will gild it [the bridle] and will delight in a third nesting."[20] If 12th-century readers assumed that the "broken pact" referred to the oaths that both Stephen and many Anglo-Norman barons had made to the Empress but failed to honor, then they might well have interpreted the bridle as the monarchial power that Matilda would make golden or perfect when she attained – through her birthright – her third "nesting" (or site of power), England, having already attained power in the Holy Roman Empire through her first husband and power over Anjou through her second. To represent Matilda as an eagle would likely have seemed both entirely appropriate and symbolically logical to an Anglo-Norman audience, given both the Empress's status as a noblewoman and her title of Empress of

---

16   *DGB*, vii.113.78; Orderic Vitalis, *Ecclesiastical History* xii.47 (iv.490–94), ed. and trans. M. Chibnall, *The Ecclesiastical History of Orderic Vitalis*, 6 vols., Oxford, 1969–80, vol. 6, pp. 384–89.

17   *DGB*, vii.113.84–85: "Catuli leonis in aequoreos pisces transformabuntur."

18   *DGB*, vii.113.85–86: "et aquila eius super montem Arauium nidificabit."

19   G. Heng discusses Mount Aravius as Snowdon in "Cannibalism, the First Crusade, and the Genesis of Medieval Romance", *Differences: A Journal of Feminist Cultural Studies* 10:1 (1998), 98–174, at pp. 118–19.

20   *DGB*, vii.113.87–114.94: "Deaurabit illud aquila rupti foederis et tercia nidificatione gaudebit."

the Romans; Geoffrey's doing so also contrasts her with Stephen as dragon/worm.[21] It is significant that Merlin's prophecies descend into obscurity after this sequence of events. The fact that symbolic representation of Matilda's future reign appears at the narrative moment at which the past becomes the present gives her a pivotal position in Geoffrey's construction of history.

Reinforcing the positive presentation of Empress Matilda in the *PM*, one unnamed female figure eliminates harms that males cannot remove, and another heals the harms that males somehow cause. The first one is a *puella*, "girl", who performs a rescuer's task that no male in the *PM* appears able to perform. After an unidentified "they" (which presumably includes or consists mainly of males) fails to hide a spring that causes sudden death and makes the burial of its victims impossible, and this "they" likewise fails to contain another spring whose water causes those who drink it to die of unquenchable thirst, this girl "will bring in/use a cure of healing".[22] Using "only her breath", she "will dry up the deadly springs".[23] Then her evidently magical "sulphurous footsteps" will produce smoke that "will provide food for underwater creatures".[24] Merlin's prophecy presents this girl as a healer who possesses powers that surpass those of males: she both prevents human deaths and supports animal life. The second female healer undoes the harms to Britain that males somehow cause. After a snake associated with a *colonus Albaniae*, "farmer of Scotland", destroys the harvest with its poison and causes the people in several cities to die, the city of Claudius sends the *remedium*, "remedy": *alumpnam flagellantis*, "the scourge's pupil or foster-daughter", who heals these harms to the natural world and its human inhabitants.[25] Whether this scourge is the farmer associated with the snake, or a different male who is this female figure's teacher or foster-father, Merlin's prophecy about her is clear: "She will carry the right balance ... of medicine, and in a short time the island will be restored."[26] Given this female healer's connection with the city of Claudius, she could be Gewissa in the *DGB*, who ends the conflict between her father and husband; therefore, Merlin's prophecy suggests that women supply the medicine of peace.[27]

---

21   M.J. Curley notes that the eagle and dragon both "stood for Roman civilization itself" in "Animal Symbolism in the Prophecies of Merlin", in W.B. Clark and M.T. McMunn (eds.), *Beasts and Birds of the Middle Ages: The Bestiary and Its Legacy*, Philadelphia, 1989, pp. 151–63, at p. 160.
22   *DGB*, vii.116.147–56: "medelae curam adhibeat".
23   *DGB*, vii.116.157: "solo anhelitu suo", "fontes nociuos siccabit".
24   *DGB*, vii.116.160–61: "passus sulphureos", "cibum submarinis conficiet".
25   *DGB*, vii.116.266–70.
26   *DGB*, vii.116.270–71: "Stateram ... medicinae gestabit et in breui renouabitur insula."
27   *DGB*, iiii.69.357–59.

Although Geoffrey's *PM* is a text with an apocalyptic ending, its references to the eagle associate Empress Matilda with the healing of Britain from the harm King Stephen has done to it. Similarly, its references to two young women associate womankind with healing Britain. Within the context of Geoffrey's diatribe about the horrors of civil war that enables him to speak in his own voice after Arthur's mortal wounding, the cataclysmic end of the world that Merlin prophesies provides a convincing demonstration of the destruction that civil war causes and the need for constructive female power.[28]

3   *De gestis Britonum*: Female Regency and Kingship as Correctives to Male Misbehavior

As noted above, the main plot of the *DGB* articulates Geoffrey of Monmouth's anti-civil-war stance more directly than the *PM*. However, as the *DGB* develops an account of the reigns of the more than 100 kings of Britain who ruled before the English gained dominion over the island, it also creates a sharper contrast between destructive male power and constructive female power. Within his narrative of early British kingship, Geoffrey reveals his "feminist" philosophy that the legitimate heir should reign – regardless of gender. He does so by including two female king-candidates who could have reigned, a female regent who admirably performs the military and political functions of a king, and two competent and moral female kings who do reign, both peacefully and successfully. Furthermore, the good qualities of the female regent and kings highlight the misconduct of male kings, misconduct that can indicate incompetence or criminality.

According to Geoffrey's version of the British past, both Helena the daughter of King Coel and the unnamed daughter of King Octavius could have – and should have – reigned as kings. Helena has the same problem that Empress Matilda had: due to her father's death, she must rely on noblemen to support her as a king-candidate. Like King Henry I, King Coel dies suddenly, leaving behind as his heir a daughter whom her father has educated so that she can rule *facilius*, "more easily", after his death.[29] This description suggests that, like Henry who made clear his intention that his daughter would reign after

---

28   *DGB*, xi.185.141–186.154.

29   *DGB*, v.78.140–42. For evidence of Matilda's preparation to rule well, see Beem, *The Lioness Roared*, pp. 35, 39–41 (political experience) and E. van Houts, "Latin and French as Languages of the Past in Normandy During the Reign of Henry II: Robert of Torigni, Stephen of Rouen, and Wace", in R. Kennedy and S. Meecham-Jones (eds.), *Writers of the Reign of Henry II: Twelve Essays*, New York, 2006, pp. 53–77, at pp. 66–69 (literacy in French, German, Latin, and possibly Italian).

him by having his barons twice swear fealty to her, Coel intends for his daughter to reign. Geoffrey even underscores Helena's right to rule by having Duke Caradocus of Cornwall refer to Coel's daughter as "Helena [whom] we cannot deny is master of this kingdom by hereditary right".[30] Helena does not reign, however, because Constantius takes the throne and marries her, begetting Constantinus upon her; for Helena, marriage denies her access to the political power her father had wanted her to have and transforms her into a receptacle for her husband's seed. The story of Octavius's daughter demonstrates that failure to support the legitimate female heir on the part of the king and his counselors results in civil war and all the unnecessary suffering it brings. First Octavius's nephew, Conanus Meriadocus, fights for the throne after Octavius gives his daughter and crown to a Roman nobleman named Maximianus; then, Conanus and Maximianus fight a series of battles in which each man causes *dampnum maximum*, "the greatest damage", to the other.[31] When Maximianus finally acquires the throne, he not only displays *saeuitia*, "savagery", by slaughtering the French, but also leaves Britain open to attack by the Huns and Picts, for he has stripped Britain of much-needed defenders.[32] These king-candidates matter in part because of precedents for female rule that Guendoloena, Cordeilla, and Marcia provide.

The story of Guendoloena, the first of Geoffrey's female figures who functions as a king, is striking for three reasons: it shows that a woman can be a more moral and more competent ruler than a man, it emphasizes her kingly functions rather than the fact that she *chooses* to step aside so that her son can rule, and it reveals Geoffrey's tendency not to villainize a female figure even when she commits a morally questionable act. In contrast to her husband Locrinus, who violates his marriage vows through a secret seven-year affair with his German mistress Estrildis, impregnates this mistress, and then tries to cast his lawful wife aside, Guendoloena fulfills her duties as queen consort: she remains faithful to her husband and gives birth to a male heir to the throne.[33] Despite exchanging the traditional gender role of queen consort for leader of troops, Guendoloena receives the support of all of the young men of Cornwall (her home region) – a detail that underscores the justice of her cause and makes her a moral reformer rather than a rebel.[34] This female leader then proves her moral superiority by becoming the apparent beneficiary of

---

30   *DGB*, v.83.291–93: "Helenam nequimus abnegare hereditario iure regnum istud possidere".

31   *DGB*, v.81.208–83.305.

32   *DGB*, v.85.331–86.359, v.88.395–405.

33   *DGB*, ii.24.40–25.53.

34   *DGB*, ii.25.53–55; K. Olson interprets Guendoloena as an invader in "Gwendolyn and Estrildis: Invading Queens in British Historiography", *Medieval Feminist Forum* 44:1 (2008), 36–52.

God's support when, on the battlefield, her husband dies after being struck by an arrow as he leads troops against Guendoloena's army.[35] For Anglo-Norman readers who noted the similarity between Locrinus's death and that of King Harold II, who reputedly died after being wounded in the eye by an arrow during the Battle of Hastings, Guendoloena would become the "Norman" (rightful) king and Locrinus the "Saxon" (illegitimate) one who loses his throne to the leader whom God has chosen to rule Britain. Geoffrey's narration emphasizes that Guendoloena performs all of the functions of a king: she gathers and leads troops, defeats her enemy in battle, and eliminates those who pose a political threat to the rightful succession of her son Maddan by having her husband's mistress and illegitimate daughter executed.[36] In a book containing many brief reigns, Guendoloena's fifteen-year reign – after her husband's ten-year one – underscores her competence to rule.[37] Geoffrey's emphasis on Guendoloena's kingly functions rather than her status as a regent continues when he describes how she *chooses* to transfer power to her son Maddan once he is *aetate adultum*, "mature in age"; after her son reaches his majority and she steps aside so that he can rule, she then reigns alone over Cornwall – the region from which Galfridian Britain draws many of its leaders – until her death.[38] Although the implication of this transfer of power from mother to son might be that a woman should not rule if there is a legitimate and morally upright male heir, her case makes clear that a woman has a right to rule when a male king proves to be immoral and incompetent.

Most striking, however, is Geoffrey's choice not to villainize this female regent even when she displays extreme anger and orders two killings. Although angered by Locrinus's misdeeds, Guendoloena's label of *indignans* denotes not only that she is "furious, raging" but also that she is "full of righteous anger".[39] Even the rage that motivates her killing of Estrildis and her daughter Habren does not become grounds for villainization, for this rage is *paterna*, "paternal", and receives the same lack of criticism that her father Corineus's anger does.[40] Furthermore, Geoffrey's phrasing presents the deaths of these two women as executions, not murders: Guendoloena [*i*]*ubet*, "orders", that they be thrown into the river.[41] This verb makes the two deaths the result of a ruler's order, an order that preserves both the Britons' ethnic purity and their sovereignty

---

35   *DGB*, ii.25.55–57.
36   *DGB*, ii.25.53–61.
37   *DGB*, ii.26.65–66.
38   *DGB*, ii.26.66–68.
39   *DGB*, ii.25.54; *DMLBS*, s.v. *indignans*, def. 5.a and b.
40   *DGB*, ii.25.58, ii.24.27–51.
41   *DGB*, ii.25.58.

over the island of Britain. The fact that Guendoloena's execution of Habren is not a shameful moral wrong becomes even more evident when Guendoloena proclaims *per totam Britanniam*, "through all Britain", that the river should be called by this young woman's name.[42] By granting to Habren the *honorem ae-ternitatis*, "honor of immortality", Guendoloena not only honors Habren's royal blood but also shifts readers' attention away from the execution itself and onto the river as a memorial for the young woman.[43] Geoffrey's first female ruler turns out to be a regent, but she is a defender of British civilization – not a villain.

In contrast to Geoffrey's circuitous presentation of Guendoloena (the seeming king who turns out to be a regent), his presentation of his first female king, Cordeilla, is straightforward: she is the worthy heir to her father's throne whose reign gains legitimacy through Geoffrey's narratorial condemnation of her nephews as barbarous specifically because they rebel against her due to her gender. Cordeilla proves herself worthy to be king when she displays moral integrity as she tries to save her father from the consequences of his poor decision-making by hinting that her sisters love his possessions rather than him.[44] She proves her worthiness again when she displays compassion and political savvy as she protects her exiled and bedraggled father from humiliation at the French court, and then works with her husband to grant Leir sovereignty over France until they can help him regain the British throne.[45] This loyal daughter accompanies Leir, perhaps as an advisor, on the military campaign against his rebellious sons-in-law that puts him back on the throne.[46] Crucially, Cordeilla reigns as a *feme sole* (a woman exercising power without a male guardian), for both her husband and father are dead when she accedes to the throne.[47] In addition, her peaceful five-year reign in a book full of civil wars provides evidence of competence.[48] Although her nephews' rebellion ends her reign, it reaffirms her right to rule because Geoffrey labels as *saeuiciae*, "savagery, barbarity", their motive for it: "they were indignant that Britain should be subject to the rule of a woman."[49] The nephews' barbarity becomes evident when, after Cordeilla brings five years of peace, they destroy provinces within

---

42 *DGB*, ii.25.60–61.
43 *DGB*, ii.25.61–62.
44 *DGB*, ii.31.151–62.
45 *DGB*, ii.31.231–49.
46 *DGB*, ii.31.252–54.
47 *DGB*, ii.31.254–56; for a full discussion of Empress Matilda as a *feme sole*, see Beem, *The Lioness Roared*, pp. 25–62.
48 *DGB*, ii.32.260.
49 *DGB*, ii.32.264–67: "indignati sunt Britanniam femineae potestati subditam esse."

their aunt's kingdom and then battle each other in a violent civil war.[50] By stating that "on account of being overwhelmed by grief after her loss of royal power, she killed herself", Geoffrey reveals that Cordeilla's personal investment in her identity as a female king is so great that she refuses to live when she can no longer wield political power.[51] Therefore, he naturalizes the exercise of political power by a woman and implies the necessity and morality of supporting a legitimate female ruler over an incompetent or immoral male.

Marcia, Geoffrey's second female king, not only proves herself to be intellectually superior to her husband and morally superior to her son, but also reigns until she dies. Geoffrey's narration favors Marcia over her husband, King Guithelinus, for the king receives the briefest of mentions as reigning *benigne et modeste*, "benevolently and with moderation", until his death.[52] In contrast, Marcia receives praise for possessing the traits that make her intellectually superior to her husband: she is learned in all arts, and she creates not only the law code called the Merchenelage but also "many and incredible things that she invented through her own natural genius".[53] After Marcia functions as her husband's partner in power who devises a law code, the British crown passes to her and her seven-year-old son, Sisillius.[54] Nevertheless, Marcia rules as a king rather than a regent, for Sisillius does not become king until after his mother "from this light had departed".[55] Geoffrey's narration suggests that, because of Marcia's *consilio*, "wisdom", and *sensu*, "moral sense", she "obtained rule over the entire island"; therefore, there is no reason for her son to govern the land until his wise mother can no longer do so.[56] Because all Geoffrey says about Sisillius is that he "took possession of the crown, assuming control of the government", Marcia apparently surpasses her son in moral sense just as she surpasses her husband in intellectual achievement.[57]

Within Geoffrey's metanarrative of kingship, female rule becomes an attractive alternative to male rule because some male monarchs are weak and foolish while others commit crimes of tyranny, warmongering, sexual misconduct, and/or murder. Guendoloena's successful 15-year reign that makes possible her son Maddan's peaceful 40-year one contrasts strongly with her husband's weak and foolish pursuit of private desire, desire that threatens the legitimate royal

---

50   *DGB*, ii.32.260–82.
51   *DGB*, ii.32.269–70: "ob amissionem regni dolore obducta sese interfecit."
52   *DGB*, iii.47.257.
53   *DGB*, iii.47.257–61: "multa et inaudita quae proprio ingenio reppererat."
54   *DGB*, iii.47.259–62.
55   *DGB*, iii.47.265–66: "ab hac luce migrasset."
56   *DGB*, iii.47.264–65: "imperium totius insulae optinuit."
57   *DGB*, iii.47.265–66: "sumpto diademate gubernaculo potitus est."

bloodline and undermines political stability.[58] It also contrasts strongly with the reign of her tyrannical successor Mempricius: he murders his own brother to obtain the throne, murders family members who might succeed him, and commits sodomy.[59] Geoffrey's report that a pack of wolves eats Mempricius underscores this tyrant's ravenous appetite for both power and illicit sex.[60] Cordeilla's predecessors highlight two of her roles: model of competent and peaceful rule, and corrector of male incompetence. First King Leil grows politically weak and neglects his duties, causing civil war to break out; then her father foolishly divides his kingdom and thereby enables his sons-in-law and two dishonest daughters to strip him of power.[61] Cordeilla's successors likewise make female rule attractive, for her nephews Marganus and Cunedagius fight a civil war, and then the brothers Ferreux and Porrex fight a civil war that triggers a chaotic period during which five kings vie for power.[62] In Marcia's case, although her predecessors Belinus and Gurguint Barbtruc establish political order, and her husband Guithelinus reigns benignly, her successors make her example of wise kingship shine more brightly. Her reign seems more impressive given that the reigns of her immediate successors (Sisillius II, Kimarus, and Danius) receive no commentary at all, while several of her later successors commit terrible crimes.[63] For example, Morvidus is a tyrant so bloodthirsty that, after he exhausts himself trying to kill every one of his Flemish enemies, he orders that the remainder be "flayed alive and, after they were flayed, burnt"; because of "these and other barbarous deeds", a monster swallows him.[64] Later, King Arthgallo loses the British throne for five years because he tries to take for himself all of his people's wealth and strives to remove nobles from their rightful positions, and then King Enniaunus is so tyrannical that he gets deposed.[65] Although there are good male kings as well as bad, all three of Geoffrey's female rulers are both competent and on the side of right – offering to readers an attractive alternative to rule by males.

---

58 *DGB*, ii.26.65–71, ii.24.40–25.53.

59 *DGB*, ii.26.73–81.

60 *DGB*, ii.26.81–84.

61 *DGB*, ii.28.115–29.117, ii.31.139–89.

62 *DGB*, ii.32.270–82, ii.33.291–304.

63 *DGB*, iii.47.265–67, iii.47.267–52.353.

64 *DGB*, iii.48.277–86: "uiuos excoriari et excoriatos comburi", "haec et alia saeuiciae suae gesta".

65 *DGB*, iii.50.298–302, iii.52.350–53.

4   *De gestis Britonum*: Empowered Arthurian Females

Although literary critics have branded Geoffrey of Monmouth the first medieval author to villainize and marginalize Arthur's queen, Ganhumara,
Geoffrey's history actually presents a "feminist" version of the Arthurian past.[66]
Geoffrey's flexible conception of gender roles and empowerment of female figures are evident in his portrayal of the marriage of Uther and Igerna, Merlin's
prophecy about Arthur and Anna, and the marriage of Arthur and Ganhumara.

Despite the fact that Uther's acquisition of Igerna through military conquest could have resulted in a loveless marriage of political necessity, Geoffrey
makes their marriage a model royal union in which the king and queen are
partners in love and perhaps in power too.[67] They offer proof of their love
(and, according to medieval lore, of Igerna's experiencing pleasure in the
royal bed) by producing children, a daughter as well as a son: "From then on,
they remained together, equally united by no small love, and they begot a son
[Arthur] and a daughter [Anna]."[68] Although the translation just offered reflects a traditional interpretation of Geoffrey's sentence, it does so because it
assumes that Igerna in particular, and medieval women in general, cannot be
in power. Nevertheless, because the word *pariter* can mean "as equals" only in
reference to feudal tenure, a resistant, feminist interpretation of this sentence
is possible – one that assumes that Igerna could wield power: "From then on,
they remained constantly as equals, with no small love uniting them, and they
begot a son [Arthur] and a daughter [Anna]." This nontraditional interpretation is plausible given that the ideals of genuine affection and partnership in
marriage appear elsewhere in Geoffrey's history. Britain's first king, Brutus, expresses affection for his homesick bride Innogin by catching her *inter brachia*,
"in [his] arms", and using both *dulces amplexus*, "gentle embraces", and *dulcia
basia*, "gentle kisses", to calm and comfort her until – exhausted with weeping –
she falls asleep.[69] Aganippus not only desires his future wife Cordeilla passion-
ately, despite her lack of dowry, but also functions as her partner in power after
they marry: they work together to restore King Leir to the throne using their
financial and military resources.[70] Within this narrative context, it is possible

---

66   L.J. Walters, "Introduction", in ead. (ed.), *Lancelot and Guinevere: A Casebook* (Arthurian
      Characters and Themes, 4), New York, 1996, pp. xiii–lxxx, at p. xv; S. Samples, "Guinevere:
      A Re-Appraisal", in Walters (ed.), *Lancelot and Guinevere*, pp. 219–28, at pp. 219–20.

67   *DGB*, viii.138.532–36.

68   *DGB*, viii.138.535–36: "Commanserunt deinde pariter non minimo amore ligati progenu-
      eruntque filium et filiam."

69   *DGB*, i.15.270–16.275.

70   *DGB*, ii.31.175–85, ii.31.237–54.

that the Uther-Igerna relationship – the only marital relationship that Geoffrey describes explicitly – offers a "feminist" model of a royal marriage, one that makes man and wife partners in both love and power.

Although Geoffrey's redactors and translators altered his "feminist" version of the Arthurian past, Geoffrey presents the children of Uther and Igerna as an expression of the equality – of love and perhaps of power – within their parents' royal marriage.[71] Merlin asserts that the son will be *potentissimum*, "most powerful", but the daughter's line will triumph over the son's, for her "sons and grandsons will possess the realm of Britain in succession".[72] The claim that Arthur will build a vast empire, yet Anna's descendants will reign over Britain, is consistent with the reigns of both the two female kings who succeed a father or husband and the three male kings who either inherit or acquire the throne through the matriline.[73]

Both Arthurian society as a whole and Arthur's court reflect the Galfridian ideas of females being active participants in society and male-female partnerships benefitting society. When Arthur rebuilds British churches that the Saxons have razed, he ensures that both female and male members of the Christian monastic community can return to their holy work; therefore, females are active participants in Arthurian society.[74] Within the royal court, noblewomen not only share a symbolic identity with their male partners through wearing clothing of the same color as the men's livery and arms, but also participate in a mutual moral improvement program, one that benefits both genders.[75] While the ladies' love stirs knights *in furiales amores*, "into frenzied passions", yet inspires them to be *probiores*, "more honest", the knights' love makes the women both *castae*, "chaste", and *meliores*, "more virtuous".[76] Geoffrey's use of the verb [e]*fficiebantur*, "they were made" – with the men and women as its joint subject – signals this mutual moral improvement.[77] At Arthur's court, women are active and visible members of the chivalric community: they are

---

71   Tolhurst, *Feminist Origins*, pp. 25–26, 55–112.

72   *DGB*, viii.133.369–72: "filii et nepotes regnum Britanniae succedenter habebunt."

73   The two female kings appear in *DGB*, ii.31.254–ii.32.270 (Cordeilla) and iii.47.261–66 (Marcia). One male king inherits the British throne through the matriline in *DGB*, v.74.32–37 (Bassianus), while two male kings legitimize their reigns through marrying a female king-candidate in *DGB*, v.78.136–43 (Constantius marries Helena, daughter of Coel) and v.83.291–95 (Maximianus marries Octavius's daughter).

74   *DGB*, ix.151.198–99.

75   *DGB*, ix.157.387–89.

76   *DGB*, ix.157.390–95.

77   *DGB*, ix.157.385–91; S. Echard notes how Geoffrey's "emphasis on the role of women in inciting knightly behaviour foreshadows the preoccupations of the vernacular romances" in "Geoffrey of Monmouth", in ead. (ed.), *The Arthur of Medieval Latin Literature: The*

not rewards for knightly valor who function as tokens of exchange between males. Women judge the value of knights, rewarding with their love only those who prove themselves *tercio in milicia*, "three times in battle".[78] These passionate partnerships of knights and their ladies link Arthur's court to that of his father Uther, who wooed his future wife Igerna with passion.[79]

The content of Ganhumara's initial description encourages readers to expect that she will wield significant power: she is of Roman lineage, has been brought up in Cornwall, and possesses great beauty – beauty that Geoffrey describes using phrasing nearly identical to that with which he describes Igerna's.[80] Because the Romans are the standard by which Geoffrey measures British civilization and power, marrying a woman of Roman descent unites two bloodlines (Roman and British) that, in the *DGB*, share a common Trojan origin.[81] Significantly, Ganhumara's Romanness likens her to Empress Matilda who "began to share the emperor's throne and public life" when she married Emperor Henry V at the age of 11; "undertook the formal duties of government", until her widowhood at the age of 23, in a German empire that its leaders saw as the heir of the ancient Roman empire; and then retained her title as a consecrated empress until her death.[82] Ganhumara's upbringing by Cador, duke of Cornwall, suggests both a virtuous nature and the potential to wield power, for Cornwall is the region that produces many outstanding individuals who aid or rule Britain.[83] Finally, by likening Ganhumara to Igerna through the phrase "she surpassed the women of the island with respect to beauty", Geoffrey sets the expectation that Ganhumara's relationship with Arthur will resemble that of Igerna and Uther.[84]

Development and Dissemination of the Arthurian Legend in Medieval Latin (Arthurian Literature in the Middle Ages, 6), Cardiff, 2011, pp. 45–66, at p. 56.

78   *DGB*, ix.157.389–90.

79   *DGB*, viii.137.454–60.

80   *DGB*, ix.152.208–11, viii.137.455–56.

81   *DGB*, iiii.54.6–15.

82   M. Chibnall, *The Empress Matilda: Queen Consort, Queen Mother and Lady of the English*, Oxford and Cambridge, MA, 1991, pp. 26, 33, 42; Beem, *The Lioness Roared*, pp. 35, 40.

83   J.S.P. Tatlock notes the pattern of Cornwall and its eponym supplying Britain with both helpers and rulers in Tatlock, *LHB*, pp. 400–01; *DGB*, i.17.330–i.21.489 (Corineus, eponym of Cornwall); ii.25.52–ii.26.68 (Guendoloena, daughter of Corineus); ii.34.305–37 (King Dunuallo Molmutius); iiii.64.267–71 (King Tenuantius); v.76.68–v.78.124 (King Asclepiodotus); v.87.366–v.88.395 (Duke [called King] Dionotus and his daughter); viii.124.138–49 (Duke Gorlois); ix.143.28–31, ix.148.133–47, x.171.338–42 (Duke Cador); xi.178.81–84 (King Constantinus III); xi.189.210–17 (Duke Bledericus).

84   *DGB*, ix.152.210–11, viii.137.455–56: "tocius insulae mulieres pulcritudine superabat."

Ganhumara fulfills this expectation by wielding both ceremonial and political power at the moment J.S.P. Tatlock calls "the structural and the dramatic climax of the entire *Historia*".[85] Her ceremonial power is evident during the crown-wearing at Caerleon, during which Geoffrey presents her as Arthur's partner in power through parallel processions, Masses, and feasts. The parallel processions display, to the nobles present, the political power of both royals; these ceremonies also suggest that the queen rules *with* the king. The king gets crowned, and then is escorted to a church by four archbishops – with four kings carrying golden swords and an assembly of clergy preceding him.[86] Ganhumara dons her regalia before she receives escort from archbishops and bishops; the four queens of the aforementioned kings – carrying doves – precede her, and all the women in attendance follow her.[87] Although the Masses occur in separate churches, they are equally impressive events, for the magnificent music and singing in both locations so enthrall the knights that "they did not know which of the churches they should seek first."[88] The knights' indecisiveness could be Geoffrey's fictionalized version of the Anglo-Norman barons' struggle to choose between the factions of Empress Matilda and King Stephen. At the parallel feasts, the greater number of the queen's attendants maintains the dignity of her feast, despite her husband's servants having expensive matching liveries.[89] Because the feast sequence segues into Geoffrey's description of the aforementioned mutual moral improvement program at Arthur's court, readers are likely to interpret the queen's celebration as rivaling the king's. Furthermore, Anglo-Norman readers who noticed that Arthur uses his marriage to confirm his status as the ruler of a newly forged European empire and raise himself to a Roman level of greatness might well have associated this celebratory plot sequence with King Henry I's use of his daughter's marriage to Emperor Henry V to confirm his own political status and access to Roman greatness.[90] Geoffrey confirms that Ganhumara wields political power when Arthur, before leaving Britain to fight the Romans, makes her co-regent with Mordred. Geoffrey's phrasing – "entrusting Britain to his nephew Mordred and to Queen Ganhumara to take care of" – presents the queen as her husband's partner in power.[91]

---

85   Tatlock, *LHB*, p. 270.
86   *DGB*, ix.157.359–64.
87   *DGB*, ix.157.364–68.
88   *DGB*, ix.157.369–71: "nescirent quod templorum prius peterent."
89   *DGB*, ix.157.375–84.
90   Chibnall, *The Empress Matilda*, p. 16.
91   *DGB*, x.164.14–15: "Modredo nepoti suo atque Ganhumarae reginae Britanniam ad conseruandam permittens".

The "feminist" nature of Geoffrey's version of the Arthurian world becomes even more evident when he condemns Mordred as the primary – and possibly the only – villain in his account of Arthur's loss of power. Ganhumara becomes a possible victim of circumstance for two reasons. One is that her status as co-regent disappears at the moment of betrayal, a detail that mitigates her responsibility for Arthur's downfall.[92] The other is that Geoffrey presents her one moral wrong, violating her marriage vows, using phrasing that makes her a grammatical object: she "had been joined to the same man [Mordred] in abominable sexual relations".[93] The passive verb form *copulatam fuisse* represents her misdeed indirectly. This choice of phrasing on Geoffrey's part can be read in both a traditional way and a resistant, feminist one. A traditional interpretation of this passage would assert that the passive verb form does not lessen the gravity of Ganhumara's offence, and therefore brands her as the root of "the negative portrayal of Guinevere, which would come to color the [Arthurian] tradition".[94] However, a resistant reading would assert that this passive form makes the queen seem less than fully responsible for her sexual relationship with her nephew, a detail consistent with the possibility that Mordred rebelled and gathered a large army to support his claim to the throne, and then gave the queen little choice but to accept his sexual advances. This possibility becomes more likely when Geoffrey's phrasing brands Mordred the villain who "had usurped [Arthur's] crown through tyranny and treachery" as well as the only traitor in this episode: Mordred is the person "into whose safekeeping [Arthur] had entrusted Britain".[95] Geoffrey further underscores the nephew's violation of his uncle's sovereignty and marital bed by breaking the narrative frame at this point to assert that he will not remain silent about this event.[96] This act of narratorial slow motion might well have caused Anglo-Norman readers to recall Stephen of Blois's decision to betray his uncle Henry I by usurping the

---

92   *DGB*, x.176.480–84.

93   *DGB*, x.176.483–84: "nefanda uenere copulatam fuisse." Wright translates *copulatam fuisse* as a deponent verb, so Ganhumara "united" with Mordred (*DGB*, x.176.484). However, I follow Fries in interpreting the verb form as passive and build upon her observation that "the passive verb makes the Queen's cooperation with the usurper [Mordred] problematic"; M. Fries, "Gender and the Grail", *Arthuriana* 8:1 (1998), 67–79, at p. 69. Given that in the seven other situations in which Geoffrey uses the verb *copulare*, not once does he use the verb as a deponent, interpreting *copulatam fuisse* as a passive form is the option most consistent with the author's pattern of usage. See *DGB*, ii.24.27; ii.31.141; ii.31.177; iii.40.105; iiii.68.330 (I interpret this form as passive); v.81.201; and v.81.225.

94   Walters, "Introduction", in ead. (ed.), *Lancelot and Guinevere*, p. xv.

95   *DGB*, x.176.481–83: "eiusdem diademate per tirannidem et proditionem insignitum esse", "cuius tutelae permiserat Britanniam."

96   *DGB*, xi.177.1–5.

throne the king had left to his daughter Empress Matilda. The possibility that
Ganhumara is her nephew's victim rather than his co-conspirator becomes
even more likely when Geoffrey labels Mordred *sceleratissimus proditor ille*,
"that most criminal traitor" – a superlative adjective he has already applied to
the murderous Giant of Mont-Saint-Michel – and the queen as *desperans*, "de-
spairing", as she flees to a convent after hearing that her nephew is approaching Winchester.[97] Mordred's epithet [*p*]*eriurus*, "the perjurer", makes readers
wonder whether the queen flees at the thought of Mordred gaining permanent
possession of both her and the kingdom.[98]

Ganhumara is striking because she is complex in her characterization: she
is a powerful queen who breaks her marriage vows and fails to produce an
heir. However, what distinguishes her from the versions of Arthur's queen that
Geoffrey's translators and other successors created is that she is a female figure
whom Geoffrey chooses *not* to villainize, despite her committing the moral
wrong of adultery that (because her spouse is King Arthur) constitutes treason.[99]
Furthermore, Ganhumara's case reveals that Geoffrey does not blame female
figures' moral failings on supposed feminine weakness. In addition, he tends to
create portraits of female moral strength, dignity, and heroism.

Both Helena, the niece of Hoelus, and Helena's nursemaid suffer acts of violence perpetrated by the Giant of Mont-Saint-Michel; nevertheless, Geoffrey
assigns to each of these female figures a brand of heroism that proves her
moral strength and gives her dignity despite her victimization. In contrast to
Arthur who displays traditional male heroism when he kills the giant with a
skull-splitting sword stroke, the nursemaid displays knightly heroism.[100] At
first she seems to be a victim, for she enters the narrative as "an old woman
crying and wailing" and expresses to Beduerus her feelings of pain and sorrow
in response to the giant's crimes: kidnapping both her and Helena, attempting
to rape Helena, and raping her.[101] However, the nursemaid soon proves her
moral strength by taking on a knightly function, for she not only risks dismem-
berment by the giant as much as Arthur or Beduerus does but also takes on
the role of the knightly hero by protecting Beduerus from a terrible fate. The
nursemaid tries to prevent Beduerus's "death of indescribable sufferings" by
advising him to flee before the giant can tear his body to pieces "in miserable

97   *DGB*, xi.177.10, x.165.58, xi.177.33–34.
98   *DGB*, xi.177.32–35.
99   Tolhurst, *Feminist Origins*, pp. 55–112.
100 *DGB*, x.165.90–91.
101 *DGB*, x.165.52, x.165.55–67: "anum flentem et eiulantem".

massacre", then consume him while he is in "the flower of [his] youth".[102] In this interaction, she functions as a knight, for she protects someone whom she describes using imagery often associated with female virgins. The nursemaid's humble and willing sacrifice to protect one of Arthur's men constitutes an alternative to the brutal and selfish heroism of the king and gives her dignity even as she reports the violation she has suffered.[103] Helena's brand of heroism defeats the Giant of Mont-Saint-Michel through an act of will despite her fear: she denies him the prize of her virginity as a virgin martyr-saint would. Like Dionotus's daughter and her female companions, who experience great fear at the hands of barbarians but choose death over sexual violation, Helena suffers *timore*, "fear", when the giant embraces her; nevertheless, she dies before he can sexually violate her – and precisely because she fears being violated by such a creature.[104] Helena's apparent inability to accept the possibility of losing her virginity through an act of violence makes her a model of moral strength, a secularized version of the medieval virgin martyr-saint. Geoffrey celebrates Helena's brand of heroism by inventing the etymology for the place he calls Helena's Tomb, the site of her burial.[105] In this way, her heroism becomes part of the landscape of Normandy.

5   The *Vita Merlini*: Female Power Validated

Geoffrey of Monmouth claims in the opening line of his *VM*, composed *c*.1150, that this poem will focus on "the madness of the prophetic seer", yet the prominent and varied roles of its female figures reveal a different focus: female power.[106] Here, as in the *PM* and the *DGB*, Geoffrey depicts female figures in mostly positive ways while assigning to them both male and female roles. Strikingly, the only major character whom Geoffrey adds to the Arthurian material he reworks in this poem is Morgen, a sorceress and ruler.[107] Furthermore,

---

102   *DGB*, X.165.55–57, X.165.66–67: "inenarrabiles mortis poenas", "miserabili caede", "florem iuuentutis".

103   J.J. Cohen, "Decapitation and Coming of Age: Constructing Masculinity and the Monstrous", *The Arthurian Yearbook* 3 (1993), 173–92, at p. 179, citing M. Kundera, "The Traffic in Women: Notes on the 'Political Economy' of Sex", in R.R. Reiter (ed.), *Toward an Anthropology of Women*, New York, 1975, pp. 157–210.

104   *DGB*, v.88.373–95, x.165.61–66.

105   L. Thorpe, "Le Mont Saint-Michel et Geoffroi de Monmouth", in R. Foreville (ed.), *Vie montoise et rayonnement intellectuel du Mont Saint-Michel* (Millénaire monastique du Mont Saint-Michel, 2), Paris, 1967, pp. 377–82, at pp. 380–82.

106   *VM*, l. 1: "[f]atidici vatis rabiem".

107   B. Clarke notes this fact in the introduction to the *VM*, pp. vii–50, at p. 4.

Geoffrey invents the figure of Merlin's wife Guendoloena and transforms the figure of Merlin's sister into her brother's rival, one who eventually succeeds to Merlin's position as prophet of the Britons and Geoffrey's position as author.[108]

Like Geoffrey's history, his Arthurian poem both critiques the princely power that, through military action, has devastated cities full of civilians and celebrates female power in gender-bending ways.[109] The figure now known as Morgan le Fay enters the Arthurian literary tradition as one of nine sisters who enforce a *geniali lege*, "friendly law", upon visitors to Avalon, although Morgen surpasses her siblings in both beauty and skill in healing.[110] As Fries has noted, Geoffrey's introduction of Morgen and the land she rules in "positive and even ... androgynous" terms, as well as his presentation of her as ruling without "a male consort", contrasts sharply with Morgen's later incarnation – the "tramp": a sexually active, then incestuous, and finally rather pathetic figure who (lacking magical powers of her own) uses magical skills to entrap men in order to satisfy her lust.[111] Within the context of medieval authors' erosion of both her powers and her goodness, Geoffrey's Morgen is a standout. She bends the rules of traditional gender roles in part because she is a sorceress, yet her magical powers of shapeshifting and flying are presented matter-of-factly – not with the moral ambiguity that antifeminist authors tend to assign to sorceresses.[112] Morgen also bends these rules by teaching *mathematicam*, "mathematics, astrology" (a scientific field traditionally dominated by males)

---

108 B. Clarke states in his name notes index to the *VM* that "Guendoloena, Merlin's wife, is a new character without direct antecedents"; *VM*, pp. 156–226, "Guendoloena", at p. 186. N. Tolstoy agrees with Clarke that "There can be no doubt that Geoffrey invented the character of Guendoloena" in "Geoffrey of Monmouth and the Merlin Legend", *AL* 25 (2008), 1–42, at p. 37.

109 *VM*, ll. 23–25.

110 *VM*, ll. 916, 918–19.

111 M. Fries, "From The Lady to The Tramp: The Decline of Morgan le Fay in Medieval Romance", *Arthuriana* 4:1 (1994), 1–18, at p. 2. Fries, at pp. 3–5, traces this decline: Chrétien de Troyes' *Erec and Enide* assigns Morgan her first lover, Guiomar; 13th-century French prose romances transform this affair into the incestuous and shameful cause of her exile from Arthur's court as well as her motivation for exploiting Merlin's love for her to gain knowledge of enchantment; later French romances transform her into an evil sorceress who tries to entrap Guiomar and other lovers, thereby fulfilling her sexual desire and destroying them, yet must now learn magic from a male; the *Prose Merlin* presents her as attending a convent school; Hartmann von Aue reduces her to the supplier of a healing plaster for Erec's wounds; and then the *Prose Lancelot*, *Prose Tristan*, and Thomas Malory's *Morte D'Arthur* reduce the means of her sorcery to drugging wine or using a "magic potion or powder".

112 *VM*, ll. 920–25; S. Echard, *Arthurian Narrative in the Latin Tradition* (Cambridge Studies in Medieval Literature, 36), Cambridge, 1998, p. 153.

to her sisters.[113] Morgen's androgyny is evident in the combination of roles she plays: the safely feminine ones of fertility goddess, healer, and beauty, and the traditionally masculine ones of teacher of mathematics and/or astrology and ruler.[114] Morgen's place of residence supports Geoffrey's positive presentation of her power. "The Fortunate Island" (Island of Apples), which Michael J. Curley identifies as "a variation on the topos of a lost paradise or Golden Age" present in both Ovid's *Metamorphoses* and Celtic mythology, is a female-run second Eden.[115] This paradise not only replaces the Edenic island of Britain idealized at the beginning of the *DGB* but also provides a model of feminine stability and peace – one that contrasts with the political instability and civil wars that fill Geoffrey's history of early Britain.[116]

Geoffrey's Morgen takes on greater significance both because her powers surpass those of Merlin (normally the dominant magical figure in Arthurian literature), and because she contributes to a pro-female pattern at work in the poem. In Geoffrey's history, Merlin possesses both engineering skill and the gift of prophecy; in his Arthurian poem, Merlin still possesses the gift of prophecy, despite going mad in response to the terrible loss of life caused by a civil war.[117] Nevertheless, Morgen surpasses Merlin when she resolves the situation with which the Arthurian section of the *DGB* ends: the mortally wounded King Arthur gets carried to the island of Avalon for healing.[118] She, unlike her male counterpart, has the power to heal the king's mortal wound.[119] After Morgen declares that she can cure Arthur only if he remains under her care for a long time, the *VM* explains that the Britons leave her presence rejoicing – apparently confident that she will heal their king.[120] Geoffrey's artistic choice of creating this connection between Morgen and the mortally wounded king constitutes part of a pro-female pattern at work in the poem: Morgen heals Arthur of a physical wound, and Ganieda heals Merlin of a psychological wound.[121]

---

113   *VM*, ll. 926–28.
114   *VM*, ll. 908–28.
115   M.J. Curley, *Geoffrey of Monmouth* (Twayne's English Authors Series, 509), New York, 1994, p. 126; *VM*, ll. 908–17.
116   *DGB*, i.5.24–38.
117   *DGB*, viii.128.212–130.279, vii.111.25–117.304, viii.133.355–72; *VM*, ll. 1–2, 19–76.
118   *DGB*, xi.178.81–84.
119   *VM*, ll. 929–38.
120   *VM*, ll. 936–40.
121   For Geoffrey of Monmouth's invention of Morgen's link with the wounded Arthur, see Clarke's name notes index to the *VM*, "Morgen", *VM*, p. 203 and A.O.H. Jarman, "The Merlin Legend and the Welsh Tradition of Prophecy", in R. Bromwich, A.O.H. Jarman, and B.F. Roberts (eds.), *The Arthur of the Welsh: The Arthurian Legend in Medieval Welsh Literature* (Arthurian Literature in the Middle Ages, 1), Cardiff, 1991, pp. 117–45, at p. 133. For Ganieda's healing of Merlin, see *VM*, ll. 165–209.

Both Geoffrey's invention of a wife for Merlin and his choice of having her contribute to the poem's dramatic intensity show that he deliberately included prominent female figures in his works throughout his career; however, Guendoloena's displacement and dismissal reveal Geoffrey's favoring of female figures who play nontraditional gender roles. Because Guendoloena asserts an emotional claim on her husband that competes with Ganieda's claim, this traditional wife-figure contributes to the poem's dramatic intensity: "They doubled the force of their kisses in competition with each other and, moved by great tenderness, wrapped their arms around the man's neck."[122] Nevertheless, Geoffrey not only gives Guendoloena less narrative space than Ganieda but also signals his higher level of interest in nontraditional females by displacing, and then dismissing, this figure whom Basil Clarke describes as a "faithful tearful dependant".[123] Ganieda proves herself to be the dominant female figure of the *VM* even before her sister-in-law collapses under the weight of unbearable grief, grief due to Merlin's harsh rejection of her: Ganieda does so by bringing Merlin's behavior back into conformity with courtly norms and by restoring him to sanity.[124] In addition, she displaces Guendoloena by speaking for her – articulating Guendoloena's desire to go with Merlin as well as asking him whether Guendoloena has his permission to remarry.[125] Merlin's words and actions, however, dismiss Guendoloena. Although Ganieda sends for her sister-in-law so that she can help Ganieda prevent Merlin's departure for the woods, Guendoloena's pleas neither change Merlin's plans nor receive his usual kindly look.[126] Crucially, Merlin's strongest emotion during this interchange with the two women is distaste for his wife. He implies that his wife's weeping repulses him when he says, "I do not want, sister, a sheep that pours out water in a spring's gaping cleft that is as wide-open as the Virgin's Urn during flood."[127] Both by characterizing his wife as a (presumably dull-witted) sheep and by using the word *hiatus*, "space (between parts)" or "cleft", a word that can have off-color connotations, Merlin expresses distaste.[128] His comment that he will not become an Orpheus – meaning he would rather leave his wife in Hades than try to rescue her – constitutes implicit rejection of his wife.[129] His lack of

---

122 *VM*, ll. 217–18: "Oscula certatim geminant et brachia circum / colla viri flectunt tanta pietate moventur."

123 Clarke, name notes index to the *VM*, "Guendoloena", *VM*, p. 186.

124 *VM*, ll. 357–61, 122–26, 165–212.

125 *VM*, ll. 362–67.

126 *VM*, ll. 354–59.

127 *VM*, ll. 369–70: "Nolo soror pecudem patulo que fontis hiatu / Diffundit latices ut uirginis urna sub estus."

128 *DMLBS*, s.v. *hiatus*, def. 1 and short definition.

129 *VM*, ll. 371–73.

emotional attachment to his wife becomes evident in his willingness to provide a dowry so that Guendoloena can marry whomever she wishes.[130] Setting
Guendoloena aside enables Geoffrey to focus on Ganieda, a character who
plays both male and female roles.

Although Clarke has dubbed Ganieda "after Merlin the best-realised character in [the] *VM*", the variety of roles Ganieda plays gives her character
a complexity that might make her better realized than Merlin.[131] When she
rescues and restores Merlin, she plays the role of female hero. After learning
that her brother has gone mad following the loss of his close companions in a
Briton-Scot civil war, Ganieda sends retainers to bring Merlin back to the royal
court over which she presides with her husband, King Rodarchus of Cumbria.[132]
Given that Ganieda's messenger returns her brother to sanity using a song about
how Merlin's sister and wife mourn for him with equal intensity, Ganieda heals
her brother by providing both the physician (the messenger) and the cure (the
content of the song).[133] This song restores the prophet to his true self, for it
restores his ability to think rationally and reject his other, mad self whom *odit*,
"he hates" – a self that is "other" because it cannot be "moved by the devotion/
compassion of his sister and wife".[134]

Ganieda gains additional complexity because she functions as a female
counter-hero, yet Geoffrey does not villainize her.[135] Even when Geoffrey
marks Ganieda as an adulteress through a leaf that got caught in her hair during a sexual encounter with her lover, he neither labels her a villain in this
part of the plot sequence, nor makes a disparaging comment about women
in general based on the moral wrong she has committed.[136] Although a reader
might explain and excuse her sexual activities by categorizing Ganieda as a
"fairy-mistress", Geoffrey's neutral narration is striking – especially given that
Merlin's laughing scornfully at his sister and identifying her action as illicit
provide an obvious opportunity for misogynistic comments.[137] More importantly, both Geoffrey and Merlin blame males for the problems at Rodarchus's
court. When Merlin relapses into madness after returning to court, Geoffrey
could disparage Ganieda for both orchestrating the prophet's return to court

---

130   *VM*, ll. 375–76, 381–84.
131   Clarke, name notes index to the *VM*, "Ganieda", *VM*, p. 184.
132   *VM*, ll. 121–26.
133   *VM*, ll. 165–209.
134   *VM*, ll. 207–11: "motus pietate sororis / uxorisque".
135   Clarke acknowledges Ganieda's complexity, name notes index to the *VM*, "Ganieda", *VM*,
      p. 184.
136   *VM*, ll. 258–61, 285–93.
137   On Ganieda as fairy-mistress, see L.A. Paton, "Merlin and Ganieda", *Modern Language
      Notes* 18:6 (1903), 163–69, at p. 167; *VM*, ll. 262, 285–93.

and corrupting the court through her immorality. Instead, Geoffrey blames this madness on "such great crowds of people", crowds that must include males.[138] Merlin then suggests that the materialism of King Rodarchus is the root cause of the court's corruption, for he both rejects the king's attempt to bribe him into remaining at court using clothes, horses, and treasure and associates the king's gifts with corruption; Rodarchus's attempt to cheer Merlin up by sending him to a marketplace only underscores the king's materialism.[139] Rodarchus seems even more blameworthy when he resorts to chains to restrain the unbribable Merlin, yet Merlin must also shoulder some blame because he is determined to return to the woods and remain a mad, distorted version of his true self.[140]

Geoffrey presents positively even Ganieda's role as trickster, despite her undermining Merlin through this role. Although Rodarchus turns his face from her and curses the day he married her after learning that she has lain outdoors with her lover, Ganieda not only uses her womanly charm to claim her innocence but also tricks her brother into uttering three different prophecies about a single boy by twice disguising the child; consequently, she discredits her *furenti*, "raving", brother as a witness against her.[141] Strikingly, Geoffrey expresses admiration for this female trickster who functions here as a counter-hero, saying, "This ingenious woman, as soon as she saw [the boy], immediately formulated an unusual trick by which she could vanquish her brother."[142] Her triumph becomes complete when Rodarchus feels vexed that he *condempnarat amantem*, "condemned his lover", and then Ganieda grants her husband *veniam*, "pardon", kisses and caresses him, and restores him to *letum*, "happiness".[143] Assuming that Geoffrey knew a Lailoken tale in which the queen plots the prophet's murder because he has used the leaf in her hair to reveal her adultery, this joyful resolution of the adultery plot suggests that Geoffrey selectively edited the Merlin tradition to shape his Ganieda into a positive female figure.[144]

When the death of her husband King Rodarchus frees her from earthly concerns, Ganieda appropriates a male role by becoming first a political, and then a Christian, philosopher. In a 35-line speech, Ganieda articulates her transformation from widow into philosopher.[145] As she eulogizes her husband,

---

138 *VM*, ll. 221–22: "tantas hominum ... turmas".
139 *VM*, ll. 232–45, 272–77, 485–89.
140 *VM*, ll. 246–53, 272–79.
141 *VM*, ll. 294–343.
142 *VM*, ll. 306–07: "Hunc cum prospiceret convolvit protinus artem / ingeniosa novam qua vult convincere fratrem."
143 *VM*, ll. 344–46.
144 Jarman, "The Merlin Legend", pp. 122–23, 134.
145 *VM*, ll. 693–727.

Ganieda expresses the essence of the political philosophy central to Geoffrey's *DGB*: that a good king loves peace, brings peace between warriors, respects the clergy, gives justice to both the highborn and the lowly, and is generous.[146] Ganieda states that Rodarchus's body must rot in the ground, and that the glory of the world is fleeting.[147] By implicitly critiquing her husband's pursuit of worldly power, Ganieda takes on a role like that of the three female rulers in the *DGB* who correct the foolish and inappropriate behavior of males and enable men to lead better lives; therefore, Geoffrey's Arthurian poem – like his history – can be read as a mirror for princes. As the first character in the *VM* to mention Jesus Christ, Merlin's sister then articulates the Christian philosophical position that people will gain happiness – and Christ will grant them *perpetuo ... honore*, "an eternal reward" – if they *perstant*, "remain steadfast", in both their piety and service to God, and then leave their earthly lives.[148] After transitioning into her role as philosopher, Ganieda asserts that the primary relationship in her life is the one she has with her brother, and she pledges to live with him, wearing a black cloak and joyfully worshipping God.[149]

When Ganieda succeeds Merlin as prophet of the Britons, Geoffrey shows that his Arthurian poem resembles his history: it presents female power as an attractive alternative to male power. Ganieda starts off as the facilitator of her brother's prophecies. After she provides Merlin with both the space in which to prophesy and the secretaries to record his words, he utters a prophecy that takes the Anglo-Normans to task for fighting a civil war.[150] Nevertheless, Ganieda has the last prophetic word in the *VM*.[151] Geoffrey prepares for Ganieda's replacement of the often-acerbic Merlin by having her join an all-male spiritual fellowship, one that includes both her brother and his companion Telgesinus, but excludes the leaders present at Maeldinus's healing.[152] Because her prophetic utterance is the only one in the poem about the political landscape of Geoffrey's present and recent past, it has the greatest relevance to Geoffrey's Anglo-Norman audience. Through this prophecy, Ganieda replaces Merlin as prophet, yet her acquisition of her brother's position seems natural: she utters prophecies when she rises *ad alta spiritus*, "to spiritual heights", possessing an altered state of consciousness like that of both Merlin and the oracles of the ancient world.[153] It also seems natural because she begins to prophesy

---

146   *VM*, ll. 693–702.
147   *VM*, ll. 703–14.
148   *VM*, ll. 720–23.
149   *VM*, ll. 724–27.
150   *VM*, ll. 555–66, 654–80.
151   *VM*, ll. 1474–1517.
152   *VM*, ll. 1461–65.
153   *VM*, ll. 1469–70.

while standing in her brother's *aula* – a word with the basic meaning of "hall", but whose additional meanings – "royal ... favour, usage", "hall of justice", and "demesne" – connote aristocratic power, power she is in the process of acquiring from her brother.[154] Merlin himself declares that his sister has become spiritual royalty when he acknowledges her as the prophetic voice of the Britons, willingly conferring all his power upon her: "Is it you, sister, the breath [of prophecy] has preferred to foretell future things, and closed my mouth and little book? Therefore, this undertaking is given to you. Rejoice in it and assert all things faithfully through my authority."[155] Although Ganieda's gift of prophecy stuns her friends into silence, her brother not only congratulates her but also tells her to rejoice in the gift she has received.[156]

This smooth transfer of power reveals that the Merlin-Ganieda relationship frees Ganieda from normative gender roles, for it lacks the tension typical of brother-sister relationships in mythology. Merlin and Ganieda have both *Einverständnis*, "mutual understanding", and *Austauschbarkeit ihrer prophetischen Funktion*, "interchangeability of their prophetic function".[157] This relationship between equals liberates the female character to exercise power without being branded an extraordinary woman. Ignoring medieval literary norms, Geoffrey naturalizes the transfer of vaticinal power from a male to a female character; to take a prominent example, Dante Alighieri demonizes the prophet Tiresias whose body changes from male to female and back again.[158] Geoffrey's flexible approach to gender roles positions him outside of – and in opposition to – the medieval antifeminist tradition.

Geoffrey's willingness to embrace female power becomes all the more evident when he announces the end of his own career as a writer immediately after Merlin announces the end of his career as a prophet. Geoffrey ends his poem with the assertion, "Britons, give a laurel wreath to Geoffrey of Monmouth. He is indeed yours, for at one time he sang of your battles and those of your leaders, and he wrote a little book that today people call *The Deeds of the Britons* – deeds that are celebrated throughout the world."[159] Geoffrey's use of

---

154   *DMLBS*, s.v. *aula*, def. 1, 3, 4, and 5b.

155   *VM*, ll. 1521–24: "Tene, soror, voluit res precantare futuras / spiritus osque meum compescuit atque libellum? / Ergo tibi labor iste datur. Leteris in illo / auspiciisque meis devote singula dicas."

156   *VM*, ll. 1518–24.

157   I. Vielhauer-Pfeiffer, "Merlins Schwester: Betrachtungen zu einem keltischen Sagenmotiv", *Inklings: Jahrbuch für Literatur und Ästhetik* 8 (1990), 161–79, at p. 178.

158   Dante Alighieri, *Inferno* Canto 20, ll. 40–45, trans. R. and J. Hollander, *Dante. The Inferno*, New York, 2000, pp. 362–63.

159   *VM*, ll. 1525–29: "Britanni, / laurea serta date Gaufrido de Monemuta. / Est etenim vester, nam quondam prelia vestra / vestrorumque ducum cecinit scripsitque libellum / quem nunc Gesta vocant Britonum celebrata per orbem."

the verb *canere*, that denotes both singing and foretelling, allies him with his three characters who sing their prophecies: Telgesinus, Merlin, and Ganieda.[160] Furthermore, his announcement means that Ganieda is the only prophet and potential author at the end of the *VM*: she has inherited Merlin's role as the recipient of spiritual wisdom and, as prophet, can continue to sing of the future after Geoffrey withdraws from Anglo-Norman politics. At the end of the *VM*, Ganieda is in charge of receiving spiritual wisdom and disseminating it to the Britons, and her voice finally replaces the voices of both her brother and the author who created her.

6   Conclusion

The extant works of Geoffrey of Monmouth are examples of medieval "feminism" because they resist the antifeminist tradition in several ways. The *PM*, *DGB*, and *VM* all assign pivotal roles to female figures and present female figures in predominantly positive ways – even when they are involved in potentially damning situations. As a narrator, Geoffrey consistently chooses not to villainize powerful females, whether they appropriate male roles as Morgen, Ganieda, and his female rulers do, or commit moral wrongs as both Ganhumara and Ganieda do. In addition, he creates a variety of female heroes in characters such as Helena, niece of Hoelus, and her nursemaid, and celebrates the cleverness of a female counter-hero, Ganieda. Even when a female character suffers victimization, he gives her moral strength and dignity. Geoffrey's willingness to use female figures to critique the misconduct of male kings might well be a reaction to King Stephen's usurpation of the English throne and weaknesses as a ruler. Although Geoffrey's history could be dismissed as a piece of propaganda that prepares for the future reign of Empress Matilda as England's first female king, his *VM* reveals that all of this author's extant works reflect the same tendencies: to allot more narrative space to powerful female figures playing nontraditional roles than to powerless ones playing traditional roles, to empower females to correct male misdeeds, and to present female power as both natural and as an attractive alternative to male tyranny. Geoffrey's consistently "feminist" agenda merits both further study of his works and continued efforts to identify other male authors who resist the medieval antifeminist tradition.

---

160   *DMLBS* defines *canere* as "to sing" and "to recite", but it does not link this verb with the idea of foretelling, s.v. 1 *canere* v.1 and 5. However, that meaning is present in classical Latin; see *The Oxford Latin Dictionary*, ed. P.G.W. Clare, Oxford, 1982, s.v. *cano*, def. 8. Geoffrey's knowledge of classical Latin literature would have made invoking these two meanings of the verb natural to him.

CHAPTER 13

Geoffrey of Monmouth and Race

Coral Lumbley

1   Introduction to Medieval Race

Geoffrey of Monmouth's *De gestis Britonum* abounds with human collectivities which he variously identifies as *nationes, gentes,* and *populi.* An abbreviated list of the text's cast of collectivities includes Trojans, Britons, Romans, Saracens, Burgundians, Huns, Basques, Irish, Scythians, Picts, Scots, Flemings, Armoricans, Africans, Saxons, Normans, and Christians, a group that, for Geoffrey, is theoretically synonymous with the *humanum genus,* the "human race", as a whole.[1] This capacious representation of Britain's history, in which the eponymous Britons develop a sophisticated civilization through interaction with a diverse set of peoples, revolutionized historical writing in Britain. We know that Geoffrey wrote for an elite Anglo-Norman audience in the early 1130s, and that his work, shedding (fictional) light on the mysterious lost history of the Welsh, was wildly popular among Welsh, Anglo-Norman, and, eventually, English audiences. The socio-political agenda of Geoffrey's intervention in the Anglocentric histories of Britain available to Anglo-Norman newcomers in Britain, however, is less understood. Did Geoffrey's text serve to denigrate the Welsh or to elevate their status? Did Geoffrey support Anglo-Norman colonialism in Britain or did he critique it? Was Geoffrey Welsh, Anglo-Norman, or both, and how did his own identity inform his historiography? While these questions cannot be answered simply, we may better understand Geoffrey's intervention in the socio-political shifts of his time through analysis of the racial logics undergirding his work.[2] Such an analysis reveals that Geoffrey

---

1   *DGB*, iiii.64.276. D.K. Buell notes that "class, ethnicity, and gender are ... specifically singled out as the divisions overcome by redemption in Christ", but that this idea saw only theoretical development and little praxis. See *Why This New Race: Ethnic Reasoning in Early Christianity*, New York, 2005, p. x.

2   Geoffrey of Monmouth's career is an important touchstone for scholarship on medieval race. According to T. Hahn, "The Difference the Middle Ages Makes: Color and Race before the Modern World", *JMEMS* 31 (2001), 1–38, at p. 8, "Geoffrey of Monmouth's *History of the Kings of Britain* (1135), which has been called the most influential book written during the European Middle Ages, displaces English and Norman antagonisms onto the ancient clash of Britons and Germanic invaders, and in the process it renders racial antagonism a crucial component of any larger vision of natural history." Indeed, Hahn states that "the frameworks, the terms,

---

contributes to Norman colonialism by establishing a system of race in which hybridization operates as a useful tool in empire-building.[3] Simultaneously, he establishes a binary between a new European civilization and the old Roman world with its allies and re-orients both Saxon and Roman identities, grouping them with Eastern and African alterities to establish a new Eurocentric focus for British historiography.

The multilingual and multicultural milieu of 12th-century Britain necessitates scholarship which accounts for various systems of differentiation between peoples.[4] Building upon the advent of medieval postcolonial studies, two systems of differentiation, those of ethnicity and of race, have recently entered the literary critical field with force.[5] The use of ethnicity as an analytic category by which to study premodern texts is decidedly less controversial than that of race. Modern ethnicity operates as a horizontal system of human classification and refers to an individual's or group's ancestrally inherited cultural practices, including but not limited to religious practices, language/dialect spoken, national origins/citizenship, dwelling modes and places, clothing and hairstyles worn, food preparation, and food consumption. Ethnicity is sometimes used as a synonym for race, but it is perhaps best characterized as one element of race, as I discuss below.[6]

The concept of a group of people lacking any ethnicity has permeated popular American thought, especially in Anglo-American circles. It was once

the very peoples devised by ... Geoffrey define specific and distinctive medieval engagements with race." See D. Kim, "Introduction to Literature Compass Special Cluster: Critical Race and the Middle Ages", *Literature Compass* 16:9–10 (2019), 1–16.

3   On the de/merits of various types of hybridities as contemporary and historical critical concepts, see J. Nederveen Pieterse, *Globalization and Culture: Global Mélange*, 2nd ed., Lanham, 2009, pp. 97–101.

4   M. Chibnall, *Anglo-Norman England, 1066–1166*, Oxford, 1986, p. 208, identifies Geoffrey's time and place in history as messily multi-racial, a characterization which Hahn echoes in "Difference", p. 7.

5   For foundational work on postcolonial studies, see F. Fanon, *The Wretched of the Earth*, trans. C. Farrington, New York, 1968; E.W. Said, *Orientalism*, London, 2003; and G.C. Spivak, "Can the Subaltern Speak?" in C. Nelson and L. Grossberg (eds.), *Marxism and the Interpretation of Culture*, London, 1988, pp. 271–316. For foundational work on medieval postcolonialism, see J.J. Cohen (ed.), *The Postcolonial Middle Ages*, New York, 2000; id., *Hybridity, Identity, and Monstrosity in Medieval Britain: On Difficult Middles*, New York, 2006; id. (ed.), *Cultural Diversity in the British Middle Ages: Archipelago, Island, England*, New York, 2008; P.C. Ingham, *Sovereign Fantasies: Arthurian Romance and the Making of Britain*, Philadelphia, 2001; and M.R. Warren, *History on the Edge: Excalibur and the Borders of Britain, 1100–1300* (Medieval Cultures, 22), Minneapolis, 2000.

6   See R. Bartlett, *The Making of Europe: Conquest, Colonization and Cultural Change 950–1350*, Princeton, 1994, as well as Buell, *Why This New Race*.

common for the term "ethnic people" or the slur "ethnics" to refer to minorities or people of color, in a problematic attempt to refer to peoples of color as one large group. This verbiage indicates that white "Caucasians" see themselves as lacking cultural practices or physiological traits which signify ethnicity. Despite this disavowal of ethnicity in some areas of the modern world, the category remains useful in a sociological sense, showing that self-identification can reveal useful perceptions about group identity while remaining potentially flawed in logic. Groups that fit into the category of "white Caucasian" (or white European with a specific set of assimilated cultural practices) but are distinguishable based on cultural practices include, for example, Irish Americans, Italian Americans, and German Americans.[7] The horizontal category of ethnicity has been applied to medieval texts with relatively little controversy.[8] For example, scholars have identified the Normans and the Saxons as two discrete ethnic groups and faced little argument. However, these groups were seen as *hierarchically* different by some medieval writers, including Geoffrey, troubling the modern concept of whiteness as a pan-ethnic, unified category in the Middle Ages.

Indeed, Dorothy Kim has shown that what we call ethnicity also seems to operate as a component of medieval race itself.[9] Rather than removing the subject of ethnicity from the study of medieval race, or ignoring race in favor of ethnicity, we can treat ethnicity as a collection of embodied cultural givens (including social systems such as government, codes of conduct, and economies) which were used by medieval thinkers to develop and enforce social hierarchies based on embodied essentialisms, or race.[10] For example, Welsh dependence on pastoralism and transhumance was used by Anglo-Norman

---

7   R.F. Kennedy, C.S. Roy, and M.L. Goldman (eds.), *Race and Ethnicity in the Classical World: An Anthology of Primary Sources in Translation*, Indianapolis, 2013, p. xiii, differentiate between modern race and modern ethnicity: "In the post-Enlightenment world, a 'scientific,' biological idea of race suggested that human difference could be explained by biologically distinct groups of humans, evolved from separate origins, who could be distinguished by physical differences, predominantly skin color. Ethnicity, on the other hand, is now often considered a distinction in cultural practice within the same race." L. Ramey, *Black Legacies: Race and the European Middle Ages*, Gainesville, FL, 2014, p. 25, takes a similar viewpoint, suggesting that that "race" refers to "a group that shares some socially selected *physical* traits, as opposed to 'ethnicity,' which is defined by socially selected *cultural* traits". On race-making, "ethnic" whiteness, and modern Irish, see N. Ignatiev, *How the Irish Became White*, New York, 1995 (repr. 2009).

8   See W.C. Jordan, "Why 'Race'?" *JMEMS* 31:1 (2001), 165–74 and M. Eliav-Feldon, B. Isaac, and J. Ziegler (eds.), *The Origins of Racism in the West*, Cambridge, 2009.

9   D. Kim, "Reframing Race and Jewish/Christian Relations in the Middle Ages", *transversal: Journal for Jewish Studies*, 13:1 (2015), 52–64.

10   Buell, *Why This New Race*, p. x, uses the two terms interchangeably in a conscious provocation of how modern readers think about Christianity as an identity. R. Bartlett, "Medieval

chroniclers to scaffold beliefs and practices placing the English as the supreme race of Britain. What would be considered elements of ethnicity today (heavy dependence on livestock instead of agrarianism, consumption of meat and milk rather than bread, non-participation in seasonal agricultural activities) were racialized (essentialized and used as justification for hierarchization) by Anglo-Norman and English writers.

Race as an analytic category for the Middle Ages has faced considerable resistance by some medievalists, many of whom voice desire to avoid presentism and anachronism.[11] In the modern world, race as a social category is frequently signified by and interpreted according to physiognomic traits, especially skin color and genetic descent, making modern critical race studies seemingly difficult to apply to premodern texts. Indeed, the case against medieval race is founded upon the entirely accurate fact that modern race is largely the product of post-medieval phenomena. Key events in the formation of modern race include the trans-Atlantic slave trade and African diaspora, Enlightenment thought, global colonialism, and pseudo-scientific rationalization of hierarchical classifications of genetic traits such as skin color. Indeed, modern race is not a horizontal system but a vertical one, couched in the notion that an individual's external appearance reflects one's blood and therefore one's ability to function in an ideal (frequently Anglo American), "modern" society. Therefore, careless application of modern notions of race to the Middle Ages can generate anachronistic readings. To put it simply, modern whiteness is not identical to medieval forms of whiteness; modern blackness is not identical to medieval ideas of blackness.[12]

However, Geraldine Heng's paradigm-shifting work, as well as the work of many scholars of color in both print and digital spaces,[13] has shown that hierarchical views of peoples based on cultural practices and embodied characteristics, or at least perceptions of essentialized, embodied characteristics, existed in the Middle Ages; thus, "race is a structural relationship for the articulation and management of human differences, rather than a substantive content."[14]

and Modern Concepts of Race and Ethnicity", *JMEMS* 31 (2001), 39–56, at pp. 41–42, also treats them as synonyms.

11   See M. Chibnall, "'Racial' Minorities in the Anglo-Norman Realm", in S.J. Ridyard and R.G. Benson (eds.), *Minorities and Barbarians in Medieval Life and Thought*, Sewanee, 1996, pp. 49–62, at p. 49.

12   See C. Whitaker, "Black Metaphors in the *King of Tars*", *JEGP* 112:2 (2013), 169–93; id., "Race-ing the dragon: the Middle Ages, Race and Trippin' into the Future", *postmedieval* 6:1 (2015), 3–11; Ramey, *Black Legacies*; and Eliav-Feldon et al. (eds.), *Origins of Racism*.

13   See J. Hsy and J. Orlemanski, "Race and Medieval Studies: A Partial Bibliography", *postmedieval* 8:4 (2017), 500–31.

14   G. Heng, *The Invention of Race in the European Middle Ages*, Cambridge, 2018, p. 19. Also see the argument for "race" instead of "otherness" or "prejudice" on p. 27. J. Tanner, "Race and

Varieties of race proliferated in the premodern world, with Heng demonstrating that religious, cartographic, colonial, and epidermal racial systems manifest across the biopolitics and sociopolitics of medieval time and space.[15]

We must also recognize that, as modern race, white supremacy, and ethnonationalism are deeply significant issues within academic and popular discourse communities, medieval scholarship must generate understandings of medieval race.[16] This is not to say that we can apply modern critical race theory to medieval circumstances in a seamless or simple fashion. Just as modern concepts such as ethnicity, class, gender, and sexuality must be adjusted when applied to medieval contexts (which certainly contain social dynamics related to these modern systems of human categorization), so must medieval critical race develop as a study related to, though not synonymous with, modern critical race. It is for these reasons that medieval race can indeed serve as a useful category in medieval scholarship.

It follows, then, that there are situations in which race ought to be used as a medieval category. Just as modern racial discourse is founded upon notions of blood-based group identity, as evidenced in the "one-drop rule" in the United States, so do medieval writers look to blood-based identity in classifications of people. Just as race today is mainly treated as being embodied and corporeal (located mainly in recognizable skin color, hair color and texture, facial characteristics, and other physiological traits), so is medieval race deeply corporeal. For medieval writers, race could be defined through the theory of

---

Representation in Ancient Art: Black Athena and After", in D. Bindman and H.L. Gates, Jr. (eds.), *The Image of the Black in Western Art*, new ed., Cambridge, MA, 2010, pp. 1–40, at p. 15, notes that that "modern Euro-American 'scientific' racism is just one type of racism, and it is analytically unhelpful to treat this single historically specific model of racism as a conceptual norm." To do so implies that "modern Euro-American racism is somehow, in contrast to its classical antique counterparts, genuinely intellectually coherent and scientifically well grounded."

15 Heng, *Invention*, p. 27.

16 See S. Lomuto, "White Nationalism and the Ethics of Medieval Studies", *In the Middle*, 5 December 2016, <http://www.inthemedievalmiddle.com/2016/12/white-nationalism-and-ethics-of.html> (accessed 26 May 2019) and "Public Medievalism and the Rigor of Anti-Racist Critique", *In the Middle*, 4 April 2019, <http://www.inthemedievalmiddle.com/2019/04/public-medievalism-and-rigor-of-anti.html> (accessed 26 May 2019); D. Kim, "Teaching Medieval Studies in a Time of White Supremacy", *In the Middle*, 28 August 2017, <http://www.inthemedievalmiddle.com/2017/08/teaching-medieval-studies-in-time-of.html> (accessed 26 May 2019) and *Digital Whiteness & Medieval Studies*, Leeds, 2019; M. Rambaran-Olm, "Misnaming the Medieval: Rejecting 'Anglo-Saxon' Studies", *History Workshop*, 4 November 2019 <http://www.historyworkshop.org.uk/misnaming-the-medieval-rejecting-anglo-saxon-studies/> (accessed 13 February 2020); and N. Lopez-Jantzen, "Between Empires: Race and Ethnicity in the Early Middle Ages", *Literature Compass* 16:9–10 (2019), 1–12.

geohumoralism, the theory of peoples receiving their physiognomic and hu-
moral traits from their natural environments. Isidore's *Etymologies* codified the
work of Aristotle and Galen for a medieval audience, stating that "[p]eople's
faces and coloring, the size of their bodies, and their various temperaments
correspond to various climates. Hence we find that the Romans are serious,
the Greeks easy-going, the Africans changeable, and the Gauls fierce in nature
and rather sharp in wit, because the character of the climate makes them so."[17]
Isidore also transmits the concept that races form by taking upon themselves
the characteristics of their geographies. In fact, "Some suspect that the Britons
were so named in Latin because they are brutes. Their nation is situated with
the Ocean, with the sea flowing between us and them, as if they were outside
our orbit."[18]

Setting geohumoralism to one side, the argument has been made that medieval race was merely religious difference. However, Geraldine Heng reminds
us that modern race is increasingly located in religion, with re-emergences of
anti-Semitism, despite many Jewish people being classified as racially white,
and Islamophobia becoming ideological standards in the political policies of
Christian-majority countries. As medieval hierarchical organizations of peoples were frequently based on religion, the gap between modern and medieval
race is diminishing.[19]

Ultimately, we would do well to make medieval race a point of deeper investigation. Because the hierarchical classification of peoples based on corporeal
and cultural practices is an ageless phenomenon, the study of race should be
as well. Claims of anachronism may be rooted in good faith understandings of
how modern race works; however, these claims ultimately serve only to foreclose vital discussions about how humans have divided and ranked one another throughout time. If discussions of medieval race are shut down before they
have begun, valuable knowledge about the social matrices of the medieval
world is simply rejected. Medieval race may differ from modern race, but pre-
modernists can certainly participate in the academy's recuperation of histories

---

17   Isidore of Seville, *Etymologies* IX.ii.105, ed. W.M. Lindsay, *Isidori Hispalensis Episcopi
     Etymologiarum sive Originum Libri XX*, 2 vols., Oxford, 1911 (repr. 1989): "Secundum diver-
     sitatem enim caeli et facies hominum et colores et corporum quantitates et animorum
     diversitates existunt. Inde Romanos graves, Graecos leves, Afros versipelles, Gallos na-
     tura feroces atque acriores ingenio pervidemus, quod natura climatum facit", Isidore of
     Seville, *Etymologies*, trans. S.A. Barney, W.J. Lewis, J.A. Beach, O. Berghof, and M. Hall, *The
     Etymologies of Isidore of Seville*, Cambridge, 2006.
18   Isidore of Seville, *Etymologies* IX.ii.102, ed. Lindsay: "Brittones quidam Latine nominatos
     suspicantur, eo quod bruti sint, gens intra Oceanum interfuso mari quasi extra orbem
     posita. De quibus Vergilius (Ecl. I, 66): Toto divisos orbe Britannos", trans. Barney et al.
19   See G. Heng, *Empire of Magic: Medieval Romance and the Politics of Cultural Fantasy*, New
     York, 2001, p. 12. Heng's observations have become increasingly relevant over time.

of race throughout time. Toni Morrison's 1992 call to change is still relevant today. There is a racial, academic problem in that "in matters of race, silence and evasion have historically ruled literary discourse"; indeed, claims of anachronism resonate with the problem of silence that Morrison identifies.[20] Fear of anachronism is partially responsible for the problem of scholarly evasion of the issue of race, as is concern about re-entrenching modern racist systems.[21] Ultimately, this fear impoverishes medieval scholarship more than it benefits our academic enterprise, which must account for the social realities of racism and race in both modern and medieval ages.[22]

2 Hybridity and Empire

Geoffrey of Monmouth's intellectual milieu included both learned, theological considerations of race codified by Isidore and situationally-specific representations of race by his contemporaries. It has long been acknowledged that Geoffrey's personal investment in the racial politics of Britain seems to have stemmed from his own hybrid identity.[23] Geoffrey has been identified as ethnically hybrid, a Norman with Welsh or Breton descent and/or affiliation; although little is known of his family, he has been treated as a border figure, hailing from Monmouth in the Welsh Marches.[24] Scholarship has long speculated that Geoffrey was, in fact, Breton, as his work shows great admiration for the deeds of ancient Bretons, who are originally Britons and thus Trojans, sharing

---

20 T. Morrison, *Playing in the Dark: Whiteness and the Literary Imagination*, New York, 1992, p. 10.

21 Proponents of using the term in scholarship note that its ability to induce discomfort is part of its usefulness: Buell, *Why This New Race*, p. 21, argues that "because our interpretive models for studying the ancient past have been formulated and revised within racist cultures, we need to keep the term active so as to be able to examine how our interpretive models encode, and thus perpetuate, particular notions about race." J.J. Cohen, "Race", in M. Turner (ed.), *A Handbook of Middle English Studies*, Hoboken, 2013, pp. 109–22, at p. 116, notes that "taxonomies of differentiation are hierarchical – not equalizing", and thus "race captures the differentiation of medieval peoples far better than more innocuous terms."

22 See D. Armenti and N.I. Otaño Gracia, "Constructing Prejudice in the Middle Ages and the Repercussions of Racism Today", *Medieval Feminist Forum* 53:1 (2017), 176–201. See also the ongoing work of the Medievalists of Color collective, housed digitally at <medievalists ofcolor.com> (accessed 18 April 2019).

23 On Geoffrey's identity, see the Introduction to this volume.

24 As Bartlett has established, Anglo-Norman creation of the Marches of Ireland and Wales brought together senses of identity tied to French, English, Flemish, Welsh, Irish, and Latin languages. Geoffrey's linguistic affinities are far easier to comprehend than his ethnic ones, to the extent that ethnicity and language can viewed as separate. See R. Bartlett, *Gerald of Wales, 1146–1223*, Oxford, 1982, p. 14.

equally in the admirable descent of the peoples of Cornubia (Cornwall, named
for the valiant Corineus), Loegria (England, for Locrinus), Kambria (Wales, for
Kamber), and Albania (Scotland, for Albanactus).[25] Whether Welsh, Breton, or
even Cornish, Geoffrey emphasizes the kinship of Breton and Welsh peoples
and gives us evidence for his investment in both cultures. Thus, whether Welsh
or Breton, Geoffrey's hybrid identity is a key element of his authorial identity
for both medieval and modern scholars. It is little surprise that racial and ethnic identities manifest as key issues in Geoffrey's work.

Geoffrey's own intervention in the discourse of race in Britain is of massive
significance, considering how influential his *DGB* became in the centuries following its completion. Not only did the text establish a founding mythology
for Britain, but it established conventions of the discourse of race. Ultimately,
Geoffrey develops a new model of race in the deep history of Britain, thus in-
novating a system for a new, postcolonial Britain.[26]

Geoffrey's representation of race departs from his models in that he is
highly interested in the malleable and generative nature of race. Rather than
providing a rote account of how the world's peoples separated from one another and crystallized into their current states, his narrative is about the creative possibilities of hybridity. Of course, there are caveats to this statement:
some races are more prestigious than others, and the ability to effect organized
colonization is a key elevating factor in a group's status. For Geoffrey, race is
highly malleable, but still reveals the impossibility for some peoples (such as
Africans, Huns, Goths, and Saxons) to integrate into the heights of European
civilization.[27] Geoffrey's concern with what constitutes correct forms of colonization in his narrative reveals motivation for why he portrays race as he does.
In providing admirable models of ethnic hybridity in ancient Britain, Geoffrey
paves the way for himself and the Anglo-Norman elite, including his patron,
Robert of Gloucester, to push forward the colonizing efforts begun by Henry I.
In praising the glorious possibilities of hybridity, Geoffrey campaigns for a

25   Tatlock, *LHB*, pp. 19 and 443, argues strongly for Geoffrey's Breton heritage. See Joshua
      Byron Smith's Introduction to this volume for an overview of this debate.
26   Although many medieval writers display disbelief or discomfort with racial mixing,
      Geoffrey's *DGB* seems to be somewhat of an outlier. J.J. Cohen in "Hybrids, Monsters,
      Borderlands: The Bodies of Gerald of Wales", in id. (ed.), *The Postcolonial Middle Ages*,
      pp. 85–104, at p. 96, points to the work of Gloria Anzaldúa for a model of medieval hy-
      bridity; G. Anzaldúa, in *Borderlands/La Frontera: The New Mestiza*, San Francisco, 1987;
      H.K. Bhabha, *The Location of Culture*, London and New York, 1994.
27   S. Kinoshita, *Medieval Boundaries: Rethinking Difference in Old French Literature*,
      Philadelphia, 2006, p. 5, argues that Geoffrey's "representations of alterity were notably
      more fluid and less marked by the racializing discourses typical of later centuries than we
      sometimes assume".

specific brand of colonialism, one which uses intermarriage and cultural appropriation to facilitate assimilation.[28] Arthur's wondrous square loch in Moray, Scotland is exceptional because its inhabitants are fully segregated; four types of fish swim there, but never stray from their own corners.[29] For Geoffrey, the notion of living beings maintaining the integrity of their own group identities throughout time is a wondrously improbable concept.

Following Bede, Geoffrey sets up his narrative by listing the *quinque ... populis*, "five peoples", who inhabit Britain, the *insularum optima*, "best of islands": the *Normannis ... atque Britannis, Saxonibus, Pictis, et Scotis*, "Normans and Britons, Saxons, Picts, and Scots".[30] Rather than listing five languages like Bede and Henry of Huntingdon, he lists five peoples. This choice allows him to maintain Bede's five-part form while shifting focus from languages to types of people occupying Britain and to exchange the cosmopolitan Latin language for the Norman people.[31] Also significant is the fact that for Bede, the Saxons were the group holding pride of place as the first group to be listed, whereas for Geoffrey it is the Normans. If Geoffrey's affiliation and alliances were not made sufficiently clear in his Prologus, they are in the "Descriptio Insulae".

Almost instantly after presenting the current races of Britain, Geoffrey begins his narrative with an account of Aeneas, pulling the current affairs of Britain into the classical world. While Aeneas's descendants have found a home in Italy, the descendants of Priam are in thrall to the Greeks when Brutus finds himself in their midst. Like a new Moses, Brutus is viewed as a salvific figure to the enslaved Trojans, who "began to flock to him, asking that he be their leader and free them from their bondage to the Greeks".[32] Geoffrey's first

---

28   As S. Kinoshita observes in "Translatio/n, Empire, and the Worlding of Medieval Literature: the Travels of *Kalila wa Dimna*", *Postcolonial Studies* 11:4 (2008), 371–85, at p. 122, imperialism hybridizes itself as a means of spreading and consolidating power.

29   *DGB*, ix.150.179–83: "Erat quippe haut longe illinc, latitudinem habens uiginti pedum eademque mensura longitudinem cum quinque pedum altitudine; in quadrum uero siue hominum arte siue natura constitutum, quatuor genera piscium infra quatuor angulos procreabat, nec in aliqua partium pisces alterius partis reperiebantur", "Quite near [another loch], it was twenty feet wide, twenty feet long and five feet deep; square in shape, either by the hand of man or naturally, it supported in its four corners four species of fish, none of which ever strayed into the space of the other three."

30   *DGB*, i.5.42–44.

31   Like Bede, Henry of Huntingdon categorizes Britain's peoples by language: "Quinque autem linguis utitur Britannia, Britonum uidelicet, Anglorum, Scotorum, Pictorum et Latinorum", "Five languages are in use in Britain: those of the Britons, the English, the Scots, the Picts, and also of the Latins." See Henry of Huntingdon, *History of the English* i.8, ed. and trans. D. Greenway, *Henry, Archdeacon of Huntingdon: Historia Anglorum. The History of the English People*, Oxford, 1996, pp. 24–25.

32   *DGB*, i.7.76–77: "coeperunt ad eum confluere, orantes ut ipso duce a seruitute Graecorum liberarentur."

hybrid hero emerges here as Brutus's lieutenant Assaracus. Assaracus is a *nobil-issimus iuuenis*, "most noble youth", who is the son of a Greek man and Trojan woman.[33] Being sympathetic to the Trojan cause, this figure becomes a pivotal figure in Briton history. Assaracus's doubled, or hybrid, identity results in his poor treatment at the hands of the Greeks:

> For he was in dispute with his brother over three castles that their father had granted to Assaracus on his deathbed, which his brother was trying to take from him because his mother had been a concubine. The brother by contrast was Greek on both sides and had induced the king and the other Greeks to support his faction.[34]

This passage portrays Greece not merely as a multiethnic place, but as a multiracial one, where one group of people have posited inborn racial superiority over another. Assaracus's mother comes from a low caste, and not merely because she is a prostitute. Her Greekness and her status as a sex worker combine to give her son a racial identity a cut below that of his full-blooded Greek brother. Geoffrey's portrayal of Assaracus as a "most noble youth" calls the Greek perception of hybridity as negative into question. Rather than diminishing his status, Assaracus's doubled identity makes him uniquely qualified to take up the vital task of leading Trojans to a new and better land. Thanks to Assaracus's assistance, Brutus executes a massively successful military ambush against the Greeks, freeing the Trojans from their bondage. The Trojans make their way westward, garnering honorable victories against various groups as they travel and land at the island of Albion, "which was inhabited by none except a few giants".[35]

Alternating periods of strife and peace between Britain and Rome occupy a significant portion of the *DGB*, and are important moments for Geoffrey's development of his model of race. Even though Julius Caesar acknowledges the ancient kinship between Romans and Britons, calling the Britons his own *cognati*, "cousins", he orders the rulers of Britain to submit to his supremacy, just like *ceterae ... gentes*, "other nations".[36] According to Caesar, the Britons

---

33   *DGB*, i.7.79–80.
34   *DGB*, i.7.80–85: "Ex Troiana namque matre natus erat fiduciamque in illis habebat maximam ut auxilio eorum inquietudini Graecorum resistere quiuisset. Arguebat enim eum frater suus propter tria castella quia sibi moriens pater donauerat et ea auferre conabatur quia ex concubina natus fuerat. Erat autem frater patre et matre Graecus asciueratque regem ceterosque Graecos parti suae fauere."
35   *DGB*, i.21.453–54: "quae a nemine, exceptis paucis gigantibus, inhabitabatur".
36   *DGB*, iiii.54.14; 13.

have fallen from their glorious Trojan origins: "Unless I am mistaken, they are no longer our equals and have no idea of soldiering, since they live at the edge of the world amid the ocean."[37] For Caesar, the Britons' ethnic identity has shifted fundamentally thanks to their relocation away from the center of human civilization. Therefore, they are racially inferior to the Romans, who have maintained the higher racial status of the Trojans. Geoffrey quickly shows that Caesar is mistaken, elevating the Britons to the very status which Caesar believes they have lost.

King Cassibellaunus refutes Caesar's accusation and shames the emperor for his belief in the Britons' racial degeneration, saying, "Your request disgraces you, Caesar, since Briton and Roman share the same blood-line from Aeneas, a shining chain of common ancestry which ought to bind us in lasting friendship."[38] Cassibellaunus goes on to prove his worth by successfully defending Britain from the yoke of Rome, humiliating Caesar in military defeat. Caesar retreats to Rome, knowing he would not survive another engagement with such a *feroci populo*, "fierce people".[39] When Caesar returns two years later, Cassibellaunus routs him a second time. This series of victories demonstrate the valiant nature of the Britons, a nature which Geoffrey's audience would not have attributed to the modern Welsh.[40] At this point in time, the Britons and the Romans are equally prestigious. No external force can topple their power; indeed, it takes internal strife to bring Britain under the sway of the Roman empire.

---

37   *DGB*, iiii.54.9–10: "Sed nisi fallor ualde degenerati sunt a nobis nec quid sit milicia nouerunt, cum infra occeanum extra orbem commaneant."

38   *DGB*, iiii.55.23–26: "Opprobrium itaque tibi petiuisti, Caesar, cum communis nobilitatis uena Britonibus et Romanis ab Aenea defluat et eiusdem cognationis una et eadem catena praefulgeat, qua in firmam amicitiam coniungi deberent."

39   *DGB*, iiii.58.92.

40   For studies of negative portrayals of the Welsh in Norman Latinate circles of Britain, see M.A. Faletra, *Wales and the Medieval Colonial Imagination: The Matters of Britain in the Twelfth Century*, New York, 2014; R. Kennedy and S. Meecham-Jones (eds.), *Authority and Subjugation in Writing of Medieval Wales*, New York, 2008; A. Plassmann, "Gildas and the Negative Image of the Cymry", *CMCS* 41 (2001), 1–15; J. Gillingham, *The English in the Twelfth Century*; and W.R. Jones, "England Against the Celtic Fringe: A Study in Cultural Stereotypes", *Journal of World History* 13:1 (1971), 155–71. For a discussion of how classical representations of a universal model of cultural development were used as secular justification for Norman expansionism, see S. Khanmohamadi, *In Light of Another's Word: European Ethnography in the Middle Ages*, Philadelphia, 2013. Of course, expansionism could result in coexistence, whether peaceful or tense; see R.R. Davies, "Race Relations in Post-Conquest Wales: Confrontation and Compromise", *Transactions of the Honourable Society of Cymmrodorion* (1974–75), 32–56.

After the conversion, the rule of the island comes into question, threatening to throw Britain's government into disarray. The man who emerges victorious from this complication is the second of Geoffrey's conspicuously heroic hybrids: Maximianus. When the aging king Octavius must select an heir, having no son of his own, an advisor suggests that Octavius give his *filiamque ei cum regno*, "his daughter and crown", to Maximianus.[41] According to Geoffrey, this suggestion is ideal, as

> Maximianus had a British father ... while his mother and his nation were Roman, so that he was of royal blood on both sides. Hence Caradocus could promise peace, since he knew that Maximianus' claim to Britain rested both on imperial descent and British birth.[42]

Geoffrey emphasizes Maximianus's royal descent, but calls special attention to his mixedness, which makes him uniquely qualified for kingship. Although Romans and Britons share ancestors, they have developed into new races, separated by a deep rift which can only be mended by Maximianus. On his deathbed, Octavius is reassured by an advisor who says, "See now, God has deigned to send you this young man, of Roman blood and descended from the British royal family."[43] By logic of his hybrid descent, Maximianus will ensure peace for the Britons.

Both Maximianus and Assaracus are hybrids whose qualifications are largely those of blood; because they have doubled parentage, they seem to be doubly useful to the Britons' enterprise of nation-building. The *DGB*'s focus on the history of Geoffrey's home island and its original occupants building a civilization at the edge of world means that its portrayal of hybridity focuses on how a doubled identity can solidify political and military power. Indeed, our two key hybrids intervene in turning points in the political history of Britain; Assaracus facilitates the Britons' exodus from Greece and their subsequent transformation from a race of slaves to a sovereign nation. Maximianus transforms Britain from a province of the Roman empire to a conquering nation in its own right.[44]

---

41   *DGB*, v.81.203.

42   *DGB*, v.81.203–08: "Erat autem patre Brittannus ... ipsum genuerat; matre uero et natione Romanus ex utroque sanguine regalem ferebat procreationem. Iccirco igitur stabilitatem pacis promittebat quia sciebat illum et ex genere imperatorum et ex origine Britonum ius in Britanniam habere."

43   *DGB*, v.83.287–88: "Ecco ergo tibi dignatus est subuectare Deus iuuenem istum, et ex genere Romanorum et ex regali prosapia Britonum creatum."

44   See M.J. Curley, "Conjuring History: Mother, Nun, and Incubus in Geoffrey of Monmouth's *Historia Regum Britanniae*", *JEGP* 114:2 (2015), 219–39, at p. 237, for Merlin as a positive hybrid figure.

Because Geoffrey has set up a model of positive hybridity, the undesirable results of racially homogenizing policies come as little surprise in Book v of the *DGB*. In fact, an attempt to engineer a settlement upon the principle of racial purity results in one of the text's most tragic events. Having grown bored in his kingdom, the king sails to conquer Armorica (Brittany) with Octavius's nephew Conanus. Maximianus pledges to create a new Britain for Conanus, saying, "I shall make you the ruler of this kingdom; we shall drive out its inhabitants, and it will be another Britain, occupied by our people."[45] Lust for riches corrupts the noble king, whose conquering policies are unnecessarily cruel and involve slaughtering all men of the lands he conquers. He pauses only to undertake the settler colonialist occupation of Armorica, filling it with a *Britannico populo*, "British population", which he presents to Conanus.[46]

Conanus seeks to continue the project of engineering a racially pure colony by rewarding his British soldiers with wives: "To avoid intermarriage with the French he ordered that women should come from the island of Britain to be their brides."[47] Conanus instructs the regent king of Britain, Dionotus, to export women to the colony, hoping that Dionotus's beautiful daughter Ursula will be included in the shipment.[48] The plan to prevent a hybrid generation of Britons is carried out without delay. Dionotus "gather[s] 11,000 noblemen's daughters, as well as sixty thousand girls of common birth" and ships them from London to Armorica.[49]

The Britons' conquest of Armorica occurs under unsavory circumstances, but Conanus's attempt to import a wholesale shipment of British wives worsens the situation. Most of the women object to the arrangement, preferring virginity or their *parentes et patriam*, "parents and country", to seeking wealth through marriage in the new Britain.[50] Geoffrey notes that their various preferences soon become moot, since the ships are swiftly wrecked by storms. Most women drown and "[t]he few women who escaped the danger were driven to foreign islands, where they were butchered or enslaved by an unknown

---

45 *DGB*, v.84.324–26: "Promouebo etenim te in regem regni huius, et erit haec altera Britannia, et eam ex genere nostro expulses indigenis repleamus."

46 *DGB*, v.86.349.

47 *DGB*, v.87.365–66: "Et ut nullam commixtionem cum Gallis facerent, decreuit ut ex Britannia insula mulieres uenirent quae ipsis maritarentur."

48 This episode is an adaptation of the legend of St Ursula and the 11,010 virgins. In the legend, Ursula is sent across the sea to wed the pagan Attila, alongside other reluctant maidens. A shipwreck results in their attempted rapes and deaths at the hands of Huns. See Tatlock, *LHB*, pp. 236–41.

49 *DGB*, v.88.373–74: "collegit per diuersas prouintias filias nobilium numero undecim milia, de ceteris ex infima gente creatis sexaginta milia."

50 *DGB*, v.88.378–80.

people."[51] The survivors refuse sex with foreign soldiers they encounter and are killed. Little known to the women themselves, their killers are revealed to have been Hun and Pictish forces, sent by Rome to eradicate British invaders of the Continent. The very women meant to serve as vessels for a pure British civilization are subjected to horrific deaths in foreign lands. Rather than kill the British men, the Huns and Picts eradicate the possibility of British racial homogeneity in Armorica. The text leaves the audience to assume that the British inhabitants of Armorica intermarry with the French women of the area. Given Geoffrey's consistent praise of the Bretons, it seems that this intermarriage yielded fortunate results.[52] The glorious career of Maximianus becomes a lesson about the impossibility of racial purity in expansionist projects, with the narrative hinging upon the racialized villainy of Huns and Picts, two peoples whom Geoffrey excludes entirely from the possibility of incorporation.

The culminating point of Geoffrey's colonialist agenda, favorable as it is toward the idea of mixedness, is in the court of King Arthur itself. Although Arthur ensures that his own royal British family members are restored to their ancestors' seats as kings of Britain, he desires Britain to become a cosmopolitan center. Thus he "began to increase his household by inviting all the best men from far-off kingdoms and conducted his court with such charm that he was envied by distant nations".[53] Arthur fosters ethnic diversity, not racial seclusion, within his court, resulting in global fear and respect for his excellence. In turn, Arthur sets and fulfills the goal of uniting one third of the world, Europe, under his rule,[54] with his success illustrated by the sheer number of nobles present at his coronation at Caerleon. Lords from the whole of Britain, Ireland, Iceland, Gotland, the Orkneys, Norway, Denmark, Flanders,

---

51   *DGB*, v.88.386–87: "Quae uero tantum periculum euaserunt appulsae sunt in barbaras insulas et ab ignota gente siue trucidatae siue mancipatae."

52   The Welsh account of this tale provides a more explicit, and disturbing, ending to the story of Brittany's founding. See *Breudwyt Maxen Wledic*, ed. B.F. Roberts, Dublin, 2005, pp. 10–11; *The Mabinogion*, trans. S. Davies, Oxford, 2007, pp. 103–10, at p. 110.

53   *DGB*, ix.154.225–27: "inuitatis probissimis quibusque ex longe positis regnis, coepit familiam suam augmentare tantamque faceciam in domo sua habere ita ut aemulationem longe manentibus populis ingereret."

54   *DGB*, ix.154.229–36: "Denique, fama largitatis atque probitatis illius per extremos mundi cardines diuulgata, reges transmarinorum regnorum nimius inuadebat timor ne inquietatione eius oppressi nationes sibi subditas ammitterent ... Cumque id Arturo notificatum esset, extollens se quia cunctis timori erat, totam Europam sibi subdere affectat", "As his reputation for generosity and excellence spread to the farthest corners of the world, kings of nations overseas became very frightened that he would attack and deprive them of their subjects ... When Arthur learned of this, he exulted at being universally feared and decided to conquer all Europe."

Boulogne, Normandy, Anjou, Armorica, and the twelve peers of France attend, with all peoples present expressing their love for Arthur and his world-famous largesse.[55] The sophistication and ostentation of the coronation celebrations are apparently indescribable, but Geoffrey does provide one detail of the feast, reminding readers of why the Britons are deserving of political supremacy and the love of their conquered subjects. Arthur's court observes the "old Trojan custom" of holding separate feasts for men and women.[56] This fact, presented as a bit of historical curiosity for Geoffrey's readers, has little consequence for the narrative. It serves mainly to recall the glorious ancestry of the British people, an ancient race deserving of admiration and study.

Geoffrey's admirable hybrid figures and the diversification of Arthur's court through his conquest of Europe suggest that the *DGB* represents race as malleable in the service of an imperial agenda. At Arthur's court, racial difference becomes a non-issue in a unified Europe where all peoples serve Arthur without reservation. However, Geoffrey's very description of peace is fraught with the specters of those not present at the joyous events at Caerleon. According to the *DGB*, some *populi* seem to exist outside the pale. While racial difference can be overcome and even deployed to individual or group advantage through hybridity, some peoples exist outside the acceptable range of racial difference.

3   The Limits of Hybridity

The crowning at Caerleon includes a wide range of peoples, but Spain emerges as the point of delimitation for Arthur's empire. According to Geoffrey, "there was no prince worth his salt this side of Spain who did not answer such a call" to the high court in Britain.[57] This geographical limit reveals a Eurocentric focus to Geoffrey's narrative. The *DGB* is the tale of British supremacy over one third of the tripartite world, with Asia and Africa remaining in the distance beyond Spain. The text's focus on Britain's history and the relationships between European peoples means that, for Geoffrey, this piece is a form of self-definition. This definitional mode necessitates the use of alterities; while Geoffrey's colonialist narrative supports multiethnic scenarios as a solution to

---

55   *DGB*, ix.156.306–55.

56   *DGB*, ix.157.375–76: "antiquam namque consuetudinem Troiae".

57   *DGB*, ix.156.353–54: "non remansit princeps alicuius precii citra Hispaniam quin ad istud edictum ueniret." Geoffrey's multiple negative associations with Spain diverge dramatically from Isidore's complimentary description of his homeland. See Isidore of Seville, *History of the Kings*, trans. G. Doninini and G.B. Ford, Jr., *Isidore of Seville's History of the Kings of the Goths, Vandals, and Suevi*, Leiden, 1966, pp. 1–2.

racial hostilities, representations of Asian and African influences emerge as convenient narrative Others for British history. Furthermore, Geoffrey innovates a history linking the Saxons to non-European alterity, establishing them as outsiders of Arthur's glorious European empire.

The issues of the conspicuous absence of non-European peoples at Arthur's crowning is soon resolved when a messenger from the Roman Lucius Hiberius arrives, demanding tribute. In response, Arthur assembles a pan-European army and marches to Rome where he meets Lucius's army of African and Asian kings, including forces from Greece, Africa, Spain, Parthia, Media, Libya, Iturea, Egypt, Babylon, Bithynia, Phrygia, Syria, Boetia, and Crete.[58] Lucius's army comes from the "other" side of Spain, from which no princes had come to Arthur's court. The *DGB*'s Eurocentric focus means that this army is not defined, but operates as an intimidating force of 460,100 soldiers.[59] Rather than provide ethnographic descriptions of this non-European, threatening army, Geoffrey deploys a giant to stand in for the racial alterities which Arthur faces. Echoing the duel with Frollo, whose Gaulish forces lurk behind him, Arthur duels a racialized figure in the form of a giant while Lucius's army assembles in the distance.[60]

It has come to be widely theorized that racial difference was popularly represented as what modern scholarship might call a difference in species; thus, a monstrous, or gigantic, body often stands in for a racially marked body.[61] Geoffrey's giants operate as racialized Others of various identifications, with the defeat of the giants signifying British triumphs over unassimilable difference. The first fact that we learn about the *magnitudinis gigantem*, "huge giant", is that he *ex partibus Hispaniarum aduenisse*, "had come from Spain".[62] The giant's geographic identity, combined with his grotesque corporeality, operating in the context of the *DGB*'s use of Spain as a point of delimitation for Arthur's established European empire, points to the giant's racialization. The specter of the menacing Other, particularly the Muslim, operates in the giant

---

58   *DGB*, X.163.1–11.

59   *DGB*, X.163.10–11.

60   Arthur's duel with Frollo is not racialized as is his battle with the giant of Mont-Saint-Michel, but narrative parallels are evident. *DGB*, X.155.250–305.

61   See Cohen, "Race", pp. 109–10; G. Guzman, "Reports of Mongol Cannibalism in the Thirteenth Century", in S.D. Westrem (ed.), *Discovering New Worlds: Essays on Medieval Exploration and Imagination*, New York, 1991, pp. 31–68; D.H. Strickland, *Saracens, Demons, Jews: Making Monsters in Medieval Art*, Princeton, 2003; Heng, *Empire of Magic*, pp. 23 and 36–37; Warren, *History on the Edge*, p. 34; S. Huot, *Outsiders: The Humanity and Inhumanity of Giants in Medieval French Prose Romance*, Notre Dame, 2016, p. 8; Whitaker, "Black Metaphors", pp. 169–93.

62   *DGB*, X.165.33; 33–34. On the term "Saracen", see S. Rajabzadeh, "The Depoliticized Saracen and Muslim", *Literature Compass* 16:9–10 (2019), 1–8.

of Mont-Saint-Michel. For Geoffrey and his readers, the "Saracen" was a racial type, bound up in religious, ethnic, and geographic identities. In a historical text concerned with wondrous natural phenomena and deeds, Geoffrey offers us a larger-than-life iteration of the Muslims populating Lucius's army. This figure of alterity, unlike the Europeans conquered and integrated into Arthur's empire, must be extinguished altogether.

This giant also carries associations with the first giant to appear in the *DGB*, Goemagog of Britain. According to Geoffrey, Britain was populated with barbaric giants before Brutus and his people arrived, whose central purpose in the *DGB* is to provide an indigenous race for the Trojans to conquer, cementing British identity as an imperial force with which to be reckoned. (Indeed, as Michael Faletra shows in this volume, Geoffrey's giants are a race designed to be colonized). Goemagog is a spectacle of physical alterity to the noble British leaders Brutus and Corineus. Geoffrey's description goes as thus: "One of these Cornish giants was a monster called Goemagog, twelve cubits tall and so strong that he could loosen and uproot an oak tree as if it were a twig of hazel."[63] Goemagog's corporeal form is as impressive in death as it was in life; after Corineus wrestles with him and casts him off a sea cliff, "he was torn into a thousand pieces and stained the sea red with his blood."[64] This intensely embodied giant establishes a pattern of giants operating as racialized bodies in the *DGB*. In naming his first giant, Geoffrey taps into a well-established literary tradition of Gog and Magog. These unclean tribes of indefinite origins operated as eschatological specters for Geoffrey's audience. Biblical, classical, and Arabic sources describe Gog and Magog as monstrous races lurking in the Caucasus mountains, only temporarily imprisoned there by a massive wall and/or God's will.[65] The *DGB* harnesses these references for a learned, Latinate audience and presents the giant Goemagog as a racial body requiring extermination if a European empire is to succeed.

Gog and Magog have been associated with different groups throughout history, leading to the question of how Geoffrey and his audience may have read

---

63   *DGB*, i.21.469–72: "Erat ibi inter ceteros detestabilis quidam nomine Goemagog, staturae duodecim cubitorum, qui tantae uirtutis existens quercum semel excussam uelut uirgulam corili euellebat."

64   *DGB*, i.21 486–87: "in mille frustra dilaceratus est et fluctus sanguine maculauit."

65   See A.R. Anderson, *Alexander's Gate, Gog and Magog and the Inclosed Nations*, Cambridge, MA, 1932, for a full, if dated, study of the tradition of Alexander's encounter with the tribes of Gog and Magog. For biblical references to Gog and Magog, see Ez. 38 and 39 and Rev. 20. For Arabic references, see *The Qur'ān: New Annotated Translation*, trans. A.J. Droge, Sheffield, 2013, 18:92–98 and Ibn Fadlān, *Ibn Khurradādhbih on Sallām the Interpreter and Alexander's Wall 844*, trans. P. Lunde and C. Stone, *Ibn Fadlān and the Land of Darkness: Arab Travellers in the Far North*, London, 2012, pp. 99–104.

Goemagog.[66] Ultimately, the ambiguity characterizing Goemagog's identity as it relates to Geoffrey's contemporary audience is generative. Goemagog's fundamental corporeal and cultural alterity harnesses the concept of racial difference to portray monstrosity. The giant poses a racial alterity on the very land to which he is indelibly tied and deserves a highly public extermination in service to the new empire forming in Britain. For Geoffrey, indigeneity is a signifier of racial inferiority, one from which he distances the Welsh and other worthy cultures.[67]

Goemagog serves as an important cognitive precedent for the reader of the *DGB*, bringing his valences of meaning to bear upon the unnamed giant of Mont-Saint-Michel. Like Goemagog, the unnamed giant is impossibly, grotesquely embodied. He kidnaps and attempts to rape a maiden. When she perishes of terror, rather than submit to the giant's attack, the giant sexually assaults her elderly attendant. When Arthur and his knights approach him, the giant is revealed to be as repugnant as the stories about him would suggest. Indeed, he is massively, repulsively corporeal: "The monster was by the fire, his mouth smeared with the blood of half-devoured pigs, some of which he had eaten, some of which, fixed on spits, he was roasting over coals."[68] Medieval giants are not human, nor fully inhuman; they are a manifestation of a racial fantasy, wherein racial difference is marked clearly upon a body and can be understood and manipulated by a hegemonic power. Geoffrey's giants signify undefined racial alterity, obviated as both giants are slain by supreme figures of Euro-Christian British excellence.

After dealing with the Spanish giant, Arthur moves on to deal with Lucius and his pan-Asian and African army. As Arthur's men slash through the enemy,

---

66   Tatlock, *LHB*, p. 50, notes that many early medieval writers discuss Magog, son of Japhet, and Gog and Magog as creatures shut up in the Caucasus mountains, to be released at some apocalyptic moment in the future. The legend is likely of Jewish origin and was picked up by Isidore, Nennius, Bede, and Haimo of Halberstadt, to name a few writers. Tatlock also notes that these mysterious figures have been interpreted as Scythians, Goths, Tartars, Turks, and Muslims. Tatlock concludes, "At any rate for a thousand years they were identified with various barbarous peoples who were threatening Christendom" (p. 54). Tatlock also stated that there is no reason to believe that Geoffrey's giants have anything to do with any of these peoples (p. 55).

67   For an introduction to the concept of indigeneity, as it intersects with Spivak's notion of subalternity, see J.A. Byrd and M. Rothberg, "Between Subalternity and Indigeneity: Critical Categories for Postcolonial Studies", *Interventions: International Journal of Postcolonial Studies* 13:1 (2011), 1–12. On medieval indigeneity, see A. Miyashiro, "Our Deeper Past: Race, Settler Colonialism, and Medieval Heritage Politics", *Literature Compass* 16:9–10 (2019), 1–11.

68   *DGB*, x.165.74–76: "Aderat autem inhumanus ille ad ignem, illitus ora tabo semesorum porcorum, quos partim deuorauerat, partim uero uerubus infixos subterpositis prunis torrebat."

we are reminded of British racial superiority through a statement formulated in religious terms. Arthur personally kills two non-Christians, one of the last moments of the battle which Geoffrey narrates in detail: "He cut off the heads of two kings who were unlucky enough to meet him, Sertorius of Libya and Politetes of Bithynia, and dispatched them to hell."[69] Not only are these men unable to resist Arthur's relentless attacks, they do not even die honorable deaths in battle. As Arthur and his superior British race press forward against the African and Asian troops of Lucius, Geoffrey pauses to remind his readers that there is a fundamental racial-religious rift between the two sides. This castigation operates in religious terms, but is accompanied by a racial stereotype pointing to Britons' perception of non-Europeans as essentially different.

This racist stereotype is embedded in multiple narrative layers. The rallying speech which Arthur uses to spur on his pan-European army focuses largely upon the wrongdoings of the Romans, who he characterizes as *semi-viros*, "effeminates".[70] Arthur places an imagined insult against of the Britons in their mouths, ventriloquizing for rhetorical effect: "Clearly they considered you to be as cowardly as easterners when they planned to exact tribute from your country and make you slaves."[71] By having Arthur himself vocalize a racist stereotype, Geoffrey gives prominence and credence to the convention of portraying peoples of the East as racially inferior. In essence, Arthur's rallying speech appeals to a racial stereotype rooted in geohumoral essentialism. While Geoffrey's text is radical in its portrayal of European racial politics, it makes use of conventional, contemporary beliefs about races outside Christian Europe to elevate the status of the Britons within the European world.

Perhaps Geoffrey's most radical intervention in the racial discourse of 12th-century Britain is his denigration of the Saxons, assigning to them racializing stereotypes which his contemporaries assign to the Welsh. In postcolonial terms, Geoffrey relegates the Saxons to what we might label subaltern status.[72] While hybridity operates as a productive possibility across some racial divides within the *DGB*, it does not apply to barbarians like the barbarian Saxons. For Geoffrey, some European races are fundamentally flawed. The Picts and Scots, for example, are internal foreigners who are little more than pests in the *DGB*.

69 *DGB*, x.174.434–36: "Duos reges, Sertorium Libiae Bithiniaeque Politetem, infortunium ei obuios fecit, quos abscisis capitibus ad Tartara direxit."
70 *DGB*, x.169.284. Accusations of effeminacy are commonplace in many racializing rhetorics.
71 *DGB*, x.169.278–80: "Sane orientalium gentium segnitiam in uobis esse existimabant dum patriam uestram facere tributariam et uosmet ipsos subiugare affectarent."
72 In addition to Spivak on the subaltern, see R. Guha, *Writings on South Asian History and Society*, Delhi, 1984, and D. Chakrabarty, *Provincializing Europe: Postcolonial Thought and Historical Difference*, new ed., Princeton, 2008.

It is the Saxons, however, who seem to be the most fundamentally flawed group in Geoffrey's text. The text fixates not only on their religion, but on their peculiar language and treacherous character, established by their May Day slaughter of Britons, and reiterated throughout the text.[73] This portrayal elevates the history of the Britons and simultaneously justifies later Norman occupation of the island, since the glorious Britons have fallen from power and the Saxons are deeply undeserving of their erstwhile hegemony. While scholarship suggests that the binary between Saxons and Normans disappeared quickly after the Conquest, with any racial antagonism being subsumed quickly by intermarriage and linguistic assimilation, Geoffrey's text is relatively uninterested in Anglo-Norman hybridity.[74]

The *DGB* rejects outright the Anglocentric orientation of historiography in central medieval Britain, moving beyond disinterest into outright antipathy.[75] The Saxons' introduction into the narrative establishes them not only as pagans, but as a menacing racial alterity in Britain. Saxon occupation of Britain is due to Vortigern's infamous treachery, which paves the way for Horsa and Hengist to establish a Saxon presence in Britain. When Vortigern welcomes the brothers to his court, he questions them in such a way that allows Geoffrey to provide an ethnic portrait for the Saxons in their own voices. Hengist immediately explains that Saxon warships have come to Britain because of a *consuetudo*, "custom", of his people, which dictates that overpopulation be relieved by sending men abroad.[76] Hengist then describes his *deos patrios*, "native gods", establishing immediately that these men have peculiar ethnic and religious practices.[77] Geoffrey suggests it would be right to be wary of these foreigners, especially when they request land. Vortigern hesitates, saying "I am forbidden to grant such favours because you are foreigners and pagans, and I am not yet well enough acquainted with your character and customs to treat you like my fellow countrymen."[78] For Geoffrey, xenophobic policies are necessary and useful when deployed against the Saxons, as opposed to the Normans. However, Vortigern is persuaded and ceases to resist the Saxons entirely once he meets

---

73   *DGB*, vi.104.

74   This orientation operates in contrast to many of Geoffrey's contemporaries, such as William of Malmesbury and Henry of Huntingdon, who were hybrids themselves. See Cohen, *Hybridity*, pp. 43–76.

75   See Thomas's chapter in this volume; on Geoffrey's anti-Bede strategies, see Cohen, *Hybridity*, p. 65.

76   *DGB*, vi.98.262.

77   *DGB*, vi.98.277.

78   *DGB*, vi.99.320–22: "Prohibitus sum huiusmodi donaria uobis largiri, quia alienigenae estis et pagani nec adhuc mores uestros et consuetudines agnosco ut uos conciuibus meis parificem."

Hengist's daughter Ronwein. Satan, working through the pagan Saxons, causes Vortigern to be enchanted by lust for Ronwein, entrenching him in Saxon company and culture.[79]

For Geoffrey, linguistic difference between the Britons and Saxons is a key tool for illustrating racial difference, reflecting Isidore's statement that Germanic racial characteristics are represented in their language.[80] Indeed, Kim's theory of spoken language as a racializing mechanism holds true in the DGB. The Saxon language is the only "foreign" language spoken in the DGB, outside of Latin and Latinized versions of place-names, and it is entangled with the characteristic treachery of the Saxon race. Ronwein's greeting to Vortigern, "Lauerd king, wassail", and the traditional response of "drincheil", seal Vortigern's love for the Saxons.[81] His initiation into the speech and customs of the newcomers exposes Britain to a centuries-long foreign occupation. Ronwein's role in the drinking ritual by which Vortigern ensnares himself in Saxon conquest echoes through the narrative. After Vortigern's exile, Ronwein reprises her role of offering drink to men. This time, she commits murder with poison, ridding herself of her stepson Vortimer.[82]

The menacing Saxon language appears a second time, reiterating its association with betrayal and murder. Assisted by Ronwein as an informant of Vortigern's movements, Hengist invites the British king and people to a May Day parlay. In the DGB's most dramatic scene of Saxon treachery, the two sides gather and Geoffrey develops narrative tension by revealing that "Hengist, resorting to unheard-of treachery", had instructed the Saxons to prepare to slaughter the unsuspecting Britons. Indeed, "When he saw that the moment was ripe for treachery, Hengist shouted, 'nimet oure saxas' and immediately

---

79   DGB, vi.100. For more work on Vortigern's lust for the exotic pagan Ronwein, see Warren, *History on the Edge*, esp. p. 44. On colonizing Western feminization and eroticization of the East, see Heng, *Empire of Magic*, pp. 181–238. See also A. Burge, *Representing Difference in the Medieval and Modern Orientalist Romance*, New York, 2016.

80   The *inmanitas barbariae*, "monstrosity of barbarism", of Germanic peoples gives a fearsome quality even to their names. See Isidore of Seville, *Etymologies* IX.ii.97, ed. Lindsay, trans. Barney et al.

81   DGB, vi.100.346–52.

82   DGB, vi.102. Geoffrey develops exceptionally positive portrayals of female leadership, perhaps due to his support for Empress Matilda, mother of the Plantagenet dynasty and half-sister of his sometimes-patron Robert of Gloucester. The Saxon Ronwein is largely an exception to this general trend in the DGB and VM. See F. Tolhurst, *Geoffrey of Monmouth and the Feminist Origins of the Arthurian Legend*, New York, 2012; ead., *Geoffrey of Monmouth and the Translation of Female Kingship*, New York, 2013; and her contribution to this volume.

seized Vortigern and held him by his robe."[83] The Saxons follow suit and slit the throats of 450 unarmed British leaders, then banish Vortigern to Wales.

Both before and after their conversion, the Saxons are essentialized as treacherous and wicked. Their introduction to the narrative and the events leading to their establishing a Saxon presence in Britain portray the newcomers as evil foreigners, essentially corrupt in racial terms. This portrayal continues through the text. When the Saxons are unable to kill Uther Pendragon in battle, they develop a new strategy: "Resorting to their customary treachery, they plotted to kill the king by deceit."[84] Following the example of Ronwein, some *nefandi proditores*, "wicked traitors", poison Uther's spring, a *fraude*, "treacherous deed", which kills the king and 100 other men.[85] After Arthur routs the Saxons, who pledge hostages and leave Britain for Germany, the Saxons turn and attack cities along the Severn. Arthur wonders at this *facinus*, "wickedness", and announces that "Since the wicked Saxons, true to their evil repute, refuse to keep faith with me", he will keep faith with God and avenge his countrymen.[86] Mordred's betrayal of Arthur takes up the racialized valences of the concept of treachery. Like Lucius, who built an army of races outside Geoffrey's realm of acceptability, Mordred builds an army of Saxons, Scots, Picts, and Irish. With his army of racialized, inferior peoples, Mordred becomes tainted with the mark of treachery, as Geoffrey refers to him as *ille nefandus*, "the treacherous" Mordred.[87] After Arthur's death, Saxon treachery sees the island overrun by Africans: "Thanks to the Saxons' treachery, Gormundus and a hundred and sixty thousand Africans crossed to Britain, which was being laid completely waste, on the one side by the faithless Saxons, and on the other by the continual civil wars waged by its own citizens."[88] African alterity arrives in Britain in force, but it is the characteristic Saxon proclivity for treachery that results in slaughter throughout Britain. Of course, the innate Welsh tendency toward civil war is another problem altogether, one addressed below. However, while

---

83 *DGB*, vi.104.459–67: "Hengistus, noua proditione usus ... Ut igitur horam proditioni suae idoneam inspexisset Hengistus, uociferatus est 'nimet oure saxas' et ilico Vortegirnum accepit et per palliam detinuit."

84 *DGB*, viii.142.598–99: "Proditioni etiam solitae indulgentes, machinantur qualiter regem dolo interficiant."

85 *DGB*, ix.142.598, 606, 608.

86 *DGB*, ix.146.83; 89–90: "Quoniam impiissimi atque inuisi nominis Saxones fidem michi dedignati sunt tenere."

87 *DGB*, xi.178.72.

88 *DGB*, xi.184.125–28: "Exin proditione eorum cum centum sexaginta milibus Affricanorum ad Britanniam transfretauit, quam in una parte mentitae fidei Saxones, in alia uero ciues patriae, ciuilia bella inter se assidue agentes, penitus deuastabant."

the Britons are falling from grace, the Saxons remain inherently and unchangeably faithless.

Geoffrey's vision of a Saxon-African alliance draws heavily from William of Malmesbury's account of the Danish Guthrum's baptism.[89] It seems possible that the biblical metaphor which William had drawn upon to make the point that a pagan Dane's proclivities are no more changeable than the color of an Ethiopian's skin could have inspired Geoffrey's engagement with race at this moment. Of course, while William's Gormundus is metaphorically dark-skinned, Geoffrey's Gormundus is raced more concretely. His African identity (or geographic race) likely signals a "Saracen" identity, a racial-religious category that was often depicted through black or dark skin.[90] While William's Gormundus was linguistically and culturally alien, Geoffrey places his Gormundus's alterity upon the character's skin.

However, African occupation of Britain is short-lived, as King Gormundus gives Loegria to the Saxons, "through whose treachery he had landed".[91] British forces attempt to expel the Saxons, and when an opportunity for co-existence arises, the British king of Demetae, Margadud, reminds King Caduallo that "since it has been your intention to drive the entire English race from Britain's shores, why change your mind and permit them to live among us in peace? ... Ever since they first entered this land, the Saxons have always plotted to betray our race."[92] The pathos-filled speech of the exiled British King Cadualadrus recalls the *uersutae proditionis*, "deceitful treachery", of the Saxons, reminding Geoffrey's readers that the Saxons did not win Britain through noble means, and rendering their occupation of the island illegitimate. Cadualadrus, on his way to exile in Armorica, calls out for all the undeserving races who attempted to control Britain to return. The Romans, Scots, Picts, and *ambrones Saxones*, "ravenous Saxons", may as well return, since Britain is now uninhabited.

Even after Saxon conversion, Geoffrey's characterization of the Saxons is uncomplimentary. In the only episode of the *DGB* which portrays Saxon piety, Oswald, king of Northumbria, raises the cross and commands his soldiers to

---

89   William of Malmesbury, *Deeds of the English Kings* ii.121.6, ed. and trans. R.A.B. Mynors, completed by R.M. Thomson and M. Winterbottom, *William of Malmesbury: Gesta Regum Anglorum, The History of the English Kings*, 2 vols., Oxford, 1998–99.

90   Cohen gives Geoffrey's main source for Gormundus as the Old French *Gormont and Isembart*, in which Gormont is a Saracen invading England; see "Race", p. 110.

91   *DGB*, xi.186.157: "quorum proditione applicuerat".

92   *DGB*, xi.200.481–88: "quoniam omne genus Anglorum te ex finibus Britanniae expulsurum proposuisti, cur a proposito tuo diuertens ipsos inter nos in pace manere pateris ... Saxones ergo, ex quo primum patriam nostrum ingressi sunt, semper insidiantes gentem nostrum prodiderunt."

pray with him against the British king Caduallo and his Saxon ally, Peanda. Oswald wins the day, but is killed soon after.[93] For a narrative moment, Caduallo becomes an unsympathetic character, torturing men, women, and children in an attempt at genocide.[94] This reversal of Saxon and British characteristics is temporary, however. After the Britons lose their sovereignty altogether, the Saxons indulge in their *continuum morem*, "unfailing custom", and invite hordes of their Germanic countrymen to immigrate to Britain.[95] This *nefandus populus*, "wicked people", surge into the once-noble island. For Geoffrey, Saxon occupation of Britain is unjustified, regardless of the Saxon religion. The Saxon race is inherently flawed, regardless of British behavior.

Because some races are innately lower than others within Geoffrey's racial schema, it is simply impossible for Saxon-Briton mixing to work within his model of positive hybridity. As the text winds to a close, the potential for a peacefully multiethnic Britain, incorporating Britons and Saxons, is definitively foreclosed by the tale of Edwin and Caduallo.[96]

These two men, one Saxon and one Briton, respectively, are princes. Raised together in the relatively neutral territory of Armorica, Edwin and Caduallo are foster brothers who take up their thrones in mutual *amicitiam*, "friendship".[97] However, this interracial friendship comes to a swift end when Edwin asks Caduallo's permission to hold a royal crowning ceremony for himself in Northumbria. This move would signify full equality between the two kings, with Southern and Northern Britain fully divided between Saxon and British rulership. Caduallo seems amenable to the arrangement, but a queer intimacy with a fellow Briton intervenes in Caduallo's queer interracial relationship with a Saxon.

Geoffrey creates a scene of physical intimacy between Caduallo and his nephew, Brianus, while British leaders consider Edwin's request. During talks at the River Duglas, "elsewhere by the river Caduallo was reclining in the lap of a nephew of his, called Brianus."[98] This idyllic scene marks a narrative shift from sparse, chronicle-like prose to a "close-up shot" on the faces of the two men. While counselors debate among themselves, "Brianus wept and the tears he shed dripped onto the king's face and beard. Caduallo thought that rain

---

93   *DGB*, xi.199.
94   *DGB*, xi.198.
95   *DGB*, xi.204.551.
96   Of course, this portrayal is not necessarily based on historical truth. See L. Brady, *Writing the Welsh Borderlands in Anglo-Saxon England*, Manchester, 2017, esp. p. 27.
97   *DGB*, xi.191.246.
98   *DGB*, xi.191.252: "iacebat Caduallo in alia parte fluminis in gremio cuiusdam nepotis sui, quem Brianum appellabant."

was falling and raised his head, but when he saw the youth was weeping, he asked the reason for his sudden sadness."[99] Brianus's tears on Caduallo's head, which reclines on Brianus's lap, attest to the intimacy of this relationship. When Brianus reveals that the source of his sorrow is the degradation of the British people at the hands of the Saxons, Caduallo is entirely persuaded to deny Edwin's request for full sovereignty in Northumbria.

Geoffrey provides no clear moral commentary upon this decision. While the peace enjoyed between Caduallo and Edwin was portrayed positively, so is the queer relationship between Caduallo and Brianus. Because it is Brianus who is ultimately responsible for the concluding events of the DGB, it is possible that his character sheds light on how the ending of the DGB functions in racial terms. Brianus's tear-filled speech, delivered as he cradles his uncle's head, is portrayed sympathetically. The image Geoffrey conjures in this moment is that of the Virgin Mary, cradling Christ's head and bathing him in her tears, like an early iteration of the Piéta. Brianus is oriented as the long-suffering helpmeet; however, rather than using his intimate relationship with the king to weave peace, he makes an emotional appeal for war. The evocative nature of the scene carries with it an implicit approval of Caduallo's determination to make war on the Saxons.

The physical and emotional intimacy between Caduallo and Brianus intensifies during the war. After a shipwreck at the isle of Guernsey, Caduallo falls ill with "such grief and anger at the loss of his comrades that he refused to eat and lay sick in his bed for three days and nights".[100] Caduallo's love for his men is so intense that the loss of his soldiers in a shipwreck causes him intense physiological pain. Because the only food Caduallo desires is game, Brianus goes hunting the length and breadth of Guernsey with no success. In a gesture of erotic, Christ-like self-sacrifice, Brianus "cut and removed a slice from his own thigh, which he roasted on a spit and presented to the king as venison".[101] Brianus's meat revives his beloved king, who proclaims the meal to be the most delicious he had ever tasted.

---

99 DGB, xi.191.254–56: "fleuit Brianus lacrimaeque ex oculis eius manantes ita ceciderunt ut faciem regis et barbam irrorent. Qui imbrem cecidisse ratus erexit uultum suum uidensque iuuenem in fletu solutum causam tam subitae maesticiae inquisiuit."

100 DGB, xi.193.310–11: "tantus dolor et ira ob amissionem sociorum suorum ita ut tribus diebus et noctibus cibo uesci aspernaretur ac in lecto infirmatus iaceret."

101 DGB, xi.193.318–20: "'scidit femur suum et abstraxit inde frustum carnis parataque ueru torruit illud et ad regem pro uenatione portauit.'"

Racially speaking, cannibalism typically places a human race on the far end
of the spectrum between man and monster.[102] For Isidore, discussion of the
peoples of the world begins in the Mediterranean and Europe, then moves east
and south, proceeding as far as the Trochodites, Pamphagians, Icthyophagians,
and Anthropophagians (cannibals), before reaching the Antipodes.[103] In fact,
for Isidore, the Anthropophagians seem to be the most foreign race possible,
since the Antipodean people, according to him, are imaginary.[104] However,
Geoffrey portrays Brianus's offering of his thigh for Caduallo's consumption
as a novel, selfless action. Brianus takes on feminine valences of Christian
sacrifice, resembling the maternal pelican who pierces her own breast and
revives her young with her own blood.[105] Whether he is portrayed as Marian
or Christ-like, Brianus is a figure of holy femininity whose central goal is the
promotion of Caduallo and his British subjects. When the *DGB* poses the question of whether Saxon and British alliance is possible and desirable, the holy
Brianus intervenes with persuasive homoerotic, intrafamilial, and intraracial
solutions to the problem of British sovereignty.

Brianus's final, valiant deed is a racially-charged assassination. In the text's
third negative reference to Spain, we learn that the Saxon Edwin, echoing
the Saxon recruitment of the African Gormundus, has hired a Spanish augur
named Pellitus.[106] Aided by his sister, who had been kidnapped by Edwin,
Brianus locates the augur and kills him swiftly.[107] The Saxons lose their advantage: Pellitus's exotic, esoteric Spanish education.

The deeds of Caduallo and Brianus establish the impossibility of a Saxon-
Briton alliance, since their intimate relationship supersedes the fraternal
bond which Caduallo and Edwin once enjoyed. The final king of the Britons
is Caduallo's son Cadualadrus, whose own mixed parentage is provided as
an afterthought. Geoffrey states that "His mother was Peanda's paternal sister, but by a different mother, belonging to the noble line of the Gewissei."[108]
Intermarriage between the royal Saxons and Britons comes to naught, as did

102 On medieval race as a spectrum, see S.C. Akbari, *Idols in the East: European Representations of Islam and the Orient, 1100–1450*, Cornell, 2009. On cannibalism, see Heng, *Empire
of Magic*.

103 Isidore of Seville, *Etymologies* IX.ii.120–33.

104 Isidore of Seville, *Etymologies* IX.ii.132, ed. Lindsay: "Anthropophagi gens asperrima sub
regione Siricum sita, qui quia humanis carnibus vescuntur, ideo anthropophagi nominan-
tur", "Anthropophagians are a very rough tribe situated below the land of the Sirices. They
feed on human flesh and are therefore named 'maneaters'", trans. Barney et al.

105 Isidore, *Etymologies* XII.vii.26, ed. Lindsay.

106 *DGB*, xi.193.

107 *DGB*, xi.197.

108 *DGB*, xi.202.516–18: "Mater eius fuerat soror Peandae patre tantum, matre uero diuersa, ex
nobili genere Gewisseorum edita."

the fosterage of Edwin and Brianus. An angelic voice sends the last great Briton king, Cadualadrus, to be numbered among the saints and to await the prophesied return of the Britons.[109] For Geoffrey, it is not possible for Saxons and Britons to mix productively. While hybridity functioned in the deep past, facilitating the inception and growth of British civilization on both island and continent, it fails in the end.

4   Conclusion

Geoffrey famously concludes the *DGB* with a castigation of the Welsh: "As their culture ebbed, they were no longer called Britons, but Welsh, a name which owes its origin to their leader Gualo, or to queen Galaes or to their decline."[110] In characteristic fashion, Geoffrey looks to etymological reasons for the name "Welsh" and points to its derivation from the Old English term *wealh*, which varies in meaning but is often taken to mean "foreigner".[111] For Geoffrey, race is highly malleable, with the exception of some peoples. This malleability serves a highly useful purpose: that of new colonial movements in Britain.

Although the Saxons cultivate the land of Loegria, they came by the land through wickedness and treachery, traits which Geoffrey's contemporaries attributed mainly to the Welsh. By transferring these racialized traits to the Saxons and elevating the history of the Welsh, Geoffrey paves the way for the Norman colonization of Britain. In fact, Geoffrey's single, direct address to the Welsh reads as an exhortation of his own people, thus using the ancient Welsh as a metaphorical vehicle for his modern target audience: "Why, you slothful race, weighed down by your terrible sins, why with your continual thirst for civil war have you weakened yourself so much by internal strife? You once subjected far-off realms to your power, but are now unable to protect your land, wives and children from your foes, so that you resemble a vineyard once good, but now turned sour."[112] This long speech reiterates again and again the

---

109   *DGB*, xi.205.

110   *DGB*, xi.207.592–94: "Barbarie etiam irrepente, iam non uocabantur Britones sed Gualenses, uocabulum siue a Gualone duce eorum siue a Galaes regina siue a barbarie trahentes."

111   See J. Bosworth, "An Anglo-Saxon Dictionary Online", ed. T.N. Toller et al., Prague, 2010, <http://bosworth.ff.cuni.cz/034770> (accessed 31 May 2018), s.v. *wealh*, I: "a foreigner, properly a Celt (cf. the name *Volcae*, a Celtic tribe mentioned by Caesar), Walch, *barbarus*".

112   *DGB*, xi.185.141–45: "Quid, ociosa gens pondere inmanium scelerum oppressa, quid semper ciuilia proelia siciens tete domesticis in tantum debilitasti motibus, quae cum prius longe posita regna potestati tuae subdidisses nunc uelut bona uinea degenerata in amaritudinem uersa patriam, coniuges, liberos nequeas ab inimicis tueri?"

evils of civil war and the failure of imperial designs in light of internal discord. Indeed, it seems that many of Geoffrey's complaints against the Britons/Welsh operate as appeals to his contemporary Norman audience. For Geoffrey, who completed the *DGB* in 1136 under the patronage of Robert of Gloucester, a key player in the English civil war of 1135–57, internal strife was a major problem. Because of these well-documented concerns over England's sovereignty, the *DGB*'s portrayal of race cannot be extricated from its historical context. While the text's criticisms of Welsh disunity have been read as anti-Welsh, they seem to be anti-civil war, speaking to the chaos-inducing wars between Robert of Gloucester, the Empress Matilda, and Stephen of Blois. For Geoffrey, imperialism functions at its best when intermarriage allows the conquerors to mix seamlessly with the native population.[113] While some races are unworthy of such mixing, the glorious heritage of the Welsh make them worthy of hybridization with their new conquerors.

Although hybridity can be an important facilitator of empire, there are subaltern peoples who exist beyond the pale of racial acceptability in Geoffrey's world. By showing who these peoples are, and replacing the Welsh with the Saxons as internal European Other, Geoffrey negotiates the Welsh into a relatively elevated position in the growing Norman empire. Furthermore, in a tripartite world, the *DGB* develops an early model of Eurocentric history, orienting Britain as prestigious enough to take up an influential role in European government. In turn, Europe emerges as the central point of Geoffrey's history. Ultimately, Geoffrey replaces Isidore's model of geohumoral race with the concept of race as situational and malleable, legitimizing the process of hybridization, though excepting peoples beyond the pale. The various racial boundaries both deconstructed and established in the *DGB* enjoyed long afterlives, with Geoffrey's foundational text paving the way for the development of the *homo europaeus*[114] and for a nascent imperial British consciousness.

---

113   It is possible that Geoffrey's positive attitude toward intermarriage is directly related to the marriages of the Empress Matilda. See M. Chibnall, *The Empress Matilda: Queen Consort, Queen Mother and Lady of the English*, Oxford and Cambridge, MA, 1991.

114   Heng, *Invention*, p. 24.

CHAPTER 14

Religion and the Church in Geoffrey of Monmouth

Barry Lewis

Few authors inspire as many conflicting interpretations as Geoffrey of Monmouth. On one proposition, however, something close to a consensus reigns: Geoffrey of Monmouth wrote history in a manner that shows remarkable indifference toward religion and the institutional church. Antonia Gransden, in her fundamental survey of medieval English historical writing, says that "the tone of his work is predominantly secular" and even that he "abandoned the Christian intention of historical writing" and "had no moral, edificatory purpose", while J.S.P. Tatlock, author of what is still the fullest study of Geoffrey, speaks of a "highly intelligent, rational and worldly personality" who shows "almost no interest in monachism ... nor in miracles", nor indeed in "religion, theology, saints, popes, even ecclesiastics in general".[1] Yet, even if these claims reflect a widely shared view, it is nonetheless startling that they should be made about a writer who lived in the first half of the 12th century. Some commentators find Geoffrey's work so divergent from the norms of earlier medieval historiography that they are reluctant to treat him as a historian at all. Gransden flatly describes him as "a romance writer masquerading as an historian".[2] More cautiously, Matilda Bruckner names Geoffrey among those Latin historians who paved the way for romance by writing a secular-minded form of history "tending to pull away from the religious model (derived from Augustine and Orosius) that had viewed human history largely within the scheme of salvation".[3]

This Christian tradition of historiography, against which Geoffrey of Monmouth is said to have rebelled, had its origins in late antiquity in the works of Eusebius, Augustine, and Orosius. Leaving aside the important differences between these authors, their legacy may be summarized as follows. History had a clear beginning in Creation, and it would come to an equally clear end with the final Judgement. Everything that happened between those two points

---

1 A. Gransden, *Historical Writing in England, c.550–c.1307*, London, 1974, pp. 187, 204, 207; Tatlock, *LHB*, pp. 257, 446. I am grateful to Ben Guy for his comments on a draft of this article, and to Daniel Watson for references provided. The views expressed are my own.

2 Gransden, *Historical Writing in England, c.550–c.1307*, p. 202.

3 M.T. Bruckner, "The Shape of Romance in Medieval France", in R.L. Krueger (ed.), *The Cambridge Companion to Medieval Romance*, Cambridge, 2000, pp. 13–28, at p. 35.

was worthy of examination solely for what it revealed of the unfolding of God's will, and events were to be interpreted in terms of sin, punishment, and redemption. Early medieval authors adapted this framework for writing the history of individual peoples by showing how each nation achieved membership of the universal Christian church. In this providential view of history, there was room for the exemplary function – the idea that history provided models of good behavior to be imitated and of bad behavior to be avoided – but the emphasis was on the unfolding of God's plan.

In different ways, all of Geoffrey of Monmouth's predecessors – Gildas, Bede, and the author of the *Historia Brittonum* – subscribed to this tradition by setting the history of Britain within the wider story of salvation. Geoffrey, according to much modern commentary, turned away from their preoccupation with providence. He was not a preacher, nor did he attempt a church history, and while the author of the *Historia Brittonum* chose to start from the creation of the world, Geoffrey's work opens with the pagan heroes of Troy. Yet beyond the mere consensus that Geoffrey wrote a new, more secular kind of history, opinions begin to diverge sharply. If his aim was not to expound the role of God in shaping events, what was it? Some have argued for political motives, often quite incompatible ones: either to endow the Anglo-Norman kingdom of England with a lengthy and glorious past, or to justify Norman rule over Wales, or alternatively to assert the ancient dignity of the Britons and their descendants, the Welsh, or else to advance the interests of those numerous Bretons who had crossed the Channel as part of the conquering Norman aristocracy. Others emphasize intellectual, literary, and personal motives, but these too are very varied: to make a career for himself by revolutionizing the tradition of English historiography, to disparage monastic values, even just to amuse himself at the expense of his readers. A particularly influential strain of criticism sees Geoffrey's rebellion as a philosophical one. His work, so it is argued, shows how history proceeds through the interaction of human desires and weaknesses with the caprices of blind fortune. Regimes and dynasties are intrinsically fragile and prone to failure and replacement by others. In Robert Hanning's phrase, Geoffrey chose to write a story of "great men on a great wheel".[4] Siân Echard has questioned whether Geoffrey accepted that historical events reflected the workings of divine justice at all.[5]

---

4   R.W. Hanning, *The Vision of History in Early Britain: From Gildas to Geoffrey of Monmouth*, New York, 1966, p. 121.

5   S. Echard, *Arthurian Narrative in the Latin Tradition* (Cambridge Studies in Medieval Literature, 36), Cambridge, 1998, ch. 1 passim.

So closely is medieval historiography bound to the providential model that Geoffrey of Monmouth's work can appear too anomalous to discuss within the boundaries of the genre. Those who see Geoffrey as a proto-romancer and precursor of Chrétien de Troyes set him within the context of the literature of the royal and aristocratic courts of the 12th century, courts that attracted authors who, like Geoffrey, were secular clerks rather than monks. Looking to the past for models of aristocratic self-definition, they turned to the pagan antiquity described so vividly in the Latin classics. Some of the earliest romances explored the values of courtly society through the adventures of Alexander and the events of the Trojan War. If medieval historians looked to the past to discern the will of God, authors of romances reimagined it in terms of the culture and values of their aristocratic audiences. Geoffrey might be seen as a transitional figure, writing the Latin prose of the historian but conveying the spirit of the romancer. Francis Ingledew has argued that Geoffrey expresses a new "genealogical construction of history" in the service of the Anglo-Norman aristocracy, who traced their roots literally back to Troy, as did the Britons:[6] such a view would suggest that Virgil's *Aeneid* shaped Geoffrey's account of British origins more profoundly than the Old Testament.

DGB is not, however, a romance. It is in Latin, and claims for itself the genre of history: Geoffrey famously cites Gildas and Bede as his predecessors, and William of Malmesbury, Henry of Huntingdon, and Caradog of Llancarfan as his colleagues. If we wish to discuss how, or even whether, his concept of history differs from theirs, then we will have to consider the role of God in Geoffrey's narrative and the respective importance of providence, chance, and human agency in shaping the flow of events. Each one of the interpretations which I have mentioned so far concedes that Geoffrey was detached from the concerns of providential history; some even suggest that he barely allowed any role to God in guiding events. In this chapter I shall scrutinize this proposition. I shall argue that is possible to go too far in secularizing Geoffrey of Monmouth. His work, like that of his predecessors, shows a strong interest in religious history and in the place of the Britons within the unfolding story of salvation, and he does not, in the end, emancipate himself from a providential view of events.

---

6 F. Ingledew, "The Book of Troy and the Genealogical Construction of History: The Case of Geoffrey of Monmouth's *Historia regum Britanniae*", *Speculum* 69:3 (1994), 665–704.

1   **Pagan Britain**

The first four books of the *DGB* are set in the pagan past. The British nation is
traced back to Brutus, a great-grandson of Aeneas. Brutus is born in Italy but
is exiled after he accidentally kills his father with an arrow. He visits Greece,
Africa, and Aquitaine, winning battles and gaining supporters on the way. On
an island called Leogetia he discovers a temple of Diana and receives from the
goddess a prophecy that he will found a second Troy in an island in the ocean,
that is, in Britain. Brutus and his followers duly land in Britain, clear it of the
giants who were its only inhabitants, and found a kingdom. Brutus and his successors rule for many centuries. During this time, all of them are pagans and
are presented as such; occasional synchronisms with biblical events remind
us that this all happens long before the time of Christ. Geoffrey accepts the
paganism of his characters without comment or explicit disapproval. Among
the achievements of his British kings he notes the building of temples and
the proper conduct of sacrifices. At least one king, Belinus, is cremated. The
influence of classical texts is apparent in these early books, especially Virgil's
Aeneid. Such texts provided ample sources for pagan ritual, so that Geoffrey
was able to describe sacrifices in some detail, notably when Brutus and his
companions worship Jupiter, Mercury, and Diana on Leogetia.[7] In contrast,
the burial of several of the kings within cities, and even in or near temples,
is a medieval Christian conception, for in pagan times bodies were buried in
cemeteries outside city walls and would have been regarded as a pollution in
spaces consecrated to the gods.[8] Geoffrey resembles other 12th-century authors in showing a strong tendency to view the pagan past as analogous in
many respects to the Christian present.[9] This extends to the occasional reference within these early chapters to God or to a single creator.[10] Similarly,
pagan figures are judged by the same moral standards as contemporary ones.
So Geoffrey's good kings are notable for pursuing justice, passing equitable
laws, making peace between disputants, laying out roads, and founding cities

7   *DGB*, i.16.280–315. For discussion, see Tatlock, *LHB*, p. 261.
8   Tatlock, *LHB*, p. 260. An example is Dunuallo Molmutius, buried in Trinovantum "prope
     templum Concordiae", "near the temple of Harmony" (*DGB*, ii.34.336–37).
9   On this phenomenon see H. Phillips, "Medieval Classical Romances: The Perils of
     Inheritance", in R. Field, P. Hardman, and M. Sweeney (eds.), *Christianity and Romance in
     Medieval England*, Cambridge, 2010, pp. 13–25.
10   *DGB*, iii.41.134, 57.76, and iv.63.255–57. J. Marenbon, *Pagans and Philosophers: The Problem
     of Paganism from Augustine to Leibnitz*, Princeton and Oxford, 2015, p. 70 has character-
     ized Geoffrey's treatment of paganism, like that in many romances, as "incidental": that
     is, he does not raise any of the theological and moral difficulties that Marenbon gathers
     under the heading "the Problem of Paganism".

and temples. Bad kings engage in sodomy and are ripped to pieces by wolves, or practice necromancy and fall to their deaths.[11] Even in these cases, Geoffrey avoids explicit moralizing, simply allowing the fate that befell these kings to speak for itself. Of course, the pagan kings of Britain lived in the period before Christ and could not know the truth, though they might pursue natural justice; Marcia, queen to the equitable king Guithelinus, for instance, creates her "Marcian Law" *proprio ingenio*, "through her own devising".[12] This allows their achievements to be safely claimed for the British nation: the founding of famous cities such as London and Leicester, the development of roads, even the sanctuary rights of churches, which are supposed to derive from similar rights assigned to the pagan temples by King Dunuallo.[13] Only with the conversion of the Britons to Christianity does a clearly negative view of paganism emerge.

2   Conversion to Christianity, and the Establishment of a British Church

At the end of Book IIII, at a date still deep within the period of Roman domination, the Britons convert to Christianity. Learning of the miracles being performed by Christians in other lands, the British king Lucius writes to Pope Eleutherius asking for a mission. In response, the pope sends two teachers named Faganus and Duvianus, who baptize both the king and his people. The pagan temples are turned into churches. Geoffrey asserts that there was already a religious hierarchy in pagan Britain, consisting of twenty-eight *flamines* overseen by three *archiflamines* whose seats were at London, York, and Caerleon in Wales. In classical times, a *flamen* was a priest who served a particular pagan deity, but here he is a figure who has authority over lesser religious functionaries (described as "the remaining spiritual advisors and temple-servants") and thus foreshadows the role of the Christian bishop.[14] The *archiflamen* (not a classical term) in turn resembles a Christian archbishop. Indeed, upon conversion each *flamen* is replaced by a bishop, and each *archiflamen* by an archbishop. Once this arrangement has received the pope's approval, King Lucius further demonstrates his piety by handing over the landed wealth of the temples to the new churches.

---

11   *DGB*, ii.26.80–84 (Mempricius), 30.130–34 (Bladud).
12   *DGB*, iii.47.258.
13   *DGB*, ii.34.328–33.
14   *DGB*, iiii.72.415–16: "ceteri iudices morum atque phanatici".

Geoffrey's account of the conversion of the Britons is a developed form of
the Lucius legend. The story that a British king called Lucius wrote a letter
to the pope first appeared in the collection of short papal biographies known
as the *Book of the Popes* (*Liber Pontificalis*), from where it was taken up in the
8th century by Bede.[15] By the early 9th century the story had found its way to
Wales: it appears in the *Historia Brittonum* of 829 or 830, probably drawn from
Bede.[16] As is now well established, the real Lucius was a king of Edessa in Syria,
and the connection with Britain is spurious.[17] The Lucius legend filled a gap
in the historiography of the Britons by offering a legend of conversion on the
typical medieval model: a top-down, king- and missionary-centered account
in which the ruler's conversion is followed naturally by the conversion of his
whole realm and the founding of churches. It is the model familiar from Bede's
description of the conversion of the English kingdoms. Bede, however, had allowed Lucius a mere few lines, dismissed the Britons as defective Christians,
and devoted the rest of his work to the new, orthodox church of the English.
Geoffrey provides the entire British people with a church with claims to roots
older than those of its English supplanter and a hierarchy more venerable than
anything that derived from the mission of Augustine to Kent in 597.

The Lucian mission secured the claim of the British church to antiquity and
to Roman orthodoxy. Geoffrey, though, was concerned with more than these
requirements: he wanted to reconstruct the organization of the ancient British
church. It has been shown that his source for the older pagan hierarchy of
flamines and *archiflamines* and their replacement by Christian bishoprics was
probably the 9th-century Pseudo-Isidorian *Decretals*, mediated through some
text of canon law.[18] Such an idea would interact powerfully with Geoffrey's own
interest in ancient British geography. Throughout the *DGB*, Geoffrey attempts
to reverse what he saw as the developments since the English conquests, so
as to return to a presumed earlier dispensation. Thus, places with obvious

15   Bede, *Ecclesiastical History* i.4 and v.24, ed. and trans. B. Colgrave and R.A.B. Mynors,
     Bede's Ecclesiastical History of the English People, Oxford, 1969, rev. ed., Oxford, 1991,
     pp. 24-25 and 562-63, and *On the Reckoning of Time* lxvi.331, ll. 1164-65, ed. C.W. Jones,
     Bedae Venerabilis opera, VI: *Opera didascalia* 2, Turnhout, 1977, pp. 239-545, at p. 501.
16   *Historia Brittonum* §22, ed. Faral, *LLA*, vol. 3, pp. 2-62, at p. 19; D.N. Dumville, "*Historia
     Brittonum*: An Insular History from the Carolingian Age", in A. Scharer and G. Scheibelreiter
     (eds.), *Historiographie im frühen Mittelalter*, Wien, 1994, pp. 406-34, at pp. 432-44, dis-
     cusses the likely influence of Bede over the *Historia Brittonum*, though not this passage.
17   A. Harnack, "Der Brief des britischen Königs Lucius an den Papst Eleutherus",
     Sitzungsberichte der königlich-preussischen Akademie der Wissenschaften (1904), 909-16.
18   E. Jones, "Geoffrey of Monmouth's Account of the Establishment of Episcopacy in
     Britain", *JEGP* 40 (1941), 360-63; S. Williams, "Geoffrey of Monmouth and the Canon Law",
     Speculum 27:2 (1952), 184-90.

upstanding Roman remains, but which were of little consequence in Geoffrey's time, could be rehabilitated as great centers of ancient British life: Silchester and Caerleon are examples. Another key source was the list of the 28 cities of Britain, found in *Historia Brittonum*.[19] That bishoprics should be established in major towns was a well-known principle in Geoffrey's time. By combining this idea with the evidence for earlier cities, both written and archaeological, Geoffrey was able to locate the ancient bishoprics of the Britons in centers where no bishop sat in his day. The idea that the metropolitans should be in London and York was derived from Bede.[20] Like the rest of the geography of the *DGB*, Geoffrey's church hierarchy appears at once familiar and strange. Its foreignness to the actual hierarchy of the 12th century subtly undermines the authority of the English dispensation.

A further striking feature is the third province, covering Wales. The existence of such a province was a matter of lively dispute in Geoffrey's time. The see of St Davids, in south-west Wales, had a long-standing claim to lead a separate Welsh province. It was a central argument of the *Life of St David*, composed by Rhygyfarch in the 1080s or 1090s, that David had been elevated to an archbishopric, either by the Patriarch of Jerusalem, or at a famous synod held at Llanddewibrefi in mid-Wales, at which David preached against the Pelagian heretics and was acknowledged to be head of the British church.[21] The first Norman bishop of St Davids, Bernard (1115–48), made a determined effort to secure recognition as metropolitan of a Welsh province. His efforts were resisted, however, by the south-eastern Welsh see of Llandaff. A Llandaff text, *De primo statu Landavensis ecclesie* ("On the First Condition of the Church of Llandaff"), written probably in the 1120s, insisted that Llandaff's first bishop, Dubricius (Welsh *Dyfrig*), ruled a province extending over all of South Wales.[22]

---

19   *Historia Brittonum* §66a, ed. Faral, LLA, vol. 3, pp. 57–58.

20   Bede, *Ecclesiastical History* i.29, ed. and trans. Colgrave and Mynors, pp. 104–07. These were the locations originally selected by Pope Gregory, though political realities led to a different arrangement.

21   See Rhygyfarch ap Sulien, *Life of St David* §46, ed. and trans. R. Sharpe and J.R. Davies, "Rhygyfarch's *Life* of St David", in J.W. Evans and J.M. Wooding (eds.), *St David of Wales: Cult, Church and Nation*, Woodbridge, 2007, pp. 107–55, at pp. 140–41, for the patriarch making David an archbishop, but there are signs that this is a clumsy alteration from Rhygyfarch's earlier version in which he was merely made a bishop, cf. §49, so that the granting of the archbishopric was reserved for the Synod of Brefi (§53); this better suits the structure of the *Life*, which presents the synod as the climax of his career.

22   *De primo statu Landavensis ecclesie*, ed. J.G. Evans and J. Rhŷs, *The Text of the Book of Llan Dâv: Reproduced from the Gwysaney Manuscript*, Oxford, 1893, pp. 68–71, at p. 69. For the date, see W. Davies, "*Liber Landavensis*: its Construction and Credibility", EHR 88 (1973), 335–51, at pp. 338–39.

Further, and very powerful, opposition came from Canterbury, which claimed the Welsh sees for itself. In the end, it would be Canterbury that emerged as the victor, terminating hopes for a separate Welsh province, but that outcome was far from settled when Geoffrey wrote.

If the Welsh province was an idea current in Geoffrey's time, his decision to place its see in Caerleon was definitely not. Why did Geoffrey make such a drastic intervention in the ecclesiastical history of Wales? No source is known, but Shafer Williams pointed out that texts of canon law, such as undoubtedly supplied the pseudo-historical terms *flamen* and *archiflamen*, were often accompanied by lists of bishops' sees.[23] It is conceivable that, if Geoffrey encountered such a list, it may have contained a name bearing some resemblance to *Urbs Legionum* (Caerleon). On the other hand, Geoffrey had already attached great importance to Caerleon during the pagan period, and famously he would also choose it as the location of Arthur's magnificent feast, the culmination of his reign.[24] The place undoubtedly mattered greatly to Geoffrey. John Gillingham has argued that he had an eye on political developments in south-east Wales, especially after the death of Henry I; in 1136 a local Welsh dynasty captured Caerleon and re-established Welsh power in a region that had seemed lost to Anglo-Norman encroachment.[25] This may well have been a factor, though it is plausible that he had already been led to ponder on the place by the remarkable upstanding Roman remains, which he mentions ("in Caerleon, whose site beside the river Usk in Glamorgan is marked by ancient walls and buildings").[26] Add to this the fact that *Urbs Legionum* is one of the very few places mentioned by Gildas, in connection with the martyrdom of SS Julius and Aaron, and the temptation to make it a place of major importance may have been great.[27] As a choice, it is quite consistent with Geoffrey's general use of textual and archaeological evidence to redraw the map of ancient Britain.

---

23   S. Williams, "Geoffrey of Monmouth", pp. 188–89, n. 17.

24   *DGB*, iii.44.218–23 and ix.156–62.

25   J. Gillingham, "The Context and Purposes of Geoffrey of Monmouth's *History of the Kings of Britain*", *Anglo-Norman Studies* 13 (1990), 99–118 (repr. in id. (ed.), *The English in the Twelfth Century: Imperialism, National Identity and Political Values*, Woodbridge, 2000, pp. 19–39, at pp. 35–36).

26   *DGB*, iiii.72.419–21: "in Vrbe Legionum, quam super Oscam fluuium in Glamorgantia ueteres muri et aedificia sitam fuisse testantur".

27   Gildas, *The Ruin of Britain* i.10, ed. and trans. M. Winterbottom, *Gildas: The Ruin of Britain and Other Works* (Arthurian Period Sources, 7), Chichester, 1978, p. 92. In *DGB*, ix.156.318–22 these two saints are the dedicatees of two magnificent churches at Caerleon.

Christopher Brooke viewed the choice of Caerleon as so bizarre as to suggest that Geoffrey was deliberately mocking both St Davids and Llandaff.[28] From our viewpoint the choice is indeed historically inaccurate, but we have seen that Geoffrey had his reasons. Nothing suggests that Caerleon was chosen to slight any other place. Llandaff, it is true, was bound to suffer in comparison because it was too near to Caerleon, and too lacking in obvious Roman credentials, to be imagined as a bishop's seat in its own right. Hence Geoffrey appropriated its founder-saint, Dyfrig, to be his archbishop of Caerleon, and demoted the other important Llandaff saint, Teilo, from a bishop to *illustris presbyter Landaviae*, "distinguished priest of Llandaff".[29] St Davids, on the other hand, could have found little in the *DGB* to complain about. It is described very positively as David's favorite monastery, founded by no less a figure than St Patrick, while David too receives lavish praise.[30] Moreover, the *PM* indicates that St Davids inherited the glorious primatial tradition that Geoffrey created for Caerleon.[31] Accepting these ideas would compel considerable, and no doubt painful, surgery to St Davids' own traditions, as we shall see presently, but there is no case for saying that the *DGB* sets out to denigrate St Davids or to cast doubt on its right to lead a Welsh province. The essence of Geoffrey's claim is that the British church was much older and more venerable than the English one, and that led him to trace its structures back far earlier than the 6th-century David. The geography of Geoffrey's British church is not, I suggest, a challenge to any of the Welsh churches of the day. It is a challenge to Bede and to the English viewpoint that he represented.

3   Geoffrey's Conversion Story in the Light of Other 12th-Century Versions

Thus far it has been assumed that Geoffrey's account of the British church was his own creation. I believe this to be essentially correct, but the Lucius legend was topical in Geoffrey's time, so the question of what he may have drawn from the work of others must be addressed. Bede simply stated that Lucius

---

28   C.N.L. Brooke, *The Church and the Welsh Border in the Central Middle Ages*, ed. D.N. Dumville (Studies in Celtic History, 8), Woodbridge, 1986, p. 24.

29   *DGB*, ix.158.407–08. Note, though, that Teilo is treated with great respect and is made arch-bishop of Dol in Brittany, an idea that is implied in the Book of Llandaff *Life of St Teilo*, ed. J.G. Evans and J. Rhŷs, *The Text of the Book of Llan Dâv: Reproduced from the Gwysaney Manuscript*, Oxford, 1893, pp. 97–117, at p. 112, ll. 5–6.

30   *DGB*, ix.158.405–06 (on David); xi.179.90–93 (on St Davids).

31   *DGB*, vii.112.48–49.

obtained what he had requested, but 12th-century writers add that a mission was sent from Rome to Britain and are interested in the names and activities of the missionaries. The relations between the various accounts have proved to be contentious. Here the question is whether Geoffrey responded to Bede alone or whether he had seen more recent versions of the story.

One of these new versions is given by William of Malmesbury in his *The Early History of Glastonbury* (c.1129). Unfortunately, the *Early History* was heavily interpolated during the 13th century, making it difficult to be certain how much of the account is William's own, but an excerpt added to some manuscripts of his *Deeds of the English Kings* allows us to be fairly certain of his original wording, in this section at least.[32] William makes no mention of a church hierarchy: his only interest is in the belief that the missionaries sent to Lucius founded the first church at Glastonbury, on account of which their fame shall endure, even though the passage of time has carried away their names. This absence of names suggests that the tale was still very much under development when William of Malmesbury wrote, for the other versions are not shy to name the men in question. There is nothing in William's account which suggests that Geoffrey drew on it in particular.

A second account forms the opening section of the anonymous *De primo statu Landavensis ecclesie*, mentioned earlier.[33] This tract from Llandaff names the missionaries as *Elvanus* and *Meduuinus* and insists that they were Britons sent to Rome as part of Lucius's original delegation. Unlike William of Malmesbury, the author of the *De primo statu* does not explicitly link the missionaries to the church on whose behalf he was writing. Nevertheless, Medwin may be associated with Llanfedw, near Llandaff, though Elfan has not been identified.[34] The *De primo statu* employs the Lucius story as a kind of preamble to its main matter, which is an account of the later mission of St Germanus of Auxerre and St Lupus of Troyes to Britain in 429 in order to combat the Pelagian heresy. It is to St Germanus, not the earlier Lucian mission, that Llandaff and

---

32 A reconstruction of William's original wording is given in William of Malmesbury, *The Early History of Glastonbury*, ed. J. Scott, *The Early History of Glastonbury: An Edition, Translation and Study of William of Malmesbury's De Antiquitate Glastonie Ecclesie*, Woodbridge, 1981, p. 168. For the much expanded later text see ibid., pp. 46–51; parts of this derive from Geoffrey.

33 *De primo statu Landavensis ecclesie*, ed. Evans and Rhŷs, p. 68.

34 Early attestations of *Llanfedw*, e.g. *Landivedon* (1281), seem to contain the hypocoristic element *ty-*, thus suggesting that the rest is a saint's name rather than the common noun *bedw* "birch trees". See the Melville Richards archive of Welsh place-names, *Cronfa Ddata Enwau Lleoedd: Archif Melville Richards* [Place-name database: the Melville Richards archive], <http://www.e-gymraeg.co.uk/enwaulleoedd/amr> (accessed 27 March 2017), s.v. *Llanfedw*.

its privileges are traced. Even so, the Lucian preamble conveys the idea that British Christianity had a continuous history from ancient times, a theme which is developed far more explicitly by Geoffrey. It also broaches the idea of a church hierarchy, but it offers no detail beyond the bare statement that an *ecclesiasticum ordinem*, "ecclesiastical structure", was founded and bishops ordained; it lacks any mention of Geoffrey's *flamines* or *archiflamines*. In both Geoffrey and the *De primo statu* the number of missionaries is two, a figure which does not appear in the uninterpolated *Early History of Glastonbury*. This suggests some kind of link between Geoffrey and the Llandaff document. Bafflingly, the names of the missionaries are different, and yet those given by Geoffrey still suggest Llandaff influence. His *Faganus* is certainly Ffagan of St Fagan's, a parish that borders on Llandaff, and *Duvianus* is in all likelihood Dyfan of Merthyr Dyfan, a few miles to the south-west. It is hard to see these names as other than chosen in the interests of Llandaff, yet in Llandaff's own account, as we have just seen, the missionaries are called Medwin and Elfan.[35] There is no obvious reason why Geoffrey should have altered the names, so the conclusion suggests itself that he was following a different source, not now extant, but which should also have come from Llandaff. Why there should be two different sets of names for the Lucian missionaries, both apparently invented to suit Llandaff, remains a mystery.

Yet another version of the Lucius legend is found in a letter apparently sent by the chapter of the cathedral of St Davids to Pope Honorius II (1124–30).[36] The letter sets out the claims of St Davids to be an archbishopric and the metropolitan see of Wales. It calls the Lucian missionaries *Faganus* and *Duvianus*, as in Geoffrey. Unlike Geoffrey, it identifies the third, Welsh archbishopric with St Davids, a decision which leads the writer into considerable historical difficulties. Nevertheless, the letter's insistence that St Davids was founded during the Lucian mission establishes primacy over Llandaff which, as we saw above, did not make such a grandiose claim. To judge by the dates of Pope Honorius, this letter precedes Geoffrey by some years. Indeed, it could be the lost source followed by Geoffrey; this was the conclusion accepted by Christopher Brooke

---

35 Neither St Fagan's nor Merthyr Dyfan is attested until after Geoffrey's time, so the possibility must be admitted that they took their names from Geoffrey; in which case, Geoffrey's source is wholly obscure. However, Merthyr Dyfan belongs to a type of name that was obsolescent in the 12th century (D. Parsons, *Martyrs and Memorials: Merthyr Place-Names and the Church in Early Wales*, Aberystwyth, 2013, p. 40), and is most unlikely to be a late coinage.

36 Gerald of Wales, *Invectives* ii.10, ed. W.S. Davies, "De Invectionibus", *Y Cymmrodor* 30 (1920), 1–248, at pp. 143–46.

and later by John Reuben Davies.[37] The implications are profound, for the letter contains many more similarities to Geoffrey's account, such as the story of the replacement of the pagan hierarchy and the idea that there were three archbishoprics. If Geoffrey took from the letter not only the minor detail of *Faganus* and *Duvianus*, but these important ideas as well, then most of his vision of the early British church would have to be seen as a St Davids invention.

There are compelling reasons for rejecting this theory. The letter is extant only in a collection made by Gerald of Wales in the early 13th century. Why would a writer, working in the 1120s in the interests of St Davids, choose the names *Faganus* and *Duvianus* which take us so infallibly back to Llandaff? The likelihood must be that the author found them in an existing source and felt compelled to use them. That points to Llandaff – or to Geoffrey. It is possible that the St Davids writer used the same, lost Llandaff source that, I have argued above, lies behind Geoffrey's account. However, further problems in the letter point to Geoffrey himself as the source. In Geoffrey's scheme, the Welsh archbishopric lay at Caerleon and only later passed to St Davids; David himself was archbishop of Caerleon, not St Davids, which was merely a favorite monastery of his, and he was himself preceded in the archbishopric by St Dyfrig. In contrast, St Davids' tradition, as seen in Rhygyfarch's *Life of St David*, was that David first founded his church and that it was later elevated to the status of an archbishopric on account of David's stellar performance at the Synod of Brefi. The letter-writer has sacrificed these cherished ideas in order to accommodate what Geoffrey says. He does not mention Caerleon by name nor refer to the transfer of the archbishopric. That allows him to imply that St Davids was the seat of the Welsh archbishops from the beginning and to accommodate the idea that Dyfrig was David's predecessor, but it forces him to abandon the idea that David founded St Davids.[38] The whole story of the Synod of Brefi is also lost since it could not sit with the idea of a much older, Lucian archbishopric. The writer has done a heroic job of absorbing the DGB and turning it to his own purposes, but the costs were severe. When we see that the letter explicitly refers to the Welsh archbishopric as the third *in textu historiarum*, it

---

37   Brooke, *The Church and the Welsh Border*, p. 22 and n. 26; J.R. Davies, *The Book of Llandaf and the Norman Church in Wales*, Woodbridge, 2003, p. 110. Davies has become less sure in "Cathedrals and the Cult of Saints in Eleventh- and Twelfth-Century Wales", in P. Dalton, C. Insley, and L.J. Wilkinson (eds.), *Cathedrals, Communities and Conflict in the Anglo-Norman World*, Woodbridge, 2011, pp. 99–115, at pp. 102–03, esp. n. 103, where he cautiously acknowledges that the letter is indebted to Geoffrey.

38   Gerald of Wales, *Invectives* ii.10, ed. Davies, p. 143: "Ad cuius sedem ... beatus Dauid ... legitur fuisse archipresul consecratus", "to which see ... we read that the blessed David ... was consecrated archbishop".

is hard to avoid the conclusion that the author is citing Geoffrey's book, which does indeed name Caerleon in third place.[39] It is conceivable that parts of Geoffrey's work were already circulating in the late 1120s, in time to be used by the writer of the letter to Honorius; certainly Geoffrey's views on the status of Caerleon must have been formed by the time he came to write the *PM*, since it is mentioned in it, and the prophecies circulated a few years before *DGB* was finished around 1138. More likely, however, is that the letter as we have it is a later product, and suspicion must fall on Gerald of Wales.[40]

The theory that the St Davids letter was Geoffrey's main source throughout his account of the conversion must be rejected. It seems rather that he used a version of the Lucius legend from Llandaff, containing the names *Faganus* and *Duvianus*, but otherwise probably similar to the existing *De primo statu Landavensis ecclesie*, hence the importance of St Dyfrig in Geoffrey's vision. The hierarchy, especially the three metropolitan sees, was his own creation, for the same text shows that Llandaff never evolved a clear sense of itself at the head of a Welsh province; that was a St Davids concept, but one which Geoffrey transformed following his own priorities. Geoffrey, too, was the first author explicitly to trace the Welsh hierarchy as far back as the time of King Lucius. What emerges, then, is that Geoffrey was neither a passive recipient of the church history written by his contemporaries, nor an irreligious joker intent on subverting it. Rather, he had a coherent vision of the early British church, formed by reading his sources in a spirit of opposition, or at least one-upmanship, with regard to the English church. His vision was serious enough to persuade a later advocate of St Davids to recast the traditions of his church as profoundly as we see in the so-called "letter to Pope Honorius".

---

39   Thus I would translate *in textu historiarum* as "in the text of the *Histories*", cf. *DGB*, ix.156.321–22, 332–33: "terciam metropolitanam sedem Britanniae habebat ... Trium etiam metropolitanarum sedium archipraesules, Lundoniensis uidelicet atque Eboracensis nec non et ex Vrbe Legionum Dubricius", "Britain had three metropolitan sees ... also the three archbishops of the metropolitan sees, namely, of London and York, and also from Caerleon, Dubricius" (translation adapted from Wright). See also *St Davids Episcopal Acta, 1085–1280*, ed. J. Barrow, Cardiff, 1998, p. 4, who also regards the letter as dependent on Geoffrey.

40   This is denied by Brooke, *The Church and the Welsh Border*, p. 22, n. 26. He acknowledges that the letter diverges greatly from other St Davids sources, but does not account for the divergence. I suggest that the writer was assimilating a rival version that was too influential to ignore. That is a fair description of the status of Geoffrey's work c.1200, but it is doubtful whether it would be the case before the full publication of the *DGB*. Gerald's use of Geoffrey is well-attested, notably in the account of Welsh Christian origins which he wrote himself (Gerald of Wales, *Invectives* ii.1, ed. Davies, pp. 130–35).

4   The Continuity of the British Church

The unbroken tradition of the British church is a major theme of Geoffrey's
DGB. Repeatedly, at points in his story where his sources raised uncomfortable
hints of discontinuity, Geoffrey took pains to smooth over the cracks. Recasting
Gildas's account of the Diocletianic persecution, he attributes the blame for carrying out the persecution in Britain to a Roman official, Maximianus Herculius,
implicitly exonerating the British king Asclepiodotus who was reigning at the
time.[41] Another awkward moment was the mission of Germanus and Lupus,
who came to Britain to combat the Pelagian heresy in 429. The mission occupies four chapters in Bede, but Geoffrey ruthlessly disposes of it in a few lines,
incidentally shifting part of the blame for the poor state of British Christianity
onto the Saxon pagans.[42]

It is, however, in Geoffrey's long account of the battle for supremacy between the Britons and the Saxon invaders that the unbroken thread of British
Christianity is to be seen most clearly. From the outset, great emphasis is laid
on the pagan religion of the newcomers. The moment when the British king
Vortigern learns that they are not Christians is described vividly: Hengist states
that "Mercury" led them to Britain, and Vortigern, hearing the name, lifts up
his head with sudden attention and asks what religion they follow. On learning
that they worship many gods, and Mercury or Woden above all, he says: "Your
faith, or rather faithlessness, makes me truly sorry. Your coming, however, fills
me with joy, since God or some other has brought you at an opportune time
for my needs."[43] Hengist, by his own reckoning, had been guided to Britain by
his god Mercury or Woden. Vortigern doubts whether Mercury is a god or rather some other kind of power (*siue deus, siue alius* – I would translate *deus* as
"a god", without capitalization, here) yet he eagerly accepts the help of the pagans, hard pressed as he is by Pictish attacks and by the threat of invasion from
Brittany. Vortigern is not a pagan himself: of that Geoffrey leaves no doubt. He
is, rather, a Christian who deliberately allies himself with a pagan under the
control of demonic forces. Already Vortigern has shown great wickedness, first
in elevating the monk Constans to the throne against his monastic vows, and
then in having Constans murdered and usurping the throne himself. Allying
himself with Hengist, even while acknowledging the possibility that a demonic

---

41   *DGB*, v.77.103ff.

42   *DGB*, vi.101; Bede, *Ecclesiastical History* i.17–22, ed. and trans. Colgrave and Mynors,
      pp. 54–69.

43   *DGB*, vi.98.285–87: "De credulitate uestra, quae pocius incredulitas dici potest, uehement-
      er doleo. De aduentu autem uestro gaudeo, quia in congruo tempore uos necessitati meae
      siue deus siue alius optulit."

being lay behind his coming to Britain, marks a further step down into depravity. Yet Geoffrey sets the final descent into evil in Vortigern's sexual desire for Hengist's daughter, Ronwein. Again, Geoffrey leaves no room for ambiguity:

> Vortigern became drunk on various kinds of liquor and, as Satan entered into his heart, asked her father for the girl he loved. Satan, I repeat, had entered into his heart, for despite being a Christian he wanted to sleep with a pagan woman.[44]

Through Vortigern, a usurper who was never accepted as legitimate by a consensus of the Britons, but who tricked his way to the throne under a cloud of suspicion, the pagans are admitted into the Christian land of Britain. It is made clear that they could never have fought their way in against the united resistance of the Britons, neither were they accepted by the British people. Vortigern's role in the story is to be the tool of Satan whose sinful weakness explains how God's people came to be led astray in this way. It is a view already expressed in the 9th-century *Historia Brittonum*, to which Geoffrey's portrait of Vortigern is heavily indebted, but Geoffrey has enlarged on Vortigern's downward descent into evil.[45]

The subsequent struggle between the Britons and the Saxons is cast in terms both patriotic and religious, and amounts at times to holy war. The first leader of the British resistance is Vortigern's own son, Vortimer. He almost succeeds in expelling the Saxons entirely, but again the devil himself intervenes to cut short his success. The next deliverer, Aurelius Ambrosius, laments the fact that the Saxons have "destroyed our holy churches and wiped out the Christian faith almost from shore to shore".[46] Repeatedly, the victory of the Saxons is postponed. Vortimer restores the churches of Britain. Aurelius restores them again. The greatest of all the British leaders is, of course, Arthur. Before his great victory at Badon, Arthur himself assures his men that they will be victorious through the aid of Christ. Then Archbishop Dubricius addresses the army, employing all the rhetoric of the Crusade. Death in battle against pagans is no death, for it brings certainty of eternal life: such martyrdom washes away

---

44   *DGB*, vi.100.357–60: "Vortigernus autem, diuerso genere potus inebriatus, intrante Sathana in corde suo, amauit puellam et postulauit eam a patre suo. Intrauerat, inquam, Sathanas in corde suo quia cum Christianus esset cum pagana coire desiderabat."

45   Cf. *Historia Brittonum* §37, ed. Faral, *LLA*, vol. 3, p. 29: "intravit Satanas in corde Guorthigirni", "Satan entered into Vortigern's heart."

46   *DGB*, viii.119.49–50: "sacras ecclesias destruxit, et Christianitatem fere a mari usque ad mare deleuit."

all sins.[47] Now Arthur arms himself with his shield, on which is painted an image of the Virgin Mary, "to keep her memory always before his eyes".[48] Hard pressed at the crisis of the battle, Arthur triumphs when he calls out the name of the Virgin. He is the third, following Vortimer and Aurelius, to restore the churches of Britain after they have been devastated by the pagans.

As is the case in much other literature of the time, hatred of paganism does not preclude respect for the prowess and chivalry of the pagans. Often the Saxons are depicted as fighting bravely. Yet this merely magnifies all the more the Christians who vanquish them. Only during the reign of the disastrous tyrant Kareticus do the Saxons, aided by the African king Gormundus, finally overrun England and send the archbishops of London and York fleeing into Wales, Cornwall, and Brittany with the relics of their saints. Even then continuity is preserved in those marginal regions,[49] and there is to be one final flourish of British rule, under Caduallo and Cadualadrus, before the end.

The advent of Christianity among the Saxons was a moment fraught with difficulty for Geoffrey. Thus far, his treatment of the Saxons could follow familiar lines. They could either be dismissed as utter barbarians, or treated as individual men of honor and courage and as worthy opponents of the Britons, but still ultimately damned to hell. From this point, however, the religious chasm could not be so easily exploited. Geoffrey deals with the difficulty by a drastic rewriting of Bede's account.[50] The actual conversion of the English is dealt with as summarily as possible, and then the narrative moves immediately to the British church and its relations with the missionary who came to the English, Augustine. Bede had condemned the Britons for refusing to help Augustine to evangelize the English, and later, when many British monks of Bangor are slaughtered by the pagan Æthelfrith of Northumbria, Bede portrayed this as no more than divine justice. Contrast Geoffrey here: in his account, Augustine finds the British church to be flourishing, correctly organized, and distinguished by great sanctity. Augustine is not allowed any dialogue: all the talking is done by Abbot Dinoot of Bangor. The Britons' refusal to help in

---

47   *DGB*, ix.147.94–105.

48   *DGB*, ix.147.110: "ipsum in memoria ipsius saepissime reuocabat".

49   *DGB*, xi.188.178–80: "in parte autem Britonum adhuc uigebat Christianitas, quae a tempore Eleutherii papae habita numquam inter eos defecerat", "It [Christianity] still flourished in the British part, never having wavered since it was introduced in pope Eleutherius' time."

50   Compare *DGB*, xi.188–89 with Bede, *Ecclesiastical History* ii.2, ed. and trans. Colgrave and Mynors, pp. 134–43. Wright, "Geoffrey of Monmouth and Bede", pp. 35–41, gives a detailed comparison and very lucidly reveals Geoffrey's pro-British bias. See further M.J. Curley, *Geoffrey of Monmouth* (Twayne's English Authors Series, 509), New York, 1994, pp. 102–08. This episode is also discussed by Rebecca Thomas in her contribution to this volume.

the conversion of the Saxons is explained on the reasonable basis that the latter were mortal enemies who were occupying most of their land. The killing of the British monks is martyrdom and they "won their place in the kingdom of heaven".[51] Finally, the massacre of the monks is avenged by a wholly fictitious British victory over the Saxon army.

A further difficult matter which Geoffrey inherited from Bede was the career of the Christian king of Northumbria, Oswald.[52] In Bede's account, the Welsh king Cadwallon of Gwynedd attacked Northumbria, killed its king Edwin and ravaged the kingdom sorely. He was met in battle at Denisesburn by Oswald, and fell (c.633). Some years later (642), Oswald himself was killed in another battle by King Penda of Mercia. Bede presented Oswald in strongly hagiographical terms: his victory is won under the sign of the Cross and through trust in God, whereas his British opponent Cadwallon was denigrated as a Christian in name only. Oswald was a famous and widely venerated saint, and it would appear that Geoffrey was unable or unwilling to eliminate Bede's positive, hagiographical portrait of him.[53] Geoffrey's expedient was to remove his hero Caduallo from the battle altogether. Making clever use of the information which he found in Bede, who said that Cadwallon allied himself with Penda of Mercia, Geoffrey made Penda into the opponent whom Oswald defeated. Instead of falling in battle against the English king, Caduallo dies in his bed after a long and glorious reign. Penda, meanwhile, fights Oswald a second time and kills him; again, Geoffrey makes sure to state that Caduallo was elsewhere. If the English saint could not be eliminated, his opponent could still be rescued from the role of villain in Oswald's hagiography.

5   Saints, Churchmen, and Monks

Geoffrey's history concentrates on kings and military leaders, and this is an important part of the secularism which critics have attributed to him. Bishops appear largely as adjuncts to kings, though Guithelinus, Germanus, and Dubricius have some important agency of their own. Guithelinus and Dubricius, especially, are fighting prelates, but even their role is largely that of inserting some

---

51   *DGB*, xi.189.210: "martirio decorati regni caelestis adepti sunt sedem."

52   *DGB*, xi.199; contrast Bede, *Ecclesiastical History* ii.20 and iii.1–2, ed. and trans. Colgrave and Mynors, pp. 202–07 and 212–19.

53   Cf. N. Wright, "Geoffrey of Monmouth and Bede", *AL* 6 (1986), 27–59, at p. 43. He suggests that Geoffrey retained Oswald's saintly characteristics as a "foil" for the later British saint Cadwaladr. It is more likely that Oswald was simply so well-established as a saint that he had to be accommodated.

backbone into the secular power when it seems to be *fainéant*. Dubricius, the Welsh Dyfrig, seems to have inherited the role of St Germanus as war-leader of the Britons against the pagans, for his harangue of the British army before Badon recalls the role of Germanus in the famous Alleluia victory.[54] The message, however, is notably different. The hagiographical picture of Germanus allows no room for any other agency than God working through the saint, and so the pagan army turns and flees without a drop of blood being spilt. Geoffrey's Dubricius, in contrast, urges the Britons to fight to the last extremity, and they do. The saint's part in the battle is limited to exhortation. The victory, it should be noted, is still God's: the tide of battle only turns in the Britons' favor when Arthur invokes the names of the Virgin Mary and then God himself, at which point he becomes irresistibly powerful.[55] Yet the battle was won through the courage and valor of God's servants, not by a miracle.

No other saint in Geoffrey's *DGB* quite matches Dubricius. Eldadus, bishop of Gloucester, is described as *beatus* and as a man of the greatest wisdom and devotion.[56] He buries the dead British leaders after the treachery of the long knives, attends the council of Aurelius Ambrosius, makes a speech which ensures that the Saxon leader Hengist is executed and another which secures mercy for the remaining Saxons, and finally escorts Aurelius to the burial place of the British leaders at Ambrius's monastery.[57] Eldadus is Geoffrey's own invention, as Tatlock showed.[58] His connection with Gloucester plausibly reflects Geoffrey's hopes for the patronage of Robert, earl of Gloucester. Another quite prominent saint is David, who succeeds Dubricius at Caerleon. Uncle of Arthur, teacher and leader of an exemplary life, he dies in the reign of Constantinus, in Menevia (now St Davids), a monastery of his own within his diocese.[59] He loved Menevia because it had been founded by Patrick, who prophesied his birth. There, too, he was buried at the order of King Maelgwn. As was noted earlier, some of this material diverges from the traditions of

---

54   *DGB*, ix.147; cf. Bede, *Ecclesiastical History* i.20, ed. and trans. Colgrave and Mynors, pp. 62–65. Geoffrey omits all mention of the Alleluia victory from the *DGB*.

55   *DGB*, ix.147.126–28: "Quemcumque attingebat Deum inuocando solo ictu perimebat, nec requieuit impetum suum facere donec quadringentos septuaginta uiros solo Caliburno gladio peremit", "As he called on God, he killed any man he touched with a single blow and pressed forward until with Caliburnus alone he had laid low four hundred and seventy men."

56   *DGB*, viii.125.159.

57   *DGB*, viii.104.470–73, 125.162–66, 126.182–86, 127.204.

58   Tatlock, *LHB*, p. 242.

59   *DGB*, ix.158.405–06 and xi.179.89–94.

St Davids itself. In Rhygyfarch's *Life of St David*, Patrick relinquishes the site to David, to whom is reserved the honor of founding the church.[60]

David, the exemplary monk-archbishop, reminds us that the *DGB* offers no real evidence of hostility to monks or monasticism. The reminder is needed, for it has been argued that Geoffrey wrote in a spirit of secular distrust for cloistered monks.[61] It should be noted that "devout [*religiosi*] communities of men and women [who] serve God according to the Christian tradition" are cited as a praiseworthy feature of Britain's great cities, while the monks of Bangor are praised for their devotion and for sustaining themselves through their own labors.[62] True, the monk Constans makes a terrible king, being entirely unprepared for rule on account of his cloistered life,[63] but that is not a criticism of monasticism in itself but of the breaking of monastic vows. The last British king, Cadualadrus, renounces the world to die as a penitent.[64]

In Geoffrey of Monmouth's view of history it is rulers, rather than churchmen, who dominate events. Yet if history is rooted in this world, it is still written with an acceptance that secular rulers, too, have to look forward to the next world. This will become particularly apparent in the last two sections of this essay, which are devoted to how Geoffrey ended his history and to the rethinking of his great work which he undertook in the later *VM*.

6   The Ending of British Rule and the Hope for a Future Restoration

As we approach the end of the *DGB*, so the tone becomes more and more colored by the kind of providential history that Geoffrey is supposed by many modern commentators to have left behind. A long speech by Caduallo injects a tone of moral judgement into this final section of the book.[65] Addressing Salomon of Brittany, Caduallo blames the weakness of his own people on their degeneracy. His speech is an adaptation of Gildas's powerful diatribe against the sins of the Britons. Indeed, Caduallo mentions Gildas by name, and unusually among Geoffrey's appeals to that author, the citation is honest. The subsequent loss of much of Britain is in accordance with the will of God. Caduallo, however, is not prepared to abandon the fight. He still believes that God's

---

60 Rhygyfarch, *Life of St David* §3 and §15, ed. Sharpe and Davies, pp. 110–13 and 120–21.
61 E.g. V.I.J. Flint, "The *Historia Regum Britanniae* of Geoffrey of Monmouth: Parody and its Purpose. A Suggestion", *Speculum* 54:3 (1979), 447–68.
62 *DGB*, i.5.40–42; xi.188.180–87.
63 *DGB*, vi.95.168–69.
64 *DGB*, xi.206.583.
65 *DGB*, xi.195.

favor can be turned back to the Britons if they fight bravely and nobly for their
country, and even if not, the reputation of the Britons should still be saved by
the bravery of their resistance. Here we see the contradictory tendencies in
Geoffrey: on the one hand the Gildasian inheritance of sin and repentance,
but on the other the aristocratic values of courage and glory. No resolution is
offered: Caduallo embarks on his war of reconquest, and is spectacularly successful. Yet he manages only to stave off defeat, not to prevent it altogether.
Under his successor, Cadualadrus, the Britons are finally deprived of the sovereignty of Britain by the will of God, which is visited upon them in the shape
of plague and famine; no military power, insists Geoffrey, could have prevailed
over them in this way, but against the will of God there can be no victory. They
themselves are to blame for their plight, which is a punishment for their many
great sins. The Saxons, however, are only able finally to occupy what is now
England because all of its British inhabitants have abandoned it for fear of the
anger of God. It is left to Cadualadrus, last British king of Britain, in another of
the great speeches from Book XI, to tell his fellow-countrymen that they have
lost their age-old battle:

> Woe to us sinners for the terrible crimes with which we never ceased to
> offend God when we had time to repent. His mighty retribution is upon
> us, to uproot from our native soil us whom neither the Romans once nor
> later the Scots, the Picts or the deceitful treachery of the Saxons could
> drive out. In vain have we so often recovered our native land from them,
> since it was not God's will that we should reign there for ever.[66]

It is difficult to see how else Geoffrey could have handled this crucial moment
of the loss of sovereignty. Throughout the DGB, the Britons are portrayed as for-
midable warriors. Again and again, they prevail against invaders and conquer
foreign lands. Geoffrey has repeatedly postponed the evil moment of their defeat far beyond the point where the preceding English historians had placed
it; now, finally, it has to be faced. How could he account for the final loss of
Britain without undermining everything he has said so far? His answer is this
Gildasian turn which absolves the Britons of failure as warriors and elevates

---

66   DGB, xi.203.532–37: "Vae nobis peccatoribus ob immania scelera nostra quibus Deum
      offendere nullatenus diffugimus dum paenitentiae spatium habebamus. Incumbit ergo
      illius potestatis ultio, quae nos ex natali solo extirpat, quos nec Romani nec deinde
      Scoti uel Picti nec uersutae proditionis Saxones exterminare quiuerunt. Sed in uanum
      patriam super illos totiens recuperauimus, cum non fuit Dei uoluntas ut in ea perpetue
      regnaremus."

their fate to the realm of divine providence, which – so the hope is expressed – may in future encompass their restoration.

The close dependency on Gildas in the last part of the *DGB* has been noted and discussed by Neil Wright.[67] As he observes, Geoffrey's greater sympathy for the Britons caused him to postpone this kind of rhetoric to a very late stage in his history. The postponement allows for a lengthy development of the Britons' heroic resistance. Nevertheless, the moment of judgement comes, and the Britons are found lacking, as even their leaders can see. It is no coincidence that these purple passages are put into the mouths of characters. The set-piece speech was a convention of historiography inherited from the classical historians, a device that allowed passages of emotionally charged language to be accommodated within the much more neutral style of history. Most of Geoffrey's book is told in the smooth, objective-sounding style of the historian. These dense recapitulations of Gildas's highly-charged rhetoric could only be accommodated as direct speech. The important point, however, is that they are accommodated.

Along with the language of providential history, we find the language of hagiography appearing, too, in the figure of Cadualadrus. Geoffrey's last king of Britain ends his life in Rome as a penitent who had "renounced the world for the sake of the Lord's eternal kingdom".[68] Cadualadrus is a composite of a king Cadwaladr of Gwynedd and of Bede's Cædwalla, a king of Wessex who died in Rome in 688. The very meager early sources for Cadwaladr of Gwynedd show that his reign was already regarded as historically significant before Geoffrey; in the probably 10th-century prophetic poem *Armes Prydein Vawr* ("The Great Prophecy of Britain"), he appears as one of two heroes who will return to lead the Britons to victory.[69] It seems to have been Geoffrey who turned this hope for Cadwaladr's return into an expectation that his relics would be brought back from Rome: the Cadwaladr of *Armes Prydein* is a vengeful war leader, not a penitent, and still less a set of bones. This opens the difficult question of whether Cadwaladr was regarded as a saint before Geoffrey. There are several churches called Llangadwaladr in Wales, notably one in Anglesey which contains a memorial to Cadwaladr's grandfather, Cadfan.[70] Yet, none of the Welsh texts that call him *Cadwaladr Fendigaid*, "the Blessed", is earlier than Geoffrey, and his credentials as a saint in the *DGB* appear to rest on his pilgrimage and

---

67   N. Wright, "Geoffrey of Monmouth and Gildas", *AL* 2 (1982), 1–40, at pp. 12–14, 21, 39–40.
68   *DGB*, xi.206.583: "abiectis mundialibus propter Dominum regnumque perpetuum".
69   See Ben Guy's chapter in this volume.
70   N. Edwards, *A Corpus of Early Medieval Inscribed Stones and Stone Sculpture in Wales*, 3: *North Wales*, Cardiff, 2013, pp. 180–83.

death in the holy city, features actually taken from the career of Cædwalla of Wessex. Unless the conflation of the two men is older than the *DGB*,[71] it would seem that Geoffrey at the very least strengthened the sanctity of Cadwaladr, if he did not reinterpret a wholly secular figure. By accepting the will of God, and renouncing the world, Geoffrey's holy St Cadualadrus brings the story of the Britons to a fitting conclusion. The only remedy for their plight is penance, and their last king shows them the way to redemption. Symbolically, when the time of their penance comes to an end, St Cadualadrus (in the shape of his relics) will again lead them to victory.[72]

The end of Geoffrey's book should warn us against dismissing providential history. Hanning's powerful argument that Geoffrey saw history as a series of cycles of rise and decline, symbolized for him by Fortune's wheel, might lead us to ignore the very deliberate choices made by Geoffrey in this last section. I would not wish to deny that cyclical history governed by fortune is an important concept in the *DGB*, but it does not replace providential history. Rather, both co-exist in an uneasy tension which is not resolved. This difficulty can be seen in Hanning's treatment of the ending. Insisting that the Britons' plight was the result of their own internal strife, he offered a resolutely secular reading which brushed aside the religious language of sin and penitence which is so notable in the *DGB* from the disastrous reign of Kareticus onwards. His dismissal of the providential turn as a "convenience" on the part of Geoffrey is perhaps the weakest part of his whole argument.[73] Hanning also underestimated the emotional importance of British identity; indeed, his focus on

---

71   D.N. Dumville, "Brittany and *Armes Prydein Vawr*", *Études celtiques* 20 (1983), 145–59, at p. 154 is open to the idea that the conflation predated Geoffrey, but on the grounds of a doubtful biblical parallel. In *Trioedd Ynys Prydein: The Triads of the Island of Britain*, ed. and trans. R. Bromwich, 4th ed., Cardiff, 2014, Bromwich also argues that the conflation is old because Bede calls Cadwaladr's father, Cadwallon, by the English form *Cædwalla*. That does not show when Cadwaladr himself was confused with Cædwalla of Wessex specifically. Wright, "Geoffrey of Monmouth and Bede", pp. 50–52 tends to see Geoffrey as the originator. As he notes, the conflation can hardly be a blunder.

72   The motif of Cadualadrus's relics is rather reminiscent of the fate of many such relics in the face of violent events like the Scandinavian raids of the 9th and 10th centuries: to be withdrawn to a place of safety in the hope that they might one day return in triumph to their proper home. See, for a general discussion, R. Bartlett, *Why Can the Dead Do Such Great Things? Saints and Worshippers from the Martyrs to the Reformation*, Princeton, 2013, pp. 290–92. Cadualadrus is slightly unusual, though, in making provision for their safety before he actually died.

73   Hanning, *Vision*, p. 140 and also p. 232, n. 85. His argument that the angelic voice announces just one more stage in the "eternal cycle" of "Fortune's Wheel", rather than having providential meaning, does not convince. The fact that he returns to the problem suggests a continuing difficulty for his interpretation.

fortune and cyclicality in Geoffrey's thought at times comes close to treating the case of the Britons as no more than an exemplum that could have been replaced by any other. The intensity of Geoffrey's partisanship, revealed in his savage rewriting of Bede, tells another story. Far from secularizing Gildas, as Hanning claims,[74] Geoffrey in the end finds no alternative to him, for in no other way could the failure of the Britons be explained nor, perhaps, be made emotionally bearable.

7   Prophecy, History, and the *Vita Merlini*

British history, as presented in the *DGB*, is a fulfilment of prophecy. The glorious future of the Britons is foretold to Brutus on Leogetia in Book I, and their rule over Britain ends with another prophecy, that they will recover the island only when God is pleased to allow that to happen. Book VII, the *PM*, which also circulated independently, is given over entirely to prophecies told by Merlin to Vortigern. Initially these cover events in the *DGB* from the time of Merlin to the end, and then they continue through what can be recognized as oblique references to subsequent Saxon and Norman history, through Geoffrey's own time and beyond, to the moment when British rule over the island would be renewed. Beyond that point, again, they continue in a series of fantastically obscure images, culminating in the disturbance of the stars and planets which will precede the Day of Judgement and the end of time.

Though history and prophecy appear so closely linked in the *DGB*, the nature of prophetic inspiration is not questioned. Brutus is not sure whether to believe that a goddess has indeed spoken to him,[75] yet the prophecy is clearly fulfilled by subsequent events. Those who witness Merlin's ecstasy believe that "he was inspired" – *numen esse in illo* – but the source of that inspiration is not stated.[76] Later, Merlin himself speaks of a spirit who instructs him and would abandon him if he abused the gift for frivolous purposes.[77] At least the prophecy given to Cadwaladr is unambiguously transmitted by an angelic voice and thus of divine origin. The angel's words are checked against older prophecies by Alanus, ruler of Brittany, and found to be in agreement with them. It has been suggested that this shows a certain skepticism toward the divine origin

---

74   Hanning, *Vision*, pp. 137–38.
75   *DGB*, i.17.313–14.
76   *DGB*, vi.108.577.
77   *DGB*, viii.128.228–30.

of the prophecy,[78] but arguably the opposite is true: the angel's voice is veri-
fied as authentic because previous prophecies, too, were believed somehow to
come from God. Perhaps the question looms larger for modern readers than
for medieval ones. Such has been argued by Julia Crick, who pointed out that
12th-century churchmen were heavily involved with writing and interpreting
prophetic texts.[79] Geoffrey himself tells us that he first "translated" the *PM* on
behalf of Alexander, bishop of Lincoln. That Merlin's vision ends with the es-
chatology of the Last Judgement is another indication that the prophet spoke
in accordance with God.[80] As Richard Southern pointed out, most medieval
commentators were ready to acknowledge that prophetic inspiration, though
it originated in God, could be manifested in apparently unworthy or even non-
Christian individuals.[81] Merlin was the son of an incubus, and both Southern
and Crick discuss evidence that his nature was a matter of concern for some
medieval readers,[82] but there is nothing in the *DGB* that requires us to take him
as an explicitly pagan prophet.

Geoffrey returned to the figure of the prophet in his later work, the *VM*. This
text may not have been as popular or influential as the *DGB*, to judge by the
smaller number of surviving manuscript copies, but it should not be neglected.
The story is set many decades after the time in which Merlin was active according to the *DGB*, and thus Merlin's lifespan is greatly expanded. Here, he is
a Welsh king and prophet who fights in a battle in northern Britain and goes

78   Curley, *Geoffrey of Monmouth*, p. 107.
79   J. Crick, "Geoffrey of Monmouth, Prophecy and History", *Journal of Medieval History*
     18:4 (1992), 357–71 traces the reception of the prophecies; see also her "Geoffrey and
     the Prophetic Tradition", in S. Echard (ed.), *The Arthur of Medieval Latin Literature: The
     Development and Dissemination of the Arthurian Legend in Medieval Latin* (Arthurian
     Literature of the Middle Ages, 6), Cardiff, 2011, pp. 67–82.
80   Hanning, *Vision*, pp. 171–72 interprets this quite differently, seeing "no divine providence,
     no judgement"; "the impersonal universe ... will lose control of itself and history will dis-
     solve into nothingness." Yet Merlin refers quite clearly to the resurrection of the dead,
     which in Christian belief will precede Judgement.
81   R.W. Southern, "Aspects of the European Tradition of Historical Writing, 3: History as
     Prophecy", *Transactions of the Royal Historical Society*, fifth series, 22 (1972), 159–80 (repr.
     in R.J. Bartlett (ed.), *History and Historians: Selected Papers of R.W. Southern*, Oxford, 2004,
     48–65, at pp. 49, 54–56).
82   Southern, "Aspects of the European Tradition of Historical Writing, 3", pp. 55–56; Crick,
     "Geoffrey of Monmouth, Prophecy and History", esp. pp. 358, 362, 370. The commentary
     on the prophecies attributed to Alan admits that some people worried that Merlin was a
     pagan, and cites the Lucius legend to show that he must, as a Briton, have been a Christian
     (Alan of Lille, *Interpretation of the Prophecy of Merlin*, ed. Ioachim Bratheringii, *Prophetia
     anglicana: Merlini Ambrosii britanni ... vaticinia et praedictiones a Galfredo Monemutensi
     latine conversae una cum septem libris explanationum in eamdem prophetiam ...*, Frankfurt,
     1603 and 1608, pp. 4–5).

mad with grief. He spends many years living as a wild man in the wilderness of what is now south-west Scotland and north-west England. Twice he is temporarily cured, but twice he suffers a relapse. Finally, he recovers his senses after drinking from a spring of pure water. This leads to the loss of his prophetic spirit, which passes to his sister Ganieda. The work ends with Merlin, Ganieda, the poet Telgesinus, and another former madman, Maeldinus, all abandoning the world to live together as hermits in the wilderness.

The *VM* appears a rather disjointed poem, but if it is seen as a reconsideration of Geoffrey's earlier work, then its force becomes more apparent. The *DGB* shows the great sweep of history, the rise and fall of peoples and dynasties. The scale of the *VM* is smaller. Most of its action takes place during the short reign of the usurper Conanus, at a time when the fortune of the Britons is at a low ebb. Though Merlin briefly prophesies the restoration of British power, the focus is very much on political and moral failure, on a kingdom brought low by internecine strife. The parallel with Geoffrey's own time is apparent, for the *VM* was composed during the civil war that erupted after the death of Henry I in 1135. Events in that war are foretold by Ganieda at the end of the poem. The *VM* is a study in personal and religious retreat. It follows Merlin into the wilderness, and comes to the conclusion that life is preferable there. In marked contrast to the *DGB*, the *VM* relegates the world of kings and battles to the background. The response of the individual to events is the theme here: the political consequences of the battle are ignored in favor of Merlin's overwhelming grief for his fallen brothers, with which we may compare Ganieda's sadness after the passing of King Rodarchus. Ultimately, the individual's best response to the transience of worldly life is to retreat into a closer relationship with God. Merlin, having previously been compelled into the wilderness by his madness, rationally chooses the ascetic life, refusing the chance to take up his kingship again. The other madman, Maeldinus, is cured by the same spring as Merlin, and makes the same choice. Ganieda joins her brother after the death of her husband, King Rodarchus; her lament for him is full of the topoi of renunciation of the world.[83] Telgesinus, finally, abandons what I take to be his secular verse to live under Merlin's guidance.[84] Though it may seem that the four retreat into a small world of their own, the long discourses of Telgesinus and Merlin on creation set their decision in a much broader context, *sub specie*

---

83   *VM*, ll. 693–731.

84   *VM*, l. 1458: "despecto themate mundi"; Clarke's translation, "turning away from the traffic of the world", is too general given Taliesin's role as a poet; I suggest "turning away from the [poetic] theme of this world".

aeternitatis. They choose the life to come over the disappointments and failures of this life.

Though the *VM* explores the complexity of the prophetic role to much greater degree than the *DGB*, it remains ambiguous regarding Merlin's inspiration. This seems to accompany his loss of reason, and yet he is specifically called a *vates* even before the fateful battle. This Latin term for a poet always implies a figure who has access to higher or divine inspiration. Moreover, Merlin welcomes the return of his reason, even though the price he must pay is the loss of his prophetic gift, and he thanks God for granting him the change, as if his former state were not so much a gift as a burden.[85] Yet having regained his reason, Merlin promptly chooses to remain in the wilderness as a hermit. Merlin's remarkable knowledge of birds is gained (so he claims) while he lives as a wild man, yet Telgesinus's equally thorough knowledge of creation and geography derives from study, probably under his master Gildas in Brittany, and so the relative merits of reason and inspiration are left unstated.[86] Ziolkowski has suggested that this reflects the incomplete amalgamation of contradictory traditions – a shamanism which he attributes to Celtic tradition, political prophecy, and the idea of Christian prophecy – but he also tries to argue that Merlin progresses from one to the next, from an initial state of faithlessness to an acceptance of Christian revelation.[87] Yet Merlin is clearly a Christian from the beginning,[88] and it is possible to see the different sources of knowledge, namely inspiration and the scholarly study of creation, as complementary rather than opposed to one another. Merlin begins not in a state of faithlessness, but in an attachment to worldliness which is overcome by the end of the poem.[89]

Geoffrey's portrait of Merlin in the *VM* bears strong resemblances to the northern wild man, Lailoken, known from Scottish sources. It has been plausibly argued that Geoffrey appropriated the Lailoken figure and re-identified

---

85   *VM*, ll. 1156–75.

86   *VM*, ll. 1298–1386 (Merlin on birds), 737–940 (Telgesinus on creation, waters, and islands), 1179–1253 (on waters again); for Telgesinus studying under Gildas, see ll. 685–88.

87   J. Ziolkowski, "The Nature of Prophecy in Geoffrey of Monmouth's *Vita Merlini*", in J.L. Kugel (ed.), *Poetry and Prophecy: The Beginnings of a Literary Tradition*, Ithaca, 1990, pp. 151–62.

88   Cf. his invocation of Christ in *VM*, l. 87.

89   For an interpretation on these lines, see P.B.R. Doob, *Nebuchadnezzar's Children: Conventions of Madness in Middle English Literature*, New Haven, 1974, pp. 153–58. Echard, *Arthurian Narrative in the Latin Tradition*, pp. 214–31 offers a very different reading of the *VM* as "an almost nihilistic appraisal of the abilities of man to understand or control his destiny".

him with his southern Welsh prophet.[90] Lailoken was associated with the patron saint of Glasgow, St Kentigern, from whom he receives the sacrament just before his death. Kentigern was also the supposed founder of the see of St Asaph in north-east Wales, to which Geoffrey was elected bishop in 1151. It is tempting to make some connection between this fact and his reception of the northern material, for Geoffrey may have come across the wild man material while researching the career of Kentigern. However, there is such a dearth of early sources from St Asaph that it is impossible to establish whether the cult of Kentigern was present there in Geoffrey's time. Indeed, an alternative and very plausible suggestion is that Geoffrey himself was responsible for introducing the cult of Kentigern to St Asaph.[91] Certainly the connection of the Glasgow saint with north-east Wales seems fanciful enough to be the product of his imagination: compare his removal of Dubricius and David from their acknowledged churches to his imaginary see of Caerleon. If, as seems likely, the material on the northern wild man came to him already attached to traditions of St Kentigern, it is notable that Geoffrey has completely excised the saint from the narrative.[92] In choosing to close his poem with Merlin's embrace of the hermit life rather than his death, Geoffrey left no room for the saint in reconciling the wild man to reason and salvation. Perhaps, as is hinted, a prophet needed no mediator with God.[93]

8   Conclusion

Some readings of Geoffrey of Monmouth come close to regarding him as entirely detached from the religious culture of his day. Robert Hanning made

---

90   Most thoroughly by O.J. Padel, "Geoffrey of Monmouth and the Development of the Merlin Legend", *CMCS* 51 (2006), 37–65. But see also N. Tolstoy, "Geoffrey of Monmouth and the Merlin Legend", *AL* 25 (2008), 1–42, reasserting the view that Myrddin was already a northern figure in Welsh tradition before Geoffrey.

91   Clarke in *VM*, pp. 33–34; in more detail J.R. Davies, "Bishop Kentigern among the Britons", in S. Boardman, J.R. Davies, and E. Williamson (eds.), *Saints' Cults in the Celtic World* (Studies in Celtic History, 25), Woodbridge, 2009, pp. 67–99, at pp. 85–87.

92   Clarke believed that Kentigern is mentioned obliquely in the elegy for King Rodarchus in *VM*, ll. 698–99: "Tractabat sanctum justo moderamine clerum, / jure regi populos summos humilesque sinebat", which he translated as "He treated the holy priest with due consideration and made the rule of law available to high and low alike." The interpretation of *sanctum ... clerum* as "holy priest" is forced. It is more likely to be a reference to the clergy in general, see also other examples of the combination of *clerus* and *populus* in ll. 11, 1059, 1082.

93   Cf. *VM*, ll. 1156–75, where Merlin gives thanks to God for curing him.

him an intellectual revolutionary who developed the secularizing trend in
12th-century historiography to the furthest extreme imaginable. Christopher
Brooke, influenced by Hanning's secularizing approach, saw in Geoffrey's
works only humor and the desire for personal advancement, not the serious
pursuit of an idea, while more recently Siân Echard seems poised between seeing Geoffrey as either a philosophical or a literary revolutionary.[94] We should
beware, however, the danger of considering British history as little more than
a vehicle through which Geoffrey expressed his philosophy or, alternatively, an
object upon which he exercised his literary playfulness. That does not do justice to the intensely partisan manner in which Geoffrey refashioned his sources, nor to the pervasive religious element in his works. I have argued, instead,
that Geoffrey presents the fate of the Britons in moral, exemplary terms, and
that he treats their rise, fall, and future return to power as part of the inscru-
table providence of God. This consideration should also weigh on any political
interpretation. That Geoffrey could be critical of the Britons, and especially of
the Welsh, needs to be seen in the light of the exemplary function of history
and the concepts of sin, repentance, and redemption. Geoffrey was not a modern nationalist, concerned to whitewash every blemish. National history could
not be divorced from salvation history, nor from the reality of human weakness. British defeat was a fact which demanded an interpretation in moral
terms, but the *PM* left open the possibility that the Britons would recover from
their state of sin and be allowed once again to rule their own island. History,
of course, would not end at that point, and neither did Merlin's prophecies:
there would still be sin, and change, and tumult, until all would be resolved in
Judgement. If Geoffrey struggled to resolve the tension between the providential model and the fickleness of events in this world, it may be suggested that
his *VM* offers trust in God as his response.

---

94   Compare Echard, *Arthurian Narrative in the Latin Tradition*, ch. 1 with her "'Hic est Artur':
Reading Latin and Reading Arthur", in A. Lupack (ed.), *New Directions in Arthurian
Studies*, Cambridge, 2002, pp. 49–67.

PART 4

Reception

∴

The Medieval Reception of Geoffrey of Monmouth

Georgia Henley and Joshua Byron Smith

Geoffrey of Monmouth's work was read, adapted, and translated throughout Europe. The articles in this section provide an overview of this far-reaching reception in as many cultural traditions as possible. We have requested that contributors focus on the reception of Geoffrey's work proper, as opposed to the general efflorescence of Arthurian literature – a distinction that is admittedly not always easy to make. These articles are meant as points of entry into larger bodies of scholarship and are intended to stimulate further research. To that end, we have favored concision instead of comprehensiveness. In organizing the following essays under cultural and linguistic rubrics, we have relied on our contributors' expertise and our own judgment; readers are asked not to place too much importance on the various categories. Italy as we know it, for example, did not exist as such in the Middle Ages, and here Italy and other distinctions like it should be understood merely as convenient shorthand for the modern researcher. Finally, in spite of our best efforts, we suspect that we have omitted some aspect or another of Geoffrey's influence. Geoffrey's work might have been known in Poland, for example, or in the Hebrew language.[1] And while multiple correspondents informed us that there was no Arabic reception, more research might prove otherwise. Unfortunate omissions are perhaps expected in such a large project, but we hope that these may be balanced by the wealth of information brought together here, much of it put in dialogue for the first time.

---

1 M. Schlauch, "Geoffrey of Monmouth and Early Polish Historiography: A Supplement", *Speculum* 44 (1969), 258–63.

CHAPTER 15

Geoffrey of Monmouth's Byzantine Reception

Thomas H. Crofts

That the Matter of Britain had reached, at a relatively early date, not only the Western Mediterranean but also Asia Minor and the Middle East, we have the testimony of a (possibly pseudo-) Alan of Lille, whose commentary on the *Prophetiae Merlini* is found with Geoffrey's DGB in Valenciennes, Bibliothèque Municipale, 792:[1]

> Whither has winged fame not conveyed and published the name of Arthur the Briton even as far as Christian rule extends? Who, I say, does not speak of Arthur the Briton, when he is considered almost more famous among the peoples of Asia than among the Britons, as our pilgrims returning from the East tell us? The eastern peoples speak of him, the Western peoples speak of him, with the whole world stretching between them. Egypt speaks of him; nor is the sheltered Bosporus silent. Rome, the queen of cities, sings of his deeds; nor are Arthur's battles unknown to her former rival Carthage. Antioch, Armenia, and Palestine praise his exploits.[2]

While the evidence tends to bear out this wide geographical swath of early Arthurian reception, research has in fact yielded no direct proof of Geoffrey of Monmouth's reception on "the sheltered Bosporus". Despite the wide and immediate success of the DGB, there is no trace of this book, or of Geoffrey's name, in the Byzantine record. This will be unsurprising if just a few things are borne in mind. First, the list of Western medieval – or classical Latin for that

---

1 No. 211 in Crick, *SC*.

2 Alan of Lille, *Interpretation of the Prophecy of Merlin*, ed. Ioachim Bratheringii, *Prophetia anglicana: Merlini Ambrosii britanni ... vaticinia et praedictiones a Galfredo Monemutensi latine conversae una cum septem libris explanationum in eamdem prophetiam ...*, Frankfurt, 1603 and 1608, pp. 22–23: "Quo enim Arturi Britonis nomen fama volans non pertulit et vulgavit: quousque Christianum pertingit imperium? Quis inquam Arturum Britonem non loquatur, cum pene notior habeatur, Asiaticis gentibus, quam Britannis; sicut nobis referunt Palmigeri nostri de orientis partibus redeuntes? Loquuntur illum orientales, loquuntur occidui, toto terrarum orbe divisi. Loquitur illum Aegyptus, Bosforus exclusa non tacet. Cantat gesta eius domina civitatum Roma, nec emulam quondam eius Carthaginem, Arturi praelia latent. Celebrat actus eius Antiocha, Armenia, Palaestina." My translation.

matter – authors who were read or translated by Byzantines is extremely short, and of that list, Western imaginative literature makes up a very small portion; medieval Latin historiography is entirely absent from it. As Elizabeth A. Fisher observes,

> The literature of other cultures did not attract the scholars or savants of Byzantium, nor did the effort of translating Latin literature into Greek appeal to them. The Greek literary inheritance from antiquity provided abundant resources in *belles lettres*, biography, historical writing, and technical treatises. This rich inheritance satisfied Byzantine aesthetic, scholarly, and practical needs and supplied literati both with abundant literary models and with virtually inexhaustible subjects for scholarly study.[3]

It was ordinary for Byzantine clergy and intellectuals to have little or no knowledge of Latin. Reinforcing this indifference to Western literature were the Catholic Crusades, which did nothing to enamor the Latin world to the Greeks, and which, with the Fourth Crusade, put a decisive end to whatever polite commerce might have existed between the Latin West and the Greek East. The half-century of Latin rule which followed the events of 1204 only confirmed for the Byzantines what Anna Komnena had written (based on her father Alexios I's experience of them during the First Crusade): "The officers of the Celts ["Celt" and "Norman" were for Anna pretty much synonymous] are characteristically impudent and rash, money-grubbing by nature, and excessive in their physical appetites; they also exceed all races of men in their verbosity", to say nothing of the gruesome atrocities they committed in war: while ravaging Nicaea, she writes, the Normans "tore some newborn babes limb from limb, others they impaled on spits and roasted over a fire; and every kind of torture was visited upon the elderly".[4] It was within twelve years of Anna's writing that Geoffrey of Monmouth completed the *DGB*.

It is unsurprising, then that Geoffrey's work, so universally popular in the West, should have left no trace in Byzantine textual culture. Of the more than

3 E.A. Fisher, "Planoudes, Holobolos, and the Motivation for Translation", *Greek, Roman, and Byzantine Studies* 43:1 (2002/03), 77–104, at p. 77.

4 *Annae Comnenae Porphyrogenitae Alexias* [The Alexias of Anna Komnena, Porphyrogenita] II.241–42, II.77, ed. A. Reifferscheid, 2 vols., Leipzig, 1884: "οἱ δὲ Κελτοὶ κόμητες φύσει μὲν τὸ ἀναίσχυντον καὶ ἰταμὸν ἔχοντες, φύσει δὲ τὸ ἐρασιχρήματον καὶ πρὸς πᾶν τὸ αὐτοῖς βουλητὸν ἀκρατὲς καὶ πολυρρῆμον ὑπὲρ πᾶν γένος ἀνθρώπων ...", "τῶν τε γὰρ βρεφῶν τὰ μὲν ἐμελίζον, τὰ δὲ ξύλοις περιπείροντες ὤπτιζον ἐν πυρί, πρὸς δὲ τοὺς τῷ χρόνῳ προσήκοντας πᾶν εἶδος ποινῆς ἐπεδείκνυντο." My translation.

200 copies and fragments of the *DGB*, only one manuscript (Vatican City, Biblioteca Apostolica Vaticana, Ottoboni lat. 3025) contains any writing in Greek, but it is a composite and apparently athematic manuscript.[5] The Greek section (at fols. 38r–44r), which I have investigated, contains notes and documents related to various ecumenical councils.

Signs of *indirect* reception of Geoffrey's work, in the form of Arthurian art and literature, may be found in Greek-speaking territories from south-eastern Italy to Cyprus. These occurrences are usually attributable to Latin occupation: the geography of "Alain", quoted above, tellingly alights on the Crusader-states of Antioch, Armenian Cilicia, and Jerusalem. Since Geoffrey of Monmouth, in spirit at least, may have touched down anywhere the Crusaders set foot, there are many examples of Arthurian literature being read or enjoyed in the Greek-speaking eastern Mediterranean, especially in Cyprus.[6] But in these cases – all occurring in one or another Crusader court – no true Byzantine reception of the material can be measured.

But there are instances – however isolated – of the influence of Western practice and ideology in Byzantine society, and these instances may constitute, at a third remove, a possible register of Byzantine reception of Geoffrey of Monmouth. In southeastern Italy – under Byzantine control *c*.871–1071 – the floor of the Norman cathedral of Otranto is paved with an enigmatic Byzantinesque mosaic (*c*.1165) showing, as part of a pictorial universal history, a king identified as *Rex Arturus* riding a goat into the underworld even as he confronts a monstrous cat. The narrative pictured seems distinctly more Welsh than Anglo-Norman, more supernatural than historiographical, since the cat must be an incarnation of the monstrous Cath Palug from the 10th- or 11th-century dialogue-poem found in the Black Book of Carmarthen,[7] and glimpsed again in the "Three Powerful Swineherds" triad of *Trioedd Ynys Prydein* ("The Triads of the Island of Britain").[8] Arthur's supposed entry into Hell may be

---

5   Crick, *SC*, pp. 326–28.

6   D. Jacoby, "Knightly Values and Class Consciousness in the Crusader States of the Eastern Mediterranean", *Mediterranean Historical Review* 1 (1986), 158–86.

7   Black Book of Carmarthen, Poem 31 (*Pa gur yv y porthaur*): "Kei win a aeth von / y dilein lleuon / y iscuid oed mynud / erbin cath paluc", "Cai the Fair went to Anglesey / to destroy lions. / His shield was polished / against the Clawing Cat [*Cath Palug*]". Text from *Trioedd Ynys Prydein: The Triads of the Island of Britain*, ed. and trans. R. Bromwich, 4th ed., Cardiff, 2014, p. 473; translation by J.K. Bollard, "Arthur in the Early Welsh Tradition", in N.J. Lacy and J.J. Wilhelm (eds.), *The Romance of Arthur: An Anthology of Medieval Texts in Translation*, 3rd ed., Abingdon, 2013, pp. 9–27, at p. 16.

8   *Trioedd Ynys Prydein*, ed. and trans. Bromwich, Triad 26, pp. 51–58, at pp. 51–52, ll. 22–26: "Ac yn Llaneuir yn Aruon adan y maen du y dotwes ar geneu kath, ac y ar y maen y b6ryoed y g6rueichat yn y mor, a meibion Paluc yMon a'e magassant, yr dr6c vdunt. A honno vu

related to a legend current in medieval Sicily that King Arthur lived under Mount Etna. Such manifestations may provide evidence of Arthurian narratives having spread to southern Italy independently of Geoffrey's texts, and probably by oral transmission.

In the realm of military and social practice – and also but indirectly related to Geoffrey's *oeuvre* – the following two items may be observed: first, as a facet of his well-known fascination with Western chivalry, Emperor Manuel I Komnenos (1118–80) outfitted his cavalry with body-length shields (as opposed to the traditional small, round buckler) and long lances, and had them trained in jousting, with the emperor himself taking part in the exercises.[9] Secondly, the word καβαλλάριος (kavallarios) entered Greek usage after 1204, and continued in use after the Paleologan restoration (1261); significantly, the term was not typically a pejorative one, but, like its Latin counterpart *miles* – and as distinct from the Greek "cavalry soldier", ἱππεύς (hippeus) – signified a Western knight's military function and elevated social rank. Future research into Byzantine Italy may yield further and more definite points of contact between Geoffrey's textual tradition and Byzantine culture, since even after the fall of the Byzantine "Regno" (which included most of southern Italy) in 1071, and throughout the Hohenstaufen period (1197–1266), Greeks in Sicily and southern Italy were strong allies of the "Latin" (though really German) kings and emperors, especially in their common resistance to papal power. Frederick II's laws, for example, were issued in Greek as well as Latin.

In this context, it is worth mentioning that Frederick II, according to a letter of 1240, commissioned a romance called *Palamedes* from one "Johannes Romanzor"; no other testimony of this text or of Romanzor survives. Again, the author, or redactor, of the Neapolitan version of the Byzantine *Tale of Achilles*, which is essentially a medieval romance, mentions "Palamedes" as a part of his narrative repertoire ("… or I can tell of Palamedes", … ἢ λέγω Παλαμήδη); but again, no Greek "Palamedes" is extant.[10]

The one Greek Arthurian text to survive – a fragmentary 307-line poem in Byzantine "political" meter – is the translation into high-literary "Atticizing"

Gath Baluc. Ac a uu vn o Deir Prif Ormes Mon a uagwyt yndi", "And at Llanfair in Arfon under the Black Rock, [Henwen] brought forth a kitten, and the Powerful Swineherd threw it from the Rock into the sea. And the sons of Palug in Anglesey fostered it in Môn, to their own harm: and that was Palug's Cat, and it was one of the Three Great Oppressions of Môn, nurtured therein." Translation by Bromwich. For discussion see ead., pp. 473–76; see also H. Nickel, "About Palug's Cat and the Mosaic of Otranto", *Arthurian Interpretations* 3:2 (1989), 96–105.

9   *DGB*, ix.217–87.
10   K. Mitsakis, "Palamedes", *Byzantinische Zeitschrift* 59 (1966), 5–7.

(as opposed to "demotic", or spoken) Greek of the opening adventure of Rustichello da Pisa's 13th-century Arthurian *Compilazione*, an episodic prose romance fashioned as a prequel to the enormous Prose *Tristan*. Untitled in the manuscript (Vatican City, Biblioteca Apostolica Vaticana, Vat. gr. 1822), but generally called "The Old Knight" (Ἱππότης ὁ Πρεσβύτης), the Greek poem relates the adventures of an elderly knight, later revealed to be Branor le Brun, who comes to Arthur's court and effortlessly unhorses all the great knights ("Gaoulvanos", "Tristanos", "Lanselottos ek Limnēs", and "Palamedes" himself) and pledges his service to "Rex Artouzos", before riding to the aid of a maiden whose castle is under siege by a "King with a Hundred Knights". The origin and audience of this anonymous text remain something of a mystery, but the single surviving copy (dating from the mid- to late 15th century) shows every sign of belonging to one of the *ad hoc* Greek anthologies used by expatriate Greek professors and their Italian students during the Northern Italian renaissance. Its studied use of Homeric diction and syntax could have had both satirical and pedagogical application. The poem could very likely have been used as a specimen of the 15-syllable political verse-form, or as a reading exercise using subject matter familiar to an Italian student; copies of Rustichello's book were certainly available at that time and place.[11] At all events, it was written by a Greek who had a respectable gift for verse storytelling.

While "The Old Knight" – and Rustichello's *Compilazione*, for that matter – could have been written by someone who had never read Geoffrey of Monmouth, it does represent the only extant treatment in medieval Greek of the Matter of Britain, and is notable for its trenchant, mock-heroic critique both of Arthurian romance, and of Western chivalry itself.

---

11 T.H. Crofts, "The Old Knight: An Edition of the Greek Arthurian Poem of Vat. gr. 1822", *AL* 33 (2016), 158–217.

CHAPTER 16

The *De gestis Britonum* in Castile

Paloma Gracia

The influence of the *De gestis Britonum* in Castile was profound and extensive. There are two characters in particular that truly transcend and are recreated again and again in different ways: one is Brutus, whose story is incorporated to a greater or lesser extent in different works, among which stands out the *General estoria* of Alfonso X; the other is Merlin, in his capacity as a prophet, particularly because the collection of prophecies inserted in the *DGB* is incorporated, almost in its entirety, into the *Baladro del sabio Merlín con sus profecías* published in 1498 and in the version edited in 1535. Even if we were to leave aside any short or superficial echo of the *DGB*, of which there are many, the influence of the *DGB* in Castilian historiography and in Arthurian romance was very important; the connection between Brutus and the Trojan myth expanded the influence of the *DGB*, and Merlin's reputation as a necromancer revived a lagging, though interesting, prophetic genre.

1   De gestis Britonum

The moment in which the *DGB* was introduced to Castile, as well as the route of its diffusion, is in truth unknown. Traditional scholarship, which begins with Entwistle (1922), connects this moment to the marriage alliances of the kings Alfonso VII of León and Castile (1105–57) and Alfonso VIII of Castile (1155–1214), who became fathers-in-law of Louis VII and Louis VIII of France by marrying off their daughters Constance of Castile (c.1136–60) and Blanche of Castile (1188–1252), respectively. Alfonso VII was the son of Raymond of Burgundy and Alfonso VIII was the husband of Eleanor of England (or Eleanor Plantagenet), daughter of Eleanor of Aquitaine.[1] Later scholarship reconsiders

---

1   This essay is indebted, in some paragraphs, to the one published as P. Gracia, "Arthurian Material in Iberia", in D. Hook (ed.), *The Arthur of the Iberians: The Arthurian Legends in the Spanish and Portuguese Worlds* (Arthurian Literature in the Middle Ages, 8), Cardiff, 2015, pp. 11–32. The founding scholarship on this topic is the essay by W.J. Entwistle, "Geoffrey of Monmouth and Spanish Literature", *Medieval Literature Review* 17:4 (1922), 381–91, although many of his essential points have been disputed, particularly by L. Kasten, "The Utilization of the *Historia Regum Britanniae* by Alfonso X", *Hispanic Review* 38:5 (1970),

the role of Eleanor of England's literary patronage in the Castilian courts, limiting her influence to the concession that it may have been particularly easy to acquire a copy of the *DGB* in the Castilian court under her literary patronage. The *Anales navarro-aragoneses* (1196) and the *Anales toledanos primeros* (1219) mention the battle that took place between Arthur and Mordred in Camlan: both give the event the same date of 542 AD; the *Anales toledanos primeros* mention that Mordred is Arthur's nephew.[2]

Eleanor could also have had something to do with the interest that her grandson, King Alfonso X, showed toward Geoffrey's text. The inclusion of the *DGB* in the *General estoria* ("The Universal History") could have also been suggested by French historiography, which had already incorporated materials derived from the work of Geoffrey: thus the *Histoire ancienne jusqu'à César* ("Ancient History According to Caesar"), used by Alfonso X himself, was a structural and ideological model for his *General estoria*.[3]

Four parts (*partes*) of the *General estoria* draw from the *DGB*. The group constitutes what Alfonso X calls the *Estoria de las Bretannas* ("The History of the Britons"), which is unevenly distributed among the different parts: it begins at the end of part II, by inserting the story of Brutus into the thread of 1 Kings, and ends in part V, when the compilation narrates the time period of Julius Caesar. The references to biblical passages that Alfonso X finds in the *DGB* determine the insertion point of the different materials from Geoffrey's text. The

---

97–114, and A. Deyermond, "Problems of Language, Audience, and Arthurian Source in a Fifteenth-Century Castilian Sermon", in A. Torres-Alcalá et al. (eds.), *Josep María Solà-Solé: homage, homenaje, homenatge: miscelánea de estudios de amigos y discípulos* (Biblioteca Universitaria Puvill. V, Estudios misceláneos, 1), Barcelona, 1984, pp. 43–54. Kasten disagreed with the reason given to explain how Alfonso X acquired a copy of the *DGB*, as well as the way in which he adapted the work. Deyermond's observations have more reach, covering the entire period the *DGB* was in use and discussing the role of Eleanor of Aquitaine in its introduction, which Entwistle had deemed decisive; Deyermond's consideration that the first text containing material derived from the *DGB* is the *Corónicas navarras* led him to restrict the role of Eleanor in the dissemination of Geoffrey's work. In Deyermond's opinion, Eleanor would have limited herself to encouraging, in Castile, an interest that had arisen previously in Navarre that was strengthened by certain historical events concerning Alfonso X.

2 A.P. Hutchinson, "Reading between the Lines: A Vision of the Arthurian World Reflected in Galician-Portuguese Poetry", in B. Wheeler (ed.), *Arthurian Studies in Honour of P.J.C. Field*, Cambridge, 2004, pp. 117–32; "*Anales navarro-aragoneses hasta 1239*: edición y estudio", ed. F. Bautista, *e-Spania* 26 (2017), <http://journals.openedition.org/e-spania/26509> (accessed 30 May 2018).

3 P. Gracia, "Hacia el modelo de la *General estoria*. París, la *translatio imperii et studii* y la *Histoire ancienne jusqu'à César*", *Zeitschrift für romanische Philologie* 122 (2006), 17–27. For the edition, see Alfonso X, *General estoria*, ed. P. Sánchez Prieto-Borja, A. Cabrejas, and M. Belén, *General estoria. Segunda Parte*, 2 vols., Madrid, 2009.

incorporation is done carefully, avoiding inconsistencies and redundancies and working in harmony with Alfonso's project, both in terms of structural complexity and in terms of ideological purpose. The compilation is especially interested in problems related to dynastic succession, such as the partition of Britain into three regions, one for each of Brutus's children, and the female succession of King Lear. Geoffrey's text enjoyed absolute credibility and the only probable reason that the *General estoria* does not include more sections of the *DGB* is that, although Alfonso X desired that the chronicle should conclude with an account of his own reign, the extant manuscripts abruptly end at the lives of the Virgin Mary's parents, and so it is not possible to know the full extent of the compilation.

The success of the Trojan material, the influence of the *General estoria*, and the desire of King Pedro I of Castile to emulate his father, King Alfonso XI, were the main motivations for the adaptation of the *DGB* in 14th-century Castile. Pedro I of Castile, aiming to surpass the version of the *Crónica troyana* composed during the reign of Alfonso XI, which was fundamentally a prose version of the *Roman de Troie*, promoted a new version of the *Historia troyana*, composed between 1365 and 1369. The *Historia Troyana* of Pedro I includes new material, interspersed throughout the *Roman de Troie*, that comes from Alfonso's *General estoria*, although not directly from the extant compilation, but from an independent, lost copy of the *Libro de Troya*.[4] The updated *Historia Troyana* deals especially with what happened after the fall of Troy, generously accepting the events of Aeneas and Brutus derived from an account in the *DGB*, perhaps through a French intermediary version. Thus, based on the *DGB*, the insertions tell the story of Brutus from his birth to the episode about Pandrasus's court, where the story stops, due to the loss of the last folios of the single manuscript that preserves this section (Madrid, Biblioteca Nacional de España, 10146); but it is presumed that the original story also would have covered the conquest of Britain.

Later, the story of Brutus would be included in many historiographical texts of the late Middle Ages, although Geoffrey's Latin original was replaced by the adaptations of the *DGB* that were already available in Iberian romances and in Wace's *Roman de Brut*: this is the case for the *Crónica de 1404*, the *Libro de las generaciones*, the *Sumas de la historia troyana*, and the *Victorial* by Gutierre Díaz de Games. Sometimes, if the passage is short, it is difficult to discern whether the source is an Iberian synthesis of the *DGB* or of the *Roman de Brut*.

---

4   R. Pichel Gotérrez, "*Lean por este libro que o acharam mays complidamente …*: del *Libro de Troya* alfonsí a la *Historia troyana* de Pedro I*", *Troianalexandrina: Anuario sobre literatura medieval de materia clásica* 16 (2016), 55–180.

2   Prophetiae Merlini

In addition to the historiographical texts and materials derived from the so-called *Post-Vulgate* Arthurian cycle, Castile enjoyed a wide tradition of prophecies attributed to Merlin, which circulated as a collection and were incorporated into different works.[5] *Baladro del sabio Merlín con sus profecías* ("The Cry of Merlin the Wise and his Prophecies") was published in 1498: it is the first printed version of the Arthurian *Merlin* and the *Post-Vulgate Suite du Merlin*, and was published in Burgos. Later, under the global title of *La Demanda del Sancto Grial con los maravillosos fechos de Lançarote y de Galaz su hijo. 1535* ("The Quest for the Holy Grail with the Marvelous Deeds of Lancelot and his son Galahad. 1535"), a printer in Seville published two books: a *primero libro de la "Demanda del Sancto Grial"*, which was a text closely related to the *Baladro* from Burgos, and a *segundo libro de la "Demanda del Sancto Grial"*, derived from the *Queste del Saint Graal* of the same cycle. Both editions (1498 and 1535, respectively) insert the prophetic sections of the *DGB* in the same place as Geoffrey added them, that is, after Vortigern asks about the meaning of the dragons. It is difficult to determine the moment when these prophecies were incorporated into the Peninsular versions of the *Merlin* of the *Post-Vulgate*, although the Vindel manuscript of the *Crónica de 1404* (New York, Hispanic Society of America, B2278) suggests the possibility that the prophecies were already part of a *Libro del Valadro de Merlim* (a certain "Book of the Cry of Merlin") by the first third of the 15th century. In addition, although the prophetic collection is a direct translation of the Latin original, it is possible that there was a French translation of the prophecies that perhaps – although it did not serve as an original translation – inspired the addition of the prophecies.

To the prophecies derived from the *DGB*, essentially the same ones offered by the *Baladro* from Burgos, *La Demanda del Sancto Grial* of 1535 adds two collections of prophecies attributed to Merlin but of Peninsular origin: one short and the other extensive, located between the first and second books. This is because once the narration of the death of Merlin is finished, the publication offers one last chapter titled *De algunas profecías que el sabio Merlín dixo antes de su muerte* ("On Some Prophecies Which Merlin the Wise Told Before his Death") which contains a long, extensive collection of prophecies concerning events tied to Castilian politics, the most modern of which dates to 1467. This

---

5   P. Cartelet, "Capítulo VIII. Las profecías interpoladas del *Baladro del sabio Merlín*: la ambición de una enciclopedia merliniana", in *'Fágote de tanto sabidor.' La construcción del motivo profético en la literatura medieval hispánica (siglos XIII–XV)*, Les Livres d'e-Spania "Études", 2016, <http://journals.openedition.org/e-spanialivres/1044> (accessed 24 June 2019).

collection of prophecies attributed to Merlin constitutes an amalgam of materials whose origin, dating, and purpose are diverse; hence the difficulty they
offer, both in terms of understanding the facts they allude to and in terms of
their reading and editing. The most extensive collection preserved is that which
is inserted under the heading *Aquí comiençan las profecías del sabio Merlín,
profeta digníssimo*, "Here begin the prophecies of Merlin the Wise, a most worthy prophet." Several key parts stand out in this collection: the so-called *Visión
de Alfonso en la ciudad de Sevilla*, "The vision of Alfonso in the city of Seville",
for which there is also a Catalan version, in which an angel reveals to the king
that the curse he has uttered will cause the loss of his lineage up to four generations; the *Profecías que revela Merlín a Maestre Antonio*, "Prophecies that
Merlin revealed to Master Antonio", which begin with the loss of Spain by King
Rodrigo; and the *Profecías de Merlín cerca de la ciudad de Londres*, "Merlin's
prophecies about the city of London", which allude to Alfonso x, Alfonso xi,
Pedro i, and Enrique ii, and extend to the year 1377. This last group in the collection was translated into Catalan, and is preserved in Barcelona, Biblioteca
de Catalunya, 271, copied at the beginning of the 15th century. This manuscript
offers a version of the prophecies that is better than the ones in the Sevillian
Demanda del Sancto Grial: they are more correct and contain elements that the
Castilian edition printed in 1535 has lost. The prophecies attributed to Merlin
and related to this tradition or collection served as a model for those contained
in the *Poema de Alfonso XI*, the *Crónica del rey don Pedro*, and the *Cancionero
de Baena* ("The Songbook of Baena").

Translated from Spanish by Nahir I. Otaño Gracia

CHAPTER 17

The Reception of Geoffrey of Monmouth in the Crown of Aragon

Nahir I. Otaño Gracia

The reception of Geoffrey of Monmouth in Catalonia and the Crown of Aragon demonstrates that the *De gestis Britonum* was an important component in the creation of a textual, historical, and mythical Catalan identity. Despite the dearth of primary materials available, scholars have found information derived from the DGB in several texts produced by the Crown of Aragon.[1] These texts include a partial translation into Catalan of the DGB as well as other historiographical records and the *Crónicas* of Ramon Muntaner (1325–28). The use of the DGB in these contexts connect Geoffrey's work with the creation of a mythical and historical lineage for the Crown of Aragon. Some scholars, including myself, suggest that the use of the DGB in the 13th and 14th centuries helped legitimize the ideologies of expansion of the Crown of Aragon.[2] The historiographical records follow a pattern from other Christian Peninsular texts to create a Spanish genealogy, and the *Crónicas*, an account of Catalan chivalry, aim to demonstrate Catalan superiority.[3] This entry contextualizes

---

1 I use Ernst Kantorowicz's definition of the Crown, which does not only include the king but those who work alongside the king to protect the kingdom. He defines the Crown as a "composite body, an aggregate of the king and those responsible for maintaining the inalienable rights of the Crown and the kingdom. As a perpetual minor, the Crown itself had corporational character – with the king as its guardian, though again not with the king alone, but with that composite body of king and magnates who together were said to be, or to represent, the Crown"; E.H. Kantorowicz, *The King's Two Bodies: A Study in Medieval Political Theology*, Princeton, 1957, repr. 1997 with a new preface, p. 381.

2 See D. Abulafia, "La Corona de Aragón en la Época de *Tirant Lo Blanc*, 1392–1516", in E. Mira (ed.), *Joanot Martorell y el otoño de la Caballería*, Valencia, 2011, pp. 47–60, at p. 49; J. Aurell, *Authoring the Past: History, Autobiography, and Politics in Medieval Catalonia*, Chicago, 2012, pp. 192–93; and J. Izquierdo, "Traslladar la memòria, traduir el món: la prosa de Ramon Muntaner en el context cultural i literari romànic", *Quaderns de filologia. Estudis literaris* 8 (2003), 189–244 for some examples of the use of Arthuriana in Catalonian affairs. My own forthcoming research on Catalan Arthurian manuscripts shows that texts such as *La Faula* (1370–74), *Curial e Güelfa* (1440–60), and *Tirant lo Blanc* (1490) also claim that Catalan knights are better than Arthurian knights in order to support chivalric ideologies of expansion.

3 The terms Iberia, Al-Andalus, and Spain are interrelated concepts that define different aspects of the Peninsula. Iberia corresponds to the entire Peninsula. Al-Andalus encompasses

---

the reception of the *DGB* in the history of the Crown of Aragon and delves into the extant materials and their role in Catalan affairs.

The reception of Geoffrey of Monmouth must be understood through several geographical frameworks. They include the south of France (known as Occitania), the Iberian Peninsula, and the Mediterranean world.[4] The similar cultures of Occitania and Catalonia in the 12th century and the easy movement of the Occitan and Catalan troubadours throughout the Pyrenees means that the troubadours from both Occitania and Catalonia treated the literature very similarly.[5] The integration of Catalonia and the kingdom of Aragon combined the maritime and inland territories of the Aragon courts and the Catalan dynasty, creating the Crown of Aragon and expanding the territories of the Catalans into the Peninsula and the Mediterranean.[6] The acquired status of the Crown as an up-and-coming kingdom redefined the ways the Catalan courts understood themselves. The *Deeds of the Counts of Barcelona* (*Gesta comitum Barcinonensium*, 1180), for example, was written to create a Catalan genealogy as a response to the Catalan courts' central position in Occitania, the Peninsula, and the Mediterranean.[7] The Albigensian Crusade of 1212, however, changed the needs of the Crown of Aragon once again and they began to prioritize expansion in the Mediterranean, breaking the ties that united the Crown of Aragon with Occitania.[8]

Muslim-controlled territories between 711–1492. Spain encompasses Christian-controlled territories now associated with the Spanish state (Castile, Navarre, Aragon, Catalonia, and so on). See T.F. Glick, *Islamic and Christian Spain in the Early Middle Ages*, Princeton, 1979, pp. 13–15.

4   The introduction of Arthurian motifs to Catalan literature and culture begins with the cultural and political connections between Catalonia and Occitania. See A.J. Kosto, *Making Agreements in Medieval Catalonia: Power, Order, and the Written Word, 1000–1200*, Cambridge, 2001, p. 9; L. Patterson, *The World of the Troubadours*, Cambridge, 1993, pp. 1–3; L. Soriano Robles, "The *Matière de Bretagne* in the Corona de Aragón", in D. Hook (ed.), *The Arthur of the Iberians: The Arthurian Legends in the Spanish and Portuguese Worlds* (Arthurian Literature in the Middle Ages, 8), Cardiff, 2015, pp. 165–86, at p. 162.

5   For the francophone reception of Geoffrey, see Chapter 20, which indicates that there is no extant Occitan reception of Geoffrey.

6   In 1137 Ramon Berenguer IV, Count of Barcelona (1131–62), was betrothed to Petronilla of Aragon (1136–76), gaining control not only of the territories of the counts of Barcelona, but also of the kingdom of Aragon. Alfonso II (1162–96), child of Petronilla and Ramon, became the first king of what is known as the Crown of Aragon.

7   See J. Aurell, "From Genealogies to Chronicles: the Power of the Form in Medieval Catalan Historiography", *Viator* 36 (2005), 235–64, at p. 238; and S.M. Cingolani, "De historia privada a historia pública y de la afirmación al discurso: Una reflexión en torno a la historiografía medieval catalana (985–1288)", *Talia Dixit* 3 (2008), 51–76.

8   M. Vanlandingham, *Transforming the State: King, Court and Political Culture in the Realms of Aragon (1213–1387)*, Leiden, 2002, p. 9.

The inclusion of the *DGB* in the textual production of the Crown of Aragon is discernable after the break between Occitania and Catalonia because the Crown saw Spain and the Mediterranean as their new sources for European growth economically and culturally. This historical context serves as a backdrop for the reception of Geoffrey of Monmouth in the Crown of Aragon. The Catalan Crown saw itself as a young kingdom, and because they saw themselves as young, they began to build their own historical and mythical past as a response to their relatively new position within Spanish and European affairs. In addition, it is also imperative to know that the connection between the history of the Crown of Aragon and Spain is also the reason for the dearth of materials for analysis. Both the Inquisition and the advent of the printing press greatly diminished the extant medieval texts available for study in Spain. The latter used manuscripts of the common variety for bookbinding; the former made keeping texts of entertainment dangerous. The end result is that many manuscripts were lost, including manuscripts that would have included the work of Geoffrey of Monmouth, making any assessment of the Catalan reception of the text incomplete.[9]

Despite the difficulties in assessing the reception of Geoffrey of Monmouth's *DGB* in the Crown of Aragon, the impact of the text is discernable. The *Anales navarro-aragoneses*, also known as the *Crónicas navarras*, was written c.1196 in Latin and Navarre-aragonese.[10] The historiographical text mentions the death

---

9   J.M. Lucía Megías explains that "the success of the printed romances of chivalry, which
       would become one of the staples of the burgeoning Hispanic publishing industry, would
       lead to many of the common chivalric manuscript codices being replaced by printed edi-
       tions ... To this factor, which we may class as an aesthetic consideration, there was added
       another, as the Counter-Reformation gave impetus to methods of control over what was
       published and what was kept in the noble libraries of Spain: there was an increasing ten-
       dency to remove the literature of entertainment from these collections" ("The Surviving
       Peninsular Arthurian Witnesses: A Description and an Analysis", in Hook (ed.), *The Arthur
       of the Iberians*, pp. 33–57, at pp. 50–51). The loss of Catalan Arthurian texts becomes ap-
       parent when we compare the extant manuscripts of Arthurian romance with their men-
       tions in the chancery registers. The Catalan registers mention five copies of *Merlí* (from
       1383–1459), 18 copies of *Lançalot* (from 1319–1488), 13 copies of *Saint Graal* (from 1342–
       1600), three copies of *Mort Artu* (from 1349–1422), and 22 copies of *Tristan en Prose* (from
       1315–1467). By contrast the extant Catalan manuscripts of these romances include no cop-
       ies of *Merlí*, two copies of *Lançalot*, two copies of *Saint Graal*, one of *Mort Artu*, and three
       of *Tristan en Prose* (S.M. Cingolani, "'Nos en leyr tales libros trobemos plazer e recreation'.
       L'estudi sobre la difusió de la literatura d'entreteniment a Catalunya els segles XIV i XV",
       Llengua & Literatura 4 (1990–91), 39–127, at pp. 74–92).
10   The *Anales navarro-aragoneses* were written in the kingdom of Navarre which neighbors
       the kingdom of Aragon. The use of Navarre-aragonese is a testament to the connections
       between the two kingdoms in the early history of the Peninsula.

of Arthur and gives the same date as the *DGB*. The *Anales* state that "It was in the year D.LXXX that King Arthur and Mordret made battle in Quibleno."[11] It is clear that the information derives from Geoffrey's work (either from a copy of the text or an indirect source). The *Anales navarro-aragoneses* inspired both directly and indirectly Christian Iberian historiographic tradition. Historiographic texts from the Christian courts of the Peninsula such as *Fuero de Navarra* (c.1205), *The Book of Kings* (*Liber regum*) or *Chronicon Villarense* (c.1211), *Anales toledanos primeros* (c.1217), and *General estoria* (c.1270–80) all mention the battle between Arthur and Mordred using Geoffrey's dating of the event.[12]

The role of the *DGB* as part of Catalan historiography is apparent in Paris, Bibliothèque nationale de France, esp. 13 (1385–1430) which is a compilation of historiographic texts, including Gauchier de Denain's *Compendi historial*, Rodrigo Jiménez de Rada's *Crónica d'Espanya*, and Jaume Domènech's *Genealogia dels reis d'Aragó*. Folios 83v–97v in particular contain a translation of the *DGB* into Catalan.[13] Pere Bohigas argues that this compilation of historiographic texts is one of the sources used by the Catalan chronicler Juan Fernández de Heredia (1310/15–1396), who incorporates parts of the *DGB* into the *Grant Crónica d'Espanya* found in Madrid, Biblioteca Nacional de España, 10133.[14] Fernández de Heredia was Master of the Order of St John of Jerusalem and an influential force in the Crown of Aragon and Europe in general.[15] Fernández de Heredia continues the tradition of other agents of the Christian courts of the Peninsula who used the *DGB* as part of their historiography.

---

11   "Era D.LXXX aynos fizo la bataylla el rey Artus con modret en Quibleno." My translation. Cited from C. Alvar, "The Matter of Britain in Spanish Society and Literature from Cluny to Cervantes", in Hook (ed.), *The Arthur of the Iberians*, pp. 187–270, at p. 234. See also *Corónicas navarras*, ed. A. Ubierto Arteta (Textos Medievales, 14), Zaragoza, 1989, p. 40.

12   As in the British Isles, the *DGB* was incorporated into chronicles and annals throughout the Peninsula. See Chapter 25 of this volume as well as P. Gracia, "Arthurian Material in Iberia", in Hook (ed.), *The Arthur of the Iberians*, pp. 11–32, at pp. 15. The *Anales Toledanos I* give the same date as the *DGB* but change Arthur's name to Rey Zitus. The annal states that "Lidió el Rey Zitus con Modret su sobrino en Camblenc, Era DLXXX", "King Zitus fought with his nephew Modret in Camblenc, it was DLXXX" (*Anales Toledanos I*, ed. E. Flórez, *España Sagrada* (*XXIII*), Madrid, 1767, p. 381, my translation).

13   P. Bohigas, *Sobre manuscripts i bibliotheques* (Textos i Estudis de Cultura Catalana, 10), Barcelona, 1985, pp. 123–32, 180–203; Soriano Robles, "*Matière de Bretagne*", p. 170.

14   Bohigas, *Sobre manuscripts i bibliotheques*, p. 179. A digital copy of the manuscript *Grant Crónica d'Espanya* is available online at <http://bdh-rd.bne.es/viewer.vm?id=0000008341&page=1> (accessed 16 March 2018).

15   L. Badia and I. Grifoll, "Language: From the Countryside to the Royal Court", in F. Sabaté (ed.), *The Crown of Aragon: A Singular Mediterranean Empire* (Brill's Companions to European History, 12), Leiden, 2017, pp. 361–86, at pp. 380–81.

Regarding the Crown of Aragon in particular, Fernández de Heredia used the *DGB* to solidify a mythical and historical past for the Crown.

The use of Geoffrey's work in historiographic records is an example of the ways the Crown of Aragon enhanced its standing within a European setting. The *Crónicas* of Ramon Muntaner and Bernat Desclot (1283–88) continue the tradition of using the *DGB* in the construction of a Catalan identity.[16] Both texts use *DGB* and Arthuriana to enhance the narration of Jaume's birth found in his own *Crónica*.[17] They specifically use the birth of Arthur in the *DGB* and the birth of Galahad in the *Vulgate* to create an association between Jaume, Arthur, and Galahad as the best kings/knights in Christian Europe in order to solidify Jaume's claim to the throne.[18] Muntaner's *Crónica* in particular substitutes Jaume for Arthur and the Duke of Tintagel for Uther Pendragon.[19]

Although these examples are few, they demonstrate that the *DGB*, especially the character of Arthur as represented in the *DGB*, was one of the ways that the Crown of Aragon created their own historical and mythical past in order to claim their own Europeanness. This is consistent with the use of Arthuriana in the Catalan courts to claim that the Crown of Aragon was the future of chivalric conquest in Europe.

---

16   J. Aurell, *Authoring the Past*, pp. 40–42.

17   Known in English as James I the Conqueror, Jaume was born in 1198. In 1213 he became king of the Crown of Aragon after his father, Piere le Catholic (1196–1213), died at the battle of Muret. James I is known for his ambitious policies of expansion in the Peninsula and the Mediterranean Sea. Following his grandfather's footsteps, Alfonso II, who commissioned the *Gesta comitum* and gave his patronage to the troubadour poets in order to create a Catalan genealogy, Jaume dictates *El Llibre dels fets del rei en Jaume* ("The Book of the Deeds of King James"), the first of the *Quatre Grans Chròniques* ("Four Great Chronicles"), to celebrate the deeds of the Crown of Aragon. For more information see J. Aurell, *Authoring the Past*, pp. 39–54.

18   P. Bohigas, *Aportació a l'estudi de la literature catalana*, Monserrat, 1982, p. 280; J.M. Pujol, *La memòria literària de Joanot Martorell: Models i scriptura en el 'Tirant lo Blanc'*, Barcelona, 2002; A.G. Elliot, "The Historian as Artist: Manipulation of History in the Chronicle of Desclot", *Viator* 14 (1983), 195–209.

19   M. Montoliu, "Sobre els elements èpics, principalment asturians, de la Crònica de Jaume I", in n.n. (ed.), *Homenaje ofrecido a Menéndez Pidal: miscelánea de estudios lingüísticos, literarios e históricos*, 3 vols., Madrid, 1924, vol. 1, pp. 698–712.

CHAPTER 18

The Middle Dutch Reception of Geoffrey of Monmouth

David F. Johnson

Before discussing the traces of Geoffrey's works that have been identified in the vernacular literature of the medieval Low Countries, it may be useful to briefly review the highpoints of the Latin context for their reception in this region.

1   Pre-Galfridian References to King Arthur in the Medieval Low Countries

Anyone interested to learn whether Geoffrey of Monmouth's Latin writings were known in the medieval Low Countries[1] may be surprised to discover that not only was this indeed the case, but that Arthur appears in Latin texts in the Low Countries even before Geoffrey published his famous *De gestis Britonum* c.1138.[2] The two most notable such mentions of King Arthur in works penned in Latin by authors from the medieval Low Countries are found in Herman of Tournai's (also Herman of Laon, or in Dutch, Herman van Doornik) *On the Miracles of St Mary of Laon* (*De miraculis S. Mariae Laudunensis*), and in Lambert of St Omer's famous encyclopedia, the *Liber Floridus*. In the latter,

---

1   I use "Low Countries", "Netherlandic", and "The Netherlands" in their historical sense, to refer to what at the time was known as "Germania Inferior". As P.F.J. Obbema points out, this is the region comprising "what is now Belgium, the Netherlands, and the bordering Rhineland"; see "The Rooklooster Register Evaluated", *Quaerendo* 7 (1977), 326–53, at p. 330.

2   For information on the Latin Arthurian tradition in the medieval Low Countries, I have leaned heavily on two articles by G. Tournoy: "De Latijnse Artur in de Nederlanden", in W. Verbeke, J. Janssens, and M. Smeyers (eds.), *Arturus Rex: Koning Artur en de Nederlanden: la matière de Bretagne et les anciens Pays-Bas* (Mediaevalia Lovaniensia, Series 1, Studia 16), Leuven, 1987, pp. 147–88 and "A First Glance at the Latin Arthur in the Low Countries", in W. Van Hoecke, G. Tournoy, and W. Verbeke (eds.), *Arturus Rex: Acta Conventus Lovaniensis 1987* (Mediaevalia Lovaniensia, Series 1, Studia 17), Leuven, 1991, pp. 215–21. For an exhaustive overview of the vernacular chronicle tradition in this region more broadly, see especially G.H.M. Claassens, "Niederländische Chronistik im Mittelalter", in G. Wolf and N.H. Ott (eds.), *Handbuch Chroniken Des Mittelalters*, Berlin, 2016, pp. 577–608.

published in 1121, Lambert draws on the *Historia Brittonum*, among other sources, for material concerning Arthur that he includes in two chapters in this famous work (chapter 52, *On the Marvels of Britain* (*De mirandis Britannie*), and chapter 57, *The History of the English* (*Historia Anglorum*)). In chapter 52, Lambert recounts two legends concerning Arthur, the first of which tells of the stone in which is found the footprint of his dog, Cabal. Attempts to move the stone from atop its cairn are fruitless: no matter where one tries to hide it, by the third day one will find it back on top of the pile of stones Arthur himself had placed there. The second legend deals with the tomb erected by Arthur for his son Antyr, a tomb that yields different dimensions each time it is measured. Both of these were drawn from the *Historia Brittonum*, but Tournoy sees in Lambert's excision of the detail that it was Arthur himself who slew his son an intentional move to portray Arthur in a more positive light.[3] A bit further on in this same chapter Lambert provides a description of Arthur's palace, which includes a sculptural depiction of his victories. According to Tournoy, this detail does not appear in any of the known redactions of the *Historia Brittonum*, nor may it be found in any of Lambert's other usual sources, which may or may not point in the direction of originality on the part of this author from the medieval Low Countries, though it does demonstrate a genuine pre-Galfridian interest in Arthur in the region.[4] In chapter 57, Lambert repeats the account of Arthur's twelve victories under the heading *Historia Anglorum*.[5] The *De miraculis S. Mariae Laudunensis* is a saint's life written in 1142 by Herman van Doornik, abbot of St Martin's Abbey in Doornik/Tournai until 1136. Herman wrote it at the behest of the bishop of Laon, and it contains an account of the journeys of a number of canons of Laon through France and England to raise money to rebuild the cathedral of Laon, which was destroyed by fire in 1112. While traveling through Devonshire they are shown Arthur's chair and oven, and the travelers are told that they are in "Arthur's country". The relics the canons carry with them perform several miracles, but they fail to heal a local who argues with the French delegation, contending that Arthur still

---

3   See Tournoy, "De Latijnse Artur", pp. 149–50. For more on the autograph manuscript of Lambert's *Liber Floridus*, see especially A. Derolez, *The Making and Meaning of the Liber Floridus: A Study of the Original Manuscript Ghent, University Library MS 92* (Studies in Medieval and Early Renaissance Art History, 76), London, 2015. The entire manuscript, Ghent, University Library, 92, is available in high resolution facsimile online at <https://lib.ugent.be/catalog/rug01:000763774> (accessed 31 May 2018).

4   Tournoy, "De Latijnse Artur", p. 150.

5   Tournoy, "De Latijnse Artur", p. 150, and see Ghent, University Library, 92, fol. 72v for the passage in question.

lives.[6] If nothing else, these few references to King Arthur in the pre-Galfridian Latin writings of authors from the Low Countries demonstrate that the region would prove to be a fertile ground for the reception of Geoffrey's *DGB* and *PM*. There is other evidence that speaks to the presence of a pre-Galfridian (oral) Arthurian tradition in this region as well, most notably a witness to a grant dating to 1118 by the name of "Walewein van Melle".[7]

2   The Reception of Geoffrey's Works in the Medieval Low Countries – the Manuscripts

In his preliminary review of manuscripts with a Netherlandish provenance containing either the *DGB* or the *PM*, Tournoy arrives at a total of some 20. He concludes that it is impossible to know how many there were in the region from the 12th century on, or how many have been lost. His review of published wills and testaments from the period turned up no references to copies of these works, and only one from a library catalogue from one of the seven collegiate churches of Liège, St Paul's. Records from the largest medieval libraries in the region – the monastic libraries – are more often than not very late and incomplete. The catalogues published by Antonius Sanderus in his *Bibliotheca Belgica Manuscripta* (Rijsel, 1641–44) list a number of tantalizing entries for manuscripts in some 11 Netherlandic monastic libraries, with titles that suggest copies, in whole or part, of Geoffrey's *DGB* and *PM*. Unfortunately, in most cases we have no way of knowing when or where these manuscripts were written, or even which versions of the texts in question they contain. Equally tantalizing are references found in the monumental composite catalogue known as the *Rooklooster Register*, a manuscript that collects information from booklists compiled from 100 individual religious institutions in the medieval Low Countries. As Tournoy points out, the entry (under the sub-heading "Authors") on fol. 141v of this manuscript attributes texts that were most likely Geoffrey's *DGB* and *PM* to "*Galfridus viterbiensis*", which the compiler has corrected by consulting a manuscript in the Rooklooster itself: *Nos habemus "Gaufridus*

---

6   Tournoy, "De Latijnse Artur", pp. 147–48. See also A. Breeze, "Arthur in Early Saints' Lives", in S. Echard (ed.), *The Arthur of Medieval Latin Literature: The Development and Dissemination of the Arthurian Legend in Medieval Latin* (Arthurian Literature in the Middle Ages, 6), Cardiff, 2011, pp. 26–41, at p. 26, as well as J.S.P. Tatlock, "The English Journey of the Laon Canons", *Speculum* 8:4 (1933), 454–65.

7   For more on this *Vualauuaynus*, and further references, see G.H.M. Claassens and D.F. Johnson (eds.), *King Arthur in the Medieval Low Countries* (Mediaevalia Lovaniensia, Series 1, Studia 28), Leuven, 2000, pp. 4–5.

monemutensis", "We have 'a Geoffrey of Monmouth'".[8] In the margin the scribe tells us that four other libraries owned exemplars of these texts, as well. Again, even if the information provided by these catalogues and booklists is sketchy and incomplete, it testifies to the presence and popularity of Geoffrey's Latin works. We are of course on much firmer ground when it comes to the manuscripts containing Geoffrey's works that are still preserved in archives and libraries in the Netherlands today, and Tournoy describes 11 of these that are known to have been compiled and to have resided in the medieval Low Countries.[9] There is one further striking Latin text that deserves mention here, for it comprises an instance of an author from the Low Countries adapting Geoffrey's DGB to his own ends, and in Tournoy's words, constitutes "the only attempt in the Latin literature of the Low Countries at a more personal re-working of Arthurian material".[10] An otherwise unknown copyist by the name of Bernardus transcribed *The Fall of Troy* of Dares Phrygius and the DGB at some point in the second half of the 12th century. He is thought to have been the one to insert a prologue and an epilogue, as well as a summary in leonine hexameters at the end of each one of the nine books of the DGB, after which he appends a summary of the legend of Brutus. In the prologue to this adaptation of the DGB, Bernardus tells his audience just how silly the idea is that Arthur will ever return.[11]

3   Geoffrey of Monmouth in Middle Dutch: Jacob van Maerlant and the *Spiegel historiael*

So far as we know, no integral translations of the DGB or the PM into Middle Dutch were ever produced. The reasons for this are unclear, though in the end

---

8   Tournoy, "De Latijnse Artur", p. 153. For more information on the *Rooklooster Register* and an ongoing project to publish this important manuscript online, see *The Rooklooster Register Unveiled*, Cartusiana and Österreichische Nationalbibliothek, 2009–13, <http://rrkl.cartusiana.org/?q=node/7> (accessed 31 May 2018). The entry on fol. 141v may be consulted at <http://rrkl.cartusiana.org/?q=image/view/354/_original> (accessed 31 May 2018). For a good introduction to the manuscript in English, see Obbema, "The Rooklooster Register".

9   Tournoy, "De Latijnse Artur", pp. 153–55. All 11 of these manuscripts are more fully described in Crick, *SC*.

10   Tournoy, "A First Glance at the Latin Arthur", p. 216, and id., "De Latijnse Artur", pp. 155–56.

11   See J. Hammer, "Some Leonine Summaries of Geoffrey of Monmouth's *Historia Regum Britanniae* and Other Poems", *Speculum* 6:1 (1931), 114–23. The attribution of all of the leonine verses that appear in these two manuscripts (Douai, Bibliothèque municipale, 880 and 882) to Bernardus is called into question, however, by Crick, *DR*, p. 79.

it may simply be because Geoffrey's chronicle concerned mainly British history, and while it enjoyed a certain popularity in the medieval Low Countries in Latin, other chronicles and historiographical works, especially vernacular ones, took precedence over Geoffrey's work throughout the period.[12] The road that leads to one of the most comprehensive incorporations of Geoffrey's *DGB* in a Middle Dutch text actually begins with another Netherlandic chronicler, Sigebert of Gembloux, whose Latin *Chronicle* enjoyed wide circulation during the Middle Ages after his death in 1112.[13] According to Geoffrey Ashe, Geoffrey of Monmouth may have borrowed the name of the Roman emperor Lucius from Sigebert's chronicle.[14] Next we find that an anonymous monk from Ourscamp (near Beauvais) expanded Sigebert's *Chronicle* by adding material from the *DGB* to produce the *Auctarium Ursicampinum*.[15] Sometime after it was completed, this expanded version of Sigebert's *Chronicle* was then used by Vincent of Beauvais in composing his *Speculum historiale*, a text that brings us full circle back to the medieval Low Countries, for it was this work that the Flemish poet Jacob van Maerlant translated and reworked into his own vernacular *Spiegel historiael* ("Mirror of History"). When around 1283 Maerlant began work on an account of the history of the world in vernacular verse, which he dedicated to the man he hoped would become his patron, Floris V, count of Holland, he had already composed poems in Middle Dutch concerning that part of British history which involves the Arthurian legend, namely in his translations of the Old French Vulgate Cycle prose renderings of Robert de Boron's *Estoire del Saint Graal* and *Estoire de Merlin*. These works became known as the *Merlijn*, which consists of two parts, the first part as the *Historie van den Grale*, and the second under the title *Boek van Merline*.[16] What concerns us here is that the version of history represented in the French works he adapted was something that Maerlant later came to distrust, and he includes many criticisms of his French sources in the text of his adaptive translation. By the time he began work on the *Spiegel historiael*, Maerlant had come to regard verse romances in French as lies and fables, and believed that if he could not find a source for something

---

12   See Claassens, "Niederländische Chronistik im Mittelalter", pp. 577–608.

13   See J. Deploige, "Sigebert of Gembloux", in R.G. Dunphy (ed.), *Encyclopedia of the Medieval Chronicle*, 2 vols., Leiden, 2010, vol. 2, pp. 1358–61, who notes that "in all, 65 manuscripts have been attested, of which more than 44 are preserved" (p. 1358).

14   Tournoy "A First Glance at the Latin Arthur", p. 218.

15   See Tournoy, "A First Glance at the Latin Arthur", pp. 218–19 for analysis of this monk's changes to the *DGB* in his efforts to incorporate it into Sigebert's chronicle.

16   These texts have been most recently edited by T. Sodmann: Jacob van Maerlant, *Historie van den Grale* and *Boek van Merline*, ed. T. Sodmann, *Jacob van Maerlant: Historie van den Grale und Boek van Merline* (Niederdeutsche Studien, 26), Cologne and Vienna, 1980.

in Latin, it could not be true.[17] Moreover, writing this history of the world for a secular court audience, he realized that he both had to trim his main source, Vincent of Beauvais' *Speculum historiale*, of much of its theological material, and look for a more expansive treatment of Arthurian history than was available in the *Speculum historiale*.[18] Vincent of Beauvais seems not to have had a copy of the *DGB* at his disposal, although his account of Arthurian history is ultimately based on it, being mediated through his main source, the expanded *Chronicon* of Sigebert of Gembloux, or *Auctarium Ursicampinum*. Maerlant, however, did have a copy of the *DGB* to hand, and with the aid of this he expanded the brief Arthurian passage in Vincent of Beauvais' text – some 1500 words – to no fewer than 1500 lines of verse.[19] Most of the material Maerlant took from the *DGB* to extend Vincent's terse treatment occurs in Books I, V, and VI of the *Spiegel historiael*. Of the seven chapters he devotes to Brutus in Book I, five contain material he drew from the *DGB*. In Chapter VII of Book V, Maerlant takes up the story of the *Adventus saxonum*, followed by other Arthurian highlights taken from Geoffrey such as Vortigern, the coming of Merlin, Aurelius Ambrosius, the death of Uther Pendragon, Arthur's accession to the throne, his subsequent conquests, his famous court, and his war with the Romans. Finally, it is in chapters 29 and 30 of Book VI that we find the account of the civil war between Arthur and Mordred, and the fateful battle on Salisbury Plain.[20]

---

17 For this aspect of his adaptation of these works, see especially W.P. Gerritsen, "Jacob van Maerlant and Geoffrey of Monmouth", in K. Varty (ed.), *An Arthurian Tapestry: Essays in Memory of Lewis Thorpe*, Glasgow, 1981, pp. 369–76. See also Claassens and Johnson (eds.), *King Arthur*, pp. 1–5.

18 Gerritsen, "Jacob van Maerlant", p. 377.

19 Gerritsen, "Jacob van Maerlant", pp. 378–79. In a note Gerritsen observes that he can find no material in the *Speculum historiale* that can be directly derived from the *DGB*. He notes Vincent's own admission that he lacked British sources to take his account of the English kings any further than 735 (p. 386, n. 39).

20 For an analysis of select passages influenced by the *DGB* in Maerlant's *Spiegel historiael*, see Gerritsen, "Jacob van Maerlant", pp. 380–83. The chapters containing the material from the *DGB* are found in Jacob van Maerlant, *Spiegel historiael* [Mirror of history], ed. M. De Vries and E. Verwijs, *Jacob van Maerlant, Philip van Utenbroeke, and Lodewijk van Velthem, Jacob van Maerlant's Spiegel historiael: met de fragmenten der later toegevoegde gedeelten* [Jacob van Maerlant's Mirror of history: with the fragments of its later additions], 4 vols., Gravenhage, 1861–79 (repr. Utrecht, 1982), vol. 2, III *Partie*, I *Boek*, pp. 47–56; III *Partie*, V *Boek*, pp. 277–82, 333–43; and III *Partie*, VI *Boek*, pp. 386–88.

4   Geoffrey of Monmouth and the Lanceloet Compilation

There is one further instance in Middle Dutch literature where Geoffrey's *DGB* makes an appearance: the translation and adaptation of the *Mort Artu* in the final text in the so-called *Lancelot Compilation: Arturs doet*. The compiler of this manuscript took an existing translation into Middle Dutch of the Old French *La Mort le Roi Artu* and modified it to fit in his own Middle Dutch version, much expanded, of the Old French Vulgate Cycle.[21] Here the compiler has removed the original passage concerning the battle between Arthur and the Romans he encountered in his exemplar, and replaced it, nearly verbatim, with its counterpart from Jacob van Maerlant's *Spiegel historiael*.[22] Why he should have done so is a matter of debate. Gerritsen believes that it was out of deference for the more historically "accurate" version represented by Maerlant's translation of a Latin authority, whereas De Graaf maintains that its inclusion heightened the religious aspect of the text, a feature emphasized at the outset of this version of the story of Arthur's death with the addition of a prologue, unique to the Dutch text, redolent with religious meaning.[23]

---

21   For a convenient overview in English of this manuscript and the texts it contains, as well as its place in the landscape of Middle Dutch romance, see Claassens and Johnson (eds.), *King Arthur*, pp. 1–33.

22   *Roman van Lancelot*, ed. W.J.A. Jonckbloet, *Roman van Lancelot (XIIIᵉ eeuw). Naar het (eenig-bekende) handschrift der Koninklijke Bibliotheek, op gezag van het Gouvernement uitgegeven door Dr. W.J.A. Janckbloet* [The romance of Lancelot (13th century). Edited from the (only known) manuscript in the Royal Library, under the auspices of the government and edited by Dr. W.J.A. Janckbloet], 2 vols., Gravenhage, 1846–49, vol. 2, pp. 187–275, ll. 9683–10128. Compare Jacob van Maerlant, *Spiegel historiael*, ed. De Vries and Verwijs, vol. 2, pp. 335–43.

23   For the interpolation of this passage into *Arturs doet*, see especially K. de Graaf, "De episode van Arturs oorlog tegen de Romeinen", in *Hoe Artur sinen inde nam: Studie over de Middelnederlandse ridderroman Arturs doet*, Door een werkgroep van Groninger neerlandici ["The episode of Arthur's battle against the Romans" in *How Arthur met his end: studies on the Middle Dutch romance* Arturs doet, by a work group of medievalists at the University of Groningen], Groningen, 1983, pp. 207–14, and W.P. Gerritsen, "L'épisode de La Guerre Contre Les Romains Dans La Mort Artu Néerlandaise", in n.n. (ed.), *Mélanges de Langue et de Littérature Du Moyen Age et de La Renaissance Offerts à Jean Frappier*, 2 vols., Geneva, 1970, vol. 1, pp. 337–49. For more on the unique prologue at the outset of *Arturs doet*, see especially B. Besamusca and O.S.H. Lie, "The Prologue to *Arturs doet*, the Middle Dutch Translation of *La Mort le Roi Artu* in the *Lancelot Compilation*", in E. Kooper (ed.), *Medieval Dutch Literature in its European Context* (Cambridge Studies in Medieval Literature, 21), Cambridge, 1994, pp. 96–112.

CHAPTER 19

The English Reception of Geoffrey of Monmouth

Elizabeth Bryan

1 De gestis Britonum

Historical narratives in Middle English that translated or incorporated matter from Geoffrey of Monmouth's *DGB* began as early as 1185, continued to be composed throughout the 13th, 14th, and 15th centuries, and were consulted by Tudor readers and historians of England across the 16th century.[1] The earlier Middle English texts duplicated the historical span of the *DGB*, but by the end of the 13th century, the Geoffrey-derived history of ancient Britain began to appear in English as the first section of longer histories of Anglo-Saxon, Anglo-Norman, and Plantagenet England. Some translations of Geoffrey's work into Middle English altered the position of the *DGB* as providing a history of origins for the British (i.e. Britons), transposing that history into a teleological history of the English, to whom dominion over the island of Britain explicitly belonged. The collective term "Brut tradition" (referring to any history based on Brutus, Geoffrey's Trojan-descended, legendary founder of ancient Britain), has been applied to any and all of these texts, but the nomenclature of "Brut" can be ambiguous and scholars must remain alert to possible confusion in the literature about which text, or genre, is actually under discussion.[2] Whereas Geoffrey's *DGB* was a significant catalyst for writing in Middle English from the 12th through the 15th centuries, many Middle English "Brut" histories

---

1 An essential resource for Middle English chronicles is E.D. Kennedy, *Chronicles and Other Historical Writing* (A Manual of the Writings in Middle English, 8), New Haven, 1989, especially Chapter 2, "*Brut* Chronicles", pp. 2611–47 (discussion) and 2781–2845 (bibliography). See also R.G. Dunphy (ed.), *Encyclopedia of the Medieval Chronicle*, 2 vols., Leiden, 2010.

2 For example, "Brut" chronicles listed in inventories in wills surveyed by L.M. Friedman were (erroneously) assumed to be all by Laȝamon, according to a personal communication from Friedman as reported by Carole Weinberg at the 1998 Laȝamon's *Brut* conference in St John, New Brunswick, Canada, whereas some of these book legacies were more likely Prose *Brut* manuscripts or other chronicles. See L.M. Friedman, *Dead Hands: A Social History of Wills, Trusts, and Inheritance Law*, Stanford, 2009. For some issues raised by critics' differing uses of the term "Brut" and difficulties of "Brut" nomenclature, see *The Abridged English Metrical Brut: British Library MS Royal 12 C. XIII*, ed. U. O'Farrell-Tate (Middle English Texts, 32), Heidelberg, 2002, pp. 14–17.

---

were drawn most directly from intermediary Anglo-Norman French iterations of Geoffrey's DGB, especially Wace's *Roman de Brut*, from which the Middle English texts Laʒamon's *Brut*, Robert Mannyng of Brunne's *Chronicle* (1338), and London, College of Arms, Arundel 22 were directly translated.

The earliest of the DGB-derived Middle English histories was Laʒamon's *Brut (fl.*1185–1216 or ?1236).[3] Laʒamon, a secular cleric at Areley Kings near Worcester, likely drew directly on the DGB as well as Wace's *Roman de Brut*, though systematic study of his direct use of the DGB is needed.[4] Only one of the Middle English histories, the anonymous *Castleford's Chronicle* (*c.*1327), translated the entire DGB, including Merlin's prophecies, directly from Geoffrey's Latin to Middle English.[5] The most widely read Brutus-based history in English was the 15th-century anonymous Middle English Prose *Brut*, which in various continuations took the history as far as 1461.[6] Its prolific manuscript production (over 183 manuscripts survive) mirrored, in the 15th century, the explosion of readership that Geoffrey's DGB, its remote textual ancestor in Latin, had enjoyed in the 12th.

Verse, in a significant variety of Middle English prosodies, was the prevalent form in 12th- and 13th-century DGB-derived English-language history texts;

---

3   Laʒamon, *Brut*, ed. G.L. Brook and R.F. Leslie, *Layamon: Brut. Edited from British Museum MS Cotton Caligula A ix and British Museum MS Otho C xiii*, 2 vols., London, 1963–78; vol. 3 is in preparation by R. Allen and L. Perry. Also useful, especially for its notes, is Laʒamon, *Brut*, trans. R. Allen, *Lawman: Brut*, London, 1992. A facing-page edition and translation is Laʒamon, *Brut*, ed. and trans. W.R.J. Barron and S.C. Weinberg, *Laʒamon: Brut, or Hystoria Brutonum*, New York, 1995. See K. Tiller, *Laʒamon's Brut and the Anglo-Norman Vision of History*, Cardiff, 2007, for the most recent book-length study of Laʒamon's *Brut*, including an argument for 1185 as the earliest date of composition.

4   See F.H.M. Le Saux, *Layamon's Brut. The Poem and its Sources* (Arthurian Studies, 19), Cambridge, 1989, for claims that Laʒamon drew from the *PM* and *VM*. Occasional details or wording in Laʒamon's *Brut* correlate better with the DGB than with Wace's *Roman de Brut*; Laʒamon's direct use of Geoffrey's work is in need of further study.

5   *Castleford's Chronicle, or, The Boke of Brut*, ed. C.D. Eckhardt, 2 vols., Oxford and New York, 1996. E.D. Kennedy, *Chronicles*, pp. 2624–25, 2809–11 uses the title "Thomas Bek of Castleford's Chronicle of England". *Castleford's Chronicle* adds hagiographic material to the DGB matter.

6   *The Brut; or, The Chronicles of England*, ed. F.W.D. Brie (Early English Text Society, 131, 136), London, 1906, 1908 (repr. Woodbridge, 2000). Essential studies are F.W.D. Brie, *Geschichte und Quellen der mittelenglischen Prosachronik. The Brute of England oder The Chronicles of England*, Marburg, 1905; L. Matheson, *The Prose "Brut": The Development of a Middle English Chronicle* (Medieval & Renaissance Texts & Studies, 180), Tempe, 1998; and J. Marvin, *The Construction of Vernacular History in the Anglo-Norman Prose Brut: the Manuscript Culture of Late Medieval England*, York, 2017.

prose was introduced in 14th- and 15th-century "Brut" texts, though some verse continued as well.[7]

In chronological order, the Middle English narratives derived indirectly or directly from Geoffrey's *DGB* are:

- Laȝamon, *Brut*, surviving in two copies, London, British Library, Cotton Otho C. xiii (*s.* xiii^{ex}–xiv^{in}) and London, British Library, Cotton Caligula A. ix (*s.* xiii$^{3-4}$)
- Robert of Gloucester, *Metrical Chronicle* (*s.* xiii^{ex}–*s.* xiv^{in})[8]
- *Short English Metrical Chronicle* (*c.*1307; Auchinleck version, 1330–40)[9]
- *Castleford's Chronicle* (also Thomas Bek of Castleford, *Chronicle of England*) (*c.*1327)
- Robert Mannyng of Brunne, *Chronicle* (1338)
- "History of the Kings of Britain" attributed to Walter, archdeacon of Oxford and Wace ("Gnaor" or "Guace") in London, College of Arms, Arundel 22, fols. 8r–8ov
- Middle English Prose *Brut*
- John Trevisa's translation of Ranulph Higden's *Polychronicon* makes use of details from the *DGB*
- Genealogical rolls in Middle English form another significant medium for the English-language reception of the *DGB*[10]

---

7   T. Summerfield, *The Matter of Kings' Lives: Design of Past and Present in the Early Fourteenth-Century Verse Chronicles by Pierre de Langtoft and Robert Mannyng*, Amsterdam and Atlanta, 1998, argues that in England, poetry was an authoritative form for history in vernacular English and French languages, whereas prose was privileged in Latin histories. When gauging the historiographical seriousness of a text on the basis of a historian's choice of verse or prose, the critic must weigh whether to privilege clerical and scholastic Latin expectations alone. It is no longer adequate to assume that formal "verse" is equivalent to generic "romance".

8   Robert of Gloucester, *Chronicle*, ed. W.A. Wright, *The Metrical Chronicle of Robert of Gloucester*, 2 vols., London, 1887. There are at least 14 manuscripts in at least two recensions, plus a prose paraphrase. See also Robert of Gloucester, *Chronicle*, ed. T. Hearne, *Robert of Gloucester's Chronicle*, 2 vols., Oxford, 1724.

9   *The Abridged English Metrical Brut*, ed. O'Farrell-Tate; see also *An Anonymous Short English Metrical Chronicle*, ed. E. Zettl (Early English Text Society, 196), London, 1935. There are seven manuscripts plus one manuscript of an Anglo-Norman version. At least nine different titles have been used by editors and critics to refer to this text, including *Chronicle of England*, *Anonymous Riming Chronicle*, *Short Metrical Chronicle*, *Short English Metrical Chronicle*, and *Anonymous Short English Metrical Chronicle*.

10   See, for example, J. Rajsic, "Looking for Arthur in Short Histories and Genealogies of England's Kings", *Review of English Studies* 68:285 (2017), 448–70.

2   Prophetiae Merlini

In the *DGB*, Merlin prophesies on four occasions, and a Merlinian prophecy to Arthur is recalled at the end of the history.[11] Wace's *Roman de Brut* famously omitted Geoffrey's *PM*, but reinserted the individual prophecy that Arthur's end would be doubtful as commentary at Arthur's death.[12]

La3amon's *Brut* (*fl.*1185–1216 or ?1236), the earliest Middle English translation (via Wace) of Geoffrey's matter, reinstated from the *DGB* quite a few more individual prophecies than Wace did.[13] La3amon's source had to be either the *DGB*, *PM*, and/or possibly a manuscript of Wace (such as Lincoln, Cathedral Library, 104 or Durham, Cathedral Library, C.IV.27) in which Geoffrey's Latin prophecies had been restored. La3amon interpolated these Geoffrey-derived prophecies structurally and poetically across the career of King Arthur and at the history's conclusion, adding Merlinian prophecies at Arthur's conception,[14] the creation of the round table,[15] and war with Mordred.[16] A manuscript variant at Arthur's passing (l. 14297), which asserts a Merlinian prediction (possibly an adaptation of the *DGB*, xi.205.563–73) of a specifically Arthurian return to help either the "Bruttes" (BL Cotton Otho C. xiii) or the "Anglen" (BL Cotton Caligula A. ix), has provoked critical debate about the political stance of La3amon and/or his text's audience(s).[17]

Castleford's Chronicle (c.1327) is the only English *Brut* chronicle to have translated the entirety of Geoffrey's prophecies into Middle English, as part of its direct translation of the entire *DGB* into Middle English rhyming couplets.[18] Its prophecies omit only the final lines of the *DGB*, vii.117.295–304, where Geoffrey's prophecies turn from planets to zodiac signs and constellations;

---

11   *DGB*, vi.108.563–64, 567–68, 573–74; vii.112–117.304. The prophecies also circulated separately as the *PM*, as Geoffrey explains in *DGB*, vii.109–110; viii.118.4–5, 7–21; viii.133.361–72; xi.205.564–73.

12   Wace, *Roman de Brut*, ed. I.D.O. Arnold, *Le Roman de Brut de Wace*, 2 vols., Paris, 1938–40, vol. 2, p. 694, l. 13286; *DGB*, vii.112.42. Wace also interpolated a claimed Merlinian prophecy that Gurmund would be a pirate (*Roman de Brut*, ed. Arnold, vol. 2, p. 699, ll. 13401–02), which is not in the *DGB* nor La3amon's *Brut*.

13   *DGB*, vii.112.39–43, 115.129–31, 116.166–67, 118.20–21; viii.133.369–72; xi.205.563–73.

14   La3amon, *Brut*, ed. Brook and Leslie, vol. 2, pp. 489–90, ll. 9398–9423, cf. *DGB*, vii.112.36–43, 115.129–31.

15   La3amon, *Brut*, ed. Brook and Leslie, vol. 2, pp. 601–2, ll. 11494–11517, cf. *DGB*, vii.112.41–43, 115.129–31; viii.133.369–71; xi.205.563–73.

16   La3amon, *Brut*, ed. Brook and Leslie, vol. 2, pp. 743–46, ll. 14161–14202, cf. *DGB*, vii.116.165–72.

17   La3amon, *Brut*, ed. Brook and Leslie, vol. 2, p. 751, l. 14297. See, for example, D. Donoghue, "La3amon's Ambivalence", *Speculum* 65:3 (1990), 537–63.

18   *Castleford's Chronicle*, ed. Eckhardt, vol. 1, pp. 414–51, ll. 15364–16731.

Castleford's Chronicle reads at that point, *þarof na mare to lerne*, "there is no more to learn about that."[19]

One other significant Middle English transmission of the *PM* is a 15th-century selection of 37 prophecies with commentaries on how these predictions were fulfilled in Anglo-Norman England, rendered in Middle English prose. Eckhardt has edited the unique manuscript, University Park, Pennsylvania State University, Pattee Library, PS. v-3, and observes that "complete English prose translations [of Geoffrey's *PM*] were apparently not made until the seventeenth century."[20]

3   Vita Merlini

Le Saux argues that Laȝamon drew on the *VM* for his elaboration of Merlin's encounter with a hermit, but otherwise few studies exist of the possible influence of the *VM* on Middle English writing.[21]

---

19   *Castleford's Chronicle*, ed. Eckhardt, vol. 1, p. 451, l. 16731.
20   *The Prophetia Merlini of Geoffrey of Monmouth: A Fifteenth-Century English Commentary*, ed. C.D. Eckhardt (Speculum Anniversary Monographs, 8), Cambridge, MA, 1982, p. 4.
21   Le Saux, *Layamon's Brut*, pp. 110–17.

CHAPTER 20

The Anglo-Norman and Continental French Reception of Geoffrey of Monmouth's Corpus from the 12th to the 15th Centuries

Jean Blacker

Although[1] there were pockets of resistance, particularly regarding the work's reliability – the most notable from William of Newburgh[2] – acceptance of Geoffrey of Monmouth's *De gestis Britonum* (*c.*1123–39)[3] (hereafter *DGB*) was brisk and strong; the current count of manuscript witnesses in Latin is over 225, with nearly 50 manuscripts from the 12th century alone.[4] The *Prophetiae*

---

1 Given space restrictions, the lists, notes, and references presented here cannot be exhaustive, but are intended to suggest future paths of research.

2 Henry, archdeacon of Huntingdon, was amazed (*stupens*) to have discovered it at Le Bec in the company of Robert de Torigni, and treated it with caution in his adapted abbreviation of Geoffrey's *DGB*, the *Epistola ad Warinum* (*c.*1139); see Henry of Huntingdon, *History of the English*, ed. and trans. D. Greenway, *Henry, Archdeacon of Huntingdon: Historia Anglorum. The History of the English People*, Oxford, 1996, pp. 558–83, at p. 558; and N. Wright, "The Place of Henry of Huntingdon's *Epistola ad Warinum* in the Text-History of Geoffrey of Monmouth's *Historia regum Britannie*: a Preliminary Investigation", in G. Jondorf and D.N. Dumville (eds.), *France and the British Isles in the Middle Ages and Renaissance: Essays by Members of Girton College, Cambridge, in Memory of Ruth Morgan*, Woodbridge, 1991, pp. 71–113. Alfred of Beverley repeated much of Geoffrey's account of the history of the Britons in his *Annales* (*c.*1143), but noted that no contemporary Saxon or Roman historians had commented on Arthur's conquests: *Annales* v, ed. T. Hearne, *Aluredi Beverlacensis Annales, sive historia de gestis regum Britanniae, libris IX E. codice pervetusto ...*, Oxford, 1716, p. 76. William of Newburgh's scathing criticism of what he considered Geoffrey's mendacious propaganda is the most well-known; on William's criticism, and that of Gerald of Wales (each of whom were writing in the 1190s, and the latter who evinced some ambivalence toward the Galfridian material), see, for example, K. Robertson, "Geoffrey of Monmouth and the Translation of Insular Historiography", *Arthuriana* 8:4 (1998), 42–57. See also S. Meecham-Jones, "Early Reactions to Geoffrey's Work", pp. 181–208 in this volume.

3 Most recently edited as the *De gestis Britonum*, ed. M. Reeve and trans. N. Wright, *Geoffrey of Monmouth, The History of the Kings of Britain: An Edition and Translation of De gestis Britonum [Historia Regum Britanniae]*, Woodbridge, 2007; for dating, see p. vii. See also *Bern*, ed. Wright; and *The First Variant Version*, ed. Wright.

4 Crick, *SC* and Crick, *DR*; for references to Crick's updates in the count, as well as Reeve's own discoveries, see *DGB*, pp. vii–viii, n. 5. See also J. Tahkokallio, "Update to the List of Manuscripts of Geoffrey of Monmouth's *Historia regum Britanniae*", *AL* 32 (2015), 187–203; id., "Early Manuscript Dissemination", in this volume, who counts nearly 80 manuscripts

Merlini (*c*.1130–35), which circulated separately, as well as part of the *DGB*, is extant in over 70 manuscripts as an independent text;[5] the *Vita Merlini* (*c*.1148–55) was less widely known, or at least less widely copied, with fewer than a dozen manuscripts, many fragmentary.[6]

However, reception can also be gauged by the number of translations and adaptations, in addition to Latin recopyings; the term "adaptations" here is used to mean texts in another language that can conform closely to the original, though more broadly based than translations; practically speaking, the almost innumerable isolated or episodic borrowings of characters, events or places, from Galfridian material inserted into Arthurian or other romances, for example, are excluded from consideration here. Measured in terms of translations and adaptations, the French-language reception of Geoffrey's work (primarily the *DGB* and the *PM*), both in continental dialects and Anglo-Norman, was very enthusiastic, most likely second only to the English tradition(s) of adapted (or "translated") versions of those two works. As noted below, much work remains to be done, particularly on the interrelationships among these texts across these very rich French-language traditions.[7]

---

before *c*.1210, pp. 155–80; for the *PM* see M.B. McInerney's "Riddling Words: The *Prophetiae Merlini*" in this volume, pp. 129–52.

5 *The Prophetia Merlini of Geoffrey of Monmouth: A Fifteenth-Century English Commentary*, ed. C.D. Eckhardt (Speculum Anniversary Monographs, 8), Cambridge, MA, 1982, p. 10. See also Alan of Lille, *Interpretation of the Prophecy of Merlin*, ed. and trans. C. Wille, *Prophetie und Politik: Die 'Explanatio in Prophetia Merlini Ambrosii' des Alanus Flandrensis*, 2 vols. (Lateinische Sprache und Literatur des Mittelalters, 49), Bern, 2015, vol. 1, pp. 5–18; and G. Veysseyre and C. Wille, "Les commentaires latins et français aux *Prophetie Merlini* de Geoffroy de Monmouth", *Médiévales* 55 (2008), 93–114.

6 *VM*, pp. 43–45.

7 For an overview of the European reception of the *DGB*, see H. Tétrel and G. Veysseyre, "Introduction", in ead. (eds.), *L'Historia regum Britannie et les "Bruts" en Europe, Tome I, Traductions, adaptations, réappropriations (XIIᵉ–XVIᵉ siècle)* (Rencontres 106, Civilisation médiévale, 12), Paris, 2015, pp. 9–37. Occitan reception (in terms of translations or adaptations rather than treatments of Arthurian myths or isolated characters such as appear in the romance *Jaufré* for example [ed. C. Brunel, Paris, 1943]) appears non-existent, though recent discoveries of previously unknown texts such as the anonymous Anglo-Norman verse *Brut* in London, College of Arms, 12/45A (scroll) (see I.A.b.3 [*DGB*, translations (verse), anonymous, number 3] below, and n. 15), suggest, as always, that there may be unknown Occitan texts still buried in manuscripts awaiting discovery. The same may be true for 12th- to 15th-century French/Occitan versions of the *VM* as well, of which there are currently no known vernacular copies.

I   *De gestis Britonum*

A. Translations (verse): Keeping in mind that medieval authors had a different view of "translation" than moderns, a view – and practice – that often admitted some adaptation, interpretation, and original contributions, the following texts were most likely intended to "reproduce" to a considerable extent the vulgate *DGB* or the First Variant version, or a combination, revealing more consistent "faithfulness" to the Latin originals than a significant number of the works listed under "Adaptations" (I.B) (the greater portion of which are prose texts).[8]

a) Known authors:

1)   Gaimar, *Estoire des Bretuns* – no longer extant; known only from references in Gaimar's *Estoire des Engleis* [Dean 1],[9] oldest extant French-language chronicle (*c.*1135–40); octosyllabic; Anglo-Norman[10]

2)   Wace, *Roman de Brut* (1155) [Dean 2]; octosyllabic; earliest extant, most well-known and frequently copied of the French-language *DGB* translations; omits book of Prophecies[11]

---

8   On "translation" in 12th-century French chronicles, see especially P. Damian-Grint, *The New Historians of the Twelfth-Century Renaissance: Inventing Vernacular Authority*, Woodbridge, 1999, pp. 16–32.

9   Numbers within square brackets refer to items (or references [r] attached to items) in R.J. Dean, with the collaboration of M.B.M. Boulton, *Anglo-Norman Literature: A Guide to Texts and Manuscripts* (Anglo-Norman Text Society Occasional Publications Series, 3), London, 1999. See also n. 33 below for multiple references in Dean to the Anglo-Norman Prose *Brut* traditions.

10   Geffrei Gaimar, *Estoire des Engleis*, ed. A. Bell, *L'Estoire des Engleis by Geffrei Gaimar* (Anglo-Norman Texts, 14–16), Oxford, 1960 (repr. New York, 1971); Geffrei Gaimar, *Estoire des Engleis*, ed. and trans. I. Short, *Estoire des Engleis / History of the English*, Oxford, 2009. In an article which has significant bearing on the early vernacular reception of the *DGB*, Short suggests a narrower window for the composition of the *Estoire des Engleis*, March 1136–April 1137 ("Gaimar's Epilogue and Geoffrey of Monmouth's *Liber vetustissimus*", *Speculum* 69:2 (1994), 323–43); cf. P. Dalton, "The Date of Geoffrey Gaimar's *Estoire des Engleis*, the Connections of his Patrons, and the Politics of Stephen's Reign", *The Chaucer Review* 42:1 (2007), 23–47, and R.W. Leckie, Jr., *The Passage of Dominion: Geoffrey of Monmouth and the Periodization of Insular History in the Twelfth Century*, Toronto, 1981, pp. 78–86. See also Geffrei Gaimar, *Estoire des Engleis*, ed. and trans. J. Wogan-Browne, T. Fenster, and D. Russell, "Gaimar, *L'Estoire des Engleis*", in J. Wogan-Browne, T. Fenster, and D. Russell (eds.), *Vernacular Literary Theory from the French of Medieval England, Texts and Translations, c. 1120–c. 1450*, Cambridge, 2016, pp. 99–103 [two extracts], and I. Short, "What was Gaimar's *Estoire des Bretuns*?" *Cultura Neolatina* 71:1 (2011), 143–45.

11   For extensive manuscript details and copious variants, see Wace, *Roman de Brut*, ed. I.D.O. Arnold, *Le Roman de Brut de Wace*, 2 vols., Paris, 1938–40; see also Judith Weiss's presentation of Arnold's text, with emendations: Wace, *Roman de Brut*, trans. J. Weiss, *Wace's Roman de Brut: A History of the British: Text and Translation* (Exeter Medieval Texts and Studies), Exeter, 1999, rev. ed. 2002. My as-yet-unpublished findings suggest that Wace

b) Anonymous:[12]

Octosyllabic:

1) London, British Library, Harley 4733, late 12th century; 250 lines, with gaps (§§143–47, Arthur's coronation, pursuit of Saxons to Somerset) [Dean 1r, 17][13]

2) Munich, Bayerische Staatsbibliothek, Gall. 29, early 13th century (continental); 4182 lines (§§5–32, description of Britain, arrival of Brutus to battle at Tours)[14]

---

did not translate the First Variant version as exclusively or consistently as has been previously thought, and that the *Brut* is more alternately reliant on the vulgate *DGB* and the First Variant; this has been argued very recently by L. Mathey-Maille, "De la Vulgate à la *Variant Version* de l'*Historia regum Britannie*: *Le Roman de Brut* de Wace à l'épreuve du texte source", in Tétrel and Veysseyre (eds.), *L'Historia regum Britannie*, pp. 129–39. On Wace's decision to omit the Prophecies as found in both the vulgate and First Variant, see J. Blacker, "'Ne vuil sun livre translater': Wace's Omission of Merlin's Prophecies from the *Roman de Brut*", in I. Short (ed.), *Anglo-Norman Anniversary Essays* (Anglo-Norman Text Society Occasional Publications Series, 2), London, 1993, pp. 49–59. Manuscripts of Wace's *Brut* are almost equally divided between continental and Anglo-Norman – although given a broad range of factors, not the least Wace's Norman-based *Schriftsprache*, the poem should not be thought of as Anglo-Norman. However, in terms of cultural associations, Wace is most frequently viewed as being in the Plantagenet sphere, rather than in the French. On Wace's life and works, see Wace, *Conception Nostre Dame*, trans. J. Blacker, G.S. Burgess, and A.V. Ogden, *Wace, The Hagiographical Works: The 'Conception Nostre Dame' and the Lives of St Margaret and St Nicholas* (Studies in Medieval and Reformation Traditions, 169 / Texts and Sources, 3), Leiden, 2013, pp. 1–9.

12   Each of these anonymous verse translations of the *DGB* has been identified as Anglo-Norman except the Bekker fragment and the Munich *Brut*; none contain the Prophecies except London, British Library, Harley 1605 (among the others, only Royal and Egerton treat material in proximity to the Prophecies (*DGB* §§112–17), but they exclude them); many, if not all of the texts, with the likely exception of Egerton, date from the 12th century (the approximate manuscript dating is given here). The anonymous verse translations of the *PM* – all of which are also Anglo-Norman – appear below in II.A. See n. 17 below on the unique nature of the Egerton *Brut*.

13   "A 12th-century Anglo-Norman *Brut* Fragment (MS BL Harley 4733, f. 128)", ed. P. Damian-Grint, in I. Short (ed.), *Anglo-Norman Anniversary Essays* (Anglo-Norman Text Society Occasional Publications Series, 2), London, 1993, pp. 87–104.

14   "An Edition of the Munich *Brut*", ed. P.B. Grout, unpublished PhD thesis, University of London, 1980; ead., "The Author of the Munich *Brut*, his Latin Sources and Wace", *Medium Ævum* 54:2 (1985), 274–82. For a published edition, see *Der Münchener Brut*, ed. K. Hofmann and K. Vollmöller, *Der Münchener Brut, Gottfried von Monmouth in französischen Versen des xii. Jahrhunderts*, Halle, 1877; for a description of the manuscript, see P.B. Grout, "The Manuscript of the Munich *Brut* (Codex Gallicus 29 of the Bayerische Staatsbibliothek, Munich)", in S.B. North (ed.), *Studies in Medieval French Language and Literature presented to Brian Woledge* (Publications Romanes et Françaises, 180), Geneva, 1988, pp. 49–58.

3)   London, College of Arms, 12/45A (scroll), late 13th century; approx. 2500
     lines (§§23–133, with numerous lacunae; Prophecies omitted) [Dean 6r][15]

4)   London, British Library, Arundel 220, early 14th century; 258 lines (§§106–
     08, Vortigern's tower, discovery of Merlin) [Dean 22][16]

5)   London, British Library, Egerton 3028, mid-14th century; 2914 lines (not
     including 354-line continuation of English history to 1338–40) (§§65–
     205, sons of Cymbeline to almost conclusion, many lacunae); Prophecies
     omitted [Dean 50][17]

6)   London, British Library, Royal 13. A. xxi, first half of the 14th century;
     6237 lines (§§6–137, Aeneas's marriage to Uther's arrival at Tintagel);
     Prophecies omitted [Dean 3][18]

---

15   Discovered by O. de Laborderie, "'Ligne de reis': Culture historique, représentation du
     pouvoir royal et construction de la mémoire nationale en Angleterre à travers les généalo-
     gies royales en rouleau du milieu du 13ᵉ siècle au milieu du 15ᵉ siècle", unpublished PhD
     thesis, École des Hautes Études en Sciences Sociales, Paris, 2002, pp. 380–85 (revised in
     Histoire, mémoire et pouvoir: Les généalogies en rouleau des rois d'Angleterre (1250–1422)
     (Bibliothèque d'histoire médiévale, 7), Paris, 2013); excerpts edited by I. Short, "Un *Roman
     de Brut* anglo-normand inédit", *Romania* 126 (2008), 273–95. Short observes that, given
     that the other verse versions are from the 12th century (except for Egerton) and that this
     text also demonstrates older usages, it is also likely from the 12th century; it has approxi-
     mately 2500 lines, corresponding to lines 1293–8338 of Wace, thus a significant reduction
     of both the French poet's text and the Latin (p. 275).

16   See J. Koch, "Anglonormannische Texte in Ms. Arundel 220 des Britischen Museums",
     Zeitschrift für romanische Philologie 54 (1934), 20–56, and *I Fatti di Bretagna*, ed.
     M.L. Meneghetti, *I Fatti di Bretagna: Cronache genealogiche anglo-normanne dal XII al
     XIV secolo* (Vulgares Eloquentes, 9), Padua, 1979, pp. 33–43. See also R. Trachsler, "Du *libel-
     lus Merlini* au *livret Merlin*: Les traductions françaises des *Prophetiae Merlini* dans leurs
     manuscrits", in C. Croizy-Naquet, M. Szkilnik, and L. Harf-Lancner (eds.), *Les Manuscrits
     médiévaux témoins de lectures*, Paris, 2015, pp. 67–87, esp. pp. 72–73.

17   Although an anonymous verse *Brut*, the Egerton *Brut* (composed likely around the time
     the extant manuscript was assembled with its illustrating miniatures, late 1330s–early
     1340s) is *sui generis* in that it is an abridgment of Wace's *Brut*, not a "translation" of
     Geoffrey's *DGB*. See "An Anglo-Norman Metrical 'Brut' of the 14th century (British Museum
     Ms Egerton 3028)", ed. V. Underwood, unpublished PhD thesis, University of London, 1937,
     and J. Blacker, "Courtly Revision of Wace's *Roman de Brut* in British Library Egerton MS
     3028", in K. Busby and C. Kleinhenz (eds.), *Courtly Arts and the Art of Courtliness: Selected
     Papers from the Eleventh Triennial Congress of the International Courtly Literature Society,
     University of Wisconsin-Madison, 29 July–4 August 2004*, Cambridge, 2006, pp. 237–58; see
     also A. Stones, "The Egerton *Brut* and its Illustrations", in G.S. Burgess and J. Weiss (eds.),
     *Maistre Wace: A Celebration: Proceedings of the International Colloquium held in Jersey,
     10–12 September 2004*, St Helier, 2006, pp. 167–76.

18   The Royal *Brut* is inserted into Wace's *Brut*, in place of lines 53–8728; *An Anglo-Norman
     Brut (Royal 13.A.xxi)*, ed. A. Bell (Anglo-Norman Text Society, 21–22), Oxford, 1969. See
     also A. Bell, "The Royal *Brut* Interpolation", *Medium Ævum* 32:3 (1963), 190–202, and
     P. Damian-Grint, "Redating the Royal *Brut* Fragment", *Medium Ævum* 65:2 (1996), 280–85.

7)   New Haven, Beinecke Library, Takamiya 115 (*olim* Martin Schøyen 650), c.1225–75; 168 lines (end of §§142–43, Uther's death, Arthur's coronation, battle against Colgrin and Saxons, Scots and Picts at York) [Dean 16][19]

Decasyllabic (only Prophecies; see ii.A.ii below)
Alexandrine:

1)   Krakow, Jagiellonian University Library, Gall. fol. 176, late 12th century (continental) (Bekker fragment); 136 lines (§§127–30, assembling Stonehenge)[20]

2)   London, British Library, Harley 1605, mid-13th century; 3361 lines (in five fragments)
       [Dean 15 and 20]:[21]
   i)   1280 lines (§§73–94, death of King Lucius to arrival of Hengist)
   ii)   1279 lines (§§113–36, an incomplete text of the Prophecies [missing §112; begins at Lincoln's l. 73], to beginning of Uther's reign; see ii.A.iii.1 and n. 41 below)
   iii)   80 lines (§§152–54, reinstatement of Loth)
   iv)   81 lines (§§155–56, Bedevere, Kay enfeoffed, feast at City of Legions)
   v)   641 lines (§§165–69, Mont-Saint-Michel giant, first encounter of Arthur and Emperor Lucius)

B. Adaptations, that is, works containing sections of the *DGB* which were either
a)   Translated, sometimes rather faithfully, but often interspersed with either original passages or passages taken from other recognizable works (as in Sébastien Mamerot's version of the *Neuf Preux* which also intersperses its closely translated sections from the *DGB* with lengthy passages from romances such as the vulgate *Mort la roi Artu*);
       or

---

19   See Dean no. 16, p. 16; Bernard Quaritch (Firm), *Catalogue 1147: Bookhands of the Middle Ages. Part V: Medieval Manuscript Leaves*, London, 1991, pp. 82–83, item 101; online at <https://brbl-dl.library.yale.edu/vufind/Record/4428130> (accessed 21 May 2018).

20   "Le fragment Bekker et les anciennes versions françaises de l'*Historia Regum Britanniae*", ed. S. Lefèvre, *Romania* 109 (1988), 225–46.

21   "The Harley *Brut*: An Early French Translation of Geoffrey of Monmouth's *Historia Regum Britanniae*", ed. B. Blakey, *Romania* 82 (1961), 401–08; B. Barbieri, "La *Geste de Bretuns* en alexandrins (Harley *Brut*): Une traduction de l'*Historia* aux teintes épiques", in Tétrel and Veysseyre (eds.), *L'Historia regum Britannie*, pp. 141–55, and her edition *Geste des Bretuns en alexandrins ou Harley Brut*, ed. B. Barbieri (Textes littéraires du Moyen Âge, 37), Paris, 2015 and F. Le Saux, "Romance", in this volume, p. 250, n. 58.

b)   adapted, some more strictly (but not translated "verbatim"), some more
      loosely, in order to be fit into larger works "needing" a section on the his-
      tory of the Britons, and the life of Arthur.[22]

Except for the first item – the *Estoire des Bretons* (recently edited as the *Estoire
de Brutus*) – the following texts are listed here without precisely distinguishing
where they fall on the "translation to adaptation" continuum, leaving those
questions of definition to scholars working on these specific texts [*n.b.*: for
works extant in multiple manuscripts, not all manuscripts are listed here]:

i. **Continental Chronicles and Romances:**

1)   *Estoire des Bretons*: oldest French prose translation of the *DGB*, from §§6–
      188, with short lacunae; pre-1300, possibly pre-1280; in the only manu-
      script which contains it, the *Estoire des Bretons* is inserted into the *Histoire
      ancienne jusqu'à César*, Paris, Bibliothèque nationale de France, fr. 17177,
      fols. 82vb–108rb[23]

2)   *Perceforest*, originally composed between *c.*1330–40, reworked in the 15th
      century; translation of §§6–52 (preceded by a description of the island,
      but not Geoffrey's); largely prose (some octosyllables, decasyllables);
      opening section is the beginning of a much larger text[24]

---

22   As in the case of the anonymous verse *Bruts* and verse Prophecies, further work remains
      in order to establish the interrelationships among the texts in this list of prose adapta-
      tions of the *DGB*.

23   G. Veysseyre, "Geoffroy de Monmouth, *Historia regum Britanniae*, 1135–1139", in C. Galderisi
      et al. (eds.), *Translations médiévales, Cinq siècles de traductions en français au Moyen Âge
      (XIᵉ–XVᵉ siècles): Étude et Répertoire*, 2 vols. in 3 [1, II.1, and 2], Turnhout, 2011, vol. II.1,
      no. 237, pp. 459–60, and *L'Estoire de Brutus. La plus ancienne traduction en prose française
      de l'Historia regum Britannie de Geoffroy de Monmouth*, ed. G. Veysseyre (Textes littéraires
      du Moyen Âge, 33), Paris, 2014, pp. 180–84.

24   In fact, the *Perceforest*'s most recent English translator has gone as far as to remark that
      "indeed, on one level almost the whole of *Perceforest* can be seen as a vast interpola-
      tion into Geoffrey's *Historia* between the reigns of kings Pir and Capoir"; see *Perceforest*,
      trans. N. Bryant, *Perceforest, The Prehistory of King Arthur's Britain* (Arthurian Studies,
      77), Cambridge, 2011. However, although Kings Pir and Capoir both appear at the end
      of the *DGB* §52, Capoir appears as Scapiol in *Perceforest*, and the narrative that follows
      his eventual appearance up to the end of the text bears little resemblance to anything
      in the *DGB*. For a detailed overview of the different redactions and numerous intra- and
      inter-textual complexities of this enormous narrative, see R. Trachsler, "Le *Perceforest*", in
      R. Trachsler (ed.), *Disjointures-Conjointures: Étude sur l'interférence des matières narratives
      dans la littératures française du Moyen Âge*, Tübingen and Basel, 2000, pp. 239–81; see also
      J.H.M. Taylor, "Introduction", in ead. (ed.), *Le Roman de Perceforest, première partie* (Textes
      littéraires français, 279), Geneva, 1979, pp. 11–58; *Perceforest*, ed. G. Roussineau, *Le Roman
      de Perceforest, quatrième partie*, 2 vols. (Textes littéraires français, 343), Geneva, 1987, vol. 1,
      pp. ix–xxxv; and G. Veysseyre, "L'*Historia regum Britannie* ou l'enfance de Perceforest", in
      D. Hüe and C. Ferlampin-Acher (eds.), *Enfances arthuriennes: Actes du 2ᵉ Colloque arthu-
      rien de Rennes, 6–7 mars 2003*, Orleans, 2006, pp. 99–126.

3) *Croniques des Bretons*, anonymous 15th-century prose text; first section based on both the DGB and Wace's *Roman de Brut*; remaining sections based on the DGB; circulated separately, then as the *incipit* to Jean de Wavrin's *Croniques et anchiennes istories de la Grant Bretaigne, a present nommé Engleterre*[25]

4) Jehan Wauquelin, *Roman de Brut*, 1444–45[26]

5) Jean de Wavrin, opening section of the *Recueil des croniques et anchiennes istories de la Grant Bretaigne, a present nommé Engleterre*, c.1455[27]

6) Pierre Le Baud, *Compillacion des Chroniques et Ystoires des tresnobles roys et princes de Bretaigne armoricque jadis extraitz et descenduz de ceulx de Bretaigne insulaire*, 15th century; the whole of this work, dedicated to Jean de Derval in 1480, treats the history of Britain from its origins to 1458; the opening section contains a résumé of the DGB[28]

7) Sébastien Mamerot, the Arthurian section of the *Histoire des Neuf Preux et des Neuf Preuses*, 1460; contains a "traduction intégrale" of the DGB, with numerous changes and lacunae, among the most important of which is the elimination of Merlin's Prophecies[29]

8) *Les Neuf Preux*, Paris, Bibliothèque nationale de France, fr. 12598; 18th-century paper manuscript reflecting a 15th-century text; fols. 219a–231a containing an "Arthurian section" corresponding to the DGB §§92–132[30]

9) "Fourth redaction" of the *Histoire ancienne jusqu'à César*; 15th century; inserted Brutus section[31]

---

25 Veysseyre, "Geoffroy de Monmouth", p. 461.

26 Including the Prophecies. As Gilles Roussineau reports, the text "traduit … dans son intégralité, l'*Historia regum Britannie*"; see "Jehan Wauquelin et l'auteur de *Perceforest* traducteurs de l'*Historia regum Britannie* de Geoffroy de Monmouth", in M.-C. de Crécy (ed.), with the collaboration of G. Parussa and S. Hériché Pradeau, *Jean Wauquelin de Mons à la cour de Bourgogne* (Burgundica, XI), Turnhout, 2006, pp. 5–23, at p. 6. According to Veysseyre, this text contains a literal translation of the DGB, with no substantial borrowings from Wace; see "Geoffroy de Monmouth", p. 462.

27 Jean de Wavrin, *Recueil des croniques et anchiennes istories de la Grant Bretaigne*, ed. W. Hardy, *Recueil des croniques et anchiennes istories de la Grant Bretaigne, à présent nommé Engleterre, I: From Albina to A.D. 688*, London, 1864. Frequently referred to by the shortened title *Chronique d'Angleterre*.

28 See Veysseyre, "Geoffroy de Monmouth", p. 463.

29 See R. Trachsler, *Clôtures du cycle arthurien: Étude et textes* (Publications Romanes et Françaises, 215), Geneva, 1996, for a discussion of the text (pp. 297–313) and an edition of the sections corresponding to the DGB §§158–80 (pp. 419–64); see also A. Salamon, "Sébastien Mamerot, traducteur de l'*Historia regum Britannie*", in Tétrel and Veysseyre (eds.), *L'Historia regum Britannie*, pp. 211–30.

30 The "Arthurian section" in this manuscript also contains numerous elements from Wace; Trachsler, *Clôtures*, pp. 298–302.

31 Text named by J.H. Kaimowitz, "A Fourth Redaction of the *Histoire ancienne jusqu'à César*", in D.F. Bright and E.S. Ramage (eds.), *Classical Texts and Their Traditions: Studies in Honor*

  a)   New York, Public Library, Spencer 41
  b)   Paris, Bibliothèque de l'Arsenal, 5078

ii. **Anglo-Norman Chronicles:**

1)   Peter Langtoft, *Chronicle*, late 13th-early 14th century; the first of three
      sections contains a condensed adaptation of the *DGB*; monorhymed al-
      exandrine laisses [Dean 66][32]

2)   Anglo-Norman Prose *Brut*, 13th–14th century:[33]

  a)   The *Anglo-Norman Prose Brut to 1272*: the original form of the text,
        also referred to as the Common Text [Dean 42][34]

---

of C.R. *Traham*, Chico, CA, 1984, pp. 75–87; Kaimowitz discusses New York, Public Library,
Spencer 41, including the "detailed account of Brutus [fols. 71r–80v], the source of which
is identified in the text (f. 71r) as the *Brut*" (p. 78); Kaimowitz speculates that the *Brut*
was Wace's but also states that the text is "heavily and directly indebted" to the *DGB*. On
both that manuscript and Arsenal 5078 with respect to their translation(s) of the *DGB*, see
R. Trachsler, "L'*Historia regum Britannie* au XVᵉ siècle: Les manuscrits New York, Public
Library, Spencer 41 et Paris, Bibliothèque de l'Arsenal, 5078", in Tétrel and Veysseyre (eds.),
L'Historia regum Britannie, pp. 193–209.

32   Peter Langtoft, *Chronicle*, ed. J.-C. Thiolier, *Édition critique et commentée de Pierre de
      Langtoft, Le Règne d'Édouard Ier, tome premier*, Créteil, 1989–. See also T. Summerfield,
      *The Matter of Kings' Lives: Design of Past and Present in the Early Fourteenth-Century Verse
      Chronicles by Pierre de Langtoft and Robert Mannyng*, Amsterdam and Atlanta, 1998.

33   Extant in at least 50 manuscripts in the various textual families, the Anglo-Norman Prose
      Brut was revised and added to during the ensuing 50 years. The following abbreviated list
      of the families and earlier development of the Anglo-Norman Prose *Brut* is based primar-
      ily (though not exactly) on H. Pagan, "What is the Anglo-Norman Brut?" <https://www
      .univ-brest.fr/digitalAssets/36/36991_Heather-Pagan-com.pdf> (accessed 19 March 2018),
      pp. 1–7, at pp. 3–4, and L. Matheson, *The Prose "Brut": The Development of a Middle English
      Chronicle* (Medieval & Renaissance Texts & Studies, 180), Tempe, 1998, p. 4. The Prose *Brut*
      tradition is very difficult to describe, given not only its complexity and heterogeneity, but
      also because scholars are not in agreement as to what constitutes a *Brut* text, ranging
      from the use of the term "Brut" to refer to a group of texts almost as if they constituted a
      genre (as could be construed from P. Meyer's observation that "plusieurs des compilations
      historiques en vers ou en prose où l'*Historia Britonum* [*DGB*] a été employée portent le
      titre de *Brut*"; "De Quelques chroniques anglo-normandes qui ont porté le nom de *Brut*",
      Bulletin de la SATF 4 (1878), 104–45, at p. 105) to those referring to specific works. On the
      difficulties of definition, see in particular D. Tyson, "Handlist of Manuscripts Containing
      the French Prose *Brut* Chronicle", *Scriptorium* 48 (1994), 333–44 and H. Pagan, "When is
      a Brut no Longer a Brut?: The example of Cambridge, University Library, Dd. 10. 32", in
      Tétrel and Veysseyre (eds.), *L'Historia regum Britannie*, pp. 179–92. For further information
      on these texts, individual manuscripts, and related traditions, see Dean nos. 36, 42–49,
      and 52–53 (pp. 24–27, 30–34, and 35–36). Many of the Prose *Brut*s and related texts have
      yet to be edited.

34   Julia Marvin considers the major sources of the Oldest Version of the Prose *Brut* (which
      Pagan and Matheson refer to as the "Common Text") to include Wace's *Roman de Brut* and
      Gaimar's *Estoire des Engleis*, while the "chronicle also appears to draw directly, though

b)   The Common Text/Oldest Version, with a continuation to 1307 (end of the reign of Edward I of England; sometimes called the First Continuation)[35]

c)   Second Continuation:

    i)   Short Version (including the *Anglo-Norman Prose Brut to 1332*) [Dean 45]:[36]

        a)   The Common Text to 1307, plus the Short Continuation to 1333 (ending with an English raid on Haddington Fair, Scotland) [Dean 36]

        b)   Addition of verse prologue (in some manuscripts)[37]

    ii)   Long Version: the Common Text to 1307, much revised, including the addition of prophecies attributed to Merlin;[38] addition of prose prologue; and the Long Continuation to 1333 (ending with the battle of Halidon Hill) [Dean 46]

---

less extensively" on Geoffrey's *DGB* ("Arthur Authorized: The Prophecies of the Prose *Brut* Chronicle", *AL* 22 (2005), 84–99, at p. 84); *The Oldest Anglo-Norman Prose Brut Chronicle: An Edition and Translation*, ed. and trans. ead. (Medieval Chronicles, 4), Woodbridge, 2006; see also Marvin's description of the development of the *Brut* tradition(s) in ead., *The Construction of Vernacular History in the Anglo-Norman Prose Brut: the Manuscript Culture of Late Medieval England*, York, 2017, esp. pp. 1–15, 8, n. 22, 131–62, and 231–50; and J. Spence, *Reimagining History in Anglo-Norman Prose Chronicles*, York, 2013, esp. pp. 1–21.

35   This category may be the most debated by scholars, and ultimately prove to be more of a useful theoretical construct than an actual stage represented by manuscripts. Only a detailed, methodical examination of all the 50 or so manuscripts will explain how the text developed between the "Oldest Version" and the "Long" and "Short" versions, here listed under the rubric of the "Second Continuation" (if only to distinguish how their narratives diverge from 1307 onward, with significant variations). For further analysis, see T.R. Smith, "National Identity, Propaganda, and the Ethics of War in English Historical Literature, *c.* 1327–77", unpublished PhD thesis, University of Leeds, 2018, including appendix entries for "*The Brut*", "*Long Anglo-Norman Prose Brut*", and "*Short Anglo-Norman Prose Brut*".

36   *Prose Brut to 1332*, ed. H. Pagan (Anglo-Norman Texts, 69), Manchester, 2011.

37   According to Lister Matheson, at this stage of the development of the Short Version of the Anglo-Norman Prose *Brut* a metrical prologue was added recounting the Albina foundation myth; this prologue is an abbreviated redaction of the Anglo-Norman poem, *Des grantz geanz*, ed. G.E. Brereton, *Des Grantz Geanz: An Anglo-Norman Poem* (Medium Ævum Monographs, 2), Oxford, 1937; a prose prologue based on this same poem was also added; see Matheson, *The Prose "Brut"*, pp. 4–5 and 33–34. See also Dean nos. 36–41 (pp. 24–30), and J. Marvin, "Albine and Isabelle: Regicidal Queens and the Historical Imagination of the Anglo-Norman Prose *Brut* Chronicles", *AL* 18 (2001), 143–83.

38   The "prophecies" here are to be distinguished from the Prophecies (that is, Geoffrey's *PM*) since "the prophecies brought into the [Long Version] are not the Galfridian ones themselves, but a version of the *Prophecy of the Six Kings to Follow John*"; Marvin, *The Construction of Vernacular History*, p. 240 and n. 33.

3) *Le Livere de reis de Brittanie*, 13th century; begins with a summary of the history of England to the overthrow of the Britons, based on the *DGB* (and not on Wace) [Dean 13][39]

4) *Le Livere de reis de Engleter(r)e*, 13th century; the very short summary of the history of Britain with which the work begins is drawn from both Geoffrey and Bede [Dean 23][40]

II   *Prophecies of Merlin*

A. Verse translations:[41]

i. *Octosyllabic*:

1) London, British Library, Additional 48212.O, mid-14th century; 117 lines (*DGB* §116:33–42), Prophecies fragment, from the awakening of the Daneian forest to the heron's three eggs [Dean 21]

ii. *Decasyllabic* [Dean 19]:[42]

1) Cambridge, Fitzwilliam Museum, 302, second half of the 13th century: 668 lines (§§112–17), Prophecies preceded by 166 lines of the preamble

2) Oxford, Bodleian Library, Hatton 67, second half of the 13th century: 668 lines (§§112–17), Prophecies preceded by 172-line preamble

---

39   *Le Livere de Reis de Brittanie e Le Livere de Reis de Engletere*, ed. J. Glover, London, 1865; the most recent edition of both texts appears in C. Foltys, "Kritische Ausgabe der anglo-normannische Chroniken: Brutus, Li rei de Engleterre, Le Livere de Reis de Engleterre", unpublished inaugural dissertation, Freie Universität Berlin, 1961.

40   Bede, *Ecclesiastical History*, ed. and trans. B. Colgrave and R.A.B. Mynors, *Bede's Ecclesiastical History of the English People*, Oxford, 1969. For continuations of the *Livere de reis de Engleter(r)e*, see Dean nos. 26 and 27, p. 21.

41   All of the following are Anglo-Norman. In line 1 of the unique prologue in Lincoln, Cathedral Library, 104, a certain "Willelme" names himself as responsible for the Prophecies text in that manuscript, but he remains as yet unidentified, as is the "Helias" to whom the Durham and Fitzwilliam manuscripts appear to be attributed; all other witnesses are anonymous/without attribution. On the decasyllabic and alexandrine Prophecies, see "Anglo-Norman Verse Prophecies of Merlin", ed. and trans. J. Blacker, *Arthuriana* 15:1 (2005), 1–125, rev. ed. *Anglo-Norman Verse Prophecies of Merlin*, Dallas, 2005; on the attributions, see pp. 4–86. The Durham manuscript is the base manuscript for the decasyllabic version (and English translation) and the Lincoln manuscript, for the alexandrine version.

42   While the decasyllabic witnesses of the Prophecies have many similarities among them, as do the alexandrine, more work remains to be done to establish exact descendance (e.g., which is the earliest of the versions, what is the relationship between the different witnesses).

3)   Durham, Cathedral Library, c.IV.27, late 12th–early 13th century; Wace, *Brut* + interpolated Prophecies: 668 lines (§§112–17), preceded by 172-line preamble

4)   Cologny-Geneva, Fondation Martin Bodmer, Cod. Bodmer 67, second half of the 13th century; Wace, *Brut* fragment + Prophecies: 668 lines (§§112–17), preceded by ll. 63–172 of preamble

iii. *Alexandrine* [Dean 20]:

1)   London, British Library, Harley 1605, mid-13th century (second fragment contains most of the Prophecies; see I.A.b.2 [Alexandrine] above)

2)   Lincoln, Cathedral Library, 104, second half of the 13th century; Wace, *Brut* + interpolated Prophecies: 587 lines (§§112–17)

3)   London, British Library, Additional 45103, late 13th century; Wace, *Brut* + interpolated Prophecies: 587 lines (§§112–17)

B. Prose translations:[43]

1)   Paris, Bibliothèque nationale de France, fr. 17177 (*Estoire des Bretons*) Prophecies with occasional glosses (see I.B.i.1 above)[44]

---

43   In addition to these more comprehensive versions, there are also isolated prophecies found in a variety of texts, particularly in commentaries on the *PM*, a substantial tradition unto itself that cannot be addressed here; on the interrelationships of the various Merlin traditions including the commentaries, see especially *Prophetia Merlini*, ed. Eckhardt, pp. 1–15. In addition, there are romances that contain prophecies that came to be associated with Merlin, but also more direct borrowings from the *DGB*. For example: 1) The *Prophéties de Merlin* dating from the late 13th century and attributed (within the text) to a certain Richard d'Irlande, purportedly translated from the Latin, should more probably be considered a French Arthurian romance, with prophecies running through it as a narrative thread. See *Les Prophecies de Merlin, edited from MS. 593 of the Bibliothèque Municipale de Rennes*, ed. L.A. Paton, 2 vols. (Modern Language Association of America Monograph Series, 1), New York and London, 1926–27 (repr. New York, 1966); *Les Prophéties de Merlin (Cod. Bodmer 116)*, ed. A. Berthelot (Bibliotheca Bodmeriana Textes, 6), Cologny-Geneva, 1992; and N. Koble, *"Les Prophéties de Merlin" en prose: le roman arthurien en éclats* (Nouvelle Bibliothèque du Moyen Âge, 92), Paris, 2009; and 2) the more substantial interpolation of Galfridian prophecies in the Didot-*Perceval*; see *The Didot Perceval, according to the manuscripts of Modena and Paris*, ed. W. Roach, Philadelphia, 1941; and especially J. Abed, "La Traduction française de la *Prophetia Merlini* dans le Didot-*Perceval*", in R. Trachsler (ed.), with the collaboration of J. Abed and D. Expert, *Moult obscures paroles: Études sur la prophétie médiévale*, Paris, 2007, pp. 81–105.

44   See G. Veysseyre, "'Mettre en roman' les prophéties de Merlin. Voies et détours de l'interprétation dans trois traductions de l'*Historia regum Britannie*", in Trachsler (ed.), *Moult obscures paroles*, pp. 107–66.

2)   Jean de Wavrin, *Chronique d'Angleterre*, Prophecies with occasional gloss-
     es (see I.B.i.5)[45]

3)   Jean Wauquelin, *Roman de Brut*, Prophecies with occasional glosses (see
     I.B.i.4)

Although a superficially simple pattern emerges from the table above – 1) that
the verse translations are almost always in Anglo-Norman and appear earlier
than the prose translations; and 2) that the prose translations (but more often
adaptations) fall into two distinct groups, a) the Anglo-Norman prose chronicles which are more loosely based on Galfridian texts, and b) the continental, more of whose authors are known by name, and whose texts tend to stick
closer to the Galfridian sources – when one dives into the texts themselves,
many more questions arise than have yet been answered regarding the comparative nature of these traditions, to each other, and to the works of Geoffrey
of Monmouth. More fundamentally still, as Sylvie Lefèvre[46] notes in her recent
"call to editors", "so much remains to be done in order for the landscape to be
finally more accessible to [lit., more readable for] all of us."[47]

---

45   Richard Trachsler reports that at least three manuscripts in the Bibliothèque nationale
     de France appear to contain a text "proche ou identique" to that found in de Wavrin's
     Chronique d'Angleterre: Paris, Bibliothèque nationale de France, fr. 2806, fr. 5621, and
     fr. 16939; see "Des *Prophetiae Merlini* aux *Prophecies Merlin* ou comment traduire les va-
     ticinations de Merlin", in C. Galderisi and G. Salmon (eds.), *Actes du colloque "Translatio"
     médiévale, Mulhouse, 11–12 mai 2000* (Perspectives médiévales, supplément au numéro
     26), Paris, 2000, pp. 105–24, cited at p. 121, n. 44. As Trachsler remarks, there may of course
     be others (p. 121).

46   S. Lefèvre, "Conclusions: L'*Historia regum Britannie* entre éternels retours et complex-
     es détours", in Tétrel and Veysseyre (eds.), L'*Historia regum Britannie*, pp. 299–303, at
     p. 303: "Appel aux éditeurs": "L'ultime enseignement pourrait bien être l'absolue nécessité
     d'éditer tant de versions, traductions, adaptations encore inédites, souvent connus des
     seuls spécialistes de ce volume. Certaines entreprises sont en cours: réédition de Wace à
     partir de la copie Guiot; travaux des directrices de l'ouvrage, Hélène Tétrel et Géraldine
     Veysseyre, mais il reste beaucoup à faire pour que le paysage tout entier soit enfin plus
     lisible pour tous".

47   I would like to express my gratitude to Jane H.M. Taylor and Richard Trachsler for their
     advice in the preparation of this article, and to Heather Pagan, Trevor Smith, and Julia
     Marvin for their guidance through the complexities of the Anglo-Norman Prose *Brut* tra-
     ditions. Any errors that remain are my own responsibility.

CHAPTER 21

The German Reception of Geoffrey of Monmouth

Joshua Byron Smith

Geoffrey's German reception appears meagre in light of what we might expect.[1] No vernacular translation exists, and the number of manuscripts connected to German libraries is comparatively small, with only seven in Crick's *Summary Catalogue*.[2] Of course, Arthurian literature was popular in German-speaking lands, but, with very few exceptions, the intermediary sources seem to have been French. Indeed, one reads with regularity statements like the following: "There is little reason to doubt that the German authors who introduced Arthurian romance in southern Germany in the years around 1200 were indeed working from French sources."[3] However, two somewhat recent studies have suggested that Geoffrey's Latin works did have an influence, however small, on popular German literature. Hartmann von Aue might have used Geoffrey's *DGB* as a source for some of the names in *Erek*, though the poor textual transmission of this important work makes it difficult to say anything with certainty.[4] Another vernacular work that might betray Geoffrey's influence is Wirnt von Grafenberg's *Wigalois*. *Wigalois* contains a full-on military expedition and siege, matters which are usually not present in Arthurian romance, but a recent study has attempted to rehabilitate this narrative "defect" by arguing that Wirnt took inspiration from the *DGB*'s description of King Arthur's military campaign against Rome.[5] Both studies acknowledge the tension between Geoffrey's wider popularity and his lack of overt influence on vernacular German literature: "Although there are no marked intertextual references to Geoffrey's work in German-language Arthurian romances, the

---

1   My sincere thanks to Joseph M. Sullivan for providing references to me and for general advice on this article.

2   See Crick, *SC*, nos. 15, 56, 75, 183, 205, 213, 216. An abridgement is also present in Berlin, Staatsbibliothek, Phillipps 1880; see Crick, *SC*, p. 330. See also Jaakko Tahkokallio's chapter in this volume.

3   W.H. Jackson and S.A. Ranawake, "Introduction", in W.H. Jackson and S.A. Ranawake (eds.), *The Arthur of the Germans: The Arthurian Legend in Medieval German and Dutch Literature* (Arthurian Literature in the Middle Ages, 3), Cardiff, 2000, pp. 1–18, at p. 4.

4   C.J. Steppich, "Geoffrey's 'Historia Regum Britanniae' and Wace's 'Brut': Secondary Sources for Hartmann's 'Erec'?" *Monatshefte* 94 (2002), 165–88.

5   R. Brockwyt, "Ein Artusritter im Krieg. Überlegungen zur Namûr-Episode im Wigalois des Wirnt von Grafenberg aus intertextueller Perspektive", *Neophilologus* 94 (2010), 93–108.

© THE AUTHOR, 2020 | DOI:10.1163/9789004410398_024

breadth and scope of the distribution of his manuscripts in German-speaking territory could speak to a high degree of familiarity, among the literati at least."[6] In this regard, the German reception mirrors the Dutch: Geoffrey's Latin history, though available, did not excite the minds of German romance writers. Moreover, no known manuscript of Geoffrey's *PM* currently resides in a German archive, which seems to reflect a lack of medieval interest in the text. Indeed, while the *PM* was popular elsewhere in Europe, especially in those areas under Norman influence, German speakers paid them little heed, and the most complete survey of later medieval prophetic writing in the High German regions does not even mention Geoffrey's name.[7] In sum, Geoffrey's popularity waned east of the Rhine. Perceptive readers of this article will note its small size and the fact that one of the editors – who is not a Germanicist – has written it, which suggests that more work needs to be done on Geoffrey's German reception, if only to speculate on reasons why German readers chose not to take inspiration from him.

---

6 Brockwyt, "Ein Artusritter im Krieg", p. 98, n. 23: "Obwohl es keine markierten intertextuellen Bezüge in den deutschsprachigen Artusromanen auf Geoffreys Werk gibt, könnte die Weite und Dichte seiner handschriftlichen Verbreitung auch im deutschsprachigen Raum für einen hohen Bekanntheitsgrad zumindest unter den litterati sprechen."

7 F.C. Kneupper, *The Empire at the Edge of Time: Identity and Reform in Late Medieval German Prophecy*, Oxford, 2016. I would like to thank Frances Courtney Kneupper for confirming that Geoffrey's *PM*, and prophecies attributed to Merlin in general, was not as popular in medieval Germany as in other parts of Europe. See ch. 24 for Frederick II and Merlin.

CHAPTER 22

The Old Icelandic "Brut"

Hélène Tétrel

Breta Sögur, or *The Saga of the Britons*, is more or less extant in several manu-scripts, all of Icelandic origin.[1] They are supplemented by a series of fragments and paper copies. It is commonly accepted that there are two versions of the *Breta Sögur*. The so-called "shorter version", found in a 14th-century manu-script called *Hauksbók*, is described as an abridged version. The so-called "lon-ger version", transmitted principally in Copenhagen, Arnamagnæan Institute, AM 573 4to, is said to be closer to Geoffrey's *De gestis Britonum* than the shorter version, and more interested in chivalrous narrative developments. These as-sumptions are partially true but need to be studied further. It is, indeed, sim-plifying to refer to these two manuscripts as "two versions", and the qualifiers ("shorter" as opposed to "longer") do not always do justice to the text copied in both manuscripts. Moreover, other important witnesses of the *Breta Sögur* need to be taken into account. There are two 19th-century editions of the *Breta Sögur*, but neither, though very useful, offers a complete synoptic view.[2] This is unfortunate, since the saga is an important witness to the *DGB*'s transmission in northwestern medieval Europe.

Hauksbók (hereafter "Hb") is a codex divided into three parts. The part bear-ing shelfmark AM 544 4to contains, among other materials, a translation of *The Fall of Troy* by Dares Phrygius and a "Brut" starting with a Virgilian prologue. This version (and this version only) includes a versified translation of the *PM* called *Merlínusspá*, written by the Icelandic monk Gunnlaugr Leifsson around

---

1 *La Saga des Bretons*, ed. and trans. H. Tétrel (forthcoming, Classiques Garnier); S. Gropper, "Breta Sögur and Merlínusspá", in M.E. Kalinke (ed.), *The Arthur of the North: The Arthurian Legend in the Norse and Rus' Realms* (Arthurian Literature in the Middle Ages, 5), Cardiff, 2011, 48–60; J. Louis-Jensen, "Breta Sögur", in P. Pulsiano and K. Wolf et al. (eds.), *Medieval Scandinavia, An Encyclopedia*, New York, 1993, 57–58; A.G. Van Hamel, "The Old Norse Version of the *Historia Regum Britanniae* and the Text of Geoffrey of Monmouth", *Études celtiques* 1 [1936], 197–247.

2 *Hauksbók, udgiven efter de arnamæanske håndskrifter n° 371, 544 og 675 4to samt forskellige pa-pirhåndskrifter* [*Hauksbók*, edited from manuscripts n° 371, 544 og 675 4to and paper copies], ed. F. Jónsson and E. Jónsson, Copenhagen, 1892–96; *Annaler for nordisk Oldkyndighed og historie* [Annals for Nordic antiquities and history], ed. J. Sigurðsson, Copenhagen, 1848–49.

1200.[3] This part of the codex is now kept in Reykjavik at the Árni Magnússon Institute. It was compiled in the 14th century by an Icelandic historiographer, Haukr Erlendsson, who wrote a part of the book and had other parts written by Norwegian and Icelandic scribes. *The Saga of the Britons*, though not always closely translated, is complete in this manuscript.

AM 573 4to is an Icelandic manuscript kept in Copenhagen at the Arnamagnæan Institute; it was written in the 14th century and contains a translation of *The Fall of Troy*, a translation of the DGB §§6–178 starting with a Virgilian prologue and concluding at the end of Arthur's reign, and a small excerpt of the part of the *Conte du Graal* called *Valverspáttr* ("the story of Gawain") which breaks off abruptly with the manuscript itself. Two parts (and two hands) appear in this manuscript (hereafter "573A" and "573B"). Hand 1 wrote *The Saga of the Trojans* and *The Saga of Aeneas and the Briton Kings* until King Uther's reign.[4] About this scribe (a man or a woman, see below), it is essential to note that he/she also wrote the Galfridian section in Copenhagen, Arnamagnæan Institute, AM 764 4to. Hand 2 copied the text from the beginning of Uther's reign to the end of Arthur's and the small portion of Gawain's story. 573B is the part that includes original narrative developments which must have been influenced by chivalric literature.

AM 764 4to (hereafter "764") is a universal history compiled at the end of the 14th century in Iceland and attributed to a group of scribes (Icelandic male scribes working in collaboration with the abbey of women at Reynistaður), a part of which is now lost.[5] In it, an abridged Galfridian translation is interlaced with other historical materials; only two small sections of this translation are still extant: a brief but complete "Aeneas-Brut" paragraph adapting the DGB until the Incarnation, and an acephalous rendering of the end of the DGB (§196 to §208), kept on a now loose folio. The former was cut voluntarily: in this book, the histories of all *regna* are developed in parallel until the Incarnation. The latter, on the other hand, is accidentally deprived of its beginning. Since part of the codex is now lost, we cannot be sure of its original content, but it is very likely that more Galfridian material was contained in it.

3   *Merlínusspá*, ed. and trans. R. Poole, "Merlínusspá", in M. Clunies Ross (ed.), *Skaldic Poetry of the Scandinavian Middle Ages, VII: Poetry in Fornaldarsögur*, Turnhout, 2017, pp. 38–189.

4   *Trójumanna Saga*, ed. J. Louis-Jensen, *Trójumanna Saga* (Editiones Arnamagnæanæ. Series A, 8), Copenhagen, 1963; *Isländische Antikensagas, Die Saga von den Trojanern, die Saga von den Britischen Königen, die Saga von Alexander dem Grossen*, trans. S. Würth (Gropper), Munich, 1996.

5   S. Óskarsdóttir, "Universal History in Fourteenth-century Iceland, Studies in AM764 4to", unpublished doctoral dissertation, University College, London, 2000.

Stockholm, Royal Library, Icelandic Papp. 58 (hereafter "O1") is a paper copy of *Ormsbók*, a lost Icelandic 14th-century codex, made in 1690 by an Icelander. In O1, *The Saga of the Britons* starts with a Virgilian prologue and ends within the DGB §79 in the middle of a sentence. Like the others, this version is preceded by a translation of *The Fall of Troy*.

A fragment of a 14th-century copy of the Icelandic "Brut" has been used in the binding of a book now kept in Dublin, Trinity College Library, under shelfmark 1023a. It contains partly legible fragments of the DGB §106 and §107. Finally, there are modern copies of Hb of various interest at the National Library in Reykjavik and three in Dublin, Trinity College Library.

The "Aeneas-Brut" combination, including the specific Virgilian prologue, that is found in all these versions was probably already available in the Latin exemplar, since a similar arrangement can be found in French texts.[6] Besides, the Virgilian narrative was used by the author of the Icelandic *Veraldar Saga*, who also mentions the Trojan war. Since all the Icelandic texts share the same version of *The Fall of Troy* and the same version of the Virgilian narrative, the probability that a Latin manuscript containing a complete cycle ("Troy-Aeneas-Brut") came into the hands of a translator seems higher than that of a separate transmission.

The part of *The Saga of the Britons* that is common to Hb, 573A, 764, and O1 corresponds to the Virgilian prologue and the DGB §§6–64. The DGB §§64–79 are rendered in Hb, 573A and B, and O1. A collation of these two parts of the *Breta Sögur* with the edited texts of the DGB revealed that all Icelandic texts probably derive from the same original translation.

The part of the saga represented by Hb and 573A alone (DGB §§80–134) betrays use of the same source; so does the part represented by Hb and 573B (DGB §§135–96), though one would expect the use of a different model with the change of hands in 573. The collation of Hb with 764, fol. 38r on the DGB §§196–208 brought the same result. There is therefore no reason to believe that another Galfridian source was used other than the common one by any of the Icelandic redactors or copyists, though this does not preclude personal knowledge and, therefore additions, by one or several of the copyists/authors.

573A and 764 have been copied by the same hand and belong to the same environment; collation has confirmed they are closer to one another than each one is to Hb. A further comparison showed that O1 is closer to 573A than to Hb. Therefore, the *stemma codicum* can be roughly described as such: all versions

---

6   H. Tétrel, "Trojan Origins and the Use of the Æneid and Related Sources in the Old Icelandic Brut", *JEGP* 109:4 (2010), 490–514.

derive from the same source (the first translation into Old Norse, from a Latin text which most probably contained the entire "Troy-Aeneas-Brut" cycle); 573A and B, 764, and O1 are different but closely related (the situation of "573B" is less certain) while Hb stands on its own. Therefore, a subdivision in "two versions" is only partially true. It is still unknown where the Dublin fragments must be positioned.

It is difficult to know if the *PM* was included in the Latin source, since it is a separate text in Icelandic. Gunnlaugr Leifsson's *Merlínusspá* could have been adapted from an independent *libellus*, "little book", from the same model as the one that was used by the first translator of the *DGB*, or it could have been translated from another *DGB* text.[7]

Unlike Wace's *Roman de Brut*, but like the majority of the "Bruts" in Europe, *The Saga of the Britons* derives from a standard ("Vulgate") version of the *DGB*. It belongs, more precisely, to the "Sexburgis" family of the Vulgate *DGB* texts,[8] although some readings could point to a First Variant Version (or to a mixed version).[9] It is not irrelevant to underline that the saga shares this particularity with the Llanstephan 1 version of the Welsh *Brut y Brenhinedd* ("History of the Kings").[10]

Finally, it is difficult to decide when the first translation was made, but 1200, as Steffanie Würth already suggested, is a likely hypothesis.[11]

The Icelandic "Brut", as represented by all its versions, shows interesting particularities. Some additions are probably derived from the Latin source, some of them may have taken place in the first, now lost, Icelandic translation, and some of them may have been introduced by the redactors of the Icelandic versions that have come down to us.

DGB §5 has been replaced by a Virgilian prologue which is not translated from the *Aeneid* but from a shorter, glossed version of it. Long enough to form

---

7   R. Poole, "The Textual Tradition of Gunnlaugr Leifsson's *Merlínusspá*", in H. Tétrel and G. Veysseyre (eds.), *L'Historia regum Britannie et les Bruts en Europe, Tome II, Production, circulation et reception (XIIe–XVIe siècles)* (Rencontres 349, Civilisation médiévale, 32), Paris, 2018, pp. 195–223.

8   See Crick, *DR*, p. 93 and M.D. Reeve, "The Transmission of *the Historia regum Britanniae*", *Journal of Medieval Latin* 1 (1991), 73–117, at p. 91.

9   *First Variant Version*, ed. Wright.

10   B. Roberts, "*Brut y Brenhinedd* ms. National Library of Wales, Llanstephan 1 version", in H. Tétrel and G. Veysseyre (eds.), *L'Historia regum Britannie et les "Bruts" en Europe, Tome I, Traductions, adaptations, réappropriations (XIIe–XVIe siècle)* (Rencontres 106, Civilisation médiévale, 12), Paris, 2015, pp. 71–80, at p. 79.

11   S. Würth, *Der "Antikenroman" in der isländischen Literatur des Mittelalters. Eine Untersuchung zur Übersetzung und Rezeption lateinischer Literatur im Norden* (Beiträge zur nordischen Philologie, 26), Basel: Frankfurt am Main, 1998, p. 81.

an independent narrative, this prologue shows an obvious interest in battles, heroes, and even pagan gods, at least in the 573 and *Ormsbók* versions, where gods and goddesses appear as characters. This prologue discarded Canto VI, a choice that seems relevant to its historical perspective. It also contains a few interesting additional passages; one of them, found in all redactions, tells about Pallas's tomb and its epitaph.[12] Hb and 573/*Ormsbók* have a different version of this famous passage originally found in William of Malmesbury's *Deeds of the English Kings*, but the addition must have been already interpolated in the Latin source.

Another difference from the *DGB*, common to Hb and 573B but probably due to the first Icelandic translator, is the reorganization of the *DGB* §§155–56. Both Icelandic versions have a new development telling about Arthur's fight against giant Ritho. In Geoffrey's narrative, this episode is briefly referred to at the end of §165. The fame of the episode might explain why it is given a particular role in the *Saga*. On closer look, nevertheless, it does not show use of any source other than the *DGB* §165. It is sensible to ascribe this invention to the first Icelandic translator, whereas, in the case of the Virgilian prologue, similarities in the French "Brut" tradition point to the Latin source.

Hb is said to be shorter than 573, but this is not always true. It sometimes displays episodes which have been discarded by other Icelandic versions. This is the case with the episode of the giant stones raised by Merlin in the *DGB* §§128–30. In this part of the saga, only 573A and Hb are available. 573A does not have any trace of the *DGB* §§127–30. Hb, on the other hand, has kept the story, although it is a rather short recension of it. Another example showing that Hb does not look for brevity at all costs is the reinsertion of *Merlínusspá*.

However, it is true that 573B contains several longer narrative additions which are not shared by Hb. Two original amplifications draw attention. The first one appears shortly after the beginning of 573B and tells about King Uther's treasonous seduction of Igerna (*DGB* §137). In this version, a new development occurs: Igerna refuses to accept Uther as her husband, and Uther is forced to ask Merlin to concoct a love-potion. Another addition appears at the end of 573B and deals with the relationship between Guinevere and Mordred. Neither of them display evidence of the use of another source than the *DGB*, but, together with other particularities (for example, the fact that 573B stops rendering the *DGB* after Arthur's reign, that it is followed by an episode of the *Conte du Graal*, etc.), they increase the reader's impression of a more chivalric version of the text. It is important to remember that this part of the manuscript

---

12   R. Patzuk-Russell, "The Legend of Pallas' Tomb and its Medieval Scandinavian Transmission", *JEGP* 118:1 (2019), 1–30.

is copied by hand B and is only concerned with Arthurian times. Though there is no evidence of a Galfridian source other than Hb's in this part of the saga, it is obvious that the narrative is meant for an Arthurian readership. Since only 573B and Hb have this part, it is hard to tell if 573B is responsible for the additions, or if these additions were included in the first Icelandic translation and discarded by Hb. Marianne Kalinke has suggested that some of the additions included in the Arthurian part of 573 derive from the first Icelandic translation and were influenced by Wace's *Brut*.[13] I would be more tempted (without certainty) to ascribe these additions, if they come from Wace, to the redactor of 573B, who wrote at a time when Wace's *Brut* had overwhelmed the Anglo-Norman and French "Brut" tradition, rather than to a translator from the end of the 12th century. But it is difficult to tell if *The Saga of Arthur* (573B) displays evidence of external Arthurian influence, and if so, when those influences took place. Research on this corpus, when entirely edited, should bring some answers.

---

13   M. Kalinke, "Arthur, king of Iceland", *Scandinavian Studies* 87 (2015), 8–32.

CHAPTER 23

The Reception of Geoffrey of Monmouth in Ireland

Joshua Byron Smith

Geoffrey of Monmouth's works did not appeal to the Irish as they did to the other peoples of the North Sea.[1] Although English, Welsh, French, and Norse translations of the *DGB* exist, no Middle Irish translation is extant, nor is there any evidence that there ever was one. Latin manuscripts of the *DGB* did circulate in Ireland, though in many cases it is difficult to know exactly when they reached their current archival homes in Ireland.[2] Nonetheless, in comparison with Britain and northern France, the *DGB* does not seem to have been a particularly popular text. Uncovering Geoffrey's influence in Ireland is also difficult because the figure of King Arthur – by whose presence Geoffrey's influence is often revealed – was already known in early Ireland.[3] A few scholars have thought it possible that British influence, possibly stemming from Geoffrey of Monmouth, can be detected in the *Acallam na Sénorach* ("The Colloquy of the Ancients"), a large Middle Irish compilation of Fénian stories.[4] And it has been ventured that a lost Irish tale, the *Aigidecht Arthúir* ("The Hospitality of Arthur"), could be related to Geoffrey's work.[5] Finally, late medieval Ireland did witness a flourishing of Arthurian literature, but here the influence seems to have been through romance and not from direct engagement with Geoffrey's work.[6]

There is comparatively little written on Geoffrey's reception (or lack thereof) in Ireland. It may be that some parts of Geoffrey's work, in particular the

---

1   I would like to thank Patrick Wadden for his insightful comments and suggestions on this entry.

2   Crick, *SC*, lists the following as having Irish associations: nos. 1, 61, 62, 63, 64, 65, 66, and 67.

3   A. Dooley, "Arthur of the Irish: A Viable Concept?" *AL* 21 (2004), 9–28.

4   Dooley, "Arthur of the Irish", pp. 22–23. An edition and translation of the Arthurian episode can be found in the same volume, pp. 24–28.

5   Dooley, "Arthur of the Irish", pp. 20–21; P. Mac Cana, *The Learned Tales of Medieval Ireland*, Dublin, 1980, p. 108, n. 107. The *Aigidecht Arthúir* appears in the A version of the Irish tale list in the Book of Leinster, which was written in the late 12th century. This gives a tight, though not impossible, timeline for Galfridian influence, and, besides, it is unwise to infer too much from a title alone.

6   J.F. Nagy, "Arthur and the Irish", in H. Fulton (ed.) *A Companion to Arthurian Literature*, Oxford, 2009, pp. 117–27. Also useful for Arthurian literature in Ireland is J. Carey (ed.), *The Matter of Britain in Medieval Ireland: Reassessments*, London, 2017.

non-Arthurian sections, exercised some influence on medieval Irish literature that has so far remained undetected. However, it is just as possible that the Irish simply did not accept Geoffrey's history because they already had their own accounts of early Insular history in the *Lebor Bretnach* (the Irish translations and adaptations of the *Historia Brittonum*) and the *Lebor Gabála Érenn* ("The Book of the Takings of Ireland"). Indeed, Geoffrey's history may have been felt to be too close for comfort: both traditions make claims to an august classical past in similar ways, especially since one of Geoffrey's major influences was the *Historia Brittonum*. Moreover, Geoffrey's account drips with anti-Irish sentiment.[7] It portrays the Irish as barbarous enemies allied with other perpetually troublesome peoples. More disturbing is the fact that the British are said to have conquered Ireland – on two separate occasions no less – long before the arrival of the Normans in the 12th century, giving the events of the 12th century historical precedence.[8] Indeed, Gerald of Wales explicitly lists Arthur's conquest of Ireland as one of the five reasons English kings have a legal right to hold Ireland.[9] No wonder, then, that Gaelic Ireland did not welcome Geoffrey's history with the zeal that their Insular neighbors did. But could these very characteristics have made Geoffrey's history appealing to the Anglo-Irish nobility, one of the audiences that Gerald of Wales had in mind for his *Conquest of Ireland*? Further research in this area would be welcomed.

---

7 Tatlock, *LHB*, pp. 78–80.
8 Once under Arthur's leadership (*DGB*, ix.153.212–24) and once under Malgo's (*DGB*, xi.183.115–21).
9 Gerald of Wales, *The Conquest of Ireland* ii.6, ed. J.F. Dimock, *Giraldi Cambrensis Opera*, 8 vols., London, 1861–91, vol. 5, pp. 207–414, at pp. 319–30.

CHAPTER 24

The Reception of Geoffrey of Monmouth's Work in Italy

Fabrizio De Falco

The reception of Geoffrey of Monmouth's work in medieval Italy is an integral part of two fascinating veins of inquiry: the early appearance of the Matter of Britain in Italy and its evolution in various social, political, and cultural contexts around the Peninsula.[1] At the beginning of the 12th century, before the *De gestis Britonum* was written, an unedited Arthurian legend was carved on Modena Cathedral's *Portale della Pescheria*, a stop for pilgrims headed to Rome along the Via Francigena.[2] Remaining in the vicinity of Modena, the only continental witness of the First Variant Version of the *DGB* (Paris, Bibliothèque de l'Arsenal, 982) can be connected to Nonantola Abbey.[3] Moving to the kingdom of Sicily, in 1165 the archbishop of Otranto commissioned an enormous mosaic for the cathedral, and Arthur is depicted in one of the various scenes, astride a goat, fighting a large cat.[4] To describe Geoffrey of Monmouth's reception in

---

1 E.G. Gardener, *The Arthurian Legend in Italian Literature*, London and New York, 1930; D. Delcorno Branca, "Le storie arturiane in Italia", in P. Boitani, M. Malatesta, and A. Vàrvaro (eds.), *Lo spazio letterario del Medioevo, II. Il Medioevo volgare, III: La ricezione del testo*, Rome, 2003, pp. 385–403; G. Allaire and G. Paski (eds.), *The Arthur of the Italians: The Arthurian Legend in Medieval Italian Literature and Culture* (Arthurian Literature in the Middle Ages, 7), Cardiff, 2014.

2 In this version, Gawain is the protagonist and Arthur is not yet king. R. Lejeune and J. Stennon, "La legende arthurienne dans la sculpture de la cathedrale de Modène", *Cahiers de Civilisation Medievale* 6 (1963), 281–96; L.M. Gowan, "The Modena Archivolt and the Lost Arthurian Tradition", in W. Van Hoecke, G. Tournoy, and W. Webecke (eds.), *Arturus Rex, Vol. II. Acta Conventus Lonvaliensis 1987*, Leuven, 1991, pp. 79–86.

3 D. Delcorno Branca, "Diffusione della materia arturiana in Italia: per un riesame delle 'tradizioni sommerse'", in P. Benozzo (ed.), *Culture, livelli di cultura e ambienti nel Medioevo occidentale: atti del IX Convegno della Società italiana di filologia romanza, Bologna 5–8 ottobre 2009*, Rome, 2012, pp. 321–40, at p. 323; For Italian manuscripts, see the catalogue in Crick, *DR*, nos. 71, 72, 109, 163, 172, 181, 182.

4 It is the demon Cath Palug from the Welsh tradition. The story of his battle with Arthur appears in French romances from the late 12th and early 13th centuries. Its presence in Otranto illustrates the ties between the Norman Kingdom of Sicily and northern Europe. Cf. C. Settis Frugoni, "Per una lettura del mosaico pavimentale della cattedrale di Otranto", *Bullettino dell'Istituto Storico Italiano per il Medio Evo* 80 (1968), 213–56; H. Nickel, "About Palug's Cat and the Mosaic of Otranto", *Arthurian Interpretations* 3:2 (1989), 96–105.

Italy, one must address two topics: the development of the Italian Arthurian tradition – as well as its polemical and political use – and the diffusion of the *DGB* along with its fascinating historiography.

In the courtly contexts of the Empire and the Kingdom of Sicily in the 12th and 13th centuries, we can already see how ephemeral the line was between medieval historiography's interest in the *DGB* and the use of the Matter of Britain in political battles. The first accurate tradition of Geoffrey of Monmouth's work in Italy was at the Hohenstaufen Imperial Court, when Geoffrey of Viterbo used the *DGB* in writing his *Pantheon* (*c*.1185–90), a universal story in prose and verse intended for the court of the emperor Henry VI. Lucienne Meyer's work on the sources Geoffrey used underlines how the section regarding the history of Britain is a selection of passages from the *DGB* ending at the prophecy of Arthur's return.[5] According to Paul Zumthor and Donald Hoffman, Geoffrey of Viterbo initiated the use of Merlin's prophecies in Imperial circles. The prophecies were later used widely in the milieu surrounding Frederick II.[6] During the same years, in the Kingdom of Sicily's struggle between the Norman nobility and the Empire, the Matter of Britain thoroughly entered the realm of political battle. In 1189, Tancred of Lecce, the natural son of Ruggero II of Altavilla, was crowned king of Sicily by the Norman nobility, in opposition to the rights claimed by Emperor Henry VI by marriage to Costanza d'Altavilla, the heir named by the deceased King William II. While traveling in Sicily in 1191, Richard the Lionheart gave Tancred a sword said to be Excalibur.[7] In this gift

5 Godfrey of Viterbo, *Pantheon*, ed. G. Waitz (Monumenta Germaniae Historica, Scriptores, 22), Hanover, 1872, pp. 107–307; L. Meyer, *Les légendes des Matières de Rome, de France et de Bretagne dans le "Pantheon" de Godefroi de Viterbe*, Paris, 1933, pp. 190–223. The study, however, has various lacunae, cf. F.P. Magoun, Jr., "Les Légendes des matières de Rome, de France et de Bretagne dans le 'Pantheon' de Godefroi de Viterbe by Lucienne Meyer", *Speculum* 11:1 (1936), 144–46. On Geoffrey of Viterbo as Imperial historian: L.J. Weber, "The Historical Importance of Godfrey of Viterbo", *Viator* 25:2 (1994), 153–95; K. Hering, "Godfrey of Viterbo: Historical Writing and Imperial Legitimacy at the Early Hohenstaufen Court", in T. Foerster (ed.), *Godfrey of Viterbo and His Readers: Imperial Tradition and Universal History in Late Medieval Europe*, Farnham, 2015, pp. 47–66.

6 P. Zumthor, *Merlin le Prophète, un thème de la littérature polémique, de l'historiographie et des romans*, Lausanne, 1943, p. 97; D.L. Hoffman, "Was Merlin a Ghibelline? Arthurian Propaganda at the Court of Frederick II", in M.B. Shichtman and J.P. Carley (eds.), *Culture and the King: The Social Implications of the Arthurian Legend, Essays in Honor of Valerie M. Lagorio*, Albany, 1994, pp. 113–28. This theme is also addressed in E. Kantorowicz, *Federico II Imperatore*, Milan, 1976, p. 369.

7 Benedict of Peterborough, *The Deeds of King Henry II*, ed. W. Stubbs, *Gesta Regis Henrici Secundi Benedicti Abbatis. The Chronicle of the Reigns of Henry II, and Richard I, AD. 1169–1192: Known commonly under the Name of Benedict of Peterborough*, 2 vols., London, 1867, vol. 2, p. 169.

it is possible to see Richard taking a political position in favor of Tancred and hostile to the Hohenstaufen.[8] A few years later, Otto of Brunswick's Imperial Court saw the birth of the fascinating legend, studied for the first time by Arturo Graf, in which Arthur seeks refuge in Sicily after his final battle.[9] In the *Otia Imperialia* ("Entertainment for an Emperor", *c.*1210), Gervase of Tilbury – followed by other authors[10] – identified Arthur's final refuge as the bowels of Mount Etna, transforming Sicily into Avalon. Gervase of Tilbury was educated at the court of Henry II of England, and Arthur's return – in a work dedicated to Otto IV of Brunswick, grandson of Henry II and enemy of Frederick II – can be seen as a preview of the way in which, later, the Guelf and Ghibelline factions made broad use of the Matter of Britain.

From the 13th to the 15th century, Merlin was the protagonist in a florid tradition independent from Geoffrey of Monmouth, and numerous prophecies attributed to him were written in Italy.[11] These prophecies referred primarily to Frederick II. The emperor, protagonist of the 13th century prophetic writing, was described, depending on the faction, as the Savior or the Antichrist.[12] After their initial use in imperial circles, Merlin's prophecies took on increased importance in the Guelf party's polemical output.[13] The most well-known

---

8   H. Bresc, "Excalibur en Sicilie", *Medievalia* 7 (1987), 7–21; M.R. Warren, "Roger of Howden Strikes Back: Investing Arthur of Brittany with the Anglo-Norman Future", *Anglo-Norman Studies* 21 (1998), 261–72; E. D'Angelo, "Re Artù ed Excalibur dalla Britannia romana alla Sicilia normanna", *Atene e Roma* 3:4 (2007), 137–58.

9   A. Graf, "Artù nell'Etna", in id. (ed.), *Miti, leggende e superstizione nel medioevo*, Milan, 1984, pp. 321–38.

10   Gervase of Tilbury, *Recreation for an Emperor*, ed. and trans. S.E. Banks and J.W. Binns, *Otia imperialia. Recreation for an Emperor*, Oxford, 2002, pp. 334–37; Cesarius of Heisterbach, *Dialogus miraculorum* (1219–23); Stephen of Bourbon, *Tractatus de diversis materiis predicabilibus* (1250–61); *Florian et Florete* (1250–70); *Il detto del gatto lupesco* (s. xiii). See A. Pioletti, "Artù, Avalon, l'Etna", *Quaderni Medievali* 28 (1989), 6–35.

11   Zumthor, *Merlin le Prophète*; D. Hoffman, "Merlin in Italian Literature", in P. Goodrich and R.H. Thompson (eds.), *Merlin: A Casebook*, New York, 2003, pp. 186–96; C. Daniel, *Les prophéties de Merlin et la culture politique (XIIe–XVIe siecles)*, Turnhout, 2006.

12   Cf. G. Podestà, "Roma nella Profezia (secoli XI–XIII)", in n.n. (ed.), *Roma antica nel Medioevo: mito, rappresentazioni, sopravvivenze nella 'Respublica Christiana' dei secoli IX–XIII, atti della quattordicesima Settimana internazionale di studio, Mendola, 24–28 agosto 1998*, Milan, 2001, pp. 356–98; F. Delle Donne, *Il potere e la sua legittimazione: letteratura encomiastica in onore di Federico II di Svevia*, Arce, 2005.

13   Cf. n. 8 of this chapter; P. Ménard, "Les Prophéties de Merlin et l'Italie au XIIIe siècle", in K. Busby, B. Guidot, and L.E. Whalen (eds.), *"De sens rassis". Essays in Honor of Rupert T. Pickens*, Amsterdam and Atlanta, 2005, pp. 431–44; C. Daniel, *Les prophéties de Merlin*, pp. 341–68.

cases that present Frederick as the Antichrist are the *Verba Merlini* (*c.*1240)[14] and a prophetic text falsely attributed to Gioacchino da Fiore: *Abbot Joachim's Exposition of the Sibyls and Merlin* (*Expositio abbatis Joachimi super Sibillis et Merlino, c.*1240).[15] Following this, Merlin's prophecies became an integral part of the internal struggle in various Italian cities between the Guelfs and the Ghibellines. In the boarder district of Treviso, Merlin's prophecies were used to legitimize Ezzelino da Romano's consolidation of power. Ezzelino, the Lord of Padua, was an ally of Frederick II.[16] *Prophéties de Merlin* (*c.*1276), written in French by a certain "Richart d'Irlande", who Lucy Paton identifies as a Venetian Guelf, was one of the most widely disseminated texts.[17] Involved in the struggle between the Guelfs and the Ghibellines, Merlin was distanced from Geoffrey of Monmouth, becoming part of a rich textual tradition that has not yet been studied in its entirety.[18]

Regarding the dissemination of Geoffrey of Monmouth's work, it is important to address the attention the humanists and their predecessors paid him. His work was known by the Italian intellectual elite and already used as a historic source by Paolino Veneto, who collected passages by Geoffrey of Monmouth and Gervase of Tilbury to write his *Compendium* (1321–23).[19] Paolino drew a connection between Geoffrey of Monmouth and Boccaccio, which illustrates the importance given to the DGB in medieval historiography.[20] Daniela Delcorno Branca's work shows how Boccaccio used the DGB to write the *Fall of Princes* (*c.*1355–70)[21] and, specifically, the chapter *De Arturo*

14   The text appears, with some variants, in Salimbene de Adam, *Chronicle*, ed. O. Holder-Egger, *Salimbene de Adam, Chronica fratris Salimbene de Adam ordinis Minorum* (Monumenta Germaniae Historica, Scriptores, 32), Hanover, 1905–13, p. 360.

15   O. Holder-Egger, "Italienische Prophetieen des 13. Jahrhunderts. I.", *Neues Archiv der Gesellschaft für ältere deutsche Geschichtskunde zur Beförderung einer Gesamtausgabe der Quellenschriften deutscher Geschichten des Mittelalters* 15 (1889), 142–78. The *Expositio* is unedited; for a list of manuscripts, see M. Reeves, *The Influence of Prophecy in the Later Middle Ages. A Study in Joachimism*, Oxford, 1969, p. 520.

16   Zumthor, *Merlin le Prophète*, pp. 101–02.

17   *Les Prophecies de Merlin, edited from MS. 593 of the Bibliothèque Municipale de Rennes*, ed. L.A. Paton, 2 vols. (Modern Language Association of America Monograph Series, 1), New York and London, 1926–27 (repr. New York, 1966), vol. 1, p. 58.

18   For more on the various cities, see C. Daniel, *Les prophéties de Merlin*, pp. 277–86.

19   Cf. M. Di Cesare, "Problemi di autografia nei testimoni del Compendium e della Satirica Ystoria di Paolino Veneto", *Res Publica Litterarum* 30 (2007), 39–49.

20   D. Delcorno Branca, *Boccaccio e le storie di re Artù*, Bologna, 1991, p. 69.

21   Giovanni Boccaccio, *On the Fates of Famous Men*, ed. P.G. Ricci and V. Zaccaria, *Tutte le Opere di Giovanni Boccaccio*, gen. ed. V. Branca, 10 vols., Milan, 1967–98, vol. 9; V. Zaccaria, "Le due redazioni del De Casibus", *Studi sul Boccaccio* 10 (1977–78), 1–26.

Britonum Rege.[22] Boccaccio added a number of variants and omitted all fairy-tale elements. This omission demonstrates his intent to use the DGB as a histo-riographic instrument, a *modus operandi* also used in writing his *De montibus* (begun c.1355)[23] where Geoffrey of Monmouth served as a reference for his de-scription of British geography. The use of the DGB as a historic source is high-lighted in Alessandro Malanca's recent work on Galasso da Correggio's *Historia Anglie* (c.430).[24] This work, a reworking of the DGB, was dedicated to Count Filippo Maria Anglo Visconti with the encomiastic intent of recalling the leg-end of the Trojan origins of the Visconti.[25] The count was a passionate reader of history pertaining to illustrious men, and Galasso da Correggio wished to offer him a synthesis between aristocratic cultural fashion and the humanist ideal. Thus intending to write a *Historia* as opposed to the *fabulae* that were in vogue, Galasso drew inspiration from the work of Geoffrey of Monmouth, just as Boccaccio had done before him.

We have seen how, on the one hand, the political use of the Matter of Britain transformed some characters but on the other, the DGB in its original form had a recognized historiographic value. The interaction between these two themes is essential for anyone who wishes to study Geoffrey of Monmouth's reception in medieval Italy. This little-addressed field of study would certainly benefit from further investigation.

Translated from Italian by Lauren Jennings

---

22   Giovanni Boccaccio, *On the Fates of Famous Men* viii.19–20, ed. Ricci and Zaccaria, pp. 729–41; Delcorno Branca, *Boccaccio*, pp. 69–112.

23   Boccaccio worked on *De Montibus* for his whole life. Giovanni Boccaccio, *De montibus, sil-vis, fontibus, lacubus, fluminibus, stagnis seu paludibus et de diversis nominibus maris* [On mountains, forests, fountains, lakes, rivers, swamps or marshes, and on the many names for the sea], ed. M. Pastore Stocchi, *Tutte le Opere di Giovanni Boccaccio*, gen. ed. V. Branca, 10 vols., Milan, 1967–98, vol. 8; M. Pastore Stocchi, *Tradizione medievale e gusto umanistico nel "De montibus" del Boccaccio*, Florence, 1963; Delcorno Branca, *Boccaccio*, pp. 115–26.

24   The work is contained in the following manuscripts: Paris, Bibliothèque nationale de France, lat. 6041D; Palermo, Biblioteca Comunale, 2 Qq C 102; and Correggio, Biblioteca Comunale, 33. See A. Malanca, "Le armi e le lettere. Galasso Da Correggio: Autore dell'Historia Anglie", *Italia Medioevale e Umanistica* 48 (2007), 1–57; id., "Le fonti della materia di Bretagna nell'opera di Galasso da Correggio", *Giornale Italiano di Filologia* 61 (2009), 271–98.

25   E. Pellegrin, *La bibliothèque des Visconti et des Sforza ducs de Milan au XVe siècle*, Paris, 1955; M. Zaggia, "Appunti sulla cultura letteraria in volgare a Milano nell'età di Filippo Maria Visconti", *Giornale storico della letteratura italiana* 170 (1993), 161–219, 321–82.

CHAPTER 25

Geoffrey of Monmouth in Portugal and Galicia

Santiago Gutiérrez García

The dissemination of the works of Geoffrey of Monmouth in medieval Portugal must be analyzed, aside from its peculiarities, within the broader context of the Hispanic kingdoms. Knowledge of Geoffrey's works in Portuguese lands accords with the dynamics of dissemination and circulation of texts in the central and western areas of the Iberian Peninsula, and shows strong connections to events happening in the neighboring kingdom of Castile-León. As in Castile-León, no copies of Geoffrey's work are documented in Portugal during the Middle Ages, while there are only a few allusions to his work that allow scholars to indirectly establish the presence of his work in West Iberia. This situation is somewhat paradoxical, since scholars have considered Portugal one of the main points of entry of the Matter of Britain into the Peninsula. There is no doubt, in fact, that the Atlantic coast of the Portuguese kingdom generated contact by sea with the peoples of northwestern Europe, especially those of Britain.[1] Thus, for example, Portuguese ports were on several occasions layovers for Crusader expeditions on their way to the Mediterranean, or for Crusaders participating in the conquest of cities in central and south Portugal, such as Lisbon, which were taken with the help of the British in particular. And, in the same manner, the alliances that the kings of Portugal established with England – think, for example, of the wedding between João I and Philippa of Lancaster in 1387 – not only consolidated Portugal's recent independence from the kingdom of Castile-León, but also fostered Anglo-Portuguese commercial and cultural exchanges.

Nevertheless, despite the close contacts between northwest Europe and Portugal, the first evidence of Geoffrey's corpus in the kingdom is linked to the center of the Peninsula, as it derives from historiographical texts created in Castile, such as that of Alfonso X *el Sabio* ("the wise"). This monarch used the *DGB* to write the *General estoria* (1270–84), which he referred to as the *Estoria de las Bretannas*.[2] The title could be a reference to the *DGB* directly or to some other history derived from Geoffrey's. Both options seem possible, because the

---

1   As a matter of fact, according to the Trojan origin story of the British people, the Portuguese coast was on the route that the Trojans would have taken on their way to Britain.

2   For additional discussion, see Paloma Gracia's contribution to this volume.

General estoria makes note of a history of Britain written in Latin, from which Alfonso X took verbatim quotations.[3] See, for example, the following passage, in which Brutus's visit to the temple of Diana is described: "and those words of Brutus's prayer are in that history of Britain in Latin, like all the other material from that book, and it reads as follows: *Mighty goddess of the forest, terror of woodland boars ...*"[4] Galfridian accounts are scattered in succeeding passages throughout sections II to V of the *General estoria*, although, due to the unfinished nature of Alfonso's chronicle, they only go as far as the expedition of Julius Caesar.

Be that as it may, the *General estoria* did not take long to circulate throughout the westernmost of the Hispanic kingdoms, both in Spanish and in translations into Portuguese. Proof of the chronicle's dissemination is the several copies found in Portuguese libraries, such as the manuscript of the Public Library of Évora written in Castilian, or the manuscript of the Arquivo Distrital de Castelo Branco, and the five manuscripts of the Arquivo da Torre do Tombo de Lisbon – all written in Portuguese.[5] Although the transmission of such an extensive text as the *General estoria* was carried out in a very fragmented way, and the extant copies found in Portugal do not contain the passages taken from the *DGB*, it is logical to suppose that the chronicle of Alfonso X spread the passages to the kingdom just as it served as a model for 14th-century Portuguese historiography.

One of the works that follows Alfonso's model is the *Crónica Geral de Espanha de 1344* ("The 1344 General History of Spain"), composed *c.*1344 by Pedro Afonso (1287–1350), Count of Barcelos (henceforth referred to as D. Pedro) and son of King Dinis I.[6] This chronicle has not survived in its original form, but in a redaction (*c.*1400) that has significant modifications. The redactor eliminated all

---

3   F. Gómez Redondo, "La materia de Bretaña y los modelos historiográficos: el caso de la *General estoria*", *e-Spania* 16 (2013), <https://journals.openedition.org/e-spania/22707> (accessed 30 May 2018), §14.

4   Alfonso X, *General estoria*, ed. P. Sánchez Prieto-Borja, A. Cabrejas, and M. Belén, *General estoria. Segunda Parte*, 2 vols., Madrid, 2009, vol. 2, p. 512. The manuscript states: "e aquellas palavras de la oración de Bruto son en aquella estoria de Bretaña en latín, como todas las otras razones d'ese libro, e dizen d'esta guisa: *Diva potens nemorum, terror silvestribus apris ...*" The italics in the body of the text and the translation are my own, signaling that the manuscript shifts languages from Spanish to Latin. The translation of the Latin is that of Neil Wright; see *DGB*, i.16.294.

5   Évora, Public Library, CXXV 2/3; Castelo Branco, Arquivo Distrital, CNCVL/01/LV014; Lisbon, Arquivo da Torre do Tombo, Fragmentos, cx. 13, mç. 10, n° 30, Fragmentos, cx. 21, n° 29, Fragmentos, cx. 21, n° 30, Fragmentos, cx. 21, n° 31, Fragmentos, cx. 21, n° 32.

6   Count Pedro of Barcelos, *Crónica de 1344*, ed. L.F. Lindley Cintra, *Crónica geral de Espanha de 1344*, Lisbon, 1952.

the materials that were considered unrelated to the Hispanic kings. Those re-moved chapters would have included a brief summary of the history of Britain based on the *DGB*. The narration has been preserved in a Castilian transla-tion of the original *Crónica*, available in Salamanca, University of Salamanca Library, 2656. In just one chapter, CCCXXI, the author outlines a tight summary of the last section of Geoffrey's *DGB*, from the death of Arthur and the succes-sion to the throne of Lot de Leonís (Loth) and Constantín (Constantinus), until the lineage of the kings of Britain is extinguished after the death of Cavadres (Cadualadrus). The author ends the narration by recalling the ties between the monarchs of Britain and the kings of Troy, but not without cause, since his mo-tive in including this summary is to relate the origins of the great European lin-eages and dynasties, and in this context he can insert the lineage of the kings of Spain.

A similar goal is found in the inclusion of another summary of the *DGB*, spe-cifically in section II of the *Livro de linhagens* ("Book of Lineages") written by D. Pedro between 1340 and 1344. In this case, the account goes back to the reign of Dardanus of Troy, linking Priam, Aeneas, and Brutus with the lineage of the kings of Britain, and extends as far as the death of Cavadres (Cadualadrus) and the conquest of the island by the Saxons. It is, therefore, a summary of the whole of the *DGB* except for the *PM*, which are not documented in Portugal. Its purpose would be the same as that of the Galfridian passages used in the *Crónica Geral de Espanha de 1344*, although this time with the intention of ex-alting noble Portuguese families.

In view of the details contained in these two excerpts, it can be concluded that D. Pedro did not use Geoffrey's *DGB* directly, but some intermediate ver-sion, whose identification has caused some controversy among scholars. The successive contributions of Manuel Serrano y Sanz, Luís Filipe Lindley Cintra, and Diego Catalán have established that D. Pedro used a version of the *Liber regum* ("The Book of Kings"), a historiographical work written in Navarre between 1196 and 1209.[7] Specifically, it is believed that he could have drawn on the *Libro de las generaciones* (c.1256–70), a composition derived from the

---

7   M. Serrano y Sanz, "*Cronicón Villarense (Liber Regum)*. Primeros años del siglo XIII. La obra histórica más antigua en idioma español", *Boletín de la Real Academia Española*, 6 (1919), 192–220 and 8 (1921), 367–82; L.F. Lindley Cintra, "O *Liber Regum* e outras fontes do *Livro de Linhagens* do Conde D. Pedro", *Boletim de Filologia*, 11 (1950), 224–51; id., "Uma tradução galego-portuguesa desconhecida do *Liber Regum*", *Bulletin Hispanique*, 52 (1950), 27–40; Count Pedro of Barcelos, *Crónica de 1344*, ed. Lindley Cintra; D. Catalán Menéndez-Pidal, *De Alfonso X al Conde de Barcelos: cuatro estudios sobre el nacimiento de la historiografía romance en Castilla y Portugal*, Madrid, 1962.

oldest version of the *Liber regum*.[8] Nevertheless, it cannot be ruled out that D. Pedro handled more than one version of the latter work or even a compilation based on another edited version of the *Liber regum*, the so-called *Liber regum toletanus* ("The Toledo Book of Kings", c.1220). Catalán himself proposed that this compilation could have been made in Mondoñedo, a city in northern Galicia with ecclesiastical links to the Portuguese town of Braga.[9] Catalán did so by taking into account certain linguistic features and allusions from the texts, but above all he took into account the similarities that D. Pedro's narration of Galfridian episodes had with other works composed in the Iberian northwest – such as the *Crónica de 1404* or the Galician version of the *Crónica de Castilla*. More recently, Bautista has reiterated the Galician origin of the supposed compilation, although proposing Santiago de Compostela as its place of origin.[10]

Another indirect reference reaffirms the difficulties of studying the dissemination of Geoffrey's corpus in Portugal because of its elusive nature and the scarcity of data on its circulation. Box and Deyermond, for example, call attention to a comment in chapter CXII of the *Livro de Jose de Arimateia* ("The Book of Joseph of Arimathea") made to a certain Mestre Baqua, "who translated the History of Britain into French from Latin".[11] The figure in question is Wace, who adapted the DGB into French as the *Roman de Brut*. These two scholars mention the originality of the reference, since it is not found in other French or English versions of the work, and therefore cannot come from a foreign source. With some caution, they deduce that the mention of Wace does not imply a thorough knowledge of his work nor its direct handling. It would be enough for the Portuguese redactor to know of the importance of Wace in the dissemination of Arthuriana if he were searching for a prestigious reference with which to compare his own work. Be that as it may, the knowledge, even indirect, of Wace as the adapter of Geoffrey's DGB into French demonstrates a certain familiarity with texts associated with Geoffrey's corpus on the part of authors in

---

8   Catalán Menéndez-Pidal, *De Alfonso X*, p. 365.

9   D. Catalán Menéndez-Pidal, *De la silva textual al taller historiográfico alfonsí. Códices, crónicas, versiones y cuadernos de trabajo*, Madrid, 1997, p. 343.

10   F. Bautista, "Original, versiones e influencia del *Liber regum*: estudio textual y propuesta de *stemma*", *e-Spania* 9 (2010), <https://journals.openedition.org/e-spania/19884> (accessed 30 May 2018), §36.

11   *Estória do Santo Graal*, ed. J.C. Ribeiro Miranda, *Estória do Santo Graal. Livro Português de José de Arimateia. Manuscrito 643 do Arquivo Nacional da Torre do Tombo*, Porto, 2016, p. 330. The manuscript says "*que traladou a Estoria de Brutos em framces de latim*". See J.B.H. Box and A. Deyermond, "Mestre Baqua and the Grail Story", *Revue de Littérature Comparée* 51 (1977), 366–70.

the Iberian Peninsula, who might have also used the author of the *Roman de Brut* to enhance their own prestige.

In contrast, studies of the dissemination of Geoffrey of Monmouth's work in Portugal have privileged the search for texts written in Portuguese, paying less attention to medieval Latin texts. Nevertheless, an analysis of the works in Latin found in Portuguese libraries that would have circulated during the Middle Ages can shed additional light to the data exposed so far. To give just one example, the *Speculum historiale* by Vincent de Beauvais (1240–60) used the *DGB* as one of its sources. Several copies of the work of this French Dominican are kept in Portuguese libraries, both as manuscripts (Lisbon, National Library of Lisbon, Il.135, Il.126–128, and Il.130–131), as well as incunables in the Public Library of Évora, the National Library of Lisbon, the University Library of Coimbra, and the Arquivo Municipal de Castelo Branco. There are also incunable copies of the *Chronicon* by Antoninus of Florence (1477) in the National Library of Lisbon and the Public Library of Évora. Antoninus took as his main source the *Speculum historiale* and, through it, repeated many passages from Geoffrey, thus contributing, albeit indirectly, to the dissemination of his work.

The above information allows us to conclude that in Portugal, Geoffrey was known in an indirect and partial way, which demonstrates, paradoxically, how the immense popularity of his *DGB* achieved great geographical reach, disseminated in a wide variety of ways.

Translated from Spanish by Nahir I. Otaño Gracia

CHAPTER 26

The Scottish Reception of Geoffrey of Monmouth

Victoria Shirley

Medieval Scottish historians had a complex relationship with Geoffrey of Monmouth and his *De gestis Britonum*. Geoffrey was a source of authority on British history who was worthy of respect; however, his idea of Insular union could not always be reconciled with Scottish national history, which advocated Scotland's independence from England. Geoffrey's narrative of British history was contested in official letters, legal documents, and Latin historiography produced in Scotland between the 14th and 15th centuries. Such national rewritings of the *DGB* are exemplified by the *Instructiones* (1301) and the *Processus* (1301) by Baldred Bisset – a lawyer who was also a canon of Caithness and rector of Kinghorn in the St Andrews diocese – and the *Chronicle of the Scottish People* by John of Fordun (1384 × 1387), which was continued by the Augustinian canon and abbot of Inchcolm, Walter Bower, in his *Scotichronicon* (1440 × 1447). These texts reimagine the political geography of Britain in the *DGB* to articulate Scottish resistance to English imperial conquest.

In the *DGB*, Geoffrey of Monmouth uses the story of Locrinus, Albanactus, and Kamber to explain the tripartite division of Britain into England, Scotland, and Wales. After the death of their father, Brutus of Troy, Geoffrey writes that

> Locrinus, the first-born, received the central part of the island, afterwards called Loegria after him; Kamber received the region across the river Severn, now known as Wales, which for a long time was named Kambria after him, and for this reason the inhabitants still call themselves Cymry in British; Albanactus the youngest received the region known today as Scotland, which he named Albania after himself.[1]

---

1 *DGB*, ii.23.5–10: "Locrinus, qui primogenitus fuerat, possedit mediam partem insulae, quae postea de nomine suo appellata est Loegria; Kamber autem partem illam quae est ultra Sabrinum flumen, quae nunc Gualia uocatur, quae de nomine ipsius postmodum Kambria multo tempore dicta fuit, unde adhuc gens patriae lingua Britannica sese Kambro appellat; at Albanactus iunior possedit patriam quae lingua nostra his temporibus appellatur Scotia et nomen ei ex nomine suo Albania dedit."

According to Geoffrey, Britain is a single kingdom, and the different regions – or parts of Britain – are not individual sovereign states; rather, they are merely separate parts of the whole island.

The division of Britain in the DGB was used to support different political and national agendas during the First War of Scottish Independence (1296–1328).[2] In a letter to Pope Boniface VIII, Edward I used the story of Brutus's sons to assert that England held sovereignty over Scotland; however, the Scottish lawyer Baldred Bisset demonstrated how Edward had revised the story for his own purposes. Meanwhile, in the late 14th century, the Scottish historian, John of Fordun, challenged and contested the geopolitical construction of Britain in Geoffrey's DGB. In the *Chronicle of the Scottish People* (1384 × 1387), which was the first narrative of the history of Scotland from its foundation by Scota and Gaythelos to the death of King David I in 1153, John revised and rewrote the division of Britain in the DGB to determine Scotland's independence from England. John was also one of the first Scottish chroniclers to challenge the legitimacy of King Arthur, and he promoted the sons of Anna – Gawain and Mordred – as the rightful heirs to the British throne.[3] Later writers, such as Walter Bower, the author of the *Scottis Originale*, John Major, and Hector Boece, continued to question Arthur's right of succession, and presented him as a bastard, a traitor and a tyrant. From the 14th to the 16th centuries, Scottish historians used legal discourse and rhetorical argumentation to interrogate the authority of Geoffrey's narrative of British history, and to address their own ideas about nation, territory, and political sovereignty.

In his letter of 1301 to Pope Boniface VIII, Edward I uses the division of Britain in the DGB to explain England's right to hold Scotland. The letter subtly rewrites the story of Brutus's sons in the DGB to emphasize the power of Locrinus, the eldest son, over his brothers Albanactus and Kamber. The text states that

> Afterwards he [Brutus] divided his realm among his three sons, that is he gave to his first born, Locrine, that part of Britain now called England, to the second, Albanact, that part then known as Albany, after the name of Albanact, but now as Scotland, and to Camber, his youngest son, the part then known by his son's name as Cambria and now called Wales,

2   See R.J. Goldstein, *The Matter of Scotland: Historical Narrative in Medieval Scotland*, Lincoln, 1993.
3   See J. Wood, "Where Does Britain End? The Reception of Geoffrey of Monmouth in Scotland and Wales", in R. Purdie and N. Royan (eds.), *The Scots and Medieval Arthurian Legend*, Cambridge, 2005, pp. 9–24.

the royal dignity being reserved for Locrine, the eldest. Two years after the death of Brutus there landed in Albany a certain king of the Huns, called Humber, and he slew Albanact, the brother of Locrine. Hearing this, Locrine, the king of the Britons, pursued him, and he fled and was drowned in the river from which his name is called Humber, and thus Albany reverted to Locrine.[4]

Locrinus is clearly the most powerful of Brutus's sons, and he is fashioned as *rex Britonum*, "king of the Britons"[5] – such an epithet was never ascribed to him in Geoffrey's *DGB*. Edward uses a passive grammatical construction to describe Scotland's submission to England: Albania (or Scotland) is the patient subject; *reveritur* (from *reverto*) is the passive verb; and Locrinus is the active subject (or agent). As the successor of Locrinus, Edward insists that Scotland should be subjugated to England, and that he should have control of the whole island.

In response to Edward's letter to Boniface, the Scottish lawyer Baldred Bisset prepared two letters, known as the *Instructiones* and the *Processus*, which established Scotland's independence from England. These letters, which are extant in Book XI of Walter Bower's *Scotichronicon*, contest the veracity of Edward's version of the foundation and division of Britain by Brutus of Troy. The *Instructiones* addresses the silences and omissions in Edward's version of the Brutus story. The text states that "the king omitted to write down the truth about what happened, touching only on what seemed to suit his purpose and suppressing the rest of the truth."[6] The *Instructiones* acknowledges that Britain was divided between Brutus's sons, and that the regions were named Cambria, Albany, and Loegria; however, the text also asserts that, when the Scots arrived in Britain, they drove the Britons out of Albany and renamed it Scotland:

---

4   *Anglo-Scottish Relations, 1174–1328: Some Selected Documents*, ed. and trans. E.L.G. Stones, Oxford, 1970, pp. 194–97: "Et postea regnum suum tribus filiis suis divisit, scilicet Locrino primogenito illam partem Britannie que nunc Anglia dicitur et Albanacto secundo natu illam partem que tunc Albania a nomine Albanacti nunc vero Scocia nuncupatur, et Cambro filio minori partem illam nomine suo tunc Cambria vocatam que nunc Wallia vocatur, reservata Locrino seniori regia dignitate. Itaque biennio post mortem Bruti applicuit in Albania quidam rex Hunorum nomine Humber et Albanactum fratrem Locrini occidit, quo audito Locrinus rex Britonum prosecutus est eum qui fugiens submersus est in flumine quod de nomine suo Humber vocatur et sic Albania revertitur ad dictum Locrinum."

5   *Anglo-Scottish Relations*, ed. and trans. Stones, pp. 194–95: "rex Britonum".

6   Walter Bower, *Scotichronicon* xi.49.28–29, ed. D.E.R. Watt and trans. N.F. Shead, W.B. Stevenson, and D.E.R. Watt, *Scotichronicon: in Latin and English*, 9 vols., Aberdeen, 1987–98, vol. 6, pp. 140–43: "rei geste veritatem scribere rex omisit, ea tangens solummodo que suo viderentur proposito convenire, reliqua veritate suppressa."

When these Britons had been driven from Albany in this way by the Scots, along with their king and the laws, language and customs of the Britons, it is well known that the name of Albany was banished along with the former lordship held by the Britons. The place of the name Albany was taken by the new name Scotland along with the new people, the Scots, with their rites, language and customs – regarding which the Scots have nothing in common with the Britons – and with their king and the new lordship of the Scots. And for this reason, this part of the island of Britain previously called Albany, as the king has written, was from then on inviolably and unshakeably always called Scotland thereafter, since conditions changed along with the name.[7]

Bisset constructs the Britons and the Scots as two separate peoples, with their own laws, rites, language, and customs, and he argues the first Scots claimed Scotland "by the same right and title as that by which Brutus had earlier occupied the whole of Britain".[8] The change of name from Albany to Scotland symbolizes the transfer of power from the Britons to the Scots. Furthermore, the creation of a Scottish monarchy separates the new kingdom of Scotland from the rest of Britain, and establishes the limits of British power across the island.

In the more rhetorically advanced *Processus*, Bisset challenges Edward's version of the Brutus story on legal grounds. As in the *Instructiones*, Bisset aims to discredit Edward as he gives evidence "in his own case",[9] and he directly contests Edward's account of the division of Britain between Locrinus, Albanactus, and Kamber. He writes that

The king [Edward] says that Brutus held that monarchy as a whole, and that he had divided it among his sons: we do not disagree about that. But we utterly deny that he made his division in such a way that the brothers were made subordinate to him for three reasons. First because, whatever the king states, division means equal shares in consequence, when there

---

7   Walter Bower, *Scotichronicon* xi.49.59–69, ed. Watt and trans. Shead et al., vol. 6, pp. 142–43: "Quibus exactis tali modo Britonibus de Albania per Scotos cum suo rege, legibus, lingua et moribus Britonum, exulavit et inde notorie nomen Albanie cum dominio pristino Britonum; in locumque eiusdem nominis Albanie nomen successit novum Scocie, una cum Scotorum nova gente suisque ritibus, lingua et moribus (quibus nichil commune est cum Britonibus) unaque cum suo rege et dominio novo Scotorum. Et hec pars insule Britannie dicta prius Albania, ut rex scripsit, extunc mutatis condicionibus cum nomine vocata est Scocia ista de causa semper postea inviolabiliter et inconcusse."

8   Walter Bower, *Scotichronicon* xi.49.54–55, ed. Watt and trans. Shead et al., vol. 6, pp. 142–43: "jure eodem et titulo quo Brutus totam prius occupaverat Britanniam".

9   Walter Bower, *Scotichronicon* xi.60.33, ed. Watt and trans. Shead et al., vol. 6, pp. 178–79: "in sua propria causa".

is no evidence to the contrary; hence it is that where there are not several shares, one share is defined as a half. Second, because matters which are uncertain should if possible be brought into line with common law, by which one king is not subject to another, nor one kingdom to another, as mentioned above. Third, because a father's division of his property of the kind is usually arranged so as to avoid the possibility of jealousy between the children after the father's death.[10]

In contrast to Edward, who simply relied on the narrative of the *DGB* to support his argument, Bisset's uses the laws of inheritance to legitimize his claim. He points out that Scotland "would not fall to Locrinus himself by right of succession unless there was a failure in all the other levels of the family tree".[11] As a result of Albanactus's death, Bisset implies that Scotland should have been divided between two remaining brothers – namely, Locrinus and Kamber. Bisset is clearly the more skilled rhetorician who is able to point out the flaws of his opponent's argument. Moreover, by demonstrating that Edward's argument has several false premises, Bisset strengthens his claim that Scotland should be an independent nation, and so he presents a more persuasive case to his recipient, Pope Boniface.

In the 14th century, Scottish lawyers and historians rewrote the myth of the Egyptian princess Scota and her Greek husband Gaylethos to explain how Scotland had been founded before Brutus arrived and established Britain.[12] Like Bisset, John of Fordun also critically evaluates the reliability of the Brutus story. Although John subverts Geoffrey's account of Brutus of Troy using the legend of Scota and Gaythelos, his approach to the division of Britain between Brutus's sons is more nuanced. In Book Two of his *Chronicle*, John mentions Albanactus, who "gained possession of the land which in our day is called

---

10   Walter Bower, *Scotichronicon* xi.61.13–25, ed. Watt and trans. Shead et al., vol. 6, pp. 180–81: "Nam dicit Brutum illam monarchiam integram habuisse et quod diviserit inter filios suos: non diffitemur ad presens. Sed, quod sic diviserit quod alii subicerentur sibi, plane negamus. Triplici racione: tum quia divisio dicit partes ergo equales, cum non appareat de contrario, quicquid ipse scribat. Hinc est quod appellacione partis, ubi non sunt plures partes, dimidia continetur. Tum quia omnia non liquida, si possint, ad jus commune debent redigi, per quod rex regi, seu regnum regno, non subest, ut superius est notatum. Tum quia divisiones huiusmodi paterne solent fieri ut occasio invidie inter liberos post mortem patris evitetur."

11   Walter Bower, *Scotichronicon* xi.61.33–35, ed. Watt and trans. Shead et al., vol. 6, pp. 180–81: "jure successionis, nisi omnes alii gradus et stirpes deficerent ... ad ipsum Locrinum non posset obvenire".

12   See K.H. Terrell, "Subversive Histories: Strategies of Identity in Scottish Historiography", in J.J. Cohen (ed.), *Cultural Diversity in the British Middle Ages: Archipelago, Island, England*, New York, 2008, pp. 153–72.

Scotland. He gave it the name Albany after his own name."[13] This chapter also includes several quotations from Bede and Geoffrey that affirm that Scotland was part of Britain (albeit when it was called Albion), and it is designed to be read in dialogue with the two preceding chapters, which quote the same historians, in order to show how these authorities also seem to support the independence of Scotland from Britain. The purpose of this contrast is to cast considerable doubt over the authority of these historians, and, by extension, John also questions Albanactus's right to Scotland. By demonstrating that the works of earlier historians contain irreconcilable differences, John can use these discrepancies to suit his own argument concerning the relationship between Albion and Britain. He asserts that

> whatever varying description of this sort is found in the histories for the boundaries of Britain because of writers' inadequacy, the commonly held opinion at the present time indicates that the whole of Albion is to be called Britain from [the name of] Brutus, who had settled none of it except for its southern regions.[14]

Written history has little credence here, and it is public opinion that has the most authority. The people confirm that Albion is Brutus's territory; but John is careful to indicate that he only conquered the south of the island, and renamed it Britain. The careful negotiation between the terms Albion and Britain allows John to demonstrate that Britain was not a unified island, and that Scotland was beyond British control.

The doubts that John raised about Geoffrey's narrative also allowed him to reimagine the geopolitical landscape of Britain. He contests the division of Britain into three separate nations – England, Scotland, and Wales:

> Loegria was the kingdom of Locrinus beginning in the southern region of the island, that is on the shore of Totnes, and finishing at the river

---

13   Walter Bower, *Scotichronicon* ii.4.16–18, ed. Watt and trans. J. and W. MacQueen, vol. 1, pp. 174–75: "possedit patriam, que nostris temporibus Scocia vocatur, cui nomine ex nomine suo dedit Albaniam." The passages from Book II of the *Scotichronicon* that are quoted throughout this essay were directly copied by Walter Bower from John of Fordun's *Chronicle of the Scottish People*. D.E.R. Watt's edition of the *Scotichronicon* includes extensive notes that indicate the material that Walter Bower added to the material from John of Fordun's *Chronicle*.

14   Walter Bower, *Scotichronicon* ii.4.32–37, ed. Watt and trans. J. and W. MacQueen, vol. 1, pp. 176–77: "Verum quicquid huiusmodi varie diffinicionis finium Britannie scriptorum vicio reperiatur historiis, vulgaris opinio moderni temporis omnem Albionem a Bruto qui [nichil] preter australes eius regiones cultura redigerat dici velit Britanniam." I have altered the translation thanks to the advice of an anonymous reader.

Humber and the river Trent in the north. Then Cambria the region of the
younger brother Camber lies adjacent to the kingdom of Loegria, not at
its southern boundary as certain authorities declare, nor at its northern
boundary, but on its western side, divided from it by mountains and the
Severn Estuary, side by side with it as it were, and facing towards Ireland.
Albany, the kingdom of Albanactus and the third region of the kingdom
of the Britons, had its beginning at the same river Humber and the tidal
reaches of the river Trent and the ends of the northern extremity of
Britain, as was explained above. The Britons at one time held only lordship over all the provinces of this region of Albany that were between
the Humber and the Firth of Forth, and they never had any possession
further north in Albion.[15]

This division of Britain in the *Chronicle* is based on the natural landscape, and
it is more detailed than Geoffrey's account in the *DGB*. Indeed, John provides a
brief survey of Britain and shows how the kingdoms of Locrinus, Kamber, and
Albanactus are positioned against one another. The rivers of Britain become
part of its political geography, and they are used to demarcate the boundaries
between the three separate territories. However, in this account of the division of Britain, Albanactus is not given Scotland: instead he inherits the north
of Britain, which is distinct from Locrinus's kingdom in the south. By rewriting Geoffrey's original narrative, the Scots reimagine the landscape of Britain,
and they also reject Albanactus as the founder of their nation. Scotland is conceived as a separate territory with its own inhabitants.

The works of Baldred Bisset and John of Fordun demonstrate how Geoffrey
of Monmouth's *DGB* was received, and subsequently rewritten, in 14th-century
Scotland. While Bisset refuted Edward's claims of political sovereignty, John
subverted Geoffrey's vision of Insular unity. Both writers used the division of
Britain between Locrinus, Albanactus, and Kamber to emphasize the political,
geographical, and national differences between England and Scotland.

---

15   Walter Bower, *Scotichronicon* ii.6.16–30, ed. Watt and trans. J. and W. MacQueen, vol. 1,
        pp. 178–79: "Loegria vero Locrini regnum ad meridianam insule plagam, Totonensis sci-
        licet litus, incipiens ad Humbri flumen versus boream, et ad ampnem de Tharent finem
        habet. Cambria deinde fratris quoque junioris Cambri regio connexa Loegrie regno jacet
        non ad australem eius finem, ut quidam autumant, neque borealem sed ad ipsius latus
        occiduum, ab eo montibus marique Sabrino divisa, quasi collateralis ei versus Hiberniam
        ex opposito. Albania siquidem regnum Albanacti tercia regio regni Britonum ad idem
        Humbri flumen et gurgitem ampnis de Tharent habens inicium, in fine boreali Britannie,
        sicut superius expressum est, terminatur. Huius autem Albanie regionis provincias, que-
        cumque fuerint, que sunt inter Humbrum et mare Scoticum, olim Britones dominio tan-
        tum et nichil umquam possessionis amplius in Albione versus boream habuerunt."

CHAPTER 27

The Reception of Geoffrey of Monmouth in Wales

Ben Guy

The influence of Geoffrey of Monmouth on medieval Welsh vernacular literature was pervasive. Since many of the themes, characters, and events in Geoffrey's work had been drawn in the first instance from stories and texts emanating from medieval Wales, it was natural that the Welsh should feel an immediate affinity with Geoffrey's writings. Although Geoffrey openly disparages the latter-day Welsh at the end of the *De gestis Britonum*, he did succeed in providing them with a long and glorious past in which the ancestors of the Welsh, the Britons, were associated with the original founding and naming of the kingdom of Britain. Geoffrey helped to confirm prior Welsh historical assumptions and to provide a coherent organizational framework for the mass of inherited Welsh literary-historical tradition.

An early manifestation of Geoffrey's influence may be seen in the pedigree of the kings of Gwynedd and Deheubarth, which absorbed some of Geoffrey's legendary kings of Britain within only a few decades of the completion of Geoffrey's *DGB* around 1138.[1] But it was only with the translation of Geoffrey's *DGB* into medieval Welsh that his work began to infiltrate popular conceptions of Welsh and British history at a more fundamental level. The translation process may have begun with an attempt to identify Welsh equivalents for the many characters named in the work, as may be evidenced in a poem composed by Cynddelw Brydydd Mawr around 1187.[2] By no later than *c.*1250, however, there had been several attempts at translating the entirety of Geoffrey's *DGB* into Welsh. These translations are known collectively as *Brut y Brenhinedd* ("History of the Kings").

---

1   B. Guy, "Gerald and Welsh Genealogical Learning", in G. Henley and A.J. McMullen (eds.), *Gerald of Wales: New Perspectives on a Medieval Writer and Critic*, Cardiff, 2018, pp. 47–61, at pp. 50–55.

2   P. Sims-Williams, *Rhai Addasiadau Cymraeg Canol o Sieffre o Fynwy* [Some Middle Welsh adaptations of Geoffrey of Monmouth], Aberystwyth, 2011, pp. 6–9; B. Guy, "Constantine, Helena, Maximus: on the Appropriation of Roman History in Medieval Wales, *c.*800–1250", *Journal of Medieval History* 44 (2018), 381–405, at pp. 400–01.

At least four versions of *Brut y Brenhinedd* survive from the 13th century: the Llanstephan 1 version (earliest manuscript s. xiii[med]),[3] the Peniarth 44 version (earliest manuscript s. xiii[med]), the Dingestow version (earliest manuscript s. xiii[2]),[4] and the *Liber Coronacionis Britanorum* (earliest manuscript s. xiii/xiv).[5] Other versions appeared later: the idiosyncratic Cotton Cleopatra version (earliest manuscript c.1330)[6] and the derivative Red Book of Hergest version (earliest manuscripts s. xiv[2]),[7] both probably prepared in the first half of the 14th century, and *Brut Tysilio* (earliest manuscript s. xvi[med]), an abbreviation redacted in the 15th or early 16th century.[8] None of these versions is entirely independent of the others.[9] For example, they all draw upon the same translation of the *PM*, one seemingly created prior to the first full translation of the *DGB* itself.[10] Although it is therefore clear that successive redactors of *Brut y Brenhinedd* were guided by the work of their predecessors, supported by

3   Discussed, with edited excerpts, in *Brut y Brenhinedd: Llanstephan MS. 1 Version*, ed. B.F. Roberts (Mediaeval and Modern Welsh Series, 5), Dublin, 1971, and again in B. Roberts, "*Brut y Brenhinedd* ms. National Library of Wales, Llanstephan 1 version", in H. Tétrel and G. Veysseyre (eds.), *L'Historia regum Britannie et les "Bruts" en Europe, Tome I, Traductions, adaptations, réappropriations (XIIe–XVIe siècle)* (Rencontres 106, Civilisation médiévale, 12), Paris, 2015, pp. 71–80.

4   Edited in *Brut Dingestow*, ed. H. Lewis, Cardiff, 1942, and discussed in B. Roberts, "Fersiwn Dingestow o Brut y Brenhinedd" [The Dingestow version of *Brut y Brenhinedd*], BBCS 27 (1976–78), 331–61.

5   Edited and discussed in *Liber Coronacionis Britanorum*, ed. P. Sims-Williams, 2 vols., Aberystwyth, 2017.

6   Edited and translated in *Brut y Brenhinedd: Cotton Cleopatra Version*, ed. and trans. J.J. Parry, Cambridge, MA, 1937 (the only full translation of *Brut y Brenhinedd* into English) and discussed in B.F. Roberts, "*Ystoriaeu Brenhinedd Ynys Brydeyn*: a fourteenth-century Welsh Brut", in J.F. Eska (ed.), *Narrative in Celtic Tradition: Essays in Honor of Edgar M. Slotkin* (CSANA Yearbook, 8–9), Hamilton, NY, 2011, pp. 215–27, and in P.-Y. Lambert, "À propos de la traduction galloise du ms. London, British Library, Cotton Cleopatra B.V", in Tétrel and Veysseyre (eds.), *L'Historia Regum Britannie*, pp. 81–103.

7   Text from the Red Book of Hergest edited in *The Text of the Bruts from the Red Book of Hergest*, ed. J. Rhŷs and J.G. Evans, Oxford, 1890, and the version is discussed in B.F. Roberts, "The Red Book of Hergest Version of *Brut y Brenhinedd*", *Studia Celtica* 12/13 (1977–78), 147–86.

8   Discussed in B.F. Roberts, *Brut Tysilio*, Swansea, 1980.

9   For a recent discussion of the textual relationships, see Sims-Williams, *Rhai Addasiadau*, which is updated, abbreviated, and translated into English in id., "The Welsh Versions of Geoffrey of Monmouth's 'History of the Kings of Britain'", in A. Harlos and N. Harlos (eds.), *Adapting Texts and Styles in a Celtic Context: Interdisciplinary Perspectives on Processes of Literary Transfer in the Middle Ages. Studies in Honour of Erich Poppe*, Münster, 2016, pp. 53–74.

10   B. Roberts, "Copïau Cymraeg o *Prophetiae Merlini*" [Welsh copies of *Prophetiae Merlini*], *National Library of Wales Journal* 20 (1977), 14–39.

continued deferral to multiple versions of the original Latin text, it nevertheless remains true that each version has its own distinct flavor.[11]

The proliferation of versions of *Brut y Brenhinedd* is indicative of the high
popularity attained by the text. It survives in more medieval Welsh manuscripts
than any text aside from the Laws of Hywel Dda.[12] Many of these manuscripts
were written in Cistercian monasteries, which became the central nodes of
Welsh-language culture between the 13th and 16th centuries. Through its Welsh
versions, Geoffrey's *DGB* had a profound effect on other types of Welsh literature. It inspired the writing of the short prose tale *Lludd and Llefelys*, which is
often found inserted into copies of *Brut y Brenhinedd* (though it is also found
independently).[13] In some manuscripts, *Brut y Brenhinedd* became the center-
piece for a sequence of Welsh prose texts telling the history of the Britons from
the fall of Troy to 1282: it is often prefaced by *Ystorya Dared*, the medieval Welsh
version of Dares Phrygius's *The Fall of Troy*, and followed by *Brut y Tywysogyon*
("History of the Princes"), which became the standard vernacular account of
Welsh history from *c.*682 to 1282.[14] The original compiler of the latter text clearly conceived the work as a continuation of Geoffrey's *History*, because the annalistic account begins explicitly with the death of Cadwaladr and the Britons'
loss of sovereignty over Britain. *Brut y Brenhinedd* similarly infiltrated the triadic and genealogical literature, to the extent that new versions of those types
of texts tended to follow Geoffrey's account of the British past in preference
to other accounts.[15] It is no surprise that even the genealogist of Llywelyn ap
Gruffudd, prince of Gwynedd (1255–82), should be confident that a reference
to a genealogical variant found in the "Hystoria" would be understood, without
further specification, as a reference to Geoffrey's *DGB*.[16]

By the 14th and 15th centuries, Geoffrey's account of British history had
been normalized to a considerable degree in Welsh writing. This is demonstrated by the constant references to events and characters of Geoffrey's *DGB*

---

11   The characteristics of the versions are summarized in *Brut y Brenhinedd*, ed. Roberts,
      pp. xxiv–xxxi.

12   D. Huws, *Medieval Welsh Manuscripts*, Aberystwyth, 2000, pp. 12 and 40–41.

13   Edited in *Cyfranc Lludd and Llefelys*, ed. B.F. Roberts (Mediaeval and Modern Welsh
      Series, 7), Dublin, 1975, and translated in *The Mabinogion*, trans. S. Davies, Oxford, 2007,
      pp. 111–15.

14   H. Fulton, "Troy Story: The Medieval Welsh *Ystorya Dared* and the *Brut* Tradition of British
      History", in J. Dresvina and N. Sparks (eds.), *The Medieval Chronicle VII*, Amsterdam, 2011,
      pp. 137–50.

15   *Trioedd Ynys Prydein: The Triads of the Island of Britain*, ed. and trans. R. Bromwich,
      4th ed., Cardiff, 2014, pp. lxvi–lxix.

16   D.E. Thornton, "A Neglected Genealogy of Llywelyn ap Gruffudd", *CMCS* 23 (1992), 9–23, at
      pp. 13–15.

in strict-meter poetry. Geoffrey's *PM* became similarly integrated into main-stream poetic, and especially prophetic, discourse, supported no doubt by the 13th-century Welsh commentary on the text.[17] Likewise, the 14th-century Welsh prose text on the birth of Arthur twice refers its readers to "Ystoria y Brytaniett" ("The History of the Britons") for further information on Uthyr's death, and draws many incidental details from the *Brut*.[18] The trend continued into the 15th century. The text concerning the "Twenty-Four Knights of Arthur's Court" contains an indiscriminate blend of elements from Welsh legend, Geoffrey's *DGB*, the Welsh-language *Y Seint Greal* (translated in the 14th century from two French prose Grail romances), and the 13th-century French Vulgate cycle of Arthurian romances.[19] By the end of the 15th century, Geoffrey's account of British history still provided the undisputed master narrative for the Welsh past and for the literary works predicated on it, and it continued to find adherents in Wales down to the 19th century.[20]

---

17   R.W. Evans, "Prophetic Poetry", in A.O.H. Jarman and G.R. Hughes (eds.), *A Guide to Welsh Literature 1282–c. 1550: Volume II*, rev. D. Johnston, Cardiff, 1997, pp. 256–74, esp. pp. 262 and 264; B. Roberts, "Esboniad Cymraeg ar broffwydoliaeth Myrddin" [A Welsh commentary on the prophecy of Merlin], *BBCS* 21 (1964–66), 277–300.

18   C. Lloyd-Morgan, "Blending and Rebottling Old Wines: the Birth and Burial of Arthur in Middle Welsh", in Harlos and Harlos (eds.), *Adapting Texts and Styles*, pp. 155–75, at pp. 158–60.

19   *Trioedd Ynys Prydein*, ed. and trans. Bromwich, pp. cx–cxiii and 266–69.

20   For the debate about Geoffrey's authenticity in Wales down to the 19th century, see *Brut y Brenhinedd*, ed. Roberts, pp. 55–74.

Bibliography

Primary

Note on the citation of primary sources in this bibliography: primary sources are listed here in alphabetical order by first name of author. If first name of author is not known (as is often the case with medieval texts), the source is listed in alphabetical order by medieval title, translated into English in most cases. Please see our Note on Translations at the front of the volume for our policy on the translation of medieval titles of works. If neither author nor medieval title are known, the source is listed by the title of the modern edition.

The Abridged English Metrical Brut: British Library MS Royal 12 C. XIII, ed. U. O'Farrell-Tate (Middle English Texts, 32), Heidelberg, 2002.

The Acts of Welsh Rulers, 1120–1283, ed. H. Pryce, Cardiff, 2005.

Adam Usk, *Chronicle*, ed. C. Given-Wilson, *The Chronicle of Adam Usk*, Oxford, 1997.

Alan of Lille, *Interpretation of the Prophecy of Merlin*, printed by Ioachim Bratheringii, *Prophetia anglicana: Merlini Ambrosii britanni ... vaticinia et praedictiones a Galfredo Monemutensi latine conversae una cum septem libris explanationum in eamdem prophetiam ...*, Frankfurt, 1603 and 1608.

Alan of Lille, *Interpretation of the Prophecy of Merlin*, ed. and trans. C. Wille, *Prophetie und Politik: Die 'Explanatio in Prophetia Merlini Ambrosii' des Alanus Flandrensis*, 2 vols. (Lateinische Sprache und Literatur des Mittelalters, 49), Bern, 2015.

Alfonso X, *General estoria*, ed. P. Sánchez Prieto-Borja, A. Cabrejas, and M. Belén, *General estoria. Segunda Parte*, 2 vols., Madrid, 2009.

Alfred of Beverley, *Annals*, ed. T. Hearne, *Aluredi Beverlacensis Annales, sive historia de gestis regum Britanniae, libris IX E. codice pervetusto ...*, Oxford, 1716.

"*Anales navarro-aragoneses hasta 1239*: edición y estudio", ed. F. Bautista, *e-Spania* 26 (2017), <http://journals.openedition.org/e-spania/26509> (accessed 30 May 2018).

Anales toledanos primeros, ed. E. Flórez, *España Sagrada (XXIII)*, Madrid, 1767.

An Anglo-Norman Brut (Royal 13.A.xxi), ed. A. Bell (Anglo-Norman Text Society, 21–22), Oxford, 1969.

"An Anglo-Norman Metrical 'Brut' of the 14th century (British Museum Ms Egerton 3028)", ed. V. Underwood, unpublished PhD thesis, University of London, 1937.

"Anglo-Norman Verse Prophecies of Merlin", ed. and trans. J. Blacker, *Arthuriana* 15:1 (2005), 1–125, rev. ed., *Anglo-Norman Verse Prophecies of Merlin*, Dallas, 2005.

The Anglo-Saxon Chronicle: a Collaborative Edition. Vol. 7: MS. E, ed. S. Irvine, Cambridge, 2004.

Anglo-Scottish Relations, 1174–1328: Some Selected Documents, ed. and trans. E.L.G. Stones, Oxford, 1970.

Annae Comnenae Porphyrogenitae Alexias [The Alexias of Anna Komnena, Porphyrogenita], ed. A. Reifferscheid, 2 vols., Leipzig, 1884.

Annaler for nordisk Oldkyndighed og historie [Annals for Nordic antiquities and history], ed. J. Sigurðsson] Copenhagen, 1848–49.

Annales Cambriae, AD 682–954: Texts A–C in Parallel, ed. and trans. D.N. Dumville, Cambridge, 2002.

"Annales Londonienses", ed. W. Stubbs, *Chronicles of the Reigns of Edward I and Edward II*, 2 vols., London, 1882–83, vol. 1, pp. 1–251.

An Anonymous Short English Metrical Chronicle, ed. E. Zettl (Early English Text Society, 196), London, 1935.

Armes Prydein Vawr, ed. and trans. I. Williams and R. Bromwich, *Armes Prydein: The Prophecy of Britain from the Book of Taliesin*, Dublin, 1972.

Arthur and Gorlagon, ed. G.L. Kittredge, *Arthur and Gorlagon: Versions of the Werewolf's Tale*, New York, 1966 (repr. from *Harvard Studies and Notes in Philology and Literature* 8 (1903), 149–275).

Asser, *Life of King Alfred*, ed. W.H. Stevenson, *Asser's Life of King Alfred. Together with the Annals of Saint Neots*, Oxford, 1959.

Bede, *Ecclesiastical History*, ed. and trans. B. Colgrave and R.A.B. Mynors, *Bede's Ecclesiastical History of the English People*, Oxford, 1969, rev. ed., Oxford, 1991.

Bede, *On the Reckoning of Time*, ed. C.W. Jones, *Bedae Venerabilis opera*, VI: *Opera didascalia* 2, Turnhout, 1977, 239–545.

Benedict of Peterborough, *The Deeds of King Henry II*, ed. W. Stubbs, *Gesta Regis Henrici Secundi Benedicti Abbatis. The Chronicle of the Reigns of Henry II, and Richard I, AD. 1169–1192: Known commonly under the Name of Benedict of Peterborough*, 2 vols., London, 1867.

Brenhinedd y Saesson: or, The Kings of the Saxons. BM Cotton MS. Cleopatra B v and the Black Book of Basingwerk, NLW MS. 7006, ed. and trans. T. Jones (History and Law Series, 25), Cardiff, 1971.

Breudwyt Maxen Wledic, ed. B.F. Roberts, Dublin, 2005.

Breudwyt Ronabwy: allan o'r Llyfr Coch o Hergest [The Dream of Rhonabwy, from the Red Book of Hergest], ed. M. Richards, Cardiff, 1948.

Breviate chronicle (B-text), ed. H. Gough-Cooper, *Annales Cambriae: A, B and C in Parallel, from St Patrick to AD 954*, 2016, <http://croniclau.bangor.ac.uk/editions.php.en> (accessed 4 August 2017).

The Brut; or, The Chronicles of England, ed. F.W.D. Brie (Early English Text Society, 131, 136), London, 1906, 1908 (repr. Woodbridge, 2000).

Brut Dingestow, ed. H. Lewis, Llandysul, 1942.

Brut y Brenhinedd: Cotton Cleopatra Version, ed. and trans. J.J. Parry, Cambridge, MA, 1937.

Brut y Brenhinedd: Llanstephan MS. 1 Version, ed. B.F. Roberts (Mediaeval and Modern Welsh Series, 5), Dublin, 1971.

Brut Tysilio, ed. B.F. Roberts, Swansea, 1980.

Brut y Tywysogyon: or, The Chronicle of the Princes. Peniarth MS. 20 Version, trans. T. Jones (History and Law Series, 11), Cardiff, 1952.

Brut y Tywysogyon: or, The Chronicle of the Princes. Red Book of Hergest Version, ed. and trans. T. Jones (History and Law Series, 16), Cardiff, 1955, 2nd ed., 1973.

Brut y Tywysogyon, Peniarth MS. 20, ed. T. Jones (History and Law Series, 6), Cardiff, 1941.

"Y Canu Lladin er Cof am yr Arglwydd Rhys" [The Latin poetry commemorating the Lord Rhys], ed. H. Pryce, in N.A. Jones and H. Pryce (eds.), *Yr Arglwydd Rhys*, Cardiff, 1996, 212–23.

Cartae et alia munimenta quae ad dominium de Glamorgancia pertinent, ed. G.T. Clark, 6 vols., 2nd ed., Cardiff, 1910.

Castleford's Chronicle, or, The Boke of Brut, ed. C.D. Eckhardt, 2 vols., Oxford and New York, 1996.

Chartes anciennes du Prieuré de Monmouth en Angleterre, ed. P. Marchegay, Les Roches-Baritaud, 1879.

Chrétien de Troyes, *Le Chevalier de la charrette*, ed. and trans. C. Méla, *Le Chevalier de la charrette ou le Roman de Lancelot*, Paris, 1992.

Chrétien de Troyes, *Yvain*, ed. and trans. D.F. Hult, *Le Chevalier au lion ou Le Roman d'Yvain. Édition critique d'après le manuscript B.N. fr. 1433*, Paris, 1994.

Chrétien de Troyes, *Le Chevalier de la charrette*, ed. and trans. C. Méla, *Le Chevalier de la charrette ou le Roman de Lancelot*, Paris, 1992.

Corónicas navarras, ed. A. Ubierto Arteta (Textos Medievales, 14), Zaragoza, 1989.

Cottonian chronicle (C-text), ed. H. Gough-Cooper, *Annales Cambriae: A, B and C in Parallel, from St Patrick to AD 954*, 2016, <http://croniclau.bangor.ac.uk/editions .php.en> (accessed 4 August 2017).

Count Pedro of Barcelos, *Crónica de 1344*, ed. L.F. Lindley Cintra, *Crónica geral de Espanha de 1344*, Lisbon, 1952.

Cronica de Wallia, ed. T. Jones, "'Cronica de Wallia' and other documents from Exeter Cathedral Library MS. 3514", *BBCS* 12 (1946), 27–44.

Culhwch and Olwen, ed. R. Bromwich and D.S. Evans, *Culhwch ac Olwen: an Edition and Study of the Oldest Arthurian Tale*, Cardiff, 1992.

Cyfoesi Myrddin a Gwenddydd ei Chwaer [The prophecy of Myrddin and Gwenddydd his sister], ed. M.B. Jenkins, "Aspects of the Welsh Prophetic Verse Tradition: Incorporating Textual Studies of the Poetry from 'Llyfr Coch Hergest' (Oxford,

Jesus College, MS cxi) and 'Y Cwta Cyfarwydd' (Aberystwyth, National Library of Wales, MS Peniarth 50)", unpublished PhD thesis, University of Cambridge, 1990, 33–90.

Cyfranc Lludd and Llefelys, ed. B.F. Roberts (Mediaeval and Modern Welsh Series, 7), Dublin, 1975.

Cynddelw Brydydd Mawr, *Opus*, ed. N.A. Jones and A.P. Owen, *Gwaith Cynddelw Brydydd Mawr I–II* [The work of Cynddelw Brydydd Mawr I–II] (Cyfres Beirdd y Tywysogion, 3–4), 2 vols., Cardiff, 1991.

Dante Alighieri, *Inferno*, trans. R. and J. Hollander, *Dante. The Inferno*, New York, 2000.

Dares Phrygius, *The Fall of Troy*, ed. F. Meister, *Daretis Phrygii. De excidio Troiae historia*, Leipzig, 1873.

De primo statu Landavensis ecclesie, ed. J.G. Evans and J. Rhŷs, *The Text of the Book of Llan Dâv: Reproduced from the Gwysaney Manuscript*, Oxford, 1893, 68–71.

The Didot Perceval, according to the manuscripts of Modena and Paris, ed. W. Roach, Philadelphia, 1941.

Distichs of Cato, ed. M. Boas, *Disticha Catonis recensuit et apparatu critico instruxit Marcus Boas*, Amsterdam, 1952.

Dudo of St Quentin, *The Customs and Deeds of the First Dukes of the Normans*, ed. J. Lair, *De moribus et actis primorum Normanniae ducum auctore Dudone Sancti Quintone decano*, Caen, 1865.

Early Welsh Genealogical Tracts, ed. P.C. Bartrum, Cardiff, 1966.

"An Edition of the Munich *Brut*", ed. P.B. Grout, unpublished PhD thesis, University of London, 1980.

Episcopal Acts and Cognate Documents relating to Welsh Dioceses 1066–1272, ed. J.C. Davies, 2 vols., Cardiff, 1946–48.

L'Estoire de Brutus. La plus ancienne traduction en prose française de l'Historia Regum Britannie de Geoffroy de Monmouth, ed. G. Veysseyre (Textes littéraires du Moyen Âge, 33), Paris, 2014.

Estória do Santo Graal, ed. J.C. Ribeiro Miranda, *Estória do Santo Graal. Livro Português de José de Arimateia. Manuscrito 643 do Arquivo Nacional da Torre do Tombo*, Porto, 2016.

Facsimiles of Early Charters in Oxford Muniment Rooms, ed. H.E. Salter, Oxford, 1929.

I Fatti di Bretagna, ed. M.L. Meneghetti, *I Fatti di Bretagna: Cronache genealogiche anglo-normanne dal XII al XIV secolo* (Vulgares Eloquentes, 9), Padua, 1979.

Flores Historiarum, ed. H.R. Luard, 3 vols., London, 1890.

The Four Ancient Books of Wales Containing the Cymric Poems Attributed to the Bards of the Sixth Century, Volume I, trans. W.F. Skene, Edinburgh, 1868.

"Le fragment Bekker et les anciennes versions françaises de l'*Historia Regum Britanniae*", ed. S. Lefèvre, *Romania* 109 (1988), 225–46.

Geffrei Gaimar, *Estoire des Engleis*, ed. A. Bell, *L'Estoire des Engleis by Geffrei Gaimar* (Anglo-Norman Texts, 14–16), Oxford, 1960 (repr. New York, 1971).

Geffrei Gaimar, *Estoire des Engleis*, ed. and trans. I. Short, *Estoire des Engleis / History of the English*, Oxford, 2009.

Geffrei Gaimar, *Estoire des Engleis*, ed. and trans. J. Wogan-Browne, T. Fenster, and D. Russell, "Gaimar, *L'Estoire des Engleis*", in J. Wogan-Browne, T. Fenster, and D. Russell (eds.), *Vernacular Literary Theory from the French of Medieval England, Texts and Translations, c. 1120–c. 1450*, Cambridge, 2016, 99–103.

Geoffrey of Monmouth, *De gestis Britonum*, trans. M.A. Faletra, *The History of the Kings of Britain, Geoffrey of Monmouth*, Peterborough, Ontario, 2007.

Geoffrey of Monmouth, *De gestis Britonum*, ed. A. Griscom, *The Historia Regum Britanniae of Geoffrey of Monmouth with Contributions to the Study of its Place in early British History with a Literal Translation of the Welsh Manuscript No. LXI of Jesus College Oxford*, London, 1929.

Geoffrey of Monmouth, *De gestis Britonum*, ed. J. Hammer, *Geoffrey of Monmouth. Historia regum Britanniae. A variant version edited from manuscripts*, Cambridge, MA, 1951.

Geoffrey of Monmouth, *De gestis Britonum*, ed. M. Reeve and trans. N. Wright, *Geoffrey of Monmouth, The History of the Kings of Britain: An Edition and Translation of De gestis Britonum* [*Historia Regum Britanniae*], Woodbridge, 2007.

Geoffrey of Monmouth, *De gestis Britonum*, trans. L. Thorpe, *Geoffrey of Monmouth: The History of the Kings of Britain*, London, 1966.

Geoffrey of Monmouth, *De gestis Britonum*, ed. N. Wright, *The Historia regum Britanniae of Geoffrey of Monmouth, vol. I: Bern, Burgerbibliothek, MS. 568*, Woodbridge, 1984.

Geoffrey of Monmouth, *De gestis Britonum*, ed. N. Wright, *The Historia regum Britannie of Geoffrey of Monmouth, vol. II: The First Variant Version: a critical edition*, Woodbridge, 1988.

Geoffrey of Monmouth, *Life of Merlin*, ed. B.F.L. Clarke, *Life of Merlin: Vita Merlini*, Cardiff, 1973.

Gerald of Wales, *The Conquest of Ireland*, ed. J.F. Dimock, *Giraldi Cambrensis Opera*, 8 vols., London, 1861–91, vol. 5, 207–414.

Gerald of Wales, *The Description of Wales*, ed. J.F. Dimock, *Giraldi Cambrensis Opera*, 8 vols., London, 1861–91, vol. 6, 153–228.

Gerald of Wales, *Invectives*, ed. W.S. Davies, "De Invectionibus", *Y Cymmrodor* 30 (1920), 1–248.

Gerald of Wales, *The Journey Through Wales*, ed. J.F. Dimock, *Giraldi Cambrensis Opera*, 8 vols., London, 1861–91, vol. 6, 3–152.

Gerald of Wales, *The Journey Through Wales* and *The Description of Wales*, trans. L. Thorpe, *Gerald of Wales: The Journey through Wales / The Description of Wales*, Harmondsworth, 1978.

Gerald of Wales, *The Journey Through Wales* and *The Description of Wales*, trans. W.L. Williams, *The Itinerary Through Wales and the Description of Wales*, London, 1908.

Gerald of Wales, *The Journey Through Wales* and *The Description of Wales*, rev. T. Wright, trans. R.C. Hoare, *The Itinerary through Wales, and the Description of Wales, translated by Sir Richard Colt Hoare, Bart.*, London, 1863.

Gerald of Wales, *Retractions*, ed. J.S. Brewer, *Giraldi Cambrensis Opera*, 8 vols., London, 1861–91, vol. 1, 425–27.

Gerald of Wales, *The Rights and Status of the Church of St Davids*, ed. J.S. Brewer, *Giraldi Cambrensis Opera*, 8 vols., London, 1861–91, vol. 3, 99–373.

Gerald of Wales, *The Topography of Ireland*, ed. J.F. Dimock, *Giraldi Cambrensis Opera*, 8 vols., London, 1861–91, vol. 5, 3–204.

Gervase of Canterbury, *Chronicle*, ed. W. Stubbs, *The Historical Works of Gervase of Canterbury*, 2 vols., London, 1879–80.

Gervase of Tilbury, *Recreation for an Emperor*, ed. and trans. S.E. Banks and J.W. Binns, *Otia imperialia. Recreation for an Emperor*, Oxford, 2002.

Gesta abbatum monasterii Sancti Albani, a Thoma Walsingham, regnante Ricardo Secundo, ejusdem ecclesiæ præcentore, compilata, ed. H.T. Riley, London, 1867–69.

Geste des Bretuns en alexandrins ou Harley Brut, ed. B. Barbieri (Textes littéraires du Moyen Âge, 37), Paris, 2015.

Gildas, *The Ruin of Britain*, ed. and trans. M. Winterbottom, *Gildas: The Ruin of Britain and Other Works* (Arthurian Period Sources, 7), Chichester, 1978.

Giovanni Boccaccio, *De montibus, silvis, fontibus, lacubus, fluminibus, stagnis seu paludibus et de diversis nominibus maris* [On mountains, forests, fountains, lakes, rivers, swamps or marshes, and on the many names for the sea], ed. M. Pastore Stocchi, *Tutte le Opere di Giovanni Boccaccio*, gen. ed. V. Branca, 10 vols., Milan, 1967–98, vol. 8.

Giovanni Boccaccio, *On the Fates of Famous Men*, ed. P.G. Ricci and V. Zaccaria, *Tutte le Opere di Giovanni Boccaccio*, gen. ed. V. Branca, 10 vols., Milan, 1967–98, vol. 9.

Godfrey of Viterbo, *Pantheon*, ed. G. Waitz (Monumenta Germaniae Historica, Scriptores, 22), Hanover, 1872, 107–307.

Des grantz geanz, ed. G.E. Brereton, *Des Grantz Geanz: An Anglo-Norman Poem* (Medium Ævum Monographs, 2), Oxford, 1937.

"The Harley *Brut*: An Early French Translation of Geoffrey of Monmouth's *Historia Regum Britanniae*", ed. B. Blakey, *Romania* 82 (1961), 44–70.

Hauksbók, udgiven efter de arnamœanske håndskrifter n° 371, 544 og 675 4to samt forskellige papirhåndskrifter [*Hauksbók*, edited from manuscripts n° 371, 544 and 675 4to and paper copies], ed. F. Jónsson and E. Jónsson, Copenhagen, 1892–96.

Henry of Huntingdon, *History of the English*, ed. and trans. D. Greenway, *Henry, Archdeacon of Huntingdon: Historia Anglorum. The History of the English People*, Oxford, 1996.

Historia Brittonum, ed. E. Faral, *La légende arthurienne: études et documents*, 3 vols., Paris, 1929, vol. 3, 2–62.

Historia Brittonum, ed. T. Mommsen, *Chronica Minora saec. IV. V. VI. VII. Vol. 3* [Minor Chronicles of the 4th, 5th, 6th, 7th centuries, Vol. 3] (Monumenta Germaniae Historica, Auctores Antiquissimi, 13), Berlin, 1898.

Historia Brittonum, ed. and trans. J. Morris, *Nennius: British History and the Welsh Annals* (Arthurian Period Sources, 8), London, 1980.

Historia Gruffud vab Kenan, ed. D.S. Evans, *Historia Gruffud vab Kenan, gyda rhagymadrodd a nodiadau gan D. Simon Evans* [Historia Gruffudd ap Cynan, with introduction and notes by D. Simon Evans], Cardiff, 1977.

The historie of Cambria, now called Wales, ed. D. Powel, London, 1584.

The History of the Kings of Britain: The First Variant Version, ed. and trans. D.W. Burchmore, Cambridge, MA, 2019.

Ibn Fadlān, *Ibn Khurradādhbih on Sallām the Interpreter and Alexander's Wall 844*, trans. P. Lunde and C. Stone, *Ibn Fadlān and the Land of Darkness: Arab Travellers in the Far North*, London, 2012, 99–104.

Ἱππότης ὁ Πρεσβύτης [The Old Knight], ed. T.H. Crofts, "The Old Knight: An edition of the Greek Arthurian poem of Vat. gr. 1822", *AL* 33 (2016), 158–217.

Isidore of Seville, *Etymologies*, trans. S.A. Barney, W.J. Lewis, J.A. Beach, O. Berghof, and M. Hall, *The Etymologies of Isidore of Seville*, Cambridge, 2006.

Isidore of Seville, *History of the Kings*, trans. G. Doninini and G.B. Ford, Jr., *Isidore of Seville's History of the Kings of the Goths, Vandals, and Suevi*, Leiden, 1966.

Isidore of Seville, *Etymologies*, ed. W.M. Lindsay, *Isidori Hispalensis Episcopi Etymologiarum sive Originum Libri XX*, 2 vols., Oxford, 1911 (repr. 1989).

Isländische Antikensagas, Die Saga von den Trojanern, die Saga von den Britischen Königen, die Saga von Alexander dem Grossen, trans. S. Würth (Gropper), Munich, 1996.

Jacob van Maerlant, *Historie van den Grale* and *Boek van Merline*, ed. T. Sodmann, *Jacob van Maerlant: Historie van den Grale und Boek van Merline* (Niederdeutsche Studien, 26), Cologne and Vienna, 1980.

Jacob van Maerlant, *Spiegel historiael* [Mirror of history], ed. M. De Vries and E. Verwijs, *Jacob van Maerlant, Philip van Utenbroeke, and Lodewijk van Velthem, Jacob van Maerlant's Spiegel historiael: met de fragmenten der later toegevoegde gedeelten* [Jacob van Maerlant's Mirror of history: with the fragments of its later additions], 4 vols., Gravenhage, 1861–79 (repr. Utrecht, 1982).

Jehan Bodel, *La chanson des Saisnes*, ed. A. Brasseur, *La chanson des Saisnes* (Textes littéraires français, 369), 2 vols., Geneva, 1989.

Jean de Wavrin, *Recueil des croniques et anchiennes istories de la Grant Bretaigne*, ed. W. Hardy, *Recueil des croniques et anchiennes istories de la Grant Bretaigne, à présent nommé Engleterre, I: From Albina to A.D. 688*, London, 1864.

John Peckham, *Epistles*, ed. C.T. Martin, *Registrum Epistolarum Fratris Johannis Peckham, Archiepiscopi Cantuariensis*, 3 vols., London, 1882–85.

John Prise, *Historiae Britannicae Defensio*, ed. and trans. C. Davies, *Historiae Britannicae Defensio. A Defense of the British History*, Oxford and Toronto, 2015.

King Arthur: A Casebook, ed. E.D. Kennedy, New York, 1996.

King Artus, ed. C. Leviant, *King Artus. A Hebrew Arthurian Romance of 1279*, Syracuse, 2003.

Laȝamon, *Brut*, trans. R. Allen, *Lawman: Brut*, London, 1992.

Laȝamon, *Brut*, ed. G.L. Brook and R.F. Leslie, *Layamon: Brut. Edited from British Museum MS Cotton Caligula A ix and British Museum MS Otho C xiii*, 2 vols., London, 1963–78.

Laȝamon, *Brut*, ed. and trans. W.R.J. Barron and S.C. Weinberg, *Laȝamon: Brut, or Hystoria Brutonum*, New York, 1995.

The Laws of Hywel Dda: Law Texts from Medieval Wales, ed. D. Jenkins, Llandysul, 1986.

Lebor Bretnach: The Irish Version of the Historia Brittonum Ascribed to Nennius, ed. A.G. Van Hamel, Dublin, 1932.

Liber Coronacionis Britanorum, ed. P. Sims-Williams, 2 vols., Aberystwyth, 2017.

The Life of Gruffudd ap Cynan, ed. P. Russell, *Vita Griffini Filii Conani. The Medieval Latin Life of Gruffudd ap Cynan*, Cardiff, 2005.

Life of St Gildas, ed. and trans. H. Williams, *Two Lives of Gildas: By a Monk of Ruys, and Caradoc of Llancarfan*, Felinfach, 1990, 36–37 (repr. from H. Williams, ed., *Gildas*, 2 parts (Cymmrodorion Record Series, 3), London, 1899–1901, vol. 2, 315–420).

Life of St Teilo, ed. J.G. Evans and J. Rhŷs, *The Text of the Book of Llan Dâv: Reproduced from the Gwysaney Manuscript*, Oxford, 1893, 97–117.

Le Livere de Reis de Brittanie e Le Livere de Reis de Engletere, ed. J. Glover, London, 1865.

Llandaff Episcopal Acta, 1140–1287, ed. D. Crouch, Cardiff, 1989.

Llawysgrif Hendregadredd [The Hendregadredd manuscript], ed. J. Morris-Jones and T.H. Parry-Williams, Cardiff, 1933.

Llyfr Colan: y Gyfraith Gymraeg yn ôl Hanner Cyntaf Llawysgrif Peniarth 30 [The *Llyfr Colan*: Welsh law according to the first half of manuscript Peniarth 30], ed. D. Jenkins, Cardiff, 1963.

Llyfr Du Caerfyrddin: gyda Rhagymadrodd, Nodiadau Testunol, a Geirfa [The Black Book of Carmarthen: with introduction, textual notes, and vocabulary], ed. A.O.H. Jarman, Cardiff, 1982.

Llywarch ap Llywelyn, *Opus*, ed. E.M. Jones and N.A. Jones, *Gwaith Llywarch ap Llywelyn, 'Prydydd y Moch'* [The work of Llywarch ap Llywelyn, 'Prydydd y Moch'] (Cyfres Beirdd y Tywysogion, 5), Cardiff, 1991.

Llywelyn Fardd I, *Opus*, ed. C. McKenna, "Gwaith Llywelyn Fardd I" [The work of Llywelyn Fardd I], in M.E. Owens et al. (eds.), *Gwaith Llywelyn Fardd I ac Eraill o Feirdd y Ddeuddegfed Ganrif* [The work of Llywelyn Fardd I and other poets of the 12th century] (Cyfres Beirdd y Tywysogion, 2), Cardiff, 1994, 1–100.

Llywelyn Fardd II, *Opus*, ed. C. McKenna, "Gwaith Llywelyn Fardd II" [The work of Llywelyn Fardd II], in N.G. Costigan et al. (eds.), *Gwaith Dafydd Benfras ac Eraill o Feirdd Hanner Cyntaf y Drydedd Ganrif ar Ddeg* [The work of Dafydd Benfras and other poets of the first half of the 13th century] (Cyfres Beirdd y Tywysogion, 6), Cardiff, 1995, 99–157.

Lucan, *The Civil War*, trans. J.D. Duff, *Lucan. The Civil War*, Cambridge, MA, 1928.

Lucan, *The Civil War*, ed. A.E. Housman, *M. Annaei Lucani Belli civilis libri decem*, Oxford, 1950.

The Mabinogion, trans. S. Davies, Oxford, 2007.

Macrobius, *Saturnalia*, ed. J. Willis, *Ambrosii Theodosii Macrobii Saturnalia*, 2nd ed., Leipzig, 1970.

Madog ap Gwallter, *Opus*, ed. R.M. Andrews, "Gwaith Madog ap Gwallter" [The work of Madog ap Gwallter], in R.M. Andrews et al. (eds.), *Gwaith Bleddyn Fardd a Beirdd Eraill Ail Hanner y Drydedd Ganrif ar Ddeg* [The work of Bleddyn Fardd and other poets of the second half of the 13th century] (Cyfres Beirdd y Tywysogion, 7), Cardiff, 1996, 345–92.

Marie de France, *Lais*, ed. K. Warnke and trans. L. Harf-Lancner, *Lais de Marie de France*, Paris, 1990.

"Mawl Hywel ap Goronwy" [In prase of Hywel ap Goronwy], ed. R.G. Gruffydd, *Gwaith Meilyr Brydydd a'i Ddisgynyddion* [The work of Meilyr Brydydd and his descendants] (Cyfres Beirdd y Tywysogion, 1), ed. J.E.C. Williams, P. Lynch, and R.G. Gruffydd, Cardiff, 1994, 1–21.

Merlínusspá, ed. and trans. R. Poole, "Merlínusspá", in M. Clunies-Ross (ed.), *Skaldic Poetry of the Scandinavian Middle Ages, VII: Poetry in Fornaldarsögur*, Turnhout, 2017, 38–189.

Der Münchener Brut, ed. K. Hofmann and K. Vollmöller, *Der Münchener Brut, Gottfried von Monmouth in französischen Versen des xii. Jahrhunderts*, Halle, 1877.

The Myvyrian Archaiology of Wales, ed. O. Jones, E. Williams, and W.O. Pughe, 3 vols., Denbigh, 1801–07.

The Oldest Anglo-Norman Prose Brut Chronicle. An Edition and Translation, ed. and trans. J. Marvin (Medieval Chronicles, 4), Woodbridge, 2006.

Orderic Vitalis, *Ecclesiastical History*, ed. and trans. M. Chibnall, *The Ecclesiastical History of Orderic Vitalis*, 6 vols., Oxford, 1969–80.

Original Letters Illustrative of English History, ed. H.F. Ellis, second series, 4 vols., London, 1827.

Ovid, *Epistulae ex Ponto*, ed. S.G. Owen, *P. Ovidi Nasonis Tristium Libri Quinque Ibis Ex Ponto Libri Quattuor Halieutica Fragmenta*, Oxford, 1915.

Ovid, *Heroides*, ed. and trans. G. Showerman (rev. J.P. Gould), *Ovid Heroides and Amores*, 2nd ed., Cambridge, MA, 1977.

Peirian Vaban, ed. A.O.H. Jarman, "Peirian Vaban", *BBCS* 14 (1950–52), 104–08.

Perceforest, ed. G. Roussineau, *Le Roman de Perceforest, quatrième partie*, 2 vols. (Textes littéraires français, 343), Geneva, 1987.

Perceforest, trans. N. Bryant, *Perceforest, The Prehistory of King Arthur's Britain* (Arthurian Studies, 77), Cambridge, 2011.

Peter Langtoft, *Chronicle*, ed. J.-C. Thiolier, *Édition critique et commentée de Pierre de Langtoft, Le Règne d'Édouard Ier, tome premier*, Créteil, 1989–.

Les Prophecies de Merlin, edited from MS. 593 of the Bibliothèque Municipale de Rennes, ed. L.A. Paton, 2 vols. (Modern Language Association of America Monograph Series, 1), New York and London, 1926–27 (repr. New York, 1966).

The Prophetia Merlini of Geoffrey of Monmouth: A Fifteenth-Century English Commentary, ed. C.D. Eckhardt (Speculum Anniversary Monographs, 8), Cambridge, MA, 1982.

Les Prophéties de Merlin (Cod. Bodmer 116), ed. A. Berthelot (Bibliotheca Bodmeriana Textes, 6), Cologny-Geneva, 1992.

Prose Brut to 1332, ed. H. Pagan (Anglo-Norman Texts, 69), Manchester, 2011.

The Qur'ān: New Annotated Translation, trans. A.J. Droge, Sheffield, 2013.

Regesta regum Anglo-Normannorum, 1066–1154, ed. H.W.C. Davis, et al., 4 vols., Oxford, 1913–69.

Rhyddiaith Gymraeg 1300–1425 [Welsh prose 1300–1425], ed. D. Luft, P.W. Thomas, and D.M. Smith, Cardiff, 2007–13, <http://www.rhyddiaithganoloesol.caerdydd.ac.uk/> (accessed 3 August 2017).

Rhygyfarch ap Sulien, *Life of St David*, ed. and trans. R. Sharpe and J.R. Davies, "Rhygyfarch's *Life* of St David", in J.W. Evans and J.M. Wooding (eds.), *St David of Wales: Cult, Church and Nation*, Woodbridge, 2007, 107–55.

Rhygyfarch ap Sulien, *Planctus*, ed. M. Lapidge, "The Welsh-Latin Poetry of Sulien's Family", *Studia Celtica* 8/9 (1973–74), 68–106.

The Rise of Gawain, Nephew of Arthur, ed. M.L. Day, New York, 1984.

Robert of Gloucester, *Chronicle*, ed. T. Hearne, *Robert of Gloucester's Chronicle*, 2 vols., Oxford, 1724.

Robert of Gloucester, *Chronicle*, ed. W.A. Wright, *The Metrical Chronicle of Robert of Gloucester*, 2 vols., London, 1887.

Robert of Torigny, *Chronicle*, ed. R. Howlett, *Chronicles of the Reigns of Stephen, Henry II and Richard I, Vol. IV*, London, 1889.

Le Roi Leïr. Versions des XIIe et XIIIe siècles, ed. F. Zufferey and trans. G. Nussbaumer, Paris, 2015.

The Romance of Merlin: An Anthology, ed. P. Goodrich, New York, 1990.

Les Romans d'Alexandre: aux frontières de l'épique et du romanesque, ed. C. Gaullier-Bougassas (Nouvelle bibliothèque du Moyen Age, 42), Paris, 1998.

Le Roman de Thèbes, ed. and trans. F. Mora-Lebrun, Paris, 1995.

Roman van Lancelot, ed. W.J.A. Jonckbloet, *Roman van Lancelot (XIIIᵉ eeuw). Naar het (eenig-bekende) handschrift der Koninklijke Bibliotheek, op gezag van het Gouvernement uitgegeven door Dr. W.J.A. Janckbloet* [The romance of Lancelot (13th century). Edited from the (only known) manuscript in the Royal Library, under the auspices of the government and edited by Dr. W.J.A. Janckbloet], 2 vols., Gravenhage, 1846–49.

La Saga des Bretons, ed. and trans. H. Tétrel (forthcoming, Classiques Garnier).

Salimbene de Adam, *Chronicle*, ed. O. Holder-Egger, *Salimbene de Adam, Chronica fratris Salimbene de Adam ordinis Minorum* (Monumenta Germaniae Historica, Scriptores, 32), Hanover, 1905–13.

Seneca the Elder, *Suasoriae*, ed. M. Winterbottom, *The Elder Seneca, Declamations: Controversiae and Suasoriae*, 2 vols., Cambridge, MA, 1974.

St Davids Episcopal Acta, 1085–1280, ed. J. Barrow, Cardiff, 1998.

The Story of Meriadoc, King of Cambria, ed. M.L. Day, New York, 1988.

The Canterbury Professions, ed. M. Richter, Torquay, 1973.

The Text of the Book of Llan Dâv: Reproduced from the Gwysaney Manuscript, ed. J.G. Evans and J. Rhŷs, Oxford, 1893.

Text of the Bruts from the Red Book of Hergest, ed. J. Rhŷs and J.G. Evans, Oxford, 1890.

Trioedd Ynys Prydein: The Triads of the Island of Britain, ed. and trans. R. Bromwich, 4th ed., Cardiff, 2014.

Trójumanna Saga, ed. J. Louis-Jensen, *Trójumanna Saga* (Editiones Arnamagnæanæ. Series A, 8), Copenhagen, 1963.

"A 12th-century Anglo-Norman *Brut* Fragment (MS BL Harley 4733, f. 128)", ed. P. Damian-Grint, in I. Short (ed.), *Anglo-Norman Anniversary Essays* (Anglo-Norman Text Society Occasional Publications Series, 2), London, 1993, 87–104.

Vera Historia de Morte Arthuri, ed. M. Lapidge, "An Edition of the *Vera Historia de Morte Arthuri*", *AL* 1 (1981), 79–93.

Virgil, *Aeneid*, trans. R. Fagles, New York, 2006.

Virgil, *Aeneid*, ed. R.A.B. Mynors, *P. Virgili Maronis Opera*, Oxford, 1969.

Virgil, *Eclogues*, ed. R.A.B. Mynors, *P. Virgili Maronis Opera*, Oxford, 1969.

Virgil, *Georgics*, ed. R.A.B. Mynors, *P. Virgili Maronis Opera*, Oxford, 1969.

Vitae Sanctorum Britanniae et Genealogiae: The Lives and Genealogies of the Welsh Saints, ed. A.W. Wade-Evans, Cardiff, 1944.

Vitae Virgilianae Antiquae, ed. G. Brugnoli and F. Stok, Rome, 1997.

Wace, *Conception Nostre Dame*, trans. J. Blacker, G.S. Burgess, and A.V. Ogden, *Wace, The Hagiographical Works: The 'Conception Nostre Dame' and the Lives of St Margaret and St Nicholas* (Studies in Medieval and Reformation Traditions, 169 / Texts and Sources, 3), Leiden, 2013.

Wace, *Roman de Brut*, ed. I.D.O. Arnold, *Le Roman de Brut de Wace*, 2 vols., Paris, 1938–40.

Wace, *Roman de Rou*, ed. A.J. Holden, *Le Roman de Rou de Wace*, 2 vols., Paris, 1973.

Wace, *Roman de Brut*, trans. J. Weiss, *Wace's Roman de Brut: A History of the British: Text and Translation* (Exeter Medieval English Texts and Studies), Exeter, 1999, rev. ed. 2002.

Walter Bower, *Scotichronicon*, ed. D.E.R. Watt and trans. N.F. Shead, W.B. Stevenson, and D.E.R. Watt, *Scotichronicon: in Latin and English*, 9 vols., Aberdeen, 1987–98.

Walter Map, *The Courtiers' Trifles*, ed. and trans. M.R. James, revised by C.N.L. Brooke and R.A.B. Mynors, Oxford, 1983.

The Waverley Chronicle, ed. H.R. Luard, *Annales Monastici*, 5 vols., London, 1864–69, vol. 2, 129–411.

William of Malmesbury, *The Contemporary History*, ed. E. King, trans. K.R. Potter, *William of Malmesbury. Historia novella: The Contemporary History*, Oxford, 1998.

William of Malmesbury, *Deeds of the English Kings*, ed. and trans. R.A.B. Mynors, completed by R.M. Thomson and M. Winterbottom, *William of Malmesbury: Gesta Regum Anglorum, The History of the English Kings*, 2 vols., Oxford, 1998–99.

William of Malmesbury, *The Early History of Glastonbury*, ed. J. Scott, *The Early History of Glastonbury: An Edition, Translation and Study of William of Malmesbury's De Antiquitate Glastonie Ecclesie*, Woodbridge, 1981.

William of Newburgh, *The History of English Affairs*, ed. and trans. P.G. Walsh and M.J. Kennedy, *William of Newburgh: The History of English Affairs, Book I (Edited with Translation and Commentary)*, Warminster, 1988.

William Rishanger, *Chronicle*, ed. H.T. Riley, *Willelmi Rishanger, quondam monachi S. Albani, et quorundam anonymorum, chronica et annales, regnantibus Henrico tertio et Edwardo primo*, London, 1865.

William of St Albans, *Life of St Alban*, trans. T. O'Donnell and M. Lamont, in J. Wogan-Browne and T.S. Fenster (eds.), *The Life of St. Alban by Matthew Paris*, Tempe, 2010, 133–65.

Ymddiddan Myrddin a Thaliesin (o Lyfr Du Caerfyrddin) [The Conversation of Myrddin and Taliesin (from the Black Book of Carmarthen)], ed. A.O.H. Jarman, Cardiff, 1951.

Secondary

Abed, J., "La Traduction française de la *Prophetia Merlini* dans le Didot-*Perceval*", in R. Trachsler (ed.), with the collaboration of J. Abed and D. Expert, *Moult obscures paroles: Études sur la prophétie médiévale*, Paris, 2007, 81–105.

Abulafia, D., "La Corona de Aragón en la Época de *Tirant Lo Blanc*, 1392–1516", in E. Mira (ed.), *Joanot Martorell y el otoño de la Caballería*, Valencia, 2011, 47–60.

Akbari, S.C., *Idols in the East: European Representations of Islam and the Orient, 1100–1450*, Ithaca, 2009.

Allaire, G., and Paski, G. (eds.), *The Arthur of the Italians: The Arthurian Legend in Medieval Italian Literature and Culture* (Arthurian Literature in the Middle Ages, 7), Cardiff, 2014.

Allen, V., "Ekphrasis and the Object", in A.J. Johnston, E. Knapp, and M. Rouse (eds.), *The Art of Vision. Ekphrasis in Medieval Literature and Culture*, Columbus, 2015, 17–35.

Alvar, C., "The Matter of Britain in Spanish Society and Literature from Cluny to Cervantes", in D. Hook (ed.), *The Arthur of the Iberians: The Arthurian Legends in the Spanish and Portuguese Worlds* (Arthurian Literature in the Middle Ages, 8), Cardiff, 2015, 187–270.

Anderson, A.R., *Alexander's Gate, Gog and Magog and the Inclosed Nations*, Cambridge, MA, 1932.

Anzaldúa, G., *Borderlands/La Frontera: The New Mestiza*, San Francisco, 1987.

Armenti, D., and Otaño Gracia, N.I., "Constructing Prejudice in the Middle Ages and the Repercussions of Racism Today", *Medieval Feminist Forum* 53:1 (2017), 176–201.

Ashe, G., "'A certain very ancient book': Traces of an Arthurian Source in Geoffrey of Monmouth's History", *Speculum* 56:2 (1981), 301–23.

Ashe, L., *Early Fiction in England from Geoffrey of Monmouth to Chaucer*, London, 2015.

Aurell, J., *Authoring the Past: History, Autobiography, and Politics in Medieval Catalonia*, Chicago, 2012.

Aurell, J., "From Genealogies to Chronicles: the Power of the Form in Medieval Catalan Historiography", *Viator* 36 (2005), 235–64.

Aurell, M., *La légende du Roi Arthur: 550–1250*, Paris, 2007.

Avril, F., "À quand remontent les premiers ateliers d'enlumineurs laïcs à Paris", *Les Dossiers de l'archéologie* 16 (1976), 36–44.

Badia, L., and Grifoll, I., "Language: From the Countryside to the Royal Court", in F. Sabaté (ed.), *The Crown of Aragon: A Singular Mediterranean Empire* (Brill's Companions to European History, 12) Leiden, 2017, 361–86.

Banniard, M., "Du latin des illettrés au roman des lettrés. La question des niveaux de langue en France (VIII\ᵉ–XIIᵉ siècle)", in P. Von Moos (ed.), *Entre Babel et Pentecôte, Différences linguistiques et communication orale avant la modernité (VIIIᵉ–XVIᵉ s.)*, Berlin, 2008, 269–86.

Barber, R., "The Manuscripts of the *Vera Historia de Morte Arthuri*", *AL* 6 (1986), 163–64.

Barbieri, B., "La *Geste de Bretuns* en alexandrins (Harley *Brut*): Une traduction de l'*Historia* aux teintes épiques", in H. Tétrel and G. Veysseyre (eds.), *L'Historia regum Britannie et les "Bruts" en Europe, Tome I, Traductions, adaptations, réappropriations (XII–XVIᵉ siècle)* (Rencontres, 106, Civilisation médiévale, 12), Paris, 2015, 141–55.

Barbieri, B., "'Una traduzione anglo-normanna dell'*Historia Regum Britannia*': la *geste des Bretuns* in alessandrini (*Harley Brut*)", *Studi mediolatini e volgari* 57 (2011), 163–76.

Barrett, A.A., "Saint Germanus and the British Missions", *Britannia* 40 (2009), 197–217.

Barron, J., "The Augustinian Canons and the University of Oxford: the Lost College of St George", in C.M. Barron and J. Stratford (eds.), *The Church and Learning in Later Medieval Society: Essays in Honour of R.B. Dobson*, Donington, 2002, 228–54.

Barrow, G., "Wales and Scotland in the Middle Ages", *WHR* 10 (1980–81), 303–19.

Barrow, J., *The Clergy in the Medieval World: Secular Clerics, Their Families and Careers in North-Western Europe c.800–c.1200*, Cambridge, 2015.

Bartlett, R., *England Under the Norman and Angevin Kings, 1075–1225*, Oxford, 2000.

Bartlett, R., *Gerald of Wales, 1146–1223*, Oxford, 1982.

Bartlett, R., *The Making of Europe: Conquest, Colonization and Cultural Change 950–1350*, Princeton, 1994.

Bartlett, R., "Medieval and Modern Concepts of Race and Ethnicity", *JMEMS* 31 (2001), 39–56.

Bartlett, R., *Why Can the Dead Do Such Great Things? Saints and Worshippers from the Martyrs to the Reformation*, Princeton, 2013.

Bartrum, P.C., *A Welsh Classical Dictionary: People in History and Legend up to about A.D. 1000*, Aberystwyth, 1993.

Bates, D., "Robert of Torigni and the *Historia Anglorum*", in D. Roffe (ed.), *The English and Their Legacy, 900–1200. Essays in Honour of Ann Williams*, Woodbridge, 2012, 175–84.

Bautista, F., "Original, versiones e influencia del *Liber regum*: estudio textual y propuesta de *stemma*", *e-Spania* 9 (2010), <https://journals.openedition.org/e-spania/19884> (accessed 30 May 2018).

Beem, C., *The Lioness Roared: The Problems of Female Rule in English History*, New York, 2006.

Bell, A., "The Royal *Brut* Interpolation", *Medium Ævum* 32:3 (1963), 190–202.

Bennett, J.M., *Ale, Beer, and Brewsters in England: Women's Work in a Changing World, 1300–1600*, Oxford, 1996.

Bennett, J.M., "Medievalism and Feminism", *Speculum* 68:2 (1993), 309–31.

Bernau, A., "Beginning with Albina: Remembering the Nation", *Exemplaria* 21:3 (2009), 247–73.

Besamusca, B., and Lie, O.S.H., "The Prologue to *Arturs doet*, the Middle Dutch Translation of *La Mort le Roi Artu* in the *Lancelot Compilation*", in E. Kooper (ed.), *Medieval Dutch Literature in its European Context* (Cambridge Studies in Medieval Literature, 21), Cambridge, 1994, 96–112.

Beschorner, A., *Untersuchungen zu Dares Phrygius*, Tübingen, 1992.

Bezant, J., "The Medieval Grants to Strata Florida Abbey: Mapping the Agency of Lordship", in J. Burton and K. Stöber (eds.), *Monastic Wales: New Approaches*, Cardiff, 2013, 73–87.

Bhabha, H.K., *The Location of Culture*, London and New York, 1994.

Binski, P., & Zutshi, P., *Western Illuminated Manuscripts: A Catalogue of the Collection in Cambridge University Library*, Cambridge, 2011.

Blacker, J., "Courtly Revision of Wace's *Roman de Brut* in British Library Egerton MS 3028", in K. Busby and C. Kleinhenz (eds.), *Courtly Arts and the Art of Courtliness: Selected Papers from the Eleventh Triennial Congress of the International Courtly Literature Society, University of Wisconsin-Madison, 29 July–4 August 2004*, Cambridge, 2006, 237–58.

Blacker, J., *The Faces of Time: Portrayal of the Past in Old French and Latin Historical Narrative of the Anglo-Norman Regnum*, Austin, 1994; rev. epub ed. 2019, with new Introduction, to be posted at https://utpress.utexas.edu/books/blafac.

Blacker, J., "'Ne vuil sun livre translater': Wace's Omission of Merlin's Prophecies from the *Roman de Brut*", in I. Short (ed.), *Anglo-Norman Anniversary Essays* (Anglo-Norman Text Society Occasional Publications Series, 2), London, 1993, 49–59.

Blacker, J., "Where Wace Feared to Tread: Latin Commentaries on Merlin's Prophecies in the Reign of Henry II", *Arthuriana* 6:1 (1996), 36–52.

Blacker, J., with the collaboration of G.S. Burgess, *Wace: A Critical Bibliography*, St Helier, 2008.

Bogdanow, F., and Trachsler, R., "Rewriting Prose Romance: The post-vulgate *Roman du Graal* and related texts", in G.S. Burgess and K. Pratt (eds.), *The Arthur of the French. The Arthurian Legend in Medieval French and Occitan Literature* (Arthurian Literature in the Middle Ages, 4), Cardiff, 2006, 342–92.

Bohigas, P., *Aportació a l'estudi de la literature catalana*, Monserrat, 1982.

Bollard, J.K., "Arthur in the Early Welsh Tradition", in N.J. Lacy and J.J. Wilhelm (eds.), *The Romance of Arthur: An Anthology of Medieval Texts in Translation*, 3rd ed., Abingdon, 2013, 9–27.

Bollard, J.K., "Myrddin in Early Welsh Tradition", in P. Goodrich (ed.), *The Romance of Merlin: An Anthology*, New York, 1990, 13–54.

Booth, J., and Maltby, R. (eds.), *What's in a Name? The Significance of Proper Names in Classical Latin Literature*, Swansea, 2006.

Bosworth, J., "An Anglo-Saxon Dictionary Online", ed. T.N. Toller et al., Prague, 2010, <http://bosworth.ff.cuni.cz/034770> (accessed 31 May 2018).

Bougard, F., Petitmengin, P., & Stirnemann, P., *La bibliothèque de l'abbaye cistercienne de Vauluisant*, Paris, 2012.

Bourgain, P., "Un nouveau manuscrit du text tronqué de la Chronique d'Adhemar de Chabannes", *Bibliothèque de l'École des chartes* 143 (1985), 153–59.

Bourgeois-Lechartier, M., & Avril, F., *Le Scriptorium du Mont Saint-Michel*, Paris, 1967.

Boutemy, A., "Note sur l'origine et la date du *Status Imperii Iudaici*", *Scriptorium* 1 (1946/47), 66–69.

Box, J.B.H., and Deyermond, A., "Mestre Baqua and the Grail Story", *Revue de Littérature Comparée* 51 (1977), 366–70.

Brady, L., "Antifeminist Tradition in *Arthur and Gorlagon* and the Quest to Understand Women", *Notes and Queries* 59:2 (2012), 163–66.

Brady, L., "Feminine Desire and Conditional Misogyny in *Arthur and Gorlagon*", *Arthuriana* 24:3 (2014), 23–44.

Brady, L., *Writing the Welsh Borderlands in Anglo-Saxon England*, Manchester, 2017.

Breeze, A., "*Armes Prydein*, Hywel Dda, and the Reign of Edmund of Wessex", *Études celtiques* 33 (1997), 209–22.

Breeze, A., "Arthur in Early Saints' Lives", in S. Echard (ed.), *The Arthur of Medieval Latin Literature: The Development and Dissemination of the Arthurian Legend in Medieval Latin* (Arthurian Literature in the Middle Ages, 6), Cardiff, 2011, 26–41.

Brenner, B., *Manuscript Painting in Paris during the Reign of Saint Louis: a Study of Styles*, Berkeley, 1977.

Bresc, H., "Excalibur en Sicilie", *Medievalia* 7 (1987), 7–21.

Brett, C., "Breton Latin Literature as Evidence for Literature in the Vernacular, A.D. 800–1300", *CMCS* 18 (1989), 1–25.

Brett, C., "The Prefaces of Two Late Thirteenth-Century Welsh Latin Chronicles", *BBCS* 35 (1988), 63–73.

Brett, C., "Soldiers, Saints, and States? The Breton Migrations Revisited", *CMCS* 61 (2011), 1–56.

Brie, F.W.D., *Geschichte und Quellen der mittelenglischen Prosachronik. The Brute of England oder The Chronicles of England*, Marburg, 1905.

Brockwyt, R., "Ein Artusritter im Krieg. Überlegungen zur Namûr-Episode im Wigalois des Wirnt von Grafenberg aus intertextueller Perspektive", *Neophilologus* 94 (2010), 93–108.

Bromwich, R., "Cyfeiriadau Traddodiadol a Chwedlonol y Gogynfeirdd" [Traditional and mythological references in the work of the Gogynfeirdd], in M.E. Owen and B.F. Roberts (eds.), *Beirdd a Thywysogion: Barddoniaeth Llys yng Nghymru, Iwerddon a'r Alban* [Poets and princes: court poetry in Wales, Ireland, and Scotland], Cardiff, 1996, 202–18.

Bromwich, R., Jarman, A.O.H., and Roberts, B.F. (eds.), *The Arthur of the Welsh: The Arthurian Legend in Medieval Welsh Literature* (Arthurian Literature in the Middle Ages, 1), Cardiff, 1991.

Brooke, C., "The Archbishops of St Davids, Llandaff, and Caerleon-on-Usk", in N.K. Chadwick et al. (ed.), *Studies in the Early British Church*, Cambridge, 1958, 201–42 (repr. in *The Church and the Welsh Border in the Central Middle Ages*, ed. D.N. Dumville (Studies in Celtic History, 8), Woodbridge, 1986, 16–49).

Brooke, C., Highfield, R., & Swaan, W., *Oxford and Cambridge*, Cambridge, 1988.

Brooke, C.N.L., *The Church and the Welsh Border in the Central Middle Ages*, ed. D.N. Dumville (Studies in Celtic History, 8), Woodbridge, 1986.

Brooke, C.N.L., "Geoffrey of Monmouth as a Historian", in C.N.L. Brooke, D. Luscombe, G. Martin, and D. Owen (eds.), *Church and Government in the Middle Ages: Essays Presented to C.R. Cheney on his 70th Birthday*, Cambridge, 1976, 77–91 (repr. in *The Church and the Welsh Border in the Central Middle Ages*, ed. D.N. Dumville (Studies in Celtic History, 8), Woodbridge, 1986, 95–107).

Bruce, J.D., *The Evolution of Arthurian Romance from the Beginnings down to the Year 1300*, Baltimore, 1928 (repr. Gloucester, MA, 1958).

Bruckner, M.T., "*Le Chevalier de la Charrette*: That Obscure Object of Desire, Lancelot", in N.J. Lacy and J.T. Grimbert (eds.), *A Companion to Chrétien de Troyes*, Cambridge, 2005, 137–55.

Bruckner, M.T., "The Shape of Romance in Medieval France", in R.L. Krueger (ed.), *The Cambridge Companion to Medieval Romance*, Cambridge, 2000, 13–28.

Bruckner, M.T., and Burgess, G.S., "Arthur in the Narrative Lay", in G.S. Burgess and K. Pratt (eds.), *The Arthur of the French. The Arthurian Legend in Medieval French and Occitan Literature* (Arthurian Literature in the Middle Ages, 4), Cardiff, 2006, 186–214.

Buell, D.K., *Why This New Race: Ethnic Reasoning in Early Christianity*, New York, 2005.

Burge, A., *Representing Difference in the Medieval and Modern Orientalist Romance*, New York, 2016.

Burgess, G.S., "Women in the Works of Wace", in G.S. Burgess and J. Weiss (eds.), *Maistre Wace. A Celebration: Proceedings of the International Colloquium held in Jersey, 10–12 September 2004*, St Helier, 2006, 91–106.

Burns, E.J., *Bodytalk: When Women Speak in Old French Literature*, Philadelphia, 1993.

Burnyeat, A., "'Wrenching the club from the hand of Hercules': Classical Models for Medieval Irish *compilation*", in R. O'Connor (ed.), *Classical Literature and Learning in Medieval Irish Narrative* (Studies in Celtic History, 34), Woodbridge, 2014, 196–207.

Burrow, J.W., *A History of Histories: Epics, Chronicles, Romances and Inquiries from Herodotus and Thucydides to the Twentieth Century*, London, 2008.

Bynum, C.W., *Jesus as Mother: Studies in the Spirituality of the High Middle Ages*, Berkeley, 1982.

Byrd, J.A., and Rothberg, M., "Between Subalternity and Indigeneity: Critical Categories for Postcolonial Studies", *Interventions: International Journal of Postcolonial Studies* 13:1 (2011), 1–12.

Campbell, J., "Some Twelfth-Century Views of the Anglo-Saxon Past", *Peritia* 3 (1984), 131–50 (repr. in id. (ed.), *Essays in Anglo-Saxon History*, London, 1986, 209–28).

Carey, J. (ed.), *The Matter of Britain in Medieval Ireland: Reassessments*, London, 2017.

Carley, J.P., "Arthur in English History", in W.R.J. Barron (ed.), *The Arthur of the English: The Arthurian Legend in Medieval English Life and Literature* (Arthurian Literature of the Middle Ages, 2), Cardiff, 1999, 47–57.

Carley, J.P., "Polydore Vergil and John Leland on King Arthur: The Battle of the Books", *Arthurian Interpretations* 15:2 (1984), 86–100 (repr. in E.D. Kennedy (ed.), *King Arthur: A Casebook*, New York, 1996, 185–204).

Carley, J.P., and Crick, J., "Constructing Albion's Past: An Annotated Edition of *De Origine Gigantum*", *AL* 13 (1995), 41–114.

Carlson, D.R., *John Gower, Poetry and Propaganda in Fourteenth-Century England*, Cambridge, 2012.

Carruthers, M., *The Book of Memory: A Study of Memory in Medieval Culture*, Cambridge, 1990.

Cartelet, P., "Capítulo VIII. Las profecías interpoladas del *Baladro del sabio Merlín*: la ambición de una enciclopedia merliniana", in *'Fágote de tanto sabidor'. La construcción del motivo profético en la literatura medieval hispánica (siglos XIII–XV)*, Les Livres d'e-Spania "Études", 2016, <http://journals.openedition.org/e-spanialivres/1044> (accessed 24 June 2019).

Catalán Menéndez-Pidal, D., *De Alfonso X al Conde de Barcelos: cuatro estudios sobre el nacimiento de la historiografía romance en Castilla y Portugal*, Madrid, 1962.

Catalán Menéndez-Pidal, D., *De la silva textual al taller historiográfico alfonsí. Códices, crónicas, versiones y cuadernos de trabajo*, Madrid, 1997.

Chadwick, H.M., & Chadwick, N.K., *The Growth of Literature*, 3 vols., Cambridge, 1932–40.

Chadwick, N.K., "The Conversion of Northumbria: A Comparison of Sources", in ead. (ed.), *Celt and Saxon: Studies in the Early British Border*, Cambridge, 1963, 138–66.

Chakrabarty, D., *Provincializing Europe: Postcolonial Thought and Historical Difference*, new ed., Princeton, 2008.

Charles, B.G., "The Welsh, their Language and Place-Names in Archenfield and Oswestry", in *Angles and Britons: O'Donnell Lectures*, Cardiff, 1963, 85–110.

Charles-Edwards, T.M., "Bede, the Irish and the Britons", *Celtica* 15 (1983), 42–52.

Charles-Edwards, T.M., *Early Christian Ireland*, Cambridge, 2000.

Charles-Edwards, T.M., *Wales and the Britons, 350–1064*, Oxford, 2013.

Chauou, A., *L'Idéologie Plantagenêt: Royauté arthurienne et monarchie politique dans l'espace Plantagenêt (XIIe–XIIIe siècles)*, Rennes, 2001.

Chibnall, M., *Anglo-Norman England, 1066–1166*, Oxford, 1986.

Chibnall, M., *The Empress Matilda: Queen Consort, Queen Mother and Lady of the English*, Oxford and Cambridge, MA, 1991.

Chibnall, M., "'Racial' Minorities in the Anglo-Norman Realm", in S.J. Ridyard and R.G. Benson (eds.), *Minorities and Barbarians in Medieval Life and Thought*, Sewanee, 1996, 49–62.

Chism, C., "'Ain't gonna study war no more': Geoffrey of Monmouth's *Historia regum Britanniae* and *Vita Merlini*", *The Chaucer Review* 48:4 (2014), 458–79.

Cingolani, S.M., "De historia privada a historia pública y de la afirmación al discurso: Una reflexión en torno a la historiografía medieval catalana (985–1288)", *Talia Dixit* 3 (2008), 51–76.

Cingolani, S.M., "'Nos en leyr tales libros trobemos plazer e recreation'. L'estudi sobre la difusió de la literatura d'entreteniment a Catalunya els segles XIV i XV", *Llengua & Literatura* 4 (1990–91), 39–127.

Claassens, G.H.M., "Niederländische Chronistik im Mittelalter", in G. Wolf and N.H. Ott (eds.), *Handbuch Chroniken Des Mittelalters*, Berlin, 2016, 577–608.

Claassens, G.H.M., and Johnson, D.F. (eds.), *King Arthur in the Medieval Low Countries* (Mediaevalia Lovaniensia, Series 1, Studia 28), Leuven, 2000.

Clancy, T.O., "Scotland, the 'Nennian' Recension of the *Historia Brittonum*, and the *Lebor Bretnach*", in S. Taylor (ed.), *Kings, Clerics and Chronicles in Scotland 500–1297: Essays in Honour of Marjorie Ogilvie Anderson on the Occasion of her Ninetieth Birthday*, Dublin, 2000, 87–107.

Clarke, C.A.M., "Writing Civil War in Henry of Huntingdon's *Historia Anglorum*", *Proceedings of the Battle Conference on Anglo Norman Studies* 30 (2009), 31–48.

Cobban, A.B., *The Medieval English Universities: Oxford and Cambridge to c.1500*, Berkeley, 1988.

Cohen, J.J. (ed.), *Cultural Diversity in the British Middle Ages: Archipelago, Island, England*, New York, 2008.

Cohen, J.J., "Decapitation and Coming of Age: Constructing Masculinity and the Monstrous", *The Arthurian Yearbook* 3 (1993), 173–92.

Cohen, J.J., *Hybridity, Identity, and Monstrosity in Medieval Britain: On Difficult Middles*, New York, 2006.

Cohen, J.J., "Hybrids, Monsters, Borderlands: The Bodies of Gerald of Wales", in id. (ed.), *The Postcolonial Middle Ages*, New York, 2000, 85–104.

Cohen, J.J., "Monster Culture: Seven Theses", in id. (ed.), *Monster Theory: Reading Culture*, Minneapolis, 1996, 3–25.

Cohen, J.J., *Of Giants: Sex, Monsters, and the Middle Ages* (Medieval Cultures, 17), Minneapolis, 1999.

Cohen, J.J. (ed.), *The Postcolonial Middle Ages*, New York, 2000.

Cohen, J.J., "Race", in M. Turner (ed.), *A Handbook of Middle English Studies*, Hoboken, NJ, 2013, 109–22.

Constantine, M.A., *The Truth against the World: Iolo Morganwg and Romantic Forgery*, Cardiff, 2007.

Conte, G.B., *The Rhetoric of Imitation: Genre and Poetic Memory in Virgil and Other Latin Poets*, Ithaca, 1986.

Coote, L.A., *Prophecy and Public Affairs in Later Medieval England*, Woodbridge, 2000.

Copeland, R., and Sluiter, I. (eds.), *Medieval Grammar and Rhetoric. Language Arts and Literary Theory, AD 300–1475*, Oxford, 2009.

Cowley, F.G., *The Monastic Order in South Wales 1066–1349* (Studies in Welsh History, 1), Cardiff, 1977.

Crawford, T.D., "On the Linguistic Competence of Geoffrey of Monmouth", *Medium Ævum* 51 (1982), 152–62.

Crick, J., "The British Past and the Welsh Future: Gerald of Wales, Geoffrey of Monmouth and Arthur of Britain", *Celtica* 23 (1999), 60–75.

Crick, J., "Geoffrey of Monmouth, Prophecy and History", *Journal of Medieval History* 18:4 (1992), 357–71.

Crick, J., "Geoffrey and the Prophetic Tradition", in S. Echard (ed.), *The Arthur of Medieval Latin Literature: The Development and Dissemination of the Arthurian Legend in Medieval Latin* (Arthurian Literature of the Middle Ages, 6), Cardiff, 2011, 67–82.

Crick, J., "The Power and the Glory: Conquest and Cosmology in Edwardian Wales (Exeter, Cathedral Library, 3514)", in O. Da Rold and E. Treharne (eds.), *Textual Cultures: Cultural Texts*, Cambridge, 2010, 21–42.

Crick, J., "Two Newly Located Manuscripts of Geoffrey of Monmouth's *Historia regum Britanniae*", *AL* 13 (1995), 151–56.

Crick, J.C., *The Historia regum Britanniae of Geoffrey of Monmouth, vol. III: A Summary Catalogue of the Manuscripts*, Woodbridge, 1989.

Crick, J.C., *The Historia regum Britannie of Geoffrey of Monmouth, vol. IV: Dissemination and Reception in the later Middle Ages*, Woodbridge, 1991.

Crick, J.C., "Monmouth, Geoffrey of (d. 1154/5)", *Oxford Dictionary of National Biography*, Oxford University Press, 2004, <http://www.oxforddnb.com/view/article/10530> (accessed 27 June 2018).

Crofts, T.H., "The Old Knight: An Edition of the Greek Arthurian Poem of Vat. gr. 1822", *AL* 33 (2016), 158–217.

Cronfa Ddata Enwau Lleoedd: Archif Melville Richards [Place-name database: the Melville Richards archive], <http://www.e-gymraeg.co.uk/enwaulleoedd/amr> (accessed 27 March 2017).

Crouch, D., *The Reign of King Stephen 1135–1154*, New York, 2000.

Crouch, D., "Robert, earl of Gloucester and the Daughter of Zelophehad", *Journal of Medieval History* 11:3 (1985), 227–43.

Crouch, D., "The Transformation of Medieval Gwent", in R.A. Griffiths, T. Hopkins, and R. Howell (eds.), *The Gwent County History vol. 2: the Age of the Marcher Lords, c.1070–1536*, Cardiff, 2008, 1–45.

Curley, M.J., "Animal Symbolism in the Prophecies of Merlin", in W.B. Clark and M.T. McMunn (eds.), *Beasts and Birds of the Middle Ages: The Bestiary and Its Legacy*, Philadelphia, 1989, 151–63.

Curley, M.J., "Conjuring History: Mother, Nun, and Incubus in Geoffrey of Monmouth's *Historia Regum Britanniae*", *JEGP* 114:2 (2015), 219–39.

Curley, M.J., *Geoffrey of Monmouth* (Twayne's English Authors Series, 509), New York, 1994.

Curley, M.J., "A New Edition of John of Cornwall's *Prophetia Merlini*", *Speculum* 57:2 (1982), 217–49.

Dalton, P., "The Date of Geoffrey Gaimar's *Estoire des Engleis*, the Connections of his Patrons, and the Politics of Stephen's Reign", *The Chaucer Review* 42:1 (2007), 23–47.

Dalton, P., "The Topical Concerns of Geoffrey of Monmouth's *Historia Regum Britannie*: History, Prophecy, Peacemaking, and English Identity in the Twelfth Century", *Journal of British Studies* 44:4 (2005), 688–712.

Damian-Grint, P., "Arthur in the *Brut* tradition", in G.S. Burgess and K. Pratt (eds.), *The Arthur of the French. The Arthurian Legend in Medieval French and Occitan Literature* (Arthurian Literature in the Middle Ages, 4), Cardiff, 2006, 101–11.

Damian-Grint, P., *The New Historians of the Twelfth-Century Renaissance: Inventing Vernacular Authority*, Woodbridge, 1999.

Damian-Grint, P., "Redating the Royal *Brut* Fragment", *Medium Ævum* 65:2 (1996), 280–85.

Damian-Grint, P., "Vernacular History in the Making: Anglo-Norman Verse Historiography in the Twelfth Century", unpublished PhD thesis, University of London, 1994.

Damongeot-Bourdat, M.-F., "Le roi Arthur et le Mont-Saint-Michel", *Les Amis du Mont-Saint-Michel* 115 (2010), 36–41.

D'Angelo, E., "Re Artù ed Excalibur dalla Britannia romana alla Sicilia normanna", *Atene e Roma* 3:4 (2007), 137–58.

Daniel, C., "L'audience des prophéties de Merlin: entre rumeurs populaires et textes savants", *Mediévales: Langues, Textes, Histoire* 57 (2009), 33–51.

Daniel, C., *Les prophéties de Merlin et la culture politique (XIIe–XVIe siècles)*, Turnhout, 2006.

Daniel, E.R., "Joachim of Fiore's Apocalyptic Scenario", in C.W. Bynum and P. Freedman (eds.), *Last Things: Death and the Apocalypse in the Middle Ages*, Philadelphia, 2000, 124–39.

D'Arcier, L.F., *Histoire et Géographie d'un Mythe: La Circulation des Manuscrits du* De Excidio Troiae *De Darès le Phrygien (viiie–xve siècles)*, Paris, 2006.

Davies, J., *A History of Wales*, Harmondsworth, 2007.

Davies, J.R., "Bishop Kentigern among the Britons", in S. Boardman, J.R. Davies, and E. Williamson (eds.), *Saints' Cults in the Celtic World* (Studies in Celtic History, 25), Woodbridge, 2009, 67–99.

Davies, J.R., *The Book of Llandaf and the Norman Church in Wales*, Woodbridge, 2003.

Davies, J.R., "Cathedrals and the Cult of Saints in Eleventh- and Twelfth-Century Wales", in P. Dalton, C. Insley, and L.J. Wilkinson (eds.), *Cathedrals, Communities and Conflict in the Anglo-Norman World*, Woodbridge, 2011, 99–115.

Davies, R.R., *The Age of Conquest: Wales, 1063–1415*, Oxford, 2000.

Davies, R.R., *Conquest, Coexistence and Change: Wales, 1063–1415*, Oxford, 1987.

Davies, R.R., *The Matter of Britain and the Matter of England: An Inaugural Lecture Delivered Before the University of Oxford on 29 February 1996*, Oxford, 1996.

Davies, R.R., "Race Relations in Post-Conquest Wales: Confrontation and Compromise", *Transactions of the Honourable Society of Cymmrodorion* (1974–75), 32–56.

Davies, R.R., *The Revolt of Owain Glyn Dŵr*, Oxford, 1995.

Davies, W., "*Liber Landavensis*: its Construction and Credibility", *EHR* 88 (1973), 335–51.

de Graaf, K., "De episode van Arturs oorlog tegen de Romeinen", in *Hoe Artur sinenen inde nam: Studie over de Middelnederlandse ridderroman Arturs doet*, Door een werkgroep van Groninger neerlandici ["The episode of Arthur's battle against the Romans" in *How Arthur met his end: studies on the Middle Dutch romance Arturs doet*, by a work group of medievalists at the University of Groningen], Groningen, 1983, 207–14.

De Hamel, C., *Glossed Books of the Bible and the Origins of the Paris Booktrade*, Woodbridge, 1984.

de Laborderie, O., *Histoire, mémoire et pouvoir: Les généalogies en rouleau des rois d'Angleterre (1250–1422)* (Bibliothèque de l'histoire médiévale, 7), Paris, 2013.

de Laborderie, O., "'Ligne de reis': Culture historique, représentation du pouvoir royal et construction de la mémoire nationale en Angleterre à travers les généalogies royales en rouleau du milieu du 13e siècle au milieu du 15e siècle", unpublished PhD thesis, École des Hautes Études en Sciences Sociales, Paris, 2002.

de Winter, P.M., "Copistes, éditeurs et enlumineurs de la fin du XIVe siècle: la production à Paris de manuscrits à miniatures", in *Actes du Congrès national des sociétés savantes: Section d'archéologie et d'histoire de l'art*, Paris, 1978, 173–98.

Dean, R.J., with the collaboration of M.B.M. Boulton, *Anglo-Norman Literature: A Guide to Texts and Manuscripts* (Anglo-Norman Text Society Occasional Publications Series, 3), London, 1999.

Delany, S., "'Mothers to Think Back Through': Who Are They? The Ambiguous Example of Christine de Pizan", in L.A. Finke and M.B. Shichtman (eds.), *Medieval Texts & Contemporary Readers*, Ithaca, 1987, 177–97.

Delcorno Branca, D., *Boccaccio e le storie di re Artù*, Bologna, 1991.

Delcorno Branca, D., "Diffusione della materia arturiana in Italia: per un riesame delle 'tradizioni sommerse'", in P. Benozzo (ed.), *Culture, livelli di cultura e ambienti nel Medioevo occidentale: atti del IX Convegno della Società italiana di filologia romanza, Bologna 5–8 ottobre 2009*, Rome, 2012, 321–40.

Delcorno Branca, D., "Le storie arturiane in Italia", in P. Boitani, M. Malatesta, and A. Vàrvaro (eds.), *Lo spazio letterario del Medioevo, II. Il Medioevo volgare, III: La ricezione del testo*, Rome, 2003, 385–403.

Delle Donne, F., *Il potere e la sua legittimazione: letteratura encomiastica in onore di Federico II di Svevia*, Arce, 2005.

Deploige, J., "Sigebert of Gembloux", in R.G. Dunphy (ed.), *Encyclopedia of the Medieval Chronicle*, 2 vols., Leiden, 2010, vol. 2, 1358–61.

Derolez, A., *The Making and Meaning of the Liber Floridus: A Study of the Original Manuscript Ghent, University Library MS 92* (Studies in Medieval and Early Renaissance Art History, 76), London, 2015.

Deyermond, A., "Problems of Language, Audience, and Arthurian Source in a Fifteenth-Century Castilian Sermon", in A. Torres-Alcalá et al. (eds.), *Josep María Solà-Solé: homage, homenaje, homenatge: miscelánea de estudios de amigos y discípulos* (Biblioteca universitaria Puvill. V, Estudios misceláneos, 1), Barcelona, 1984, 43–54.

Di Cesare, M., "Problemi di autografia nei testimoni del Compendium e della Satirica Ystoria di Paolino Veneto", *Res Publica Litterarum* 30 (2007), 39–49.

Dictionary of Medieval Latin from British Sources, ed. R.E. Latham, London, 1975–, <https://logeion.uchicago.edu/> (accessed 28 May 2018).

Dinshaw, C., *Chaucer's Sexual Poetics*, Madison, 1989.

Dinshaw, C., "Medieval Feminist Criticism", in G. Plain and S. Sellers (eds.), *A History of Feminist Literary Criticism*, Cambridge, 2007, 11–26.

"Disasters! War! Recession! More! 7 Forbidden Prophecies: Mystic Merlin's Secrets Come True", *Sun*, 11 September 2010.

Ditmas, E.M.R., "Geoffrey of Monmouth and the Breton families in Cornwall", *WHR* 6 (1972–73), 451–61.

Doble, G.H., *Lives of the Welsh Saints*, ed. D.S. Evans, Cardiff, 1971.

Donoghue, D., "Laȝamon's Ambivalence", *Speculum* 65:3 (1990), 537–63.

Doob, P.B.R., *Nebuchadnezzar's Children: Conventions of Madness in Middle English Literature*, New Haven, 1974.

Dooley, A., "Arthur of the Irish: A Viable Concept?" *AL* 21 (2004), 9–28.

Dronke, P., "Medieval Sibyls: Their Character and their 'Auctoritas'", *Studii Medievali* 36:2 (1995), 581–615.

Dumville, D.N., "The Anglian Collection of Royal Genealogies and Regnal Lists", *Anglo-Saxon England* 5 (1976), 23–50.

Dumville, D.N., "Brittany and *Armes Prydein Vawr*", *Études celtiques* 20 (1983), 145–59.

Dumville, D.N., "Celtic-Latin Texts in Northern England, c. 1150–c. 1250", *Celtica* 12 (1977), 19–49.

Dumville, D.N., "The Chronology of *De Excidio Britanniae*, Book I", in M. Lapidge and D.N. Dumville (eds.), *Gildas: New Approaches*, Woodbridge, 1984, 61–84.

Dumville, D., "An Early Text of Geoffrey of Monmouth's *Historia regum Britanniae* and the Circulation of some Latin Histories in Twelfth-Century Normandy", *AL* 4 (1985), 1–36.

Dumville, D.N., "*Historia Brittonum*: An Insular History from the Carolingian Age", in A. Scharer and G. Scheibelreiter (eds.), *Historiographie im frühen Mittelalter*, Wien, 1994, 406–34.

Dumville, D.N., *Historia Brittonum 3: The "Vatican" Recension*, Cambridge, 1985.

Dumville, D.N., "The Historical Value of the *Historia Brittonum*", *AL* 6 (1986), 1–26.

Dumville, D.N., "An Irish Idiom Latinised", *Éigse* 16 (1975/76), 183–86.

Dumville, D.N., "The *Liber Floridus* of Lambert of Saint-Omer and the *Historia Brittonum*", *BBCS* 26 (1975), 103–22.

Dumville, D.N., "'Nennius' and the *Historia Brittonum*", *Studia Celtica* 10/11 (1975–76), 78–95.

Dumville, D.N., "On the North British Section of the *Historia Brittonum*", *WHR* 8 (1977), 345–54.

Dumville, D.N., "The Origin of the C-Text of the Variant Version of the *Historia regum Britannie*", *BBCS* 26 (1974–76), 315–22.

Dumville, D.N., "Some Aspects of the Chronology of the *Historia Brittonum*", *BBCS* 25 (1972–74), 246–51.

Dumville, D.N., "The Textual History of the *Lebor Bretnach*: a Preliminary Study", *Éigse* 16 (1976), 255–73.

Dumville, D.N., "The Textual History of the Welsh-Latin *Historia Brittonum*", 3 vols., unpublished PhD thesis, University of Edinburgh, 1975, <https://www.era.lib.ed.ac.uk/handle/1842/8972> (accessed 22 June 2019).

Dunbabin, J., "The Maccabees as Exemplars in the Tenth and Eleventh Centuries", in K. Walsh and D. Greenway (eds.), *The Bible in the Medieval World: Essays in Memory of Beryl Smalley* (Studies in Church History, Subsidia 4), Oxford, 1985, 31–41.

Dunphy, R.G. (ed.), *Encyclopedia of the Medieval Chronicle*, 2 vols., Leiden, 2010.

Echard, S., *Arthurian Narrative in the Latin Tradition* (Cambridge Studies in Medieval Literature, 36), Cambridge, 1998.

Echard, S., "Geoffrey of Monmouth", in ead. (ed.), *The Arthur of Medieval Latin Literature: The Development and Dissemination of the Arthurian Legend in Medieval Latin* (Arthurian Literature in the Middle Ages, 6), Cardiff, 2011, 45–66.

Echard, S., "'Hic est Artur': Reading Latin and Reading Arthur", in A. Lupack (ed.), *New Directions in Arthurian Studies*, Cambridge, 2002, 49–67.

Echard, S., "Palimpsests of Place and Time in Geoffrey of Monmouth's *Historia regum Britannie*", in G. Dinkova-Bruun and T. Major (eds.), *Teaching and Learning in Medieval Europe: Essays in Honour of Gernot R. Wieland*, Turnhout, 2017, 43–59.

Echard, S., "Remembering Brutus: Aaron Thompson's *British History* of 1718", *AL* 30 (2013), 141–69.

Echard, S., "'Whyche thyng semeth not to agree with other histories ...': Rome in Geoffrey of Monmouth and his Early Modern Readers", *AL* 26 (2009), 109–29.

Eckhardt, C.D., "The Date of the *Prophetia Merlini* Commentary in MSS Cotton Claudius BVII and Bibliothèque Nationale Fonds Latin 6233", *Notes and Queries*, new series, 23 (1976), 146–47.

Edel, D., "Geoffrey's So-Called Animal Symbolism and Insular Celtic Tradition", *Studia Celtica* 18/19 (1983/84), 96–109.

Edwards, N., *A Corpus of Early Medieval Inscribed Stones and Stone Sculpture in Wales*, 3: *North Wales*, Cardiff, 2013.

Eliav-Feldon, M., Isaac, B., and Ziegler, J. (eds.), *The Origins of Racism in the West*, Cambridge, 2009.

Elliot, A.G., "The Historian as Artist: Manipulation of History in the Chronicle of Desclot", *Viator* 14 (1983), 195–209.

Emanuel, H.D., "An Analysis of the Composition of the 'Vita Cadoci'", *National Library of Wales Journal* 7 (1952), 217–27.

Entwistle, W.J., "Geoffrey of Monmouth and Spanish Literature", *Medieval Literature Review* 17:4 (1922), 381–91.

Etchingham, C., "Viking-Age Gwynedd and Ireland: Political Relations", in K. Jankulak and J. Wooding (eds.), *Ireland and Wales in the Middle Ages*, Dublin, 2007, 149–67.

Evans, D.F., "Talm o Wentoedd: the Welsh Language and its Literature c.1070–c.1530", in R.A. Griffiths, T. Hopkins, and R. Howell (eds.), *The Gwent County History vol. 2: the Age of the Marcher Lords, c.1070–1536*, Cardiff, 2008, 280–308.

Evans, R., "Gigantic Origins: An Annotated Translation of *De Origine Gigantum*", *AL* 16 (1998), 197–211.

Evans, R.W., "Prophetic Poetry", in A.O.H. Jarman and G.R. Hughes (eds.), *A Guide to Welsh Literature 1282–c. 1550: Volume II*, rev. D. Johnston, Cardiff, 1997, 256–74.

Faletra, M.A., "Merlin in Cornwall: The Source and Contexts of John of Cornwall's *Prophetia Merlini*", *JEGP* 111:3 (2012), 303–38.

Faletra, M.A., "Narrating the Matter of Britain: Geoffrey of Monmouth and the Norman Colonization of Wales", *The Chaucer Review* 35:1 (2000), 60–85.

Faletra, M.A., *Wales and the Medieval Colonial Imagination: The Matters of Britain in the Twelfth Century*, New York, 2014.

Fanon, F., *The Wretched of the Earth*, trans. C. Farrington, New York, 1968.

Faral, E., "Geoffrey of Monmouth: les faites et les dates de sa biographia", *Romania* 53 (1927), 1–42.

Faral, E., *La légende arthurienne: études et documents*, 3 vols., Paris, 1929.

Farmer, D.H., "William of Malmesbury's Life and Works", *Journal of Ecclesiastical History* 13 (1962), 39–54.

Federico, S., *New Troy: Fantasies of Empire in the Late Middle Ages*, Minneapolis, 2003.

Feuerherd, P.O., *Geoffrey of Monmouth und das Alte Testament mit berücksichtigung der Historia Britonum des Nennius*, Halle, 1915.

Field, P.J.C., "Nennius and his History", *Studia Celtica* 30 (1996), 159–65.

Finke, L., "The Rhetoric of Marginality: Why I Do Feminist Theory", *Tulsa Studies in Women's Literature* 5:2 (1986), 251–72.

Finke, L.A., & Shichtman, M.B., *King Arthur and the Myth of History*, Gainesville, 2004.

Fisher, E.A., "Planoudes, Holobolos, and the Motivation for Translation", *Greek, Roman, and Byzantine Studies* 43:1 (2002/03), 77–104.

Fleuriot, L., *Dictionnaire des gloses en vieux Breton*, Paris, 1964.

Fleuriot, L., "Langue et société dans la Bretagne ancienne", in J. Balcou and Y. Le Gallo (eds.), *Histoire littéraire et culturelle de la Bretagne*, 3 vols., Paris, 1987, vol. 1, 7–28.

Flint, V.I.J., "The *Historia Regum Britanniae* of Geoffrey of Monmouth: Parody and Its Purpose. A Suggestion", *Speculum* 54:3 (1979), 447–68.

Flood, V., *Prophecy, Politics and Place in Medieval England: From Geoffrey of Monmouth to Thomas of Erceldoune*, Cambridge, 2016.

Foley, W.T., and Higham, N., "Bede on the Britons", *Early Medieval Europe* 17 (2009), 54–185.

Foltys, C., "Kritische Ausgabe der anglonormannische Chroniken: Brutus, Li rei de Engleterre, Le Livere de Reis de Engleterre", unpublished inaugural dissertation, Freie Universität Berlin, 1961.

Foreville, R., "L'École de Caen au XIe siècle et les origines normandes de l'université d'Oxford", in *Études médiévales offertes à M. le Doyen Augustin Fliche de l'Institut*, Montpellier, 1952, 81–100.

Fowler, D.C., "Some Biblical Influences on Geoffrey of Monmouth's Historiography", *Traditio* 14 (1958), 378–85.

Frakes, J.C., *Early Yiddish Epics*, Syracuse, 2014.

Friedman, L.M., *Dead Hands: A Social History of Wills, Trusts, and Inheritance Law*, Stanford, 2009.

Fries, M., "Female Heroes, Heroines and Counter-Heroes: Images of Women in Arthurian Tradition", in S.K. Slocum (ed.), *Popular Arthurian Traditions*, Bowling Green, OH, 1992, 5–17.

Fries, M., "Gender and the Grail", *Arthuriana* 8:1 (1998), 67–79.

Fries, M., "From The Lady to The Tramp: The Decline of Morgan le Fay in Medieval Romance", *Arthuriana* 4:1 (1994), 1–18.

Fulton, H., "History and Myth: Geoffrey of Monmouth's *Historia Regum Britanniae*", in ead. (ed.), *A Companion to Arthurian Literature*, Chichester, 2008, 44–57.

Fulton, H., "Tenth-Century Wales and *Armes Prydein*", *Transactions of the Honourable Society of Cymmrodorion*, new series, 7 (2001), 5–18.

Fulton, H., "Troy Story: The Medieval Welsh *Ystorya Dared* and the *Brut* Tradition of British History", in J. Dresvina and N. Sparks (eds.), *The Medieval Chronicle VII*, Amsterdam, 2011, 137–50.

Funkenstein, A., *Heilsplan und natürliche Entwicklung: Formen der Gegenartsbestimmung im Geschichtsdenken des hohen Mittelalters*, Sammlung Dialog 5, Munich, 1965.

Gallagher, N., "The Franciscans and the Scottish Wars of Independence: An Irish Perspective", *Journal of Medieval History* 32 (2006), 3–17.

Galliou, P., & Jones, M., *The Bretons*, Oxford, 1991.

Galloway, A., "Writing History in England", in D. Wallace (ed.), *The Cambridge History of Medieval English Literature*, Cambridge, 1999, 255–83.

Galyon, A., "*De Ortu Walwanii* and the Theory of Illumination", *Neophilologus* 62:3 (1978), 335–41.

Gamper, R., Knoch-Mund, G., & Stähli, M., *Katalog der mittelalterlichen Handschriften der Ministerialbibliothek Schaffhausen*, Dietikon-Zürich, 1994.

Gardener, E.G., *The Arthurian Legend in Italian Literature*, London and New York, 1930.

Gerritsen, W.P., "Jacob van Maerlant and Geoffrey of Monmouth", in K. Varty (ed.), *An Arthurian Tapestry: Essays in Memory of Lewis Thorpe*, Glasgow, 1981, 369–76.

Gerritsen, W.P., "L'épisode de La Guerre Contre Les Romains Dans La Mort Artu Néerlandaise", in n.n. (ed.), *Mélanges de Langue et de Littérature Du Moyen Age et de La Renaissance Offerts à Jean Frappier*, 2 vols., Geneva, 1970, vol. 1, 337–49.

Gillingham, J., "The Context and Purposes of Geoffrey of Monmouth's *History of the Kings of Britain*", *Anglo-Norman Studies* 13 (1990), 99–118 (repr. in id. (ed.), *The English in the Twelfth Century: Imperialism, National Identity and Political Values*, Woodbridge, 2000, 19–39).

Gillingham, J., *The English in the Twelfth Century: Imperialism, National Identity, and Political Values*, Woodbridge, 2000.

Gillingham, J., "Henry of Huntingdon in His Time (1135) and Place (between Lincoln and the Royal Court)", in K. Stopka (ed.), *Gallus Anonymous and His Chronicle in the Context of Twelfth-Century Historiography from the Perspective of the Latest Research*, Krakow, 2010, 157–72.

Gillingham, J., "Henry of Huntingdon and the Twelfth-Century Revival of the English Nation", in S. Forde, L. Johnson, and A. Murray (eds.), *Concepts of National Identity in the Middle Ages*, Leeds, 1995, 75–101 (repr. in id. (ed.), *The English in the Twelfth Century: Imperialism, National Identity and Political Values*, Woodbridge, 2000, 123–44).

Gillingham, J., "The Historian as Judge: William of Newburgh and Hubert Walter", *EHR* 119:484 (2004), 1275–87.

Given-Wilson, C., *Chronicles: The Writing of History in Medieval England*, London and New York, 2004.

Glick, T.F., *Islamic and Christian Spain in the Early Middle Ages*, Princeton, 1979.

Godman, P., *The Silent Masters: Latin Literature and its Censors in the High Middle Ages*, Princeton, 2000.

Golding, B., "Gerald of Wales and the Cistercians", *Reading Medieval Studies* 21 (1995), 5–30.

Goldstein, R.J., *The Matter of Scotland: Historical Narrative in Medieval Scotland*, Lincoln, 1993.

Gómez Redondo, F., "La materia de Bretaña y los modelos historiográficos: el caso de la *General estoria*", e-*Spania* 16 (2013), <https://journals.openedition.org/e-spania/22707> (accessed 30 May 2018).

Gough-Cooper, H., *Annales Cambriae: A, B and C in Parallel, from St Patrick to AD 954*, 2016, <http://croniclau.bangor.ac.uk/documents/AC_ABC_to_954_first_edition.pdf> (accessed 30 April 2017).

Gowan, L.M., "The Modena Archivolt and the Lost Arthurian Tradition", in W. Van Hoecke, G. Tournoy, and W. Webecke (eds.), *Arturus Rex, Vol. II. Acta Conventus Lonvaliensis 1987*, Leuven, 1991, 79–86.

GPC Online, University of Wales Centre for Advanced Welsh and Celtic Studies, Aberystwyth, 2014, <http://www.geiriadur.ac.uk/> (accessed 30 April 2017).

Gracia, P., "Arthurian Material in Iberia", in D. Hook (ed.), *The Arthur of the Iberians: The Arthurian Legends in the Spanish and Portuguese Worlds* (Arthurian Literature in the Middle Ages, 8), Cardiff, 2015, 11–32.

Gracia, P., "Hacia el modelo de la *General estoria*. París, la *translatio imperii et studii* y la *Histoire ancienne jusqu'à César*", *Zeitschrift für romanische Philologie* 122 (2006), 17–27.

Graf, A., "Artù nell'Etna", in id. (ed.), *Miti, leggende e superstizione nel medioevo*, Milan, 1984, 321–38.

Gransden, A., "The Growth of the Glastonbury Traditions and Legends in the Twelfth Century", *The Journal of Ecclesiastical History* 27 (1976), 337–58 (repr. in J.P. Carley (ed.), *Glastonbury Abbey and the Arthurian Tradition*, Cambridge, 2001, 29–53).

Gransden, A., *Historical Writing in England, c.550–c.1307*, London, 1974.

Gransden, A., *Historical Writing in England, II: c. 1307 to the Early Sixteenth Century*, London, 1982.

Gransden, A., review of R.W. Hanning, *The Vision of History in Early Britain: From Gildas to Geoffrey of Monmouth*, *Catholic History Review* 55 (1969), 272–73.

Greenway, D., "Authority, Convention and Observation in Henry of Huntingdon's *Historia Anglorum*", *Anglo-Norman Studies* 18 (1995), 105–21.

Greenway, D., *Henry, Archdeacon of Huntingdon: Historia Anglorum. The History of the English People*, Oxford, 1996.

Greenway, D., "Henry (c. 1088–c. 1157), Historian and Poet", *Oxford Dictionary of National Biography*, <https://doi.org/10.1093/ref:odnb/12970> (accessed 18 May 2019).

Gresham, C.A., *Medieval Stone Carving in North Wales*, Cardiff, 1968.

Griffiths, M.E., *Early Vaticination in Welsh with English Parallels*, Cardiff, 1937.

Gropper, S., "Breta Sögur and Merlínusspá", in M.E. Kalinke (ed.), *The Arthur of the North: The Arthurian Legend in the Norse and Rus' Realms* (Arthurian Literature in the Middle Ages, 5), Cardiff, 2011, 48–60.

Grout, P.B., "The Author of the Munich *Brut*, his Latin Sources and Wace", *Medium Ævum* 54:2 (1985), 274–82.

Grout, P.B., "The Manuscript of the Munich *Brut* (Codex Gallicus 29 of the Bayerische Staatsbibliothek, Munich)", in S.B. North (ed.), *Studies in Medieval French Language and Literature presented to Brian Woledge* (Publications Romanes et Françaises, 180), Geneva, 1988, 49–58.

Guha, R., *Writings on South Asian History and Society*, Delhi, 1984.

Guillotel, H., "Une famille bretonne au service du Conquérant: Les Baderon", in *Droit privé et institutions régionals: Etudes historiques offertes à Jean Yver*, Paris, 1976, 361–66.

Guy, B., "The Breton Migration: a New Synthesis", *Zeitschrift für celtische Philologie* 61 (2014), 101–56.

Guy, B., "Constantine, Helena, Maximus: on the Appropriation of Roman History in Medieval Wales, c.800–1250", *Journal of Medieval History* 44 (2018), 381–405.

Guy, B., "The Earliest Welsh Genealogies: Textual Layering and the Phenomenon of 'Pedigree Growth'", *Early Medieval Europe* 26 (2018), 462–85.

Guy, B., "Gerald and Welsh Genealogical Learning", in G. Henley and A.J. McMullen (eds.), *Gerald of Wales: New Perspectives on a Medieval Writer and Critic*, Cardiff, 2018, 47–61.

Guy, B., *Medieval Welsh Genealogy: An Introduction and Textual Study*, Woodbridge, 2020.

Guy, B., "Medieval Welsh Genealogy: Texts, Contexts and Transmission", 2 vols., unpublished PhD thesis, University of Cambridge, 2016.

Guy, B., "'O herwyd yr Istoria': The Appropriation of Geoffrey of Monmouth's British History in Medieval Welsh Genealogy", unpublished paper delivered at the International Medieval Congress, University of Leeds, 8 July 2015.

Guy, B., "The Origins of the Compilation of Welsh Historical Texts in Harley 3859", *Studia Celtica* 49 (2015), 21–56.

Guy, B., "A Welsh Manuscript in America: Library Company of Philadelphia, 8680.O", *National Library of Wales Journal* 36 (2014), 1–26.

Guzman, G., "Reports of Mongol Cannibalism in the Thirteenth Century", in S.D. Westrem (ed.), *Discovering New Worlds: Essays on Medieval Exploration and Imagination*, New York, 1991, 31–68.

Hahn, T., "The Difference the Middle Ages Makes: Color and Race before the Modern World", *JMEMS* 31 (2001), 1–38.

Hammer, J., "Geoffrey of Monmouth's Use of the Bible in the *Historia Regum Britanniae*", *Bulletin of the John Rylands Library* 30 (1947), 293–311.

Hammer, J., "Some Leonine Summaries of Geoffrey of Monmouth's *Historia Regum Britanniae* and Other Poems", *Speculum* 6:1 (1931), 114–23.

Hanawalt, B.A., *"Of Good and Ill Repute": Gender and Social Control in Medieval England*, Oxford, 1998.

Hanning, R.W., *"Inventio Arthuri*: a Comment on the Essays of Geoffrey Ashe and D.R. Howlett", *Arthuriana* 5:3 (1995), 96–99.

Hanning, R.W., *The Vision of History in Early Britain: From Gildas to Geoffrey of Monmouth*, New York, 1966.

Harnack, A., "Der Brief des britischen Königs Lucius an den Papst Eleutherus", *Sitzungsberichte der königlich-preussischen Akademie der Wissenschaften* (1904), 909–16.

Harris, S., *The Linguistic Past in Twelfth-Century Britain*, Cambridge, 2017.

Harris, S., "Liturgical Commemorations of Welsh Saints II: St. Asaf", *Journal of the Historical Society of the Church in Wales* 6 (1956), 5–24.

Haycock, M., *Legendary Poems from the Book of Taliesin*, Aberystwyth, 2007.

Haycock, M., *Prophecies from the Book of Taliesin*, Aberystwyth, 2013.

Haycock, M., "Taliesin's 'Lesser Song of the World'", in T. Jones and E.B. Fryde (eds.), *Ysgrifau a cherddi cyflwynedig i Daniel Huws. Essays and Poems Presented to Daniel Huws*, Aberystwyth, 1994, 229–50.

Heng, G., "Cannibalism, the First Crusade, and the Genesis of Medieval Romance", *Differences: A Journal of Feminist Cultural Studies* 10:1 (1998), 98–174.

Heng, G., *Empire of Magic: Medieval Romance and the Politics of Cultural Fantasy*, New York, 2001.

Heng, G., *The Invention of Race in the European Middle Ages*, Cambridge, 2018.

Henley, G., "From 'The Matter of Britain' to 'The Matter of Rome': Latin literary culture and the reception of Geoffrey of Monmouth in Wales", *AL* 33 (2016), 1–28.

Hering, K., "Godfrey of Viterbo: Historical Writing and Imperial Legitimacy at the Early Hohenstaufen Court", in T. Foerster (ed.), *Godfrey of Viterbo and His Readers: Imperial Tradition and Universal History in Late Medieval Europe*, Farnham, 2015, 47–66.

Higham, N.J., *The English Conquest: Gildas and Britain in the Fifth Century*, Manchester, 1994.

Higham, N.J., "Historical Narrative as Cultural Politics: Rome, 'British-ness' and 'English-ness'", in id. (ed.), *The Britons in Anglo-Saxon England*, Woodbridge, 2007, 68–79.

Higham, N.J., *King Arthur: Myth-Making and History*, London, 2002.

Hinds, S., *Allusion and Intertext: Dynamics of Appropriation in Roman Poetry*, Cambridge, 1998.

Hoffman, D., "Merlin in Italian Literature", in P. Goodrich and R.H. Thompson (eds.), *Merlin: A Casebook*, New York, 2003, 186–96.

Hoffman, D.L., "Was Merlin a Ghibelline? Arthurian Propaganda at the Court of Frederick II", in M.B. Shichtman and J.P. Carley (eds.), *Culture and the King: The*

Social Implications of the Arthurian Legend, Essays in Honor of Valerie M. Lagorio, Albany, 1994, 113–28.

Holder-Egger, O., "Italienische Prophetieen des 13. Jahrhunderts. I.", *Neues Archiv der Gesellschaft für ältere deutsche Geschichtskunde zur Beförderung einer Gesamtausgabe der Quellenschriften deutscher Geschichten des Mittelalters* 15 (1889), 142–78.

Hsy, J., and Orlemanski, J., "Race and Medieval Studies: A Partial Bibliography", *postmedieval* 8:4 (2017), 500–31.

Hughes, K., *Celtic Britain in the Early Middle Ages, Studies in Scottish and Welsh Sources*, ed. D.N. Dumville (Studies in Celtic History, 2), Woodbridge, 1980.

Hunt, T., and Bromiley, G., "The Tristan Legend in Old French Verse", in G.S. Burgess and K. Pratt (eds.), *The Arthur of the French. The Arthurian Legend in Medieval French and Occitan Literature* (Arthurian Literature in the Middle Ages, 4), Cardiff, 2006, 112–34.

Huot, S., *Outsiders: The Humanity and Inhumanity of Giants in Medieval French Prose Romance*, Notre Dame, 2016.

Hurley, M., *Geoffrey of Monmouth*, New York, 1994.

Hutcheon, L., *A Theory of Parody: The Teachings of Twentieth-Century Art Forms*, London, 1985.

Hutchinson, A.P., "Reading between the Lines: A Vision of the Arthurian World Reflected in Galician-Portuguese Poetry", in B. Wheeler (ed.), *Arthurian Studies in Honour of P.J.C. Field*, Cambridge, 2004, 117–32.

Hutson, A.E., *British Personal Names in the Historia regum Britanniae*, Berkeley, 1940.

Hutson, A.E., "Geoffrey of Monmouth", *Transactions of the Honourable Society of Cymmrodorion* (1937), 361–73.

Huws, D., "Llyfr Coch Hergest", in I. Daniel, M. Haycock, D. Johnston and J. Rowland (eds.), *Cyfoeth y Testun: Ysgrifau ar Lenyddiaeth Gymraeg yr Oesoedd Canol*, Cardiff, 2003, 1–30.

Huws, D., "The Manuscripts", in T.M. Charles-Edwards, M.E. Owen, and D.B. Walters (eds.), *Lawyers and Laymen: Studies in the History of Law Presented to Professor Dafydd Jenkins on his Seventy-Fifth Birthday, Gŵyl Ddewi 1986*, Cardiff, 1986, 119–36.

Huws, D., *Medieval Welsh Manuscripts*, Aberystwyth, 2000.

Huws, D., *A Repertory of Welsh Manuscripts and Scribes*, forthcoming.

Huygens, R.B.C., "*Otia de Machomete* [A poem on Muhammad], Gedicht von Walter von Compiegne", *Sacris erudiri* 8 (1956), 287–328.

Ignatiev, N., *How the Irish Became White*, New York, 1995 (repr. 2009).

Ingham, P.C., *Sovereign Fantasies: Arthurian Romance and the Making of Britain*, Philadelphia, 2001.

Ingledew, F., "The Book of Troy and the Genealogical Construction of History: The Case of Geoffrey of Monmouth's *Historia regum Britanniae*", *Speculum* 69:3 (1994), 665–704.

Isaac, G., "*Armes Prydain Fawr* and St David", in J.W. Evans and J.M. Wooding (eds.), *St David of Wales: Cult, Church and Nation*, Woodbridge, 2007, 161–81.

Izquierdo, J., "Traslladar la memòria, traduir el món: la prosa de Ramon Muntaner en el context cultural i literari romànic", *Quaderns de filologia. Estudis literaris* 8 (2003), 189–244.

Jackson, K.H., "On the Northern British Section in Nennius", in N.K. Chadwick (ed.), *Celt and Saxon: Studies in the Early British Border*, Cambridge, 1963, rev. ed. 1964, 20–62.

Jackson, W.H., and Ranawake, S.A., "Introduction", in W.H. Jackson and S.A. Ranawake (eds.) *The Arthur of the Germans: The Arthurian Legend in Medieval German and Dutch Literature* (Arthurian Literature in the Middle Ages, 3), Cardiff, 2000, 1–18.

Jacoby, D., "Knightly Values and Class Consciousness in the Crusader States of the Eastern Mediterranean", *Mediterranean Historical Review* 1 (1986), 158–86.

Jaeger, C.S., "Pessimism in the Twelfth-Century 'Renaissance'", *Speculum* 78:4 (2003), 1151–83.

Jankulak, K., "Carantoc alias Cairnech? British Saints, Irish Saints, and the Irish in Wales", in K. Jankulak and J.M. Wooding (eds.), *Ireland and Wales in the Middle Ages*, Dublin, 2007, 116–48.

Jankulak, K., *Geoffrey of Monmouth*, Cardiff, 2010.

Jarman, A.O.H., "Y Ddadl Ynghylch Sieffre o Fynwy" [The debate surrounding Geoffrey of Monmouth], *Llên Cymru* 2 (1952), 1–18.

Jarman, A.O.H., "Early Stages in the Development of the Myrddin Legend", in R. Bromwich and R.B. Jones (eds.), *Astudiaethau ar yr Hengerdd / Studies in Old Welsh Poetry: Cyflwynedig i Syr Idris Foster* [Studies in Old Welsh poetry presented to Sir Idris Foster], Cardiff, 1978, 326–49.

Jarman, A.O.H., *The Legend of Merlin*, Cardiff, 1960.

Jarman, A.O.H., "The Merlin Legend and the Welsh Tradition of Prophecy", in R. Bromwich, A.O.H. Jarman, and B.F. Roberts (eds.), *The Arthur of the Welsh: The Arthurian Legend in Medieval Welsh Literature* (Arthurian Literature in the Middle Ages, 1), Cardiff, 1991, 117–45.

Jarman, A.O.H., "The Welsh Myrddin Poems", in R.S. Loomis (ed.), *Arthurian Literature in the Middle Ages*, Oxford, 1959, 20–30.

Jenkins, M.B., "Aspects of the Welsh Prophetic Verse Tradition: Incorporating Textual Studies of the Poetry from 'Llyfr Coch Hergest' (Oxford, Jesus College, MS cxi) and 'Y Cwta Cyfarwydd' (Aberystwyth, National Library of Wales, MS Peniarth 50)", unpublished PhD thesis, University of Cambridge, 1990.

Jones, A.L., *Darogan: Prophecy, Lament and Absent Heroes in Medieval Welsh Literature*, Cardiff, 2013.

Jones, E., "Geoffrey of Monmouth's Account of the Establishment of Episcopacy in Britain", *JEGP* 40 (1941), 360–63.

Jones, N.A., "Llywelyn Fardd I, II, III?" *Llên Cymru* 29 (2006), 1–12.

Jones, O.W., "*Brut y Tywysogion*: the History of the Princes and Twelfth-Century Cambro-Latin Historical Writing", *Haskins Society Journal* 26 (2014), 209–27.

Jones, O.W., "O Oes Gwrtheyrn: a Medieval Welsh Chronicle", in B. Guy, G. Henley, O.W. Jones, and R.L. Thomas (eds.), *The Chronicles of Medieval Wales and the March: New Contexts, Studies and Texts* (Medieval Texts and Cultures of Northern Europe), Turnhout, forthcoming.

Jones, R., *The Theme of Love in the Romans d'Antiquité*, London, 1972.

Jones, W.R., "England Against the Celtic Fringe: A Study in Cultural Stereotypes", *Journal of World History* 13:1 (1971), 155–71.

Jordan, W.C., "Why 'Race'?" *JMEMS* 31:1 (2001), 165–74.

Kaimowitz, J.H., "A Fourth Redaction of the *Histoire ancienne jusqu'à César*", in D.F. Bright and E.S. Ramage (eds.), *Classical Texts and Their Traditions: Studies in Honor of C.R. Traham*, Chico, CA, 1984, 75–87.

Kalinke, M., "Arthur, king of Iceland", *Scandinavian Studies* 87 (2015), 8–32.

Kantorowicz, E., *Federico II Imperatore*, Milan, 1976.

Kantorowicz, E.H., *The King's Two Bodies: A Study in Medieval Political Theology*, Princeton, 1957; repr. 1997 with a new preface.

Kasten, L., "The Utilization of the *Historia Regum Britanniae* by Alfonso X", *Hispanic Review* 38:5 (1970), 97–114.

Keats-Rohan, K.S.B., "The Bretons and Normans of England 1066–1154: the Family, the Fief and the Feudal Monarchy", *Nottingham Medieval Studies* 36 (1992), 42–78.

Keats-Rohan, K.S.B., *Domesday People: A Prosopography of Persons Occurring in English Documents, 1066–1166. I. Domesday Book*, Woodbridge, 1999.

Keats-Rohan, K.S.B., "What's in a Name? Some Reflections on Naming and Identity in Prosopography", in A.M. Jorge, H. Vilar, and M.J. Branco (eds.), *Carreiras Eclesiásticas no Ocidente Cristão (séc. XII–XIV). Ecclesiastical Careers in Western Christianity (12th–14th c.)*, Lisbon, 2007, 331–47.

Keats-Rohan, K.S.B., "William I and the Breton Contingent in the Non-Norman Conquest 1060–1087", *Anglo-Norman Studies* 13 (1991), 157–72.

Keeler, L., *Geoffrey of Monmouth and the Late Latin Chroniclers, 1300–1500*, Berkeley, 1946.

Keen, M., *Chivalry*, Bath, 1984.

Kelly, D., "Chrétien de Troyes", in G.S. Burgess and K. Pratt (eds.), *The Arthur of the French. The Arthurian Legend in Medieval French and Occitan Literature* (Arthurian Literature in the Middle Ages, 4), Cardiff, 2006, 135–85.

Kempshall, M., *Rhetoric and the Writing of History, 400–1500*, Manchester, 2011.

Kennedy, E.D., *Chronicles and Other Historical Writing* (A Manual of the Writings in Middle English, 8), New Haven, 1989.

Kennedy, R., and Meecham-Jones, S. (eds.), *Authority and Subjugation in Writing of Medieval Wales*, New York, 2008.

Kennedy, R.F., Roy, C.S., and Goldman, M.L. (eds.), *Race and Ethnicity in the Classical World: An Anthology of Primary Sources in Translation*, Indianapolis, 2013.

Ker, N., *Medieval Libraries of Great Britain: A List of Surviving Books*, London, 1964.

Keynes, S., "Anglo-Saxons, Kingdom of the", in M. Lapidge, J. Blair, S. Keynes and D. Scragg (eds.), *The Blackwell Encyclopaedia of Anglo-Saxon England*, 2nd ed., Chichester, 2014, 40.

Keynes, S., "Bretwalda or *Brytenwalda*", in M. Lapidge, J. Blair, S. Keynes and D. Scragg (eds.), *The Blackwell Encyclopaedia of Anglo-Saxon England*, 2nd ed., Chichester, 2014, 76–77.

Keynes, S., & Lapidge, M., *Alfred the Great: Asser's Life of King Alfred and Other Contemporary Sources*, Harmondsworth, 1983.

Khanmohamadi, S., *In Light of Another's Word: European Ethnography in the Middle Ages*, Philadelphia, 2013.

Kim, D., *Digital Whiteness & Medieval Studies*, Leeds, 2019.

Kim, D., "Reframing Race and Jewish/Christian Relations in the Middle Ages", *transversal: Journal for Jewish Studies* 13:1 (2015), 52–64.

Kim, D., "Introduction to Literature Compass Special Cluster: Critical Race and the Middle Ages", *Literature Compass* 16:9–10 (2019), 1–16.

Kim, D., "Teaching Medieval Studies in a Time of White Supremacy", *In the Middle*, 28 August 2017, <http://www.inthemedievalmiddle.com/2017/08/teaching-medieval-studies-in-time-of.html> (accessed 26 May 2019).

Kinoshita, S., *Medieval Boundaries: Rethinking Difference in Old French Literature*, Philadelphia, 2006.

Kinoshita, S., "Translatio/n, Empire, and the Worlding of Medieval Literature: the Travels of *Kalila wa Dimna*", *Postcolonial Studies* 11:4 (2008), 371–85.

Kneupper, F.C., *The Empire at the Edge of Time: Identity and Reform in Late Medieval German Prophecy*, Oxford, 2016.

Knowles, D., *The Monastic Order in England*, 2nd ed., Cambridge, 1963.

Koble, N., *"Les Prophéties de Merlin" en prose: le roman arthurien en éclats* (Nouvelle Bibliothèque du Moyen Âge, 92), Paris, 2009.

Koch, J., "Anglonormannische Texte in Ms. Arundel 220 des Britischen Museums", *Zeitschrift für romanische Philologie* 54 (1934), 20–56.

Koch, J.T., "*Llawr en asseð* (CA 932) 'The laureate hero in the war-chariot': Some Recollections of the Iron Age in the *Gododdin*", *Études celtiques* 24 (1987), 253–78.

Koch, J.T., "A Welsh Window on the Iron Age: Manawydan, Mandubracios", *CMCS* 14 (1987), 17–52.

Kosto, A.J., *Making Agreements in Medieval Catalonia: Power, Order, and the Written Word, 1000–1200*, Cambridge, 2001.

Krueger, R.L., *Women Readers and the Ideology of Gender in Old French Verse Romance*, Cambridge, 1993.

Kundera, M., "The Traffic in Women: Notes on the 'Political Economy' of Sex", in R.R. Reiter (ed.), *Toward an Anthropology of Women*, New York, 1975, 157–210.

Lacy, N.J., "The Arthurian Legend Before Chrétien de Troyes", in N.J. Lacy and J.T. Grimbert (eds.), *A Companion to Chrétien de Troyes*, Cambridge, 2005, 43–51.

Lambert, P.-Y., "À propos de la traduction galloise du ms. London, British Library, Cotton Cleopatra B.V", in H. Tétrel and G. Veysseyre (eds.), *L'Historia regum Britannie et les "Bruts" en Europe, Tome I, Traductions, adaptations, réappropriations (XIIe–XVIe siècle)* (Rencontres 106, Civilisation médiévale, 12), Paris, 2015, 81–103.

Lapidge, M., "Additional Manuscript Evidence for the *Vera Historia de Morte Arthuri*", *AL* 2 (1982), 163–68.

Lapidge, M., "The Welsh-Latin Poetry of Sulien's Family", *Studia Celtica* 8 (1973–74), 68–106.

Larkin, P., "A Suggested Author for *De ortu Waluuanii* and *Historia Meriadoci*: Ranulph Higden", *JEGP* 103:2 (2004), 215–31.

Laurent, F., *Plaire et édifier: Les récits hagiographiques composés en Angleterre aux XIIe et XIIIe siècles*, Paris, 1998.

Laurent, F., Mathey-Maille, L., and Szkilnik, M., "L'hagiographie au service de l'histoire: enjeux et problématique", in F. Laurent, L. Mathey-Maille, and M. Szkilnik (eds.), *Des saints et des rois. L'hagiographie au service de l'histoire*, Paris, 2014, 9–21.

Lausberg, H., *Handbook of Literary Rhetoric*, trans. M.T. Bliss et al., Leiden, 1998.

Leckie, Jr., R.W., *The Passage of Dominion: Geoffrey of Monmouth and the Periodization of Insular History in the Twelfth Century*, Toronto, 1981.

Lefèvre, S., "Conclusions: L'*Historia regum Britannie* entre éternels retours et complexes détours", in H. Tétrel and G. Veysseyre (eds.), *L'Historia regum Britannie et les "Bruts" en Europe, Tome I, Traductions, adaptations, réappropriations (XIIe–XVIe siècle)* (Rencontres 106, Civilisation médiévale, 12), Paris, 2015, 299–303.

Legge, M.D., *Anglo-Norman Literature and its Background*, Oxford, 1963.

Legge, M.D., "Master Geoffrey Arthur", in K. Varty (ed.), *An Arthurian Tapestry: Essays in Memory of Lewis Thorpe*, Glasgow, 1981, 22–27.

Lehmann, C., "The End of Augustan Literature: Ovid's *Epistulae ex Ponto* 4", unpublished PhD thesis, University of Southern California, 2018.

Lejeune, R., and Stennon, J., "La legende arthurienne dans la sculpture de la cathedrale de Modène", *Cahiers de Civilisation Medievale* 6 (1963), 281–96.

Lerner, R.E., "Antichrists and Antichrist in Joachim of Fiore", *Speculum* 60:3 (1985), 553–70.

Le Saux, F., *A Companion to Wace*, Cambridge, 2005.

Le Saux, F., "La Grande Bretagne, patrie des sciences? La représentation des technologies scientifiques dans Geoffroy de Monmouth et Layamon", in H. Tétrel and G. Veysseyre (eds.), *L'Historia regum Britannie et les "Bruts" en Europe, Tome I, Traductions, adaptations, réappropriations (XIIᵉ–XVIᵉ siècle)* (Rencontres 106, Civilisation médiévale, 12), Paris, 2015, 157–75.

Le Saux, F., "Wace as Hagiographer", in G.S. Burgess and J. Weiss (eds.), *Maistre Wace. A Celebration: Proceedings of the International Colloquium held in Jersey, 10–12 September 2004*, St Helier, 2006, 139–48.

Le Saux, F.H.M., *Layamon's Brut. The Poem and its Sources* (Arthurian Studies, 19), Cambridge, 1989.

Lindley Cintra, L.F., "O *Liber Regum* e outras fontes do *Livro de Linhagens* do Conde D. Pedro", *Boletim de Filologia*, 11 (1950), 224–51.

Lindley Cintra, L.F., "Uma tradução galego-portuguesa desconhecida do *Liber Regum*", *Bulletin Hispanique*, 52 (1950), 27–40.

Lloyd, D.M., "Madog ap Gwallter", in J.E. Lloyd, R.T. Jenkins, and W.L. Davies (eds.), *Y Bywgraffiadur Cymreig Hyd 1940* [Welsh biography up to 1940], London, 1953, 571–72.

Lloyd, J.E., "Geoffrey of Monmouth", *EHR* 57 (1942), 460–68.

Lloyd, J.E., *A History of Wales from the Earliest Times to the Edwardian Conquest*, 2 vols., 2nd ed., London, 1912; 3rd ed., 1939.

Lloyd, J.E., *The Welsh Chronicles*, The Sir John Rhys Memorial Lecture, British Academy, London, 1928, also printed in *Proceedings of the British Academy* 14 (1928), 369–91.

Lloyd-Morgan, C., "Blending and Rebottling Old Wines: the Birth and Burial of Arthur in Middle Welsh", in A. Harlos and N. Harlos (eds.), *Adapting Texts and Styles in a Celtic Context: Interdisciplinary Perspectives on Processes of Literary Transfer in the Middle Ages. Studies in Honour of Erich Poppe*, Münster, 2016, 155–75.

Lochrie, K., *Margery Kempe and Translations of the Flesh*, Philadelphia, 1991.

Lomperis, L., and Stanbury, S. (eds.), *Feminist Approaches to the Body in Medieval Literature*, Philadelphia, 1993.

Lomuto, S., "Public Medievalism and the Rigor of Anti-Racist Critique", *In the Middle*, 4 April 2019, <http://www.inthemedievalmiddle.com/2019/04/public-medievalism-and-rigor-of-anti.html> (accessed 26 May 2019).

Lomuto, S., "White Nationalism and the Ethics of Medieval Studies", *In the Middle*, 5 December 2016, <http://www.inthemedievalmiddle.com/2016/12/white-nationalism-and-ethics-of.html> (accessed 26 May 2019).

Loomis, R.S., *Arthurian Tradition and Chrétien de Troyes*, New York, 1949.

Lopez-Jantzen, N., "Between Empires: Race and Ethnicity in the Early Middle Ages", *Literature Compass* 16:9–10 (2019), 1–12.

Lot, F., *Nennius et l'Historia Brittonum*, Paris, 1934.

Loth, J., *L'Émigration bretonne en Armorique du Vᵉ au VIIᵉ siècle de notre ère*, Rennes, 1883.

Louis-Jensen, J., "Breta Sögur", in P. Pulsiano and K. Wolf et al. (eds.), *Medieval Scandinavia, An Encyclopedia*, New York, 1993, 57–58.

Lovecy, I., "*Historia Peredur ab Efrawg*", in R. Bromwich, A.O.H. Jarman, and B.F. Roberts (eds.), *The Arthur of the Welsh: The Arthurian Legend in Medieval Welsh Literature* (Arthurian Literature in the Middle Ages, 1), Cardiff, 1991, 171–82.

Lucía Megías, J.M., "The Surviving Peninsular Arthurian Witnesses: A Description and an Analysis", in D. Hook (ed.), *The Arthur of the Iberians: The Arthurian Legend in the Spanish and Portuguese Worlds* (Arthurian Literature in the Middle Ages, 8), Cardiff, 2015, 33–57.

Lynch, A., "'Peace is good after war': The Narrative Seasons of English Arthurian Tradition", in C. Saunders, F. Le Saux, and N. Thomas (eds.), *Writing War: Medieval Literary Responses to Warfare*, Cambridge, 2004, 127–46.

Mac Cana, P., *The Learned Tales of Medieval Ireland*, Dublin, 1980.

Mack, S., *Patterns of Time in Virgil*, Hamden, CT, 1978.

Madan, F., Craster, H.H.E., and Denholm-Young, N., *A Summary Catalogue of Western Manuscripts in the Bodleian Library at Oxford*, vol. 2, part 2, Oxford, 1937.

Maddox, D., and Sturm-Maddox, S., "*Erec et Enide*: The First Arthurian Romance", in N.J. Lacy and J.T. Grimbert (eds.), *A Companion to Chrétien de Troyes*, Cambridge, 2005, 103–19.

Magoun, Jr., F.P., "Les Légendes des matières de Rome, de France et de Bretagne dans le 'Pantheon' de Godefroi de Viterbe by Lucienne Meyer", *Speculum* 11:1 (1936), 144–46.

Malanca, A., "Le armi e le lettere. Galasso Da Correggio: Autore dell'Historia Anglie", *Italia Medioevale e Umanistica* 48 (2007), 1–57.

Malanca, A., "Le fonti della materia di Bretagna nell'opera di Galasso da Correggio", *Giornale Italiano di Filologia* 61 (2009), 271–98.

Marenbon, J., *Pagans and Philosophers: The Problem of Paganism from Augustine to Leibnitz*, Princeton and Oxford, 2015.

Marvin, J., "Albine and Isabelle: Regicidal Queens and the Historical Imagination of the Anglo-Norman Prose *Brut* Chronicles", *AL* 18 (2001), 143–83.

Marvin, J., "Arthur Authorized: The Prophecies of the Prose *Brut* Chronicle", *AL* 22 (2005), 84–99.

Marvin, J., *The Construction of Vernacular History in the Anglo-Norman Prose Brut: the Manuscript Culture of Late Medieval England*, York, 2017.

Matheson, L., *The Prose "Brut": The Development of a Middle English Chronicle* (Medieval & Renaissance Texts & Studies, 180), Tempe, 1998.

Mathey-Maille, L., "De la Vulgate à la *Variant Version* de l'*Historia regum Britannie*: Le *Roman de Brut* de Wace à l'épreuve du texte source", in H. Tétrel and G. Veysseyre (eds.), *L'Historia regum Britannie et les "Bruts" en Europe, Tome I, Traductions, adaptations, réappropriations (XIIe–XVIe siècle)* (Rencontres 106, Civilisation médiévale, 12), Paris, 2015, 129–39.

McRae, A., and West, J. (eds.), *Literature of the Stuart Successions: An Anthology*, Manchester, 2017.

Medievalists of Color collective, <medievalistsofcolor.com> (accessed 31 May 2018).

Meecham-Jones, S., "Introduction", in R. Kennedy and S. Meecham-Jones (eds.), *Authority and Subjugation in Writing of Medieval Wales*, New York, 2008, 1–11.

Meecham-Jones, S., "Where Was Wales? The Erasure of Wales in Medieval English Culture", in R. Kennedy and S. Meecham-Jones (eds.), *Authority and Subjugation in Writing of Medieval Wales*, New York, 2008, 27–55.

Meehan, B., "Geoffrey of Monmouth, *Prophecies of Merlin*: New Manuscript Evidence", *BBCS* 28:1 (1978–80), 37–46.

Ménard, P., "Les Prophéties de Merlin et l'Italie au XIIIᵉ siècle", in K. Busby, B. Guidot, and L.E. Whalen (eds.), *"De sens rassis". Essays in Honor of Rupert T. Pickens*, Amsterdam and Atlanta, 2005, 431–44.

Merkle, S., "Telling the True Story of the Trojan War: The Eyewitness Account of Dictys of Crete", in J. Tatum (ed.), *The Search for the Ancient Novel*, Baltimore, 1994, 183–96.

Merkle, S., "The Truth and Nothing but the Truth: Dictys and Dares", in G.L. Schmeling (ed.), *The Novel in the Ancient World*, Leiden, 1996, 563–80.

Mews, C.J., "The Council of Sens 1141: Abelard, Bernard and the Fear of Social Upheaval", *Speculum* 79:2 (2002), 342–83.

Meyer, L., *Les légendes des Matières de Rome, de France et de Bretagne dans le "Pantheon" de Godefroi de Viterbe*, Paris, 1933.

Meyer, P., "De Quelques chroniques anglo-normandes qui ont porté le nom de *Brut*", *Bulletin de la SATF* 4 (1878), 104–45.

Miles, B., *Heroic Saga and Classical Epic in Medieval Ireland*, Woodbridge, 2001.

Mitsakis, K., "Palamedes", *Byzantinische Zeitschrift* 59 (1966), 5–7.

Miyashiro, A., "Our Deeper Past: Race, Settler Colonialism, and Medieval Heritage Politics", *Literature Compass* 16:9–10 (2019), 1–11.

Mommsen, T., *Chronica Minora saec. IV. V. VI. VII. Vol. 3* [Minor Chronicles of the 4th, 5th, 6th, 7th centuries, Vol. 3] (Monumenta Germaniae Historica, Auctores Antiquissimi, 13), Berlin, 1898.

Montoliu, M., "Sobre els elements èpics, principalment asturians, de la Crònica de Jaume I", in n.n. (ed.), *Homenaje ofrecido a Menéndez Pidal: miscelánea de estudios lingüísticos, literarios e históricos*, 3 vols., Madrid, 1924, vol. 1, 698–712.

Mora-Lebrun, F., *L'Énéide médiévale et la naissance du roman*, Paris, 1994.

Morgan, N., "Matthew Paris, St Albans, London, and the leaves of the 'Life of St Thomas Becket'", *Burlington Magazine* 130 (1988), 85–96.

Morrison, T., *Playing in the Dark: Whiteness and the Literary Imagination*, New York, 1992.

Mortimer, I., "The Great Magician", in id. (ed.), *The Fears of Henry IV: The Life of England's Self-Made King*, London, 2007, 226–43.

Nagy, J.F., "Arthur and the Irish", in H. Fulton (ed.) *A Companion to Arthurian Literature*, Oxford, 2009, 117–27.

Nederveen Pieterse, J., *Globalization and Culture: Global Mélange*, 2nd ed., Lanham, 2009.

Ní Mheallaigh, K., "The 'Phoenician Letters' of Dictys of Crete and Dionysius Scytobrachion", *The Cambridge Classical Journal* 58 (2012), 181–93.

Nicholson, E.W.B., "The Dynasty of Cunedag and the 'Harleian Genealogies'", *Y Cymmrodor* 21 (1908), 63–104.

Nicholson, H., "Following the Path of the Lionheart: The *De Ortu Walwanii* and the *Itinerarium Peregrinorum et Gesta Ricardi*", *Medium Ævum* 69:1 (2000), 21–33.

Nickel, H., "About Palug's Cat and the Mosaic of Otranto", *Arthurian Interpretations* 3:2 (1989), 96–105.

Nortier, G., "Les Bibliothèques médiévales des abbayes bénédictines de Normandie. IV. La bibliothèque de Saint-Evroul", *Revue Mabillon* 47 (1957), 219–44.

O'Brien, B., *Reversing Babel: Translation among the English during an Age of Conquests, c. 800 to c. 1200*, Lanham, MD and Newark, 2011.

O'Hara, J.J., *True Names. Vergil and the Alexandrian Tradition of Etymological Wordplay*, Ann Arbor, 1996.

O'Reilly, J., "The Art of Authority", in T. Charles-Edwards (ed.), *After Rome* (Short Oxford History of the British Isles), Oxford, 2003, 141–90.

Obbema, P.F.J., "The Rooklooster Register Evaluated", *Quaerendo* 7 (1977), 326–53.

Olson, K., "Gwendolyn and Estrildis: Invading Queens in British Historiography", *Medieval Feminist Forum* 44:1 (2008), 36–52.

Óskarsdóttir, S., "Universal History in Fourteenth-century Iceland, Studies in AM764 4to", unpublished doctoral dissertation, University College, London, 2000.

Otter, M., "Functions of Fiction in Historical Writing", in N. Partner (ed.), *Writing Medieval History*, London, 2005, 109–30.

Otter, M., *Inventiones: Fiction and Referentiality in Twelfth-Century English Historical Writing*, Chapel Hill, 1996.

Owen, A.P., "Cynddelw Brydydd Mawr a'i Grefft" [Cynddelw Brydydd Mawr and his craft], in M.E. Owen and B.F. Roberts (eds.), *Beirdd a Thywysogion: Barddoniaeth Llys yng Nghymru, Iwerddon a'r Alban* [Poets and princes: court poetry in Wales, Ireland, and Scotland], Cardiff, 1996, 143–65.

Owen, M.E., "Royal Propaganda: Stories from the Law-Texts", in T.M. Charles-Edwards, M.E. Owen, and P. Russell (eds.), *The Welsh King and his Court*, Cardiff, 2000, 224–54.

Owens, B.G., "Y Fersiynau Cymraeg o Dares Phrygius (Ystorya Dared): eu Tarddiad, eu Nodweddion a'u Cydberthynas" [The Welsh versions of Dares Phrygius (Ystorya Dared): their origin, their attributes, and their interrelationships], unpublished MA thesis, University of Wales, 1951.

The Oxford Latin Dictionary, ed. P.G.W. Clare, Oxford, 1982.

Pace, E., "Geoffrey of Monmouth's Sources for the Cador and Camblan Narratives", *Arthuriana* 24 (2014), 45–78.

Padel, O.J., *Arthur in Medieval Welsh Literature*, Cardiff, 2000.

Padel, O.J., "Geoffrey of Monmouth and Cornwall", *CMCS* 8 (1984), 1–28.

Padel, O.J., "Geoffrey of Monmouth and the Development of the Merlin Legend", *CMCS* 51 (2006), 37–65.

Padel, O.J., "Recent Work on the Origins of the Arthurian Legend: A Comment", *Arthuriana* 5:3 (1995), 103–14.

Pagan, H., "What is the Anglo-Norman Brut?" <https://www.univ-brest.fr/digitalAssets/36/36991_Heather-Pagan-com.pdf> (accessed 19 March 2018), 1–7.

Pagan, H., "When is a Brut no Longer a Brut?: The example of Cambridge, University Library, Dd. 10. 32", in H. Tétrel and G. Veysseyre (eds.), *L'Historia regum Britannie et les "Bruts" en Europe, Tome I, Traductions, adaptations, réappropriations (XIIᵉ–XVIᵉ siècle)* (Rencontres 106, Civilisation médiévale, 12), Paris, 2015, 179–92.

Page, W. (ed.), *The Victoria History of the County of Oxford: Volume II*, London, 1907.

Paris, G., "La Borderie, *L'Historia Britonum*", *Romania* 12 (1883), 367–76.

Parkes, M., *Pause and Effect: An Introduction to the History of Punctuation in the West*, Berkeley, 1993.

Parry, J.J., *The Vita Merlini* (University of Illinois Studies in Language and Literature, 10.3), Urbana, IL, 1925.

Parry, J.J., "The Welsh Texts of Geoffrey of Monmouth's *Historia*", *Speculum* 5:4 (1930), 424–31.

Parsons, D., *Martyrs and Memorials: Merthyr Place-Names and the Church in Early Wales*, Aberystwyth, 2013.

Partner, N.F., *Serious Entertainments: The Writing of History in Twelfth-Century England*, Chicago and London, 1977.

Pastore Stocchi, M., *Tradizione medievale e gusto umanistico nel "De montibus" del Boccaccio*, Florence, 1963.

Paton, L.A., "Merlin and Ganieda", *Modern Language Notes* 18:6 (1903), 163–69.

Patterson, L., *The World of the Troubadours*, Cambridge, 1993.

Patzuk-Russell, R., "The Legend of Pallas' Tomb and its Medieval Scandinavian Transmission", *JEGP* 118:1 (2019), 1–30.

Pearson, M.J. (ed.), "St Asaph: Bishops", *Fasti Ecclesiae Anglicanae 1066–1300: Volume 9, the Welsh Cathedrals (Bangor, Llandaff, St Asaph, St Davids)*, London, 2003, 33–36, British History Online, <http://www.british-history.ac.uk/fasti-ecclesiae/1066-1300/vol9/pp33-36> (accessed 6 May 2019).

Pellegrin, E., *La bibliothèque des Visconti et des Sforza ducs de Milan au XVᵉ siècle*, Paris, 1955.

Peyrafort-Huin, M., *La bibliothèque médiévale de l'Abbaye de Pontigny (XIIᵉ–XIXᵉ siècles)*, Paris, 2001.

Phillimore, E., "The *Annales Cambriæ* and the Old-Welsh Genealogies from *Harleian MS. 3859*", *Y Cymmrodor* 9 (1888), 141–83 (repr. in J. Morris (ed.), *Genealogies and Texts* (Arthurian Period Sources, 5), Chichester, 1995, 13–55).

Phillips, H., "Medieval Classical Romances: The Perils of Inheritance", in R. Field, P. Hardman, and M. Sweeney (eds.), *Christianity and Romance in Medieval England*, Cambridge, 2010, 13–25.

Pichel Gotérrez, R., "*Lean por este libro que o acharam mays complidamente ...*: del *Libro de Troya* alfonsí a la *Historia troyana* de Pedro I", *Troianalexandrina: Anuario sobre literatura medieval de materia clásica* 16 (2016), 55–180.

Pickens, R.T., Busby, K., and Williams, A.M.L., "Perceval and the Grail: The Continuations, Robert de Boron and *Perlesvaus*", in G.S. Burgess and K. Pratt (eds.), *The Arthur of the French. The Arthurian Legend in Medieval French and Occitan Literature* (Arthurian Literature in the Middle Ages, 4), Cardiff, 2006, 213–73.

Piggott, S., "The Sources of Geoffrey of Monmouth: I. The 'Pre-Roman' King-List", *Antiquity* 15 (1941), 269–86.

Piggott, S., "The Sources of Geoffrey of Monmouth: II. The Stonehenge Story", *Antiquity* 15 (1941), 305–19.

Pioletti, A., "Artù, Avalon, l'Etna", *Quaderni Medievali* 28 (1989), 6–35.

Plassmann, A., "Gildas and the Negative Image of the Cymry", *CMCS* 41 (2001), 1–15.

Podestà, G., "Roma nella Profezia (secoli XI–XIII)", in n.n. (ed.), *Roma antica nel Medioevo: mito, rappresentazioni, sopravvivenze nella 'Respublica Christiana' dei secoli IX–XIII, atti della quattordicesima Settimana internazionale di studio, Mendola, 24–28 agosto 1998*, Milan, 2001, 356–98.

Pohl, B., "*Abbas qui et scriptor*? The Handwriting of Robert of Torigni and his Scribal Activity as Abbot of Mont-Saint-Michel (1154–1186)", *Traditio* 69 (2014), 45–86.

Poole, R., "The Textual Tradition of Gunnlaugr Leifsson's *Merlínússpá*", in H. Tétrel and G. Veysseyre (eds.), *L'Historia regum Britannie et les Bruts en Europe, Tome II, Production, circulation et reception (XIIᵉ–XVIᵉ siècles)* (Rencontres 349, Civilisation médiévale, 32), Paris, 2018, 195–223.

Poppe, E., "*Imtheachta Aeniasa* and its Place in Medieval Irish Textual History", in R. O'Connor (ed.), *Classical Literature and Learning in Medieval Irish Narrative* (Studies in Celtic History, 34), Woodbridge, 2014, 25–39.

Porter, D., "The *Historia Meriadoci* and Magna Carta", *Neophilologus* 76:1 (1992), 136–46.

Press, A., "The Precocious Courtesy of Geoffrey Gaimar", in G.S. Burgess (ed.), *Court and Poet: Selected Proceedings of the Third Congress of the International Courtly Literature Society*, Liverpool, 1981, 267–76.

Pryce, H., "British or Welsh? National Identity in Twelfth-Century Wales", *EHR* 116 (2001), 775–801.

Pryce, H., "Yr Eglwys yn Oes yr Arglwydd Rhys" [The church in the age of the Lord Rhys], in N.A. Jones and H. Pryce (eds.), *Yr Arglwydd Rhys* [The Lord Rhys], Cardiff, 1996, 145–77.

Pryce, H., "Esgobaeth Bangor yn Oes y Tywysogion" [The diocese of Bangor in the age of the princes], in W.P. Griffith (ed.), *"Ysbryd Dealltwrus ac Enaid Anfarwol": Ysgrifau ar Hanes Crefydd yng Ngwynedd* ["Enlightened spirit and eternal soul": essays on the history of religion in Gwynedd], Bangor, 1999, 37–57.

Pryce, H., *J.E. Lloyd and the Creation of Welsh History: Renewing a Nation's Past*, Aberystwyth, 2011.

Pryce, H., "J.E. Lloyd's *History of Wales* (1911)", in N. Evans and H. Pryce (eds.), *Writing A Small Nation's Past: Wales in Comparative Perspective, 1850–1950*, Farnham, 2013, 49–64.

Pujol, J.M., *La memòria literària de Joanot Martorell: Models i scriptura en el 'Tirant lo Blanc'*, Barcelona, 2002.

Putter, A., "Arthurian Literature and the Rhetoric of Effeminacy", in F. Wolfzettel (ed.), *Arthurian Romance and Gender: Masculin/feminine dans le roman arthurien medieval*, Amsterdam and Atlanta, 1995, 34–49.

Quaritch, Bernard (Firm), *Catalogue 1147: Bookhands of the Middle Ages. Part V: Medieval Manuscript Leaves*, London, 1991.

Rajabzadeh, S., "The Depoliticized Saracen and Muslim", *Literature Compass* 16:9–10 (2019), 1–8.

Rajsic, J., "Looking for Arthur in Short Histories and Genealogies of England's Kings", *Review of English Studies* 68:285 (2017), 448–70.

Rambaran-Olm, M., "Misnaming the Medieval: Rejecting 'Anglo-Saxon' Studies", *History Workshop*, 4 November 2019 <http://www.historyworkshop.org.uk/misnaming-the-medieval-rejecting-anglo-saxon-studies/> (accessed 13 February 2020).

Ramey, L., *Black Legacies: Race and the European Middle Ages*, Gainesville, FL, 2014.

Ray, R., "Historiography", in F.A.C. Mantello and A.G. Rigg (eds.), *Medieval Latin: An Introduction and Bibliographical Guide*, Washington, 1996, 639–49.

Ray, R.D., "Medieval Historiography Through the Twelfth Century", *Viator* 5 (1974), 33–59.

Reeve, M.D., "The Transmission of the *Historia regum Britanniae*", *Journal of Medieval Latin* 1 (1991), 73–117.

Reeves, M., *The Influence of Prophecy in the Later Middle Ages. A Study in Joachimism*, Oxford, 1969.

Reeves, M., *The Prophetic Sense of History in Medieval and Renaissance Europe*, Aldershot, 1999.

Reiss, E., "The Welsh Versions of Geoffrey of Monmouth's *Historia*", *WHR* 4 (1968/9), 97–127.

Richter, M., *Giraldus Cambrensis: The Growth of the Welsh Nation*, Aberystwyth, 1972.

Rigg, A.G., *A History of Anglo-Latin Literature 1066–1422*, Cambridge, 1992.

Roberts, B., "*Brut y Brenhinedd* ms. National Library of Wales, Llanstephan 1 version", in H. Tétrel and G. Veysseyre (eds.), *L'Historia regum Britannie et les "Bruts" en Europe, Tome I, Traductions, adaptations, réappropriations (XIIe–XVIe siècle)* (Rencontres 106, Civilisation médiévale, 12), Paris, 2015, 71–80.

Roberts, B., *Brut Tysilio*, Swansea, 1980.

Roberts, B., "Copiau Cymraeg o *Prophetiae Merlini*" [Welsh copies of *Prophetiae Merlini*], *National Library of Wales Journal* 20 (1977), 14–39.

Roberts, B., "Esboniad Cymraeg ar broffwydoliaeth Myrddin" [A Welsh commentary on the prophecy of Merlin], *BBCS* 21 (1964–66), 277–300.

Roberts, B., "Fersiwn Dingestow o Brut y Brenhinedd" [The Dingestow version of *Brut y Brenhinedd*], *BBCS* 27 (1976–78), 331–61.

Roberts, B.F., "Astudiaeth Destunol o'r Tri Cyfieithiad Cymraeg Cynharaf o *Historia regum Britanniae* Sieffre o Fynwy, Yngyd ag 'Argraffiad' Beirniadol o Destun Peniarth 44" [A textual study of the three earliest Welsh translations of Geoffrey of Monmouth's *Historia regum Britanniae*, together with a critical edition of the Peniarth 44 text], unpublished PhD thesis, University of Wales, 1969.

Roberts, B.F., "Geoffrey of Monmouth and Welsh Historical Tradition", *Nottingham Medieval Studies* 20 (1976), 29–40.

Roberts, B.F., "Geoffrey of Monmouth, *Historia regum Britanniae*, and *Brut y Brenhinedd*", in R. Bromwich, A.O.H. Jarman, and B.F. Roberts (eds.), *The Arthur of the Welsh: The Arthurian Legend in Medieval Welsh Literature* (Arthurian Literature in the Middle Ages, 1), Cardiff, 1991, 97–116.

Roberts, B.F., "Glosau Cymraeg *Historia Regum Britanniae* Dulyn, Coleg y Drindod, llsgr. 515 (E.5.12)" [Welsh glosses on the *Historia Regum Britanniae* in Dublin, Trinity College, manuscript 515 (E.5.12)], *Studia Celtica* 37 (2003), 75–80.

Roberts, B.F., "Un o Lawysgrifau Hopcyn ap Tomas o Ynys Dawe" [One of the manuscripts of Hopcyn ap Tomas of Ynys Dawe], *BBCS* 22 (1966–68), 223–28.

Roberts, B.F., "The Red Book of Hergest Version of *Brut y Brenhinedd*", *Studia Celtica* 12/13 (1977–78), 147–86.

Roberts, B.F., "Sylwadau ar Sieffre o Fynwy a'r *Historia Regum Britanniae*" [Remarks on Geoffrey of Monmouth and the *Historia Regum Britanniae*], *Llên Cymru* 12 (1972–73), 127–45.

Roberts, B.F., "Testunau Hanes Cymraeg Canol" [Middle Welsh historical texts], in G. Bowen (ed.), *Y Traddodiad Rhyddiaith yn yr Oesau Canol* [The prose tradition in the Middle Ages], Llandysul, 1974, 274–302.

Roberts, B.F., "The Treatment of Personal Names in the Early Welsh Versions of *Historia Regum Britanniae*", *BBCS* 25 (1973), 274–89.

Roberts, B.F., "Ymagweddau at *Brut y Brenhinedd* hyd 1890" [Attitudes toward *Brut y Brenhinedd* until 1890], *BBCS* 24 (1971), 122–38.

Roberts, B.F., "*Ystoriaeu Brenhinedd Ynys Brydeyn*: a fourteenth-century Welsh Brut", in J.F. Eska (ed.), *Narrative in Celtic Tradition: Essays in Honor of Edgar M. Slotkin* (CSANA Yearbook, 8–9), Hamilton, NY, 2011, 215–27.

Robertson, E., "Medieval Feminism in Middle English Studies: A Retrospective", *Tulsa Studies in Women's Literature* 26:1 (2007), 67–79.

Robertson, K., "Geoffrey of Monmouth and the Translation of Insular Historiography", *Arthuriana* 8:4 (1998), 42–57.

The Rooklooster Register Unveiled, Cartusiana and Österreichische Nationalbibliothek, 2009–13, <http://rrkl.cartusiana.org/?q=node/7> (accessed 31 May 2018).

Rouse, M., and Rouse, R., "The Book Trade at the University of Paris, ca. 1250–ca. 1350", in L. Bataillon, B. Guyot, and R. Rouse (eds.), *La Production du livre universitaire au moyen âge*, Paris, 1988, 41–114.

Rouse, M., and Rouse, R., *Manuscripts and Their Makers: Commercial Book Producers in Medieval Paris, 1200–1500*, 2 vols., Turnhout, 2000.

Roussineau, G., "Jehan Wauquelin et l'auteur de *Perceforest* traducteurs de l'*Historia regum Britannie* de Geoffroy de Monmouth", in M.-C. de Crécy (ed.), with the collaboration of G. Parussa and S. Hériché Pradeau, *Jean Wauquelin de Mons à la cour de Bourgogne* (Burgundica, XI), Turnhout, 2006, 5–23.

Rowland, J., *Early Welsh Saga Poetry: A Study and Edition of the Englynion*, Cambridge, 1990.

Russell, P., *Celtic Word Formation: The Velar Suffixes*, Dublin, 1990.

Russell, P., "'Go and Look in the Latin Books': Latin and the Vernacular in Medieval Wales", in R. Ashdowne and C. White (eds.), *Latin in Medieval Britain* (Proceedings of the British Academy, 206), London, 2017, 213–46.

Russell, P., "*Priuilegium Sancti Teliaui* and *Breint Teilo*", *Studia Celtica* 50 (2016), 41–68.

Russell, P., *Reading Ovid in Medieval Wales*, Columbus, 2017.

Russell, P., *Vita Griffini Filii Conani. The Medieval Latin Life of Gruffudd ap Cynan*, Cardiff, 2005.

Said, E.W., *Orientalism*, London, 2003.

Salamon, A., "Sébastien Mamerot, traducteur de l'*Historia regum Britannie*", in H. Tétrel and G. Veysseyre (eds.), *L'Historia regum Britannie et les "Bruts" en Europe, Tome I, Traductions, adaptations, réappropriations (XIIe–XVIe siècle)* (Rencontres 106, Civilisation médiévale, 12), Paris, 2015, 211–30.

Salter, H.E., "Geoffrey of Monmouth and Oxford", *EHR* 34 (1919), 382–85.

Samples, S., "Guinevere: A Re-Appraisal", in L.J. Walters (ed.), *Lancelot and Guinevere: A Casebook* (Arthurian Characters and Themes, 4), New York, 1996, 219–28.

Scherb, V.I., "Assimilating Giants: the Appropriation of Gog and Magog in Medieval and Early Modern England", *JMEMS* 32 (2002), 59–84.

Schichtman, M.B., "Gawain in Wace and Layamon: A Case of Metahistorical Evolution", in L.A. Finke and M.B. Schichtman (eds.), *Medieval Texts and Contemporary Readers*, Ithaca, NY and London, 1987, 103–19.

Schlauch, M., "Geoffrey of Monmouth and Early Polish Historiography: A Supplement", *Speculum* 44 (1969), 258–63.

Scott, J., *The Early History of Glastonbury: An Edition, Translation and Study of William of Malmesbury's De Antiquitate Glastonie Ecclesie*, Woodbridge, 1981.

Serrano y Sanz, M., *"Cronicón Villarense (Liber Regum).* Primeros años del siglo XIII. La obra histórica más antigua en idioma español", *Boletín de la Real Academia Española*, 6 (1919), 192–220 and 8 (1921), 367–82.

Settis Frugoni, C., "Per una lettura del mosaico pavimentale della cattedrale di Otranto", *Bullettino dell'Istituto Storico Italiano per il Medio Evo* 80 (1968), 213–56.

Shercliff, R., "Arthur in *Trioedd Ynys Prydain*", in C. Lloyd-Morgan and E. Poppe (eds.), *Arthur in the Celtic Languages: The Arthurian Legend in Celtic Literatures and Traditions* (Arthurian Literature in the Middle Ages, 9), Cardiff, 2019, 173–86.

Short, I., "Gaimar's Epilogue and Geoffrey of Monmouth's *Liber vetustissimus*", *Speculum* 69:2 (1994), 323–43.

Short, I., "Patrons and Polyglots: French Literature in 12th-Century England", *Anglo-Norman Studies* 14 (1992), 229–49.

Short, I., "Un *Roman de Brut* anglo-normand inédit", *Romania* 126 (2008), 273–95.

Short, I., "What was Gaimar's *Estoire des Bretuns*?" *Cultura Neolatina* 71:1 (2011), 143–45.

Shwartz, S.M., "The Founding and Self-Betrayal of Britain: An Augustinian Approach to Geoffrey of Monmouth's *Historia Regum Britanniae*", *Medievalia et Humanistica* 10 (1981), 33–58.

Sidhu, N.N., "Love in a Cold Climate: The Future of Feminism and Gender Studies in Middle English Scholarship", *Literature Compass* 6:4 (2009), 864–85.

Sims-Williams, P., "The Early Welsh Arthurian Poems", in R. Bromwich, A.O.H. Jarman, and B.F. Roberts (eds.), *The Arthur of the Welsh: The Arthurian Legend in Medieval Welsh Literature* (Arthurian Literature in the Middle Ages, 1), Cardiff, 1991, 33–61.

Sims-Williams, P., "The Emergence of Old Welsh, Cornish and Breton Orthography, 600–800: the Evidence of Archaic Old Welsh", *BBCS* 38 (1991), 20–86.

Sims-Williams, P., "Some Functions of Origin Stories in Early Medieval Wales", in T. Nyberg (ed.), *History and Heroic Tale: a Symposium*, Odense, 1985, 97–131.

Sims-Williams, P., *Rhai Addasiadau Cymraeg Canol o Sieffre o Fynwy* [Some Middle Welsh adaptations of Geoffrey of Monmouth], Aberystwyth, 2011.

Sims-Williams, P., "The Welsh Versions of Geoffrey of Monmouth's 'History of the Kings of Britain'", in A. Harlos and N. Harlos (eds.), *Adapting Texts and Styles in a Celtic Context: Interdisciplinary Perspectives on Processes of Literary Transfer in the Middle Ages. Studies in Honour of Erich Poppe*, Münster, 2016, 53–74.

Smith, D.M., "Alexander (*d.* 1148)", *Oxford Dictionary of National Biography*, Oxford University Press, 2004, <http://www.oxforddnb.com/view/article/324> (accessed 13 March 2017).

Smith, J. Beverley, "The 'Cronica de Wallia' and the Dynasty of Dinefwr: a Textual and Historical Study", *BBCS* 20 (1962–64), 261–82.

Smith, J. Beverley, *Llywelyn ap Gruffudd, Prince of Wales*, Cardiff, 1998.

Smith, J. Beverley, *Yr Ymwybod â Hanes yng Nghymru yn yr Oesoedd Canol: Darlith Agoriadol/The Sense of History in Medieval Wales: an Inaugural Lecture*, Aberystwyth, 1989.

Smith, J. Byron, "Feasting on the Past: Madog of Edeirnion's Version of the *Historia Regum Britanniae*", unpublished paper delivered at the Celtic Studies Association of North America annual meeting, St Francis Xavier University, Antigonish, Nova Scotia, 5 May 2016.

Smith, J. Byron, *Walter Map and the Matter of Britain*, Philadelphia, 2017.

Smith, T.R., "National Identity, Propaganda, and the Ethics of War in English Historical Literature, *c.* 1327–77", unpublished PhD thesis, University of Leeds, 2018.

Soriano Robles, L., "The *Matière de Bretagne* in the Corona de Aragón", in D. Hook (ed.), *The Arthur of the Iberians: The Arthurian Legends in the Spanish and Portuguese Worlds* (Arthurian Literature in the Middle Ages, 8), Cardiff, 2015, 165–86.

Southern, R.W., "Aspects of the European Tradition of Historical Writing, 1: The Classical Tradition from Einhard to Geoffrey of Monmouth", *Transactions of the Royal Historical Society*, fifth series, 20 (1970), 173–96 (repr. in R.J. Bartlett (ed.), *History and Historians: Selected Papers of R.W. Southern*, Oxford, 2004, 11–29).

Southern, R.W., "Aspects of the European Tradition of Historical Writing, 3: History as Prophecy", *Transactions of the Royal Historical Society*, fifth series, 22 (1972), 159–80 (repr. in R.J. Bartlett (ed.), *History and Historians: Selected Papers of R.W. Southern*, Oxford, 2004, 48–65).

Southern, R.W., "Aspects of the European Tradition of Historical Writing, 4: The Sense of the Past", *Transactions of the Royal Historical Society*, fifth series, 23 (1973), 243–63 (repr. in R.J. Bartlett (ed.), *History and Historians: Selected Papers of R.W. Southern*, Oxford, 2004, 66–86).

Southern, R.W., *Medieval Humanism and Other Studies*, Oxford, 1970.

Sønnesyn, S.O., *William of Malmesbury and the Ethics of History*, Woodbridge, 2012.

Spence, J., *Reimagining History in Anglo-Norman Prose Chronicles*, York, 2013.

Spetia, L., *Li conte de Bretagne sont si vain et plaisant. Studi sull'Yvain e sul Jaufre*, Soveria Mannelli, 2012.

Spivak, G.C., "Can the Subaltern Speak?" in C. Nelson and L. Grossberg (eds.), *Marxism and the Interpretation of Culture*, London, 1988, 271–316.

Stacey, R.C., *Law and the Imagination in Medieval Wales*, Philadelphia, 2018.

Stancliffe, C., "Where was Oswald killed?" in C. Stancliffe and E. Cambridge (eds.), *Oswald: Northumbrian King to European Saint*, Stamford, 1995, 84–96.

Staunton, M., "Did the Purpose of History Change in England in the Twelfth Century?" in L. Cleaver and A. Worm, *Writing History in the Anglo-Norman World. Manuscripts, Makers, and Readers, c.1066–c.1250*, Woodbridge, 2018, 7–28.

Stein, R.M., *Reality Fictions: Romance, History, and Governmental Authority, 1025–1180*, Notre Dame, 2006.

Stephens, T., *The Literature of the Kymry: being a critical essay on the history of the language and literature of Wales during the twelfth and two succeeding centuries*, Llandovery, 1849.

Stephens, W., *Giants in Those Days: Folklore, Ancient History, and Nationalism*, Lincoln, NE, 1989.

Stephenson, D., *Medieval Powys: Kingdom, Principality and Lordships, 1132–1293*, Woodbridge, 2016.

Steppich, C.J., "Geoffrey's 'Historia Regum Britanniae' and Wace's 'Brut': Secondary Sources for Hartmann's 'Erec'?" *Monatshefte* 94 (2002), 165–88.

Stirnemann, P., "Les bibliothèques princières et privées aux XIIe et XIIIe siècles", in A. Vernet (ed.), *Histoire des bibliothèques françaises, Tome 1. Les bibliothèques médiévales du VIe à 1530*, [Paris], 1989, 173–91.

Stirnemann, P., "Fils de la vierge. L'initiale à filigranes parisiennes: 1140–1340", *Revue de l'Art* 90 (1991), 58–73.

Stirnemann, P., "Où ont été fabriqués les livres de la glose ordinaire dans la première moitié du xiie siècle?" in F. Gasparri (ed.), *Le xiie siècle: mutations et renouveau 1120–1150*, Paris, 1994, 257–85.

Stirnemann, P., *Quelques bibliothèques princières et la production hors scriptorium au XIIe siècle*, Paris, 1984.

Stock, B., *The Implications of Literacy: Written Language and Models of Interpretation in the Eleventh and Twelfth Centuries*, Princeton, 1983.

Stones, A., "The Egerton *Brut* and its Illustrations", in G.S. Burgess and J. Weiss (eds.), *Maistre Wace: A Celebration: Proceedings of the International Colloquium held in Jersey, 10–12 September 2004*, St Helier, 2006, 167–76.

Stones, A., "Secular Manuscript Illumination in France", in C. Kleinhenz (ed.), *Medieval Manuscripts and Textual Criticism*, Chapel Hill, 1976, 83–102.

Strickland, D.H., *Saracens, Demons, Jews: Making Monsters in Medieval Art*, Princeton, 2003.

Stubbs, W., "Preface", in id. (ed.), *Willelmi Malmesbiriensis monachi De gestis regum Anglorum libri quinque*, 2 vols., London, 1887–89, vol. 1, ix–cxlvii.

Summerfield, T., *The Matter of Kings' Lives: Design of Past and Present in the Early Fourteenth-Century Verse Chronicles by Pierre de Langtoft and Robert Mannyng*, Amsterdam and Atlanta, 1998.

Sutton, A.F., and Visser-Fuchs, L., "The Dark Dragon of the Normans: A Creation of Geoffrey of Monmouth, Stephen of Rouen, and Merlin Silvester", *Quondam et Futurus: A Journal of Arthurian Interpretations* 2:2 (1992), 1–19.

Tahkokallio, J., *The Anglo-Norman Historical Canon: Publishing and Manuscript Culture* (Cambridge Elements in Publishing and Book Culture), Cambridge, 2019.

Tahkokallio, J., "Fables of King Arthur. Ailred of Rievaulx and Secular Pastimes", *Mirator* 9:1 (2008), 19–35.

Tahkokallio, J., "Monks, Clerks and King Arthur: Reading Geoffrey of Monmouth in the Twelfth and Thirteenth Centuries", unpublished PhD dissertation, University of Helsinki, 2013.

Tahkokallio, J., "Update to the List of Manuscripts of Geoffrey of Monmouth's *Historia regum Britanniae*", *AL* 32 (2015), 187–203.

Tanner, J., "Race and Representation in Ancient Art: Black Athena and After", in D. Bindman and H.L. Gates, Jr. (eds.), *The Image of the Black in Western Art*, new ed., Cambridge, MA, 2010, 1–40.

Tatlock, J.S.P., "Caradoc of Llancarfan", *Speculum* 13:2 (1938), 139–52.

Tatlock, J.S.P., "The Dates of the Arthurian Saints' Legends", *Speculum* 14:3 (1939), 345–65.

Tatlock, J.S.P., "The English Journey of the Laon Canons", *Speculum* 8:4 (1933), 454–65.

Tatlock, J.S.P., "Geoffrey of Monmouth's Motives for Writing His *Historia*", *Proceedings of the American Philosophical Society* 79:4 (1938), 695–703.

Tatlock, J.S.P., *The Legendary History of Britain: Geoffrey of Monmouth's Historia regum Britanniae and Its Early Vernacular Versions*, Berkeley, 1950.

Tausendfreund, H., *Vergil und Gottfried von Monmouth*, Halle, 1913.

Taylor, A.J., *Welsh Castles of Edward I*, Bristol, 1986.

Taylor, J.H.M., "Introduction", in ead. (ed.), *Le Roman de Perceforest, première partie* (Textes littéraires français, 279), Geneva, 1979, 11–58.

Taylor, R., *The Political Prophecy in England*, New York, 1911.

Terrell, K.H., "Subversive Histories: Strategies of Identity in Scottish Historiography", in J.J. Cohen (ed.), *Cultural Diversity in the British Middle Ages: Archipelago, Island, England*, New York, 2008, 153–72.

Tétrel, H., "Trojan Origins and the Use of the Æneid and Related Sources in the Old Icelandic Brut", *JEGP* 109:4 (2010), 490–514.

Tétrel, H. and Veysseyre, G., "Introduction", in ead. (eds.), *L'Historia regum Britannie et les "Bruts" en Europe, Tome I, Traductions, adaptations, réappropriations (XIIᵉ–XVIᵉ siècle)* (Rencontres 106, Civilisation médiévale, 12), Paris, 2015, 9–37.

Thacker, A.T., "Bede, the Britons and the Book of Samuel", in S. Baxter et al. (eds.), *Early Medieval Studies in Memory of Patrick Wormald*, Ashgate, 2009, 129–47.

Thomas, N., "The Celtic Wildman Tradition and Geoffrey of Monmouth's *Vita Merlini*", *Arthuriana* 10:1 (2000), 27–42.

Thomson, R.M., "William of Malmesbury: Life and Works", in id. in collaboration with M. Winterbottom, *William of Malmesbury: Gesta Regum Anglorum, The History of the English Kings, Volume II. General Introduction and Commentary*, Oxford, 1999, xxxv–xlv.

Thomson, R.M., *William of Malmesbury*, Woodbridge, 2003.

Thomson, R.M., and Winterbottom, M., "Introduction", in William of Malmesbury, *The History of the English Kings*, ed. and trans. R.A.B. Mynors, completed by R.M. Thomson and M. Winterbottom, *William of Malmesbury: Gesta Regum Anglorum, The History of the English Kings*, 2 vols., Oxford, 1998–99, vol. 1, xiii–xxviii.

Thornton, D., "The Genealogy of Gruffudd ap Cynan", in K.L. Maund (ed.), *Gruffudd ap Cynan: A Collaborative Biography*, Woodbridge, 1996, 79–108.

Thornton, D.E., "Glastonbury and the Glastening", in L. Abrams and J.P. Carley (eds.), *The Archaeology and History of Glastonbury Abbey: Essays in Honour of the Ninetieth Birthday of C.A. Ralegh Radford*, Woodbridge, 1991, 191–203.

Thornton, D.E., "A Neglected Genealogy of Llywelyn ap Gruffudd", *CMCS* 23 (1992), 9–23.

Thorpe, L., "The last years of Geoffrey of Monmouth", in n.n. (ed.), *Mélanges de langue et littérature françaises du moyen âge offerts à Pierre Jonin*, Aix-en-Provence, 1979, 663–72.

Thorpe, L., "Le Mont Saint-Michel et Geoffroi de Monmouth", in R. Foreville (ed.), *Vie montoise et rayonnement intellectuel du Mont Saint-Michel* (Millénaire monastique du Mont Saint-Michel, 2), Paris, 1967, 377–82.

Tiller, K., *Laȝamon's Brut and the Anglo-Norman Vision of History*, Cardiff, 2007.

Tolhurst, F., *Geoffrey of Monmouth and the Feminist Origins of the Arthurian Legend*, New York, 2012.

Tolhurst, F., *Geoffrey of Monmouth and the Translation of Female Kingship*, New York, 2013.

Tolstoy, N., "Geoffrey of Monmouth and the Merlin Legend", *AL* 25 (2008), 1–42.

Tolstoy, N., "When and Where was *Armes Prydein* Composed?" *Studia Celtica* 42 (2008), 145–49.

Tournoy, G., "A First Glance at the Latin Arthur in the Low Countries", in W. Van Hoecke, G. Tournoy, and W. Verbeke (eds.), *Arturus Rex: Acta Conventus Lovaniensis 1987* (Mediaevalia Lovaniensia, Series 1, Studia 17), Leuven, 1991, 215–21.

Tournoy, G., "De Latijnse Artur in de Nederlanden", in W. Verbeke, J. Janssens, and M. Smeyers (eds.), *Arturus Rex: Koning Artur en de Nederlanden: la matière de Bretagne et les anciens Pays-Bas* (Mediaevalia Lovaniensia, Series 1, Studia 16), Leuven, 1987, 147–88.

Trachsler, R., *Clôtures du cycle arthurien: Étude et textes* (Publications Romanes et Françaises, 215), Geneva, 1996.

Trachsler, R., "L'*Historia regum Britannie* au XVe siècle: Les manuscrits New York, Public Library, Spencer 41 et Paris, Bibliothèque de l'Arsenal, 5078", in H. Tétrel and G. Veysseyre (eds.), *L'Historia regum Britannie et les "Bruts" en Europe, Tome I, Traductions, adaptations, réappropriations (XIIe–XVIe siècle)* (Rencontres 106, Civilisation médiévale, 12), Paris, 2015, 193–209.

Trachsler, R., "Du *libellus Merlini* au *livret Merlin*: Les traductions françaises des *Prophetiae Merlini* dans leurs manuscrits", in C. Croizy-Naquet, M. Szkilnik, and L. Harf-Lancner (eds.), *Les Manuscrits médiévaux témoins de lectures*, Paris, 2015, 67–87.

Trachsler, R., "Le *Perceforest*", in R. Trachsler (ed.), *Disjointures-Conjointures: Étude sur l'interférence des matières narratives dans la littératures française du Moyen Âge*, Tübingen and Basel, 2000, 239–81.

Trachsler, R., "Des *Prophetiae Merlini* aux *Prophecies Merlin* ou comment traduire les vaticinations de Merlin", in C. Galderisi and G. Salmon (eds.), *Actes du colloque "Translatio" médiévale, Mulhouse, 11–12 mai 2000* (Perspectives médiévales, supplément au numéro 26), Paris, 2000, 105–24.

Trachsler, R., "*Vaticinium ex eventu*, ou comment prédire le passé: observations sur les prophéties de Merlin", *Francofonia* 45 (2003), 91–108.

Tudor, V., "Reginald's *Life of Oswald*", in C. Stancliffe and E. Cambridge (eds.), *Oswald: Northumbrian King to European Saint*, Stamford, CT, 1995, 178–94.

Tyson, D., "Handlist of Manuscripts Containing the French Prose *Brut* Chronicle", *Scriptorium* 48 (1994), 333–44.

Van Hamel, A.G., "The Old Norse Version of the *Historia Regum Britanniae* and the Text of Geoffrey of Monmouth", *Études celtiques* 1 [1936], 197–247.

van Houts, E., "Historical Writing", in C. Harper-Bill and E. van Houts (eds.), *A Companion to the Anglo-Norman World*, Woodbridge, 2003, 103–22.

van Houts, E., "Latin and French as Languages of the Past in Normandy During the Reign of Henry II: Robert of Torigni, Stephen of Rouen, and Wace", in R. Kennedy and S. Meecham-Jones (eds.), *Writers of the Reign of Henry II: Twelve Essays*, New York, 2006, 53–77.

Vanlandingham, M., *Transforming the State: King, Court and Political Culture in the Realms of Aragon (1213–1387)*, Leiden, 2002.

Veysseyre, G., "Geoffroy de Monmouth, *Historia regum Britanniae*, 1135–1139", in C. Galderisi et al. (eds.), *Translations médiévales, Cinq siècles de traductions en français au Moyen Âge (XIe–XVe siècles): Étude et Répertoire*, 2 vols. in 3 [I; II.1 and 2], Turnhout, 2011, vol. II.1, no. 237, 459–60.

Veysseyre, G., "L'*Historia regum Britannie* ou l'enfance de Perceforest", in D. Hüe and C. Ferlampin-Acher (eds.), *Enfances arthuriennes: Actes du 2e Colloque arthurien de Rennes, 6–7 mars 2003*, Orleans, 2006, 99–126.

Veysseyre, G., "'Mettre en roman' les prophéties de Merlin. Voies et détours de l'interprétation dans trois traductions de l'*Historia regum Britannie*", in R. Trachsler (ed.), with the collaboration of J. Abed and D. Expert, *Moult obscures paroles: Études sur la prophétie médiévale*, Paris, 2007, 107–66.

Veysseyre, G., and Wille, C., "Les commentaires latins et français aux *Prophetie Merlini* de Geoffroy de Monmouth", *Médiévales* 55 (2008), 93–114.

Vielhauer-Pfeiffer, I., "Merlins Schwester: Betrachtungen zu einem keltischen Sagenmotiv", *Inklings: Jahrbuch für Literatur und Ästhetik* 8 (1990), 161–79.

Wade-Evans, A.W., "The Brychan Documents", *Y Cymmrodor* 19 (1906), 18–48.

Walker, D., "Nicholas ap Gwrgan (d. 1183), bishop of Llandaff", *Oxford Dictionary of National Biography*, Oxford University Press, 2014, <http://www.oxforddnb.com/view/article/20086> (accessed 26 June 2018).

Walters, L.J., "Introduction", in ead. (ed.), *Lancelot and Guinevere: A Casebook* (Arthurian Characters and Themes, 4), New York, 1996, xiii–lxxx.

Ward, E.J., "Verax historicus Beda: William of Malmesbury, Bede and Historia", in R.M. Thomson, E. Dolmans, and E.A. Winkler (eds.), *Discovering William of Malmesbury*, Woodbridge, 2017, 175–87.

Warren, M.R., *History on the Edge: Excalibur and the Borders of Britain, 1100–1300* (Medieval Cultures, 22), Minneapolis, 2000.

Warren, M.R., "Roger of Howden Strikes Back: Investing Arthur of Brittany with the Anglo-Norman Future", *Anglo-Norman Studies* 21 (1998), 261–72.

Waswo, R., "Our Ancestors, The Trojans: Inventing Cultural Identity in the Middle Ages", *Exemplaria* 7:2 (1995), 269–90.

Watkins, P.A., "The Problem of Pendar: a Lost Abbey in Medieval Senghenydd and the Transformation of the Church in South Wales", unpublished MPhil thesis, University of Wales, Lampeter, 2015, <http://repository.uwtsd.ac.uk/647/1/Paul%20Anthony%20Watkins%20MPhil%20FINAL%20Thesis%20%281%29.pdf> (accessed 25 September 2017).

Watson, A., *Descriptive Catalogue of the Medieval Manuscripts of All Souls College, Oxford*, Oxford, 1997.

Weber, L.J., "The Historical Importance of Godfrey of Viterbo", *Viator* 25:2 (1994), 153–95.

Weldon, J., "Fair Unknown", in S. Echard and R. Rouse (eds.), *The Encyclopedia of Medieval Literature in Britain*, 4 vols., Chichester, 2017, vol. 2, 783–87.

Werner, W., *Die mittelalterlichen nichtliturgischen Handschriften des Zisterzienserklosters Salem*, Wiesbaden, 2000.

West, G.D., "L'uevre Salomon", *Modern Language Review* 49 (1954), 176–82.

Wheatley, A., "Caernarfon Castle and its Mythology", in D.M. Williams and J.R. Kenyon (eds.), *The Impact of the Edwardian Castles in Wales: the Proceedings of a Conference Held at Bangor University, 7–9 September 2007*, Oxford, 2010, 129–39.

Wheeler, G., "Kingship and the Transmission of Power in Geffrei Gaimar's *Estoire des Engleis*", unpublished PhD thesis, University of Sheffield, 2017.

Whitaker, C., "Black Metaphors in the *King of Tars*", *JEGP* 112:2 (2013), 169–93.

Whitaker, C., "Race-ing the dragon: the Middle Ages, Race and Trippin' into the Future", *postmedieval* 6:1 (2015), 3–11.

Wilhelm, F., "Antike und Mittelalter. Studien zur Literaturgeschichte. I. Ueber fabulistische quellenangaben", *Beiträge zur Geschichte der deutschen Sprache und Literatur* 33 (1908), 286–339.

Williams, D.H., "Fasti Cistercienses Cambrenses", *BBCS* 24 (1971), 181–229.

Williams, D.H., *The Welsh Cistercians: written to commemorate the centenary of the death of Stephen William Williams (1837–1899)* (*The father of Cistercian archaeology in Wales*), Leominster, 2001.

Williams, G.A., *The Last Days of Owain Glyndŵr*, Talybont, 2017.

Williams, G., *The Welsh Church from Conquest to Reformation*, 2nd ed., Cardiff, 1976.

Williams, G.J., *Traddodiad Llenyddol Morgannwg* [The literary tradition of Morgannwg], Cardiff, 1948.

Williams, I., "Cyfeiriad at y Brawd Fadawg ap Gwallter?" [A reference to Brother Madog ap Gwallter?], *BBCS* 4 (1928), 133–34.

Williams, J.E.C., "Brittany and the Arthurian Legend", in R. Bromwich, A.O.H. Jarman, and B.F. Roberts (eds.), *The Arthur of the Welsh: The Arthurian Legend in Medieval Welsh Literature* (Arthurian Literature in the Middle Ages, 1), Cardiff, 1991, 249–72.

Williams, M., *Fiery Shapes: Celestial Portents and Astrology in Ireland and Wales, 700–1700*, Oxford, 2010.

Williams, S., "Geoffrey of Monmouth and the Canon Law", *Speculum* 27:2 (1952), 184–90.

Wood, J., "Virgil and Taliesin: The Concept of the Magician in Medieval Folklore", *Folklore* 94:1 (1983), 91–104.

Wood, J., "Where Does Britain End? The Reception of Geoffrey of Monmouth in Scotland and Wales", in R. Purdie and N. Royan (eds.), *The Scots and Medieval Arthurian Legend*, Cambridge, 2005, 9–24.

Woolf, A., "Geoffrey of Monmouth and the Picts", in W. McLeod (ed.), *Bile ós Chrannaibh: A Festschrift for William Gillies*, Ceann Drochaid, 2010, 269–80.

Wormald, P., "Bede, the *Bretwaldas* and the Origin of the *Gens Anglorum*", in P. Wormald et al. (eds.), *Ideal and Reality in Frankish and Anglo-Saxon Society*, Oxford, 1983, 99–129.

Wright, N., "Geoffrey of Monmouth and Bede", *AL* 6 (1986), 27–59.

Wright, N., "Geoffrey of Monmouth and Gildas", *AL* 2 (1982), 1–40.

Wright, N., "Geoffrey of Monmouth and Gildas Revisited", *AL* 5 (1985), 155–63.

Wright, N., "The Place of Henry of Huntingdon's *Epistola ad Warinum* in the Text-History of Geoffrey of Monmouth's *Historia regum Britannie*: a Preliminary Investigation", in G. Jondorf and D.N. Dumville (eds.), *France and the British Isles in the Middle Ages and Renaissance: Essays by Members of Girton College, Cambridge, in Memory of Ruth Morgan*, Woodbridge, 1991, 71–113.

Wright, N. (ed.), and Crick, J., *The Historia regum Britannie of Geoffrey of Monmouth*, 5 vols., Woodbridge, 1985–91.

Würth, S., *Der "Antikenroman" in der isländischen Literatur des Mittelalters. Eine Untersuchung zur Übersetzung und Rezeption lateinischer Literatur im Norden* (Beiträge zur nordischen Philologie, 26), Basel and Frankfurt am Main, 1998.

Zaccaria, V., "Le due redazioni del De Casibus", *Studi sul Boccaccio* 10 (1977–78), 1–26.

Zaggia, M., "Appunti sulla cultura letteraria in volgare a Milano nell'età di Filippo Maria Visconti", *Giornale storico della letteratura italiana* 170 (1993), 161–219, 321–82.

Ziolkowski, J.M., "The Nature of Prophecy in Geoffrey of Monmouth's *Vita Merlini*", in J.L. Kugel (ed.), *Poetry and Prophecy: The Beginnings of a Literary Tradition*, Ithaca, 1990, 151–62.

Ziolkowski, J.M., & Putnam, M.C.J., *The Virgilian Tradition. The First Fifteen Hundred Years*, New Haven, 2008.

Zumthor, P., *Merlin le Prophète, un thème de la littérature polémique de l'historiographie et des romans*, Lausanne, 1943.

Manuscripts

General Index

247, 251, 253, 255, 339, 434, 450, 452, 456,
458n.15, n.17, n.18, 461, 462n.34, 465, 472,
474, 485; *Roman de Rou* 247–48
Waleran of Meulan 68–69, 71, 76, 167–70,
292n.2
Wales Edwardian conquest of, 187, 197, 287,
289, 323, 496. *See also* Anglesey,
Deheubarth, Dyfed, Glamorgan,
Gwent, Gwynedd, Powys, Snowdon,
Snowdonia, Welsh, Welsh language.
Walter Bower, *Scotichronicon* 487–93
Walter Espec 162–63, 164–65, 170, 271
Walter Giffard 240
Walter Map 25–26, 137–38, 193
Walter of Coutances, bishop of Lincoln,
archbishop of Rouen 205–06
Walter, archdeacon of Oxford 8, 21–24,
35–36, 41, 67, 236, 238, 295, 305, 314,
328, 451
Walwanus. *See* Gawain.
Wars of the Roses 185, 234
Welsh as degenerated from Britons, 33–39,
108, 241, 285, 299, 325, 376, 395, 418;
discourse of racial inferiority, 199–200,
379, 387, 390; history writing themes,
258–70; prophetic literature, 49, 64–65,
136, 151, 194, 197, 258, 259n.8, 277, 288,
336, 422. *See also* Armes Prydein Vawr;
reception of Geoffrey, 25, 195–97,
270–90; Roman inheritance of, 151,
204, 207, 259–61, 287, 379, 402–05
Welsh language 14, 20, 39–42, 269; Old
Welsh, 38, 41, 54, 55
werewolf 227. *See also* Arthur and
Gorlagon.
Westminster Cathedral, 10; Treaty of, 10,
326

whiteness 370–72
Whitland Abbey 174, 259, 272, 282, 285, 286
Wihenoc of La Boussac 40, 325
William Camden, *Britannia* 215
William fitz Osbern 269
William II of Sicily 478
William Lambarde, *Perambulation of
Kent* 215
William Longchamp, bishop of Ely 205
William of Gloucester 272
William of Malmesbury *The Contemporary
History*, 158, 162, 293, 345n.13; *Deeds of the
English Kings*, 112–15, 162, 172–73, 291–313,
391, 406, 473; *The Early History of
Glastonbury*, 57, 406; *History of the English
Bishops*, 219
William of Newburgh and Geoffrey's
name, 7, 14n.51; reaction to *DGB*, 36, 185,
194–208, 223, 454n.2
William of St Albans 8n.18
William Rishanger, chronicle of 284
William Rufus 78, 144, 239–40, 320
William the Conqueror 40, 131, 167, 314n.84,
320
Wirnt von Grafenberg, *Wigalois* 467
Woden 113, 410
Wonders of the East 252
Wulfhere, son of Penda 119
Wulfred. *See* Wulfhere.
Wulfstan 17

Ymddiddan Myrddin a Thaliesin 63–64, 133
York 47, 58, 92, 121, 162–65, 205, 403,
409n.39, 412, 459
Ystorya Dared 81, 196, 259, 286, 496. *See also*
Dares Phrygius.

Printed in the United States
By Bookmasters